1 & 2 CHRONICLES

KERUX COMMENTARIES

1 & 2 CHRONICLES

A Commentary for Biblical Preaching and Teaching

JOSHUA E. WILLIAMS

CALVIN F. PEARSON

KREGEL
MINISTRY

1 & 2 Chronicles: A Commentary for Biblical Preaching and Teaching
© 2024 by Joshua E. Williams and Calvin F. Pearson

Published by Kregel Ministry, an imprint of Kregel Publications, 2450 Oak Industrial Dr. NE, Grand Rapids, MI 49505-6020.

Library of Congress Cataloging-in-Publication Data
Names: Williams, Joshua E.– author. | Pearson, Calvin F.– author.
Title: 1 & 2 Chronicles : a commentary for biblical preaching and teaching / Joshua E. Williams, Calvin F. Pearson.
Other titles: One and two Chronicles
Description: First edition. | Grand Rapids : Kregel Ministry, [2024] |
    Series: Kerux commentaries | Includes bibliographical references.
Identifiers: LCCN 2023049734; Subjects: LCSH: Bible. Chronicles—Commentaries.
Classification: LCC BS1345.53 .W55 2024 | DDC 222/.607—dc23/eng/20231214
LC record available at https://lccn.loc.gov/2023049734

ISBN 978-0-8254-5848-4

Printed in China
24 25 26 27 28 / 5 4 3 2 1

Contents

REIGNS OF JUDAH'S KINGS (2 CHRONICLES 10:1–36:23)

PUBLISHER'S PREFACE TO THE SERIES

Since words were first uttered, people have struggled to understand one another and to know the main meaning in any verbal exchange.

The answer to what God is talking about must be understood in every context and generation; that is why Kerux (KAY-rukes) emphasizes text-based truths and bridges from the context of the original hearers and readers to the twenty-first-century world. Kerux values the message of the text, thus its name taken from the Greek *kērux*, a messenger or herald who announced the proclamations of a ruler or magistrate.

Biblical authors trumpeted all kinds of important messages in very specific situations, but a big biblical idea, grasped in its original setting and place, can transcend time. This specific, big biblical idea taken from the biblical passage embodies a single concept that transcends time and bridges the gap between the author's contemporary context and the reader's world. How do the prophets perceive the writings of Moses? How does the writer of Hebrews make sense of the Old Testament? How does Clement in his second epistle, which may be the earliest sermon known outside the New Testament, adapt verses from Isaiah and also ones from the Gospels? Or what about Luther's bold use of Romans 1:17? How does Jonathan Edwards allude to Genesis 19? Who can forget Martin Luther King Jr.'s "I Have a Dream" speech and his appropriation of Amos 5:24: "No, no, we are not satisfied, and we will not be satisfied until 'justice rolls down like waters, and righteousness like a mighty stream'"? How does a preacher in your local church today apply the words of Hosea in a meaningful and life-transforming way?

WHAT IS PRIME IN GOD'S MIND, AND HOW IS THAT EXPRESSED TO A GIVEN GENERATION IN THE UNITS OF THOUGHT THROUGHOUT THE BIBLE?

Answering those questions is what Kerux authors do. Based on the popular "big idea" preaching model, Kerux commentaries uniquely combine the insights of experienced Bible exegetes (trained in interpretation) and homileticians (trained in preaching). Their collaboration provides for every Bible book:

- A detailed introduction and outline
- A summary of all preaching sections with their primary exegetical, theological, and preaching ideas
- Preaching pointers that join the original context with the contemporary one
- Insights from the Hebrew and Greek text
- A thorough exposition of the text
- Sidebars of pertinent information for further background
- Appropriate charts and photographs
- A theological focus to passages

- A contemporary big idea for every preaching unit
- Present-day meaning, validity, and application of a main idea
- Creative presentations for each primary idea
- Key questions about the text for study groups

Many thanks to Jim Weaver, Kregel's former acquisitions editor, who conceived of this commentary series and further developed it with the team of Jeffrey D. Arthurs, Robert B. Chisholm, David M. Howard Jr., Darrell L. Bock, Roy E. Ciampa, and Michael J. Wilkins. We also recognize with gratitude the significant contributions of Dennis Hillman, Fred Mabie, Paul Hillman, Herbert W. Bateman IV, and Shawn Vander Lugt who have been instrumental in the development of the series. Finally, gratitude is extended to the two authors for each Kerux volume; the outside reviewers, editors, and proofreaders; and Kregel staff who suggested numerous improvements.

—Kregel Publications

EXEGETICAL AUTHOR'S PREFACE
TO 1 & 2 CHRONICLES

Some books of the Old Testament receive a lot of attention among church members. Christians are usually familiar with Genesis, Exodus, Joshua, Judges, 1 and 2 Samuel, 1 and 2 Kings, Proverbs, Psalms, and Isaiah, to name a few. They read these books, study them, and often hear sermons addressing them. In contrast, 1 and 2 Chronicles seems to be far more unfamiliar, except perhaps for Jabez's prayer or the occasional revival sermon addressing 2 Chronicles 7:14. For many, Chronicles is just a repeat of the books of Samuel and Kings. Even recently, an Old Testament colleague confessed that he hadn't spent much time studying or thinking about Chronicles until he was recently forced to look at it. He thought the book didn't have much to offer above Samuel and Kings. However, once he began studying it, he found the book to be fascinating and significant.

In many ways, Chronicles provides a front-row seat to one of the first Old Testament theologians—that is, one of the first to read, interpret, and bring together various threads of the Old Testament story into a coherent, theological story of its own. Chronicles shows how two main figures in the Old Testament relate to one another: Moses and David. Chronicles shows how the Law of Moses shaped Israel's history through the Davidic dynasty and the Jerusalem temple. The book reveals how an Old Testament author interpreted other Old Testament writings. The book also points the way to an ideal picture of the people of God: a people gathered to worship God properly, ruled by a Davidic heir. This portrait presses into the New Testament and the coming of Jesus, son of David, son of Abraham. In this way, the book points to the faithfulness of God toward his people and the hope that he will fully establish his rule and finally restore his people. May God hasten that day.

—Joshua E. Williams

PREACHING AUTHOR'S PREFACE
TO 1 & 2 CHRONICLES

This historical narrative teaches us to worship our Lord with a heart wholly committed to him. As we read the accounts, our hearts are encouraged when we see a king who enjoys great blessings as he follows the Lord. And we are equally discouraged when kings abandon the Lord because of a divided heart, and suffer the consequences. The book ends with a ray of hope for God's blessings, but we are left wanting a better example and an effective power to change our own divided hearts. Perhaps the first readers were left with the same longing. We now have both, example and empowerment, through Jesus. He lived a perfect exemplary life, but even more his saving work on our behalf allows us to rely upon his Spirit who can give us a whole heart devoted to God. Our sin still invokes God's hand of discipline; and by his mercy and grace, our obedience enables us to enjoy his blessings.

Anytime one preaches or teaches the Old Testament one must keep the context of the full canon in mind. However, I would suggest that one should not turn too quickly to other passages, lest you end up preaching a passage from Ephesians and only use 1 and 2 Chronicles for illustrations. If we are not careful, we could end up preaching Ephesians instead of Chronicles.

Of course, our preaching is to be Christian. Our approach is to present the message of a pericope, knowing that the message can be more personal and more fulfilling because of Christ's work for us. The message is the same for us as it was for the ancient readers, but with Christ the understanding and application becomes richer. I often mention Jesus's work specifically, but at times it is assumed.

Sermons should have a central idea, whether it is called a theme, a main idea, or a "big idea." However, such a unifying idea is only a tool to assist in communicating the text. Our purpose is to present God's living and active Word.

I like to think this work is simply my sitting down with you and dialoguing about how to preach or teach a passage. I pray that as you read what we have written, God's Spirit will be at work in you. Perhaps, he will use the commentary and the sermonic suggestions as seeds that will help grow effective structures, illustrations, and applications for your setting.

Jerusalem 2023
—Calvin F. Pearson

EXEGETICAL AUTHOR'S ACKNOWLEDGMENTS

This book is dedicated to my wife, Johnita,
and our three children, Brooke, Seth, and Luke,
who have granted me an enchanted life.

One constant through my academic career has been the book of Chronicles. Whether I have been working on Hebrew syntax, hermeneutics, biblical composition, Old Testament theology, or a host of other subjects, Chronicles has been a constant companion, shaping my views of such matters through the years. My interest in Chronicles began in a doctoral seminar under the supervision of John Sailhamer. During this seminar, we looked at Hebrew syntax through the lens of parallel passages between Samuel-Kings and Chronicles. Without that early exposure to the fine details of those texts, I don't know that the journey to this volume would have ever commenced. I am grateful to Dr. Sailhamer for his close reading of the text and his investment in me as a supervisor.

My colleagues at Southwestern Baptist Theological Seminary have refined my thinking and encouraged me along the way. My discussions with them have provided guidance when I was stuck and some challenge when I was too confident. Also, I am grateful for the sabbatical in 2022–2023 which allowed me to finish this writing project. My colleagues were ready and willing to pick up what I put down for that year. Furthermore, my time spent as a visiting scholar at Southeastern Baptist Theological Seminary in Spring 2023 provided an environment for me to finish the work well as I used their library resources and dialogued with colleagues there.

My students have been a great source of encouragement and motivation through the years. They have worked through many key passages with me in the Hebrew text. Their thoughts and questions have spurred on my own thoughts and prompted me to clarify my thinking where it has been vague.

During this process, it has been a great pleasure to work with my friend and colleague Calvin Pearson. He has been a wonderful dialogue partner and has truly taken this work to the next level. Our back-and-forth conversations have sharpened me and made this commentary better.

Finally, I owe a debt to the entire team at Kregel. When Herb Bateman asked me to contribute to this series, I was excited and nervous. Herb's consistent encouragement has gone a long way to my finishing the project. Also, Shawn Vander Lugt has been a delight to work with as the managing editor, and the rest of the editorial team has been so helpful. I pray that this volume aids the preachers and teachers of God's Word and thereby strengthens God's churches.

—Joshua E. Williams

PREACHING AUTHOR'S ACKNOWLEDGMENTS

To my wife Jan
and children: Anna, John and Janelle, Deborah and Nick

Without the Lord's empowerment and the impact of many people on my life, I would have never been able to write this volume.

First and foremost is my wife of forty-eight years, Jan, who supported, edited, and greatly encouraged me through the process.

Since my area is the preaching of the text, I am greatly indebted to all those who taught me. Five stand out: Duane Litfin, Elliot Johnson, John Reed, Haddon Robinson, and Don Sunukjian. And, I thank my students and colleagues, with whom I was privileged to co-labor,

Much of my preaching skill and style was forged through the churches which God entrusted me to pastor: Calvary Baptist, Seagoville, Texas; Bay Area First Baptist, League City, Texas; and Hopevale Church, Saginaw, Michigan.

God used so many to form me spiritually. I list some knowing that many others had and still have a profound influence on my life: Don Sims, Mickey Thompson, Jesse Outlaw, John Gaskill, Duane Garrett, Ben Crawford, Rob Morrow, Alan Deetjen, Jeannette Clift George, Larry York, my current pastor Justin Dancer, and many more than I have room to list.

Lastly, I am indebted to Joshua Williams and his reliable and usable scholarship which is the foundation for my homiletical contribution. I value his friendship, which began more than twenty years ago at Southwestern Baptist Seminary.

Thank you, to all of these and dozens of others, for being God's tool to shape and refine my homiletics and my life. May he use this volume to bring glory to himself.

A fellow servant of the Savior,
—Calvin F. Pearson

OVERVIEW OF ALL PREACHING PASSAGES

1 Chronicles 1:1–9:44

EXEGETICAL IDEA
YHWH preserved his chosen people Israel, even through their punishment, so that they would be an obedient community living in their land, worshipping him properly in Jerusalem, led by a son of David.

THEOLOGICAL FOCUS
YHWH faithfully preserves his people, even through punishment, so that they may worship him obediently.

PREACHING IDEA
Remember what defines you: God's choice and expectation.

PREACHING POINTERS
The application of this pericope is challenging, because it is not only a narrative, but a special kind of narrative. It can be helpful to put ourselves in the place of those Jews who heard it read when they returned from exile. Their lives were filled with uncertainty and they had the great challenge of rebuilding a nation. It is easy to see that they would struggle with national identity. To solidify who they were as a nation, individuals would have to remember or perhaps learn for the first time that God chose them and gave them a task. This genealogy shows that Israel was chosen and was expected to obey the God who chose them. The centrality of that obedience was worship.

Because of the world we live in and our sin nature, the church and those in the church need to be reminded of who we are, what defines us. Those in our church who have been through a crisis often will need a reminder of who they are. When you lose a spouse of forty years, when you lose a job, when you are fired, when illness hits—these are all reasons for someone to struggle with who they are. What defined them was taken away. This passage can help us grab hold of what truly defines us: God's choice of us and his assignment for us. When we remember what defines us, we should respond in worship.

1 Chronicles 10:1–14

EXEGETICAL IDEA
Because Saul was unfaithful to YHWH and broke his commandments, YHWH destroyed Saul's dynasty and turned the kingdom over to David.

THEOLOGICAL FOCUS
God desires those who are faithful to lead in his kingdom and rejects those who are not.

PREACHING IDEA
Reject rejection by embracing faithfulness.

PREACHING POINTERS
Because of the seventy years of exile, the ones who first heard this passage knew all too well that there are consequences to sin. Perhaps they wondered if God's disciplining hand was still on them. How could they be sure that they could once again be useful to build God's kingdom? If we want to be useful workers in God's kingdom, don't be like Saul. Saul was not faithful to seek God, and God rejected him as king. This passage teaches us to be faithful to YHWH through the warning that workers and leaders in God's kingdom can be put on the sidelines by God.

1 Chronicles 11:1–12:40 [HB 41]

EXEGETICAL IDEA
All Israel recognized David as king, according to David's character and YHWH's word.

THEOLOGICAL FOCUS
God's people, at their best, remain united under the authority of God's chosen king, Jesus, our Messiah.

PREACHING IDEA
We are at our best when we follow the best leader.

PREACHING POINTERS
The narrative of these two chapters is not a story with a clear plot line, but rather the celebration of David becoming king and showing the support he had in all Israel. Through this selective and overstated account of him becoming king, David is presented as the ideal king. At the beginning of this chronicling of the kings of Israel, God stirs in us this desire for a perfect leader. Though we have never written out our list, there is in each of us a picture of what the ideal leader should be like. We know that no leader is perfect, but we still have this inner standard. The great and joyful good news is that Jesus is this perfect king, the perfect leader.

1 Chronicles 13:1–14:17

EXEGETICAL IDEA
YHWH blessed David and Israel because they sought YHWH, but he struck them when they did not seek him properly.

THEOLOGICAL FOCUS
God impartially rewards or punishes his people based on their intentions and actions.

PREACHING IDEA
The bitterness of discipline, or the delight of blessing?

PREACHING POINTERS
At first glance, it is hard to see how these two chapters form a unit of thought. And yet, the concept of God breaking out against Uzzah and the Philistines shows that unity. The bitterness of YHWH breaking out against Uzzah for touching the ark is contrasted with YHWH's blessing of David by establishing his kingdom and then empowering him to break out against the Philistines. The same Lord who breaks out in discipline is the same Lord who breaks out in blessing. God is helping us get a fuller view of who he is and how we should step into his presence. Since the bitterness of discipline and the delight of blessing both come from our holy and impartial Lord, we must approach him with awe because of his holiness and assurance because of his blessing.

1 Chronicles 15:1–16:43

EXEGETICAL IDEA
David demonstrates his devotion to YHWH by transferring the ark to Jerusalem according to Mosaic law and by establishing Israel's musical worship service to praise YHWH as God of all creation and God of Israel.

THEOLOGICAL FOCUS
God deserves obedient praise because he is the God of all creation and the God of his people.

PREACHING IDEA
Give worthy worship to our worthy Lord.

PREACHING POINTERS
The postexilic community had a very difficult task in front of them. They had to rebuild the nation and the temple. As they heard of this joyful episode in the history of God's family, it taught them, and teaches us, to celebrate our Lord, even when things are not as we would like them. It is important to see David's celebration in light of the previous tragedy of forgetting about the holiness of God. For Israel, God had specific commands about the ark. Obedience to these specific commands was an expression of the heart of obedience in all areas. We have no ark, but we still need to have a heart and life of obedience. While obedience is always important, the focus of this pericope is worship. Worship must be done with obedience. In addition, at times our worship should be filled with celebration, just as Israel's was.

The question arises as to how to celebrate in the church in this century. Our worship of God is not always celebratory, but it is always in obedience to him. But when we do celebrate, what does it look like? While the specific music, atmosphere, sounds, even seating arrangement will vary with cultures, the elements that must never vary are obedience, reverence, and a singular focus upon our Lord.

1 Chronicles 17:1–27

EXEGETICAL IDEA

When David wanted to build YHWH a temple, YHWH took the initiative to build David a dynasty—one that would not only build YHWH a temple but secure Israel as YHWH's people in their land.

THEOLOGICAL FOCUS

The Lord proves he is truly God, as he chooses the Davidic line to fulfill his promises to his people and to lead them to worship him properly.

PREACHING IDEA

God has the plan—we have the worship.

PREACHING POINTERS

Every congregation, every class, every person experiences a change of plans. Often those are not pleasant and are hard to adjust to. At some level we all struggle when our plans are changed. David had his plans changed. What could be more noble and God-honoring than to build YHWH's temple? Surely God would honor this plan.

David had a plan. God had a better one. David wanted to build God a house, but God said, "No." Instead, *God* would build *David* an eternal house. While God's plans for us are not as specific as they were for David, we can still trust that they are better than our plans.

1 Chronicles 18:1–20:8

EXEGETICAL IDEA

As YHWH fulfilled part of his promise, David's reign at this point appeared ideal: David defeated his enemies, rallied competent warriors, expanded his influence in the region, increased his wealth, prepared for temple construction, organized his administration, and governed with justice.

THEOLOGICAL FOCUS

God uses the one loyal to him to fulfill his plan to bless his people.

PREACHING IDEA

To be a part of God's great work, be loyal to him.

PREACHING POINTERS

Everyone wants to be a part of something that is successful. When our team has a winning season, we are more likely to watch the games. We take a new job not only because of the direct benefits to us, but because we want to be a part of a successful company. We enter into marriage because we think it can be a success.

In these chapters we see God bringing great success to David and to Israel. The first readers wanted success in their rebuilding of Israel. They needed YHWH to work in powerful ways. The loyalty of David serves as an example of how to be a part of God's great work. God was showing the exiles that he would work to keep his promises. Their loyalty to the great God would bring them into his great plan and work. He would work; they only needed to remain loyal. What could be more successful than God keeping his promises? And what could be more glorifying to him than expressing our faith through our loyalty to him?

1 Chronicles 21:1–22:1

EXEGETICAL IDEA
YHWH selected the site for the temple after punishing Israel for David's sin.

THEOLOGICAL FOCUS
YHWH can use a tragic situation caused by sin to accomplish his plan for blessing.

PREACHING IDEA
Move on from our sin and into God's victory.

PREACHING POINTERS
This passage wonderfully shows how our great God brings blessing out of tragedy, even when that tragedy is the result of sin. One cannot mention this theme without thinking of humanity's sin of crucifying Christ and his victorious resurrection. David's sin, his exemplary repentance, and God's resulting victory give us a pattern so that we can move from our sin into God's victory.

1 Chronicles 22:2–19

EXEGETICAL IDEA
Following the pattern of Moses and Joshua, David prepared for God's task of building the temple and charged Solomon and the people to obey YHWH's instructions to succeed in finishing the task.

THEOLOGICAL FOCUS
Carrying out God's will calls for a community of devoted followers empowered by God.

PREACHING IDEA
Be a part of God's big plan.

PREACHING POINTERS
God was inviting those in David and Solomon's time, and then those after the exile, to be a part of something bigger than themselves—that is, to be a part of building his temple. The temple

was to give light to the nations, to make his glory known, to be a place of prayer and worship, and to show that forgiveness comes through sacrifice. The temple is gone, and now God is inviting us to be a part of a new building—not one constructed of rocks but one fashioned with living stones. Not a physical building, but a breathing building: the church. While there are numerous differences between the temple and Christ's church, the purpose is still the same. God's plan of dwelling in and working through the church calls for a community of people who are committed to the task, devoted to him, and empowered by him. Each of us is invited to play a part in God's big plan of working through the church to show his love for the world.

1 Chronicles 23:1–27:34

EXEGETICAL IDEA
During his last days, David promoted the worship of YHWH and the well-being of Israel by meticulously organizing the personnel to serve in the future temple and by securing a peaceful transfer of royal authority to Solomon.

THEOLOGICAL FOCUS
Worshipping YHWH is a serious task of obedience, worthy of meticulous care and consideration, resulting in blessing.

PREACHING IDEA
Meaningful corporate worship begins with meticulous work.

PREACHING POINTERS
Across the centuries, worship in Israel changed: when Israel built a permanent structure instead of a tent, when the temple was destroyed and the Babylonians took Israel into captivity, and when the exiles returned to rebuild the temple. But greater changes were in store. Jesus's death and resurrection changed everything. When we study a passage that lists the personnel for temple worship, we must remember the changes and looks for what has not changed: we still worship the same God. We are still sinful people living in a sinful world. Because of this, we need order and structure to help us as sinners come together and worship our Lord.

This passage doesn't give us direction as to what happens in worship; rather, it shows the importance of order and personnel structure. The Israelites needed meticulous work to have meaningful worship, and we need the same.

1 Chronicles 28:1–21

EXEGETICAL IDEA
YHWH chose Solomon to lead Israel in following YHWH, especially by building a temple according to a divinely revealed plan that resembled both the tabernacle and the postexilic temple.

THEOLOGICAL FOCUS
God works according to his plan to dwell with his people, to bless those loyal to him.

PREACHING IDEA

God's supreme royalty demands our complete loyalty.

PREACHING POINTERS

This narrative of motivational speeches to build the temple is more than a pep rally for Solomon and Israel. While there are charges to accomplish that task, there is a deeper lesson for us. God's character is revealed through what is said about God's choice and provision. The God-ordained task to build a temple reveals that God desires to dwell with us. As the story is presented, some of God's characteristics emerge. These characteristics are of a perfect king. We might say he alone is supreme royalty. It is his supreme royalty that commands our complete loyalty to him.

1 Chronicles 29:1–30

EXEGETICAL IDEA

The end of David's reign presented an ideal picture of all Israel: devoted to YHWH as the everlasting, universal ruler, generously supporting the temple, and experiencing a stable transition from one of YHWH's chosen kings to another.

THEOLOGICAL FOCUS

As the everlasting, universal ruler, God deserves people's full devotion and brings peace for his people.

PREACHING IDEA

As you put your hand to the task, keep your heart on the Lord.

PREACHING POINTERS

One of the great blessings of technology is that how-to videos are available for just about everything. This passage presents the key element in every task that our Lord puts in front of us. Some tasks like those that the Israelites faced are particularly hard. While working hard, having a team, and planning well are all important, it was not the focus of David or of the Israelites. Their focus was not on giving to build the temple and transitioning to a new king; instead, their focus was devotion to the Lord.

2 Chronicles 1:1–17

EXEGETICAL IDEA

Because of YHWH's promise to David, YHWH prepared Solomon, who was a true worshipper, to build the temple.

THEOLOGICAL FOCUS

According to his plan, YHWH blesses those who truly worship him in order to enable them to worship him more.

PREACHING IDEA

When our worship controls our requests, his provision is realized.

PREACHING POINTERS

Second Chronicles begins with a most encouraging event. The postexilic Jews were trying to rebuild a land that was neglected and a nation that had been destroyed. While they faced a national crisis, the individual tasks of starting again in an unfamiliar land must have compounded that crisis. They needed encouragement. They needed to know that God was faithful and that he would provide what they needed to accomplish his will. This passage shows us that YHWH is faithful and, by Solomon's example, gives us a directive to experience that faithfulness. Solomon placed a priority on worship. His worship of God enabled him to realize the amazing blessing of God that was beyond what he could ask or think.

While our crises may be different from the ancient Israelites, we are still asking the same questions and wrestling with the same challenges. How can the church continue her mission in such a difficult time? How can I, as an individual follower of YHWH, continue my mission? Will God provide? Yes, of course, we say, but our feelings may not agree. This passage helps us see that a faithful God will provide what is needed to accomplish his will in our lives.

2 Chronicles 2:1 [HB 1:18]–5:1

EXEGETICAL IDEA

As a part of God's plan, God's chosen, wise king Solomon built a great temple to worship the great God YHWH.

THEOLOGICAL FOCUS

As God, YHWH deserves the best in worship. He works in history according to his plan to enable his people to worship him appropriately in their context.

PREACHING IDEA

Worship of our great God deserves our best.

PREACHING POINTERS

The postexilic Jews had to rebuild the temple. How would they do it? Solomon had great resources that had been accumulated by his father David. These Jews had next to nothing. The land and resources were devastated. They were moving back after seventy years of exile. Why did God give them this account of the first temple being so elaborate and extravagant? Certainly, they could not duplicate what Solomon did. Putting ourselves in their shoes not only helps us see how they would apply these chapters, but also gives us a direction as to how this pericope should change our lives. As they heard about Solomon's heart to build a great house for the name of YHWH, hopefully they would want the same heart. This is not a passage about external gifts to God; this is about our working to have great worship because we worship the great God.

2 Chronicles 5:2–14

EXEGETICAL IDEA
The Jerusalem temple took over the role of the tabernacle, both as the center of all Israel's ritual worship and as the seat of YHWH's unique presence, when Israel transferred the ark according to Mosaic legislation and fulfilled the work David began.

THEOLOGICAL FOCUS
God always wants to dwell with his people and enjoy their worship.

PREACHING IDEA
When we need to feel God's presence, it is time to worship.

PREACHING POINTERS
With the advance of technology aimed at individual use, we have become more emotionally isolated. We were created with a need to be with others and with God. Though it is expressed in various ways, we all desire God's presence. This passage is about God letting Israel, and us, know that he is with us. While we should not expect another cloud, we can look for a renewed awareness of God's presence. The text shows us that Israel's proper worship led up to the cloud filling the temple. That proper worship included sacrifice, a focus on God's written covenant, and majestic music. The result was, and can be, a special awareness of God's presence.

2 Chronicles 6:1–42

EXEGETICAL IDEA
The temple was important because it was a worthy place for YHWH to dwell in hiddenness, because it fulfilled part of YHWH's promise to David, and because it would become a place for prayer.

THEOLOGICAL FOCUS
God is present and transcendent, faithful to his promises, and attentive to those who pray to him.

PREACHING IDEA
Yes, God does hear our prayers.

PREACHING POINTERS
Remember the old mobile phone commercials that featured the phrase, "Can you hear me now?" Mobile phone coverage has greatly improved, but we still experience disruption in our phone service. When driving through a hilly or rural area, we might have to ask, "Did you hear me?" This episode in the life of Israel teaches us that we don't have to ask that of God. His character and love for us leads us to pray—and he is attentive to our prayers. In

the communication of law-enforcement officers in TV series, we often hear, "Copy that." The phrase means that a person not only heard what you said but that they have also understood it. In a sense, when we pray, God says, "Copy that"—not in the sense that he is taking orders from us, but that he truly hears us and is attentive to our need.

2 Chronicles 7:1–22

EXEGETICAL IDEA
YHWH and all Israel affirmed the Jerusalem temple as the focal point for Israel's ritual worship, a place for Israel to turn for YHWH's help as long as they turned to YHWH alone.

THEOLOGICAL FOCUS
All true worship is directed to God alone as part of a relationship in which he blesses obedience and disciplines disobedience.

PREACHING IDEA
Our relationship with God is to be enjoyed, not endured.

PREACHING POINTERS
It is a clear theme throughout the Bible: we enjoy God's blessings through obedience, and we endure God's discipline when we disobey. This passage gives us a foundation for our obedience when we face a struggle. The grand celebration of God showing his coming to dwell in the temple, along with the sacrifices and feasting, gave the Israelites a wonderful experience of God's presence. This public mountaintop experience is followed by a private session in which the king is warned about the consequences of disobedience. These two events almost seem in opposition, but linking them together shows us the uniqueness of this passage. The celebration and the memory of it hopefully motivated Israel to obey God's laws. In our own lives, the memory of a special experience of God's presence can prompt us and help us to obey.

2 Chronicles 8:1–16

EXEGETICAL IDEA
Solomon built up Israel as a consequence of building the temple and prepared the temple for its continual use in worship according to Mosaic and Davidic authority.

THEOLOGICAL FOCUS
Worshipping God builds up the community when conducted properly.

PREACHING IDEA
To grow spiritually, invest in good habits of worship.

PREACHING POINTERS
Sometimes the most important events in life are the moment-by-moment activities. A marriage is built not so much on the big events, but through the daily forgiveness and acts of love that are offered each day. Growing in our walk with the Lord has the mountaintop experiences, which

need to be there, but the spiritual growth is a matter of an ongoing routine of daily practices of the spiritual disciplines. This passage presents some very normal activities. Solomon does his job as king to lead the nation in continual, ongoing worship. He does this by securing the nation and making provision for worship. These very normal activities of the king give us the assurance that great good comes out of normal, ongoing, routine habits of worship.

2 Chronicles 8:17–9:31

EXEGETICAL IDEA
Other nations acknowledged YHWH's rule and love for Israel when YHWH gave Solomon what he promised: wisdom and wealth beyond compare.

THEOLOGICAL FOCUS
God demonstrates what he is like when he faithfully fulfills his promises to his people.

PREACHING IDEA
The Lord has, and will, provide with extravagant abundance.

PREACHING POINTERS
Solomon's wealth and wisdom are presented here in such a way that it is almost surreal, even more so to modern readers. Just one of the two hundred gold decorative shields would be worth around $300,000 today. These abundant blessings that the writer is asking us to remember are based upon God being the source and God keeping his promises. And it is this same foundation of God's character that allowed Israel, and allows us, to look for a better future. God is not leading us to live in the past, but through an affirming picture of the past he is leading us to trust in him for a better future. This future will be with extravagant abundance—not necessarily in terms of gold, silver, and human wisdom, but with what he knows is the very best.

2 Chronicles 10:1–19

EXEGETICAL IDEA
Through the interactions of Rehoboam, his counselors, Jeroboam, and Israel, YHWH fulfilled his prophetic word to separate Israel into two kingdoms.

THEOLOGICAL FOCUS
God ultimately works through all circumstances to accomplish his plan.

PREACHING IDEA
God doesn't need a backup plan; he only has Plan A.

PREACHING POINTERS
As I write this, Great Britain is mourning the death of Queen Elizabeth II. She completed her reign, and her son Charles is now on the throne. She will be missed. One of the talking points of newscasters is how this will change the plans of the monarchy. What will be King Charles's emphasis? (If there is a current transfer of power that is well known by your listeners, use that instead.)

This passage gives us great comfort by assuring us that YHWH's plans and emphasis will never change, and every circumstance will be used by him to further his plan. When we look at blunders and sins in our own lives, in the lives of those around us, and in our world, God's sovereignty can comfort us, guide us, and lead us to worship him.

2 Chronicles 11:1–12:16

EXEGETICAL IDEA
When Rehoboam listened to YHWH's word, YHWH responded favorably, but when he forsook YHWH, YHWH responded with judgment.

THEOLOGICAL FOCUS
Responding to God's revelation shapes the course of human lives: accepting it leads to blessing, but rejecting it leads to disaster.

PREACHING IDEA
Obey God's Word, not to get (receive) good but because he is good.

PREACHING POINTERS
At first glance Rehoboam is a picture of each of us. Just like him, I obey; I disobey; I listen to God; I don't listen. In many ways we are like him, but he is described as evil. So, in my sympathetic identification with this very human king, how do I escape this negative and condemning description? I don't want to be called evil. The Chronicler gives the reason for the description of evil: Rehoboam did not set his heart to seek YHWH. This passage is a call to worship our great Lord. This less-than-desirable king leaves us wanting a king who has a heart of obedience and submission. Jesus is our obedient king who submitted to the Father and gives us the foundational sacrifice for our worship.

2 Chronicles 13:1–14:1a [HB 13:23a]

EXEGETICAL IDEA
YHWH strengthened Judah for legitimately worshipping and exclusively trusting him, while he brought disaster on Israel for forsaking him.

THEOLOGICAL FOCUS
God strengthens those who worship and trust him alone, but he opposes those who forsake him and trust others.

PREACHING IDEA
Face battles by seeking the face of God.

PREACHING POINTERS
We live in a world that is filled with opposition to God's kingdom and will. Broadly speaking, we see culture moving away from biblical morality. The mindset is becoming more and more materialistic. Crime seems to be on the rise. Our governmental leaders seem to be more and

more hostile toward each other. And the opposition to God's kingdom is also within each of us. The Chronicler gives us a guide as to how to face the battle that comes to us. Abijah faced opposition to God's rule and will with worship. This passage is important for us in a world filled with opposition to God and his kingdom. The way to face battles is to seek the face of God.

2 Chronicles 14:1b [HB 13:23b]–16:14

EXEGETICAL IDEA
When Asa relied on YHWH, YHWH blessed him; but when he did not, YHWH punished him.

THEOLOGICAL FOCUS
Relying on God is always right and shapes the future of one's life.

PREACHING IDEA
Don't end up an independent, grumpy old person.

PREACHING POINTERS
The essence of the message of the whole Bible is that we must depend upon God for the forgiveness of sin, through the work of Jesus on our behalf. Our salvation is completely dependent upon him and his work. This concept of dependence should continue throughout our lives, not just when we come to faith. This passage teaches us the importance of remaining dependent upon God throughout our whole lives. Asa starts out relying upon God, but ends up living independently from God. He starts out well but ends up an independent, and probably grumpy, old man.

2 Chronicles 17:1–19:3

EXEGETICAL IDEA
Jehoshaphat's sincere commitment to worship YHWH properly reduced the impact of his objectionable action to ally himself with Ahab.

THEOLOGICAL FOCUS
God blesses those who follow him exclusively and protects them from the fate of the wicked.

PREACHING IDEA
Since God is the source of our blessings, only worship him.

PREACHING POINTERS
This stage of Jehoshaphat's reign illustrates how YHWH rewards Jehoshaphat in his obedience and even mitigates his punishment for a foolish alliance. It teaches us to enjoy the blessings that come from fully embracing the worship of God through faith in his merciful sacrifice and to not seek blessings though an alliance with those who do not worship him. Since God is the source of our blessings, we only and always worship him.

2 Chronicles 19:4–21:1

EXEGETICAL IDEA
Even Jehoshaphat's righteous reforms and trust in YHWH in the face of battle could not eliminate the disastrous consequences of his alliance with a wicked nation.

THEOLOGICAL FOCUS
Justice and victory belong to God; therefore, trusting him only leads to blessing.

PREACHING IDEA
We can trust our powerful and just God.

PREACHING POINTERS
This story is astonishing. A nation goes to battle—with the choir leading the way. God, in his surprising ways, brings about victory by causing the enemies to turn upon each other. What a grand victory! Surely, we can trust our all-powerful Lord. However, this unusual victory is in the context of more normal activities: the setting up of a justice system and the disobedience of a king. The theme that is more subtle, which comes out in the fuller narrative, is that of God's justice. We can trust him because of his power and his justice. He can be trusted that he *can* and *will* do what is right.

2 Chronicles 21:2–23:21

EXEGETICAL IDEA
Because Jehoram and Ahaziah followed the wicked ways of Israel, they led the Davidic dynasty to the brink of destruction; however, Jehoiada the priest led the people to restore the Davidic king and proper worship.

THEOLOGICAL FOCUS
Even though sin threatens God's blessing, God remains faithful to his promises.

PREACHING IDEA
The darker the days, the more we need to walk in his light.

PREACHING POINTERS
Each of us has been, or is currently, in a time when God's blessings are hard to see. When the darkness comes, we begin to doubt that he will keep his promises, which can lead us to a lack of trust in his commands. When money is tight, perhaps a little unnoticed and culturally accepted stealing is in order. Adulterous thoughts come easily when a marriage is filled with conflict. When a culture is moving toward immorality, it is hard to resist moving with it. This dramatic story about the near-destruction of the Davidic line teaches us to trust our Lord even when things look very dark.

2 Chronicles 24:1–27

EXEGETICAL IDEA
While the priest Jehoiada was alive, he led Joash to obey YHWH by restoring Davidic rule and temple worship; but after Jehoiada died, Joash and Judah forsook YHWH, forgot Jehoiada, and saw their fortunes reversed.

THEOLOGICAL FOCUS
Righteous counsel leads to life, but wicked counsel to forsake God leads to disaster.

PREACHING IDEA
Listen to the one who rewards and judges.

PREACHING POINTERS
Joash's tragic story is a call to obedience in the face of ungodly counsel. Joash displays obedience for us, and the text demonstrates God's blessing of rewards. Even more vivid is the judgment that comes when Joash turns from YHWH and listens to ungodly counsel. Joash listened to a group of Judah's leaders that offered ungodly advice. Ungodly counsel still rings in our ears today. The voices in our culture can often be ungodly. This ungodly counsel can come through cultural traditions, entertainment, and through professionals such as lawyers, accountants, and counselors. It can be heard even from well-meaning family and employers. This passage reaffirms the call to obedience and focuses on the danger of listening to ungodly counsel.

2 Chronicles 25:1–26:2

EXEGETICAL IDEA
Because Amaziah did not trust YHWH completely and turned away from him, YHWH punished him with defeat and death.

THEOLOGICAL FOCUS
When God's people do not trust him completely and consistently, he disciplines them.

PREACHING IDEA
Partial trust in God leads to self-dependence and God's discipline.

PREACHING POINTERS
The unique element in Amaziah's life is his ambivalence. He is making up his mind to follow YHWH or not. His life is presented in two clearly defined parts: (1) the ambivalent section: whether to fully trust God or not; and then, (2) his descent into trusting only in himself, followed by God's discipline. This serves as a warning to us to not be half-hearted in our commitment to Christ. While Amaziah is a negative example, the writer doesn't leave us there. By mentioning that God has power to help and has "much more to give," the Chronicler gives us hope that we can have a wholehearted commitment to God.

2 Chronicles 26:3–27:9

EXEGETICAL IDEA
When Uzziah followed YHWH, YHWH helped him; when Uzziah became arrogant enough to violate YHWH's sanctity, YHWH punished him, but carried on his work through his obedient son Jotham.

THEOLOGICAL FOCUS
Although God may reward past obedience, he still disciplines those who pridefully presume upon his sanctity; however, future obedience may restore such rewards.

PREACHING IDEA
Help from God doesn't mean we can help ourselves.

PREACHING POINTERS
Uzziah should have set his pride aside when he received God's help, but he held onto it. One would think that if you open your hands for God's help you have emptied your hands of pride, but Uzziah held onto his pride. His pride provided a pathway to arrogance. In his arrogance he thought he could violate God's law. When we are given help by God, we can see that gift as a sign that we now have special privileges. It can make us think that since God helped us, we can help ourselves to whatever we want. Uzziah ignored the sanctity of the temple, and, if not careful, we can ignore the sanctity not of a place, but of a relationship. Our faith in Christ's death and resurrection brought us into a sacred relationship with God. How can we cling to prideful disobedience when we embrace the cross?

2 Chronicles 28:1–27

EXEGETICAL IDEA
When Ahaz stubbornly disobeyed YHWH, shut down YHWH's worship, and trusted in other kings and gods, he proved to be worse than the nation of Israel that listened to YHWH's warning, so YHWH punished him.

THEOLOGICAL FOCUS
Regardless of status, origin, or even past failure, God treats people according to their trust in him and obedience to him.

PREACHING IDEA
God's disciplining hand should lead us to obey.

PREACHING POINTERS
In this age of positive reinforcement in which there are no wrong answers, only those that still need some work, the harsh justice and discipline that God administers to Ahaz will be difficult to present. However, that is the thrust of the text. This is not a story that puts us over

Ahaz in judgment so that we can shake our heads and say, "Isn't he terrible?". We need to see that the story also includes the positive example of the northern leaders who obey God. This passage gives us a choice to let sin govern our lives, or to trust and obey. Sin results in God's discipline, so choose to trust and obey.

2 Chronicles 29:1–31:21

EXEGETICAL IDEA
When Hezekiah restored proper worship by addressing previous sins, uniting the people at the temple, and providing for future sacrifices, YHWH blessed all obedient Israel.

THEOLOGICAL FOCUS
God blesses worship that addresses past sins, promotes unity among believers, and provides for future ministry.

PREACHING IDEA
Restore and refresh the joy of worship.

PREACHING POINTERS
When the COVID pandemic hit, the church I was attending stopped having in-person worship services. We tried to continue to worship, sitting at home watching the leaders on a screen, listening to our own voices singing, and then working hard to stay focused on a message that seemed far away. Worship didn't stop; it was just very different. Perhaps that is the closest experience we have to the situation that Hezekiah had when he started his reign.

As the pandemic eased and in-person worship began to resume, it was like a fresh breeze. We could sing, pray, and listen to the Word with live people. Ahaz's wicked practices shut down the corporate worship of YHWH. This passage describes how worship of YHWH returned. It showed the first readers, and shows us, how our worship can be renewed and refreshed. They confessed sin, they celebrated the forgiveness and deliverance of Passover, and they provided for the advancement of future worship.

2 Chronicles 32:1–33

EXEGETICAL IDEA
YHWH acted as the true God when he responded to Hezekiah in war and sickness.

THEOLOGICAL FOCUS
YHWH is the only true God with the power to deliver those who trust him from any opposing force, whether spiritual or physical.

PREACHING IDEA
God's unending power requires our perpetual dependence.

PREACHING POINTERS

Was it too good to be true? Hezekiah's reign was filled with the obedience that came from a heart that sought after God. Would he, as other kings, become proud and end his reign in disobedience? That is what seems to have happened. The Assyrians attack—God delivers, and Hezekiah become proud. Thus, he joins the list of disappointing kings. But it doesn't end that way. He is confronted about his pride, repents, and humbles himself before YHWH. When God displays his enduring power, our response should be continued and total dependence upon him.

2 Chronicles 33:1–25

EXEGETICAL IDEA

The Lord forgave and restored King Manasseh, who directly violated God's covenant, when he humbled himself before the Lord, but did not forgive his son Amon when he did not humble himself.

THEOLOGICAL FOCUS

The Lord forgives and restores even the most disobedient when they humble themselves and repent, but judges those who arrogantly continue in sin.

PREACHING IDEA

God's grace isn't just amazing—it's astonishing.

PREACHING POINTERS

The author is proving to us that there is no evil so terrible that it is beyond God's surprising grace. It is easy to say that God forgives even the worst sin, but when faced with the extreme evil of Manasseh, do we really believe that God will forgive him? When greed overtakes one's life, when the spouse cheats again, when drugs are taken again and again, will God forgive them? When I find myself having blatantly disobeyed God in some harmful act or thought, will God forgive me? God included this story in his record to shout to us in terms we could not miss—that no matter how horrible my sin, he offers forgiveness and restoration. We can always humbly turn to him.

2 Chronicles 34:1–35:27

EXEGETICAL IDEA

Josiah followed YHWH and obeyed the law to an exemplary degree, but because of Judah's coming exile and Josiah's ignoring God's warning, Josiah experienced a surprising death instead of typical royal blessings.

THEOLOGICAL FOCUS

God accomplishes his plans in a way that is just both to his people as a whole and to individuals.

PREACHING IDEA

Don't drop the ball—trust the one who never does.

PREACHING POINTERS

At first glance, this story is only about finishing well. Josiah is wonderful up to the last few days of his life. Certainly, this is part of the message, but there is another part that is the motivation for us to finish well. This passage also teaches us that God will always accomplish his plans. Josiah's obedience or disobedience did not alter God's plans for him or for the nation. We can always trust our great God because he will always keep his promises. He will always accomplish his will, no matter what we do. God's good and just hand is not dependent upon us.

2 Chronicles 36:1–23

EXEGETICAL IDEA

Even though YHWH justly judged Judah and Jerusalem for not listening to him, he held out hope for the future.

THEOLOGICAL FOCUS

Judgment is not God's final word for his people.

PREACHING IDEA

Our sins are many; his mercy is more.

PREACHING POINTERS

The books of 1–2 Chronicles all point to God's people being able to properly worship him under the leadership of a perfect king. Jesus is our perfect eternal king who enables us to worship God as we should. This closing pericope shows us, once again, that human kings are not sufficient to lead us or enable us to properly worship God. The rebellious sins of Judah and her kings remind us that we too are sinful. Sin leads to God's sure and just judgment, but in his love God offers us mercy.

ABBREVIATIONS

GENERAL ABBREVIATIONS

ANE	Ancient Near East(ern)
B.C.	Before Christ
HB	Hebrew Bible
LXX	Septuagint (the Greek OT)
MT	Masoretic Text
NT	New Testament
OT	Old Testament

TECHNICAL ABBREVIATIONS

cf.	compare (*confer*)	impf.	imperfect
ch(s).	chapter(s)	inf.	infinitive
ed(s).	editor(s)	masc.	masculine
e.g.	for example (*exempli gratia*)	n.	note; footnote
esp.	especially	ptc.	participle
etc.	and the rest (*et cetera*)	s.v.	under the word (*sub verbo*)
Heb.	Hebrew	v(v).	verse(s)
i.e.	that is (*id est*)		

BIBLICAL SOURCES

Old Testament		*Old Testament (continued)*	
Gen.	Genesis	Neh.	Nehemiah
Exod.	Exodus	Esther	Esther
Lev.	Leviticus	Job	Job
Num.	Numbers	Ps./Pss.	Psalm(s)
Deut.	Deuteronomy	Prov.	Proverbs
Josh.	Joshua	Eccl.	Ecclesiastes
Judg.	Judges	Song	Song of Songs
Ruth	Ruth	Isa.	Isaiah
1 Sam.	1 Samuel	Jer.	Jeremiah
2 Sam.	2 Samuel	Lam.	Lamentations
1 Kings	1 Kings	Ezek.	Ezekiel
2 Kings	2 Kings	Dan.	Daniel
1 Chron.	1 Chronicles	Hos.	Hosea
2 Chron.	2 Chronicles	Joel	Joel
Ezra	Ezra	Amos	Amos

Old Testament (continued)

Obad.	Obadiah
Jonah	Jonah
Mic.	Micah
Nah.	Nahum
Hab.	Habakkuk
Zeph.	Zephaniah
Hag.	Haggai
Zech.	Zechariah
Mal.	Malachi

New Testament

Matt.	Matthew
Mark	Mark
Luke	Luke
John	John
Acts	Acts
Rom.	Romans
1 Cor.	1 Corinthians
2 Cor.	2 Corinthians

New Testament (continued)

Gal.	Galatians
Eph.	Ephesians
Phil.	Philippians
Col.	Colossians
1 Thess.	1 Thessalonians
2 Thess.	2 Thessalonians
1 Tim.	1 Timothy
2 Tim.	2 Timothy
Titus	Titus
Philem.	Philemon
Heb.	Hebrews
James	James
1 Peter	1 Peter
2 Peter	2 Peter
1 John	1 John
2 John	2 John
3 John	3 John
Jude	Jude
Rev.	Revelation

REFERENCES

BDB	Brown, Francis, S. R. Driver, and Charles A. Briggs. *A Hebrew and English Lexicon of the Old Testament.* Oxford: Clarendon, 1907.
BHS	Biblia Hebraica Stuttgartensia
GKC	Gesenius, Wilhelm. *Gesenius' Hebrew Grammar.* Edited by Emil Kautzsch. Translated by Arthur E. Cowley. 2nd ed. Oxford: Clarendon, 1910.
HALOT	Koehler, Ludwig, Walter Baumgartner, and Johann J. Stamm. *The Hebrew and Aramaic Lexicon of the Old Testament.* Translated and edited under the supervision of Mervyn E. J. Richardson. 2 vols. Leiden: Brill, 2001.

PERIODICALS

ABR	*Australian Biblical Review*
AUSS	*Andrews University Seminary Studies*
BA	*Biblical Archaeologist*
BAR	*Biblical Archaeology Review*
BASOR	*Bulletin of the American Schools of Overseas Research*
Bib	*Biblica*
BSac	*Bibliotheca Sacra*
CBQ	*The Catholic Biblical Quarterly*
HeyJ	*Heythrop Journal*
HTR	*Harvard Theological Review*
HUCA	*Hebrew Union College Annual*

JANES	*Journal of Ancient Near Eastern Studies*
JAOS	*Journal of the American Oriental Society*
JBL	*Journal of Biblical Literature*
JETS	*Journal of the Evangelical Theological Society*
JHebS	*Journal of Hebrew Scriptures*
JJS	*Journal of Jewish Studies*
JNES	*Journal of Near Eastern Studies*
JSOT	*Journal for the Study of the Old Testament*
JSQ	*Jewish Studies Quarterly*
JSS	*Journal of Semitic Studies*
JTS	*Journal of Theological Studies*
NovT	*Novum Testamentum*
OLP	*Orientalia Lovaniensia Periodica*
Or	*Orientalia* NS
RB	*Revue biblique*
SJOT	*Scandinavian Journal of the Old Testament*
TLZ	*Theologische Literaturzeitung*
TynBul	*Tyndale Bulletin*
VT	*Vetus Testamentum*
WTJ	*Westminster Theological Journal*
ZAW	*Zeitschrift für alttestamentliche Wissenschaft*

BOOK SERIES

AB	Anchor (Yale) Bible
AcBib	Academia Biblica
AIL	Ancient Israel and Its Literature
AOAT	Alter Orient und Altes Testament
AOTC	Abingdon Old Testament Commentaries
BJS	Brown Judaic Studies
BLS	Bible and Literature Series
BZAW	Beihefte zur Zeitschrift für die alttestamentliche Wissenschaft
ConBOT	Coniectanea Biblica Old Testament Series
FAT	Forschungen zum Alten Testament
FOTL	Forms of Old Testament Literature
FRLANT	Forschungen zur Religion und Literatur des Alten und Neuen Testaments
HAT	Handbuch zum Alten Testament
HBM	Hebrew Bible Monographs
HCOT	Historical Commentary of the Old Testament
HSM	Harvard Semitic Monographs
ICC	International Critical Commentary
JSOTSup	Journal for the Study of the Old Testament Supplement
LHBOTS	Library of Hebrew Bible/Old Testament Studies
NCBC	New Century Bible Commentary
NIVAC	New International Version Application Commentary

OBT	Overtures to Biblical Theology
OTL	Old Testament Library
OTS	Old Testament Studies
PBM	Paternoster Biblical Monographs
PFES	Publications of the Finnish Exegetical Society
RBS	Resources for Biblical Study
SBTS	Sources for Biblical and Theological Study
SSN	Studia Semitica Neerlandica
SymS	Symposium Series
VTSup	Vetus Testamentum Supplement
WAWSup	Writings from the Ancient World Supplement Series
WBC	Word Biblical Commentary
YNER	Yale Near Eastern Researches

BIBLE TRANSLATIONS

CSB	Christian Standard Bible
ESV	English Standard Version
HCSB	Holman Christian Standard Bible
JPS	Jewish Publication Society
KJV	King James Version
NASB	New American Standard Bible
NET	New English Translation
NIV	New International Version
NKJV	New King James Version
NLT	New Living Translation
NRSV	New Revised Standard Version

INTRODUCTION TO 1 & 2 CHRONICLES

OVERVIEW OF 1 & 2 CHRONICLES

Author: Anonymous, generally referred to as the Chronicler

Place of Writing: In or around Jerusalem

Original Readers: Jewish people living in the traditional land of Israel and in the Diaspora

Date: Late fifth/early fourth century B.C.

Historical Setting: The small sparsely populated and economically underdeveloped postexilic province of Yehud within the Persian Empire

Occasion: Amid competing religious and political centers, the book encourages the postexilic community that they are still YHWH's people, and as his people they have a responsibility to participate in and support the ritual worship of YHWH in the Jerusalem temple.

Literary Genre: Prophetic historiography

Theological Emphasis: The Chronicler emphasizes that Jerusalem is the place YHWH has chosen for the temple and that YHWH rewards all the tribes of Israel who fulfill their fundamental duty to support the Jerusalem temple and the worship that takes place there.

AUTHORSHIP OF BOOK

Who wrote 1 and 2 Chronicles? It seems this simple question should receive a simple answer. However, the answer to the question has always been a bit complicated. Like other Old Testament historical books, Chronicles is an anonymous text; nowhere does it specify who wrote it. Jewish (and Christian) tradition has identified Ezra as the author. However, the tradition is not quite so simple. For instance, the Babylonian Talmud Bava Batra 15a, one of the earliest preserved statements regarding the authorship of Chronicles, assigns Ezra authorship for part of the book but Nehemiah for the rest

(see Talshir 1988a, 359; Viezel 2009a, 244–48). Later rabbinic traditions maintain Ezra as the author, ignoring Nehemiah, but also claim that the prophets Haggai, Zechariah, and Malachi somehow assisted Ezra in writing the book (Viezel 2009b, 9–13). Although the traditions point primarily to Ezra, they do not claim that he is the sole author.

The traditions do not assign Ezra sole authorship at least in part because of the genealogy of David (1 Chron. 3:10–24). The genealogy of David extends for at least twenty-five generations. With a conservative estimate for the length of a generation, the last names of the list would occur around 425 B.C. at the earliest and more probably between 400 B.C. and 350 B.C. Therefore, the genealogy lists individuals who lived later than Ezra. For this reason, Bava Batra 15a assigns the rest of the material to Nehemiah while later traditions refer to the prophets as a means for explaining how Ezra could record genealogical information from the future (Viezel 2009b, 8–12). Unfortunately, these proposals still do not resolve all the questions raised by Ezra being the author of the book.

Comparing Chronicles to Ezra and Nehemiah raises further questions about Ezra as the author. Although the books share many features in common (e.g., postexilic outlook and characteristics of Late Biblical Hebrew), the works differ in important matters, including some specific linguistic features (Japhet 1968, 334–71; Thronveit 1982, 201–15; Williamson 1977, 52–58; but see Talshir 1988b, 168–93), compositional techniques (see Steins 2015, 245), and theological emphases (for a good summary, see Jonker 2013a, 11). This evidence points to an author other than Ezra or Nehemiah.

Unfortunately, if Ezra is not the author, there is little evidence for determining the specific identity of the author. For this reason, it has become customary to refer to the author of Chronicles as the "Chronicler." Although the content of Chronicles does not indicate a specific individual as the author, it suggests that the Chronicler was most likely a scribe (perhaps a Levite) attached in some way to the temple administration, living in or around Jerusalem.

At the same time, identifying the Chronicler simply as the author of the book can hide other complicated matters. Even though it is handy to speak of the Chronicler, one should not imagine this person sitting down to write this long text on a scroll one day. One of the key features of Chronicles is that it incorporates material from previous biblical texts into its own work. About half of Chronicles contains parallel accounts to Samuel and Kings. The genealogical

Ezra the Scribe,
Meister des Codex Amiatinus. Public domain.

information in the beginning of the book draws heavily on Genesis, Numbers, and Joshua. The hymn sung after delivering the ark to Jerusalem (1 Chron. 16) combines Psalms 96, 105, and 106. As a result, Chronicles is a complex piece of literature. Authorship in this case includes not only composing passages, but also selecting, arranging, and editing material from various kinds of sources to make a coherent account of Israel's past. As a result, the author's message is found not only in the specific claims made by the text, but also in the way that the author arranges the units of text and how he links them together. For instance, the listing of David's mighty warriors occurs toward the end of the books of Samuel (2 Sam. 23:8–39); however, it occurs immediately following the death of Saul in Chronicles (1 Chron. 11:10–47). By arranging the material in this way, the Chronicler demonstrates the support David receives from all the competent warriors of Israel from the beginning of his reign. This point contributes to the Chronicler's picture of all Israel united under Davidic leadership in worshipping YHWH.

DATE OF WRITING

Within the OT's storyline, Chronicles emerges in the final stages. The early stages consist of Israel becoming a people, securing a land, and establishing a monarchy and then two monarchies. The middle stages consist of Israel's failure toward YHWH and YHWH's judgment through exile. The final stages consist of some of Israel's leadership returning to their homeland, reconstructing its temple, and learning how to live as a distinct people within a foreign empire. One could summarize the storyline into the following three stages: possessing the land (preexilic), losing the land (exilic), and returning to the land (postexilic).

To be sure, Chronicles emerges during the postexilic period. However, the postexilic period spans centuries, and scholars have proposed dates for Chronicles ranging from approximately 500 B.C. to 150 B.C. One way to narrow down the date of Chronicles is to examine the significant imperial and cultural changes that took place during the postexilic period. During the first part of the postexilic period, the Achaemenid Empire (Persia) dominated the ancient Near East, including the land of Israel. Its imperial control of the region lasted for a couple of centuries until 330 B.C. when Alexander the Great conquered the region. In the aftermath of Persia's fall, the cultural landscape of the entire region shifted, beginning what is often called the Hellenistic period.

In Chronicles, one can find clear traces of Persian influence on the book. In terms of direct reference, the final verses record how the Persian emperor Cyrus proclaims that one belonging to YHWH's people may return to the homeland and build YHWH's temple. In terms of language, the book borrows Persian words (for details, see Kalimi 2005a, 41–42), including the name of currency (daric; 1 Chron. 29:7). In contrast, one cannot find clear traces of Hellenistic influence on the book. In terms of direct reference, the book does not plainly refer to any events of the Hellenistic period. In terms of language, the book shows no signs of Greek influence. This type of evidence favors a Persian date—or at the latest, an early Hellenistic date for the book.

Greek Influence

Although clear evidence of Greek influence upon Chronicles is difficult to find, one should not conclude that Chronicles operates in a different world than classical Greek literature. Within the ancient world of trade and commerce, it is likely that some level of cultural interaction took place within the Mediterranean world even before Alexander the Great. Some scholars (notably, Knoppers 2003b, 627–50, and Van Seters 1997, 8–54) have pointed to similarities in historiographical methods as possible evidence for such cultural interaction. However, since such interaction took place even during the Persian period, these similarities do not bear much significance for establishing the date of Chronicles.

The other factor to consider when dating the book is determining the number of generations recorded for David's genealogy. As mentioned above, the genealogy of David extends into a period beyond Ezra and Nehemiah. However, the precise number of generations following Jehoiachin/Jeconiah (1 Chron. 3:17) is not clear because of interpretive questions raised by manuscript evidence for the verses (MT suggests six while LXX suggests twelve or fourteen). As a result, if one interprets the text to record just a few generations following Jehoiachin (e.g., five), then the text points to a date around 400 B.C.; if one interprets the text to record several generations (e.g., fourteen), then the text points to a date well within the Hellenistic period. If one takes a result between the extremes, which seems likely, the lineage extends to sometime between 400–350 B.C., that is, the late Persian period.

HISTORICAL SETTING

The conditions in which the Chronicler operated were largely long-lasting aftereffects of the Babylonian exile. The Babylonians put an end to the southern kingdom Judah as a political state. They destroyed and plundered Jerusalem. They devastated the areas around Jerusalem as well. Among the key leaders of the nation, those they did not kill they exiled to Babylon. This devastation and exile had innumerable political, social, cultural, economic, and religious ramifications for the people of Judah.

First, the Babylonian exile left Jerusalem and much of the region around it in bad shape. When the Babylonian Empire fell to the Persians, matters appeared more hopeful. The Persians allowed those living in exile to return to their homeland, redevelop the former capital Jerusalem, and build a temple for their God, YHWH. Still, during the time of the Chronicler, Jerusalem was a small capital of a small, politically insignificant, and economically underdeveloped province within the Persian Empire. That province was called Yehud, recalling the legacy of the southern kingdom Judah (which is pronounced more like Yehudah in Hebrew). Despite the more favorable conditions in the Persian Empire, Yehud had no political independence and certainly no king.

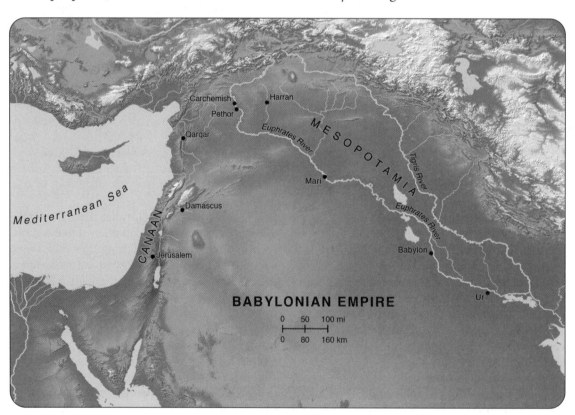

Babylonian Empire. Map by A. D. Riddle.

In contrast to Yehud, the Persian province Samaria (recalling the northern kingdom Israel) generally fared well during the period of the Babylonians and into the Persian period. As a result, the province, in many ways the inheritance of the northern tribes, possessed a larger population, greater political influence, and a more prosperous economy. The relationship between the two provinces and their populations was a question that needed to be faced as Yehud reestablished its capital and rebuilt its temple.

Yehud and Samaria

The relationship between the two provinces is quite complex. Although there appears to have been tension between the two provinces, at times, they also shared a great deal in common. As Gary Knoppers has argued, the two groups, although distinct, shared a great deal of cultural tradition. He argues that this cultural overlap cannot be explained simply from a common ancestry but requires significant interaction between the two provinces (2013, 131–34).

Second, the Babylonian exile dispersed many from Judah into lands beyond Palestine. Besides those forcibly exiled to Babylon, where they started new lives, others moved because of the conditions in Palestine. They scattered among other nations, building lives where they went. As they went, many retained their identities as those from Judah who worshipped YHWH. As a result, during the Chronicler's time one could say that the worship of YHWH had become an international religion. Even though the worshippers were almost exclusively descendants of Israel (whether from the southern or northern tribes), where they lived affected their relationship to their homeland, to Jerusalem, and to other nations. Furthermore, various communities had established temples of their own (e.g., Elephantine, Gerizim, and Leontopolis). The rebuilding of the Jerusalem temple required setting aside significant resources to maintain the worship there. In this international setting, the status of the Jerusalem temple in relation to those outside Yehud required clarification. Furthermore, given the poor conditions in

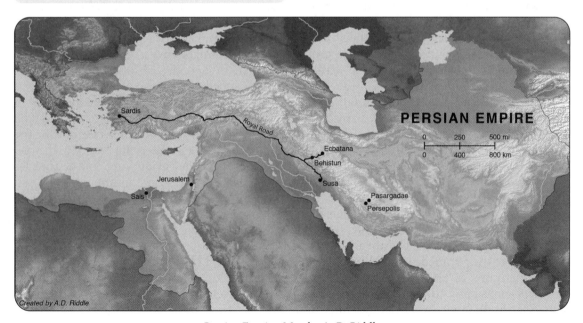

Persian Empire. Map by A. D. Riddle.

Yehud, support for the temple and its personnel required consistent encouragement, as Haggai 1 and Nehemiah 13:10–13 demonstrate. Unlike other temples in the Persian period, the Jerusalem temple did not have extensive lands used to support itself (Knoppers 2003a, 112).

Third, the areas of the southern kingdom Judah where Benjaminites lived were not hit as hard by the Babylonians. As a result, the tribe of Benjamin rose in prominence within the region during the exilic period. The Benjaminite city Mizpah functioned as an administrative capital during the exilic period, while Gibeon likely served as a center of religious activity (see Blenkinsopp 2003, 95–99; Giffone 2016, 85–99; Jonker 2013b, 92–94, 141; Lipschits 2006, 34–35). Even after the Persians allowed the exiled community to return and establish Jerusalem as a capital, the tribe of Benjamin maintained a significant population and prominent leadership in the province.

OCCASION

The book of Chronicles closes with a picture of the Babylonian destruction and exile of Judah, followed by Cyrus's proclamation inviting YHWH's people in exile to return to their homeland to build a temple in Jerusalem. The proclamation points to an occasion for the writing; however, the Chronicler produced the book several generations later. As pointed out in the Historical Setting section above, the Babylonian exile created long-lasting effects for the people of Judah, even after Cyrus's proclamation. The Babylonian exile and its aftermath raised a theological question: Are the people still YHWH's people such that he still cares for them? The Chronicler addresses this theological question by encouraging the people that they are still YHWH's people and that he has not abandoned them, despite their immediate conditions.

Furthermore, as YHWH's people they still have a responsibility toward YHWH in worship. Specifically, the Chronicler reminds the postexilic community that YHWH has chosen Jerusalem as the city for his temple. As a result the Chronicler writes to encourage the people, wherever they may live, to return to Jerusalem and support it so that the proper ritual worship of YHWH can continue. YHWH accepts this type of proper worship and will pour out blessings upon those who engage in it and support it.

Persian imperial policy would have provided another catalyst for the Chronicler's work. Not only did Persian policy allow for those exiled to return to construct the temple in Jerusalem, but it also allowed for the development and implementation of regional laws, especially those associated with the temple (although a matter of considerable debate; see Knoppers 2001, 115–34, for a discussion of the issue helpful in the context of Chronicles). An apparent desire of the Yehudite community, as shown in Ezra and Nehemiah, was to restore the former practices of their ancestors, particularly those outlined in Mosaic law (see Davis 2019, 138–42). This desire to restore the former things may have also prompted the Chronicler to survey history with a focus on Judah and its former worship practices as authorized especially by Moses and David. This survey provided a portrait of what the descendants of Israel had been so that the community might have a sense of what it could be. Even though the Chronicler's work never hints at rebellion against the Persian Empire, it does paint a picture of YHWH's people living in their land according to their tribes, worshipping YHWH at the Jerusalem temple, supporting the temple personnel, observing the Mosaic law, and being led by a Davidic king. The Chronicler encourages the postexilic community to remain faithful to YHWH through proper worship, as they wait for YHWH to bring about his blessings on the people and the land.

LITERARY GENRE

With few exceptions, Chronicles is a series of narrative accounts of past events. In other words, Chronicles is writing about history or historiography. However, to refer to the book as merely historiography does not do the book justice. First, the book includes more than just narrative accounts of the past. The first nine chapters contain genealogies peppered with information about military numbers, settlement patterns, and personal anecdotes. Within the narrative account of David's reign, the book pauses the narrative in places to include the following: a long record of military information regarding the troops supporting David (1 Chron. 11–12); a long listing of temple personnel consisting of priests, Levites, musicians, gatekeepers, judges, and other officials (1 Chron. 23–26); and a listing of leaders within David's administration (1 Chron. 27). This information is not necessary nor customary to include in a writing of history.

Second, a mere interest in the past does not drive the Chronicler to create this work. The Chronicler is interested in teaching his audience with examples from the past. As a result, he includes or removes certain details to make the teaching point clearer. One of his primary teaching aims is to illustrate and reinforce the principle that YHWH rewards obedience and punishes disobedience. In account after account, the Chronicler presents obedience immediately followed by reward, and disobedience immediately followed by punishment (e.g., for obedience, see beginning of Jehoshaphat's reign, 2 Chron. 17; for disobedience, see Ahaz's reign, 2 Chron. 28). In other passages, he states the principle explicitly (e.g., 1 Chron. 28:9; 2 Chron. 15:2). Although history itself often reveals the same principle (esp. ancient historiography), the degree to which the principle informs what is included and omitted, the sequence of the events, and the way in which the events are recounted reveals that the Chronicler intends to do more than just provide a simple account of past events—he wants to teach with them.

Third, the Chronicler presents his picture of the past as a means for pointing to the future. His work is really a call to action. As such it resembles the work of the prophets, who interpreted their past and present circumstances to discern the proper course of action to avoid a future disaster or to secure a future peace. In fact, one can see traces of prophetic influence throughout the Chronicler's work. The Chronicler draws on several prophets as sources for the accounts of Judah's kings (for an exploration of the nature of these sources, see Knoppers 2021, 137–61). Prophets occur frequently to warn someone not to keep taking their same course of action. The book even closes with a reference to the prophet Jeremiah, pointing to the future hope that Jeremiah (among other prophets) foresees.

As a result, it is appropriate to modify the genre of Chronicles from merely historiography to prophetic historiography. Chronicles draws on the prophets throughout the work as it connects "the past with the present by the interpretation of events" (Schweitzer 2011, 59). Like the prophets, the Chronicler interprets past events in light of YHWH's justice; that is, he rewards obedience and punishes disobedience. Like the prophets, the Chronicler is writing to call for action from his postexilic audience. Like the prophets, he is calling the postexilic audience to worship YHWH properly and exclusively. The book is prophetic in its sources, in its outlook, and in its purpose.

THEOLOGICAL THEMES

One can summarize the theological message by exploring the following four topics in the book: (1) covenant, (2) cult, (3) kingdom, and (4) community. Although I will treat each topic distinctly, they are not isolated from one another. Instead, they interact and interrelate in many ways and on many levels.

Covenant

The narrative of Chronicles contains a repeated, consistent plot pattern throughout its pages: obedience to YHWH leads to blessing; disobedience leads to disaster. This pattern reflects the principle of retribution that governs the Chronicler's view of Israel's past. In virtually every narrative, the Chronicler shows that the consequences follow almost immediately upon the actions (e.g., Asa's obedience leads to his success, 2 Chron. 14:3–5; Ahaz's disobedience leads to his military defeat, 2 Chron. 28:1–5). Generally, the consequences of actions do not extend beyond those who perform them. As a result, the reign of each king appears as an opportunity for Israel to start over, either toward obedience or disobedience (Ben Zvi 2006a, 166–68). To a large degree, each generation determines its own fate. At the same time, each king's reign is not completely isolated from the others (e.g., Ahaziah is buried because of his grandfather Jehoshaphat, 2 Chron. 22:9) such that Israel's disobedience eventually leads to destruction and exile for the people (Knoppers 2021, 312–52).

This principle of retribution is a consistent theological theme throughout Chronicles, but the Chronicler does not present it as some abstract immutable law of the moral order. For the Chronicler, retribution operates within YHWH's covenantal relationship with Israel (Kelly 2003, 213). The Chronicler primarily derives his understanding of the nature of that covenantal relationship from the law of Moses. Mosaic law certainly speaks to the principle of retribution (e.g., Lev. 26; Deut. 28; 30:15–18). It also points to the core of this covenant relationship: YHWH is Israel's God and Israel is YHWH's people (e.g., Exod. 19–20; Lev. 26:12). For this reason, the Chronicler repeatedly shows that worshipping YHWH exclusively and properly is obedience, but failing to worship him exclusively and properly is disobedience (see Wright 2013, 209–11). Furthermore, the law of Moses provides the standards for worshipping YHWH properly. With this covenant background in mind, obedience takes on the concrete forms of seeking YHWH by removing other gods and their implements of worship, looking after the Jerusalem temple, and following Mosaic legislation regarding the proper practices of worship. These practices

honor the covenantal relationship between YHWH and Israel as Israel treats YHWH as God and YHWH cares for his people.

Seeking YHWH

One of the Chronicler's common expressions to describe obedience to YHWH is "seeking" (דרשׁ) him. The expression represents more than a specific action or a momentary decision. As Steven McKenzie puts it, "Seeking Yahweh is perhaps the Chronicler's favorite expression for personal devotion to God" (2004, 57). In contemporary language, one might use the term "follow" in a religious sense (e.g., a Christian follows Jesus). It is an expression of a lifestyle of devotion (e.g., 1 Chron. 16:11; 22:19; 2 Chron. 12:14; 26:5). Most often, the expression carries overtones of participating properly in the ritual worship directed exclusively to YHWH. For instance, the prophet Jehu commends Jehoshaphat because he has removed items of pagan worship (Asherah poles) and committed himself to seek YHWH—that is, to worship YHWH through the proper ritual means.

Retribution is a fundamental part of almost every covenant. A covenant outlines rewards for obedience and punishments for disobedience. Chronicles demonstrates that YHWH is faithful in carrying out those terms of his covenant with Israel. At the same time, Chronicles shows that YHWH is "more than faithful." He exceeds the covenant's requirements and always does so in Israel's favor. First, even though the Chronicler usually places the consequences immediately following their actions, in cases of disobedience, the narrative often breaks between the actions and consequences to include a prophet's warning of immediate disaster (e.g., Elijah's warning to Jehoram, 2 Chron. 21:12–15; see also Japhet 2009, 138–40). YHWH sends these prophetic figures to ensure that those disobeying are aware of their obligations and aware that their actions violate those obligations. Heeding the warning avoids the disaster, but ignoring the warning brings the disaster. Such warnings go beyond covenant retribution.

Second, YHWH forgives those who repent. The reign of King Manasseh illustrates this point in the sharpest terms: even though Manasseh worships many other gods, violates numerous Mosaic stipulations, and ignores prophetic warnings, when he turns to YHWH in his distress and humbles himself, YHWH forgives him and returns him to his throne in Jerusalem (2 Chron. 33). Such forgiveness goes beyond covenant retribution.

Third, YHWH restores Israel to rebuild the Jerusalem temple. At the end of the book, YHWH stirs up Cyrus to declare a return to Jerusalem to build the temple. YHWH initiates this restoration for Israel. Again, such restoration goes beyond covenant retribution. Consequently, Chronicles shows that not only is YHWH faithful to carry out the covenant obligations of retribution, but he is also more than faithful. He is gracious. As J. G. McConville puts it, "The writer's real concern is to show that, however low the people of God sink, their cause is never totally lost, but there is always a way back, through repentance, to God's favor. Similarly, that favor can so easily be squandered by a lapse of faithfulness" (1984, 5).

Cult

Cult—that is, formal ritual worship—plays a central role in the book of Chronicles. Chronicles repeatedly points to aspects of the cult important for all Israel. First, the Chronicler understands Israel's ritual worship to be a perpetual obligation for all Israel. As Solomon says, "Look, I am ready to build a temple to honor the LORD my God and to dedicate it to him in order to burn fragrant incense before him, to set out the bread that is regularly displayed, and to offer burnt sacrifices each morning and evening, and on Sabbaths, new moon festivals, and at other times appointed by the LORD our God. This is something Israel must do on a permanent basis" (2 Chron. 2:4 [HB 3] NET). For the Chronicler,

worshipping YHWH is not just a personal or informal piety or devotion to YHWH. It has a concrete manifestation in the sacred rituals, practiced in sacred space by sacred personnel with sacred implements and sacred accoutrements. In fact, devotion to YHWH consists of respecting these matters (see esp. Abijah's words to Jeroboam in 2 Chron. 13:10–11).

Second, the Chronicler points to the exclusive nature of ritual worship. The Chronicler emphasizes that there is only one God, YHWH; one place for ritual worship, Jerusalem; one tribe to minister in the temple, the Levites; one family to offer ritual sacrifice, the Aaronic priests. This exclusive worship precludes syncretism with other religions; therefore, Israel cannot worship YHWH along with other gods or use foreign elements (idols, Asherah poles, etc.). For instance, when the Chronicler records that Ahaz worships Aramean gods, he then immediately describes how Ahaz closes the Jerusalem temple (2 Chron. 28:22–24). Ahaz cannot worship other gods and YHWH at the same time. Furthermore, the Chronicler records that when Jeroboam appoints priests from tribes other than Levi and creates the gold calves as images for YHWH, Jeroboam in fact forsakes YHWH (2 Chron. 13:8–10). Worshipping YHWH is exclusive; therefore, for the Chronicler, to worship YHWH inappropriately is not to worship him at all (see also Japhet 2009, 169–70; Lynch 2014b, 75–78).

Third, the primary source for evaluating Israel's ritual worship is the law of Moses. At the same time, the Chronicler shows how David (and his descendants, to a lesser degree) extends Mosaic stipulations to form another source for Israel's ritual worship. For instance, Mosaic law indicates that YHWH will choose a place to dwell; however, Chronicles shows how the Davidic covenant specifies the place as Jerusalem. Furthermore, Mosaic law says virtually nothing about the role of music in worship; however, David extends the law to include music as a vital part of Israel's ritual worship. In this way both

Moses and David serve as important sources for determining the shape of Israel's ritual worship (see De Vries 1988, 619–39).

Fourth, the Chronicler inextricably links ritual worship with a proper attitude of the worshipper. Three expressions capture the essence of what the Chronicler expects in the attitude of the worshipper. First, he speaks of having a "perfect heart" (לֵב/לְבָב שָׁלֵם), referring to sincere devotion to YHWH (1 Chron. 28:9; 29:9, 19; 2 Chron. 16:9; 19:9; 25:2). Second, he speaks of willingness (נדב) to support Israel's ritual worship. He recounts how Israel offers acceptable contributions for building the Jerusalem temple; they do so generously and willingly, under no compulsion (1 Chron. 29:6–17). Third, he speaks of the people's joy and rejoicing (שָׂמַח, שִׂמְחָה). Such joy accompanies various important events in Israel's ritual worship, including transferring the ark to Jerusalem (1 Chron. 15:25), offering contributions for building the temple (1 Chron. 29:9, 17; 2 Chron. 24:10), dedicating the Jerusalem temple (2 Chron. 7:10), swearing an oath to worship YHWH exclusively (2 Chron. 15:15), and celebrating Passover and the Feast of Unleavened Bread (2 Chron. 30:21–26). Often, the musical service of the temple reflects this joy as well (1 Chron. 15:16; 2 Chron. 23:13, 18; 29:30). Furthermore, the attitude of the worshipper is so important for the Chronicler that YHWH may forgive a ritual offense for those who worship with the proper attitude (see 2 Chron. 30:18–19). As McKenzie states, "For all the importance that he attaches to rules and liturgy, the Chronicler recognizes that it is not these but the attitude of the worshiper that forms the essence of religion that is pleasing to God" (2004, 50).

Kingdom

The book of Chronicles is a book about a kingdom: the kingdom of YHWH. Although the book is about this kingdom, it does not define the kingdom in abstract terms. Instead, it describes it in the concrete events and institutions of ancient Israel. As a feature of this concrete description, the book focuses its attention on the Davidic dynasty. Unlike the book of Kings, Chronicles does not address other kings, particularly kings of the northern kingdom, except as they encounter those of the Davidic line. The reason, as 2 Chronicles 13:5 explains, is that YHWH has entrusted his kingdom over Israel to the sons of David.

Chronicles presents the primary task of Israel's king as unifying all Israel to worship YHWH at the place he has chosen: the Jerusalem temple. Throughout the book, upright kings care for the temple and bring Israel together to worship YHWH properly there (for details, see Cudworth 2016, 9–91). Alongside this responsibility, the kings also play a role in organizing the worship at the temple extending, but not contradicting, Mosaic stipulations concerning worshipping YHWH properly. The kings extend these stipulations based on changing historical circumstances, such as modifying Levitical duties once the ark rests in a permanent place (e.g., 1 Chron. 23:25–26; 2 Chron. 35:3–4). The Davidic kings should be a catalyst for all Israel to worship YHWH. Furthermore, at their best, the Davidic kings' reach stretches beyond Israel to other nations. Chronicles demonstrates this point when even foreign kings acknowledge YHWH as God because of the Davidic king (e.g., Solomon and Hiram, 2 Chron. 2:12 [HB 11]; Solomon and the queen of Sheba, 2 Chron. 9:8). As a result, the Davidic king's role points to YHWH as king of Israel and the nations throughout history.

Unfortunately, many Davidic kings fail to fulfill their role. As a result Judah, the nation they rule, comes to an end in the closing chapter of Chronicles. However, the book's focus on YHWH's kingdom reassures the reader that although a Davidic king does not rule over Israel as in times past, YHWH still rules. YHWH reveals his continued rule by raising up the Persian emperor Cyrus to authorize the return to

Jerusalem and the rebuilding of the temple there (2 Chron. 36:22–23). As a result, for the Chronicler's time, even though Israel did not have a Davidic king on the throne, YHWH still ruled and worked for the benefit of his people through the Persian Empire. Ultimately, however, the Chronicler expresses hope that a Davidic king will rule in the future.

Hope for the Davidic dynasty lies, in part, in the hope for Israel. The role of the Davidic king to bring Israel together to worship YHWH in Jerusalem supports Israel's responsibility as a people to worship YHWH: "The election of the royal House of David is therefore understood in the context of Israel's election; it is part of Israel's universal task to glorify YHWH" (Koorevaar 2015, 219). Since YHWH has not abandoned Israel forever, he will not abandon the Davidic line forever.

In summary, YHWH is king. He has entrusted his rule over Israel to the Davidic dynasty from Judah. The primary responsibility of the king is to gather Israel to worship YHWH properly, especially at the Jerusalem temple. As a result, the nations will also praise YHWH. Even though the Davidic line failed to fulfill its responsibility, YHWH still rules and, from the Chronicler's point of view, will someday restore the Davidic dynasty.

Community

One might say that in the postexilic situation the Chronicler faces an identity crisis, not a crisis of his own identity but of his people's identity. Among a host of options for defining his people's identity, the Chronicler chooses to focus on the following aspects of his people. First, he identifies his community as Israel and defines this community as YHWH's people. In one sense, Israel is always YHWH's people because of the covenant relationship between YHWH and Israel (see above). In another sense, Israel must strive to be YHWH's people, pledging that they will worship him exclusively (2 Chron. 23:16–19). The Chronicler reminds his community of their identity as YHWH's people to encourage them to act as YHWH's people, even if they have not been acting that way previously.

Second, the Chronicler focuses on the continuity of Israel as YHWH's people throughout their history. The genealogies at the front of the book first point in this direction by showing how the Chronicler's people are descendants of the ancestor Israel/Jacob. Israel as a people is not some new development, even though the political form governing this people (the Persian province Yehud) may be. Israel has a long, rich heritage. At the same time, Israel's continuity consists of more than just lineage. It includes their institutions of worship. The Chronicler goes to significant lengths to present the Jerusalem temple as the continuation and fulfillment of the wilderness tabernacle (see commentary on 2 Chron. 2–4). He shows that the priests follow the instructions of their ancestor Aaron (1 Chron. 6:49; 24:19). He includes David's organizing the priests into twenty-four courses, a practice observed during the Second Temple period. As a result, the Chronicler demonstrates that despite Israel's changing historical circumstances, a thread of continuity as YHWH's people runs throughout.

Third, the Chronicler highlights that Israel as YHWH's people entails all Israel, that is, those from all the tribes, including the northern tribes. Again, the genealogies first point in this direction, since the Chronicler mentions the tribes within the lists. At the same time, the Chronicler maintains a tension throughout his work. On the one hand, the Chronicler apparently denies the northern tribes' independent political power and expresses concerns whenever the Davidic kings partner with the northern kingdom (e.g., Jehoshaphat's alliance with Ahab [2 Chron. 19:2] and Ahaziah [2 Chron. 20:37]). On the other hand, the Chronicler shows that those from the northern tribes are welcome to participate in worshipping YHWH and that many of them do. The Chronicler celebrates the major moments in Israel's history of worship when all Israel comes together to Jerusalem, such as transferring the ark (1 Chron. 13:5; 15:3), dedicating the temple (2 Chron. 7:8), and celebrating the Passover (2 Chron. 30:5). In this way, all Israel consists of all the tribes; however, their unity is not political. Instead, "their unity was to be based on their common worship of Yahweh centered in the Jerusalem temple" (Braun 1986, xxxvii).

Conclusion

In closing, the book of Chronicles addresses several theological issues important for the postexilic context of the Chronicler. At the same time, his message extends far beyond his own specific context. At the heart of his theological message is his picture of Israel, his people. The Chronicler presents Israel as YHWH's people, bound to him by a covenant that defines obedience/disobedience and describes the consequences of reward/punishment. YHWH is faithful to fulfill the terms of that covenant, but he is also more than faithful, showing mercy to those who repent and restoring his people according to his plan. As YHWH's people, Israel has an obligation to worship YHWH exclusively and properly. At its best, YHWH has used the Davidic dynasty to lead the way in that worship, especially by building and maintaining YHWH's temple in Jerusalem. Although the Chronicler did not experience a time in which a Davidic king ruled, his book shows that he awaited such a king. His book points to Israel at its best: all Israel gathered to worship YHWH at the Jerusalem temple according to Mosaic regulation, led by a Davidic king.

OUTLINE

ISRAEL AND ITS PLACE IN THE WORLD (1 CHRON. 1:1–9:44)

- Identifying Israel as a Nation Through Its Generations (1:1–9:44)

REIGN OF DAVID (1 CHRON. 10:1–29:30)

- YHWH Transfers the Kingdom to David at Saul's Death (10:1–14)
- Israel Transfers the Kingdom to David (11:1–12:40 [HB 41])
- Israel Experiences the Blessings and Dangers of YHWH's Presence (13:1–14:17)
- Israel Successfully Transfers the Ark (15:1–16:43)
- The Davidic Covenant (17:1–27)
- David Defeats Enemy Nations (18:1–20:8)
- A Sinful Census That Leads to a Sacred Site (21:1–22:1)
- David Prepares for the Temple (22:2–19)
- Organizing Israel for YHWH's Future Temple and Future King (23:1–27:34)
- YHWH Reveals the Plans for the Temple (28:1–21)
- David's Farewell (29:1–30)

REIGN OF SOLOMON (2 CHRON. 1:1–9:31)

- Worship, Wisdom, and Wealth at the Beginning of Solomon's Reign (1:1–17)
- Solomon Builds the Temple (2:1 [HB 1:18]–5:1)
- Solomon Transfers the Ark into the Temple (5:2–14)
- Solomon's Prayer of Dedication (6:1–42)
- YHWH, Solomon, and Israel Affirm the Jerusalem Temple (7:1–22)
- Solomon Completes Building the Temple (8:1–16)
- Solomon's Wisdom and Wealth (8:17–9:31)

REIGNS OF JUDAH'S KINGS (2 CHRON. 10:1–36:23)

- The Kingdom Divides (10:1–19)
- Rehoboam's Reign over Judah—YHWH's Faithfulness Expressed (11:1–12:16)
- Reign of Abijah—When Proper Worship Led to Victory (13:1–14a [HB 13:23a])
- Reign of Asa—Importance of Relying on YHWH (14:1b [HB 13:23b]–16:14)
- Reign of Jehoshaphat—Sincere Worship but a Foolish Alliance (17:1–19:3)
- Reign of Jehoshaphat—Testing Jehoshaphat's Trust (19:4–21:1)
- House of Ahab—Davidic Dynasty Saved from Destruction (21:2–23:21)
- Reign of Joash—The Difference a Priest Can Make (24:1–27)
- Reign of Amaziah—Half-Hearted Devotion Followed by Foolish Idolatry (25:1–26:2)
- Reigns of Uzziah and Jotham—The Rewards of Righteousness and Punishment of Pride (26:3–27:9)
- Reign of Ahaz—A King More Wicked Than the Wicked (28:1–27)
- Reign of Hezekiah—Promoting Proper Worship at the Temple (29:1–31:21)
- Reign of Hezekiah—YHWH Responds to Prayer in War and Sickness (32:1–33)
- Reigns of Manasseh and Amon—The Difference Humility Can Make (33:1–25)
- Reign of Josiah—A Righteous King Faces Inevitable Judgment (34:1–35:27)
- Reigns of Judah's Final Kings—Judah's Judgment and Future Hope (36:1–23)

ISRAEL AND ITS PLACE IN THE WORLD (1 CHRONICLES 1:1–9:44)

As one might expect of a historical work, Chronicles begins with an introduction to the main character: Israel. However, the modern reader may not expect that the introduction would consist of several chapters of genealogies filled with lists of names, some known and many more unknown. The genealogies begin with Adam, but they quickly move to focus on one nation composed of many tribes: Israel. Among the tribes, three are especially prominent: Judah, Benjamin, and Levi. Their placement respectively at the beginning, end, and middle of the genealogies signals their prominence. Since Judah and Benjamin occur first and last, they form a framework for Israel. However, at the center is the tribe of Levi. YHWH set Levi apart as those who would serve in his sanctuary, most notably, his temple in Jerusalem. Placing Levi at the center conveys a sense of what Chronicles envisions Israel to be as a nation: a people who worship YHWH together at the Jerusalem temple.

Beyond the lists of names, the first nine chapters contain geographical information, military notes, and numerous anecdotes. These anecdotes point to major themes within Chronicles. For instance, one can discern YHWH's blessing of obedience and his punishment for disobedience in numerous anecdotes. YHWH blesses Jabez through the power of prayer (1 Chron. 4:9–10). YHWH grants the Reubenites, Gadites, and half-tribe of Manasseh victory in battle because they trusted YHWH and cried out to him (1 Chron. 5:18–22). However, YHWH sent those same tribes into exile when they turned from YHWH and worshipped other gods.

In this way begins the story of Israel and YHWH, the God of Israel.

1 Chronicles 1:1–9:44

EXEGETICAL IDEA
YHWH preserved his chosen people Israel, even through their punishment, so that they would be an obedient community living in their land, worshipping him properly in Jerusalem, led by a son of David.

THEOLOGICAL FOCUS
YHWH faithfully preserves his people, even through punishment, so that they may worship him obediently.

PREACHING IDEA
Remember what defines you: God's choice and expectation.

PREACHING POINTERS
The application of this pericope is challenging, because it is not only a narrative, but a special kind of narrative. It can be helpful to put ourselves in the place of those Jews who heard it read when they returned from exile. Their lives were filled with uncertainty and they had the great challenge of rebuilding a nation. It is easy to see that they would struggle with national identity. To solidify who they were as a nation, individuals would have to remember or perhaps learn for the first time that God chose them and gave them a task. This genealogy shows that Israel was chosen and was expected to obey the God who chose them. The centrality of that obedience was worship.

Because of the world we live in and our sin nature, the church and those in the church need to be reminded of who we are, what defines us. Those in our church who have been through a crisis often will need a reminder of who they are. When you lose a spouse of forty years, when you lose a job, when you are fired, when illness hits—these are all reasons for someone to struggle with who they are. What defined them was taken away. This passage can help us grab hold of what truly defines us: God's choice of us and his assignment for us. When we remember what defines us, we should respond in worship.

IDENTIFYING ISRAEL AS A NATION THROUGH ITS GENERATIONS (1:1–9:44)

LITERARY STRUCTURE AND THEMES (1:1–9:44)

At first glance, Chronicles appears to be a strange book for the contemporary reader. It begins with nine chapters of genealogies, which may appear as a bewildering list of strange names referring to ancient people unknown anywhere else in the Bible. However, these lists follow certain patterns. Some of the genealogies (e.g., list of Davidic kings, 1 Chron. 3:10–14) focus on the continuous lineage from father to one son, ancestor to one descendant. These linear or vertical genealogies, as they are called, draw attention to a lineage's depth. Other genealogies (e.g., the list for the tribe of Benjamin, 1 Chron. 8:1–27) present one generation after another, listing multiple descendants in each generation. These segmented or horizontal genealogies, as they are called, draw attention to a lineage's breadth. Both types of genealogies occur repeatedly, often alongside one another, and contribute to the Chronicler's genealogical picture of Israel.

When one zooms out beyond the individual lists themselves, another pattern emerges: the genealogies reflect a concentric structure in which the first element corresponds to the last, the second to the second-to-last, the third to the third-to-last, and so forth. The first and last lists locate Israel both geographically and historically. The first element locates Israel in the world. The last element locates Israel historically by listing those returning to Jerusalem. Within this structure, three tribes stand out: Judah, Benjamin, and Levi. Judah and Benjamin form the first and last elements within Israel's genealogy.

Together they form the framework for Israel, but Judah receives preeminence (1 Chron. 5:2), as expressed through the reign of David and his descendants (1 Chron. 3:1–24). The tribe of Levi lies at the center of the genealogies. Levi's genealogy emphasizes the tribe's role as the personnel who carry out the ritual worship for YHWH at the Jerusalem temple. The focus on Levi depicts Israel as a nation centered on the proper worship of YHWH through the divinely appointed personnel at the divinely chosen sanctuary. The other lists in 1 Chronicles 1–9 (the nations surrounding Israel, Simeon and Transjordan tribes, the northern tribes, and the returnees from exile) relate to this core structure of Israel, as represented by Judah, Benjamin, and Levi.

At the same time, the genealogies consist of more than names. They often contain a mixture of information regarding genealogy, military composition, and settlement patterns. Furthermore, alongside this information, there are some anecdotes that do not seem closely related to the surrounding genealogies. This supplementary information introduces important themes that the rest of Chronicles will take up and develop.

- ***Israel in the World (1:1–54)***
- ***Israel Within Its Tribes (2:1–8:40)***
  - *Judah (2:1–4:23)*
  - *Simeon and Transjordan Tribes (4:24–5:26)*
  - *Levi (6:1–81 [HB 5:27–6:66])*
  - *Northern Tribes (7:1–40)*
  - *Benjamin (8:1–40)*
- ***Israel Returning to Jerusalem (9:1–44)***

EXPOSITION (1:1–9:44)

If first impressions determine the value of a book, most modern readers would see little value in Chronicles. The book begins with long lists of unknown people, sometimes in unknown places, with little to no information about the people or places themselves. Although Chronicles may not make a spectacular first impression for most modern readers, for the book's first readers these lists constituted a significant, even engaging, entryway into the history that follows. Following ancient practice, the lists introduce the book's main (but not most important) character: Israel. However, defining Israel is not a simple task for the first readers. For their ancestors, Israel was a state, a land, and a people. However, circumstances have changed. The past state, land, and people no longer overlap as they once did. The political state has been destroyed, the land divided and resettled, and the people scattered among surrounding nations. Relating the Israel of the past with the Israel of their present is an important question for the first readers. The Chronicler includes the opening lists of his book to contribute to an answer. He points to Israel as a people, genealogically related, settled in a land promised to their ancestors. At the same time, the Chronicler looks beyond the ethnic and geographical aspects of Israel to focus on the religious (Schweitzer 2013, 25). The Chronicler emphasizes that what ultimately defines Israel, both in the past and the present, is their relationship to YHWH. Israel is YHWH's people, and YHWH is Israel's God.

YHWH's Relations to Others

The language of Chronicles focuses on YHWH as God in relation to Israel. The expression YHWH God occurs 113 times in Chronicles. From that total, 102 refer to YHWH as God in relation to another—most often Israel, the fathers, or a specific person such as David or Hezekiah. The evidence shows that the Chronicler does not usually refer to YHWH simply as God but as the God of Israel, either as a people or an individual within Israel. This fact is interesting because during the time of the first readers, YHWH worshippers were scattered throughout the Mediterranean world. In this international setting, Chronicles did not focus on YHWH as deity in the abstract, but in his particular relationship to Israel. In Chronicles YHWH is not simply God, or even the God of heaven; he is Israel's God.

As a result, Chronicles focuses on Israel as a community that worships YHWH with the proper personnel, at the proper times, through the proper measures, in the proper location. The literary structure of these genealogies (see "Literary Structure" in the introduction) reveals the central role that Levi plays and the leading role that Judah, particularly the Davidic line, plays. The genealogies show that when the people worship YHWH in this way, they live up to all that Israel is intended to be and embody the best of what Israel has been in the past (such as during the days of David, Solomon, and other good kings).

The genealogies serve this function of defining Israel quite well. Even the scope of the material hints at this definition. In chronological terms, the genealogies move from creation (with Adam) to Israel's return to the land (1 Chron. 9). In geographical terms, the genealogies move from the world to Jerusalem and its temple. Not only does this movement focus on Israel as a worshipping community, but it also points to YHWH's rule over all history and all the world. At the same time, YHWH's attention leads to a small group in a single city. This small group is a part of YHWH's people. Although it may seem that 1 Chronicles 1–9 contains so many names, the number is an infinitesimal percentage of those who lived from creation to time of Israel's return. As a result, the genealogies point to a small group with whom YHWH has a special relationship, or for which YHWH has a special purpose. At first, this narrow focus seems to limit YHWH's attention to one ethnic group. However, the genealogies balance out the narrow selection with ethnic inclusion. In several passages, the genealogies of Israel's tribes, particularly Judah (see below), include as a part of Israel those beyond ethnic Israel. As a result, defining Israel only in ethnic terms does not do justice to the Chronicler's portrait of Israel.

Relation to Ezra and Nehemiah

The Chronicler's genealogical picture of Israel raises questions regarding Ezra and Nehemiah's understanding of who constitutes Israel. Recently, scholars have emphasized that Chronicles has a wider definition of Israel than Ezra and Nehemiah. It is not possible to address all the questions involved here; however, it is important to keep in mind a couple of points. First, both Chronicles and Ezra-Nehemiah focus on ethnic and religious factors for identifying and defining Israel. Second, Chronicles gives a general picture while Ezra and Nehemiah are dealing with specific situations and problems.

Overall, the genealogies of 1 Chronicles 1–9 show how, in the context of the world, YHWH has preserved his chosen people Israel, even beyond their exile. The genealogies point to Israel as the people of YHWH, obedient to him, living in their land, worshipping him at his temple in Jerusalem, led by Judah, particularly a Davidic descendant. The rest of Chronicles develops the story of this Israel, showing how Israel and YHWH relate to each other and how that relationship determines Israel's historical path.

Genealogies and Human Value

Beyond defining Israel, the genealogies also communicate other important theological points. For instance, the genealogies list numerous individuals, many about whom very little is known. Including their names in the Chronicler's portrait of the world implies both the significance and insignificance of each individual listed. On the one

hand, the individual forms a necessary link in preserving a people into the future; on the other hand, the individual is "but a small link" in the long chain of humankind (McConville 1984, 8). This picture gives honor to the individual, but it is not individualistic; the individual receives significance in the role played for the larger community (see also Janzen 2018, 47–52).

Israel in the World (1:1–54)

Among all the nations sharing a common humanity, Israel steps into the spotlight, not because of its position within humanity's family tree but because of God's promises to Abraham.

1:1–54. The first chapter of Chronicles focuses on Israel's place within its world. The picture begins with Adam and concludes with a list of kings and tribal leaders from Edom. The genealogy concisely traces the development of peoples in Israel's world; therefore, even when the names refer to individuals, they more importantly point to nations, peoples, tribes, and so forth (cf. sons of Canaan, 1:13–16). From generation to generation, the list addresses the secondary descendants before moving to the descendant who receives the focus (e.g., descendants of Japheth and Ham precede the descendants of Shem). In this way, the structure reveals a narrowing of focus through time. This focus corresponds to YHWH's choice in history.

When looking at the structure of the chapter, the following observations emerge. First, Israel is not alone. They are connected to the nations and peoples who surround them. Although Israel occupies the focus of the genealogies, Chronicles shows a keen interest for the surrounding nations as well. Second, Israel is a relative latecomer in history (Knoppers 2003a, 293). They do not stand out as the first of humanity or a primeval people. Therefore, YHWH's choice of Israel is not based on their status as a first people.

1:1. By starting with Adam, the Chronicler starts his history of Israel with a universal focus. Although interested in Israel, the Chronicler is not only interested in Israel. Furthermore, starting with Adam suggests that YHWH is the ruler of all nations, since all nations come from him. At the same time, the text says nothing about Adam. The text does not present him in any special way. He is simply the first name, the first human. In this way, just like the names to follow, Adam is merely human. His status, or the status of those who follow, does not determine the course of the genealogies; the Chronicler will point to other factors (cf. 1 Chron. 5:1–2).

Status of Adam

Other creation accounts and other ancient Near Eastern genealogies indicate that the first human was "of [a] special descent, bridged the divine and human spheres, functioned as either a royal priest or a prophet, enjoyed any special divine favors, or experienced any intimate relations with the gods" (Knoppers 2003a, 291).

1:10. Following Genesis 10:8, the text describes the strength of Nimrod. By mentioning Nimrod, the text may be alluding to Babylon, which Nimrod founded. If so, then this text at the beginning of the book parallels the mention of Babylon at the end of the book (2 Chron. 36:17–20, describing the destruction and exile of Jerusalem and Judah). This inclusio points to the significant role Babylon plays in exile, even as the genealogies show that exile does not essentially change what Israel is (cf. 1 Chron. 9:1–2).

1:27. The genealogy now shifts to Abraham. By referring to him as Abram and Abraham, the genealogy alludes to God's promise (Gen. 17:5) to make him a father of many nations. These nations include the Ishmaelites and Edomites, but the focus goes to the last listed: his son Isaac.

1:43–54. These verses list Edomite kings and chiefs. Two observations deserve mention. First,

the picture of Edomite leadership contrasts sharply with the Chronicler's portrait of Judah. Whereas Jerusalem remains the capital beginning with David, Edomite kings and their capitals shift many times. Second, Edom shifts from kings in the beginning of the list to chiefs after Hadad dies (1:51). Since Hadad is associated with the beginning of the Davidic dynasty, specifically with Solomon (1 Kings 11:14–22), the shift to chiefs signals that the Edomite leaders rank lower than Judah's kings (Boda 2010a, 38; Jonker 2013a, 40).

Israel Within Its Tribes (2:1–8:40)
After the Chronicler introduces a genealogical portrait of the world, he moves to the focus of his work: Israel. The following genealogies present a picture of Israel as a nation made up of its tribes. Within those tribes, Judah (at the beginning), Levi (in the center), and Benjamin (at the end) receive the most attention. In the genealogies, these tribes serve "as a framework to enclose, not a fence to exclude" (Williamson 1982, 38–39) the other tribes. Israel is a unified people, even though it consists of various tribes. Furthermore, the tribal identities extend beyond lineage; they include land. The genealogies show how the tribes live in settlements throughout the land of Israel. Many of these settlements belong to Israel's past but not the Chronicler's own postexilic situation. By mentioning them, the Chronicler points to a hope for a fully restored Israel, reflecting its previous boundaries and settlements.

Judah (1 Chron. 2:1–4:23)
The tribe of Judah, and within it the line of David, has been given prominence in Israel, and since it persevered through centuries, even through exile, it maintains hope for the future.

2:1–4:23. The Chronicler begins the portrait of Israel's tribes with Judah. Listing Judah first demonstrates the tribe's prominence within

Israel and follows the pattern set in other texts (e.g., Numbers 2:1–9 instructs Judah to lead out when Israel moves in the wilderness; Judges 1:1–2 recounts how Judah led Israel in taking the land). Judah's genealogy also brings focus to what lies at its center: the Davidic line. In this way, the genealogy narrows down to focus on a chosen line within a chosen tribe. Several elements in the genealogy, including accounts of sinful behavior (e.g., Er and Achar/Achan), point to the election of David with the tribe of Judah as well (N. Klein 2016, 220–37). At the same time, Judah's genealogy widens out to include "a range of humans—male and female, ancestor and slave, Israelite, Canaanite, Edomite, Moabite, Ishmaelite, and Egyptian—[all who] had a role to play in Judah's development" (Knoppers 2003a, 358). As examples, the genealogy points out Judah's Canaanite wife (2:3), the Ishmaelite husband of David's sister (2:17), Jarha the Egyptian slave who carries on Sheshan's lineage (2:34–35), Bithiah the daughter of Pharoah (4:18), and others. As a result, the genealogy depicts two contrasting theological ideas at the same time: election and inclusion.

Structure of Judah's Genealogy

Commentators have described the structure of Judah's genealogy as chiastic; however, not every element corresponds to a chiasm. At the same time, the structure does reveal a clear focus on the center: the Davidic line (Boda 2010a, 46).

2:1–2. These verses form the climax of the Chronicler's portrait of the world from the previous chapter. The remainder of Chronicles turns its attention to the nation Israel. It begins by listing the twelve sons of the person Israel, also known as Jacob. These sons constitute all Israel. The Chronicler's picture of Israel consists of all the tribes, including the tribes of the northern kingdom.

2:3–4. The Chronicler does not shy away from what appear to be scandalous details regarding the origins of Judah's lineage. First, Judah marries a Canaanite. Second, Judah's firstborn commits an unspecified sin for which YHWH puts him to death. Third, Judah has sons through his daughter-in-law. Recalling these details, especially with little to no comment, demonstrates that Chronicles is not idealizing Judah or his descendants.

Judah by Francisco de Zurbarán. Public domain.

2:7. The note regarding Achar points to important features of Chronicles. First, the name is an alternative spelling of Achan (עָכָן) who violated the restriction of taking plunder from Jericho (Josh. 6–7). The Chronicler's spelling (עָכָר) uses the same consonants as the verb to describe his "making trouble" (עכר; used here and Joshua 6:18; 7:25) for Israel. This small change from one consonant to another reveals more explicitly the character of the person. Second, the text mentions that Achar violates the ban. Within Chronicles, the verb used (מעל) refers to unfaithfulness, usually regarding worship, although here it refers to violating a divine sanction (see sidebar "Unfaithfulness Against YHWH" for more detail). It describes why Saul, along with his dynasty, comes to an end (1 Chron. 10:13–14) and why Judah is exiled (2 Chron. 36:14). Third, the text relates this type of violation to the well-being of Israel. Achar's violation leads to Israel's disaster. As a result, the fate of the nation lies in its proper response to God's instructions regarding proper worship. Achar's disobedience and its consequences become a pattern that plays out many times in Chronicles. Despite the trouble that comes to Israel on these occasions, YHWH still preserves Israel into future generations.

2:15. This verse lists David as Jesse's seventh son. Furthermore, David is the tenth descendant from Judah. These positions within a genealogy regularly indicate that the person has a special status within the lineage. In David's case, Chronicles focuses on his accomplishments in uniting all Israel, securing Jerusalem, transferring the ark, building a kingdom, founding a dynasty, defeating the nation's enemies, and preparing to build YHWH's temple in Jerusalem.

2:20. The text mentions Bezalel, the lead craftsman constructing the tabernacle (see esp. Exod. 31:2–11; 35:30–36:2). Later, Chronicles will present parallels between the tabernacle and the temple, presenting Solomon as a new Bezalel (see comments on 2 Chron. 2). Mentioning Bezalel here foreshadows the important role that the tribe of Judah, represented in Solomon, will play in constructing the Jerusalem temple.

3:1–24. David's line in the center of Judah's genealogy reveals an important aspect of the Chronicler's portrait of Israel. Since this lineage stretches well into the postexilic period, it most clearly reveals the Chronicler's intent to demonstrate continuity between Israel's past (portrayed in the genealogies) and his contemporary community. By tracing David's lineage into the postexilic period, the Chronicler confirms that the Davidic line endures beyond exile. At the same time, the list draws attention to the exile in several ways. First and most directly, it refers to Jeconiah (more commonly called Jehoiachin) as the captive (3:17). Second, the list also shifts from a linear genealogy to segmented genealogies after Josiah, revealing the disruption of the monarchy upon Josiah's death. Third, it presents Josiah as the forty-ninth generation from Adam, thereby making the generation of the exile the fiftieth generation. This count associates the exile with the Jubilee year and depicts the exile as a sabbath rest (cf. 2 Chron. 36:21; Jonker 2013a, 50). In other words, even though exile is YHWH's punishment on Israel, YHWH redeems the period for the land and preserves the people through it.

TRANSLATION ANALYSIS:
Some translations (e.g., NKJV) render the Hebrew (אַסִּר) as a name (Assir) rather than a noun translated "captive." Assir does occur as a name elsewhere in the genealogy of Levi (1 Chron. 6:22–23, 37 [HB 7–8, 22]), and the MT does not have an article on the word, as one might expect if it were a common noun. However, the article is likely missing due to an unintentional scribal error in transmission.

3:5–9. These verses list David's nineteen sons and one daughter. The listing does not appear to follow birth order; instead, Solomon occurs in the exact center, in the tenth position, as the focal point of the list. The list also contains a couple more interesting features. First, rather than listing Bathsheba as Solomon's mother, the text uses an alternative spelling: Bathshua (בַּת־שׁוּעַ). Second, the listing of David's children concludes with Tamar. Both Tamar and Bathshua are names associated with Judah in the genealogy (1 Chron. 2:3–4). These names together point to a strategy to relate David and Solomon to the patriarchal period (see Boda 2010a, 53).

3:19–20. The listing of Zerubbabel's children differs from those preceding it because it distinguishes two separate groups. The first group consists of three children in 3:19; the second group consists of five children in 3:20, distinguished from the other group by a closing number five. This structure parallels the listing of David's children (1 Chron. 3:1–9). Since Zerubbabel is a significant figure in the return to Israel from exile, the list likely indicates that Zerubbabel has the first group in exile and the second group upon returning to Jerusalem, just as David had the first group of children in Hebron and the second in Jerusalem. Such similarities show continuity through the Davidic line even through the exile and return.

4:1–23. Following the line of David, the genealogy restarts with Judah, but traces out different lines of descent.

4:9–10. Somewhat disconnected in context, these verses touch on an important theme running through Chronicles: the power of prayer. The brief account builds on the idea that a person's name points to the person's destiny. Jabez's name (יַעְבֵּץ), which plays on the word for pain (עֹצֶב), points to a painful life. However, when Jabez prays for YHWH's blessing and protection, YHWH grants his request and overcomes his name's destiny. The Chronicler likely includes these verses because they reflect the concerns of the vulnerable first readers who live in a small province, recovering from past pain, looking for present protection, and hoping for future prosperity. These verses present prayer as a key element to securing that hope.

4:21–23. The closing verses of Judah's genealogy point to concerns for the rest of the genealogy. First, the Chronicler addresses the reliability of his picture by pointing out that his listing is based on ancient records. Second, he focuses on the craftsmen who supported the Davidic king in the past. This concern likely lies at much of Judah's genealogy; that is, the Chronicler intends to show how the tribe of Judah supported the Davidic line in the past so that they might support the Davidic descendant in the present and/or future (a concern seen also regarding the Caleb clans in 1 Chron. 2:50–55; 4:1–4; see Boda 2010a, 47).

Simeon and Transjordan Tribes
(1 Chron. 4:24–5:26)
For Simeon and the Transjordan tribes, YHWH rewards their obedience but severely punishes their continued disobedience.

4:24–5:26. The genealogies move from Judah to Simeon and the Transjordan tribes (Reuben, Gad, and eastern Manasseh), generally following a course that goes south and then east, and back north. The tribes' lists contain similar information: descendants, settlements, genealogical records, and expansion of land (see Sparks 2008, 164–65). Furthermore, each tribe's account concludes with a conflict. These conflicts reveal an important point for the Chronicler's message. They illustrate the retribution principle that obedience leads to blessing while disobedience leads to punishment (see section "Covenant" in the introduction). Since the lists close with an account of exile, these genealogies provide a theological justification for the exile of these tribes, while also demonstrating the possibility that these tribes could succeed and expand through obedience to YHWH.

4:27, 31. These verses contain references to Judah and David. They reveal that although Simeon was a distinct tribe, it is not as large

Simeon by Francisco de Zurbarán. Public domain.

nor as significant as Judah. Even during David's time, Judah absorbed some of Simeon's cities. In this way, Simeon's well-being depends on Judah's well-being.

4:38–43. The conflicts that close Simeon's account distinguish it from Judah and from the Transjordan tribes to follow. The two conflicts portray Simeon in a violent manner. The text uses language to describe the land (quiet, wide, and peaceful), reminiscent of Dan's attacking Laish in Judges 18, and records how Simeon attacks and destroys those inhabiting the land. In contrast Judah expands peacefully (see Knoppers 2003a, 375). This picture of Simeon coincides with the image of the patriarch Simeon, who violently destroys Shechem (see Gen. 34; 49:5–7).

5:1–2. The genealogies paint a complex picture of Reuben. In the list of Israel's sons, he occurs first. Being the firstborn typically carries certain privileges: land and leadership. The firstborn receives a double portion of land among his brothers and carries out leadership within the clan. However Reuben, neither the patriarch nor the tribe, carries such significance. The text explains that the two privileges of being firstborn are transferred to others. Joseph receives the double portion of land (birthright), demonstrated by the allotments to his sons Ephraim and Manasseh; Judah receives the role of leadership, demonstrated by the Davidic line. The text explains that Reuben loses the right of the firstborn because he defiles his father's bed; that is, he has sexual relations with his father's concubine Bilhah (Gen. 35:22). In this way, the text again illustrates the retribution principle—in this case, that disobedience leads to punishment.

5:9–10. The text closes the genealogy of Reuben by recording that the tribe expands eastward. More detail is lacking; however, these verses anticipate 5:18–22, which record the expansion of all the Transjordan tribes through YHWH's help (see below).

5:18–22. To close the genealogy of Gad, the text records the expansion of Gad, along with the other Transjordan tribes, through military victory. The account of the conflict follows a pattern typical of Chronicles: a sizeable force of Israel's competent warriors engages in battle against an enemy, Israel trusts YHWH and cries out to him, YHWH hears their cries, he helps them, and he delivers their enemies into their hands, with the result that Israel carries off immense spoils of war. One may notice that even though the text mentions Israel's military strength, the battle belongs to YHWH. In one

Joseph by Francisco de Zurbarán. Public domain.

Reuben by Francisco de Zurbarán. Public domain.

sense, the army wins when it does not fight but trusts YHWH to fight for them. For the first readers living in such a vulnerable situation, this text encourages them to trust YHWH even though they do not have a great military presence.

5:25–26. Gad's genealogy closes with the expansion of the Transjordan tribes because of

Gad by Francisco de Zurbarán. Public domain.

YHWH's victory in battle for them (5:18–22). Eastern Manasseh's genealogy also closes with the movement of the Transjordan tribes; however, the movement is not expansion but exile. The text explains the reason for the change in fate. In 5:18–22 the tribes trust YHWH and cry out to him. In 5:25–26, the tribes do not trust YHWH; instead, they disobey him. How the text describes their disobedience highlights a couple of points. First, the text points toward a future exile. The text describes the tribes as being unfaithful by violating divine sanctions (מעל; see sidebar "Unfaithfulness Against YHWH"). This verb looks back to the trouble Achar caused Israel (1 Chron. 2:7) and looks forward to the future exile of all Israel (2 Chron. 36:14).

Furthermore, the text compares the tribes' activities to the nations that YHWH drove out from the land. Just as YHWH drove out nations from the land for their past transgressions, so YHWH may do to Israel. Second, the text points to the nature of Israel's relationship to YHWH. The text contrasts YHWH as "the God of their ancestors" to the "gods of the peoples of the land." Playing on a marriage metaphor, the verse describes the tribes as acting as a prostitute with the other gods who, unlike YHWH, have not had a relationship with Israel from the beginning. Israel's relationship is not something new or innovative; it rests on YHWH's presence and promise to the previous generations of Israel, as illustrated in the genealogies. Furthermore, as 5:18–22 demonstrates, in previous generations, YHWH helps the tribes as their God, listening to their cries and fighting their enemies when they trust him.

How the text describes the punishment of the tribes also highlights important points. First, the text indicates clearly that YHWH brings the punishment, even though he uses an Assyrian king to do so. The expression of "stirring up the spirit" (עור רוּחַ) relates to other texts in Chronicles in which YHWH directs a situation. YHWH stirs up the Philistines and Arabs to punish Jehoram (2 Chron. 21:16), but he also stirs up the spirit of Cyrus to declare that Israel can return to its land (2 Chron. 36:22). This expression highlights YHWH's role in directing history, whether to bring judgment or restoration. For either purpose, he directs kings, even foreign kings, to accomplish his purpose (cf. Prov. 21:1).

Name of the Assyrian King

The two names for the Assyrian king refer to the same person. Pul is a less formal, shortened name for Tiglath-pileser III. Both names occur in Kings (2 Kings 15:19, 29) and other ancient Near Eastern documents.

Second, the text indicates some lasting effects of their transgression. It lists the specific cities to which the tribes were exiled and indicates that they remained there for a long time. This information raises the question whether the tribes can ever return. What is important to note is that the exile does not reflect an inherent rejection of the tribes; 5:18–22 demonstrates such a point. The difference lies in the relationship between the tribes and YHWH: if they trust YHWH, he will secure land for them, but if not, then he will remove them from their land.

Use of the Expression "To This Day"

The text states that the tribes remain there "to this day" (עַד הַיּוֹם הַזֶּה). The expression may refer literally to the Chronicler's own day; however, it may function idiomatically to indicate something taking place for a long time after some specific point in time (see comments on 2 Chron. 8:8).

Levi (1 Chron. 6:1–81 [HB 5:27–6:66])

The genealogy of Levi points to the central role proper ritual worship plays for Israel as a people and to the properly sanctified personnel of the Levites and priests.

6:1–81 (HB 5:27–6:66). At the center of the Chronicler's genealogical picture of Israel lies Levi. The genealogy of Levi focuses on four ancestors: Aaron, and Levi's three sons (Gershon, Kohath, and Merari). Aaron's descendants, the priests, form the frame around the genealogy occurring at the beginning (6:1–15 [HB 5:27–41]) and the end (6:50–53 [HB 35–38]), thus highlighting the significance of the priests. Within

Levi by Francisco de Zurbarán. Public domain.

this frame occur two lists for each of Levi's sons, one list for the descendants with general Levitical duties and one list for the group of musicians. Following the lineages, the passage turns to the Levitical settlements.

Placing Levi at the center of the genealogies reveals an important aspect of the Chronicler's understanding of Israel: at its core, Israel is a community that engages in proper ritual worship of YHWH. Proper ritual worship requires proper personnel. The Chronicler demonstrates that the Levitical tribe constitutes the proper personnel by showing that their roles originate at key moments under key authorities in Israel's history: the period of Moses for the priests and the period of David for the musicians. As a result, when the Levitical tribe carries out the duties of ritual worship they are preserving an ancient rule and practice, whether during the Davidic monarchy or during the postexilic period.

6:3–15 (HB 5:29–41). The Levitical genealogy first focuses on the priests, the descendants of Aaron. The genealogy traces one line into the exilic period. Since this genealogy traces one line, it suggests that this line is important, perhaps even the lineage of high priests. However, the list does not contain some important priests from the narrative of Chronicles (most notably Jehoiada, 2 Chron. 23–24); therefore, it does not necessarily list high priests and certainly not all of them.

Beyond the names, the list contains two important notes: (1) it comments that Azariah served in Solomon's temple, and (2) it comments that the final priest, Jehozadak, went into exile. These comments divide the priesthood into three key moments: its founding, the construction of the temple, and the exile from the land. On the one hand, these comments bring attention to the importance of the temple in Jerusalem for the priesthood. On the other hand, they show that ritual worship by itself does not create or maintain favor

with YHWH. Being a legitimate Levitical priest does not spare one from YHWH's judgment. Throughout his work, the Chronicler maintains this type of balance regarding the Jerusalem temple and its ritual worship (e.g., see comments on 2 Chron. 2–4).

Two Azariahs

The lineage includes two Azariahs. Because of the number of generations between Zadok and the second Azariah, it is reasonable to think that the note now attached to the second Azariah properly belongs to the first Azariah; however, there is no direct textual witness supporting the reading.

6:16–30 (HB 6:1–15). After the priests, the genealogy lists other Levites according to the sons of Levi: Gershon, Kohath, and Merari. These Levites serve as assistants to the priests in Israel's ritual worship (see 6:48 [HB 33]). These lists seem to close in the period of David. The line of Kohath closes with Samuel and his sons. The line of Merari closes with Asaiah, a Levite mentioned during the ark's transfer to Jerusalem in 1 Chronicles 15:6. Closing the lists in the period of David suggests that David's reign is a key moment in Levitical history. During David's reign, the ark comes to rest in Jerusalem, with the result that the Levites receive expanded responsibilities (1 Chron. 23:26–32).

Tribal Association of Samuel

Based on other OT texts (e.g., 1 Sam. 1:1), Samuel the Levite is also an Ephraimite. For the Chronicler, Samuel's service in the sanctuary points to his inclusion within the Levitical line.

6:31–48 (HB 6:16–33). After the Chronicler traces the Levitical families from Levi to the period of David, he lists the musicians from the period of David back to Levi. When the ark comes to rest in Jerusalem, not only does David expand the responsibilities of the Levites in general, but he also assigns specific families to serve as musicians within Israel's ritual worship. The list points out that Heman from Kohath serves as the chief musician, while Asaph from Gershon and Ethan (elsewhere called Jeduthun) from Merari serve alongside him. Since David establishes the office of musicians, tracing the musicians back to Levi confirms their legitimate status within Israel's ritual worship. In other words, even though David establishes a new practice in Israel's worship, he does so within the confines of the previously given Mosaic law.

6:31–32 (HB 6:16–17). The Chronicler introduces the musicians by mentioning that David appoints them. This appointment looks forward to the transfer of the ark in 1 Chronicles 15–16. However, the verses also look forward to the transfer of the ark to Solomon's temple, recorded in 2 Chronicles 5. The deposit of the ark in Jerusalem results in a subtle change to Israel's ritual worship. In the movable tabernacle, there is no music associated with its ritual worship; however, in the permanent temple, music forms an integral part of Israel's ritual worship. As YHWH chooses Jerusalem as his dwelling place, the tabernacle of silence becomes a temple of song (Endres 2001, 179; Knoppers 2003a, 429).

6:48–49 (HB 6:33–34). Following the list of Levitical musicians, the passage describes the service of other Levites in general. They bear responsibility for various tasks in caring for the sanctuary and maintaining its ritual worship. Even though the Chronicler points out the significance of these Levites for Israel's worship, he still maintains a distinction between their duties and those of the priests. Only the priests care for the most holy place, present offerings on the altars, and make atonement for Israel. Furthermore, these priestly duties originate in Mosaic law. In the Chronicler's picture of Israel, both priests and Levites are essential for Israel's worship even though the priests occupy a central role, extending even further back into Israel's history.

In 6:48, the expression for the sanctuary is unusual: "the tabernacle of the house of God" (מִשְׁכַּן בֵּית הָאֱלֹהִים). This expression blurs the distinction between the movable tabernacle and the stationary temple, likely to show the continuity of Israel's worship, even amid changing historical circumstances.

6:50–53 (HB 6:35–38). Following the listing of priestly duties, the Chronicler includes another list of priests. Rather than extending all the way to exile (see 6:15 [HB 5:41]), the list ends one generation after Zadok, again around the time of David.

6:54–81 (HB 6:39–66). Following the lineages of Levi, the genealogy shifts to Levitical settlements. The listing of settlements reveals two important points. First, Levites and priests occupy settlements throughout Israel. Therefore, the Levites and their influence is not limited to one tribe or to a small subset of tribes. The Chronicler pictures Levites distributed throughout the land, reinforcing the Chronicler's emphasis on Israel as all Israel, not just a subset of certain tribes. Second, since the Levites live beyond Jerusalem and beyond the temple, they must serve a function beyond their service in the temple (Knoppers 2003a, 448). In fact, Chronicles later lists several Levites who serve in administrative roles in Israel (e.g., 1 Chron. 26:20–32). Therefore, the Levites constitute an essential part of Israel, in worship and beyond.

At times, the postexilic community struggled to fulfill its responsibility to the Levites (e.g., Neh. 13:10–14). The Chronicler reminds them how important the priests and Levites are for Israel as a people: they are central to the picture of Israel as a community that worships YHWH. As a result, even in the face of difficult conditions, the postexilic community needed to support the priests and Levites for Israel's well-being.

Northern Tribes (1 Chron. 7:1–40)
The genealogies of the northern tribes show that the tribes are a true part of Israel, with hope for their future even where there is past sin.

7:1–40. After addressing Levi, the Chronicler shifts to the northern tribes. In general, the listing moves from north to south (Benjamin and Asher are exceptions). Compared to the other tribes, the coverage for each tribe is limited and not all the northern tribes are included (Zebulun and Dan are missing). However, Chronicles almost entirely ignores the tribes later in the narrative, especially in comparison to the book of Kings. Furthermore, the picture of the northern tribes tends to be negative later

Zebulun by Francisco de Zurbarán. Public domain

Dan by Francisco de Zurbarán. Public domain.

in Chronicles (e.g., 2 Chron. 25:6–10). In contrast, the picture of the northern tribes in the genealogies is positive, focusing on the number of competent individuals. For this reason, it is significant that the genealogies include these tribes, even though in a limited way, and that they paint a positive picture of them. Their inclusion and portrayal signal an openness to identifying the northern tribes as Israel, even in a postexilic context.

Exclusion of Zebulun and Dan

It is possible that Zebulun and Dan dropped out of the list somewhere in the course of textual transmission. Some scholars have argued that the genealogy of Benjamin in 1 Chronicles 7:6–11 should be attributed to Zebulun, since Zebulun follows Issachar in other passages and since Benjamin has another genealogy in 1 Chronicles 8 (see Curtis and Madsen 1910, 145–49). However, the proposal is unlikely because it requires several emendations to work. For Dan, there is reason to believe that 1 Chronicles 7:12 represents the genealogy of Dan (see Knoppers 2003a, 453–54, for a convenient list). Dan would naturally be included in a listing of the sons of Bilhah (see 7:13) and precede Naphtali. Still, there is no direct manuscript evidence for this reading.

7:1–5. The list of northern tribes begins with Issachar. The genealogy presents the tribe in high regard. It emphasizes Issachar's competence and their expansion through large families. Furthermore, associating the competence of Issachar with the time of David points to the tribe as a participant of all Israel in recognizing David as king (cf. 1 Chron. 11–12).

7:6–12. Surprisingly, the genealogy of northern tribes includes Benjamin. In fact, three lists of Benjamin occur in 1 Chronicles 1–9, including all of 1 Chronicles 8. The short genealogy here noticeably differs from the other lists, suggesting that this list focuses on different families within

Benjamin. Including Benjamin among the northern tribes may reveal the nature of Benjamin as somewhat of a northern and southern tribe, a tribe on the border (Boda 2010a, 87), so that within the Chronicler's picture of Israel, Benjamin may represent a legitimate remnant of the northern kingdom.

Naphtali by Francisco de Zurbarán. Public domain.

7:14–19. The description of Manasseh covers the tribe on both sides of the Jordan, providing a more complete picture than 1 Chronicles 5, which only addresses eastern Manasseh. Two features of this genealogy deserve mention here. First, the genealogy lists several women, all of whom are Aramean. This observation reinforces the Chronicler's picture of Israel as one that allows for (at least some) ethnic diversity. Second, the genealogy refers to elements of other tribes. For instance, Makir, the father of Gilead, occurs in the genealogy of Judah (1 Chron. 2:21), while Huppim and Shuppim occur in the genealogy of Benjamin (1 Chron. 7:12). As Mark Boda states, "This pattern of interlinking the genealogy of Makir with those of two key surviving tribes of Judah and Benjamin may be the Chronicler's way of highlighting the preservation of a remnant for the key Joseph tribe of Manasseh" (Boda 2010a, 84). In other words, Manasseh survives into the days of the Chronicler himself.

7:20–29. The genealogy of Ephraim points to two themes central to Chronicles: (1) the principle of retribution, and (2) possible hope for the future. The short narrative regarding Ezer and Elead demonstrates the principle of retribution: because they attempt to steal cattle, they die. Their sin leads to punishment. Furthermore, their sin leads not only to their deaths, but it threatens the continued existence of the tribe. In response to the threat, the genealogy points to hope for the future. Ephraim has another son, Beriah, whose name plays off the expression "in pain/disaster." Similar to Jabez who was born in pain but overcomes it, Beriah continues the lineage and has a daughter who founds a city, suggesting that the future of the tribe is secure. Furthermore, the genealogy shifts to the lineage of Joshua and Ephraim's settlements, again providing a picture of Ephraim securely settled in its tribal land.

Issachar by Francisco de Zurbarán. Public domain.

Identity of Ezer and Elead
A central question for interpreting this narrative is whether to take the characters as individuals or personifications of the tribe and families within the tribe. Generally, the language is vague and could apply to an individual or a group. For instance, the picture of Ephraim mourning parallels the picture of Rachel mourning in Jeremiah 31:15, a passage in which Rachel is a personification.

For the first readers, this story of pain and hope, like that of Jabez, would be comforting. Their current circumstances due to past sin do not determine their destiny, even for the Ephraimites (cf. 2 Chron. 25:7).

7:30–40. The listing of the northern tribes concludes with Asher. Much like the account of Issachar, the genealogy emphasizes the competence of the tribe, rounding out a generally positive portrait of the northern tribes.

Benjamin (1 Chron. 8:1–40)

Benjamin, despite its failures, constitutes a vital part of Israel in preexilic, exilic, and postexilic times.

8:1–40. Rounding out the Chronicler's portrait of Israel is Benjamin. Besides the genealogies of Judah and Levi, Benjamin receives the most attention. This attention reflects the important role that Benjamin continues to play in the postexilic community of Persian Yehud. Another sign of the tribe's significance is that the genealogy concludes by focusing on the lineage of Saul. Even though the royal house of Saul ended upon his death, his lineage continued. At the same time, the Benjaminite genealogy does not appear to present "one continuous lineage stretching from a distant progenitor (Benjamin) to a particular descendant living many centuries later" (Knoppers 2003a, 488). Instead, it contains starts and restarts, undeveloped anecdotes, and a few obscurities. Therefore, attempting to provide a coherent structure for the whole proves quite difficult. One may compare the Chronicler's portrait of Benjamin to a collection of snapshots focusing on different parts of the tribe's lineage and history, without necessarily drawing the lines connecting them. Even so, the portrait depicts a large, competent tribe that forms a vital part of Israel in the past, the present, and the future.

8:6–8. These verses suggest that some elements of the tribe migrated to other areas. These migrations reveal signs of trouble. First, the forced migration to Manahath likely points to internal struggle within the tribe. Second, Shaharaim's movement to Moab reflects negatively on his decision to divorce his wives. These signs of trouble demonstrate, as seen with Judah, that the Chronicler's portrait of Israel is not idealized.

Asher by Francisco de Zurbarán. Public domain.

8:12–13. In contrast to the negative elements alluded to in 8:6–8, these verses present a positive picture of Benjamin expanding its territory. Furthermore, mentioning Beriah and Gath in the same context alludes back to Ephraim's genealogy, in which the inhabitants of Gath killed Ephraim's descendants. In this case, the tribe of Benjamin avenges

Benjamin by Francisco de Zurbarán. Public domain.

those who threatened Ephraim (Boda 2010a, 92–93).

8:28. The Chronicler points out that certain Benjaminite tribal leaders lived in Jerusalem. By mentioning these Benjaminites in Jerusalem, the text reinforces the picture of Jerusalem as belonging to Judah and Benjamin (cf. Josh. 15:63; Judg. 1:21). Furthermore, the comment reflects the situation in the preexilic and postexilic periods, drawing a line of continuity between Israel of the past and Israel of the Chronicler's present. Finally, it implies that just as Benjaminite leadership served in Jerusalem in the past, so its leadership should serve in Jerusalem for the postexilic community.

8:29–40. The lineage of Saul closes the genealogy. The genealogy portrays no interest in Saul as king; rather, it points forward to the heroic sons of Ullam, who likely lived during the final days of the kingdom of Judah or during the exile.

Israel Returning to Jerusalem (9:1–44)

The list of returnees to Jerusalem shows that YHWH preserves his people through exile and preserves the proper personnel and practices to fulfill Israel's duty to worship YHWH ritually at the Jerusalem temple.

9:1–44. After Chronicles presents all Israel according to its tribes throughout its generations, the focus shifts to the postexilic community returning to Jerusalem. The passage summarizes those who return (e.g., those from Judah, Benjamin, and Levi) and then includes some names representative of those groups. Including this list demonstrates direct continuity between Israel before exile and Israel after exile in terms of descent, location, and ritual worship: "It is thus the vital link whereby the Chronicler associates the community of his own day with the people whom he has introduced and whose history he is about to relate" (Williamson 1982,

87). The list of returnees begins and ends with the phrase "lived in Jerusalem" (9:3, 34), thus reflecting how important the Chronicler considers Jerusalem for the postexilic community. After focusing on Jerusalem, the passage turns to Gibeon to present the genealogy of Saul again (earlier presented in 1 Chron. 8:29–40).

Relation to Nehemiah 11

The list of names and the information introducing them parallels Nehemiah 11 to a large degree. The relationship between the passages is not clear. The list from Nehemiah 11 may be the source for Chronicles, or the list from Chronicles may be the source for Nehemiah. More likely, the lists draw from a common source rather than from each other directly.

9:1. This verse closes out the genealogical picture of Israel. At the same time, it looks forward to the coming list of returnees by mentioning Judah's exile, a prerequisite for the return. Furthermore, the verse presents the reason for Judah's exile: they are unfaithful (מעל; see sidebar "Unfaithfulness Against YHWH"). The word to describe their behavior alludes to Achar, the troubler of Israel (1 Chron. 2:7) and the Transjordan tribes who suffer exile for the same reason as Judah (1 Chron. 5:25–26).

9:2. Immediately following the mention of exile, the text turns to those who first return to the land. The immediate transition from exile to return may be a way of minimizing the effect of the exile, at least its effect on identity (Knoppers 2003a, 512). In other words, the exile does not change who Israel is. In fact, the list of those who return begins simply with Israel as a designation for the laity and then moves to the priests, Levites, and temple servants. Furthermore, those who return settle back into their ancestral lands and cities. This comment implies two important points. First, as seen in the genealogies, Israel is not only a nation bound by common ancestry but includes land and cities. Second, the

comment reveals that the genealogical information in chapters 2–8 (associating the tribes with certain lands and cities) functions for more than just "historical interest, but rather to provide a vision for the geographical shape of restored Israel" (Boda 2010a, 99).

9:3. This verse provides the proper heading for the following list of returnees. Two observations deserve comment. First, the list focuses on those who dwell in Jerusalem. This focus on Jerusalem highlights the Chronicler's picture of Israel as centered around Jerusalem and, based on the listing of priests and Levites to follow, the worship that takes place there. For the Chronicler, using a list of those returning to Jerusalem provides an appropriate representation of Israel as a whole. Second, the heading includes four tribes: Judah, Benjamin, Manasseh, and Ephraim. The list itself only includes Judah (9:4–6) and Benjamin (9:7–9); however, by mentioning Manasseh and Ephraim as representative of the northern tribes, the Chronicler intends to include the northern tribes in his picture of the returned Israel.

9:10–13. Following the listing of Judah and Benjamin, the text turns to the priests. Two points stand out from the list. First, Azariah serves as the official over the house of God, that is, the Jerusalem temple. The title may indicate that Azariah is the high priest; however, such is not necessarily the case (see 2 Chron. 35:8, in which three persons serve in this capacity). The specific tasks associated with the role are not clear. Second, the Chronicler describes the priests as competent to conduct the ritual worship at the temple. This note demonstrates that among those who first return to Jerusalem there is a sufficient number of competent priests to ensure that proper ritual worship is restored in Jerusalem. The continuity of proper personnel through exile was a significant concern for the first readers in the postexilic community.

9:14–16. The text shifts from the priests to the priestly assistants: the Levites. The list includes names of Levites without specialized tasks as well as some of the singers (Mattaniah and Obadiah), anticipating 9:33 toward the end of the list.

9:17–22. Some of the Levites serve as gatekeepers. Beyond listing the names and posts of the gatekeepers, the text emphasizes their role in various periods of Israel's history. First, the text focuses on the period of the wilderness. First Chronicles 9:18 states that the gatekeepers serve as keepers of the Levitical camp, an allusion to Numbers 2:17, which describes the movement of Israel along with the tabernacle. Furthermore, Phineas, the grandson of Aaron, serves as their leader. The text notes that YHWH is with Phineas, likely recalling the role Phineas plays in preventing total disaster at Baal Peor by preserving the sanctity of Israel (Num. 25:1–9). In that episode, Phineas combines "cultic and marshal duties," much like the gatekeepers (McKenzie 2004, 113).

Second, the text looks to the period of David. Even though in some sense, the gatekeepers served in the wilderness period, David and Samuel institute the office and appoint the Levites to serve in those roles. This picture anticipates what Chronicles will communicate throughout: both the wilderness period and the Davidic period emerge as key moments in Israel's ritual worship.

Third, the text looks to a past and future time when Israel will have a king. The text mentions that the gatekeepers are keepers of the King's Gate, likely a reminder of the monarchic period but also a look to the future when a Davidic king will rule again (see Ezek. 46:11–18; R. Klein 2006, 276). In this way, the Chronicler demonstrates the importance of the Levitical gatekeepers not only for what Israel has been and what Israel is, but also what Israel will be.

9:23–32. The list specifies the responsibilities of the gatekeepers (some of which they likely shared with other Levites). The way that the Chronicler communicates this information bridges his present with the past. The Chronicler speaks of the sanctuary using an unusual expression, calling it "the house of YHWH, the house of the tent." The expression refers to the temple, the house of YHWH, but it also looks back to the tabernacle. For the Chronicler, the Jerusalem temple was the logical continuation of the wilderness tabernacle. This link is important to keep in mind as the Chronicler describes the gatekeepers' responsibilities, because it shows how temple practices preserve Israel's worship practices from its earliest days as a people.

Their primary responsibilities involve opening and closing the entrances to the sanctuary, protecting the sanctity of the sanctuary, and guarding the sanctuary treasuries. In a sense, they serve as the temple security detail. Their security functions require them to remain close to the temple precincts. As a result, the chief gatekeepers remain in Jerusalem while other gatekeepers, who live beyond Jerusalem, come to the temple in weekly shifts to support them.

Alongside the task of protecting the sanctuary, they maintain the materials needed for proper ritual worship: managing the sacred utensils and various food materials used in various offerings, preparing some of the meal offerings, and preparing the shewbread. At the same time, the Chronicler clarifies that their responsibilities do not infringe on priestly rites—for instance, preparing the spice mixture for anointing oil used in worship (see Exod. 30:25). These details regarding matters of ritual worship reinforce the sense that the Jerusalem temple in the Chronicler's time preserves Israel's proper worship from long ago.

9:33. This verse addresses another specific occupation within the Levites: the singers. Although a list of singers does not follow the verse, the previous list of Levites includes some singers

(Mattaniah, 9:15; Obadiah, 9:16). More importantly, the verse indicates how importantly and how frequently the singers perform their duties. Because of their musical responsibilities, they are relieved from other regular Levitical duties and maintain their residence within the surrounding chambers of the temple. By noting their work in temple worship, the text reinforces the connection between worship in the Second Temple period and worship during the days of David and following.

9:35–44. Following the list of returnees and concluding the many chapters of genealogies, the text returns to a list already presented in the genealogy of Benjamin: the lineage of Saul beginning with Gibeon (1 Chron. 8:29–40). Repeating this material accomplishes several results. First, the material sets the stage for the following narrative describing Saul's death (1 Chron. 10) by introducing Saul's lineage. Second, the material reinforces the fact that the Benjamin tribe survives through the exile. Third, the list creates a contrast between Jerusalem (9:3, 34) and Gibeon (9:35), and by extension, between David and Saul. Later in Chronicles, the text points out that Gibeon is a legitimate place for offering sacrifices because the tent of meeting and the bronze altar reside there (1 Chron. 16:39–40; 2 Chron. 1:3–6). Even though Gibeon is a legitimate site for worship in Israel's past, the Jerusalem temple supersedes it. This point also contributes to the picture of Saul as king. The Chronicler does not present Saul as an illegitimate king; instead, Saul dies and ends his dynasty because he acts faithlessly (1 Chron. 10:6, 13–14). As a result, David supersedes him as king. In this way, the fate of Gibeon and Saul is contrasted to the fate of Jerusalem and David. The two kings and the two cities have different fates, as illustrated in the list of returnees to Jerusalem recorded in 1 Chronicles 9 (Sailhamer 1983, 27–28). For the first readers, the return to Jerusalem might signal a similar fate for the Davidic monarchy: the return of a Davidic king.

Certainly, the return demonstrated that YHWH preserved his people through exile and that they could expect him to do the same for the Davidic line, extending even into the Chronicler's own day (1 Chron. 3).

The larger list of the returnees to Jerusalem serves another important function for the first readers. The postexilic community consisted of those who worshipped YHWH in various locations far beyond Palestine. Furthermore, some of those worshippers built temples in their own locations. In this context, the Chronicler reminds worshippers that YHWH has chosen Jerusalem to dwell. The Chronicler encourages them to return to Jerusalem and support the temple and priesthood there. At the same time, the Chronicler is open to whoever comes, whether from northern or southern tribes: "The Chronicler appears to have a message to those who have not returned to the land, encouraging them to return, but also a message to those who have already returned to accept those who do come" (Boda 2010a, 101).

THEOLOGICAL FOCUS

The first chapters of Chronicles introduce the reader to the main characters of Chronicles: Israel and YHWH. YHWH is Israel's God, and Israel is YHWH's people. The chapters begin by situating Israel among the other nations of their world. The chapters close by focusing on Jerusalem as the proper place where Israel worships YHWH, led by the proper personnel following the proper practices. Between these chapters, the genealogies present a picture of Israel by its tribes, in its lands, and through the ages. The picture of YHWH and of his people points to several truths that extend beyond the historical context of the OT period.

First, the genealogies show that YHWH rules over all the nations throughout history. Not only do the genealogies begin with the various nations of the world starting with Adam, but they also include specific accounts where YHWH fulfills his plan through a foreign nation (e.g., 1 Chron.

5:26; 9:1). Even though YHWH is the God of Israel, his authority and power extend well beyond Israel, encompassing all humankind.

Second, the genealogies provide several examples of the principle of retribution—that is, YHWH rewards trust and obedience while he punishes faithlessness and disobedience. These examples include individuals (Er, 1 Chron. 2:3; Achar, 1 Chron. 2:7), tribes (Transjordan tribes, 1 Chron. 5:25–26), and the entire nation (1 Chron. 9:1). As a result, the text does not limit this principle to an individual or national scope. At the same time, the text does not suggest that every success is a result of obedience or that every difficulty is a result of disobedience. In other words, the reward or punishment are not automatic, nor do they explain every situation. Still, the principle is true, even if it is not always true in a particular context.

Third, the genealogies focus on Israel as a worshipping community centered around the proper place (Jerusalem temple) with proper personnel (priests and Levites), following proper practices (Mosaic and Davidic instruction). Although the forms change between the OT and NT, the NT reinforces these concerns in Jesus: he creates a new worshipping community, composing a new temple (where the Spirit resides), constituting new personnel (priesthood of believers), and following his instituted practices (e.g., baptism and Lord's Supper).

Fourth, the listing of God's people demonstrates YHWH has faithfully preserved his people through centuries, through differing historical situations, and through periods of obedience or even disobedience. Despite the periods of pain or punishment, YHWH still maintains Israel as a people and as his people. Furthermore, within his people, special focus lies on the tribe of Levi (especially the priests) and the tribe of Judah (especially the line of David). Regarding Levi, YHWH prepares the way for his people to worship him properly by preserving the proper personnel for Israel's ritual worship. Regarding Judah, YHWH prepares the way for the future son of David to return to his proper place of authority.

PREACHING AND TEACHING STRATEGIES

Exegetical and Theological Synthesis

As God's children, we need to be reminded of who we are. Our sin nature makes forgetting very natural for us. We forget that God chose us. Our personal loving relationship with the Lord of the universe is taken for granted. Our assignment of blessing the world with his gospel is placed on the back burner of our thoughts. And our worship gets relegated to a brief moment once a week.

For ancient Israel this relationship was linked to a people, a place, and a promise. This chosen people started with Abraham and the place was Jerusalem and the land around it. The promise was that God would send an eternal and righteous king to bless the world. For seventy years Israel had been separated from the place and many of her people had perished. Certainly, it would be natural to forget who they were. No doubt, that was part of the enemy's plan: relocate the people, and they will lose their identity. But YHWH had other plans. He miraculously returned them to their land. But would their identity return? Would they see that God's choice of them went back hundreds of years to Abraham? Would they remember what was revealed through Moses?

Then the LORD passed by in front of him and proclaimed, "The LORD, the LORD God, compassionate and gracious, slow to anger, and abounding in lovingkindness and truth; who keeps lovingkindness for thousands, who forgives iniquity, transgression and sin; yet He will by no means leave the guilty unpunished, visiting the iniquity of fathers on the children and on the grandchildren to the third and fourth generations." (Exod. 34:6–7 NASB)

First and Second Chronicles seems to have been written for the exiles to help them know who they were. They needed to be reminded of YHWH's choice to shape their ancestors into a nation through which he would bless the world. They must again grasp that he both blesses obedience and disciplines sin. Perhaps most importantly they must never forget to keep proper worship of YHWH as the central activity that governs life.

Though this purposely structured genre is very foreign to our modern ears and eyes it spoke to ancient Israel and God speaks to us through it as well. With some extra work and careful attention these lengthy lists can enliven our own identity. Because we have been grafted into Israel, these are our spiritual ancestors. These are our people. And just like them we need to be reminded of who and whose we are.

Preaching Idea

Remember what defines you: God's choice and expectation.

Contemporary Connections

Is it true?

We all have written documents that prove who we are: passports, driver licenses, birth certificates, Social Security cards, student or employee badges. We use them daily. We show them to people when requested. They open doors. They let us check out books at a library. They prove that we have a right to drive a car. They are of particular importance when we travel by air or cross a border into another nation. These cards and papers identify who we are—at least enough to satisfy some authority asking for identification.

In 1999 on a Wednesday night, a terrible tragedy happened at a student gathering held at Wedgwood Baptist Church in Fort Worth, Texas. A very sick individual shot and killed seven of those attending and then killed himself. It happened in the very room where the church gathers for worship on Sunday. This horrific event was and still is a major crisis in the affected families and in the life of the church. The commemorative granite plaques and flagpole still stand at the church. Three years after that event I attended Wedgwood and got to know the pastor, Al Meredith. When I asked him about the event, he replied with great insight that came through months and years of pain: "We will never forget what happened, but we will not let it define us." Wedgwood had to choose to remember what defined them.

The Jews had gone through a crisis that could have defined them. By God's disciplining hand they had been conquered and sent into exile hundreds of miles from their homeland. Tragedy after tragedy befell them. It had been both a personal and national crisis. Now by God's merciful hand they were returning to their land. It would be very natural to forget who they were. If they'd had them, their passports would have been from Persia, not Israel; from Babylon, not Jerusalem. God wanted to remind Israel that it was not a birth certificate nor even the past seventy years that defined them.

When we go through a crisis, we sometimes forget who we are. A job loss, a divorce, the death of a family member, an illness—each of these crises can create selective amnesia. What defines us? Is it a position of a senior vice president, a marriage of thirty-plus years, a relationship with a beloved grandparent, our living in the big house we always dreamed about, or being a student at a prestigious university? In part these do and should define us, but there is a deeper definition of who we are. There was for Israel and there is for us. The genealogy showed Israel who they truly were and teaches us who we are as well.

What does it mean?

Israel was created and chosen by God. The opening chapters of 1 Chronicles show us that Israel does have a place in the world, and it is because of God's choice. This choice extends to us

75

today. We were chosen by God to be included in his family. Just as God's choice of Abraham was related to his faith, it is still by faith that we receive this gracious gift of becoming his children. Whose we are is what defines us.

A chorus written by Pat Barret and Tony Brown helps us with our identity, putting into a few well-chosen words what this genealogy was trying to say to Israel and to us: "You're a good, good, father, that's who you are / and I am loved by you, that's who I am." When looked at as a whole, this genealogy is saying to Israel, "You are loved by God." What defines them is that they were chosen by God. God loves them. And the whole of Scripture and the cross and resurrection of Jesus are saying to us that we are loved by God and that defines us. That's who we are. Who are we? We are the ones loved by God.

Another way in which we gain a sense of identity is when we have a task, something we are assigned to do. A young man went to work for a company making a very generous salary but was frustrated because he went to meetings and discussed decisions, but didn't seem to a have a clear purpose in the company. His duties were not defined. The Chronicler mentions individuals who obeyed God and were blessed (Jabez, 4:10). He also highlights individuals who disobeyed and were disciplined (Er, 2:3). God wanted Israel to know their identity through obedience that resulted in the enjoyment of his blessings. They also knew who they were when disobedient, because God's disciplining would come upon them. Their assignment was to obey. This obedience has its high point in worship. The central point of the genealogy is the tribe of Levi—the priestly tribe. The central activity for them was worship. Worship of YHWH identified who they were. Our worship of God, both corporately and individually, gives us an identity.

Now what?

As part of an eighth-grade trip to New York City, my daughter visited Ellis Island. On the plaque that lists thousands of names of those who went through the immigration process on that historic island, she found the name of Anna Carlson, who was my great-grandmother. She emigrated from Sweden in 1890. Does that define her? In part, but is that what God wanted the Israelites to do with this list of ancestors? Did they listen for their family name and swell with pride that they were of that tribe or family? If that was the case, then why the listing of Nimrod, who is credited with founding Babylon—not to mention the kings of Edom? This genealogy shows God's choice of them in the midst of other nations.

How do we respond when we are chosen? When the boss calls us in and says there is an unusual client who requires our special skill set? When the admissions office sends the letter that says we have been accepted? When another person chooses to enter into a lifelong commitment of marriage with us? Each of these changes our identity. God's choice of me to be his child, and his assignment, gives me an unshakable identity. I will always be his child. If I obey, I see his hand of blessings. If I disobey, I see his hand of discipline. His hand is always there.

Creativity in Presentation

This is probably the most challenging passage of Scripture to present. This section of nine chapters is unusually long. The names are hard to pronounce. The structure is confusing. To be honest, we wonder why God has it as part of his revelation to us. So how do we do this?

It will require an introduction that is longer than most, in which we not only give an overview of the content but also take time to explain the different kinds of genealogies (see the commentary above). Another important element is the description of the original audience: those returning from exile. We need to try to hear the genealogies like they did, because that is how we can enter into the application for us. If we see how it applied to them, we can better apply it to ourselves.

Only select verses need to be read. If the names that are harder to pronounce are to be read, then listen to them read on a Bible app. Practice reading them. When we stumble over a pronunciation it makes the name and the person seem unimportant.

Here is one possible structure:

- Remember what defines you: God's choice and expectation.
  - His choice of us (1:1–54)
  - His expectation (2:1–9:44)
    - Obedience
      - Blessings (4:10, Jabez)
      - Discipline (9:1, the nation)
    - Worship
      - Proper personnel (6:1, appointed and qualified leaders)
      - Proper place (9:34, God's church)

Because of our own sin and the sinful world that we live in, it is a battle to remember who we are. Remember, we are God's chosen children, and he has a job for us.

DISCUSSION QUESTIONS

1. How many great-grandparents' names can you remember?

2. How many forms of identification can you list (passports, driver license, etc.)? How many do you have in your wallet?

3. List three people in your life who helped shape your identity.

4. List three things that you do that shape your identity.

5. List three events from your past that shape your identity.

6. How should being God's child affect how you think about yourself?

REIGN OF DAVID
(1 CHRONICLES 10:1–29:30)

Following the picture of Israel through its genealogies, Chronicles changes its focus to the reign of David. In contrast to the books of Samuel, Chronicles does not devote attention to David's time before he rises to the throne. Chronicles also does not address David's transgressions regarding Bathsheba and Uriah. Chronicles presents a picture of David focused on Jerusalem and pressing toward the building of the temple there.

In Chronicles, the reign of David is a story about preparing for the building of the temple in Jerusalem. The narrative shows how David prepares for the building of the temple in two primary ways: (1) he organizes Israel's worship to YHWH and (2) he secures Israel's peace from their surrounding enemies. As David organizes Israel's worship, he transfers the Ark of the Covenant to Jerusalem, establishes the musical service of worship, organizes the priests and Levites, gathers material and labor resources, and charges the next generation with building the temple. As David secures Israel's peace, he and his troops defeat numerous enemies, especially the Philistines who consistently harass Israel.

As the founder of a dynasty, David becomes a model for later kings. In his zeal to worship YHWH, David models how a king should devote himself to YHWH. When David initially fails to transfer the ark to Jerusalem, he later models how to read and implement the Law of Moses to transfer the ark properly. Finally, even when David transgresses by conducting a census, David models how to respond as a repentant sinner. In these ways, David provides a model for his descendants to follow.

1 Chronicles 10:1–14

EXEGETICAL IDEA
Because Saul was unfaithful to YHWH and broke his commandments, YHWH destroyed Saul's dynasty and turned the kingdom over to David.

THEOLOGICAL FOCUS
God desires those who are faithful to lead in his kingdom and rejects those who are not.

PREACHING IDEA
Reject rejection by embracing faithfulness.

PREACHING POINTERS
Because of the seventy years of exile, the ones who first heard this passage knew all too well that there are consequences to sin. Perhaps they wondered if God's disciplining hand was still on them. How could they be sure that they could once again be useful to build God's kingdom? If we want to be useful workers in God's kingdom, don't be like Saul. Saul was not faithful to seek God, and God rejected him as king. This passage teaches us to be faithful to YHWH through the warning that workers and leaders in God's kingdom can be put on the sidelines by God.

YHWH TRANSFERS THE KINGDOM TO DAVID AT SAUL'S DEATH (10:1–14)

LITERARY STRUCTURE AND THEMES (10:1–14)

Up to this point, through the long genealogies of 1 Chronicles 1–9, the focus has been on establishing Israel's identity and its relationship with YHWH. The genealogies establish Israel as a group of related tribes. Now, the focus turns to Israel as a kingdom. It begins with the first king of Israel, Saul, but it only covers his death. The rest of his life is passed over in silence (except for genealogical information and a couple of other comments elsewhere in Chronicles). Although it may be surprising that the narrative of Chronicles begins with the end of Saul's dynasty, such a start "in the middle of the action" is not unusual in ancient writings. Furthermore, since Chronicles only describes Saul's death, it reveals that the focus is not the kingdom of Israel as a whole, but specifically the kingdom governed by the Davidic dynasty. The narrative explains how and why David and his descendants rule over the kingdom of Israel.

The passage breaks down into three main sections. The first section reports the battle at Mount Gilboa. This section concludes by stating that Saul and his sons died, bringing an end to his dynasty. At the same time, Israelites in the area abandoned their cities, with the result that Philistines occupied those cities. The second section recounts the aftermath of the battle. The Philistines boasted in their victory by displaying the remains of Saul and his sons. However, their boasting is brief because competent warriors from Jabesh retrieve the remains, bury them properly, and mourn for their deaths. The third section explains why Saul has died. Because Saul is faithless to YHWH and disobeys him, YHWH destroys his dynasty and transfers the kingdom to David.

- **Saul's Dynasty Dies (10:1–7)**
- **Philistines Boast Briefly (10:8–12)**
- **YHWH Transfers the Kingdom to David (10:13–14)**

EXPOSITION (10:1–14)

Today, one can find dozens, even hundreds, of resources about leadership. At times, people will discuss whether a leader is born or made. In this context, a born leader is someone who naturally has the drive, personality, and/or charisma that attracts others to follow the person. In the ancient Near Eastern world, the notion of a born leader would take on a different sense. Most roles passed down from father to son, including the role of king. Therefore, the king's son is literally born a leader because, under normal circumstances, he will be king. However, normal circumstances are not guaranteed, and a royal dynasty may end. Kings from beyond the royal family can arise, depending on the circumstances.

This account shows how Saul's dynasty comes to an end when he dies at Gilboa. Furthermore, the account explains that because Saul is unfaithful to YHWH and disobeys his commandments, YHWH ends his dynasty and transfers the kingdom to David.

Saul's Dynasty Dies (10:1–7)

During the battle at Gilboa Saul dies, with consequences for his servant, sons, and kingdom.

10:1–7. The account begins by stating that the Philistines attacked Israel, forcing them to retreat as the Philistines killed many Israelites at Mount Gilboa. From this general statement concerning the entire nation, the narrative narrows the focus to Saul and his sons. During the battle, the Philistines close in on Saul and his sons. They first kill his sons and then intensify their efforts against him. As a result, the archers target and injure him. Once he is wounded, he requests that his arms-bearer kill him, because he does not want the Philistines to abuse and torture him. His arms-bearer is too afraid to do what Saul commands, so Saul kills himself. The arms-bearer follows Saul, also killing himself.

Moving from the narrow focus on Saul and his sons, the narrative zooms out again to the nation of Israel. As the arms-bearer follows Saul, so also the men of Israel who live in the valley follow the rest of Israel by fleeing from the Philistines, leaving their towns abandoned.

TRANSLATION ANALYSIS:
One may argue that the phrase "the battle intensified against Saul" (וַתִּכְבַּד הַמִּלְחָמָה עַל־שָׁאוּל) should be translated "the battle weighed heavily upon Saul," that is, "the events were closing in on Saul following the deaths of his three sons" (Knoppers 2004, 517). However, Exodus 5:9 and Judges 20:34 suggest that the expression indicates that the fighting intensifies rather than that Saul feels the effects of the battle more intensely.

Language of Saul's Request

Saul's request for his arms-bearer to kill him raises three linguistic issues. First, the role traditionally translated as "armor-bearer" (נֹשֵׂא כֵלִים) refers to a person carrying more than just armor. The person was responsible for carrying any offensive or defensive equipment needed (see Seevers 2013, 65–66). For this reason, I have used the designation "arms-bearer."

Second, Saul refers to the Philistines as uncircumcised. In several passages in the OT (Judg. 14:3;

15:18; 1 Sam. 14:6; 17:26, 36; 31:4; 2 Sam. 1:20), this word specifically designates the Philistines. It appears to be a standard derogatory term used for them.

Third, the translations treat the verb (hithpael עלל) in one of two ways. They either emphasize a sense of mockery (NRSV "make sport of me") or harsh, violent treatment (HCSB, NET, NLT "torture"; ESV "mistreat"; KJV, NASB, NIV, NKJV "abuse"). In Numbers 22:29, Balaam uses the verb to describe the way the donkey has treated him. The context does not indicate that the donkey treated Balaam violently or harshly; rather, it indicates that the donkey mocked him by refusing to follow his orders. At the same time, Judges 19:25 uses the verb to describe how the men of Gibeah abused the Levite's concubine all night, leading to her death. The ESV's translation "mistreat" does not carry the same degree of harsh, violent connotation that *hithpael* עלל carries. A translation "torture" or "abuse" captures the harsh connotation, while NLT attempts to preserve both aspects of the verb by translating it as "taunt and torture."

Since the narrative shifts its focus from Israel to Saul and his sons and then back to Israel, it reveals a point important for Chronicles: the king's actions and their results are closely tied to the nation's actions and their results (see sidebar "Relation of King to People"). In this case Saul's death has two results: (1) When Saul's arms-bearer sees that Saul is dead, he follows Saul by killing himself; and (2) when the Israelites see that Saul is dead, they abandon their cities, leaving them open for the Philistines to occupy. Saul's death and the death of his "house" (בַּיִת) leads to Israel losing some of its cities. These events foreshadow the exile coming near the end of Chronicles. Since the first readers of this text need to know why exile occurs, whether YHWH still has a future for them, and how to avoid exile from happening again, this narrative holds special importance for them. At this point, the narrative does not answer these questions; it only raises them. Later, it will provide some clues on how to answer them (see below 10:13–14).

10:6. This explanatory verse forms the climax of this section. The sentence's syntactical structure alerts the reader to its importance. The sentence summarizes the narrative's events up to this point and by summarizing provides an interpretation. The sentence states that Saul and his sons died; this point is no surprise, since the narrative has already mentioned their deaths (sons, 9:2; Saul, 9:4–5). However, the second half of the sentence interprets these events: all Saul's "house" (בַּיִת) died together. The word בַּיִת serves a critical function. On the surface, the word seems to refer to all of Saul's household, that is, himself and his heirs. However, in context the word indicates Saul's dynasty (see Japhet 1993, 224; Price 2015, 117–18; Rudolph 1955, 95; Williamson 1982, 93). For this reason, the Chronicler can say that Saul's "house" (בַּיִת) died, even while he is still aware that Saul has another son (Eshbaal) and other descendants (1 Chron. 9:39–44). The Chronicler interprets the death of Saul and his three sons Jonathan, Abinadab, Malchishua as the effective end of Saul's dynasty.

> **Linguistic Evidence for Importance of 10:6**
> The chiastic structure of *wayyiqtol* then *qatal*, using the same root, highlights this verse. Furthermore, this structure helps divide the verse into the following parts: (1) Saul and sons died, and (2) his house died together. These two parts of the statement are two ways of expressing the idea that Saul's dynasty came to an end.

Philistines Boast Briefly (10:8–12)

The Philistines humiliate Saul along with Israel and announce their victory over Saul as a victory for their gods, but the inhabitants of Jabesh undermine their announcement by recovering the bodies of Saul and his sons, burying their bodies, and mourning their deaths.

10:8–12. The next narrative section moves quickly through the aftermath of the battle. The Chronicler seems to assume some familiarity with the story from other sources (e.g., the parallel account in 1 Sam. 31) and for the most part, he focuses on Saul. For these reasons, the narrative contains several abbreviated details and gaps that only become clear in light of the entire section. As an example, the narrative only explicitly mentions that the Philistines strip Saul of his equipment and behead him. It does not mention his sons or the rest of his body; however, later in the narrative it mentions that the men of Jabesh retrieve their corpses to bury them. Interpreting the passage properly requires one to refrain from overinterpreting the abbreviated details and gaps (e.g., Japhet 1993, 228–29).

10:8–9. After the battle is over, the Philistines enter the battlefield to collect their spoils. They find the corpses of Saul and his sons among those killed in the battle. They strip them of their weapons and armor (כֵּלִים); behead Saul; and take the spoils, Saul's head, and apparently the bodies with them back to Philistine territory. When the Philistines behead Saul and take his weapons and armor, they resemble David when he had defeated the Philistine Goliath (Ackroyd 1977, 6). David beheaded Goliath and took his head to Jerusalem and his armor into his own tent (1 Sam. 17:54). In the case with Saul, the situation is reversed, since the Philistines behead the Israelite king and take his head (and armaments) back to their temples.

10:10. As the Philistines return from the battlefield, they also dispatch messengers to declare to the people and to their idols that they have defeated Israel. To commemorate and celebrate their victory further, they display Saul's armaments (weapons and armor) and his head in their temples.

The text designates two temples. Most English translations read "temple of their gods" (בֵּית אֱלֹהֵיהֶם) and "temple of Dagon" (בֵּית דָּגוֹן). The designation for the first temple (בֵּית אֱלֹהֵיהֶם) is ambiguous. The temple was most likely dedicated to a single god or goddess (1 Sam. 31:10 reads Astarte/Ashtaroth עַשְׁתָּרוֹת). At the same time, אֱלֹהֵיהֶם is a more generic term so the Chronicler does not refer to a specific name, particularly of a female deity (see Frevel 1991, 269–70), in this case. One may properly translate the phrase as "the temple of their deity" (see Judg. 9:27; 2 Kings 19:37 // 2 Chron. 32:21).

The designation for the second temple is easier to identify. Dagon is a proper name for a Philistine god also mentioned in Judges 16:23 and 1 Samuel 5. Judges 16:23 recounts that the Philistines sacrifice to Dagon because they believed he defeated Samson for them. The situation here is similar: the Philistines celebrate their victory over Saul by bringing his head before Dagon. This narrative shows how the Philistines understand their political and military affairs as religious and spiritual matters as well. First Samuel 5 describes another instance in which the Philistines attempt to celebrate their military victory before Dagon (Mosis 1973, 24–26). After the Philistines defeat Israel, they capture the ark of the covenant and display it before Dagon. However, Dagon falls headless (and armless) before the ark. With Saul, the situation is reversed. Now the head of the Israelite king hangs before the pagan god.

By designating both temples, the Chronicler creates a parallel structure in the verse. The Philistines take Saul's armor to one temple while they take his head to another. When the Philistines place Saul's head and armor in their temples, they are commemorating the fact that their gods have conquered their enemies. Saul's death not only humiliates him; it humiliates Israel and even YHWH, Israel's God. However, the Chronicler already

provides clues that the Philistines are interpreting the situation incorrectly. He refers to the Philistine gods as their idols (עֲצַבֵּיהֶם, 10:9), that is, as human-made images that are unable to do anything (1 Chron. 16:26; 2 Chron. 32:19).

10:11–12. The Chronicler continues to undermine the Philistines' interpretation by mentioning the honorable deeds of the people of Jabesh. When the inhabitants of Jabesh hear how the Philistines humiliate Saul by stripping him of his armaments, beheading him, and displaying his head and armaments in their temples, their warriors retrieve his body and the bodies of his sons to bury them in Israel's territory and mourn them in fasting. The inhabitants honor Saul by mourning for him seven days. Although these actions do not reverse the outcome of the battle, they undermine the Philistines' interpretation of what has happened since they limit Saul's humiliation, thereby limiting the extent of the Philistines' victory.

YHWH Transfers the Kingdom to David (10:13–14)

At the close of the narrative, the Chronicler explains why these events took place and provides their correct interpretation: YHWH put Saul to death for his disobedience and turned the kingdom of Israel over to David.

10:13a. Up to this point, the narrative has not provided a reason for Israel's defeat, Saul's death, or the death of his dynasty. Now, the Chronicler mentions three reasons why Saul dies. First, Saul violates his relationship with YHWH (מעל). Although the word מעל may refer to a specific transgression, such as profaning a holy object or place (e.g., 2 Chron. 26:16), in this case the Chronicler most likely uses it in a more generic sense of unfaithfulness toward YHWH (although such unfaithfulness usually includes improper worship).

Unfaithfulness Against YHWH

The Chronicler speaks often of someone's unfaithfulness against YHWH, using the term מַעַל (either as a verb or noun). Therefore, a closer look at its sense helps reveals something of the Chronicler's message. At times in the OT, the term has the more specific sense of violating what is holy; however, it also occurs as a general term for infidelity (Num. 5:12, 27). Chronicles most often uses the term for infidelity toward YHWH, almost always through improper ritual worship, either of other gods or by wrong means. Especially instructive for this purpose is the end of Joshua when the eastern tribes built a pillar, and in Ezra when the people intermarry with foreigners. Almost always it is also accompanied by "Israel's defeat by a foreign people, imprisonment or exile, loss of Judah's land or cities" (Mosis 1973, 31). See also Koch 1965, 663; *HALOT* s.v. "מַעַל" 612–13.

Second, Saul does not keep the word of YHWH. To keep the word of YHWH is to obey what YHWH commands. Usually, the word of YHWH refers to a message that he reveals through a prophet. The book of Samuel recounts two incidents in which Saul does not keep the word of YHWH: 1 Samuel 13:8–14 and 1 Samuel 15:1–35. In both cases Saul disobeys the prophet Samuel (although 1 Sam. 15 uses the same language as here; see Price 2015, 117). Throughout Chronicles, the Chronicler demonstrates that disobeying what YHWH commands through his prophets leads to disaster (e.g., 2 Chron. 24:19–24; 36:12–16; cf. Deut. 18:18–19). At the same time, the only other time the phrase occurs in Chronicles (2 Chron. 34:21) refers generically to the fact that the Israelites do not obey YHWH because they do not do what the written law of YHWH demands. In this case, the Chronicler likely alludes to Saul's disobedience, but he intends his statement to be a summary of Saul's life. Just as Saul is unfaithful (מַעַל), so also, he does not obey what YHWH commands. In this way

the Chronicler intends to show that because Saul disobeys YHWH's commands, whether ignoring the words of his prophets or the commandments written in his law (Mosis 1973, 34–35; Price 2015, 117), he dies.

10:13b–14. Third, Saul consults a medium for guidance. This third reason is a particular example following the preceding two general statements (Saul's unfaithfulness and failure to keep YHWH's word). Here, the Chronicler alludes directly to 1 Samuel 28, which recounts how Saul had consulted a medium from Endor. Mosaic law specifically condemns mediums and seeking their help (Lev. 19:31; 20:6, 27; Deut. 18:11), so the Chronicler does not need to condemn Saul's actions explicitly. However, he does draw out the results of Saul's action. Unfortunately, the break between 10:13 and 10:14 obscures the relationship between them. First Chronicles 10:14 begins by stating that Saul does not inquire of YHWH (וְלֹא־דָרַשׁ בַּיהוָה). The verb דרשׁ occurs frequently in Chronicles, usually in a general sense of following YHWH (e.g., 1 Chron. 16:11; 22:19; 2 Chron. 12:14; 26:5; see also sidebar "Seeking YHWH"). Such a sense would fit well here; however, the syntax (ב preposition attached to יהוה) suggests that the word has the sense of seeking divine guidance (Mosis 1973, 39–40). The Chronicler's point is that when Saul consults the medium, he does not consult YHWH; his point is not intended to characterize Saul's life, only comment upon his visit to the medium.

Pun on Saul's Name

The Chronicler uses a pun here: he states that Saul (שָׁאוּל, "the one who was requested") requested (שָׁאוּל) a medium to give guidance. The Chronicler, like other OT writers, often uses puns, especially with the names of people and places. For instance, Solomon (שְׁלֹמֹה) will have peace (שָׁלוֹם) during his reign (1 Chron. 22:9) while he follows YHWH with his whole heart (לְבָב שָׁלֵם, 1 Chron. 29:19). See Kalimi 1995, 37–41.

At the same time, the statement that Saul does not seek YHWH looks to other parts of the OT. In the context of Chronicles, it indicates that Israel does not care for the ark or seek YHWH during Saul's reign (see 1 Chron. 13:3 and comments regarding that passage). As a result, דרש does point to the specific situation at Endor but also characterizes Saul more generally. Beyond Chronicles, 1 Samuel 28:6 states that Saul does consult YHWH (וַיִּשְׁאַל שָׁאוּל בַּיהוָה), but YHWH does not answer. The Chronicler is not contradicting the account in Samuel; rather, he is making the point that to seek YHWH, one must do it properly. In Samuel, Saul attempts to inquire of YHWH, but YHWH does not answer. Therefore, he turns to a medium to hear from Samuel, YHWH's prophet. Saul wants to gain guidance from YHWH, but he uses an illegitimate means to do so. He tries to inquire of YHWH by taking up pagan methods. The Chronicler consistently condemns this type of syncretistic practice (Japhet 2009, 169–70; Lynch 2014b, 75–78). In fact, the point he is making here is that such "inquiring of YHWH" is not inquiring of him at all.

Because of Saul's unfaithfulness and disobedience, YHWH puts him to death. On another occasion, 1 Chronicles 2:3 records that Er, Judah's firstborn, was evil (רע), so YHWH put him to death. In both cases YHWH punishes wickedness by death. The connection between these two reveals another subtler point. The Chronicler portrays Israel's first king, a Benjaminite, in a severely negative light. In a similar way, he introduces the tribe of Judah in a severely negative light. Even though the Chronicler will present positive examples from the tribe of Judah (most notably David and Solomon), his depiction is not idealized. Furthermore, he shows that neither tribal affiliation nor birth order dictates a person's fate. Regardless of tribe or order of birth, YHWH punishes wickedness—and, as seen throughout Chronicles, blesses obedience.

Since the Chronicler records that YHWH puts Saul to death, he reveals YHWH's role in the entire narrative. Even though the narrative recounts how the Philistines pursue Saul and wound him so that he commits suicide, the Chronicler reminds the reader that YHWH directs history. Saul's death is neither the result of a series of unfortunate, random events nor the result of the power of the Philistine gods (as the Philistines interpreted it) but the consequence of YHWH's decision to punish him. This point would be especially important for those who first received this book, since they were a group of people who were trying to rebuild after they had suffered destruction and exile. The Chronicler likely points out explicitly that YHWH directs these events for two reasons: (1) to encourage the people that YHWH is in control despite the way things may look or how others may interpret them, and (2) to warn them to remain faithful to YHWH alone by obeying what he has said and seeking him in the manner he has prescribed.

The narrative regarding Saul's death concludes with a note that YHWH hands the kingdom over to David. David is not the natural heir to the throne; he is the son of Jesse, not Saul. However, as 10:6 points out, Saul's sons die in the battle, and therefore his entire house dies with them. With David there is a new beginning, a chance to follow YHWH faithfully rather than forsake him as Saul did. Following Saul's death, the Chronicler emphasizes the reign of David and his legacy through his descendants who reigned over Israel.

The first readers lived in a time without an Israelite king. On the one hand, this passage would address a question of leadership for the postexilic community. During the period before Cyrus's decree, Benjamin gained prominence in the region as Jerusalem was destroyed and many from Judah were exiled. As those from the line of Judah returned, the community had to negotiate the role that Jerusalem would play in Yehud's political and religious life as well as what role the tribes of Benjamin and Judah would play. This passage would encourage the first readers to look to Jerusalem (especially its temple) and to the tribe of Judah for leadership. At the same time, it does not ignore or condemn the role that Benjamin plays in Israel's history; it only addresses Saul's dynasty.

On the other hand, the postexilic community still had not experienced a full restoration of the land, its people, or its king. The postexilic community could see that YHWH was still directing history, as shown by Cyrus's decree (2 Chron. 36:22–23), but they still waited for YHWH to complete his plans to restore his people fully in their land with a Davidic king ruling over them. The Chronicler encourages them to look for one like David to lead them, someone faithfully worshipping God through the proper ritual practices at the Jerusalem temple. At the same time, since this narrative reflects many of their circumstances, the Chronicler shows them how to avoid YHWH's judgment even in the conditions in which they live: to remain faithful to him by obeying his word (in their context, primarily the law of Moses) and following him exclusively without incorporating pagan practices (in their context, primarily rituals like divination) or pagan objects (e.g., idols).

THEOLOGICAL FOCUS

God desires those who are faithful to lead in his kingdom, and rejects those who are not.

The primary reason the Chronicler includes this account in his work is to explain that the kingdom transfers from Saul to David because of Saul's unfaithfulness to God. Saul's character and conduct lead to his fate. Especially important for Chronicles is the comment that God puts Saul to death (10:14). As a result, Saul's death was not an accident nor the result of the Philistines' gods. Even though Saul takes his own life, his death is God's decision and his doing. This observation confirms that God is searching for someone to lead his kingdom who is not like Saul—one who is faithful, obedient to his word, and following him through proper ritual worship.

On the one hand, God finds the opposite of Saul in David. The following accounts in Chronicles show David's obedience to God's word and his concern for proper worship. On the other hand, the Chronicler awaits another like David to restore the kingdom and lead God's people in proper worship. Jesus, the descendant of David, fulfills this role. He succeeds where all other kings fail. He humbly leads an obedient life, even to his death. As a result, God grants him authority over all things, such that all will acknowledge him as Lord (Phil. 2:5–11). Furthermore, those who will lead in his kingdom are those who are like him and united with him (Eph. 1:20–21; 2:6; Col. 3:1–4; Rev. 20:4). God has chosen the faithful one to rule his kingdom and has called those who reign with him to be faithful as well.

This passage illustrates a significant theme in Chronicles: retribution. In Chronicles, retribution is the principle that God rewards obedience and punishes disobedience. Clearly, God punishes Saul for his disobedience. The language describing Saul's disobedience is instructive beyond his historical circumstances. First, the text describes Saul as being unfaithful (מעל). Even though this word carries a general sense, in Chronicles it almost always occurs in contexts involving improper ritual practices. The Chronicler points to an improper ritual practice when he speaks both of Saul's not seeking God and consulting a medium. As mentioned above, Saul does not seek God properly; therefore, the Chronicler states that Saul does not seek God at all. Today, the concern to worship God properly continues. Although practices of Christian worship may vary from place to place and time to time, incorporating practices prohibited by Scripture—even for seemingly noble purposes—will inevitably lead to disaster.

Second, the text states that Saul does not obey God's word. As mentioned above, what is in view is likely the prophetic word delivered by Samuel. In the contemporary context, the Bible is God's prophetic word. Therefore, ignoring the Bible's warnings and failing to obey its instructions for this age lead to disastrous consequences just as it did for Saul.

Beyond the passage's primary point, there are two secondary points worth mentioning. First, Saul's personal disobedience has far-reaching consequences. The punishment for his disobedience leads to his death, his servant's death, his sons' deaths, and his dynasty's demise. Furthermore, his death prompts many Israelites to flee their cities (which God granted them), with the result that Philistines occupy them. The consequences extend far beyond him to his family and his nation. The passage illustrates that the consequences of disobedience often reach much further than one may ever expect. Therefore, faithfully obeying God's instructions and addressing disobedience helps safeguard one's life, family, congregation, and community.

Second, even through punishment, God demonstrates his power. When Saul dies, the Philistines defeat Israel. As a result, the Philistines boast to their gods because of their victory. Such boasting is an insult to God. However, God works to undermine their understanding of the situation. Furthermore, during the reign of David, God will use David to defeat the Philistines thoroughly. Even though the circumstances appear to show that God is defeated, he is not. He is still working and will, at least eventually, assert his rule and power. Christians can identify with this point as Jesus's crucifixion, which appears to be his defeat, leads to his resurrection, which is his victory. Furthermore, throughout history, including today, Christians have seen periods of intense persecution; however, God continues to sustain his people around the world through the ages. Seeing his hand work in such difficult situations bolsters confidence that he will do so again.

PREACHING AND TEACHING STRATEGIES

Exegetical and Theological Synthesis

The summary verse of this chapter states that Saul died with his sons and his household (10:6). The ancient standard transition of governmental authority is particularly important in understanding this passage. This is not about God looking down from heaven and throwing the mythical lightning bolt at someone who displeases him. Saul's death, which is clearly God's doing (10:14), is not about God's revenge; it is about God rejecting him as the leader. God rejected Saul as king, but this does not mean that God rejected Saul as an individual soul. The Chronicler is not making a statement about Saul's salvation; he is making a statement about God's rejection of Saul as king. This is not to say that Saul was not rejected by God. He was. But it was not primarily because Saul was sinful. If we are to compare sins of royalty, David and Saul both had numerous and grievous sins, yet David's dynasty was chosen over Saul's. Our text explicitly says that Saul was rejected because he was not faithful in seeking God's guidance. He violated his relationship with YHWH. In contrast, David sinned but sought and worshipped only YHWH. The key lies in the relationship with YHWH. David had one; apparently, Saul did not. We can rejoice that our relationship with God is grounded in the death and resurrection of Jesus. Through faith by grace our salvation is secure, but our usefulness is another matter.

As we move into applying this passage, we learn what God expects in his kingdom workers. While none of us are called or chosen to be kings of Israel, as followers of Jesus we are all called and chosen to priests (workers) in his church and in his work in the world today.

This chapter shows us the dire consequences of disobeying and not seeking YHWH. For Saul the consequence of his unfaithfulness was rejection; for believers in this age it is God's discipline. One can be rejected by God. This doesn't mean that God will have the Philistines come and strike down church workers who are not faithful to seek and obey him. It does show us that God has expectations of workers in his kingdom. When we are not faithful and loyal to him, there will be consequences.

This chapter is a warning that we can be set on the sidelines when we should be playing in the game. It would be presumptuous to articulate what form those consequences will take. In God's mercy and omniscience, the level of discipline or rejection will be appropriate. Of course, our salvation is based upon our trust in Jesus and not on our obedience, but we must not miss the teaching of this passage: that God desires those who are faithful to lead in his kingdom and rejects those who are not.

Preaching Idea
Reject rejection by embracing faithfulness.

Contemporary Connections

What does it mean?
When we are rejected by others, it hurts. Often our first response is defensive. "This is not my fault. They shouldn't have done this." We blame the system or another person.

A young man wanted to fulfill his childhood dream of becoming a police officer, but failed the entrance test. He was rejected. A faithful and active church member who had some serious emotional issues due to combat-induced PTSD was told he shouldn't apply to be a church elder. He was rejected. A young lady was embarrassed and devastated when her fiancé broke off the relationship just two weeks before the wedding day. She was rejected. After fifteen years at a chemical plant, a single mother was laid off. She was rejected. I was denied admission to a graduate school early in my career. They told me I didn't have the right personality. I was rejected. Now after thirty-five years and multiple graduate degrees, I can see that the timing was

not right. I was young and thought much too highly of myself. God knew that I needed to be rejected.

Saul's rejection tops all of these experiences. He was rejected by God. Saul chose to reject YHWH's directives and seek a medium instead of the only true living God. The consequences were severe. He would no longer serve God as king. There would be a new dynasty. Saul's rejection was in line with his position and his sin. I was rejected—of course not at the level Saul was, but I still felt the sting of rejection.

There is a spectrum when it comes to God's rejection or discipline of his children. The pedophile must never work with children. At the other end of the spectrum, a consistently tardy preschool teacher might not be asked to be the lead teacher. God teaches us in this passage that he desires faithfulness, but he does it by showing us the disastrous results of Saul's unfaithfulness. It is a warning for us to not take sin and disobedience lightly.

Is it true?
The basketball coach controlled himself for the first half of the championship game. After numerous bad calls by the referees in the first half, he couldn't help but think that for this important game they could have found better referees. The second half started with fair calls, but as the score mounted against his team it seemed the referees got worse. At first, he only shouted, "Come on, ref!" Then he jumped up when he shouted. When his star player fouled out, he took a step on the court and got in the referee's face. The referee stood back, looked at the scorekeeper, then looked at the coach who was still shouting, and threw his finger toward the locker room and said, "Coach, you are out of the game." This passage teaches us that to varying degrees God does take people out of the game.

God wanted the exiles to rebuild the temple and the nation. For this work YHWH desired not just any workmen; he wanted faithful workers. Those who were not would, at some level, be rejected. Just as God desired faithfulness in Saul, he desires faithfulness in those who build his kingdom today. The consequences for disobedience will vary just as they did in ancient Israel. God's discipline of us will be unique for each of us. Proverbs 3 and Hebrews 12 teach us that discipline is for our good, to guide us into the life that God wants for us. This ultimate good must not cloud the teaching of this passage. When we turn from God, there are consequences. We can render ourselves useless because of sin.

Now what?
As a reminder, in preaching/teaching this passage we must distinguish that God's rejection of Saul by his death is not about his salvation. It is about usefulness.

There are two sides to the application of the principle of this passage. On the positive side there is the call for faithfulness. God desires our hearts to be exclusively faithful to him. The negative description of Saul gives us a platform to emphasize three specific actions we can take to guard our faithfulness.

Saul was rejected because of his transgression or breach of faith. This is a broad life-encompassing sin. He was not, in his heart, one who followed YHWH. Apparently, when he did obey YHWH it was only a surface obedience, but not from his heart. It was only a matter of time before he would fall away from YHWH. We need to check to be sure our hearts want to follow God. For followers of Jesus the ultimate king, this heart comes through our trusting him for our salvation, and then continuing to trust his powerful Spirit to be at work in us.

The second reason he was rejected was his failure to follow the Lord's commands. To be faithful followers, we need to know and follow God's commands. This must not become a legalistic surface checking of boxes; rather, we seek to know what God expects of us.

The third reason Saul was rejected was his specific sin of consulting a medium. The positive lesson is that we should always seek God's will and never rely upon any other spiritual authority.

The other side of the application is a harsh warning. When we are unfaithful, we will stop being useful in his kingdom work. The level of rejection varies and is from God's hand. This passage doesn't give us the details of how God disciplines in each case. Nor does it specify what form that rejection may take. The point is simply, when we face temptation, this warning should motivate us into faithful obedience. As God says later in his Word, "Consider yourselves dead to sin, but alive to God in Christ Jesus" (Rom. 6:11).

Creativity in Presentation
Caution must be taken in applying this passage to present the full passage. One could only emphasize the positive aspects about being faithful without addressing the consequences of sin. Or one could emphasize the rejection of Saul to the point that none of us would qualify for service. The desired outcome of the passage is not guilt, but faithfulness. The positive aspects of faithfulness as indicated by Saul's negative examples should be given first. The negative aspect of this chapter can be presented as a motivation to be faithful. Though that is not the only or even the best motivation, it is a motivation.

Possible structure:

- Reject rejection by embracing faithfulness.
  - Present the story of the text (10:1–14)
  - How to be faithful (10:13–14a):
    - Trust Christ for a new and faithful heart
    - Submit to his commands
    - Seek his counsel
  - Why be faithful—avoid being put on the bench (10:14b)
- Reject rejection by embracing faithfulness.

DISCUSSION QUESTIONS

1. How do we express our desire to be useful?

2. What can keep us from being useful?

3. How does being disciplined by an authority (parents, boss, police officer, teacher) feel like a rejection?

4. Describe a situation where an authority disciplines someone.

5. What are different ways that we can feel or be rejected?

6. What are some emotions we feel when we are rejected?

1 Chronicles 11:1–12:40 (HB 41)

EXEGETICAL IDEA
All Israel recognized David as king, according to David's character and YHWH's word.

THEOLOGICAL FOCUS
God's people, at their best, remain united under the authority of God's chosen king, Jesus, our Messiah.

PREACHING IDEA
We are at our best when we follow the best leader.

PREACHING POINTERS
The narrative of these two chapters is not a story with a clear plot line, but rather the celebration of David becoming king and showing the support he had in all Israel. Through this selective and overstated account of him becoming king, David is presented as the ideal king. At the beginning of this chronicling of the kings of Israel, God stirs in us this desire for a perfect leader. Though we have never written out our list, there is in each of us a picture of what the ideal leader should be like. We know that no leader is perfect, but we still have this inner standard. The great and joyful good news is that Jesus is this perfect king, the perfect leader.

ISRAEL TRANSFERS THE KINGDOM TO DAVID (11:1–12:40 [HB 41])

LITERARY STRUCTURE AND THEMES (11:1–12:40 [HB 41])

These chapters recount how Israel transfers the kingdom to David. At first, the chapters look like a narrative with a developing plotline. However, the Chronicler does not arrange the material chronologically, but geographically. Furthermore, he arranges it as a concentric structure (Williamson 1981, 168–70). He begins and ends by showing how Israel establishes David's royal authority. The other elements list military troops supporting David either as he becomes king at Hebron or even before he becomes king, at Ziklag or David's wilderness stronghold.

The Chronicler uses this structure to accomplish several goals. First, he shows that all Israel, from north to south, east to west, unanimously recognizes David as the new king. Second, he shows that David's reign is more or less inevitable, both because YHWH has chosen him as king and because, even while Saul was reigning, many Israelites recognized him as the one who should rightly rule. Third, he highlights the prophetic word, blessing all those who help David because God is helping David (1 Chron. 12:18 [HB 19]). In other words, those who support David's reign are on YHWH's side because YHWH supports David's reign. Fourth, it allows the Chronicler to acknowledge a lengthy process by which David becomes king, but also to present it as a single unit. Even though David's support grew gradually (1 Chron. 12:22 [HB 23]), the Chronicler can present this support in one listing, obscuring the chronological lines, to emphasize unified support for David's reign.

- *Establishing David's Royal Authority (11:1–9)*
- *Military Leaders Supporting David as King (11:10–47)*
- *Troops Supporting David at Ziklag (12:1–7 [HB 8])*
- *Troops from Gad Supporting David at Stronghold (12:8–15 [HB 9–16])*
- *Troops from Judah and Benjamin Supporting David at Stronghold (12:16–18 [HB 17–19])*
- *Troops Supporting David at Ziklag (12:19–22 [HB 20–23])*
- *Military Units Supporting David as King (12:23–37 [HB 24–38])*
- *Establishing David's Royal Authority (12:38–40 [HB 39–41])*

EXPOSITION (11:1–12:40 [HB 41])

In ancient Near Eastern societies, kings held positions of tremendous influence and power. For this reason, becoming a king was not always an easy task. Furthermore, demonstrating that one should remain king required some convincing. Ancient Near Eastern texts employ several common reasons for justifying a certain individual as king (for a listing, see Knapp 2015, 46–56). Two of the most common and convincing are the following: the deity chooses the person as king, and the people choose the person as king. Other reasons point to the qualities of the king himself. The new king may already possess great military strength or may have been thrust into the position of being king without doing anything to take the position by force. This passage employs these same reasons to show that David became king legitimately. This passage shows how all Israel recognized that David should be king, just as YHWH had spoken.

Establishing David's Royal Authority (11:1–9)

David rightfully secures his rule over Israel through the support of the people and the choice of YHWH.

11:1. The Chronicler hints at the main theme of this section within the first words: "All Israel gathered." All Israel gathers to make David king. The Chronicler highlights how deeply the people support David when he records that all Israel declares they are David's flesh and bone. This expression conveys a kinship relationship: all Israel identifies with David, and identifies David not as an outsider but as one of them.

> **Gathering Israel**
>
> The Chronicler marks this important event by using the word קבץ ("to gather") since the word occurs in Chronicles "at the inauguration of many important events in Israel's history" (N. Klein 2006, 298–99). See, e.g., 1 Chron. 13:2 (transfer of ark); 2 Chron. 15:9–10 (making a covenant); 20:4 (Judah's victory over large army); 23:2 (removal of Athaliah); 24:5 (repair of the temple); 32:4, 6 (Assyrian assault of Jerusalem).

11:2. Furthermore, the Chronicler reinforces how David would inevitably become king over all Israel. The people recognize that David was already serving as a military leader (expressed in the idiom "leading out and bringing in") even while Saul was king and that YHWH promised David, "You will shepherd my people Israel and be prince over my people Israel." The expression "shepherding my people" involves serving as a leader to them; this task applied to the king but was not restricted to him (see 1 Chron. 17:6).

Also, when YHWH promises that David will be a "prince" (נָגִיד), in this context, the term carries the sense of "king designate" (Mettinger 1976, 159–61; see, e.g., 1 Sam. 9:16; 10:1; 13:14; 25:30; 1 Kings 1:35; 14:7; 16:2).

> **YHWH's Promise Summarized**
>
> Even though it appears that the people introduce YHWH's promise as a direct speech, it is likely intended as a summary of what God promised. Nowhere in the OT does YHWH promise these specific words in this specific order; however, when YHWH responds to David's desire to build a temple, he promises something very similar (see 1 Chron. 17:6–7; e.g., 2 Chron. 6:1).

11:3. Therefore, since all Israel recognizes that David should be king, their elders make a covenant with David and anoint him as king. They make the covenant "before YHWH," strengthening its seriousness since YHWH serves as a witness to it. Also, they anoint David as king according to YHWH's word through Samuel. In other words, not only all Israel but YHWH himself has chosen David to be king over Israel.

11:4. The Chronicler records David's next action as leading all Israel to march against Jerusalem, otherwise called Jebus, to capture the city from the Jebusites. By mentioning the Jebusites and describing them as "the inhabitants of the land" (יֹשְׁבֵי הָאָרֶץ), the Chronicler draws on previous Scriptures to make two significant points. First, Judges 1:21 recalls that the Benjaminites were not able to drive the Jebusites from Jerusalem. When David captures Jerusalem, he does something that the Benjaminites (including Saul) could not do. Second, this expression "inhabitants of the land" (יֹשְׁבֵי הָאָרֶץ) occurs frequently to describe the nations that YHWH drives out so that Israel may possess the land (e.g., 1 Chron. 22:18; 2 Chron. 20:7; cf. Exod. 23:31; 34:12). When David captures Jerusalem, he helps fulfill YHWH's work in driving out these inhabitants. Both connections elevate David's importance and positive portrayal.

The Chronicler records the capture of Jerusalem immediately following his coronation, yet preceding Israel's celebration of his coronation (1 Chron. 12:38–40 [HB 39–41]). In this case, the Chronicler is not reporting the events in chronological order (see "Literary Structure and Themes," above). Instead, he places the capture of Jerusalem first because it "underscores the fundamental importance of Jerusalem both to David and to Israel" (Knoppers 2004, 545). As seen throughout Chronicles, Jerusalem is so important because it is the site for the future temple, the place YHWH selects for his name to dwell and where the people gather to pray (e.g., 2 Chron. 6:12–40) and worship (e.g., 2 Chron. 7:12). Even from the start of David's reign, the Chronicler reveals David's interest in Jerusalem.

11:5–8. Another purpose for including the account of Jerusalem's capture is to introduce and explain some of the people and places that occur throughout Chronicles. First, Chronicles reveals that Joab plays an important role during David's reign; however, he is not included in the following lists of military leaders in chapters 11–12. Therefore, the Chronicler introduces him as David's chief commander here. The Chronicler shows how he completes David's challenge to attack the Jebusites first, and how he restores the rest of Jerusalem after he conquers it (Ristau 2015, 134–38). Second, the Chronicler introduces the city of David. He identifies the city of David with the stronghold of Zion. Since the Chronicler mentions Zion in only one other passage (2 Chron. 5:2), it is important that he identify the city of David with Zion to reveal its connection to the temple and relate it to the psalms and prophets that continually use the word "Zion" (צִיּוֹן) to refer

to Jerusalem or the Temple Mount. He also explains that the city of David receives its name because David stays there. David even builds the area up.

11:9. After mentioning the capture and rebuilding of Jerusalem, the Chronicler states that David continues growing stronger. This comment looks back at David's success in becoming king, capturing his new capital, assigning his chief commander, and together building up the captured city. At the same time, the comment looks forward to the following lists of military officers and troops who support David as king. The lists show that David's support increases over time, beginning even while Saul was reigning and continuing through the celebration of David's coronation. Therefore, even though the lists may look like a static picture of all Israel's support at the beginning of David's reign, it reveals a more dynamic picture in which more and more of Israel recognizes that David should be the next king. At the same time, the text creates a strong impression of all Israel united in supporting David. One can see how the Chronicler here balances the historical reality with his theological purpose.

Immediately before the Chronicler records the lists of officers and troops, he comments that YHWH of hosts is with David. The Chronicler rarely uses this title for YHWH (elsewhere only in 1 Chron. 17:7, 24). Its use here makes good sense because the title here depicts YHWH as a warrior, commanding his forces in battle (see 1 Sam. 17:45). At the same time, YHWH is with David, in this case meaning that YHWH is supporting and aiding David. Although David succeeds, YHWH is the real power behind David's success. Again, this comment looks back to explain how David and Joab successfully capture Jerusalem and rebuild it. It also looks forward to the lists of military units (also called "hosts"). This connection reinforces David's claim to the throne, since both YHWH and the people support him.

Divine and Popular Support

This theme recurs throughout Chronicles with both positive and negative examples. As an example on the positive side, YHWH chooses Solomon as David's successor and all the people support him (1 Chron. 29:23–24). As an example on the negative side, YHWH removes Jehoram as king through a painful death. When he dies, no one regrets his death nor honors him during his burial (2 Chron. 21:20).

Military Leaders Supporting David as King (11:10–47)

This section presents great warriors who support David as king and some of their astounding accomplishments.

11:10–47. The rest of chapter 11 contains a list of military leaders who support David as king. The list not only names several military leaders and their places of origin, but for those leaders occurring in the first part of the list, it also includes some of their heroic accomplishments. The list depicts David's officers as brave, competent warriors who support David becoming king, as YHWH promised. The list designates specifically two or three groups among these officers: the three and the thirty and/or perhaps captains. These groups appear to represent the most elite warriors; therefore, their support in making David king carries significant weight.

Designation of Military Units

Several factors make it difficult to uncover the precise relationship between the three, thirty, and/or captains as well as the warriors who belong to each group. There are several textual variants in these verses, involving three words that are very similar in Hebrew: "three" (שָׁלֹשׁ), "thirty" (שְׁלֹשִׁים), and "captains" (שָׁלִישִׁים). Furthermore, some of these variants reflect differences between the oral (*qere*) and written (*ketiv*) transmission of the Hebrew text. This list is also partially preserved in 2 Samuel 23:8–39, with some variants between the texts. Moreover, in this context, "three" and

"thirty" are designations for military units. For this reason, they may or may not always refer to a group of exactly three or thirty warriors respectively. For instance, one will notice that the Chronicler lists far more than thirty warriors even though one should most likely identify these soldiers as members of the thirty. Despite these difficulties, the general picture that emerges from the text is clear.

11:11–25. The first four warriors to occur in the list relate in some way to the group of elite warriors, the three: Jashobeam is apparently the captain of this elite group, while Eleazar serves as the next-in-command. The text recounts heroic deeds for each warrior. Jashobeam kills three hundred enemies in one fight, while Eleazar takes his stand in a field of crops to deliver Israel from the Philistines.

TRANSLATION ANALYSIS:
Translations differ on which group Jashobeam commands: the three (ESV, NLT, NRSV), the thirty (CSB, NASB), or the captains (NET, NIV, NKJV). The reading of "three" seems most likely, because the text identifies the next warrior listed (Eleazar) explicitly as a member of the group of three and describes him as next-in-command. Therefore, it seems more likely that the list would begin with the highest-ranking officer among the three and then move to the next. The other translations differ because of textual variants (cf. "Designation of Military Units," above).

After recounting a brief narrative concerning an anonymous group of three (see below), the list continues by naming Abishai and Benaiah. Both men accomplish heroic feats and gain considerable honor. Abishai, like Jashobeam, kills hundreds of enemies with his spear, while Benaiah performs unusual feats of strength and skill. He kills two powerful warriors from Moab, kills a lion in its den on a snowy day, and beats an Egyptian (described like Goliath) with only his staff and the Egyptian's own spear. However, even though Abishai and Benaiah earn a reputation like those of the elite group of three, they do not become members of that group. By recording the individual heroic deeds of these four men, two of whom do not belong to the most elite group of warriors, the Chronicler shows how these great men support David as king, further confirming that David is the rightful king. Furthermore, it illustrates YHWH of hosts—that is, YHWH the warrior is with him, strengthening his warriors to perform such heroic feats.

TRANSLATION ANALYSIS:

Translations differ on how they render the Hebrew phrase אֵת שְׁנֵי אֲרִיאֵל. The term אֲרִיאֵל is ambiguous and its meaning disputed. Translations generally approach the verse in one of three ways. First, they treat אריאל as a proper noun, and following some LXX mss., read the text as שְׁנֵי בְנֵי אֲרִיאֵל: "two sons of Ariel" (CSB, NASB, NET, NRSV). Second, they emend the word to read אראלי and understand it to mean "warrior, champion" (ESV, NIV, NLT). Third, they draw directly on a popular etymology meaning "lion of God," to render the phrase as "two lion-like heroes" (NKJV). Since בְנֵי could easily fall out following שְׁנֵי (notice the similar endings), the first approach seems most likely.

Similarities to Goliath

Two features describing the Egyptian warrior resemble Goliath. First, the text specifies the warrior's height (five cubits), demonstrating that he is quite tall like Goliath. Goliath's height varies among manuscripts, ranging from four, five, or six cubits and a span. Second, the Egyptian's spear is similar to Goliath's weapon because both resemble a weaver's beam (כִּמְנוֹר אֹרְגִים). The comparison between the two warriors further highlights the greatness of Benaiah's triumph.

11:15–19. Beyond these warriors' individual deeds, the text also relates a story concerning an anonymous group of three warriors. The story relates how these three break through the Philistine defenses at Bethlehem to bring David some water from a well located near its gate. David verbally longs for the water, so the men secure it for him. However, when David realizes what they have done and how dangerous the task, he treats the water as though it were blood and pours it out on the ground (e.g., Deut. 12:16) as an offering to YHWH (see Boda 2010a, 116, for a different interpretation, see Jonker 2013a, 99; R. Klein 2006, 305). The story presents a clear picture of the warriors: they are brave, competent, and loyal to David, even risking their own lives to secure him water from a particular place (David's hometown). However, the picture of David is ambiguous. Is David innocently making a wishful statement, and after these loyal men risk their lives to fulfill it, refuses to drink what endangers his own men's lives? Or, is David trying to satisfy some greedy craving and comes to his senses once the men return with the water? In this context in Chronicles, it seems unlikely the Chronicler would want to present David in a negative light. Also, the issue of loyalty is important for these lists of military leaders and their troops (see below). For this reason, this episode illustrates both the loyalty of David's warriors and David's compassion toward those who risk their lives for his sake. Their loyalty and his compassion strengthen David's rightful claim to be king.

11:26–47. The rest of chapter 11 consists of names and places of origin for David's other military leaders, most likely associated with the thirty. For the most part, these warriors come from Judah, its nearby surrounding areas, or from the region across the Jordan. The list anticipates 1 Chronicles 12 in which troops from all over Israel join David.

Troops Supporting David at Ziklag (12:1–7 [HB 8])

Before David becomes king, several competent Benjaminites join David to help him in war.

12:1–7 (HB 8). At the beginning of chapter 12, the Chronicler introduces a new list. This list looks back to a previous point in David's life when Saul is still alive and threatens David's life.

During this time, David flees to the Philistines, where he finds safety, and eventually receives Ziklag as a city where he can stay (1 Sam. 27:1–6). Sometime during his time at Ziklag several Benjaminites, Saul's relatives, join David. These warriors are competent long-range fighters, able to shoot arrows and sling stones with either hand. This list introduces a term running throughout the chapter: "help" (עזר, עֵדֶר). These warriors join many others in "helping" David in combat, a sign of their loyalty to him. By mentioning these warriors as Saul's relatives (אֲחֵי שָׁאוּל) who come to help David while he is still fleeing from Saul, the Chronicler strengthens the sense that David is the inevitable king of all Israel even before Saul dies.

TRANSLATION ANALYSIS:
Translations treat the Hebrew phrase עָצוּר מִפְּנֵי שָׁאוּל in one of two ways: (1) David is banished from Saul's presence (CSB, NET, NIV), or (2) his movements were restricted (and therefore must be hidden) because of Saul (ESV, NASB, NLT, NRSV). The verb often describes a person who is confined to a certain place or under watch by some authority (Neh. 6:10; Jer. 33:1, 36:5; 39:15). The word מִפְּנֵי may signal someone's presence ("from the presence of"); however, it may also indicate the cause ("because of"). Therefore, both translations are possible; however, the scene that the Chronicler is describing seems to align more closely with the second way of translating the phrase. David is on the run from Saul. His problem is not that he cannot see Saul, but that he cannot move about in Israel because Saul is trying to kill him (see Rudolph 1955, 104).

Benjaminite Warriors

Several passages present the Benjaminites as competent long-range fighters (Judg. 23–24; 1 Chron. 8:40; 2 Chron. 14:7; 17:17). Ironically, the name "Benjamin" translates as "son of right hand," yet these warriors fight with either the left or right hand (cf. Judg. 23–24). The text indicates either that each soldier was ambidextrous, or that some of them were right-handed and some of them were left-handed. It seems more likely here that since the Chronicler presents them as such impressive warriors, he intends to communicate that they are ambidextrous.

Troops from Gad Supporting David at Stronghold (12:8–15 [HB 9–16])

Before David becomes king, several competent Gadite warriors join David's forces.

12:8–15 (HB 9–16). After listing the Benjaminites, the Chronicler lists the Gadites who join David at the wilderness stronghold. This event looks even further back in David's life, since his time in the wilderness precedes his time at Ziklag (1 Sam. 22:1–5; 23:14). The Chronicler specifies that these troops switch to David's side; that is, they transfer their loyalty from Saul to David. Furthermore, their allegiance should provide a boost for David's cause, since they are such great warriors. The Chronicler uses two comparisons to describe them: they have faces like lions and are as swift as gazelles. The OT portrays a lion as fierce and fearless (e.g., Gen. 49:9; Deut. 33:22; 2 Sam. 27:10; Ps. 17:12; see Strawn 2003, 43–49), so these warriors share those characteristics. Gazelles are swift animals, even bounding through rough terrain quickly, so these warriors are extremely quick. In fact, after listing these warriors (most likely by decreasing rank), the list concludes by describing them as equal to a hundred or even a thousand other soldiers, and by recounting one of their heroic deeds: they crossed the Jordan while it was flooding over its banks.

TRANSLATION ANALYSIS:
The text is ambiguous as it describes the greatness of warriors. Translations understand the text to mean either that these captains led military

units of hundreds and thousands or that each captain was equivalent to a hundred or even a thousand men. Since the expression uses a comparison of the least (הַקָּטָן) to the greatest (הַגָּדוֹל), the latter option is more likely. If the least is equivalent to a hundred and the greatest to a thousand, then those in the middle would be equivalent to a number between a hundred and thousand. However, the comparison does not work as well if the hundred and thousand refer to military unit designations. Furthermore, the ability of one warrior to stand against many others embodies one of God's blessings (Lev. 26:8; Deut. 32:30; Isa. 30:17). See R. Klein 2006, 319. Furthermore, as Sara Japhet points out, the sons of Israel also crossed the Jordan when it was flooding over its banks (Josh. 3:15); however, they crossed on dry land. These warriors "crossed the Jordan at the peak of its overflow, through the torrent, in a feat of human strength" (Japhet 1993, 262).

Troops from Judah and Benjamin Supporting David at Stronghold (12:16–18 [HB 17–19])

Before David becomes king, several warriors from Benjamin and Judah pledge their loyalty to David because God's spirit has affirmed that God helps David.

12:16–18 (HB 17–19). This section forms the thematic and theological center of chapters 11–12. The section describes a time while David is still running from Saul, hiding out in the wilderness. Some of the Benjaminites and Judahites approach David; thus, David questions their loyalty. The words he uses in his question signal several key themes: "peace" (שָׁלוֹם), "help" (עזר), "together" (יַחַד), and "wrong" (חָמָס). David suggests that those who come in peace to help him will be united with him. Furthermore, even though he is running from Saul he has done nothing wrong, such as trying to usurp Saul to become king.

In response to David's question, the spirit inspires one of the leaders, Amasai, to clarify and expound the significance of David's words. To summarize, Amasai affirms that the warriors are loyal to David and identify together with him ("We are yours, David"). Furthermore, he clarifies that those who support David will receive peace because YHWH helps David. In other words, YHWH has selected David as king; David has not tried to become king on his own. At the same time, YHWH will give peace (שָׁלוֹם) to those who help (עזר) David, those together (יחד) from all Israel. These points form the central themes of these chapters.

> **Connections to Amasai's Words**
>
> The way that Amasai phrases the response ("We are yours, David") looks back to 1 Chronicles 1:1, where all Israel joins together to make David king. It also looks forward to 2 Chronicles 10:16, when the northern tribes form their own nation of Israel. In both cases the Chronicler points out that YHWH is directing the events (1 Chron. 10:14; 2 Chron. 10:15).

Troops Supporting David at Ziklag (12:19–22 [HB 20–23])

More warriors join David's forces even though he never fights against Saul.

12:19–22 (HB 20–23). This section has two main points: first, to show how other tribes of Israel (specifically, Manasseh) become loyal to David to help him; and second, to show that even when David lives among the Philistines while fleeing from Saul he does not attack Israel in the battle that leads to the death of Saul and his entire house (cf. 1 Chron. 10:6). These verses look back to the events recounted in 1 Samuel 29–30. David is fleeing from Saul and finds protection among the Philistines. As the Philistines prepare to attack Israel, they decide not to allow David to join them. He returns to Ziklag to find that some Amalekites have raided the city, burning it and taking captives. Chronicles only recounts how warriors from Manasseh (successfully) attack these raiders.

12:22 (HB 23). The section concludes with a note that David's army grows to an immense size because day after day warriors come over to his side. Although syntactically the verse could apply only to warriors from Manasseh, it is more likely that the verse intends to indicate that warriors from all Israel continue to join David. In fact, the verses following confirm this impression as they list the troops who join David to support him as king. As a result of these warriors coming from all Israel, David's army grows exceptionally large. The Chronicler describes its size by using a simile: it is "like a divine army" (כְּמַחֲנֵה אֱלֹהִים). Although the Chronicler on occasion associates Israel's army with YHWH's army (cf. 2 Chron. 14:12 [HB 13]), here the point is not that David's army is God's army; instead, the phrase "like a divine army" uses the divine descriptor to indicate how large the army is (cf. Jonah 3:3).

Military Units Supporting David as King (12:23–37 [HB 24–38])
This section lists the troops from all Israel's tribes who support making David king at Hebron.

12:23–27 (HB 24–38). The Chronicler returns his attention to Hebron, where all Israel has assembled to make David king (1 Chron. 11:1–3). This list describes the troops from all Israel who come to Hebron to ensure that David is king as YHWH has commanded and to celebrate his enthronement. The text lists the troops by tribe and includes the most complete listing possible: Judah, Simeon, Levi, Benjamin, Ephraim, Manasseh (west of Jordan), Issachar, Zebulun, Naphtali, Dan, Asher, Reuben, Gad, and Manasseh (east of Jordan). The Chronicler is showing that it really is all Israel that is supporting David as king.

The numbers of troops at the beginning of the list are quite a bit smaller than the numbers

later in the list; however, the tribes at the beginning of the list are located much closer to Hebron than the tribes at the end. Ralph Klein summarizes well the relationship between these two observations: "The principle seems to be, the more remote the tribe, the larger its delegation at David's coronation" (2006, 315). In other words, David does not rally his own tribe to force himself upon the rest of the tribes; even those far away (who will later separate from Judah) recognize that YHWH has chosen David to be king, and they support him as king.

The list addresses two characteristics of the troops: their competence and their loyalty. It emphasizes, using various vocabulary, that all these troops are competent warriors, properly prepared for combat. It also points out that these troops are loyal to David. It begins by acknowledging that many Benjaminites remained loyal to Saul during his lifetime, but now they follow David (12:29 [HB 30]). The troops from Zebulun support David with undivided loyalty (12:33 [HB 34]). The troops from Issachar are "those who can discern the times in order to know what Israel should do" (12:32 [HB 33]). Even though this phrase may refer to wisdom in a general sense, in context, it likely carries a more specific reference: they know that Israel should now make David king (R. Klein 2006, 324). In other words, after they perceive that YHWH has chosen David as king, they loyally follow him and indicate that all Israel should as well.

TRANSLATION ANALYSIS:
The text uses an interesting expression: בְּלֹא־לֵב וָלֵב. The repetition of לֵב seems to indicate "two hearts" or doublemindedness. These warriors did not possess this type of doublemindedness; they were singularly focused on supporting David. A translation such as "with singleness of purpose" (ESV, NRS,V cf. CSB) emphasizes their devotion to the task of helping David. A translation such as "with undivided loyalty" (NET, NIV, cf. NLT) emphasizes the relationship to David.

Establishing David's Royal Authority (12:38–40 [HB 39–41])

All the people, including these competent warriors, gladly celebrate together in making David king of Israel.

12:38–40 (HB 39–41). The list of troops closes by recounting how they enter Hebron to ensure that David is king and to celebrate his enthronement. The text emphasizes that all these troops fully agree (בְּלֵבָב שָׁלֵם) to make David king. Furthermore, everyone else in Israel also is in full agreement (לֵב אֶחָד) with them. The troops, supported by those in the neighboring areas, enjoy a feast for three days (similar activity occurs when Solomon becomes king; 1 Chron. 29:22). In fact, the supplies for the feast are so rich in quantity and quality that every type of beast of burden is needed to carry the supplies. This celebration indicates just how much all Israel supports David as king.

12:40 (HB 41). The text closes by stating that since David has become king, there is joy in all Israel. Joy is a recurring theme in Chronicles, most often associated with temple worship (e.g., 1 Chron. 15:16; 2 Chron. 23:18; 29:30; 30:21, 23, 26). One occurrence of the word proves especially helpful for understanding its significance here: in 1 Chronicles 29:22 all Israel has great joy when they affirm Solomon as king and Zadok as priest. This verse connects the joy regarding the king with the joy regarding the priest. The Chronicler points out this joy particularly for David, because David prepares for the building of the temple. In fact, the very next passage (1 Chron. 13:1–4) recounts David's desire to transfer the ark to Jerusalem. In other words, the Chronicler is indicating that Israel's joy depends on all Israel supporting the king YHWH has chosen and worshipping in the temple YHWH has chosen.

Looking back at chapters 11–12, David rarely acts himself; he is primarily passive. The people and the troops are those gathering,

coming, enthroning, helping, and so on. They make him king. Furthermore, when the Philistines battle against Saul, the Philistines do not allow David to join them (1 Chron. 12:19 [HB 20]). David does nothing to secure the throne for himself. As David claims, he has done no wrong with his hands (12:17 [HB 18]).

These chapters repeatedly point out that YHWH has selected David as king. The chapters show that YHWH communicates this selection through various means. The text cites YHWH as he speaks to David about it (1 Chron. 11:2). It draws on the authority of the prophet Samuel (1 Chron. 11:3). It uses a general prophetic formula (1 Chron. 11:10). It recounts how the spirit envelops Amasai to bless David and those who support him (1 Chron. 12:18). Finally, it cites what comes from YHWH's mouth (1 Chron. 12:24). The number and variety of these references reveal that the Chronicler wants to emphasize that David becomes king because YHWH has chosen him, and Israel recognizes this choice.

In chapter 10, the Chronicler records how Saul dies because of his wicked behavior. He closes out that chapter by stating that YHWH transfers the kingdom to David, the son of Jesse. Then, in chapters 11–12, the Chronicler records how Israel carries out YHWH's transferring the kingdom to David. His primary concern is to show how all Israel fulfills what YHWH has said by supporting David as king. For the most part, he accomplishes this purpose by including lists of military leaders and their forces who help David as he rises in prominence and power. These lists emphasize the people's loyalty to David, helping him even before Saul dies because YHWH is already helping David as well.

The first readers might react in different ways to these chapters. The days when all Israel rallied together have passed. Who belongs to Israel as the people of God may have not been clear; however, the Chronicler seems to encourage them to include those from all Israel's tribes. Furthermore, there was no Davidic king sitting on the throne, even though the passage emphasizes that David legitimately ruled as king. However, just as David did not assert his kingship or usurp the throne, so also the first readers should not follow someone wanting to usurp the Persian king that YHWH had granted authority (see 2 Chron. 36:23). The readers would see in David's enthronement that YHWH had selected him and would establish David's rule through YHWH's means rather than through underhanded political dealings. At the same time, these chapters could provide hope that the picture of all Israel, united to support a king like David, is possible. It has already taken place in the past, and so it may happen again. The people need only to wait for YHWH to turn the kingdom over to another.

THEOLOGICAL FOCUS

God's people, at their best, remain united under the authority of God's chosen king, his Messiah.

At first glance, this passage only addresses an antiquarian concern: justify David's rule over all Israel. The focus on God's word, popular support, military strength, and David's passivity serves this purpose. However, when the Chronicler puts together this account, his pictures of David and Israel speak beyond the historical past. They present models that carry theological weight.

To begin, it is helpful to examine the Chronicler's picture of David. The passage highlights several aspects regarding David's character. First, it highlights David's concern for Jerusalem. Immediately following David's coronation, he proceeds to Jerusalem and seizes control of the city, specifically the stronghold of Zion. By mentioning Jerusalem and Zion, the Chronicler anticipates the building of the temple and subtly hints that David is first concerned with worshipping God properly. Second, the passage highlights David's competence because God helps him. David gains strength and power because YHWH of Hosts aids him (1 Chron. 11:9). Even before David

becomes king, the spirit comes upon Amasai to confirm that God helps David (1 Chron. 12:18 [HB 19]). The people recognize the power of God operating through David. Third, the passage presents David as not attempting to grasp the throne for himself; in other words, he is not thirsty for power. Instead, David becomes king because God's word is working itself out through the circumstances. Throughout the passage David remains passive while the people support him as king, according to God's word.

The Chronicler presents this portrait of David as a model for a legitimate king, either during his lifetime or in the future. A legitimate king would be concerned with properly worshipping God. A legitimate king would demonstrate God's power working through him. A legitimate king would not wrestle for rule but allow God's choice to work out on its own. The New Testament confirms that Jesus fulfills this model. Jesus is concerned for properly worshipping God and even inaugurates a new era in God's worship as he explains that proper worship no longer happens only in Gerizim or in Jerusalem but in spirit and in truth (John 4:21–24). Jesus demonstrates the power of God to cast out demons, heal diseases, forgive sins, and conquer death. Despite Jesus's rightful claim to rule, he does not grasp for earthly power. Others identify him as king; he does not announce it himself. They recognize him as king as the circumstances unfold according to God's word. In these ways, Jesus confirms that he is the legitimate king and fulfills the Chronicler's anticipated expectation. Jesus is God's chosen king, his Messiah.

The Chronicler's picture of Israel also leads to theological insight. All Israel supports David as king. This unified support is more than just a bit of historical trivia; it is a goal for the people of God. The Chronicler presents this goal in terms of all Israel's tribes. The Chronicler recognizes that the people may not have reached the goal yet, but his picture encourages them to accept one another. The New Testament expands this vision of unity beyond just the tribes of

Israel. The church is one although it consists of Jews and Gentiles (Eph. 2:14–22), so the people must strive for unity (Eph. 4:3–6). Ultimately, this goal will come about so that people from every nation, tribe (including the tribes of Israel), people, and language will praise God and the Lamb, God's chosen Messiah (Rev. 7:5–10). Therefore, God's people are at their best when they remain united under the authority of God's chosen king, his Messiah.

PREACHING AND TEACHING STRATEGIES

Exegetical and Theological Synthesis
Our linear western thinking brings confusion when we try to make sense of this passage. We assume that the Chronicler is taking us on a chronological journey into the beginning of David's reign. This pericope begins and ends with an account of David being established as king (11:1–9; 12:38–40). The first includes a covenant made with the leaders of Israel, and the second account includes a joyful celebration for all of Israel. One would expect to see a series of events that led up to the celebration. But the content of the middle section (11:10–12:37) is not a listing of events but rather a description of the mighty men who support David. The order of presentation of these supporters is not based on clans or tribes, but rather on geography. Those presented first were closer to Jerusalem. The point of these two chapters is that David is being presented as the ideal king. Those who support and follow him are successful and joyful.

This ideal king is a literary overstatement because David was not ideal in many ways, but the writer wants the exiles, and us, to long for an ideal king like David. A real king is pictured for us to affirm that this is a real desire that will be fulfilled.

God seems to be saying to Israel, "These mighty men followed a great king. Don't you want a king like this?" And to us he is saying the same thing, "Don't you want to follow someone like this?" There is something in every one of us that wants to follow a leader, but every leader we know of is not perfect, so our devotion and joy must be qualified. As we read this account God is stirring something in our hearts that he put there: a desire to be led by an ideal, perfect leader. The fulfillment of this desire is in following Christ. Jesus is not only a son of David, but also the God of David. Jesus alone is our best leader, our perfect king.

Preaching Idea
We are at our best when we follow the best leader.

Contemporary Connections

Is it true?
Like it or not, we all want to follow someone. Sounds a little archaic: Isn't this the day of choice and people being applauded for doing their own thing no matter how strange or even aberrant it might be? But even those who seem to be unique have a leader, be it a parent, close friends, or a social media virtual support group.

God designed us to follow a leader. We see this in the highest office in the United States. Every president since I have been alive (Biden, Trump, Obama, Bush . . . back to Truman) ended his oath of office with the statement "so help me God." We could dismiss this prayer for help as just being a part of the requirement of the oath of office. But it is not part of the mandated oath; it is added at the request of the incoming president. Washington, Lincoln, and others added it on their own. Now it has become routine, and it shows that, at least in the formalities, our top governmental leader wants to follow a leader.

Whether it is a high school drama club, a college volleyball team, a start-up business, a construction crew, or a military unit, when we have been a part of a group that was led well, it was a pleasure to follow a leader, and resulted in unity and effectiveness.

But then the day comes when this great leader falls. Depending upon the level of failing, we might have tolerated the shortcomings and stayed as a follower. Or, the error might be so bad and even chronic that we had to leave their influence. But in either case, it didn't change our desire for a perfect leader. The fact that we know we will never have a perfect leader doesn't erase our desire to have one.

What does it mean?

The writer gives us a picture of David's characteristics of leadership, but not in the form of a list, as he did the genealogies; his telling of the story reveals them.

David was appointed by an ultimate authority. The disappointment of January 6, 2021, when rebellious rabble stormed the US capitol, is a continual embarrassment to the United States. These people were upset because they didn't believe that the president-elect had been legally elected by the people; they doubted the veracity of the electoral process. That scar on our nation shows the importance of the leader being chosen and put in office by a trusted authority. David had the highest authority to be king. It was the according to the word of God (11:3, 10). God, through the prophet Samuel, appointed David as king. It was not that David decided that he wanted to be king and orchestrated events so that he could overthrow Saul. David was almost passive in his rise to power. The events verified that God wanted him as king.

Another characteristic that God was effectively working through his leadership is indicated by the effectiveness of those who followed him. This listing of his supporters includes descriptions of their mighty deeds, from striking down enemies to slaying a lion in a pit on a snowy day. These followers accomplished great things. The true mark of a good leader is the effectiveness of those that are being led. A sports team can have individual superstars, but if not led well they will not be a championship team. That is why effective coaches and CEOs are valued so highly. Part of the effectiveness of David's mighty men came because of David's devotion to them. This is seen in his refusing to have the pleasure of drinking of Bethlehem well water when his soldiers could not share the same joy.

The story hints at another important priority for David. One of David's first acts was to take Jerusalem. The Chronicler, knowing that later this was to be the site of the temple, is subtly showing us David's heart for worship. Whom a leader worships tells us to whom he truly submits. This shows that for David the worship of YHWH was priority.

In each case these leadership characteristics are seen in our perfect leader Jesus. Appointed by God, he effectively led and leads his followers and has worship as a priority.

Now what?

This passage not only gives us a longing for the ideal leader; it gives us a model of how we should respond. Here are some phrases that stand out as guidelines for response:

- We are yours (11:18)
- Men came to David (11:22)
- An undivided heart (12:33)
- A perfect heart or full intent (12:38)

To put it in New Testament words, we should respond with a willingness to take up our cross and follow him. To paraphrase the closing words of the hymn "When I Survey the Wondrous Cross": a leader so amazing, so divine, demands my soul, my life, my all.

We all say amen! But what does that look like? The mighty men show us. They each did what was required of them by David. The commitment to the leader is best expressed in doing what the leader assigns us to do. His commands can be very specific: be kind, don't steal, love one another. Of course, our devotion leads us to obedience in these and many other commands, but following him has broader implications.

The continued application of this passage can follow different streams depending upon the need in the congregation or class. If the group is experiencing an unusual amount of difficulties, perhaps health or financial needs or even a feeling of being defeated and depressed, then the ideal king Jesus is someone to celebrate and rejoice that the perfect king is here for us. If the congregation, for some reason, is divided and lacks unity, then the unifying effect of everyone following the king can be emphasized. If your listeners are fairly new to following Christ or have never matured in their faith, then the obedience to the detailed commands of this perfect king can be highlighted.

All three of these sample responses could be presented rather than just one. And these are just three samples; certainly, responding to the ideal leader/king could have many varied and healthy responses.

Creativity in Presentation

To help orient our listeners to the topic, pictures of famous leaders could be presented. One needs to be careful to pick leaders who have a clearly established reputation with our specific set of listeners. Whom people respect as leaders varies greatly, so try to show those who are universally approved and likewise those who are universally disdained. A list could include Washington, Lincoln, Stalin, Hitler, and Churchill. (An online search of evil/good leaders yielded many more examples.) Try to make it sensitive to your setting. For my setting in Texas, Sam Houston would fit the bill. As you show these pictures, be sure to focus on their character as expressed by their deeds. End by asking what makes an ideal leader.

Most often when a narrative is being preached, the story is presented first, followed by principles and applications that come out of the passage. This pericope, while a narrative, is not a story. Rather, it presents David as the ideal king. It might be more effective to highlight the characteristics of the ideal king first, then present the narrative. Then, when the text is presented and read, listeners will better appreciate and recognize those characteristics. The last portion of the sermon would the application. Here is one possible structure:

- Characteristics of an ideal leader
  - David's example
    - David was appointed by an ultimate authority: the Word of God (11:3, 10).
    - God was effectively working through David's leadership of the mighty men (11:10–12:37).
    - For David, the worship of YHWH was priority (11:4–9).
  - Jesus fulfills these characteristics.
- Present the story
  - Establishing David's royal authority (11:1–9)
    - Military leaders supporting David as king (11:10–47)
      - Troops support (12:1–22)
    - Military units supporting David as king (12:23–37)
  - Establishing David's royal authority (12:38–40)
- We are at our best when we follow the best leader
  - Encouragement in times of need
  - Unity within the church/class
  - Call to obedience
  - Response needed in an individual setting

DISCUSSION QUESTIONS

1. Who were your favorite bosses or teachers? Why? What do you remember about them? Did they ever disappoint you?

2. When you have an excellent leader, how does it affect your emotions? Your work? Your attitude toward others?

1 Chronicles 13:1–14:17

EXEGETICAL IDEA

YHWH blessed David and Israel because they sought YHWH, but he struck them when they did not seek him properly.

THEOLOGICAL FOCUS

God impartially rewards or punishes his people based on their intentions and actions.

PREACHING IDEA

The bitterness of discipline, or the delight of blessing?

PREACHING POINTERS

At first glance, it is hard to see how these two chapters form a unit of thought. And yet, the concept of God breaking out against Uzzah and the Philistines shows that unity. The bitterness of YHWH breaking out against Uzzah for touching the ark is contrasted with YHWH's blessing of David by establishing his kingdom and then empowering him to break out against the Philistines. The same Lord who breaks out in discipline is the same Lord who breaks out in blessing. God is helping us get a fuller view of who he is and how we should step into his presence. Since the bitterness of discipline and the delight of blessing both come from our holy and impartial Lord, we must approach him with awe because of his holiness and assurance because of his blessing.

ISRAEL EXPERIENCES THE BLESSINGS AND DANGERS OF YHWH'S PRESENCE (13:1–14:17)

LITERARY STRUCTURE AND THEMES (13:1–14:17)

This narrative unit consists of two parts. The two parts relate together logically, since the second part is a result of the first. However, they also relate literarily. In both parts YHWH bursts forth (פרץ) against someone, commemorated by changing the name of the location.

In the first part, the Chronicler illustrates David's first priority while king: transferring the ark to Jerusalem as a way to care for Israel's worship. David gathers all Israel together before transferring the ark, as David and all Israel celebrate with dancing and song. However, Israel transfers the ark on a new cart. Along the journey the ark nearly falls. Uzzah reaches out to grab it, but YHWH bursts forth against him and puts him to death. This tragic failure forces David to delay his plans to transfer the ark.

The second part follows on the first. Despite Uzzah's tragic death, YHWH exalts David's kingdom because David has sought to care for Israel's worship. The Chronicler illustrates the greatness of David's kingdom by describing David's political and personal success, followed by his military success. Politically, the text describes how Huram, a foreign king, builds David a palace. Personally, the text states that David's household grows in Jerusalem. Militarily, the text describes two encounters with the Philistines in which YHWH grants David victory. The second part concludes with a final result: David's reputation grows such that other nations are afraid to fight against him.

- *David and Israel Attempt to Transfer the Ark to Jerusalem (13:1–14)*
- *YHWH Exalts David's Kingdom (14:1–17)*

EXPOSITION (13:1–14:17)

In the ancient Near Eastern world, deities played a significant role in virtually all aspects of life, including military conflict. Many armies brought images and symbols of their god(s) to the front line of battle to signify that their god(s) fought on their behalf. Since ancient Israel (at least ideally) avoided images of YHWH, the ark appears to have served that role at certain times (e.g., capture of Jericho, Josh. 6). As a symbol of YHWH's presence and power, the Israelites thought the ark would secure their victory (1 Sam. 4:3). At the same time, the ark was a sacred object, located within the holy place of the tabernacle. As a result, it served an important role in Israel's ritual worship. In 1 Chronicles 13–14 the Chronicler shows, on the one hand, that YHWH brings blessing to David for his concern to care for the ark as an important object in Israel's worship. On the other hand, the Chronicler shows that, with or without the ark, YHWH can bring disaster on those who dishonor or oppose him.

David and Israel Attempt to Transfer the Ark to Jerusalem (13:1–14)

David attempts to transfer the ark to Jerusalem; however, because he does not use the proper means, the attempt ends in disaster.

13:1–3. After describing how troops from all Israel support making David king (1 Chron.

11–12), Chronicles records that David consults with his military leaders. David asks them to consider whether they should enlist the rest of Israel to transfer the ark to Jerusalem. Given the rest of the narrative, the real question is whether they transfer the ark, not whether they should include the rest of Israel. David specifically refers to "our brothers" (אַחֵינוּ) who remain in the territories of Israel, along with the priests and Levites. Since chapters 11–12 describe the troops from the tribes who support David as king, "our brothers" most likely refers to the members of the various tribes who are not present when David is anointed king. Furthermore, since the tribe of Levi does not have a tribal allotment, the leaders would need to visit the priests and Levites in their allotted cities throughout Israel.

David specifies two conditions and one reason for the proposal to transfer the ark. The conditions are as follows: (1) it is acceptable to the leaders, and (2) it corresponds to YHWH's will. The narrative explicitly confirms that the first condition is met: "the proposal seemed right to all the people" (NET). The narrative does not explicitly address the second condition, leaving it as an open question hanging over the narrative. The reason for the proposal is that Israel has not sought YHWH during the days of Saul. This statement is somewhat ambiguous: it is not clear whether, during Saul's reign, Israel did not seek the ark or YHWH. In this context, the two are virtually synonymous; that is, seeking the ark is also seeking YHWH.

Ambiguity of Seeking

This same ambiguity between seeking YHWH or seeking a sacred object important for worship occurs in two other places: 1 Chronicles 15:13 and 2 Chronicles 1:5. In each of these cases, seeking the object illustrates seeking YHWH. See commentary in these respective passages.

13:4–5. The assembly agrees to David's proposal. As a result, David gathers all Israel from Shihor of Egypt to the entry of Hamath. These locations correlate to the ideal boundaries of Israel's territory: Egypt to the south and Hamath to the north (cf. Num. 13:21; 34:5, 8; Josh. 13:5; 15:4; Ezek. 47:15; 48:1; see comments on 2 Chron. 7:8). The text also specifies where the ark currently remains: Kiriath-jearim.

Several noteworthy points emerge from 13:1–5. First, this narrative shows that David's concern for the ark is his priority. Immediately following the celebration of David as the new king (1 Chron. 12:38–40), David brings the military leaders together to consider bringing the ark to Jerusalem. The Chronicler arranges these events based on theme and logical sequence, not necessarily based on chronology. The Chronicler records David's concern for the ark here because he intends to show that in contrast to Saul, David cares deeply about worshipping YHWH.

Nonchronological Sequencing in Chronicles

In the preceding chapters (1 Chron. 11–12), the Chronicler does not arrange the material chronologically but chiastically (see "Literary Structure and Themes" in 1 Chron. 11–12). In the case of bringing the ark to Jerusalem, David resides in Hebron at the very beginning of his reign, since he has not yet captured Jerusalem. The Chronicler is fully aware of this fact; he has chosen to prioritize the logical sequence instead of the historical one.

Second, these verses emphasize the role that all Israel plays in properly worshipping YHWH. David does not make the decision to transfer the ark; the whole assembly does. As king, David invites the people to participate in making the decision. Furthermore, if the assembly decides to do it, he encourages them to bring even more inhabitants of Israel so that "all Israel" may participate in transferring the ark. Once the assembly agrees to the proposal, David secures participants from throughout all Israel (see Cudworth 2016, 21–25). In this way, all Israel shares the concern for Israel's ritual worship, not just the king.

Third, the text mentions the priests and Levites specifically; however, the text does not communicate that the priests and Levites are needed for the task. The priests and Levites are just included alongside the rest of Israel invited to participate in transferring the ark. Even though the text does not emphasize their role in this case, mentioning them here in 1 Chronicles 13 may foreshadow the role they will play later in the book, especially 1 Chronicles 15–16.

Fourth, these verses contrast David to Saul. When David speaks of Israel's failure to seek YHWH/ark (see comments above) during Saul's reign, David speaks in the first-person plural: "We did not seek him/it in the days of Saul." The use of the first-person plural presents David as taking a measure of responsibility for the failure and working to correct it. In contrast, Saul does not seek YHWH; instead, he seeks out a medium (1 Chron. 10:13–14). Partly for this reason, YHWH puts Saul to death and transfers (*hiphil* סבב) the kingdom over to David. In contrast, as part of David's proposed correction to the failure, David speaks of "transferring" (*hiphil* סבב) the ark to Jerusalem, sharpening the distinction between Saul and David.

In light of these observations, 13:1–5 presents David as a pious king, supported by all Israel, seeking YHWH by attempting to transfer the ark to Jerusalem. This portrait contrasts sharply with Saul, an impious king, who seeks a medium rather than YHWH, leading Israel to defeat and disgrace. These verses set the stage for Israel to transfer the ark and seek YHWH.

13:6–8. These verses recount a simple narrative. After David assembles all Israel, they proceed to Kiriath-jearim, also known as Baalah, to retrieve the ark and transfer it to Jerusalem. They load the ark onto a new cart and select two men to guide the cart. As the cart makes its way toward Jerusalem, David and all the people celebrate by singing and playing music.

TRANSLATION ANALYSIS:
Translations describe the role of Uzzah and Ahio differently. Some translations (ESV, NASB, NKJV, NRSV) translate the Hebrew word (נהג) as "drive." In most contemporary contexts, the word "drive" involves someone sitting and steering something. What is more likely in view is a scenario in which Uzzah and Ahio walk alongside the oxen, leading them along. For this reason, I prefer the translation "guide" used by several translations (CSB, NET, NIV, NLT).

Behind this simple narrative lie some subtle points. First, this text focuses on YHWH's power. One way the text accomplishes this purpose is by designating the ark with more specific terms: it is "the ark of God, YHWH, who sits upon the cherubim." The image of YHWH sitting portrays him as a king sitting upon a throne. In this case, the cherubim represent this throne, or perhaps even better, a mobile throne, elsewhere associated with YHWH's chariot (see 1 Chron. 28:18; Ezek. 10:1–22; Knoppers 2004, 934). Since the cherubim are heavenly figures, this designation emphasizes YHWH's royal authority even over the heavenly realm.

Second, the text focuses on YHWH's presence. The ark as a symbol of YHWH's power also communicates his presence. The ark is where people call upon YHWH's name. As in

Transporting the Ark to Jerusalem. Public domain.

other passages, YHWH's name here represents his presence (e.g., 1 Chron. 22:7). This verse strengthens this point by describing David and all the people celebrating "before God." As in other passages, being "before God" refers to being before the ark (1 Chron. 13:10; 16:1).

Third, the text anticipates the role that the priests and Levites will play in Israel's ritual worship. In this case, David and all the people perform the music before the ark. In the future, David will appoint the Levitical musicians and the priestly trumpeters to the task of celebrating before the ark (see 1 Chron. 16:4–7, 37–42). The list of instruments strengthens this picture since the list consists of typical instruments assigned to the Levites and priests.

TRANSLATION ANALYSIS:
The end of this verse contains a phrase that is difficult to translate. Many translations (e.g., CSB, ESV, NET, NIV, NRSV) interpret the phrase as indicating that the ark bears YHWH's name, that is, the ark is called by his name. This expression usually indicates ownership (see comments on 2 Chron. 7:14). Furthermore, the Hebrew preposition עַל occurs in these contexts; however, it does not occur in this verse. For this reason, I prefer translating the phrase as "where his name is called" (cf. NASB, NKJV). This translation does not emphasize ownership but presence. The verse intends to state that the ark is the place where people experience YHWH's presence.

Despite all the positive elements in the narrative to this point (e.g., including all Israel, seeking YHWH and his ark, and celebrating before YHWH with musical performance), the narrative creates tension as one compares how the people are transferring the ark to how Moses has commanded that they should transfer it. This tension comes to a climax in the following verses.

13:9–10. This scene provides a sharp contrast in tone to the preceding verses. David's celebration over transferring the ark suddenly turns to anger and fear. This shift takes place at the threshing floor of Kidon because Uzzah, one of those guiding the cart, stretches out his hand to grab the ark when the cattle pulling the cart shake it. According to Mosaic law, touching a sacred object, such as the ark, results in death (see Num. 4:15, 20). Consistent with the law, as soon as Uzzah stretches out his hand, YHWH becomes angry with him and puts him to death.

> **Threshing Floor as Foreshadowing**
> Mentioning the threshing floor in 13:9 may foreshadow the significant role that the threshing floor of Ornan plays later in David's life (see 1 Chron. 21–22), especially since David offers a sacrifice there so that YHWH will withdraw the hand of his angel in bringing punishment on Israel (1 Chron. 21:26–28).

TRANSLATION ANALYSIS:
The text describes the cattle's action using the term שׁמט. Many translations (e.g., CSB, ESV, NET, NIV, NKJV, NLT) render the term as "stumbled"; however, this term in Hebrew has a direct object in other occurrences. For this reason, a translation such as "shake" (NRSV) or even "upset" (NASB) is preferable. Either way the text paints a picture of the ark in which the ark itself is in danger of falling to the ground.

13:11. When YHWH becomes angry, David then becomes angry. The text explains that David becomes angry because YHWH "burst out" (פרץ) against Uzzah. Two observations are worth mentioning here. First, the word translated "burst out" in this context carries serious connotations. Elsewhere in Chronicles, the word describes assaulting a city and breaching its defenses (e.g., 2 Chron. 26:6; 32:5). Furthermore, this verb occurs in another context in which YHWH's sanctity requires careful consideration. In Exodus 19:22 YHWH warns that if the priests approach him without consecrating themselves, he will "burst out" (פרץ) against them. The use of this verb in this context conveys how seriously YHWH protects his sanctity. Second, the text remains somewhat ambiguous regarding why David becomes angry. Is David angry at YHWH because he strikes Uzzah? Is he angry at Uzzah for violating the sanctity of the ark? Given the use of the verb in similar contexts (e.g., Gen. 4:5; 1 Sam. 15:11; Jonah 4:1), the Chronicler most likely intends to show that David is reacting to the entire situation. He finds the whole situation to be awful. As a result, the place becomes known as Perez-uzzah (translated as "bursting forth on Uzzah") from then on.

13:12. David's anger then turns to fear. He is likely afraid for two reasons. First, Uzzah's death demonstrates that even for those with good intentions to seek YHWH, YHWH's holy power and presence still pose a dangerous threat. A violation of YHWH's sanctity results in disaster, in this case, Uzzah's immediate death (although, see comments on 2 Chron. 30:18–20). Second, Uzzah's death raises the question whether or not anyone can ever move the ark. The ark represents where YHWH sits enthroned and for that reason serves as a possible conduit for YHWH's blessing. At this point David does not seem to realize that improper procedure has prevented Israel from transferring the ark. Thus, he appears to be afraid that no one, much less himself, will be able to transfer the ark to Jerusalem, thereby preventing YHWH's blessing from flowing to David and all Israel. Even though David's question ("How will I bring . . . ?") conveys his fear that he may not be able to transfer the ark, it also foreshadows the real issue of this failed attempt: how to bring the ark. In this case, Israel has not followed the proper procedure for transferring the ark as outlined in Mosaic law. David discovers this truth later (see 1 Chron. 15:12–13).

TRANSLATION ANALYSIS:
Although translations render David's question with slightly different wording, they generally interpret the question as asking whether David can transfer the ark. This translation reflects the issue that faces David in this event. However, in Hebrew the wording is ambiguous; it can also indicate that the question is not whether David can transfer the ark but the process by which he should transfer it. This latter translation (cf. KJV) anticipates what happens in 1 Chronicles 15, where David answers the question regarding how to transfer the ark when he follows Mosaic legislation.

13:13–14. As a result of his fear, David halts the procession to Jerusalem and leaves the ark, probably at the nearest available place, the house of Obed-edom (Japhet 1993, 281). What the text says about Obed-edom plays an important role in addressing David's fear. During the time the ark remains with Obed-edom, YHWH blesses him. This blessing is a sign that even though the ark poses a threat, it still functions as a conduit of blessing. Uzzah's death illustrates YHWH's anger in that moment; his anger does not persist. Therefore, YHWH does not oppose transferring the ark; the question becomes how one should do so.

The choice of Obed-edom may provide a clue for determining how to transfer the ark as well. The text designates Obed-edom as a Gittite. At first glance this designation appears to identify him as a Philistine from Gath; however, other elements in Chronicles suggest that he is a Levite. For instance, later in 1 Chronicles 16:5, 38, the name Obed-edom designates a prominent member of the Levitical musicians and a Levitical gatekeeper. Furthermore, 1 Chronicles 26:4–5 lists the sons of the gatekeeper Obed-edom, concluding the list with a comment that "God blessed him." This evidence suggests that "Gittite" does not identify Obed-edom as a Philistine from Gath but more likely as someone who has resided in Gath at some point or comes from the Levitical city of Gath-rimmon (see Josh. 19:45; 21:24; and sidebar below). The fact that YHWH blesses this Levite may foreshadow the key role the Levites play in successfully transferring the ark later (1 Chron. 15–16).

Identity of Gath

Gath often refers to the Philistine city; however, Obed-edom is not a Philistine. For these reasons, Japhet argues that Obed-edom likely resided in Gath at some point so that he became associated with the location (1993, 282). On the other hand, the name may refer to Gath-rimmon. Boda comments that even though Obed-edom is likely a Levite, the irony of the designation "Gittite" is still present to a degree since "when David failed the first time to bring the Ark into Jerusalem, it ended up at the 'house' of someone from 'Gath' (ironic allusion to those who stole the Ark in the first place)" (2010a, 130).

YHWH Exalts David's Kingdom (14:1–17)

Even though Israel has not successfully delivered the ark, YHWH still blesses David with political, personal, and military success.

14:1–17. The narrative abruptly shifts from the failed attempt to transfer the ark to David's political, personal, and military successes. The Chronicler carries out two purposes by including these verses after the account regarding the ark: (1) it presents David's successes as a reward for desiring to seek YHWH by transferring the ark, even if the attempt failed, and (2) it confirms for the reader that YHWH has chosen David as king. These two aspects come together as one contrasts David to Saul. When Saul does not seek YHWH and his ark (1 Chron. 10:12–14; 13:3), Saul, his household, and Israel suffer punishment. Saul dies by his own hand; his household dies along with him (1 Chron. 10:6). The Philistines defeat Israel, driving some of the Israelites from their cities (1 Chron. 10:7). As a result, YHWH turns the kingdom over to David. Even though Uzzah's death may raise the question whether David follows in the footsteps of Saul, this chapter demonstrates that because

of David's desire to seek YHWH, David's reign will be quite different than Saul's.

14:1. This chapter begins with a brief notice that Huram, king of Tyre, sends a delegation with materials and skilled labor to build a palace for David. This brief comment serves three important purposes. First, this comment shows that David is already being recognized internationally. International fame is a common blessing for good kings in Chronicles. The narrative returns to David's fame at the end (14:17). Second, the comment confirms that YHWH has not rejected David as king. In several ancient Near Eastern texts, a king does not really establish his rule over a land until he occupies a palace (Knoppers 2004, 603). Having a palace allows the king to establish a royal court to carry out his duties as king (Boda 2010a, 133). Third, this comment anticipates other significant events in Chronicles. It anticipates David's second (and successful) attempt to transfer the ark, since David will build both his palace and a tent for housing the ark (1 Chron. 15:1). It also anticipates the role that Huram will play in building a palace for Solomon and the temple for YHWH. What Huram does for David in providing exquisite building materials and skilled laborers is a foretaste of what he will do for Solomon (2 Chron. 2–4).

14:2. Because of David's international fame and building of a palace, David recognizes that YHWH has established David's reign over Israel. The Chronicler adds an expression that provides insight into his view of the Davidic reign. He comments that YHWH has made David king "for the sake of his people Israel." In other words, the king should act to benefit all Israel. Chronicles reiterates this principle during Solomon's reign when YHWH makes Solomon king because of YHWH's love for Israel (2 Chron. 2:11 [HB 10]; 9:8). One can see this principle play out throughout Chronicles in a slightly different way when time after time the direction of the king (obedience or disobedience) coincides with the direction of the people (e.g., 2 Chron. 15:12–15; 25:20; 28:22–23; 33:9; 34:31–32). This principle also allows the Chronicler a kind of shorthand in which he can describe a blessing of the individual king as a sign of blessing the entire nation (see sidebar "Relation of King to People").

14:3–7. The text transitions to David's household. The Chronicler includes this material to signal David's blessing. Chronicles repeatedly presents many wives and children as a blessing, especially for a king (see sidebar "Large Families as Blessing"). Here the text only lists David's sons born in Jerusalem—since Jerusalem, as the site where the ark will rest, is in focus here. An earlier genealogy lists all of David's sons (1 Chron. 3:1–8). This blessing of David's household becomes another sign (alongside international fame and palace building) that YHWH has established David's kingdom.

The blessing of David's household also points back to two others: (1) Saul, and (2) Obed-edom. Unlike Saul, who lost his entire household because he did not seek YHWH (1 Chron. 10:6, 13–14), David is increasing his household because he seeks YHWH. Like Obed-edom, whose household experiences YHWH's blessing while the ark remains in his house, David's household also experiences blessing and will experience even more once the ark comes to Jerusalem (1 Chron. 16:43).

14:8–9. This section illustrates again that YHWH blesses David and exalts his kingdom, this time through military success. At first the narrative appears to move in the opposite direction. When the Philistines hear that David has become king, they seek to kill him. Furthermore, they raid the Valley of Rephaim, threatening David's rule (Knoppers 2004, 599).

These actions offer a counterbalance to David's becoming king, since being king also endangers his life. Furthermore, this picture shows that the principle of retribution in Chronicles is not simplistic (see "Covenant" section in the introduction). Certainly, YHWH rewards obedience and punishes disobedience, but Chronicles also presents some circumstances as being more complex, such as the case here.

The Valley of Rephaim

The Valley of Rephaim forms a boundary for Judah and Benjamin (Josh. 15:8; 18:16) and therefore lies fairly close to Jerusalem. Furthermore, 1 Chronicles 11:15 has already mentioned an episode with the Philistines that took place in the valley. That episode demonstrates the skill and courage of some of David's warriors, while implying the weakness and ineptitude of the Philistines.

14:10–12. The real focus of this narrative is David's response to the situation. Again, the narrative contrasts David to Saul. Unlike Saul, David does not retreat from the Philistines but goes out to confront them. Unlike Saul, David seeks YHWH regarding whether and how he should attack. When YHWH assures David that he will win the battle, David and his troops fight the Philistines and defeat them. Furthermore, David responds to the victory by declaring that YHWH defeated the Philistines using David as his agent. As the Philistines flee, they leave behind their gods, that is, their idols. David responds by ordering his troops to burn the idols rather than plunder them. David's command follows Mosaic law (Deut. 7:5, 25; 12:3). In all these ways David does what is right.

Ironic Contrast with Saul

First Chronicles 14:10 uses the term שׁאל ("ask") to describe how David inquires of YHWH. This word choice presents some irony both because Saul fails to inquire (שׁאל) of YHWH in 1 Chronicles 10:13 and because Saul's name (Heb. שׁאול) derives from this same root.

Even though this narrative focuses on David's obedience, especially in contrast to Saul, it makes significant points regarding YHWH as well. The text emphasizes that YHWH fights for Israel. David recognizes that fact: he declares that YHWH bursts forth (פרץ) against the enemies. The wording of this statement is significant. It looks back to the narrative recounting the failed attempt to transfer the ark. When Uzzah stretches out his hand to grab the ark, YHWH bursts forth (פרץ) against him, putting him to death. Both occasions are commemorated by changing the place's name (Perez-uzzah, Baal-perizim). These similarities show that YHWH is impartial: he bursts forth against those who oppose him, whether from other nations who threaten Israel or from those of Israel who commit sacrilege.

TRANSLATION ANALYSIS:
The term פרץ is difficult to translate, in part, because the text compares what *YHWH* does to the Philistines to water. In other contexts, the term may be translated as "assault," "breach," or "break through," but in the context of water these translations do not work as well. I have chosen the translation "burst forth" as a way of connecting YHWH's actions against the Philistines and Uzzah with the rush of water as it breaches a dam. For a different interpretation of this term used with water, see R. Klein 2006, 342; Seow 1989, 81–84.

Location of Baal-perizim
The location of Baal-perizim is uncertain. Isaiah 28:21 describes a past event in which YHWH arose in anger at a place called Mount Perizim. The text likely alludes to the incident recorded here, in 2 Samuel 5:20 and 1 Chronicles 14:11.

14:13–16. The narrative does not stop with just one example of David's obedience. Again, David finds himself in virtually the same situation: the Philistines are raiding the valley. David responds again by seeking YHWH regarding whether and how he should attack. YHWH provides a different set of instructions, telling David to circle around the Philistines and wait to hear the signal that YHWH is marching out against the Philistines. First Chronicles 14:16 states explicitly what the narrative unit has been illustrating: David follows YHWH's commands and, as a result, thoroughly defeats the Philistine army (from Gibeon to Gezer, i.e., beyond the Valley of Rephaim). In 1 Chronicles 10 Saul does not seek YHWH, resulting in his death, his dynasty's demise, and Israel's defeat. In 1 Chronicles 14 David seeks YHWH (as evidenced by his obedience), resulting in his blessing and Israel's victory.

During this battle, the text focuses on what YHWH says to make the point that YHWH fights the battle. YHWH delays David's attack. YHWH instructs David to circle around the Philistines and wait for a signal. The signal is a sound moving among the tops of the trees. YHWH describes this sound as "marching." In this case, the marching refers to YHWH (most likely with his troops/hosts) advancing toward the Philistine camp to defeat it. In this way the text shows clearly that YHWH fights for David and Israel as they obey his commands.

Identity of Trees
First Chronicles 14:14–15 describes the location where David should wait for YHWH's signal, using the word בְּכָאִים. Apparently this word refers to some type of plant (most likely a type of shrub or tree); however, its specific identity is uncertain. For this reason, translations vary considerably.

14:17. Since David defeats the Philistines because YHWH fights against them in battle, David's reputation spreads throughout the region. Again, Chronicles presents this type of international fame as a form of YHWH's blessing. In this narrative, the picture of David's fame returns to a theme set out at the beginning of this chapter (Huram sending his delegation to David), demonstrating the various ways that

YHWH exalts David's kingdom. Since this final comment regarding David's reputation follows the accounts of his battles against the Philistines, the text implies that at least part of David's reputation involves his strength in combat. In fact, the text explains that YHWH causes this type of dread among the nations. Elsewhere in Chronicles, the text specifies that the dread of YHWH falls on other nations (2 Chron. 14:13; 17:10; 20:29). In these contexts, the dread of YHWH either results in either the enemies not attacking Israel (2 Chron. 17:10; 20:29) or in Israel defeating their enemies (2 Chron. 14:14 [HB 13]). Since this comment precedes David's successful attempt to transfer the ark to Jerusalem (1 Chron. 15–16) and YHWH's promise to David (1 Chron. 17), it seems that at least for a moment, the enemy nations do not attack. Then, beginning in 1 Chronicles 18, the Chronicler recounts how David defeats many of his enemies.

For the first readers this narrative regarding David might seem distant. The Davidic kingdom had vanished and, along with it, the ark. How could a narrative regarding the ark and David's kingdom speak to them? First, since David prioritized taking care of the ark as his first matter of business, the text encouraged the first readers to prioritize building and maintaining the temple. Haggai recounts how the people worried about their own homes before considering YHWH's temple (Hag. 1:4–11). Instead, they needed to prioritize YHWH's worship. Second, even though the people no longer possessed the ark, Chronicles shows that the ark, along with the other items from the days of Moses (tabernacle, bronze altar, etc.), are subsumed into the temple (2 Chron. 5:4–7); therefore, when the people gathered to worship at the temple and cared for the temple and its personnel, they honored the ark (Knoppers 2004, 591–93). Third, as the community sought to worship YHWH properly under their new circumstances, the death of Uzzah would remind them of the significance of both the intent to seek YHWH but also the dangerous consequences of failing to treat YHWH as holy. Finally, the narrative encouraged the community to wait for the rise of another Davidic king. Through his obedience, this coming king would secure Israel's well-being through properly worshipping YHWH.

THEOLOGICAL FOCUS

At the literary level, the image of God's "bursting forth" holds this passage together. At the theological level, the image creates a sharp contrast pointing to God's character. On the one hand, God bursts forth against the Philistines to defeat them. The Philistines are Israel's enemies. They are uncircumcised (1 Chron. 10:4) and idol-worshippers (1 Chron. 14:12). God's action is hardly surprising. On the other hand, God bursts forth against Uzzah. Uzzah is tending to the ark while all Israel has gathered to worship. It is surprising that during the celebration God becomes angry and strikes Uzzah. However, God strikes Uzzah because he touches the holy ark.

God's response to the Philistines and to Uzzah highlights two important aspects of God's character. First, the similar response points to God's impartiality in judgment. Both Uzzah and the Philistines deserve punishment, and God carries out the same punishment for both. The Philistines deserve punishment because they worship idols of other gods and attack God's people Israel. Uzzah deserves punishment because he violates God's holiness. The differences in ethnicity, setting, status, and so on do not affect whether God judges or the severity of his judgment. God remains impartial (1 Peter 1:15–17) and expects his people to be impartial in the way they treat others (2 Chron. 19:6–7; James 2:1–4).

Second, the response points to God's holiness. In this case, the text points to the distinction between what is divine and what is common. God belongs to a separate category than the world. To treat him as ordinary dishonors him. Furthermore, because of who he is, his presence can overwhelm a person or place. Therefore, when Uzzah reaches out for the ark, he faces a double danger. On the one hand, he faces the danger of God's presence overwhelming him so that he dies, a repeated concern in the OT (e.g., Exod. 20:19; Judg. 13:22; Isa. 6:5). On the other hand, he faces the danger of God punishing him because he treats what is holy as something ordinary. God's bursting forth indicates that Uzzah dies because God punishes him.

Although in the NT period holiness does not concern specific places or items, holiness remains an important aspect of God's character. The emphasis shifts from places and items to people, specifically God's people. Believers should be holy, that is, separate in their character and conduct, reflecting Christ's character and conduct (1 Peter 1:15). They may also approach God with full access because of Christ's work on their behalf (Eph. 3:12). At the same time, treating what is holy as something common can still bring severe judgment. For instance, Hebrews warns that treating the blood of Christ as something ordinary deserves punishment even worse than what the law commands (10:28–30).

Between these two images of God's "bursting forth" comes an image of God rewarding David with royal blessings. These blessings take place even though David fails to bring the ark to Jerusalem. This period of blessing speaks to the role that intent plays in God's responses. On the one hand, God rewards David for his intent to assemble all Israel to worship YHWH by caring for the ark. Not only is his intent upright, but it consists of more than just a wish or passing thought. David acts: he assembles all Israel, leads them in worship, and begins transferring the ark so that Israel's priests and Levites can tend to it. Despite his failure to accomplish the goal of transferring the ark, God rewards him for his intended actions to lead all Israel in worship. On the other hand, God kills Uzzah for attempting to keep the ark from falling. In this case, Uzzah's intent does not mitigate the consequences of his actions. In fact, the Chronicler does not seem to

consider them relevant. When it comes to violating God's holiness like Uzzah does, the consequence is punishment regardless the intent.

The NT develops these ideas further. Jesus emphasizes the proper disposition (including intent) of worship when he speaks to the Samaritan woman concerning those who worship God in spirit and truth (John 4:20–24). As a result, the forms of worship become less important than the disposition of the worshippers. God is still holy, and his holiness ensures that no human can approach him. However, those who believe in Christ may approach this holy God, confident in Christ yet aware of the danger of approaching God outside of Christ (Heb. 10:19–31). Therefore, worship maintains a balance of assurance and reverence because of who God is and what he has done through Christ.

PREACHING AND TEACHING STRATEGIES

Exegetical and Theological Synthesis

When the exiles returned, they not only had to rebuild but also had to be sure that the worship of YHWH was done correctly. Those who were left in Israel had neglected his guidelines; other gods were still being worshipped. The importance of worshipping God in the proper way needed to be established and reinforced. As they read these two chapters, the contrast between Uzzah's death and David's blessing stands out. But it is not separate sources that are contrasted, for they have one and the same source: God. If we take Uzzah's death by itself we only see the discipline; David's blessing shows us a fuller picture of God.

The physical item that represented YHWH's presence was the ark. When Uzzah reached out to touch it, he entered into the unveiled presence of YHWH. Across time, God has shown that no one can enter into intimate fellowship with him because of man's sinful state. The whole structure of the tabernacle was a demonstration of this. The lesson for them was to follow God's directives for worshipping him at the temple. It was a motivation to get the temple built and then follow God's guidelines for worship in that temple. In that worship would be the blessing of enjoying his presence and fellowship.

This worship was to be characterized by a respectful submission to his absolute and unquestioned authority, justice, and power. This approach is still right for today. Of course, Christ's work frees us from the ritual of the temple, but we still are seeking to be close to the holy God. He has not changed, nor should our attitudes in approaching him.

Preaching Idea

The bitterness of discipline, or the delight of blessing?

Contemporary Connections

What does it mean?

We don't know how it happened. What did God use to break out and strike down Uzzah? Was there some kind of static electrical charge that the ark built up and then discharged when touched? Was it a heart attack? Surely it would not have been like the mythological bolt of lightning. How it happened may cause us to wonder, but far more bothersome and confusing to us is that God did this. The man was only trying to help. God knew his motives, so why was he punished with such finality? No second chance here. To our modern sense of justice, the punishment far outweighs the crime. Perhaps we think that God's justice has evolved across the millennia. God isn't so demanding today. Or is he?

When I began my higher education, typewriters were the standard method for putting thoughts on paper. As a very poor typist, the unforgiving nature of manual typewriters was a major problem—once an error was typed, it was a major hassle to correct. The invention of the personal computer transformed how one could write. Now corrections are not only easy but could even be done automatically. If you

misspelled, just click, and now it is corrected. This not only applies to writing, but also in playing video games. If you are about to lose a computer game you could click "redo" and start over. No penalty for mistakes or wrong moves. This atmosphere of easy-to-correct and easy-to-redo has perhaps affected how we think about God's expectations for us.

Is it true?

It is much easier to believe that God blessed David because David inquired of him. But do we also believe that this same God struck down Uzzah? Doesn't God forgive? He does, but consequences still remain. Did God forgive Uzzah? If his heart was a heart of faith as was Abraham's, then yes, Uzzah had righteousness accredited to him just as Abraham did. If he was a man of faith in YHWH, we will see him in heaven. However, we must remember that we can't approach God, can't live, can't worship him, in any way we want. We must follow God's guidelines. When we don't, there are consequences.

If a husband threatens his wife with the word "divorce" or strikes her with the back of his hand, the damage is done. There is no redo. The teenager wanting to be accepted and feel like she belongs takes the pills, and the effect on her mind follows. The drugs can't be untaken. The teacher who works more on his retirement plans than his lesson plans can't undo the fact that half of his class failed the standardized tests. If a pastor can explain the difficulties of a text but doesn't care about the difficulties in people's lives, his ministry is ineffective.

Now what?

It is easy to give the broad application that our worship of God should contain both awe and assurance. We should always approach him with these in mind. The difficulty comes when we try to specify what that looks like. The word "preference" seems to come up when this is discussed. One prefers the dim lights and haze machines. For another the older hymns, with some updating, are the most worshipful to them. How do we ensure that both awe and assurance characterize our worship?

A beginning place might be to evaluate the content and emotions of the music we sing. At a Calvary Baptist church a choir of five-year-olds participated in a worship service by singing the old hymn "At *Calvary*"— probably chosen to reflect the name of the church. Envision a precious five-year-old girl singing at the top of her voice, "Years I spent in vanity and pride." The words were beyond her comprehension. What bothers me the most about this image is that, while I can comprehend the words, I have sung them, and many other hymn lyrics, without thinking about them.

Certainly, we need to apply this proper balance of awe and assurance to corporate worship, but it also should apply to our private worship. In a real sense, all of life should be an act of worship: my private prayers, the way I treat my wife, the way I speak to neighbors. Am I thinking of God, his awe and assurance? This duo should affect how I approach each day. There can be a sense of awe that God has high expectations of me and a sense of assurance because of his grace that empowers me. Is there a sense of awe that he really expects me to love others more than I love myself? Is it a wonder to me that he expects me to put their needs above mine? Those guidelines, those commands, should strike a certain amount of fear and reverence in me. And this inadequacy should lead us to utterly depend upon him for the empowerment to follow those guidelines. In that dependence comes the assurance that he is working through us and on us.

Creativity in Presentation

It will be very important to help the congregation see the connection between these chapters. It might be wise to do this in the introduction. Show the use of the same words

in 13:11 and then in 14:11. Some of the story will need to be explained, which will take away some of the shock factor. Another way to approach the difficulty of the connection is to present chapter 13 as though it were the whole sermon, and even have a concluding thought—then explain that we need to go on the next chapter, because the author ties them together.

This passage is not often used to prompt a presentation of the gospel, but it can. The ark was the symbol of God's presence with Israel. To touch it was to step into the intimate presence of YHWH. When the boundaries of this life are lifted and we step into the presence of God, we will metaphorically touch the ark. As believers in Christ we can step into God's presence (touch the ark) because of the imputed righteousness that he gives us. We can enjoy God's intimate presence, but only because of Jesus's death and resurrection and our faith in him. But how about those who have not trusted Christ? Can they touch the ark and live? A day is coming when everyone will touch the ark whether they want to or not—that is, when they stand before a holy God, in his actual palpable presence. God has provided the way to touch him and live. God, in his love, touched us with his love when Jesus took our place and paid for our sins with his death. He then rose from the grave to offer us life. Our faith in him and his work lets us stand in God's presence and live.

Here is one possible structure:

- God's breaking out in discipline should produce awe in us (13:1–14).
  - Present the text
    - Transferring the ark to Jerusalem (13:1–14)
    - Gathering all Israel (13:1–5)
    - Transferring the ark with celebration (13:6–8)
    - Tragic failure (13:9–14)
  - Explain the text

- ◦ Apply: God will break out in discipline of his children; thus, we should be in awe.
- • God's breaking out in blessing should produce assurance in us (14:1–17).
  - ◦ Present the text
    - · The blessing of political and personal success (14:1–7)
    - · The blessing of military success (14:8–17)
  - ◦ Explain the text: emphasize that David sought YHWH
  - ◦ Apply: God will bless his children when they seek him.
- • We need to approach God with awe and assurance.

DISCUSSION QUESTIONS

1. How does our nation currently show respect for the president? How did our nation currently show respect for the president fifty years ago?

2. How would you describe respectful business dress currently? Twenty years ago? Fifty years ago?

3. What are ways to show respect?

4. Which is more often seen in your church: awe or assurance? What does it look like, in your context?

5. Which is easier to help congregations experience: awe or assurance? Why?

1 Chronicles 15:1–16:43

EXEGETICAL IDEA
David demonstrates his devotion to YHWH by transferring the ark to Jerusalem according to Mosaic law and by establishing Israel's musical worship service to praise YHWH as God of all creation and God of Israel.

THEOLOGICAL FOCUS
God deserves obedient praise because he is the God of all creation and the God of his people.

PREACHING IDEA
Give worthy worship to our worthy Lord.

PREACHING POINTERS
The postexilic community had a very difficult task in front of them. They had to rebuild the nation and the temple. As they heard of this joyful episode in the history of God's family, it taught them, and teaches us, to celebrate our Lord, even when things are not as we would like them. It is important to see David's celebration in light of the previous tragedy of forgetting about the holiness of God. For Israel, God had specific commands about the ark. Obedience to these specific commands was an expression of the heart of obedience in all areas. We have no ark, but we still need to have a heart and life of obedience. While obedience is always important, the focus of this pericope is worship. Worship must be done with obedience. In addition, at times our worship should be filled with celebration, just as Israel's was.

The question arises as to how to celebrate in the church in this century. Our worship of God is not always celebratory, but it is always in obedience to him. But when we do celebrate, what does it look like? While the specific music, atmosphere, sounds, even seating arrangement will vary with cultures, the elements that must never vary are obedience, reverence, and a singular focus upon our Lord.

ISRAEL SUCCESSFULLY TRANSFERS THE ARK
(15:1–16:43)

LITERARY STRUCTURE
AND THEMES (15:1–16:43)

After the failed attempt to transfer the ark in 1 Chronicles 13, David tries again. This time, David takes different measures preparing to carry the ark. He sets up a tent in Jerusalem to house the ark and calls on the priests and Levites to consecrate themselves so that they may carry the ark as required by Mosaic law. Next, he works with the Levites to organize the procession accompanying those carrying the ark. After the ark is successfully placed in the tent in Jerusalem and the people have offered sacrifices and feasted together, David organizes the musical worship to take place before the ark. He initiates the worship by assigning the responsibility to Levitical musicians. The musicians then perform a song of worship, as an example of this type of musical worship. This song praises YHWH as the God of Israel and of all creation. Finally, David assigns the priests and Levites to carry on this worship before the ark in Jerusalem and before the tabernacle in Gibeon.

- **Preparing to Carry the Ark (15:1–15)**
- **Carrying the Ark (15:16–16:3)**
- **Organizing Worship Before the Ark (16:4–43)**
  - *Initiating Worship (16:4–7)*
  - *Song of Worship (16:8–36)*
  - *Carrying on Worship (16:37–43)*

EXPOSITION (15:1–16:43)

In the ancient world, people understood the task of approaching a holy deity as serious business (e.g., Uzzah's death). Not only must one be devoted to the deity, but one must observe the proper rituals in the proper manner to worship properly. The people expected that approaching a deity improperly would bring disaster. Earlier, in 1 Chronicles 13, the Chronicler demonstrates that approaching Israel's God is serious, even dangerous, business. Now, the Chronicler shows that approaching YHWH is possible. In this narrative, David approaches YHWH by transferring the ark to Jerusalem. He does so successfully because he follows YHWH's instructions found in Mosaic law and provides accompanying musical celebration. As a result of successfully transferring the ark by these means, David organizes Israel's ritual worship for future generations as well. Therefore, this episode of transferring the ark speaks to the nature and purpose of Israel's ritual worship.

Preparing to Carry the Ark (15:1–15)

Unlike the first attempt to carry the ark, David prepares for the ark's transfer by setting up a tent to house it, and then by calling on the priests and Levites to handle it according to Mosaic law.

15:1. First Chronicles 14 recounts various areas of David's success (political, personal, and military), culminating in a period of peace since "YHWH caused all the nations to fear him [David]" (1 Chron. 14:17b NET). During this peace, David builds up the fortified area of Jerusalem, known as the city of David, by constructing royal buildings (see 1 Chron. 11:7–8; Knoppers 2004, 612). In Chronicles, this type of building activity, especially when related to fortifications, is typical of a good king. Furthermore, in other passages, Chronicles connects royal building projects with a concern for divine spaces. One sees this connection quite clearly during Solomon's reign, since the concern for building the temple occurs alongside the concern to build a palace (2 Chron. 2:1 [HB 1:18]; 2:12 [HB 11]; 7:11; 8:1). Here, David does not build a temple, but prepares a special structure for the ark. Chronicles includes this building report to portray David as a good king who worships YHWH.

Since Chronicles mentions the purpose for this tent, the narrative builds an expectation that David will attempt again to transfer the ark to Jerusalem. The narrative doesn't disappoint. This text also suggests that David will succeed since, unlike the first attempt, David prepares a structure specifically for the ark.

15:2. Unlike the first attempt, David assigns the task of carrying the ark to the Levites. He recognizes that only the Levites may carry the ark. The Chronicler does not specify how David discovers this regulation, but David's statement closely resembles Deuteronomy 10:8. The similarities to Mosaic law become even stronger when one realizes that David's statement also incorporates language from Deuteronomy 18:5. The text implies that David interprets Mosaic law to discover this regulation. As Knoppers puts it, "In this respect, the Chronicler presents King David as a shrewd expositor of earlier scriptures" (2004, 613).

15:3–13. Once David determines that the Levites will carry the ark, he assembles all Israel again to transfer the ark. Even though transferring the ark is a concern for all Israel, the narrative focuses on the priests and Levites. David brings together groups of Levites with their leaders to prepare them for carrying the ark. He instructs them to consecrate themselves for the task and warns them of the seriousness of their participation in it.

David's statement reveals a difference between this attempt to transfer the ark and the first attempt, while also providing an important interpretation of the previous attempt. First, unlike 1 Chronicles 13, David instructs the Levites to consecrate themselves. The text suggests that before handling a sacred item such as the ark, the Levites must ensure they are prepared. This theme of Levitical consecration recurs in Chronicles at other significant moments of worship in Jerusalem (e.g., 2 Chron. 5:11; 29:5; 30:15; 35:6). Second, David states that the earlier attempt to transfer the ark failed because of what Israel did not do. The Levites did not bring up the ark the first time, and all Israel did not seek YHWH properly. Even though David calls out the Levites (notice the pronoun "you"), he switches to the first person to describe Uzzah's death as punishment for all Israel. As Japhet puts it, "This [switch to first person] is an admission of sin and an acceptance of full responsibility" (1993, 301).

TRANSLATION ANALYSIS:
This verse presents two challenges for translation. First, the verb דרשׁ has a wide semantic range, including denotations such as the following: (1) "to inquire of (usually through a mediator)," (2) "to care for," and (3) "to venerate." Second, the verb has a pronoun (pronominal suffix) for its object. This pronoun may refer either to YHWH or to the ark. For these two reasons, translations vary widely. Many translations (e.g., CSB, NET, NIV, NKJV, NLT) interpret the expression in the sense of inquiring YHWH. A smaller number of translations (e.g., NRSV) interpret the expression in the sense of caring for the ark. Some translations (e.g., ESV, NASB) leave the translation somewhat ambiguous, since they translate the verb with the English term "seek." The verb דרשׁ occurs frequently in Chronicles in the third sense of veneration. In this case, I interpret the verb this way also. As a result, I would translate the expression, "because we did not venerate him properly," or more colloquially "because we did not follow him properly."

15:14–15. After David takes care of these preparations, the Levites begin to carry the ark. In contrast to the first attempt to transfer the ark, the Levites carry the ark in the way that Moses commanded, according to YHWH's word. In other words, the text emphasizes that Israel obeys what YHWH requires as communicated through Mosaic law. Israel obeys primarily by having only the Levites carry the ark. However, they also carry it in the right way: on their shoulders, using poles. How they carry the ark does not point back to a single specific statement in the law, but refers to an interpretation of multiple instructions. For instance, Exodus 25:14 speaks of inserting poles into the rings of the ark to carry it; Numbers 7:9 speaks of the Kohathites carrying sacred items (including the ark) on their shoulders. The Chronicler shows that this interpretation fulfills what the Mosaic law requires and conforms to YHWH's will.

Carrying the Ark (15:16–16:3)

All Israel worships with joy and music as they transfer the ark to Jerusalem under the guidance of David, the priests, and the Levites, with YHWH's help.

15:16. As the Levites pick up the ark to bring it to Jerusalem, David takes the initiative in organizing the procession to accompany the ark. He calls on the Levitical leaders to appoint musicians to accompany the ark by performing loudly and joyfully with various instruments. The Levites respond by appointing the lead musicians (Heman, Asaph, and Ethan), and assigning the musicians to the musical instruments with which they will perform (harps, lyres, and cymbals). Listing the musicians and musical instruments on this occasion sets a precedent for the rest of Israel's worship: these leaders and instruments show up in Israel's worship far beyond the days of David (e.g., 2 Chron. 5:12; 20:28; 29:14, 25; 35:15). The Chronicler shows that David's act of worship on this occasion bears consequences for Israel's future ritual worship. Because of David's desire to seek YHWH properly, David sets the shape of Israel's musical worship.

Identity of Ethan

The name Ethan (אֵיתָן) occurs only here and earlier in the genealogical section of Chronicles (1 Chron. 6:44 [HB 29]). However, the name Jeduthun (יְדוּתוּן) occurs alongside Heman and Asaph in other contexts. Perhaps the names Ethan and Jeduthun refer to the same individual, either because the person was known by both names or because scribes accidentally copied the name incorrectly.

15:17–24. In light of this event's importance, the Chronicler provides details for the organization of the procession. First, the lead musicians perform on the bronze cymbals. Second, the musicians who rank just under the lead musicians fall into two categories: most of them perform on harps, while the rest perform on lyres.

Harps and Lyres

Both harps (נְבָלִים) and lyres (כִּנֹּרוֹת) are stringed instruments. There are technical differences between the two in terms of construction and performance. First Chronicles 15:20–21 likely points to such differences, since they describe playing the harps as *alamoth* (עֲלָמוֹת) and playing the lyres as *sheminith* (שְׁמִינִית). The precise meaning of these technical terms is not known; however, the point seems to be that the instruments complemented one another well.

Third, Chenaniah serves as the Levite in charge of the entire process of transporting the ark. The text emphasizes his skill and understanding in this process, ensuring that the process will take place properly. Fourth, some Levites serve as guardians for the ark. They likely guard the ark in two senses: (1) they protect the ark from the people so that it will not be defiled, and (2) they protect the people from the ark so that YHWH will not break out against them if they touch it. Fifth, seven priestly trumpeters play their trumpets. The details of this procession point in two directions. The Chronicler emphasizes the joyful musical celebration that accompanies the ark and the concern for proper reverence in handling the sacred object.

TRANSLATION ANALYSIS:
This verse describes Chenaniah as the chief Levite responsible for "lifting up" (מַשָּׂא). This term is ambiguous. It may refer to a prophetic oracle, a transport of some object, or lifting up voices in singing. Most translations (e.g., CSB, ESV, NASB, NIV, NKJV, NLT, NRSV), along with LXX, translate the term in the sense of singing. In the context, the Levites have already appointed the lead musicians Heman, Asaph, and Ethan; Chenaniah is not included. Furthermore, 2 Chronicles 35:3 uses the term מַשָּׂא specifically to refer to transporting the ark. For these reasons, I would translate the term as "transport" (cf. NET). Chenaniah oversaw the transportation of the ark and the procession that accompanied it, which included the singers (15:27).

15:25–28. The Chronicler provides other details as the procession moves into Jerusalem. First, the Chronicler emphasizes the participation of the people by referring to their representatives: the elders and high-ranking military leaders. David and these representatives accompany the processional party. Second, the Chronicler points out the people's incredible joy on this occasion. He does so directly in 15:25, but also implies such joy in 15:28 when he describes the musical celebration that takes place. Third, the Chronicler points to YHWH's help in carrying the ark. As the first attempt to transport the ark proved, it is dangerous for an earthly human to handle such a sacred object. It takes divine help just to be able to carry the ark without dreadful consequences. As a response to this divine help, the people sacrifice seven bulls and seven rams to YHWH. Fourth, even the apparel of David

and the leaders within the procession points to the opulence and majesty of this occasion. The linen robe is an extravagant garment associated with priestly and royal spheres (see 2 Chron. 5:12; Esther 1:6; 8:15).

> **Divine Construction of the Temple**
> This comment in 15:26 likely addresses a question that becomes prominent with the temple: Can a mere human build YHWH a temple? The Chronicler is concerned to show that the temple and all the elements that go with it, including the ark, are not just the product of human hands. Instead, YHWH himself enables people (Solomon most particularly) to build the temple (see Lynch 2014b, 110–17).

15:29. The Chronicler provides details of the events that transpire when the ark enters the city of David. He includes a brief comment about Michal, Saul's daughter: as she watches David celebrate the ark's arrival, she despises him. This comment appears somewhat out of the blue, but it draws on a theme earlier in Chronicles. In 1 Chronicles 13:3, the text contrasts David to Saul: David wishes to bring the ark from Kiriath-jearim, but Saul was not concerned about the ark. Here Michal, as Saul's daughter, represents a similar attitude. The comment confirms YHWH's rejection of Saul and choice of David.

16:1–3. Following the comment regarding Michal, the text records how David and the people respond to depositing the ark in the tent David prepared for it. First, the people make offerings to YHWH, as might be expected. Chronicles repeatedly records that Israel makes offerings at significant moments of Israel's ritual worship (e.g., 1 Chron. 21:26; 29:21; 2 Chron. 1:6; 8:12; 29:27). Second, once the offerings finish, David pronounces a blessing on the people. This comment looks back to Moses and Aaron as the tabernacle is finished (Lev. 9:22–23), and forward to Solomon as the temple is finished (2 Chron.

6:3). The Chronicler connects David to both the past and the future, also connecting the wilderness tabernacle to the Jerusalem temple. Third, David distributes food to all Israel present in Jerusalem. This type of celebratory feasting also takes place when David becomes king (1 Chron. 12:39–40). On that occasion, the people provide all types of food to celebrate David's coronation. Now David provides the food for all the people. David's provision of the food may be a sign confirming what Chronicles has earlier recorded in 1 Chronicles 14:2: David's kingdom is highly exalted for the sake of Israel. In this case, as David cares for the ark, he also cares for the people.

Organizing Worship Before the Ark (16:4–43)
Once Israel deposits the ark in the place David has prepared for it, David sets up Levitical musical worship, beginning with a hymn of praise to YHWH as God.

Initiating Worship (16:4–7)
16:4. Once the procession of the ark finishes, David looks forward to Israel's perpetual musical worship. The text begins by clarifying the function of the musical service: to remind (*hiphil* זכר), to give thanks (*hiphil* ידה), and to praise (*piel* הלל). Based on the hymn that follows this passage (16:8–36), the first term primarily entails reminding Israel of the marvelous deeds YHWH has done (see 16:12, 15). The latter two terms occur frequently in Chronicles, beginning with this verse. These verbs refer to praise and thanksgiving, often accompanying the confession that YHWH is good because his faithful love (חֶסֶד) endures forever.

In the activities of reminding, giving thanks, and praising, the Levites function as attendants (*piel* ptc. שרת) to YHWH. This term occurs several times in Chronicles to describe what the priests and Levites do (1 Chron. 6:17; 23:13; 26:12; 2 Chron. 5:14; 8:14; 13:10; 23:6; 29:11; 31:2). The term is a general word for clergy service (R. Klein 2012, 417), but here it looks back

to what took place in the previous chapter: appointing Levites to serve as musicians in the procession of the ark (1 Chron. 15:2). Their appointment as musicians ultimately looks forward to the temple, since once the temple is built they will no longer need to carry the ark. However, they can still fulfill their role of attending to YHWH by performing their musical service.

16:5–6. When David appoints these musicians to perform before the ark, he follows the choice that the Levitical leaders made for the procession in 1 Chronicles 15:16–21, 24. He includes a lead musician, musicians under his direction, and two priestly trumpeters. Furthermore, the text shows that this appointment shifts from the specific event of depositing the ark in Jerusalem to the continual nature of this musical service. The Chronicler uses the term תָּמִיד ("regularly") to communicate the regular practice of musical service.

16:7. Finally, the text introduces the following hymn. David assigns Asaph and his fellow musicians the responsibility of performing such regular musical praise to YHWH. The text intends to show how the Levites shifted from transporters of the ark to musicians within Israel's ritual worship. David appoints them as musical servants during this significant event of transporting the ark, in part, because they no longer need to transport the ark (1 Chron. 6:16). Furthermore, as an introduction to the following hymn, the text implies that this hymn also serves as a model for Israel's future musical worship.

TRANSLATION ANALYSIS:
Translating this verse requires resolving several exegetical issues. First, one must determine how to interpret the expression בְּרֹאשׁ. Several translations (CSB, ESV, NASB, NET, NIV, NKJV, NLT, NRSV) interpret the phrase as "first" or "for the first time." However, when the expression occurs in Chronicles, it refers to the leader (2 Chron.

13:12; 20:27). I interpret it to describe David as the leader. Second, one must determine the object of the verb, נתן ("he gave, set"). Some translations (NET, NKJV, NLT) infer the object to be the following hymn. However, other translations (CSB, ESV, NASB, NIV, NRSV) properly understand the object of the verb to be the infinitive "to praise" (לְהֹדוֹת). Finally, the combination of נתן ("he gave, set") and בְּיַד ("in the hand of") indicates assigning someone responsibility of something or someone (cf. Gen. 27:17; 30:35; 32:17; etc.). Given these considerations, I translate the verse in the following way: "On that day, David, as the leader, assigned responsibility for praising YHWH to Asaph and his colleagues."

Song of Worship (16:8–36)

This section constitutes the hymn that the Levitical musicians sing on this occasion. The hymn itself is a compilation of verses from three psalms: 105, 96, and 106, respectively.

1 Chronicles 16 and the Psalms

The song in 1 Chronicles 16 draws on several psalms. First Chronicles 16:8–22 parallels Psalm 105:1–15; 1 Chronicles 16:23–33 parallels Psalm 96:1–13; 1 Chronicles 16:34–36 parallels Psalm 106:1, 47–48. None of the superscriptions for these psalms attributes the psalm to David or Asaph. Furthermore, there are some differences between the texts of the psalms and the text of the hymn. These changes correspond to the change in occasion between the psalm and here in Chronicles. Commentators generally address these changes and their significance in Chronicles; however, see also Butler 1978, 142–50.

Even though the hymn is a compilation of psalms, it fits the current context well and ties in well with themes that run throughout Chronicles (Butler 1978, 147–50; Watts 1992, 158–59). For instance, 16:4 specifies the task of the musicians as reminding (זכר), giving thanks (ידה), and praising (הלל). The hymn calls on the people to praise YHWH in several ways, including specifically remembering (זכר, 16:12, 15), giving thanks (ידה, 16:8, 34–35), and praising (הלל, 16:10, 25). Also, 16:11 speaks of seeking YHWH and his strength (עֹז). In this case, "his strength" most likely refers to the ark, as it does elsewhere.

The Ark as YHWH's Strength

Psalm 78:61 describes the ark's capture as YHWH allowing his strength (עֹז) to go into captivity (Knoppers 2004, 646). Furthermore, Psalm 132:8 requests, "YHWH, arise from your resting place, you and the ark of your strength [עֻזֶּךָ]." Chronicles quotes this latter verse at the conclusion of Solomon's prayer (2 Chron. 6:41), immediately after Israel deposits the ark in the temple.

16:8–12. The hymn consists of four main sections: (1) general call to praise YHWH (16:8–12), (2) praise for YHWH as God of Israel (16:13–22), (3) praise for YHWH as God of all creation (16:23–33), and (4) thanksgiving and prayer of deliverance (16:34–36). The first section focuses on the call to praise YHWH because of the wonderful deeds he has done. The text does not specify these deeds, but for the occasion they would include YHWH's making David king, defeating David's enemies, and enabling the Levites to carry the ark successfully. As a result of what YHWH has done, Israel should not only praise him but declare his praise among the nations as an international witness to the character of Israel's God.

16:13–14. The second section (16:13–22) focuses on the relationship between YHWH and Israel, particularly on the patriarchs of Israel: Abraham, Isaac, and Jacob/Israel. This section begins by reminding the people of Israel's relationship to YHWH: the people are YHWH's servants, his chosen people, while YHWH is their God. This statement shows that Israel is subject to YHWH while YHWH has initiated a special relationship with them.

16:15–22. The hymn then shifts to describe YHWH's past dealings with the patriarchs of Israel based on this special relationship. The text focuses on two aspects: (1) YHWH has made a covenant with the patriarchs to give the land of Canaan as an inheritance, and (2) YHWH has protected the patriarchs even when they did not possess that land. Through repetition, the text emphasizes the perpetual nature of the covenant. The text shows the degree of YHWH's protection for the patriarchs by describing how YHWH protected the patriarchs from powerful kings, even as a small group of wanderers, so that no harm came to them. This picture likely alludes to the stories of Pharaoh and Abimelech, in which YHWH sent plagues and/or warnings to the foreign king to return the patriarch's wife (Gen. 12:12–20; 20:2–14; 26:7–11).

Although YHWH's protection of the patriarchs applies to the occasion of transferring the ark (David will still fight against his enemies to secure the land under his rule), it fits the first readers of the postexilic community much better. Based on the hymn, this small, politically insignificant people should expect YHWH to restore Israel fully in the land because of the covenant with the patriarchs. In the meantime, they can take comfort that YHWH will protect them, even from powerful kings (such as the Persian emperors).

16:23–29. The third section of the hymn shifts from praising YHWH as Israel's God to praising YHWH as the God of all creation. The text accomplishes this task in three ways. First, it calls for everyone in the world to praise YHWH and recount his marvelous deeds. It presents YHWH as a universally sovereign king, using terms associated with royalty, such as "splendor and majesty," "glory," and "strength." Furthermore, the text calls for all the nations to bring YHWH tribute (מִנְחָה), as they do later for David (1 Chron. 18:2, 6).

Tribute as Reward for Good Kings

Chronicles records other kings who receive tribute, using the same term מִנְחָה (Solomon, 2 Chron. 9:24; Jehoshaphat, 2 Chron. 17:11; Uzziah, 2 Chron. 26:8; Hezekiah, 2 Chron. 32:23). These kings receive tribute as a reward for seeking YHWH.

16:25–26. Second, the text contrasts YHWH to other gods. At first, the text shows that YHWH should be praised (מְהֻלָּל) and revered (נוֹרָא) because he is superior to other gods. In this case, the text does not intend to communicate that YHWH should simply be revered more than other gods, but that YHWH should be revered because he is superior to other "gods" (cf. Pss. 95:3; 97:9). The text describes the nature of other gods: they are useless idols.

TRANSLATION ANALYSIS:
Most translations (CSB, NASB, NIV, NKJV, NRSV) translate the term אֱלִילִים simply as "idols." In several contexts in the OT, the term refers to human-made idols (e.g., Isa. 2:8, 18, 20; 19:1, 3; Ps. 97:7; Hab. 2:18). However, the term carries another connotation of worthlessness or uselessness. Job 13:4 describes physicians who do nothing to remedy the situation, and Jeremiah 14:14 describes a practice of divination that doesn't come about. The point in these cases is that the person or object cannot bring about any change. As a result, some translations include the connotation of worthlessness: ESV translates the term as "worthless idols"; NET takes the term as an adjective, therefore translating it as only "worthless." I prefer the English term "useless," because it communicates that these gods have no power at all.

In contrast, YHWH is the creator of heaven. At first, the contrast may seem incongruous, since the first part describes what the nations' gods are while the second describes what YHWH creates. However, one may infer other elements that complete the contrast (for an explanation of a similar procedure in Proverbs, see M. Fox 2009, 494–98): both that YHWH is powerful and that the nations' gods are human-made. With this point in mind, the contrast employs the following logic: (A) the nations' gods (B) are useless idols (C) which are made (D) by human power, but (A') YHWH (B') is the powerful God (C') who made the realm (D') beyond human power. Therefore, YHWH is superior to all things, including the gods of other nations. As a result, YHWH alone deserves loyalty and praise.

Expressions of Monotheistic Belief

In this case, the Bible demonstrates that YHWH alone is the true God by contrasting him to other gods. In 1 Chronicles 17:20 David makes the same point in a different way: he states that YHWH is the only God. For a closer look at how the OT expresses its monotheistic belief, see Lynch 2014a, 47–68.

16:30–33. Third, the text personifies the natural world as rejoicing over YHWH's universal rule. First Chronicles 16:31–33 forms two parallel statements. Both statements employ figures of speech to refer to the entire natural world: the first using the combination of sky and land, the second using the combination of sea, field, and forest. Both statements portray creation rejoicing because YHWH rules: the first by explicitly stating that YHWH is proclaimed as king among all the nations, the second by stating that YHWH is coming to "judge" (שפט). In this case the word שפט, often translated "judge," should be understood in the sense of "rule" (see 2 Chron. 1:10–11; 26:21; Merrill 2015, 215). Even though the two statements are parallel, the second adds an element: YHWH is coming to rule. In context, YHWH's coming to rule likely alludes to YHWH's entering the temple (2 Chron. 5–7), from which he will exercise his universal sovereignty.

Entering the Temple as a Paradigm

Even though 1 Chronicles 16:33 points to the temple, its application lies beyond this event. More than likely, the Chronicler intends such an event to be paradigmatic, inviting future occasions in which YHWH would come to the temple to judge the earth (cf. Mal. 3:1 and Tate 1990, 515, who interprets Psalm 96:13 as describing an eschatological scene of YHWH's judgment). The Chronicler employs another psalm in a similar way. At the end of Solomon's prayer of dedicating the temple, he quotes Psalm 132 to show how YHWH's past filling of the temple anticipates a future one. For more details, see commentary on 2 Chronicles 6; see also Barbiero 2013, 243–50; Williams 2019, 81.

16:34–36. The final section of the hymn includes two summary confessions of YHWH's praise with a prayer for deliverance between them. The first confession is a common refrain in Israel's worship: "He [YHWH] is good, for his faithful love endures forever" (e.g., 1 Chron. 16:41; 2 Chron. 5:13; 7:3, 6; 20:21; Ezra 3:11; Pss. 100:5; 106:1; 107:1; 118; 136; Jer. 33:11). The hymn calls on listeners (and readers) to give thanks to YHWH because of YHWH's goodness and faithful love. The verse fulfills the task of giving thanks that David appointed the musicians to do (16:4, 7). Furthermore, the refrain summarizes and alludes back to earlier verses in the hymn that speak of YHWH's covenant with the patriarchs. YHWH's faithfulness to protect and provide for the patriarchs illustrates "his faithful love" (חַסְדּוֹ) and provides a reason for thanksgiving. The second confession is a general statement of praise to YHWH: "May YHWH the God of Israel be praised forever and ever." This verse draws the entire hymn of praise and thanksgiving to a close.

TRANSLATION ANALYSIS:
The traditional English gloss for בָּרוּךְ is "blessed." However, the sense of this word shifts considerably, depending upon the subject and object.

When God blesses a person, he bestows upon that person some benefit or special ability. However, when a person blesses God, the person praises God, usually because God is the source of a benefit or special ability. Even though in contemporary English "bless" may carry both senses, "bless" occurs more frequently in the former sense (e.g., God bless America). At the same time, "praise" and "give thanks" occur more frequently for the latter sense. For this reason, I follow translations that render the word in terms of praise (e.g., CSB, NET, NIV, NLT).

Inserted between the two confessions is a prayer for deliverance. The prayer calls on YHWH to gather the people and deliver them from the nations. As seen previously in the hymn, this prayer applies to two contexts. In the context of the original occasion, the prayer looks forward to David's task of fighting against Israel's enemies and preparing the people to build the temple (1 Chron. 18–29). In the context of the first readers, the prayer applies to the people's domination under the Persian Empire. Israel as a people has been scattered; this prayer looks forward to a time in which all the people may return to the land under independent rule.

The placement of the prayer between the two confessions of praise reveals both the reason and the results for this prayer. YHWH's goodness and faithful love provide the reason for appealing to YHWH for help. Israel's thanksgiving and praise to YHWH become the results if YHWH fulfills their request. By including this prayer in the hymn, the Chronicler ties this hope for restoration to YHWH's past marvelous deeds and faithful character and connects it to the musical service that will eventually take place in the temple. Therefore, as the musical performance reaffirms YHWH's sovereign rule over the earth and his faithfulness toward Israel, it also provides hope for Israel's full restoration.

Finally, the Chronicler shows that this musical praise represents the praise of all Israel. Following the final confession of praise to YHWH, all the people affirm what the musicians have performed as they themselves praise YHWH.

TRANSLATION ANALYSIS:
Translations must decide whether the final two words (וְהַלֵּל לַיהוָה) are part of the quotation (e.g., CSB, NET, NIV) or not (e.g., ESV, NKJV, NLT, NRSV). The decision involves two factors. First, LXX clearly reads this phrase outside the quotation ("They praised"). Second, MT has an ambiguous form with an ambiguous function. The verb could be imperfective, in which case the phrase would be part of the quotation ("Praise YHWH"); however, the form could also be an infinitive absolute. In the latter case, the infinitive can function like a perfective verb (GKC §113z) or like an imperfective (GKC §113bb). In this case, I find it likely that this phrase occurs in the quotation because it appears to be an actualization of what Psalm 106:48 calls for (see Knoppers 2004, 651).

Carrying on Worship (16:37–43)

16:37–42. This chapter closes by describing how David sets up Israel's ritual worship at that time. Now that David has moved the ark to Jerusalem, Israel has two official sacred sites: the ark in Jerusalem and the tabernacle in Gibeon. Since both are sacred sites, the Chronicler describes how David sets up their worship in similar ways. First, he assigns musicians to each location, drawing on the priests and Levites who participated in the procession of the ark. He assigns Asaph and Obed-edom, along with their colleagues, to remain by the ark in Jerusalem. He assigns Zadok and others earlier appointed by the Levitical leaders (1 Chron. 15:16–21, 24) to tend to the tabernacle in Gibeon. Second, David assigns Levites as guardians to protect the sanctity of each site, an obvious concern after the failure of 1 Chronicles 13. Third, he establishes similar patterns for ritual worship at both sites. The personnel should perform their worship duties in the following manner: (1) before the sacred object (ark in Jerusalem; tabernacle in Gibeon), (2) regularly, and (3) according to a daily schedule.

Ambiguities in Names

The verses concerning the guardians are somewhat ambiguous. It appears that there are at least two persons named Obed-edom. One is a musician, the other a guardian. Furthermore, there appear to be two persons named Jeduthun. Again, one is a musician, the other a guardian. David assigns Obed-edom, son of Jeduthun the guardian, and Hosah to guard the location in Jerusalem. He assigns the sons of Jeduthun the guardian to guard the location in Gibeon.

These similarities highlight one significant difference: their primary means of ritual worship. At Jerusalem, David assigns the musicians to minister (שׁרת) before the ark; however, at Gibeon, David assigns the priests to sacrifice burnt offerings on the altar as YHWH's law requires. The musicians at Gibeon accompany the priests, performing the same task assigned to Asaph and his colleagues in 16:4 and 7 to give thanks to YHWH. Even though music accompanies the sacrifices, at this time Israel's worship remains divided. This situation points forward to a time when Israel's worship will be unified at one location (e.g., the temple during Solomon's reign, cf. 2 Chron. 5–7).

Following YHWH's Law

When 16:40 speaks of the morning and evening offerings, it alludes to requirements recorded in Mosaic law (e.g., Exod. 29:38–42; Num. 28:2–8). Here, Chronicles refers to this law as YHWH's law, an expression occurring a few times in Chronicles to highlight the law's divine origin (e.g., 1 Chron. 22:12; 2 Chron. 12:11; 17:9; 31:3–4; 34:14; 35:26). Chronicles mentions these required regular sacrifices related to other significant points in his narrative: construction of temple (2 Chron. 2:4 [HB 3]), desertion of the northern kingdom (2 Chron. 13:11), and restoration of proper temple worship (2 Chron. 31:3).

16:43. The entire episode of transferring the ark concludes by stating that everyone returns home. The Chronicler uses this same image of the people returning home to mark the end of other ceremonies as well (2 Chron. 7:10; 31:1). The text points out David too as returning to bless his home. This comment is a fitting end to the narrative, since the first attempt to transfer the ark ends with a statement that YHWH blessed the house of Obed-edom because the ark remains there (1 Chron. 13:14). Now, David experiences the same blessing because he had transferred the ark to the city of David. Furthermore, this statement foreshadows the next scene in which YHWH promises to establish David's dynasty and allow David's descendant to build a temple. David declares these promises to be a blessing to David's house (1 Chron. 17:27).

This passage raises two concerns for the first readers. First, this passage points to the postexilic community's need to support the musical worship at the temple. At times, the community failed to support the priests and Levites sufficiently (e.g., Neh. 13:10). Second, the passage shows that following Mosaic law as the postexilic community approached YHWH brought about joy and blessing. For a small, poor community within the Persian Empire, Mosaic law provided safe access to YHWH, the God sovereign over all creation. Therefore, they should trust him to restore their fortunes, both in the present and the future.

THEOLOGICAL FOCUS

God deserves obedient praise because he is the God of all creation and the God of his people.

These chapters recount a significant moment in Israel's ritual worship. The description highlights the demeanor of David and all Israel as they worship before God, symbolized in the ark. Three aspects of their demeanor deserve consideration. First, the people worship both joyfully and reverently. Sometimes in contemporary settings, worshippers set joyful celebration and reverent observation against one another.

On the one hand, a celebration may seem too superficial or casual. On the other hand, a reverent observation may seem too somber or boring. However, when Israel transfers the ark, they show a deep reverence for God's holiness in the way they conduct themselves, while also celebrating with loud music and singing. The model in this text balances joy with reverence.

Second, the people pay attention to the details of the worship. The text includes many details of the event that may at first seem unnecessary. However, the text shows that David conscientiously arranges all the details to prepare for transferring the ark and, after its transfer, all the details for continuing Israel's worship into the future. This conscientiousness reveals both that approaching God in worship is a serious matter and that worshipping God deserves careful attention.

Third, the people worship in accordance with God's instructions. Unlike the first attempt to transfer the ark, David ensures that the manner of transferring the ark corresponds to Mosaic instruction. The text suggests that he carefully searches the law and prepares everything so that Israel will follow the law in transferring the ark. Today, the ark no longer serves as a symbol of God's presence, and Mosaic law no longer guides worship in the same way as it did for ancient Israel. However, David's example of investigating God's instructions to worship God in an appropriate manner still serves as a valid guideline for contemporary worship.

Beyond Israel's demeanor, this passage points out some reasons that God deserves to be praised. These reasons focus on God both as the God of all creation and as the God of Israel. As the God of all creation, YHWH is distinct from all other objects of worship. These other objects of worship are human-made. In the ancient context, the objects of worship were primarily idols, representations of some deity. In the contemporary context, the objects of worship are human ideas, structures, beliefs, or practices. In either context, ultimately, they are powerless

and useless. In contrast, YHWH is truly God. He has no creator; instead, he has created. He is powerful and has ruling authority over creation. As a result, all creation through all time should praise and exalt him.

As the God of Israel, YHWH works for Israel's benefit. As the Levitical song points out, God makes promises to Abraham and his descendants in the form of an oath and covenant (1 Chron. 16:15–18). He promises to give them a land for them to live in securely. God also protects them while that promise remains unfulfilled. For the first readers, living under Persian rule, God's promises and protection would provide hope for a better future and comfort for their present difficulties. Looking at the New Testament era, God promises that he will prepare a place for his people (John 14:1–3) and protect them during their present difficulties (John 17:14–16). Therefore, just as Israel worshipped God for his faithfulness regarding his promises to them and protection for them, so the church can worship God for his faithfulness regarding his promises to them and protection for them.

PREACHING AND TEACHING STRATEGIES

Exegetical and Theological Synthesis

The narrative section gives us a specific example of worship. We must be careful in how we apply this, because this was a unique event in the life of Israel. The specific actions could not be prescriptive for the postexilic community, for they had no ark to bring into the city. Thus the lesson for them, and us, is the more general approach to a worship celebration. Bringing the ark into Jerusalem was cause of great celebration, which shows us that at times worship should be filled with exuberant celebration. Israel's obedient preparing to celebrate, organizing to celebrate, and actually celebrating our great Lord gives us an example to follow in our own worship.

The poetic section called Israel to remember YHWH's faithful work regarding his promises and protection, to seek him, and to give him thanks. This call to worship applies to us as well. God, through Jesus, has brought about the great work of salvation, and he promises protection into eternal life. We too can remember his work, seek him, and give him thanks.

The two parts of this pericope give us a natural and logical structure. The narrative is a specific example of what worship can be and at times should be. The poetic section gives the more universal application of what worship should always be. At times our worship should be very celebratory, but it always should be filled with remembering what God has done, seeking him, and giving him thanks.

Preaching Idea
Give worthy worship to our worthy Lord.

Contemporary Connections

What does it mean?
He hadn't been to church in forty years. He had occasionally thought about God, but those thoughts seemed to get lost in his passion for hunting and fishing. That changed the day when he was able to walk away from a serious traffic accident—a car had run a red light and t-boned him. The crash could have ended his life; instead, it started him thinking about eternity and God.

As a teenager he briefly attended Calvary Baptist Church, being largely motivated by the girl he was dating. The girl and the church were both like faded black-and-white pictures in his memory. He couldn't find a Calvary Baptist in his area, but he knew of Calvary Church and Faith Baptist so he decided to try them both.

He arrived at Calvary Church just before the starting time of 10:00. He found a place to sit, was greeted by a few people, and then the lights went dim and the fog began filling the stage, the multicolored light beams began whirling about, singers came on stage, and the blast of the drummer's downbeat started the first song. He didn't recognize it as a hymn, but apparently the congregation did, because they not only sang but clapped; some even seemed to be dancing. Through the words of the songs and the humble attitudes of those singing, he could see that they were certainly celebrating Jesus's work in their lives.

The next Sunday he decided to attend Faith Baptist. The faded red carpet, the tan-colored pews, the well-worn blue hymnbooks, and the choir loft behind the oversized wooden pulpit looked just like the church he had attended with his girlfriend years before. He mused to himself, perhaps his old girlfriend would show up as well. He found a seat. An older gentleman began a conversation with him, which was shortened due to a piano starting to play. A leader picked up the tempo, had everyone stand, open hymnbooks, and sing, and they did. There were no laser lights, haze, or even drums, but through the words of the songs and their humble attitudes, he could see that they were certainly celebrating Jesus's work in their lives.

Both somewhat representative styles can get in the way of celebratory worship. When worship includes fog machines and moving laser lights, the sensory overload can come across as entertainment instead of celebration. On the other hand, older formats of worship can be so routine that they are no more celebratory than a well-worn alarm clock. Both formats would have seemed odd and even unrecognizable to David and Israel. And the details of Israel's celebration—which included a procession of men carrying a golden box with a half-naked king leading the way—seem strange to us. The common element is an obedient spirit of celebration that focuses exclusively upon God.

Is it true?
The old farmer had plowed with mules all his life. He had seen tractors, but hesitated to

change his proven ways; besides, he couldn't afford it. Finally, he stepped into the twentieth century and bought one. His kids were all excited, jumping and shouting when the big red tractor was delivered. Even his wife was almost in tears when she discovered they were getting a tractor. They were all celebrating—but all that came from the old farmer was a smile and a head nod. However, this same farmer could not keep from shouting nor stay in his seat when his son's basketball team won the regional championship. We might vary on how we express our excitement, but there is a desire to celebrate in each of us.

This passage is a detailed description of Israel's celebration of the unique and pivotal event of the ark coming into Jerusalem. It shows us how they celebrated, but perhaps more importantly it shows us that they *did* celebrate. It also shows us that this celebration was in obedience to God's clear guidelines.

Celebration is part of how God made us. Every culture has its various forms. The celebrations of the British monarchy are very organized with grand processions and structures. The celebration is in the attention to detail and precise execution of the processionals. In contrast is the scene of fans spontaneously rushing from the stands onto the field when the underdog team wins the game against the national champions. This passage teaches us that it is right and godly to celebrate. The Bible closes with a grand celebration of God's new heaven and new earth. Certainly we will celebrate then, but we can celebrate even now in light of that future event.

Now what?

Some years ago a popular romantic comedy caught my attention. The plot is delightfully predicable: the girl who only plans weddings falls in love and, through a twisting plot filled with humorous misunderstandings, eventually gets to celebrate her own wedding. The story has great appeal because the sadness of only planning others' weddings turns into the celebration of her own.

The celebration that is described in our passage is a celebration for all Israel, not just a few invited guests. To heighten the emphasis on all being a part of the celebration is the inclusion of Michal's despising David as he leads the celebration. God shows us that while he wants all to celebrate, it is still our choice. God is inviting us to be a part of the celebration, but we can sit on the sidelines. All Israel was invited and expected to rejoice in God's ark coming to Jerusalem, as the text emphasizes (15:3, 28; 16:3, 36, 43). This celebration belonged to every Israelite. This could have been Michal's celebration, but rather than celebrate she chose to criticize. Worship of our great Father, his Son, and the Spirit is for all believers. But it is still a choice. We need to be careful that we participate in the celebration rather than sit on the sidelines and criticize the details of a particular style.

There is an old commercial in which an old-timer asks the listeners, "How long has it been since you had a steaming bowl of Wolf-brand Chili? Well, that's too long." So, how long has it been since you celebrated God's great work and blessings?

Creativity in Presentation

Since varying views of worship style are grounded in tradition and held with deep emotions, the presentation of this passage calls for a strategy that will help the proclamation and application of its truth. There are some who will resist the call for celebration; others might balk at becoming more organized and structured. Jesus often used parables and metaphors to allow his listeners to participate in discovering his meaning. The book of Proverbs also often illustrates a situation with the meaning being implied. A similar approach could help in presenting the truths of this passage. The bulk of the sermon/lesson will be in the presenting the text, followed by some probing questions that are not fully answered. This is not to say that the preacher/teacher is leaving the application wide open to whatever the listeners think; the questions should direct the thinking by giving possible answers that come from the text, allowing individuals to participate in coming to the point of application. The overall feel is "Our worship could be like this." And our possible structure could be like this:

- Present the text
  - Give worthy worship (15:1–16:7; 16:36b–43)
    - Worthy of preparation
      - Organization (15:4–9)
      - Consecration (15:12)
      - Obedience (15:13, 25–26)
    - Worthy of celebratory praise: music and procession (15:16)
    - Worthy of all participating
      - All the people did (16:34, 43)
      - Michal did not (15:29)
  - To our worthy Lord (16:8–36a)
    - General call to praise YHWH (16:8–12)
    - Praise for YHWH as God of Israel (16:13–22)
    - Praise for YHWH as God of all creation (16:23–33)
    - Thanksgiving and prayer of deliverance (16:34–36)
- Probing questions:
  - Is our worship worthy?
  - Are we preparing for worship?
  - Is there a submissive and dependent spirit in us that prompts reverence?
  - Is there a reverence that prompts obedience?
  - Does this reverence and obedience prompt celebration?
  - Are we giving worthy worship to our worthy Lord?

Here's another approach that could be more effective for certain congregations. The text is presented as in the example above but in an imperatival form. Rather than "here is what our worship *could* be," the text is presented as "this is what our worship *should* be."

- We must give worthy worship (15:1–16:7; 16:36b–43)
  - We must prepare to worship
    - Organization (15:4–9)
    - Consecration (15:12)
    - Obedience (15:13, 25–26)
  - We must celebrate
    - Music and procession (15:16)
  - We must strive to include all
    - All the people did (16:34, 43)
    - Michal did not (15:29)
- Our Lord is worthy of this kind of worship (16:8–36a)
  - General call to praise YHWH (16:8–12)
  - Praise for YHWH as God of Israel (16:13–22)
  - Praise for YHWH as God of all creation (16:23–33)
  - Thanksgiving and prayer of deliverance (16:34–36)
- Give worthy worship to our worthy Lord

DISCUSSION QUESTIONS

1. How is joy expressed in worship?

2. How is reverence expressed in worship?

3. What are specific elements (details) that are in most current worship services?

4. How have you seen worship change during your life?

5. How have these changes enhanced or hindered worship?

6. Do you ever feel like Michal, who chose not to worship?

7. How could she have changed?

1 Chronicles 17:1–27

EXEGETICAL IDEA

When David wanted to build YHWH a temple, YHWH took the initiative to build David a dynasty—one that would not only build YHWH a temple but secure Israel as YHWH's people in their land.

THEOLOGICAL FOCUS

The Lord proves he is truly God, as he chooses the Davidic line to fulfill his promises to his people and to lead them to worship him properly.

PREACHING IDEA

God has the plan—we have the worship.

PREACHING POINTERS

Every congregation, every class, every person experiences a change of plans. Often those are not pleasant and are hard to adjust to. At some level we all struggle when our plans are changed. David had his plans changed. What could be more noble and God-honoring than to build YHWH's temple? Surely God would honor this plan.

David had a plan. God had a better one. David wanted to build God a house, but God said, "No." Instead, *God* would build *David* an eternal house. While God's plans for us are not as specific as they were for David, we can still trust that they are better than our plans.

THE DAVIDIC COVENANT (17:1–27)

LITERARY STRUCTURE AND THEMES (17:1–27)

After David had successfully transferred the ark to Jerusalem, he noticed the discrepancy between his palace and the ark's tent. As a result, David plans to build a temple to house the ark. The rest of the chapter consists of YHWH's response to David, followed by David's response to YHWH. When YHWH responds to David, his response falls into two units, both introduced by the prophetic formula "thus says YHWH" (17:4, 7). The first unit shows that David will not build the temple. The second unit focuses on YHWH's promises to provide David a dynasty from which will arise a temple-builder. This unit begins with a look at YHWH's past activity and then turns to his future activity. At the center of describing YHWH's future activity is a short chiasm (17:12–14). At the edges of the chiasm are statements that the throne of David's heir will be established forever. In the center of the chiasm is a promise that YHWH will never withdraw his loyal love (חסד) from the Davidic heir.

David then responds to YHWH. His response also falls into two units. In the first unit David expresses his awe at YHWH's word, both because of what YHWH promises and because YHWH reveals these promises to David. In this unit David reflects on the way that YHWH has treated David and Israel in the past. YHWH's activity in the past demonstrates that YHWH is truly God. Because YHWH reveals these things to David, David then requests that YHWH will fulfill his promises. If YHWH does so, then he will receive further glory and confirm that he is God, particularly Israel's God.

- **David Plans to Build a Temple (17:1–2)**
- **YHWH Responds to David (17:3–15)**
  - *David Will Not Build a Temple (17:3–6)*
  - *YHWH Promises a Dynasty and a Temple-Builder (17:7–15)*
- **David Responds to YHWH (17:16–27)**
  - *David's Awe at YHWH's Word (17:16–22)*
  - *David's Request to YHWH (17:23–27)*

EXPOSITION (17:1–27)

In the ancient Near Eastern world, kings and deities often shared a kind of give-and-take relationship. The deities chose kings and established their rule over the people. In return, kings built monuments and temples to honor the deities that made them kings. First Chronicles 17 contrasts this picture considerably. When David considers building YHWH a temple, he does not relate it to his becoming king. There is no sense of "payback" in David's proposal.

Furthermore, YHWH rejects David's plan to build a temple. Instead, YHWH chooses to honor David, build him a dynasty, and firmly secure Israel within their land. YHWH takes initiative and acts for David's benefit rather than the other way around. Furthermore, YHWH takes responsibility for the temple, raising up one of David's descendants to build it. As a result, David acknowledges YHWH's tremendous gift and points out how YHWH's actions prove he is God, particularly to Israel and David.

David Plans to Build a Temple (17:1–2)

After successfully transferring the ark to Jerusalem, David rightly intends to build a temple for YHWH.

17:1–2. Once David settles into his palace, he recognizes the disparity between where he lives and where the ark remains. David lives in a permanent palace of exquisite cedarwood while the ark remains under a transient tent of material not worth mentioning (Boda 2010a, 154). Even though the text does not state so explicitly, it implies that David intends to build a house/temple to deposit the ark there. David communicates this idea to the prophet Nathan, apparently expecting the prophet to say whether the idea will succeed or not. Nathan responds by telling David to follow through on what he plans to do because YHWH will grant him success.

> *TRANSLATION ANALYSIS:*
> This verse uses the expression of what is in one's heart. The word "heart" (לֵבָב) in this context has more to do with what David intends to do than how he feels. Translations (e.g., NET, NIV, NLT, NRSV) that render the expression as "what you have in mind" capture this sense well.

These verses present David in a positive light. First, after 1 Chronicles 15–16 recounts how David successfully transfers the ark and institutes the Levitical musical worship, it closes with a note that David returns to bless his own house (1 Chron. 16:43). David's concern for his house turns to his concern for YHWH's house, creating a link between David's good actions in 1 Chronicles 15–16 with 1 Chronicles 17. Second, David shows concern for Israel's ritual worship, in this case, building a temple for the ark. Nathan's response to David shows that David plans to do something good, since Nathan encourages him to do it. Later in Chronicles, YHWH commends David for his desire to build a temple (2 Chron. 6:7–8). Third, Nathan tells David that God is with him. In previous passages, YHWH has been with David (1 Chron. 11:9), and in the coming verses, YHWH will affirm that he has been with David (1 Chron. 17:8).

The rest of the narrative proceeds from this positive picture and comments on David's desire to build a temple.

YHWH Responds to David (17:3–15)

YHWH responds by denying David the opportunity to build a temple, but he promises David that he will build David a dynasty and appoint a future temple-builder from David's line.

David Will Not Build a Temple (17:3–6)

17:3–4. The night after Nathan assures David that he will succeed in whatever he intends to do, YHWH addresses Nathan. YHWH states clearly that David will *not* build the temple. The text here does not provide a direct rationale for rejecting David as the temple-builder (for a rationale, see 1 Chron. 22:8; 28:3); however, there is no hint that the reason is a rejection of David in general. As mentioned above, the picture of David in this chapter so far is quite positive. Furthermore, YHWH refers to David as "my [YHWH's] servant." Such an expression in this context, coming from YHWH, points to a "closeness and honor" that YHWH has for David (Japhet 1993, 339).

> **Night Appearances in Chronicles**
> Two other passages in Chronicles record YHWH appearing at night: 2 Chronicles 1:7 and 7:12. The former verse occurs at the beginning of Solomon's reign, in preparation for building the temple. The latter occurs following the construction and dedication of the temple. All three passages (1 Chron. 17:3; 2 Chron. 1:7; 7:12) have the temple in view. The night appearances unite the reigns of David and Solomon around the temple and likely indicate the significance of these passages within the book.

> *TRANSLATION ANALYSIS:*
> Translations generally render the Hebrew word הַבָּיִת as "a house" (e.g., CSB, ESV, NASB, NET, NIV, NLT, NRSV) even though the word is

definite. There are good reasons for translating the word this way; however, the word may be definite because it has in view the Jerusalem temple as the only legitimate temple (see Nordheim 1977, 450).

17:5–6. YHWH follows up with what appears to explain why David will not build the temple. First, YHWH states that ever since the exodus from Egypt, he has not remained in a temple but has moved along with Israel "from tent to tent and from tabernacle." YHWH's presence here most likely relates to the ark and its movements with Israel. As the ark moves along with Israel, it usually accompanies the tabernacle, a tent manufactured in part to house the ark. To a degree this comment aims directly at David, since David has just moved the ark from the tent of meeting/tabernacle at Gibeon to a tent he prepared in Jerusalem.

TRANSLATION ANALYSIS:
Several translations render the final phrase of 17:5 along the lines of "from tabernacle to tabernacle" (CSB), "from dwelling to dwelling" (ESV), or something similar (cf. NASB, NIV, NKJV). This translation is often based on a supposition that a second occurrence of מִשְׁכָּן ("dwelling place/tabernacle") has dropped out. However, MT only preserves one occurrence. Nonetheless, David's transfer of the ark explains the language of MT well: from the tent of meeting to the tent in Jerusalem (so that there are multiple tents) and from the tabernacle (since there is only one tabernacle; see Friedman 1980, 245–46). Knoppers also points out that this language reflects the terminology of the Pentateuch (2004, 668).

Second, YHWH asks whether he has ever requested one of Israel's judges to build him a temple. The question seems to be directed right at David. It describes the judges as those whom YHWH commands "to shepherd my [YHWH's] people." Earlier, YHWH charged David using this exact phrase: "to shepherd my [YHWH's]

people" (1 Chron. 11:2). Furthermore, this question includes the expression "a house of cedars," the very phrase that David uses to contrast his palace with the ark's tent.

At first glance these verses seem to question whether a temple should be built at all. However, in the context of the whole chapter, these verses address other concerns in response to David's desire to build a temple. First, by aiming the comments directly at David, these verses show that YHWH will take initiative to build a temple, not David. In this way, these verses along with 17:1–2 strengthen the impression that building the temple is David's idea. In response, YHWH stops David's initiative. In the coming verses, YHWH will point to his own initiative.

Second, these verses indicate that there is no rush to build a temple for YHWH. In fact, YHWH does not need a temple to dwell among the people since he has remained among them without a temple through their history up to that time. Therefore, David does not have to be the one to build the temple.

Third, the verses point to a condition required to build the temple but that has not yet come about: Israel as a people dwelling peacefully in the land. Deuteronomy 12:9–11 points to this condition as a requirement for YHWH to choose the place where he will dwell. From the exodus through the period of the judges, this condition has not been met. David begins to meet this condition (e.g., 1 Chron. 14:8–17); however, he still has several battles to win before securing the land and bringing peace (1 Chron. 18–20). In contrast, David's son Solomon will be a man of rest and peace, as David later announces (1 Chron. 22:9).

YHWH Promises a Dynasty and a Temple-Builder (17:7–15)

17:7. After YHWH responds to David's initiative, YHWH points to his own. In fact, YHWH (most often indicated by "I") is the subject of almost every verb. YHWH begins by pointing out what he has already done and then moves to what he will do. YHWH recounts three past activities to illustrate his initiative and care toward David. First, YHWH has made David king. Pointing out that YHWH takes David from tending the sheep to being king establishes that David becomes king through divine choice rather than typical means (e.g., dynastic succession; see Knoppers 2004, 668). YHWH initiates David's rise to the throne and brings it about. In this case, the text uses the expression of being "a ruler" (נָגִיד) for David's role as king. This same language occurs back in 1 Chronicles 11:2, when Israel crowns David king over all Israel and declares that he will shepherd the people (see commentary on 1 Chron. 11:2).

17:8a. Second, YHWH is with David all along the way. This point alludes back to Nathan's initial response to David: "God is with you" (17:2). The statement communicates that YHWH favors David and provides him with success. Furthermore, even though YHWH does not allow David to build the temple, he does not reject him from being king or from experiencing YHWH's favor in other ways.

Third, YHWH conquers David's enemies. Here, the language of "enemies" most likely alludes back to the Philistines. After defeating the Philistines, in 1 Chronicles 14:11 David acknowledges that YHWH "burst out against my [David's] enemies." These activities point to YHWH's initiative in making David king and YHWH's actions in supporting him as king.

17:8b. Next, YHWH turns to what he will do. YHWH makes four promises that seem to relate to David in his lifetime. First, YHWH will make David's reputation great. Although the expression differs, this idea resembles what YHWH has promised to Abraham in Genesis 12:2. Furthermore, YHWH has already brought this about for David, at least to a degree. After defeating the Philistines, David's reputation grows among all the lands.

17:9. Second, YHWH will plant Israel within its land. Furthermore, others will no longer oppress the people as has happened before David. Although the time of oppression likely refers to the period of the judges, it also applies well to the period of Saul in which the Philistines attack Israel, kill the king, and occupy some Israelite cities (1 Chron. 10). Using the language of "planting" Israel may allude back to Exodus 15:17, a passage from Moses's song sung after the crossing of the sea. In that context, Moses foresees YHWH planting Israel at YHWH's mountain sanctuary that he establishes with his hands. The picture of the mountain sanctuary relates well to the temple in Jerusalem. It appears that this picture of Israel planted comes about during the lifetime of David, since this promise occurs within others related directly to David (see also 1 Chron. 18–20).

17:10a. Third, YHWH will subdue David's enemies. Again, YHWH has already done this work. First Chronicles 17:8 recounts how YHWH has cut off all David's enemies. Furthermore, 1 Chronicles 14:8–17 recounts how David defeats the Philistines. YHWH will continue to do this work for David, beginning immediately in the next narrative unit (1 Chron. 18–20).

17:10b. Fourth, YHWH will build David a house. This expression is ambiguous. It could refer to a palace, a household, or a dynasty. YHWH has already provided for the first two since David has a palace, and YHWH has provided David with many sons (1 Chron. 14:5–7). As the following verses show, YHWH will now build David a dynasty.

Before moving on to the dynasty, let me make four observations regarding what YHWH is promising to do. First, these promises relate to David as king. Characteristics desired for kings include a great reputation, stability for the nation, military success, and a lasting dynasty. YHWH promises each to David, even though YHWH denies David the chance to build the temple. Second, to a greater or lesser degree, these promises look back to YHWH's promises recorded earlier in Israel's history—to the Abrahamic promises of a great name, a nation, a land, and even victory over enemies (e.g., Gen. 22:17). In this way these promises to David carry forward YHWH's past promises to Israel. Third, Chronicles shows how YHWH has already completed aspects of these promises even before making them here. This fact likely points to the nature of the statements. These statements are really promises, not prophecies. As a result, YHWH may fulfill them on multiple occasions. Chronicles will show how YHWH fulfills these promises during David's lifetime, but it also shows how these promises resurface in Israel's later history (e.g., Jehoshaphat, 2 Chron. 17:1–6, 10–19; Hezekiah, 2 Chron. 32:27–30). Fourth, the promise to plant Israel marks a new stage in Israel's history: "the beginning of enduring stability" (Japhet 1993, 332).

17:11–14. YHWH's promises now shift beyond David to the house YHWH is building. These promises clarify that the house YHWH will build for David is a dynasty. YHWH begins with promises to establish that dynasty. YHWH promises to fulfill the most basic requirement for having a dynasty: preserving offspring after David's death. The text communicates this point using the language of raising up a seed. The use of "seed" recalls the promises made to Abraham (e.g., Gen. 13:6; 15:5; 17:7). At the same time, the text specifies that the seed will be one of David's sons. Although the word "son" can refer to any generation of offspring (e.g., son, grandson, great-grandson), in the context of Chronicles, it most likely looks forward to Solomon. In fact, this set of promises focuses on Solomon as the expression of David's dynasty rather than focusing on the entire future dynasty itself.

17:11. YHWH promises to fulfill the next requirement for building a dynasty: establishing the offspring's kingdom. In other words, YHWH will ensure that Israel recognizes the royal authority of David's son. YHWH has already performed this same action for David, using similar language in 1 Chronicles 14:2. By preserving David's lineage and establishing the rule of David's son, YHWH builds David a dynasty. Furthermore, this similarity between David and his son reflects a concern of Chronicles to portray the reigns of David and Solomon as linked together (see comments on Solomon's reign, esp. 2 Chron. 1).

17:12. Following the promises to build David's dynasty, YHWH promises that David's descendant will build YHWH's temple. Among all these promises, this is the only one describing the actions of someone other than YHWH. The language of this promise emphasizes that this descendant (and therefore not David) will build the temple. These promises involve the actual building of two houses: YHWH builds David's house, the dynasty, and David's descendant builds YHWH's house, the temple. In Chronicles, these first three promises point forward to Solomon. In fact, as Solomon dedicates the temple, he claims that YHWH fulfills these promises (2 Chron. 6:10).

17:13. The remainder of the promises in this section address the ongoing relationship between YHWH and the Davidic dynasty. YHWH makes three statements regarding this relationship. YHWH first describes this relationship using familial terms: YHWH is the father, and the Davidic offspring is the son. In the ancient Near Eastern context, the language of father carries numerous connotations and occurs in a variety of relationships beyond the family. Despite the diversity, the use of "father-son" language always indicates a special relationship between two parties. One can argue that the language here points to a covenantal relationship between YHWH and the Davidic dynasty.

Language of Covenant

Japhet notes that the term "covenant" does not occur in this context, calling into question whether this vision constitutes a covenant or not (2009, 353–58). Despite lacking explicit terms for covenant here, Chronicles later refers to a covenant with David, apparently referring to this vision (2 Chron. 21:7).

YHWH's second statement confirms this covenantal sense of the language because YHWH promises not to remove his חֶסֶד ("favor, loyal love"), a relational and covenantal term, from the Davidic offspring the way he removed it from the one who preceded David, presumably Saul. The term חֶסֶד is quite difficult to translate because it encompasses a wide semantic range (such as "favor," "mercy," "covenant loyalty," "loyal love"). In trying to determine its sense here, one can look at Saul. As a result of YHWH's taking away his חֶסֶד from Saul, Saul suffers the following: (1) he dies in battle against his enemies, (2) he has no son to preserve his lineage (1 Chron. 10:6), (3) he therefore has no dynasty, and (4) YHWH turns the kingdom over to David. In light of these observations, the term "favor" seems most appropriate here. Earlier in this vision, YHWH already shows such favor to David (e.g., delivering him from his enemies, 17:8) and will continue to show such favor to David (e.g., again subduing David's enemies, 17:10; raising up a seed for David and establishing David's dynasty, 17:11). Here, YHWH promises that he will not remove such favor from David's dynasty as well.

17:14. YHWH's third statement elaborates on the relationship by pointing to the Davidic offspring's role in cultic and political matters. YHWH promises to appoint the Davidic offspring in both spheres. Furthermore, YHWH points out that ultimately both cultic and political authority belong to YHWH. For this reason, YHWH refers to "my house," the temple, and to "my kingdom," YHWH's rule. Appointing the Davidic offspring in the temple entails granting him authority relating to cultic matters, although such authority is limited and does not supersede the role of the priests and Levites (see 2 Chron. 26:16–20). To a degree, David already serves in this role by introducing Levitical music into Israel's ritual worship (1 Chron. 16). At the same time, appointing the Davidic offspring over YHWH's kingdom points to YHWH's everlasting authority that transcends human political structures. The Davidic offspring functions as the human representative of YHWH's everlasting divine rule.

Finally, at the beginning and end of this section describing the nature of YHWH's relationship to the Davidic offspring, the text speaks of securing the offspring's throne forever (17:12b, 14b). This repetition points to a concentric structure. This structure is significant for two reasons. First, it highlights the central element of the structure: YHWH's "favor" (חֶסֶד) to the Davidic offspring. Second, it shows that the context for this relationship is the Davidic offspring's royal authority. In other words, YHWH exhibits his fatherhood, maintains his favor, and grants his authority to the Davidic offspring in the context of the offspring ruling forever. The end of Chronicles creates tension with this picture, since a Davidic offspring no longer rules over Israel and the temple itself is destroyed. However, unlike the situation with Saul, Chronicles leaves open the issue of a Davidic seed and seems to point forward to another who will come later to build YHWH's temple as Solomon does (see comments on 2 Chron. 36:22–23; Gilhooley 2020, 95–96).

David Responds to YHWH (17:16–27)
David responds in awe that YHWH, the incomparable God, has revealed his plan to David, a mere human servant, and prays that YHWH will accomplish what he has promised.

David's Awe at YHWH's Word (17:16–22)

17:16. After Nathan delivers YHWH's words to David, David responds in prayer. As David sits before YHWH, most likely at the tent housing the ark, he assumes the same posture as he did in 17:1; however, there he sits in his palace. This similarity draws a connection between how David responds to building a palace and now how David responds to YHWH's building him a dynasty. The first response focuses on the surprising distinction between the royal palace and the ark's tent. The second response focuses on YHWH's exalted status and the surprising way that YHWH treats David, as will be seen below.

When David responds, he focuses on the status of three parties: (1) himself, (2) YHWH, and (3) Israel. When addressing his own status, he demonstrates humility in several ways. First, David recognizes that neither his identity ("Who am I?") nor his family lineage ("Who is my house?") grants him a special status before YHWH. As a result, he is not entitled to what YHWH has already done for him, that is, making him king, delivering over his enemies, building a palace, and allowing him to transfer the ark to Zion.

Use of Rhetorical Questions

This type of rhetorical question (e.g., "Who . . . ?") occurs elsewhere with the same sense of humility (e.g., David, 1 Chron. 29:14; Solomon, 2 Chron. 1:10; 2:5). In each context, the speaker (a Davidic king) recognizes his humble status before YHWH. Furthermore, this question, as an instance of self-abasing, functions as an expression of thanksgiving that magnifies YHWH's generosity to David (see Bridge 2011, 268–73).

TRANSLATION ANALYSIS:
The text uses the term בַּיִת. As seen throughout this chapter, the term בַּיִת has a wide semantic range, referring to palace, temple, dynasty, household, and here lineage. Unlike other kings, who inherit the throne through dynastic

succession, David recognizes that YHWH has made him king through other means.

17:17. Second, even though YHWH makes David king and secures his rule, David recognizes that YHWH's future promises far exceed these present blessings. However, David does not focus on the promises themselves at this point; instead, he focuses on the fact that YHWH reveals the future to David. Despite David's humble status, YHWH shows David what lies in the distant future—a rare and undeserved privilege.

TRANSLATION ANALYSIS:
The latter part of this verse is difficult to translate. One line of translation understands the verse to communicate that YHWH has shown David the distant future even though David is a mortal (Knoppers 2004, 678). Another line of translation understands the verse to communicate that YHWH treats David as one who is highly exalted (cf. CSB, NASB, NIV, NKJV, NLT, NRSV). Although there are several textual and lexical issues in translating the verse, including issues related to the parallel in 2 Samuel, the translations differ primarily based on their understanding of the phrase כְּתוֹר הָאָדָם הַמַּעֲלָה. The final word can either function as an adjective describing the man as exalted or as an adverb locating the action in the future. The former understanding is more probable because it fits well within the immediate and distant context of Chronicles. However, regardless which line of translation one follows, the verse still communicates that despite David's humble status, YHWH performs something special when he reveals to David what will happen in the future.

17:18. Third, David acknowledges his status as YHWH's servant; therefore, David can receive no greater honor than special recognition from YHWH. In fact, when the text states that YHWH knows David, in this context, that expression means that YHWH recognizes David in a special way.

TRANSLATION ANALYSIS:
TRANSLATION ANALYSIS:
Numerous translations (CSB, ESV, NASB, NIV, NKJV, NLT, NRSV) render the latter part of 17:18 something like the following: "You [*YHWH*] know your servant." In contrast, NET translates the expression as follows: "You have given your servant special recognition." This latter translation captures the sense of the expression well.

17:19. Fourth, David recognizes that even though YHWH's promises benefit David, YHWH chooses to make these future promises and reveal them according to his own will. In other words, YHWH has not been coerced or manipulated into making these promises. They follow his plan, and he makes them freely. The chapter shows how David moves from taking initiative to acknowledging that YHWH is the one at work, and that YHWH will accomplish his plan as he intends.

17:20. After David describes his own humble status, he turns to YHWH's exalted status. The text declares that YHWH is unique since there is none like him. It also expresses in the clearest and most forceful way that YHWH is the only God. YHWH's words through Nathan to David prompt David to declare this monotheistic statement because they show that as God, YHWH has the power to establish David's rule securely over Israel into future generations and as God, YHWH has the power to reveal such future events to David. In other words, YHWH's ability to declare what will happen and YHWH's ability to make such things happen demonstrate his nature as God.

17:21. Following David's brief but significant statement regarding YHWH's nature, David turns to Israel's nature. Building on YHWH's uniqueness, David reflects on how Israel is unique (Knoppers 2004, 684). He bases Israel's uniqueness on the fact that YHWH redeems the people from Egypt and drives out other nations to settle Israel as a people in their own land. This

type of activity (i.e., snatching a nation from within another and leading them to their own land) is unheard of, especially when compared to what is said about other nations and their gods (see Deut. 4:34–35) and so confirms that both YHWH and Israel are unique.

17:22. After pointing to YHWH's historical activity in bringing about Israel as a nation, David looks to the ongoing relationship established in that work. YHWH has formed Israel as his people forever, and YHWH has become Israel's God (similar expressions occur throughout the OT, e.g., Exod. 6:7; Lev. 26:12; Deut. 29:13 [HB 12]; Jer. 7:23; 11:4; 24:7; 30:22; 31:1, 33; 32:38; Ezek. 11:20; 14:11; 36:28; 37:23, 27; Zech. 8:8). The language resembles and complements what YHWH has earlier said regarding David's offspring (17:13): YHWH will be the offspring's father while the offspring will be YHWH's son. The similar language points to an underlying connection between Israel as a nation and the Davidic dynasty. These verses suggest that YHWH's commitment to Israel as a nation mirrors YHWH's commitment to David's offspring as a dynasty. One cannot fully have one without the other.

David's Request to YHWH (17:23–27)

17:23–27. David closes out his response by requesting that YHWH do what YHWH has promised. Three significant points emerge from David's request. First, in the context of this chapter, the language of this section reveals a shift from David's initiative to YHWH's initiative. In 17:2 Nathan tells David to do as David intends. In this way, Nathan affirms David's initiative. Now after YHWH responds to David, in 17:23 David recognizes YHWH's initiative, asking YHWH to do as YHWH has promised. First Chronicles 17:1 implies that David intends to build YHWH a temple (בַּיִת), but 17:25 repeats that YHWH will build David a dynasty

(בַּיִת). In 1 Chronicles 16:43 David blesses his own household (בַּיִת), but now in 17:27 YHWH blesses David's dynasty (בַּיִת). These connections contrast David's initiative to YHWH's initiative and show that David recognizes YHWH's initiative in these matters.

17:23–24. Second, at first glance it seems strange that David requests YHWH to do what YHWH has just promised. However, David makes this request because of the promises YHWH reveals and because YHWH reveals them to David. The same qualities (i.e., YHWH's power and foresight) that earlier led David to confess that YHWH is the only God (17:19–20) here lead David to pray and make this request regarding his future dynasty. Furthermore, the language David uses here looks forward to the time of building the temple under Solomon. At that time, Solomon also will request that YHWH will establish what YHWH has promised (2 Chron. 6:16–17) even though, in Solomon, YHWH has already accomplished much of what he has promised (see 2 Chron. 1:9; 6:4–10, 15). This connection points to an underlying feature of this account in Chronicles: even though it deals with the Davidic dynasty, it focuses on Solomon as both the fulfillment of the promise and the one guaranteeing that promise into the future (see esp. Williamson 2004, 176–91).

17:24–26. Third, David's request elaborates on the relationship between David, Israel, and YHWH by addressing YHWH's identity and glory. The text points out that if YHWH does what he has promised to David regarding David's dynasty, then YHWH's name will be great—that is, YHWH's reputation will be great. This request shows how YHWH's reputation is tied to his activity and identity. By accomplishing his promises to David, YHWH demonstrates that he is Israel's God. In other words, YHWH's faithful activity toward David is also YHWH's faithful activity toward Israel. YHWH's identity

as Israel's God is then tied to YHWH's identity as David's God. As David's God, YHWH has revealed the promise to build a dynasty specifically to and for David. YHWH's promises to David lead David to proclaim that YHWH is not only Israel's God and David's God, but also God in an absolute sense, "God" (הָאֱלֹהִים). These statements show how YHWH, Israel, and David are linked together, because YHWH has taken initiative to build a Davidic dynasty.

> **YHWH as God**
>
> In this case, the word הָאֱלֹהִים is not used as a name but serves as a statement regarding YHWH's nature. YHWH is the one who exemplifies all that the idea of *god* contains. In particular, as pointed out earlier, YHWH has great power to make things happen and foresight to reveal them before they happen. See also comments regarding 2 Chronicles 33:13.

This passage records one of the most significant events in YHWH's dealings with Israel because it incorporates the Davidic dynasty into the nature of Israel as a nation. For the first readers, such a passage would be difficult to relate to their own situation. They lived after the fall of the Davidic dynasty, the destruction of the Jerusalem temple, and the dispersion of many of their ancestors. Despite these difficulties, they survived as a people. For those first readers, this text provides hope in two separate directions. First, the text builds expectation that a Davidic king and the Jerusalem temple were a part of YHWH's plan for Israel's past and are a part of YHWH's plan for Israel's future. Second, the passage demonstrates that neither the Davidic dynasty nor the Jerusalem temple are required for Israel to exist as a people. YHWH points out that Israel existed as a people even when the tabernacle was the place for YHWH's dwelling and the judges served as shepherds for Israel (17:3–6). What defines Israel as a people is the fact that YHWH is their God and they are his people (17:22). Furthermore, YHWH possesses a kingdom himself. Even though YHWH assigns the Davidic dynasty responsibility over this kingdom, YHWH's kingdom rule continues whether a Davidic descendant sits on the throne or not. In this way, Israel can be confident of the future, regardless of their present circumstances, while still maintaining their identity as YHWH's people.

THEOLOGICAL FOCUS

The Lord proves he is truly God, as he chooses the Davidic line to fulfill his promises to his people and lead them to worship him properly.

God's promises to David recorded in this passage fundamentally shape the way God relates to his people from this point on. The promises incorporate, elaborate, and expand the promises made to Abraham and the other patriarchs. The Davidic promises integrate the monarchy into the picture of the ideal Israel. They reveal that God plans to use the Davidic monarchy to establish the promises to the patriarchs. The patriarchal promises envision a blessed nation, living securely and peacefully in a designated land. More importantly, the promises speak to the special relationship between YHWH and Israel: YHWH is Israel's God, and Israel is YHWH's people.

Incorporating the Davidic promises into the patriarchal promises links the fate of Israel as a people to the fate of the Davidic line as a dynasty. The link between the people and the dynasty points in two directions. On the one hand, the Davidic promises point to the past and future. In the past, Solomon is a Davidic heir who builds a temple in Jerusalem. However, Solomon does not exhaust the Davidic promises. They point beyond Solomon to an abiding hope that through the Davidic dynasty, God's people will experience all the blessings that God has in store for them as they worship him. The New Testament testifies that the Davidic descendant to bring about these blessings is Jesus of Nazareth. In one sense, Jesus has already secured these blessings for his people, but in another

sense, Jesus will secure these blessings fully and finally in the future. Therefore, just as the first readers were waiting for the Davidic descendant to arise and restore their fortunes like the days of Solomon, so also believers have a living hope of an incorruptible inheritance that God has promised (1 Peter 1:3–5).

On the other hand, the Davidic promises point to the present time between the promise and its ultimate fulfillment. The promises highlight two aspects of this period in the middle: (1) God reigns over the world whether or not a Davidic heir currently sits on a throne in Jerusalem, and (2) the responsibility of God's people is still to worship him. For the first readers, these promises directed them to trust their God even under Persian rule as they poured their energies into the Jerusalem temple and the proper ritual worship that took place there. For contemporary readers, these promises should encourage them to trust God, even under the power of the prince of this age, and to worship God together in spirit and truth among the congregations of those who follow Jesus scattered throughout the world.

Finally, as David's prayer of response shows, the way that God works proves that he is truly God. First, God knows the future and reveals it. This knowledge points to God's omniscience but also to God's omnipotence, since God is the one accomplishing his future promises. Second, God has chosen David to be the head of a dynasty and Israel (aka Jacob) to be the father of a nation. David recognizes that neither he nor Israel deserves the great honor that God has granted them. Third, God has chosen David and Israel to bless them. God has promised great things to David in establishing a dynasty, and great things to Israel in securing them in a land. Furthermore, God continues to work in similar ways. God still knows the future, has revealed it in his Word, and is working to accomplish his promises. God has still chosen those who do not deserve the great honor granted them (Eph. 2:8–10). God has still chosen to bless (Eph. 1:3–6). His work in the past and present demonstrates that he is truly God.

PREACHING AND TEACHING STRATEGIES

Exegetical and Theological Synthesis

At first glance this chapter could be a story about another of David's wise choices. Two of these critical choices were first: his desire to build a temple for YHWH, and then his choice to be willing to take on the new assignment to make the preparations to build. However, this chapter is not primarily about David's choices. Throughout 1 and 2 Chronicles it is clear that YHWH is the one who makes the major choices. He is the initiator. A materialistic view (a dominant mindset of Western thought, and sometimes mine) would present this episode as David taking steps to build his kingdom: consolidate power, choose a capital city, choose a god, and choose to build a temple to that god. This is not about David choosing YHWH; it is about YHWH choosing David. The Chronicler then tells us of David's response to YHWH's sovereign choice.

God's two key choices expressed in this chapter are his choosing to reject David's plan to build a house for him, and then God's promise that he would build a house for David. The chapter goes on to present David's two responses, which are his humble awe at God's plan and his request that God be magnified.

While God's plan for each of us is not presented to us with this specificity, he still has a plan for each of us. This plan is his choice, not ours. We, like David, make our plans that hopefully come out of a good heart, as did his. And most often those plans are changed by a sovereign God. So how do we respond to change? The real question for David, and for us, is not "How do we respond to change?", but "How do we respond to God's sovereignty?"

Preaching Idea

God has the plan—we have the worship.

Contemporary Connections

What does it mean?

God's plans often take us down roads we hadn't seen or didn't even know were there. As a teenager I sensed that God's will for me was to prepare for and then pastor a church. In high school and college, this was a driving aim of my life. When my girlfriend (now my wife) and I talked about marriage, I told her that I had chosen to be a pastor. If we married, we would never own our own home but would live in a parsonage. I had a plan. When we started seminary my plan was to graduate and pastor the same church for thirty years.

Now, after pastoring three different churches and being on full-time faculty at two seminaries, it is clear that God's plan was different than mine. It is rare that anyone plans their life and then life follows that plan. David had a heart for God's glory and made plans to do what he thought God wanted. While God doesn't deride our plans, he really doesn't need them. What he desires is our hearts. When our plans change, our hearts need to stay the same.

As the exiles read or heard about God rejecting David's plans, perhaps they were encouraged because their plans had certainly been changed. But wasn't the exile because of sin? Was *that* part of his plan? In his great wisdom and knowledge, God even uses our sin to bring about his good plan, not that our sin was his perfect will for us. It was God's permissive will that allowed sin into the world and into my life; but in his amazing plan, Jesus came, died, and rose to forgive and redeem. God reveals and accomplishes his plans in his own time and way. Nothing can thwart his plans.

This passage teaches us that God's plans are not only different than ours, they are better. Later in his life David wrote, "Many, LORD my God, are the wonders you have done, the things you planned for us. None can compare with you; were I to speak and tell of your deeds, they would be too many to declare" (Ps. 40:5 NIV).

The question remains: How will I respond when God's plans bring about change? Will we get angry at God because our dreams are dissolving? Will disappointments bring on a pity-party depression because we didn't get our own way? Will the rejection of our good plans blind us to God's greater plans?

Is it true?

When Nathan delivered the news to David that he would not be the one building the temple, his response was exemplary. We don't hear David saying what many of us would say: If I hadn't been so warlike, if I had spent more time worshipping and less time warring, then I would have been able to build the temple. If I had brought the ark back to Jerusalem sooner . . . if I had not been so concerned about building my own house . . . if I had just . . . then I could have brought about my plan. Perhaps David did go through these feelings, but he must have worked through them because in the end the record tells of his humble acceptance and rejoicing in God's changing of plans.

A friend recently suffered a minor foot injury due to falling off a ladder. He had plans to mow grass, go for a run, visit the hardware store, work in his woodshop—that is, to live his life in a normal pattern. The injury changed his plans. God in his sovereign plan allowed this to happen. My friend's response was frustration and impatience, but after three weeks of being in a medical boot and sitting far more than he liked, a new appreciation for his wife's chronic debilitating health issues began to grow in him. God's plan was different from his, and fortunately he could see God's good hand in these new plans.

None of us would say that we can control the future, but we get all frustrated when we realize that we can't. It is harder than one would think, but we need to believe that we cannot

control our future, even though we want to. We spend a great amount of energy thinking through the future. We tell our children that they need to prepare for the future and take advantage of educational opportunities. Financial advisors tell us to invest our savings with a view toward retirement. The medical profession tells us that if we eat right and exercise, we will have better health in the future. It is right to make plans, but it is wrong to think that we have the power to ensure those plans will be fulfilled. We know that God is sovereign over this world, but often we think we are sovereign over our plans. We should make plans for the best, but we must not think that we *know* what is best.

Now what?

The popular comedian of the last century Woody Allen popularized for the masses the saying, "If you want to make God laugh, tell him your plans." I think Woody Allen was wrong. This passage presents a different view of God. When David told God his plans, God didn't laugh. Instead, God told him of a greater plan, beyond anything David could imagine. We need to remember that this greater plan of God's included the rejecting of David's plan. But the question is not how God will respond when we tell him our plans; rather, the question is how we respond when we hear God's plans for us.

The hard part comes when our plans fail or are rejected, and God's greater plan is not yet seen. David not only heard about the rejection of his plan, but also had the joy of hearing of God's amazing plan for an eternal blessing. We too have an eternal plan promised for us in Christ. And we have the promise of an abundant life here and now. To be sure, these are broad and general plans, and the specifics are not laid out for us. We need to remember that while David had these specific plans revealed to him, the rest of God's plan for his life was left broad and general.

When David's plans changed, some things didn't change. David's response to YHWH's change of plans was the same response when David had in his mind to build the temple. He wanted God to be glorified. He wanted to be obedient to YHWH. He put God's kingdom and glory ahead of his. His dream to be the one to build the temple died, but his worship and obedience lived on. When our plans dissolve, our worship and obedience should remain.

Creativity in Presentation

This text includes a spatial division, one that can aid us in giving a clear presentation of the text. The story begins with David sitting (implied) in his own house, telling Nathan that he wants to build a house for YHWH. It ends with David sitting in YHWH's temporary house, giving praise to YHWH. The word given to Nathan is in between these two places. Thus, the pulpit area can be used to add clarity to the sermon/lesson. The first section could be presented on the preacher's right-hand side of the stage. Nathan's word from God could be from the center pulpit and then the response of David could be on the left-hand side. (The visual flow is from the speaker's right to left—left to right from the congregation's vantage point.) It might be appropriate to have a chair and sit for a portion of the presentation.

Since this passage talks about change, it could be helpful to talk about various responses to change. There are many websites and books that cover this subject. By presenting various ways that people respond to change, listeners can identify struggles they have, and their responses to them. Responses could include anger because they might lose something, depression because they think they can't handle the change, or frustration because they are comfortable with the way things are. The goal is to help listeners admit that we all struggle with change. While responding to change is the beginning point, the ultimate end is responding to God's sovereignty.

At the same time, care should be taken to ensure that the subject of change doesn't get too much attention. Changes are very painful when they come because of a death, or loss of a job, or marriage, or some other crisis. Therefore, acknowledging that some changes are quite painful is important. Here is one possible structure:

- Responding to a change of plans
  - Make plans with God's glory in mind (17:1–2)
  - God's plans are better than our plans (17:3–15)
  - Plans die but worship lives on (17:16–27)
- God has the plan—we have the worship.

DISCUSSION QUESTIONS

1. What plans did you have for your life in high school ?

2. What plans did you have for yourself after high school?

3. What plans did you have a month ago? How have they changed?

4. How do you feel when your plans are changed?

5. How does our trust in God's sovereignty affect our reaction to change?

6. Which is the better image to help us think about our making plans: in ink or in pencil?

7. When God changes our plans, how does it affect our worship?

1 Chronicles 18:1–20:8

EXEGETICAL IDEA

As YHWH fulfilled part of his promise, David's reign at this point appeared ideal: David defeated his enemies, rallied competent warriors, expanded his influence in the region, increased his wealth, prepared for temple construction, organized his administration, and governed with justice.

THEOLOGICAL FOCUS

God uses the one loyal to him to fulfill his plan to bless his people.

PREACHING IDEA

To be a part of God's great work, be loyal to him.

PREACHING POINTERS

Everyone wants to be a part of something that is successful. When our team has a winning season, we are more likely to watch the games. We take a new job not only because of the direct benefits to us, but because we want to be a part of a successful company. We enter into marriage because we think it can be a success.

In these chapters we see God bringing great success to David and to Israel. The first readers wanted success in their rebuilding of Israel. They needed YHWH to work in powerful ways. The loyalty of David serves as an example of how to be a part of God's great work. God was showing the exiles that he would work to keep his promises. Their loyalty to the great God would bring them into his great plan and work. He would work; they only needed to remain loyal. What could be more successful than God keeping his promises? And what could be more glorifying to him than expressing our faith through our loyalty to him?

DAVID DEFEATS ENEMY NATIONS (18:1–20:8)

LITERARY STRUCTURE AND THEMES (18:1–20:8)

Following YHWH's promise to David in 1 Chronicles 17, the Chronicler shows how YHWH immediately began fulfilling parts of the promise. These chapters especially address YHWH's promise to subdue David's enemies (1 Chron. 17:10). At the same time, it shows how David responds by ruling justly and setting aside resources to be used in the temple construction.

The chapters fall into four main sections. The Chronicler clearly marks out three sections by beginning them with the transitional phrase "after this" (1 Chron. 18:1; 19:1; 20:4). Furthermore, these sections have elements that correspond to one another. For instance, when the first section (1 Chron. 18:1–13) describes how David defeats various enemy nations, it begins with a statement about subduing the Philistines, while the last section (1 Chron. 20:4–8) describes how David further defeats the Philistines, including a statement that the Philistines were subdued. In this way, subduing the Philistines brackets the entire narrative unit. At the same time, much of the first section describes how David fights against the Arameans, while the third section (1 Chron. 19:1–20:3) describes how David defeats the Ammonites and Arameans. This parallelism between these sections highlights a contrast between the two. The first section points out that YHWH delivers (*hiphil* ישׁע) David wherever he goes (1 Chron. 18:6, 13), while 1 Chronicles 19:19 states that the Arameans are no longer willing to deliver (*hiphil* ישׁע) the Ammonites. This contrast points to YHWH's power over the nations, even when the nations band together against Israel.

Besides the three sections marked by the phrase "after this" and dealing with David's military conflicts, the other section deals with a different subject matter. This other section (1 Chron. 18:14–17) addresses David's administration, presenting David as a just, impartial ruler.

- *David Defeats Various Enemy Nations (18:1–13)*
- *David's Administration (18:14–17)*
- *David Defeats the Ammonites and Arameans (19:1–20:3)*
- *David Further Defeats the Philistines (20:4–8)*

EXPOSITION (18:1–20:8)

Ancient Near Eastern societies had many expectations of their kings. An ideal king should be a fair, discerning judge, solving disputes impartially. An ideal king should also be a capable administrator, setting up an effective political structure without corruption. Furthermore, an ideal king should be a capable warrior and military leader, recruiting competent warriors and leading his troops to victory in battle. As a result, he should bring peace and security to the land, accumulate great wealth, and exercise authority and influence in his region.

The ability to fulfill all these expectations for ancient societies extended beyond the individual king; it pointed to some divine power understood to be behind the king. Either the king was divine (as in Egypt) or served as a type of intermediary for the deity. In either case the king's success and reputation also pointed to the success and reputation of the deity/deities supporting the king.

First Chronicles 18–20 picks up on elements of these expectations and presents David as an ideal king as he defeats his enemies in battle. YHWH has promised to subdue David's enemies (1 Chron. 17:10). In these chapters, YHWH fulfills that promise as he "delivered David everywhere he went" (1 Chron. 18:6, 13). As a result, David secures peace for Israel, increases his wealth (much of which he sets aside for building the temple), and expands his influence in the region. As David's reputation grows, so does YHWH's.

David Defeats Various Enemy Nations (18:1–13)

YHWH fulfills part of his promise to David by subduing David's enemies, expanding David's influence, and increasing David's wealth for the future temple construction.

18:1. The first verse of this narrative unit looks back to the previous chapter to show how YHWH is fulfilling part of his promise to David. The phrase translated "after this" (אַחֲרֵי־כֵן) joins this verse to the previous chapter, but only loosely. What tightly binds this verse to the previous chapter is the mention of the Philistines, David's enemies (cf. 1 Chron. 14:10–11), and the use of the word "subdue" (*hiphil* כנע). These two features relate to YHWH's promise to David that YHWH would subdue all David's enemies (1 Chron. 17:10). In this way, the Chronicler is showing that YHWH is immediately fulfilling part of his promise to David.

In this case, not only does David defeat the Philistines but he also assumes control of one of their cities, Gath, and its outskirts. This action presents a contrast to Saul, since in the Chronicler's account of Saul the Philistines seize control of some Israelite cities (1 Chron. 10:7). This verse, and its connections to previous passages in Chronicles, reaffirms that YHWH has made David king and chooses to bless him.

18:2. After addressing the Philistines, the Chronicler turns his attention to Moab. Although Moab is an enemy (cf. 1 Chron. 11:22; 2 Chron. 20:1–12), David does not seize its territory. The Chronicler provides a brief, general statement that David defeats Moab and makes them vassals who pay him tribute. The Chronicler will make similar statements about Aram (18:6) and Edom (18:13). These statements show that rather than integrating his defeated enemies into a single political state, David expands his influence among the neighboring nations (Knoppers 2004, 702). In this way Moab, Edom, and the Arameans retain their political identities, while recognizing the power and influence of David's kingdom.

TRANSLATION ANALYSIS:
The most common translation for the Hebrew word עֶבֶד is "servant" or "slave." However, as Japhet points out, that translation "is much too general for the present context." Instead, "a specific political status is denoted by the recurring Hebrew term 'vassals bearing tribute'" (1993, 347).

18:3–6. Following the brief comments regarding the Philistines and Moab, the Chronicler provides a slightly more detailed account regarding Aram. The details of the account serve to strengthen the point that YHWH is defeating David's enemies as promised. The Chronicler states that David confronts Hadadezer, the king of Zobah, as Hadadezer attempts to demonstrate his authority at the Euphrates River by setting up a monument. This description presents Hadadezer as a formidable enemy, since he is confident enough to make such an attempt at controlling the region. The Chronicler sharpens this picture by presenting the enemy's military advantage. He records the numbers of defeated enemy soldiers and chariots. Chariots, especially many of them, represent a significant military advantage over David's forces. Furthermore, David faces reinforcements from Damascus. A combined force, including the use of reinforcements, paints the picture of a formidable enemy. Despite the enemy's strength, David defeats them. Yet, it is not David alone who wins; the Chronicler explicitly states that YHWH delivers David everywhere he goes.

Setting Up a Monument

First Chronicles 18:3 speaks of setting up a monument at the Euphrates River. Ancient Near Eastern kings often used such monuments as a way of indicating their authority over a region. Two other instances in the OT point in this same direction (see 1 Sam. 15:12; 2 Sam. 18:18).

TRANSLATION ANALYSIS:

Translations render the Hebrew word יֹשַׁע (hiphil) in different ways. A traditional translation for the word is "save." In this case, the translations emphasize different connotations. Many translations (CSB, ESV, NIV, NLT, NRSV) focus on the context of defeating the enemies in battle; therefore, they translate the word along the lines of "made David victorious" (CSB, NLT) or "gave David victory" (ESV, NIV, NRSV). Other translations (NET, NKJV) render the word more generally, such as "protected" (NET) or "preserved" (NKJV). I have translated the word as "delivered" to communicate the sense of rescuing and aiding David without tying the term to the specific military context.

As YHWH fulfills his promise to defeat David's enemies he also fulfills, at least partly, his promise to establish a place for Israel where they will no longer be oppressed (cf. 1 Chron. 17:9). Mentioning the Euphrates River points in this direction because Deuteronomy 11:24 describes the land of Israel as extending to the Euphrates River. Although David does not integrate all the land of the Arameans up to the Euphrates into a single kingdom, he creates peace throughout the region and asserts his influence over it. This peace and influence over the region become important aspects of Solomon's rule, since 2 Chronicles 9:26 speaks of Solomon's authority as extending to the Euphrates River. In this way, YHWH establishes a place for Israel.

18:7–8. As the Chronicler concludes his account regarding Hadadezer, he introduces

another theme characteristic of David's reign: David's preparation for temple construction. The text specifically points out that the bronze collected from Hadadezer's cities is the material Solomon uses to construct several temple furnishings. Furthermore, even though the Chronicler does not explicitly connect the gold shields (18:7) with the future temple construction, 2 Chronicles 23:9 states that the temple contains such shields during the days of the priest Jehoiada. In other words, the text presents David as a king who dedicates to YHWH what he receives in victory to prepare for the temple construction.

TRANSLATION ANALYSIS:

Traditionally, the word שֶׁלֶט has been translated "shields" (BDB s.v. "שֶׁלֶט" 1020) The translation makes good sense as it occurs here and in 2 Chronicles 23:9. However, other linguistic evidence leads to a translation of "quivers" (HALOT s.v. "שֶׁלֶט" 1522–23). Given the use of the word both here and in 2 Chronicles 23:9, I have retained the traditional translation.

18:9–11. The theme of dedicating resources to YHWH continues as David interacts with other nations. At first, David receives treasures from one of Hadadezer's enemies: Tou, king of Hamath. Unlike the previous cases, David does not attain this wealth by attacking Hamath. Instead, King Tou, recognizing David's great victory, sends his son to offer these treasures. Then the Chronicler includes a general statement that David dedicates the precious materials that he gathers from the neighboring nations. The language refers to spoils of war (Dirksen 2005, 245) such as those attained in military conflict earlier and later in the chapter. At the same time, the statement is not intended to be chronological, since David has yet to defeat Edom or the Ammonites. As a statement out of chronological order, it emphasizes and characterizes David as a king devoted to YHWH (Knoppers 2004, 703).

TRANSLATION ANALYSIS:
Translations vary considerably in how they render the verbs for the first part of this verse. The reasons involve the functions of these verbs in different social contexts. For instance, some translations (e.g., ESV, KJV) render the phrase לִשְׁאָל־לוֹ לְשָׁלוֹם "to inquire of his health" according to the usual sense of the words. However, most translations focus on the social function of asking about one's health, that is, such an action occurs as a greeting. For this reason, several translations (e.g., CSB, NET, NIV, NKJV, NLT, NRSV) render the phrase simply as "greet." The following phrase consists of the word typically translated "bless" (ברך). However, some translations (e.g., CSB, NIV, NLT, NRSV) focus on the social function of such a blessing as a congratulation (see 1 Sam. 13:10; 25:14). I would render both expressions together as "recognize" in an attempt to capture both aspects.

18:12–13. The narrative returns to the theme of David's defeating his enemies. In this case, the narrative highlights the military success of one of David's commanders: Abishai. Even though the text does not associate the victory specifically with David, describing Abishai's victory honors David, since David is king over such a great hero (Knoppers 2004, 733–34). As a result of Abishai's victory, David expands his influence in the region by setting up garrisons and making the Edomites vassals (as he did to the Arameans, 18:6). Furthermore, as in 18:6 above, the Chronicler specifies that YHWH delivers David everywhere he goes.

David's Administration (18:14–17)
David embodies the model of a good king as he establishes a proper administration and rules with justice and righteousness.

18:14–17. At this point, the Chronicler repeats information that appears well established: David rules over all Israel. Repeating this information shifts the focus from David's military activities

to his political ones. The statement also makes sense in this context, since the Chronicler has just recorded how David secures his influence and authority throughout the entire region, ensuring that he rules over all Israel.

After addressing the extent of David's rule, the Chronicler turns to its quality: David embodies the Old Testament's "moral ideal" (Japhet 1993, 637) by acting with "justice" (מִשְׁפָּט) and "righteousness" (צְדָקָה). This activity entails protecting the most vulnerable from fraud, fighting corruption (esp. the use of bribes), and ensuring impartiality in judgment (e.g., Deut. 10:17–18; 16:18–19). This activity characterizes YHWH himself (Deut. 10:17–18; 2 Chron. 19:7; Ps. 33:5); as a result, when David rules with justice and righteousness, he reflects the way that YHWH rules (cf. Ps. 99:4).

As confirmation of David's righteous rule, the Chronicler records various officers within David's administration who ensure such justice and righteousness in Israel. The people occupying such offices would maintain close contact with the king as they oversee various areas of Israel's life. As a result, the list includes the military commander Joab alongside the priests Zadok and Ahimelek, as well as political officers.

Ahimelek as Priest
Two issues relate to Ahimelek as the name of the priest. First, MT Chronicles preserves the name as Abimelek; however, the other textual witnesses and the parallel text in 2 Samuel 8:17 read Ahimelek. Second, Ahimelek appears to be the father of Abiathar (cf. 1 Sam. 22:20; 23:6; 30:7). As Knoppers points out, papponymy (the practice of naming a son after his paternal grandfather, a practice attested during the Persian/Hellenistic period) likely explains the mention of Abiathar as the father here (2004, 705).

Some of these roles (e.g., military commander, priests) have well-established responsibilities; others do not. Although the text does not provide enough detail to ascertain the specific tasks of these latter offices, one can surmise their general responsibilities. For instance, the Cerethites and Pelethites most likely make up David's bodyguard (2 Sam. 15:18; 1 Kings 1:38, 44). The roles of "recorder" (מַזְכִּיר) and "scribe" (סֹפֵר) are difficult to distinguish since both most likely deal with records, laws, and/or foreign correspondence; however, the recorder likely has a more public role than the scribe (for suggestions of these roles based mostly on an Egyptian model, see Mettinger 1971, 25–62). Finally, David's sons seem to function as some type of advisors or administrators, probably in various areas of Israel's life.

> **Parallel in 2 Samuel 8:18**
>
> The parallel passage in 2 Samuel 8:18 identifies the king's sons as priests. More precisely, MT Samuel contains such a reading. Such a reading likely results from a mistake in textual transmission (Wenham 1975, 79–82).

David Defeats the Ammonites and Arameans (19:1–20:3)

Because of YHWH's help, David and his troops defeat the Ammonites and their mercenary allies the Arameans.

19:1–5. By using the phrase "after this" (אַחֲרֵי־כֵן), the text transitions to another example of YHWH's delivering David from his enemies. Unlike the previous chapter, the Chronicler develops the backdrop to the military conflict in greater detail. The Chronicler describes how David chooses to send messengers to comfort the new Ammonite king, Hanun, after his father's death. The text portrays David as acting honorably, seeking to respect the positive political relationship between David (and Israel) and the deceased King Nahash (and Ammon).

TRANSLATION ANALYSIS:
The text describes David as desiring to "show kindness" (CSB, ESV, NASB, NIV) or "show loyalty" (NET, NLT, NRSV). In this context, the phrase used (עָשָׂה חֶסֶד) probably intends to communicate both connotations of faithfulness and kindness.

However, based on the poor advice of the new king's advisors, King Hanun misinterprets David's honorable efforts as a plot to spy out the land for a future attack. Hanun insults David by humiliating David's messengers. Hanun has their beards shaved and their robes cut off high enough to expose the messengers' buttocks (see Isa. 7:20; 20:4; Jer. 41:5). For David's response, the Chronicler only describes how David responds to his messengers by allowing them to recover in Jericho and then return to Jerusalem. These events, in which David treats Hanun with honor but Hanun treats David with insults, set the backdrop to the ensuing military conflict.

> **Hanun and Rehoboam**
>
> Commentators have noted similarities between Hanun and Rehoboam. In both cases, a new king accepts the advice of officials to escalate tensions as a show of power; the results in both cases are disastrous (see further Japhet 1993, 356).

19:6–9. When the Ammonites realize that their actions have severed the positive relationship between Israel and Ammon, they prepare for war. The Chronicler emphasizes that the forces opposing David have the military advantage. The Ammonites hire a mercenary force composed of thousands of chariots and other soldiers from some Aramean cities. Ammonite forces join in the battle. The Ammonites and Arameans coordinate an attack so that David's forces will have to fight on two fronts. The Ammonites remain close to a city with its walls, while the Aramean forces station themselves in the open field so that David's forces, led by Joab, will march between the two. The Ammonite and Aramean forces have the clear tactical advantage.

Identity of the Walled City

Identifying the city is a challenging task. The MT reads the city's name as Medeba (מֵידְבָא). This name does occur elsewhere in the OT; however, it is associated with Moab, not Ammon (cf. Num. 21:30; Josh. 13:9; Isa. 15:2). If Medeba is a Moabite city, then the historical picture is difficult to imagine. Partly for this reason, some scholars reconstruct the place's name as "waters of Rabbah" (מֵי רַבָּה). The words closely resemble one another and Rabbah occurs again later in the same context (1 Chron. 20:1). For more information, see Knoppers 2004, 715.

TRANSLATION ANALYSIS:

This verse uses the expression of "becoming odious" (באש). In some cases, this verb describes things that spoil (e.g., manna spoils when left, Exod. 16:20). However, when referring to people, the word may describe a relationship in which hostilities are quite likely (e.g., Gen. 34:30; Exod. 5:21; 1 Sam. 13:4). The sense may be close to the English idiom of ruining or spoiling a relationship. If so, then one might translate the verse idiomatically as follows: "When the Ammonites realized that they ruined/spoiled the relationship with David."

19:10–13. Joab responds by creating a military strategy, encouraging the troops to stay strong, and leaving the results of the conflict in YHWH's hands. His strategy includes dividing his troops into two groups so that they may help each other. When he encourages the troops, he reminds them that, unlike the mercenaries on the other side, they fight for the people and the cities belonging to their God, YHWH. In other words, more is at stake than a win or loss in a single battle. The well-being of Israel and the reputation of YHWH are also at stake. Furthermore, Joab recognizes that YHWH will determine the outcome. The language provides a subtle clue that YHWH will defeat the enemy since "the good" of 19:13 likely alludes to 1 Chronicles

17:26 and "the good" YHWH promised David, which includes defeating David's enemies. The language points to the question of whether YHWH will keep this promise, regardless of military advantages or strategies.

19:14–15. The Chronicler demonstrates convincingly that YHWH will honor his promise to defeat David's enemies. Seemingly without even a fight, the Arameans flee from Joab as he prepares for battle. Once the Arameans flee, the Ammonites follow suit, retreating within their city walls. With this retreat, the immediate threat to Israel weakens. As a result, Joab returns to Jerusalem.

19:16–19. After showing how Israel initially defeats the combined forces of Aram and Ammon, the Chronicler deals with each group separately. He records how the Arameans eventually submit to David's authority after he defeats a large Aramean force made up of troops sent from far away, even beyond the Euphrates River. As a result of David's victory, the Arameans are no longer willing to aid (*hiphil* ישׁע) Ammon against David. This comment contrasts what the text says earlier regarding YHWH and David: YHWH delivered (*hiphil* ישׁע) David everywhere he went (1 Chron. 18:6, 13). This contrast again highlights that YHWH is fulfilling his promise to David by defeating David's enemies.

20:1–3. Having addressed Aram, the Chronicler turns to Ammon. Unlike Aram, Ammon does not submit to David and become his vassal. Likely for this reason, David treats them differently. David's troops ravage Ammonite territory. His troops besiege and destroy the capital Ammonite city Rabbah. David plunders Rabbah. Beyond carrying away precious materials, David also removes the crown from the head of the Ammonite king and places it on his own head. Such a gesture depicts David's strength and authority in victory.

Parallels Between Accounts with Arameans and Ammonites

These verses provide a clear picture of David's defeating the Ammonites; however, the significance of some details remains unclear, especially the location of David. First Chronicles 20:1 specifies that David remains in Jerusalem while Joab besieges Rabbah. In 20:2 David appears to be at Rabbah while in 20:3 David is returning to Jerusalem. Two factors might account for these circumstances. First, this account appears to be parallel in numerous ways to the account regarding the Arameans. During that account, Joab initially faces the Arameans and puts them to flight. When Aram appears again, David, without mentioning Joab, leads Israel in the fight against Aram. When David defeats them, they submit to be David's vassals and no longer aid Ammon. Here with Ammon, Joab leads the troops initially to besiege the city. David, without mentioning Joab, then arrives to plunder the city and set up the policy for dealing with Ammon. In both accounts the subject alternates from Joab to David. Second, some text explaining David's arrival to Rabbah may have dropped out from the Chronicles text. The parallel text in 2 Samuel 12:27–29 explains that Joab invites David to capture Rabbah so that David will claim authority over the city rather than Joab.

Finally, David institutes a devastating policy against the Ammonite cities. The nature of the policy is ambiguous. Several factors affect the picture of David's policy regarding the Ammonite cities. First, one must consider the verb. In Chronicles, the Hebrew verb (שׂוּר) is translated "to saw." However, in the parallel in 2 Samuel 12:31, the verb "to set" (שׂים) occurs, and in this context most likely carries the notion of setting the people to a task. Most translations assume that the object of the verb is the people of the city. If one accepts the Chronicles reading, then it appears David is sawing the people in pieces. For this reason, translators generally accept the Samuel reading so that David's policy entails subjecting the people to forced labor. However,

neither passage specifies the object of the verb. Since the specific tools mentioned in the verse are used to cut or remove rock or wood, the object of the verb is more likely not the people, but the city structures themselves. Therefore, David's policy involves destroying city walls and other significant structures (Knoppers 2004, 730–31). David's policy reduces the threat that Ammon poses to Israel and demonstrates David's authority over the region.

David Further Defeats the Philistines (20:4–8)

David, through his elite warriors, subdues the Philistines by killing their elite warriors.

20:4–8. This narrative concludes with the same group with which it begins: the Philistines. Both 1 Chronicles 18:1 and 1 Chronicles 20:4 state that David subdues the Philistines. The narrative here provides three specific examples of how David and the Israelites subdue the Philistines. These examples consist of one-on-one military contests between David's warriors and some Philistine champions.

The significance of these contests extends beyond the individual, beyond the military, and beyond David's warriors. First, even though the battles described in these verses are personal contests, they "have larger repercussions for the armed forces from which the heroes are drawn" (Knoppers 2004, 735). Therefore, victory over the opposing champion results in victory over the opposing army. Second, even though the battles are military contests, they point to a religious contest as well. The text points to this connection when it speaks of a Philistine champion taunting Israel (20:7). When the Philistine taunts Israel, he also taunts the God of Israel, YHWH (see 1 Sam. 17:36, 45; 2 Chron. 32:17; Prov. 14:31; 17:5). As a result, the battle is not only an assault on Israel's well-being but also an assault on YHWH's reputation. Third, even though David's warriors fight these contests, they act on behalf of David and under his authority. As a result, their victories are also his victories (1 Chron. 20:8).

In light of these observations, these verses illustrate how YHWH defeats David's enemies, fulfilling part of the promise made to David in 1 Chronicles 17:10. Further details strengthen this point.

20:4. The text gives few details regarding the battle that breaks out again between Israel and the Philistines, and the resulting contest between David's warrior Sibbecai and the Philistine champion Sippai. However, the text does point to Sippai's ancestry; he is a descendant of the Rephaim. Numerous translations (CSB, ESV, KJV, NASB, NKJV, NLT, NRSV) render the word here as "giants," following a tradition that extends back at least as far as ancient Greek translations. If one thinks of "giants" as people of extraordinary size and strength, then the translation seems appropriate, since elsewhere the OT describes the Rephaim as a group of strong and tall people who inhabit the land before Israel (e.g., Deut. 2:10–11, 20–21). By describing Sippai as a descendant of the Rephaim, the text presents him as an imposing enemy. In context this verse indicates that Sibbecai defeats Sippai based upon YHWH's power (cf. Deut. 2:21).

20:5. Another battle breaks out between Israel and the Philistines. David's warrior Elhanan (cf. 1 Chron. 11:26) defeats the Philistine champion, the brother of Goliath. In this case, the text indicates that the Philistine is an imposing enemy by pointing out his relation to Goliath and the enormous size of his weapon. As in the previous verse, the text implies that Elhanan defeats the Philistine champion based upon YHWH's power.

Elhanan and Lahmi

The text of Chronicles records that Elhanan defeated Lahmi (לַחְמִי), Goliath's brother. In contrast, the parallel text in 2 Samuel 21:19 records that Elhanan the Bethlehemite (בֵּית הַלַּחְמִי) defeated Goliath, not his brother. Sometime in the process of copying Samuel, the object marker (אֶת) replaced the word for "brother" (אָחִי) so that Elhanan defeated Goliath rather than his brother. The name Lahmi may be original to the Chronicler, but it closely resembles the latter part of "Bethlehemite" (לַחְמִי compared to הַלַּחְמִי). For this reason, some interpreters argue that Chronicles has an error in transmission here also.

20:6–7. Finally, another battle breaks out between Israel and the Philistines. Again, the text presents the Philistine as a formidable opponent. In this case, the text addresses his extraordinary size, the number of fingers and toes (twenty-four appendages total), his descent from the Rephaim, and his taunting of Israel. Despite the intimidating qualities of the Philistine, Jonathan, David's nephew, defeats the Philistine champion.

20:8. This verse consists of a summary of 20:4–7. The summary points to the common descent of the Philistine champions from the Rephaim to indicate what formidable opponents they are. Despite their extraordinary qualities, David and his warriors defeat them. Again, in this way YHWH fulfills part of his promise to David to subdue David's enemies.

For the first readers of 1 Chronicles 18–20, the narratives regarding David's military victories over the neighboring nations would have a strange, distant ring to them. No Davidic king sat upon Israel's throne for the postexilic community. There is little evidence that within the Persian Empire, Israel experienced these types of military threats from the neighboring peoples. Furthermore, the idea that the neighboring nations would serve as vassals to Israel appears to be the opposite of their situation: they are the servants of others (Neh. 9:36–37). At the same time, the picture of David's reign embodies many of the future promises that Israel awaits. Based on the words of the prophets, the postexilic community waited for a Davidic king to rule with justice and righteousness and to provide security for Israel in its land (e.g., Jer. 23:5–6; 33:15–16). In this way, the Chronicler's narrative about David's military victories provides more than a look at the past; it also provides a model for the anticipated future. The postexilic community could be assured that just as YHWH fulfilled part of his promise to David in the past, so YHWH will fulfill all his promises to David in the future.

THEOLOGICAL FOCUS

God uses the one loyal to him to fulfill his plan to bless his people.

From God's call to Abraham in Genesis 12 onward, Scripture reveals God's plan for his people Israel. Sometimes, it is easy to take for granted that from the very beginning God has intended to do what is beneficial for his people, that is, to bless them. A fundamental component of that blessing is for Israel to live securely in the land God promised to Abraham. Living securely entails both living without the fear of foreign invasion and living within a society governed by justice and righteousness. This passage picks up on both aspects of living securely to reveal both as part of God's benevolent plan for Israel.

At the same time, God does not just intend for Israel to enjoy these blessings; he actively works to provide them. Even though David and his warriors fight the battles and win the victories, the Chronicler reveals that YHWH is behind their victories (1 Chron. 18:6, 13). Because YHWH is able to fulfill his promises regardless of the opposition he faces, even when David faces formidable foes as he does in this passage, he wins. As a result, the passage presents YHWH as benevolent, powerful, and actively working to fulfill his promises.

The counterpart to YHWH in this passage is David. David is a good king. He actively works for what benefits Israel. He defeats their enemies and rules with justice and righteousness. Furthermore, he proves his loyalty to God by dedicating the spoils of war to the future temple in Jerusalem. On one hand, as a follower of God, David serves as an example for others to follow. Even though David's specific activities largely result from his unique role as king, his desire to defeat the enemies of God's people, to promote justice and righteousness, and to dedicate what he gains for God's service point to proper priorities for anyone who follows God.

On the other hand, David serves as a model for a particular person: a future Davidic descendant. Like David, this descendant will rule with justice and righteousness. Like David, he will be faithful to his God. Like David, he will fulfill God's plan. The New Testament makes it clear that this Davidic descendant is Jesus (e.g., Matt. 1:1; Rom. 1:2–4). At the same time, just like the first readers of Chronicles, Christians still await the coming of Jesus to fulfill completely all that God has promised for his people (see 1 Thess. 4:13–18). The description of David's activity in this passage encourages God's people to remember the good that God has in store for them and to long for it with the coming of Jesus (2 Tim. 4:8).

PREACHING AND TEACHING STRATEGIES

Exegetical and Theological Synthesis

God was not only keeping his promise to David; he was building the nation of Israel. God was doing great things in their world. He was preparing a nation to worship only him, and through that nation the savior of the world would come. David's part was to be the king of that nation. His loyalty is presented in this passage, and we see God's blessing through that loyalty. This loyalty is expressed when we see that God delivered David from his enemies, which implies that David depended upon God. David's just and righteous administration of the nation was loyalty expressed through obedience. The setting aside of the spoils of war to be used to build the temple for YHWH showed his loyalty to worship.

Our loyalty to God does not earn us a place in his kingdom or plan. We are brought in through his grace experienced by our faith. Just as Israel hoped for a perfect king to lead them, we hope in the Lord Jesus who is the perfect king of Israel and over all of God's family. David's loyalty allowed him to be a part of what God was doing. When we are loyal to God, it puts us in a position to be greatly used by him. We may not see how we are a part of his work, but we are. Our loyalty can be expressed just as David's was: obedience, dependence, and worship.

Preaching Idea
To be a part of God's great work, be loyal to him.

Contemporary Connections

What does it mean?
What a great blessing for David to be a part of what God was doing through Israel. When we think back to joint efforts of which we have been a part, it brings a deep satisfaction. For me, singing in the men's chorus at seminary was a great blessing. We rehearsed hours upon hours to perform at the annual Founder's Day banquet. Joining together with other voices to create a sound that was far beyond what one voice could produce brought a deep satisfaction. Likewise, a mission trip to a third-world country to help build a church building lets us feel that we are making a difference.

These chapters are about YHWH building his nation, which included establishing security from enemies and providing resources to build the temple. He chose to include David in this process. David's role was to be loyal to YHWH, as shown by his dependence upon YHWH, his integrity as an administrator, and his priority on worship. David was brought into a purpose and plan far bigger than himself.

God has a plan that he is executing on a daily basis. We seldom can see his plan, but wouldn't it be great to be a part of this grand and good plan? The path to be included in God's work is our loyalty to him. Not that our loyalty earns a position; rather, our loyalty allows us to be in a position to be used by him.

Is it true?
A man in his thirties, Clark, attends a morning small group of men. During the discussion he mentions that he is struggling with truly loving his wife and asks for prayer. He is being loyal to God by his attendance and being willing to share a need. Another man, Jared, who also is a part of the group, hears that request. Jared is silently convicted that he too needs to love his wife more. Later in the day an attractive coworker catches his attention. She compliments Jared on his appearance and then touches his hand in a way that is not seen but is clearly a flirtatious signal. At that point he recognizes the temptation and turns from it. That attack on his marriage has been turned away. God was mightily at work. The loyalty of Clark to attend the group and be humble enough to share his need was part of God's plan to save Jared's marriage. Clark never knew the full picture, but he was still a part of God's amazing powerful work.

God is at work in our local churches and ministries. Our loyalty to him in obedience, worship, and integrity puts us in a position to be greatly used. His plan and our part in it are often not fully seen, yet we still have a part.

Now what?
God presented us with specifics of David's life. Though we must be careful when we see anyone other than our savior as an example, it seems that God is giving us directives through David. David was dependent upon God's great power when he faced challenges. This was an expression of his loyalty to YHWH. Loyalty is often highlighted when it would be understandable to abandon that to which we are loyal. When our home team has a losing season, we speak of being loyal to them and cheering them on. My high school football team was never a powerhouse. Instead of our cheers being "First and ten, let's do it again," we teasingly modified the cheer, "Third and twenty-four, don't worry about the score." When challenges come, our loyalty could waver. David's didn't.

When working at the church brings conflicts and disappointments, we still need to be loyal to our God and serve as he directs. When worship services are not to our liking, we need to focus on our savior. Despite the headaches of organizing a ministry, we must continue to be loyal to administer with integrity. David depended upon God. David exercised integrity in his administration. David was always thinking about the worship of YHWH.

Creativity in Presentation

A delightful children's book and video series is *Thomas and Friends*. The creator of this series, Rev. W. Awdry, personifies train engines to teach children important moral lessons. A common theme in his writings is about being a useful engine. The little book *Thomas the Really Useful Engine* could be both a children's sermon and part of the introduction to the sermon. Though the book is far too long to be read in full, it could be summarized, with key points being read. The transition to the sermon is that we all want to be useful in some way to someone. The video version might also be used if edited properly and copyright laws observed. Using a children's book is always a win/win situation. They are simple enough for all to understand. All can identify with them. Teenagers remember them, and parents and grandparents perhaps read a children's book the night before. And, few people are threatened by a children's book.

The structure of the sermon seems to call for presenting the whole story before expanding on the application. The first part of the sermon could be spent presenting the story, followed by highlighting David's points of loyalty, leading into the application. Here is one possible structure:

- The story: Through David's loyalty, God provides powerfully for Israel, giving them safety and resources to worship.
  - David defeats various enemy nations (18:1–13)
  - David's administration (18:14–17)
    - David defeats the Ammonites and Arameans (19:1–20:3)
    - David further defeats the Philistines (20:4–8)
- The meaning: David's demonstration of loyalty to YHWH
  - David depended upon God's victory and help (18:6, 13)
    - Joab depended on God (19:13)
  - David obeyed God through just administration (18:14–17)
  - Centrality of worship: spoils went to build the temple (18:6–7, 11)
- Application
  - We need to be loyal to God in our dependence upon him.
  - We need to be loyal to God in our obedience to him.
  - We need to be loyal to God by our prioritizing worship.

The placement of the gospel message would quite naturally fit under our being dependent upon God. There is no greater reason to depend upon God than our need for forgiveness and reconciliation to him.

DISCUSSION QUESTIONS

1. What part did you play in a past event?

2. What are some ways people can be useful to an organization?

3. What are some ways that people feel like they are a part of something bigger than themselves?

4. When is it hard to be loyal? What are some hindrances to being loyal by being dependent upon God?

5. When is it hard to be righteous and just in administration? What hinders our worship?

1 Chronicles 21:1–22:1

EXEGETICAL IDEA
YHWH selected the site for the temple after punishing Israel for David's sin.

THEOLOGICAL FOCUS
YHWH can use a tragic situation caused by sin to accomplish his plan for blessing.

PREACHING IDEA
Move on from our sin and into God's victory.

PREACHING POINTERS
This passage wonderfully shows how our great God brings blessing out of tragedy, even when that tragedy is the result of sin. One cannot mention this theme without thinking of humanity's sin of crucifying Christ and his victorious resurrection. David's sin, his exemplary repentance, and God's resulting victory give us a pattern so that we can move from our sin into God's victory.

A SINFUL CENSUS THAT LEADS TO A SACRED SITE (21:1–22:1)

LITERARY STRUCTURE AND THEMES (21:1–22:1)

Following all David's success, the narrative takes a sudden turn as David sins and Israel suffers. This narrative records the situation in four main sections. The first three sections develop the plot; however, the fourth section provides a parenthetical comment that draws out the significance of the entire episode, as David recognizes Jerusalem as the future site for YHWH's temple.

The plot runs along the following lines: During the first section, David is enticed to count the people of Israel. This decision reflects his own pride: he decides to trust his own strength rather than YHWH's (which the Chronicler has highlighted in 1 Chron. 18–20). Even though Joab warns David not to conduct this census, David proceeds. As a result, the plot moves forward, showing how YHWH punishes Israel. When David confesses his wrongdoing and asks for forgiveness, YHWH allows David to choose the form of punishment. As YHWH punishes Israel, he relents from destroying Jerusalem; however, the threat of punishment remains and requires further action on David's part. David again confesses his wrongdoing and, following YHWH's command, purchases a site to build an altar (Ornan's threshing floor). After David builds that altar, YHWH sends fire from the sky to approve this action and ends the threat of punishment. The narrative draws to a close as David recognizes this place as the site for YHWH's future temple. In this way, the narrative shows how YHWH selected the site for the temple when he stopped his punishment against Israel because of David's sin.

- *David Enticed to Count the People (21:1–6)*
- *YHWH Punishes According to David's Choice (21:7–14)*
- *YHWH Relents and David Builds an Altar (21:15–27)*
- *David Recognizes Jerusalem as the Site for the Temple (21:28–22:1)*

EXPOSITION (21:1–22:1)

The first readers of Chronicles faced many challenges. Since many of Israel's previous leaders were exiled because of their unfaithfulness to YHWH, their return created tension within the Persian province of Yehud, the land associated with the earlier kingdom of Judah. Furthermore, returning Jerusalem to prominence politically and building a temple there may have intensified this tension. Within this context, the Chronicler attempts to unite all the tribes of Israel in worshipping YHWH at the Jerusalem temple. To accomplish this goal, the Chronicler must overcome some challenges. First, he must show that the Jerusalem temple is the only site for YHWH's legitimate ritual worship. To address this challenge, the Chronicler demonstrates that the site of the Jerusalem temple is not a practical human decision but the result of YHWH's choice. Second, he must navigate the tension among the tribes, particularly Benjamin. The evidence suggests that Benjamin fared better than Judah during the exile, since Mizpah and apparently Gibeon served as important administrative (Mizpah) and religious (Gibeon) cities (see Blenkinsopp 2003, 95–99; Giffone 2016, 85–99; Jonker 2013a, 92–94, 141; Lipschits 2006, 34–35). As part of navigating this challenge, the Chronicler recognizes the importance of Gibeon as a worship center in the past (because of the tabernacle), but then shows how its importance is superseded by the temple in Jerusalem.

The narrative of 1 Chronicles 21 recounts David's sin of a census and the aftermath of that sin. The narrative builds to David's recognition that Jerusalem is the site of YHWH's temple. Along the way, it addresses the Chronicler's concerns as it shows that YHWH selected the site for the temple after punishing Israel because of David's sin.

David Enticed to Count the People (21:1–6)

Despite YHWH's faithfulness to defeat David's enemies in battle (1 Chron. 18–20), David is tempted to rely on his own power by counting the number of those available to be his soldiers.

21:1. In 1 Chronicles 21, David's reign takes an unexpected turn. To this point, David has exemplified the characteristics of a faithful king for all Israel (except for the failed effort to transfer the ark in 1 Chronicles 13). However, David now falls prey to temptation, bringing disastrous consequences on all Israel.

The first issue to address is the cause of David's failure: Who or what tempts David to sin? Most English translations (e.g., CSB, ESV, NASB, NIV, NKJV, NLT, NRSV) render the first noun in 21:1 as Satan. The English name Satan is a transliteration of the Hebrew word שָׂטָן, which in other cases in the Hebrew Bible refers to an adversary or attacker. The noun may refer to a spiritual being (e.g., Job 1–2) or an individual human or national enemy (1 Kings 11:14, 23–25). For several reasons, the word in this case is more likely a common noun than a proper name (for linguistic reasons; Japhet 1993, 374). Even so, the text is not clear whether this adversary is a divine or human opponent. Given the context of 1 Chronicles 18–20, the figure is more likely a human enemy opposing Israel (see 1 Kings 5:18; 11:25).

> **Nature of Opposition to Israel**
>
> The nature of this opposition is unspecified. The phrase וַיַּעֲמֹד עַל, translated "opposed" (NET) or "stood up against" (CSB, ESV, NASB, NKJV, NRSV), may refer to a military attack (2 Chron. 20:23) or resisting someone's action (2 Chron. 26:18). In the case of Solomon in 1 Kings 11:14–25, his adversaries are political and military opponents. They appear to try to undermine Solomon's influence in the region as well as oppose him militarily.

As a result of this enemy's opposition, David is tempted to number the people. Although 21:1 does not specify the purpose for counting the people, it already presents a situation with some warning signs. First, it presents an opponent as the reason for David's numbering the people. Second, it states that through unspecified means, the opponent incites David. The term translated "incite" (סות) most often carries negative connotations (Deut. 13:6 [HB 7]; 2 Chron. 18:2; 32:11).

21:2. This verse provides clues for determining the nature of the temptation by addressing the purpose for numbering the people. Since David commands Joab and other leaders to carry out the task, the most likely purpose for this census is to determine what forces are available for David (also see the results of the census in 21:5). David requests that Joab move throughout all Israel ("from Beersheba to Dan") so that David might know his current military status.

21:3. Joab's response to David's command is the first direct sign that David is heading in the wrong direction. Joab's questions imply that this census will lead to Israel's "guilt" (אַשְׁמָה). The word often carries the sense of punishment; therefore, one should not think of this action as making Israel guilty as much as making Israel subject to punishment. However, Joab does not specify what aspect of the census will cause such punishment. Since Chronicles reports census information in other passages (e.g., 1 Chron. 11–12 [David]; 2 Chron. 14:8 [Asa]; 17:14–18 [Jehoshaphat]; 25:5 [Amaziah]; 26:11–14 [Uzziah]), it does not appear that numbering the people itself is sinful. Furthermore, since Joab expresses the wish that YHWH will multiply the number of the Israelites, possessing large numbers of troops "would be considered a good thing and would in fact result from divine blessing" (R. Klein 2006, 419).

Exodus 30:12–16 records that YHWH commands Moses to require a half-shekel ransom from every person counted by the census to avoid a plague. This money will provide what is needed to maintain the service of the tabernacle. First Chronicles 21 bears numerous similarities to the commandment in Exodus 30. For instance, both address taking a census, speak of a plague as punishment, and show concern for Israel's ritual worship. Furthermore, after 1 Chronicles 21, David turns his attention to preparing materials and personnel for constructing the temple and maintaining proper worship within it.

Despite the similarities between 1 Chronicles 21 and Exodus 30, the half-shekel ransom does not seem to be the cause of guilt for numbering the people. Joab's questions do not point to the commandment of the ransom as his concern. His questions point to the strength and loyalty of David's subjects. Therefore, even though this passage draws on Exodus 30, likely because it deals with preparing materials for maintaining Israel's ritual worship, David's failure involves trusting his military strength rather than trusting YHWH. Furthermore, David as king attempts to call up this military strength rather than allowing the people to support him (as in 1 Chron. 11–12; see Janzen 2017, 125). A focus on pride is not entirely surprising, since Chronicles provides other examples of good kings who fall into this same type of pride (e.g., Uzziah, 2 Chron. 26:16; and Hezekiah, 2 Chron. 32:25). Furthermore, this trust in David's strength provides a stark contrast to YHWH's delivering David in the past.

Two more observations regarding Joab's response deserve mentioning. First, Joab serves as a counterpart to the adversary in 21:1. Whereas the adversary incites David to number the people, Joab warns David not to do so. Chronicles repeatedly records some form of warning preceding someone's sin (see "Covenant" section in the introduction). Second, Joab's warning reveals an aspect of the relationship between the king and the people: the king's guilt may bring punishment to the people (see Leviticus 4:3 for an example regarding the priest rather than the king). As Knoppers points out, this point "reflects a cardinal tenet of ancient Near Eastern royal ideology, that a people may experience weal or woe contingent upon the standing of its king with the divine realm" (Knoppers 2004, 755; see also 1994, 572–82). Joab at least recognizes this point, and his words to David make clear that David's command to number the people will have disastrous consequences for the people.

21:4–5. Despite Joab's warning, David does not revoke his command to number the people. As a result, his command stands, so Joab carries it out. Joab travels throughout Israel before returning to Jerusalem to report the census information to David. Joab reports a large number of people available to fight for Israel. In fact, it is the largest number recorded in Chronicles for Israel's military force. This large number shows that David now knows what he hoped to discover: his own military strength.

Different Census Numbers

Second Samuel 24:9 and 1 Chronicles 21:5 report slightly different numbers for the census. Although the reasons for the variation are not clear, one likely reason is that the tribes Levi and Benjamin are not included in the final number in Chronicles.

21:6. Even though Joab carries out David's order, he does not do so fully. The Chronicler records that Joab did not include the tribes of Levi or Benjamin because he found David's command to be repulsive. More than likely these tribes were not included because of their connection to Israel's ritual worship. The law of Moses requires that Levites be excluded from a military census because they care for the tabernacle (Num. 1:47–50; see R. Klein 2006, 421). Furthermore, when these events take place, the tabernacle is in Gibeon, within Benjaminite territory. In this way, Joab appears justified in refusing to follow through completely on David's command.

Joab's Potential Guilt

Joab appears justified to leave Benjamin and Levi out of the census. Wright has argued just the opposite (1993, 87–105). He argues that Joab's failure to complete the census is the cause of the disaster that follows. He draws on many themes across Chronicles and textual details from 1 Chronicles 21, but David's admission of guilt speaks against his argument.

Therefore, despite YHWH's faithfulness to deliver David in the past and despite Joab's warning, David issues a terrible command to number the people so that he may discover his own military strength.

YHWH Punishes According to David's Choice (21:7–14)

YHWH punishes Israel for David's sin, and as a result David confesses his wrongdoing and asks that YHWH mitigate the punishment.

21:7. Just as Joab has warned, David's command brings disaster to Israel. The text states that YHWH is displeased with the census; that is, he regards the census to be something bad, wrong, or even evil. Later in 21:17, David admits that he has done what is displeasing. The language here in 21:7 anticipates David's confession and points to his responsibility in ignoring Joab's warning and ordering the census.

Since YHWH finds the census to be displeasing, he strikes Israel. YHWH has previously struck Uzzah for touching the ark (1 Chron. 13:10) and the Philistines as enemies of Israel (1 Chron. 14:15). When YHWH strikes Uzzah, it leads to death. When YHWH strikes the Philistines, it leads to defeat. Here in 21:7, the text does not specify the nature of YHWH's striking. More than likely, this striking looks forward to the punishment David will choose in the following verses. However, it is no accident that the text records this striking in 21:7 because it fits a pattern within Chronicles. In Chronicles confession and repentance follow some disaster, whether specified (e.g., 2 Chron. 7:13–14; 12:2–6; 33:11–13) or not (2 Chron. 32:25–26), although not every disaster leads to repentance (e.g., Asa, 2 Chron. 16:12; Ahaz, 2 Chron. 28:16–22). By recording that YHWH strikes Israel, the Chronicler sets the stage for David to repent (or not).

21:8. Now that the stage is set, David confesses his wrongdoing and asks for forgiveness. David uses the language of "sin" (חטא) to describe his wrongdoing, likely foreshadowing Solomon's prayer at the temple dedication (2 Chron. 6), in which Solomon describes several scenarios of disaster that result from sin (חטא). David follows his confession of wrongdoing by asking YHWH to forgive him. The expression here (*hiphil* עבר) occurs infrequently with this sense, and its use may reveal some insight regarding this passage. In 2 Samuel 12:13, after David confesses that he has sinned in the matter of Bathsheba and Uriah, Nathan assures David that YHWH has forgiven (*hiphil* עבר) his sin and that David will not die. However, David suffers other consequences for his sin (see the rest of 2 Samuel). In the case of the census, YHWH forgives David; however, the sin still brings consequences, just not David's nor the people's destruction (Boda 2010a, 177; Sklar 2005, 91–92).

Language of Wrongdoing

At first, David uses the language of "sin" (חטא). However, he also describes his wrongdoing as "acting foolishly" (*niphal* סכל). This verb does not mean that David acted ignorantly or accidentally. The verb often occurs alongside other vocabulary for wrongdoing (e.g., 1 Sam. 13:13; 26:21; 2 Chron. 16:9) and complements them by stressing that his action leads to harmful results.

21:9–12. YHWH responds to David's confession by sending David a prophetic messenger, Gad the seer. YHWH allows David to choose the form of punishment for his sin. Each form of punishment is a typical disaster (cf. 2 Chron. 6:24–28; 20:9); however, the combination of the three occurs frequently in Jeremiah as forms of punishment (e.g., 24:10; 27:8; 29:17–18; 32:24, 36; 34:17). Furthermore, one may discern several patterns in how the text presents these options. For instance, the length of each disaster becomes briefer: from three years to three months to three days. At the same time, the description of each disaster becomes longer: from three words to eight words to twelve words. This pattern suggests that the options grow progressively more severe (Japhet 1993, 382). The final option is judgment by the sword of YHWH, that is, a plague in all the land brought about by the destroying angel of YHWH. This picture of the destroying angel is reminiscent of the past Passover (Exod. 12:13, 23) and, in Chronicles, of the future destruction of the Assyrian army (2 Chron. 32:21).

One may also notice the direct contrast between the second option and the third. The second option speaks of the "sword of your [David's] enemies" while the third speaks of the "sword of YHWH." This contrast between the human and divine becomes the decisive factor in David's choice.

21:13. When David responds, he does not specify which alternative he chooses. Instead, he first states that he is in distress. In Chronicles,

the language of being in distress (צרר) occurs when someone has acted sinfully (2 Chron. 6:28; 15:4; 28:22; 33:12); the distress is a consequence of the sin. Furthermore, the distress prompts a response: either doubling down on the sinful behavior (e.g., Ahaz, 2 Chron. 28:22), or turning from it (e.g., Manasseh, 2 Chron. 33:12).

In this case, David has already confessed his wrongdoing, so he responds by resigning himself to YHWH's punishment. Building on the contrast between YHWH's sword and the enemy's sword in 21:12, David asks to "fall" into YHWH's hand rather than human hands. This same expression of falling into someone's hand occurs in the previous chapter when the Philistine champions fall into the hands of David and his servants—that is, David and his servants overcome them (1 Chron. 20:8). In contrast to the previous chapter in which YHWH caused David to overcome his enemies, now because of David's sin, YHWH will overcome David.

When David chooses to fall into YHWH's hand, to experience YHWH's sword in the land, he bases his choice on YHWH's character: YHWH is merciful. In this case, YHWH's mercy does not mean that YHWH will not punish David or the people, but it suggests that YHWH will provide some way to mitigate the punishment. David's confession sets the stage for YHWH to act mercifully, although YHWH will first punish David's sin.

21:14. YHWH follows David's choice by sending a plague (דֶּבֶר), in which seventy thousand people from Israel die (נפל). The language of this verse matches the previous verses (דֶּבֶר in 21:12 and נפל in 21:13), demonstrating that YHWH listens to David and follows through on what he has previously stated. In this way, YHWH acts as he has promised.

YHWH Relents and David Builds an Altar (21:15–27)

YHWH's mercy and David's obedience coincide, as David sacrifices on the altar that YHWH commands him to build and as YHWH accepts David's sacrifices and relents from further judgment.

21:15. YHWH has punished Israel for David's sin (21:14). Now, YHWH targets Jerusalem in particular, sending a destroying angel to devastate the city. However, before the angel strikes the city, YHWH sees the impending destruction and commands the angel to stop. This action confirms what David has just confessed regarding YHWH: YHWH is merciful (21:13). In this case YHWH relents from the disaster by preventing the angel from destroying the city and sparing Israel from any further punishment. At the same time, YHWH only pauses the judgment; the angel remains at Jerusalem with his sword drawn. The fact that YHWH pauses the punishment but leaves the angel with his sword drawn presents YHWH as merciful but also implies that something more is required before removing the threat of punishment entirely. Furthermore, the mention of the threshing floor of Ornan specifically draws attention to that location and foreshadows its role in the following narrative.

> ### YHWH's Relenting
> YHWH exhibits his mercy by stopping the angel from attacking. In this way, YHWH relents from the disaster planned for the city. This phrase relates to YHWH's forgiveness as David requests in 21:8 because it connects YHWH's forgiveness to punishment. Sometimes when YHWH forgives he foregoes punishment entirely, but more often he mitigates punishment. For instance, in Exodus 32:14 YHWH relents from destroying the people entirely; however, three thousand people still died on that day because of Israel's sinful activity. A similar situation occurs here in 1 Chronicles 21: YHWH mitigates the punishment by sparing Jerusalem entirely and by preventing the destroying angel from destroying the people entirely. See Sklar 2005, 83–85.

21:16. The narrative shifts from what YHWH sees to what David sees. David sees an impending threat to Jerusalem as the angel hangs in the air with his sword drawn and his hand outstretched as a signal for impending judgment (see Isa. 9:11, 16, 20; 10:4; 14:26–27). As a result, David and Israel's elders fall on their faces while wearing sackcloth. This action depicts their serious emotional distress as well as their reverent request for relief (for a similar example, see Josh. 7:6–9).

> *TRANSLATION ANALYSIS:*
> The text uses the expression "between earth and sky" (בֵּין הָאָרֶץ וּבֵין הַשָּׁמַיִם), most likely indicating that the angel is hanging in the air. See, e.g., the description of Absalom as he hangs from a tree (2 Sam. 18:9). At the same time, the expression indicates an area "where heavenly beings are able to carry out their mission unimpeded by earth's inhabitants" (Boda 2004, 307).

This verse also contains language and themes similar to other passages in the Old Testament, specifically Numbers 22, in which the angel of YHWH opposes Balaam with his sword drawn; and Joshua 5:13–15, in which Joshua encounters the commander of YHWH's armies with his sword outstretched. In the case of Numbers 22, the narrative shows how YHWH subverts the plot of an adversary to bless Israel (Stokes 2009, 100–102; 2019, 21–25). Although the narrative in 1 Chronicles 21 differs in many details, YHWH similarly uses the plan of an adversary to show David the location for the future temple, a source of blessing for Israel. In the case of Joshua 5, the encounter reveals that the place is holy ground. The text picks up on this theme as a way of connecting this narrative to Israel's history and foreshadowing David's discovery that the location is holy—in fact, the site for YHWH's temple (1 Chron. 22:1).

21:17–19. As David bows, he also confesses his wrongdoing again. This time his confession is more specific than 21:8 since he mentions counting the people as his sin. Furthermore, in contrast to 21:8, in which he asks for forgiveness, in this case he asks for punishment, specifically that the punishment be limited to himself and his family rather than affecting all the people (referred to as sheep). However, instead of punishing David or his family, YHWH halts the punishment altogether (21:27). YHWH provides the means for halting the punishment by commanding David to build an altar on the threshing floor of Ornan, a command that David obeys.

21:20. The narrative shifts from what David sees to what Ornan sees at the threshing floor. Ornan sees the angel but continues to thresh wheat while his sons hide. This scene resembles Gideon's encounter with YHWH's angel in Judges 6:11–24 (for details, see R. Klein 2006, 427; Willi 1972, 157; Williamson 1982, 148). At the end of that encounter, Gideon builds an altar. The connection between Gideon's encounter and Ornan's encounter accomplishes two objectives: (1) it foreshadows David's building an altar, and (2) it shows that YHWH's activity here is in line with his activity throughout Israel's history.

21:21–25. Sometime after Ornan sees the angel, David approaches Ornan so that David may purchase the threshing floor and build an altar there. David offers to purchase the site so that the plague will stop. The expression used for stopping the plague occurs in other cases where an individual performs an act on behalf of the people to stop a disaster from destroying the people. For instance, Aaron offers incense to atone for the people in light of Korah's rebellion (Num. 16:48–50 [HB 17:13–15]). Also, during the events at Baal Peor, Phinehas strikes an offending couple to stop the plague (Num. 25:8; Ps. 106:30). In this case, likely to stop the plague, Ornan offers not only the threshing floor, but also the supplies used at the site since the cattle, wheat, and equipment may be offered

as sacrifices (cattle for burnt offering, wheat for grain offering, and equipment for firewood). However, David insists on paying full price for everything. As a result, David purchases the entire site for a large sum of six hundred shekels of gold.

> **Amount for Purchasing the Site**
> Three observations regarding the amount of six hundred shekels for the purchase price are as follows: (1) the amount is larger than 2 Samuel 24:24 indicates because it involves purchasing the entire site along with its supplies, (2) the amount is the same number (although different measure) used in the holiest place in the temple, and (3) Rashi suggests that the sum represents the twelve tribes of Israel since six hundred is twelve times fifty shekels, the amount recorded in 2 Samuel 24:24. These observations point to the role the amount plays in Chronicles.

The discussion between David and Ornan closely resembles Genesis 23, where Abraham purchases the cave of Machpelah as a burial site (Williamson 1982, 149). This text likely recounts this negotiation to show that David acquires the site legitimately from its previous inhabitant (a Jebusite), just as Abraham acquired the burial site legitimately from its previous inhabitants (Hittites). This observation may also help explain why David insists on paying full price for the entire site: as the future site for the temple, it is important that the site not be a gift from a native inhabitant (cf. Gen. 14:23). In this way, David's purchase undercuts anyone else's claim on the temple site.

21:26–27. Once David acquires the site for full price, he builds an altar to obey YHWH's command. Furthermore, he makes offerings and asks for YHWH's intervention ("calls on YHWH," see 1 Chron. 4:10; 2 Chron. 6:33; 14:10). YHWH responds in two ways. First, YHWH sends fire from the sky down upon the altar. This activity points back to the inauguration of ritual worship at the tabernacle (Lev. 9:24) and forward to the inauguration of ritual worship at the temple (2 Chron. 5:13; 7:1). In this way the text shows that YHWH accepts this place and this altar as a sacred site for ritual worship. Second, YHWH ends the immediate threat to Jerusalem by commanding the angel to return his sword to its sheath. The text illustrates how a ritual sacrifice can bring an end to YHWH's judgment. This principle points to the importance of the temple, especially for the postexilic community of Israel. As they wrestled with their past failures and their current challenging circumstances, this text reminds them of the temple's importance in seeing YHWH's intervention on their behalf.

David Recognizes Jerusalem as the Site for the Temple (21:28–22:1)

David recognizes that Israel will move its ritual worship from Moses's tabernacle to the Davidic heir's temple.

21:28–22:1. These verses constitute parenthetical comments. One purpose of these comments is to demonstrate that David recognizes Ornan's threshing floor as a sacred site. The text accomplishes this purpose in three ways. First, the text points out that even after YHWH sends fire from the sky and stops the plague, David still makes sacrifices at the altar. David's sacrifices confirm that the site is an acceptable site for sacrifice. Second, the text points out that David was afraid of the angel of YHWH since his sword was drawn. From David's perspective, this comment shows that Ornan's threshing floor is the proper place to build the altar, since he could not proceed to Gibeon. Third, David says, to no one in particular (for function of this statement as a transition, see Duke 1990, 131), that the site is the location for the temple and altar. As David speaks, he addresses the future, stating that the site will be used for YHWH's temple and Israel's future altar. He is not stating that the altar he has built will be Israel's altar in the future. His comment alludes to YHWH's promise that one of his heirs will build YHWH's temple (1 Chron. 17).

Another purpose of these comments is to acknowledge the significance that Gibeon holds for Israel's ritual worship. The text accomplishes this purpose by mentioning that both the tabernacle Moses made in the wilderness and the altar for burnt offerings were at the high place at Gibeon. Since Gibeon lies within Benjaminite territory, this comment may help explain why Joab did not count Benjamin in the census (see comments on 21:6 above). Furthermore, Chronicles mentions the high place at Gibeon in three contexts: (1) the successful transfer of the ark (1 Chron. 16), (2) David's building of the altar (1 Chron. 21), and (3) Solomon's preparation for building the temple (2 Chron. 1). The mention of Gibeon here forms a link between the past (1 Chron. 16) and the future (2 Chron. 1). Despite Gibeon's importance, these comments explain why David recognizes the threshing floor as the enduring site for YHWH's temple and altar.

For the first readers, the relationship between Gibeon and Jerusalem would likely be an important one. The tribe of Benjamin appears to have played a significant role in the region during the exilic period. As a result, some Benjaminites may have been less than excited to see the rebuilding of the Jerusalem temple. However, this text, like others in Chronicles, reaches out to all Israel, especially Benjamin, to recognize their past contributions and incorporate them into God's current activity in Jerusalem (see Giffone 2016, 213–24; Jonker 2013b, 92–96).

THEOLOGICAL FOCUS

YHWH can use a tragic situation caused by sin to accomplish his plan for blessing.

In the beginning of this narrative, David finds himself in a good situation. The previous chapters have shown how David has succeeded in doing what is expected of an ancient Near

Eastern king. Surprisingly, just as the Chronicler finishes recording how David defeats his enemies, he recounts how David falls to the temptation of pride (a recurring temptation in Chronicles; see above). Even when warned, David does not change his course. Instead, he goes forward with his command and brings disaster on his people. David's actions transform a nearly ideal situation into a national tragedy. Stubborn pride is a common temptation and always eventually leads to disaster (Prov. 11:2; 16:18; 29:23; 1 John 2:16).

The text shows that the disaster that comes to Israel gets David's attention and presents him with a choice, either to stay proud or to humble himself. David humbles himself and intercedes for the people. As a result, God holds back his punishment. However, the threat of punishment remains. Not until David offers sacrifices at the proper site does God remove the threat of punishment altogether. In this case, what God requires to remove that threat is David's humble confession and proper sacrifice to God.

Theologically, David serves as a model of repentance. When David sees the effects of his actions, he confesses his sin, prays for forgiveness, leans on the mercy of God, and follows God's commands in making sacrifices. His actions and attitude exemplify what every sinner should do, with one exception: the sacrifice. Although God still requires a sacrifice to halt punishment for sin, in the contemporary age animal sacrifices are no longer required because Jesus has offered the once-for-all sacrifice for sin (Heb. 10:10–12). Because of Jesus's sacrifice, those who confess their sins will find God faithful to forgive them (1 John 1:9).

This passage reaches the climax when David realizes that the altar he has built will be the site for YHWH's temple. At the Jerusalem temple, YHWH would dwell in a special way, blessing his people through his presence. His dwelling in Jerusalem, leading to blessing for his people, was a part of his plan throughout Israel's history. For the first readers, this passage points to the exclusive legitimacy of the Jerusalem temple as the site for YHWH's ritual worship. This fact led to practical measures of visiting and supporting the Jerusalem temple in order to participate in worship and receive blessing. For contemporary readers, the legitimacy of the Jerusalem temple is not a pressing issue. However, seeing how God accomplishes his plan for Israel holds significance for any reader. God uses a sinful tragedy to accomplish his purpose. This pattern forms the heart of the story of redemption seen so clearly in the crucifixion, and then resurrection, of Jesus. Many sinned in bringing about Jesus's crucifixion, yet God used their sin to purchase redemption. Surely no deeper sins led to higher blessing. Such is the way that God works.

David's census shows how a person's pride can ruin an ideal situation and how God can use that ruin to bring about his plan for blessing. Humble confession, repentance, and sacrifice play a central role as God responds in mercy and ends the punishment. This pattern of sin-punishment-confession-relenting occurs throughout the Bible and constitutes a fundamental storyline of God's relationship with humanity.

PREACHING AND TEACHING STRATEGIES

Exegetical and Theological Synthesis

The climax of this pericope is the establishing of the place on which the temple would be built. Because of Christ's work, we now worship God in Spirit and truth and are not focused on a place. But to the Jews under the old covenant, *the place* was very important. Thus, the decision to build on the threshing floor of Ornan is of great importance and can rightly be the focus of this passage. This was the first step in the construction of the temple: establishing the place on which it will be built. While this is the climax of this pericope, the process of getting to this victory is given great attention. God had the writer give us many details about David's sin,

God's response, and David's repentance, all of which led up to the locating of the temple. The lesson is not only that God can move us from sin to his victory; he also wants us to pay attention to the process David experienced.

We are sinful people who live in a fallen world, so David's sinfulness is not unique to him. We all can identify with choosing to go against God's directives. David's sin of wanting to know the number of people is not a blatant sin against a specific command of God. After all, this is the book of Chronicles; lists and numbers play a positive role in the book's development. David's sin was the motive behind the action. As Jesus pointed out in the Sermon on the Mount, our inner thoughts are just as sinful as the action. Whom would David trust to protect Israel: his army or his God? Perhaps this experience taught him what he proclaims in Psalm 20:7, where he clearly states that he will not trust in armies, but in YHWH.

Preaching Idea
Move on from our sin and into God's victory.

Contemporary Connections

What does it mean?
"When God closes a door, He opens a window." Mother Superior and Maria say it in the musical *The Sound of Music*. It appears on inspirational calendars and on refrigerators, and it can be seen on wall hangings behind a counselor's desk. The expression reminds us that God can bring opportunity and victory where there seemed to be none. This is a good thing to remember, but what about when the door is not closed by God, but our sin is what slammed it shut?

Early one summer morning, I saw my neighbor back his pickup into his garage and start loading his tools. I went over to check on him. He clearly was upset and in a panic, trying to get as many of his tools, as fast as he could, into his truck. I asked him what was going on.

"I'm moving out." That statement hung like the dust in the air that had been stirred up from moving seldom-used tools. He went on, "I've been stupid. I just couldn't help myself." He was so intense that I wasn't sure if I should help with the portable table saw. "She saw an attorney yesterday and I'm out of here." He put the last toolbox in the bed of his truck and closed the tail gate. "It was a gal at work, and now I think she has moved on." He was mad at himself, mad at the situation, and I think a little mad at me. All he could see was a closed door that his sin had slammed shut. How could he recover? This passage gives us a pattern to move into God's good plan.

When infidelity ends in divorce. When laziness causes the loss of a job. When built-up anger leads to damaging words and accusations that end a relationship. When self-centeredness splits a church. When the door is shut as a result of sin, how do we move out of that sin into God's victory?

This passage ends with the locating of the site of the temple. This is a victory, because it is the start of the temple construction. This victorious beginning is the end of a process that David went through that began with a door being shut because of his sin.

Is it true?
On September 25, 1999, Joan Murry went for another sky-diving thrill. She had jumped dozens of times, but this jump would be very different. After free-falling from 14,500 feet, she pulled her rip cord only to have it not work; then her reserve shoot opened, only to get tangled. She hit the ground at eighty miles an hour, but somehow was not killed. Most often an impact like this causes the heart to stop beating, but hers kept beating. Later at the hospital they found hundreds of small whelps and bites all over her body; apparently, she had landed on a fire-ant bed. This sounds like adding insult to injury, but the doctors said that the ants saved her life. The

hundreds of fire-ant bites triggered adrenaline to be released in her body that caused her heart to keep beating (https://historyofyesterday.com/the-skydiver-saved-by-fire-ants). Murry literally saw the door of death closing as she fell to the ground. But the ants were the open window. Good can come in ways that we would never expect. God can bring good even out of our sin.

This is a dominant theme of the Bible: Joseph being sold as a slave only to rule Egypt, the earth being cursed and the glorious promise of a new heaven and earth. This story of David sinning and God moving him from repentance to the dedication of the ground on which the temple would be built is in tune with that theme. The zenith of this theme is Jesus's dying in our place and then rising to give us life.

God wanted us to know in detail what David did, so that when we find ourselves with a door closed because of our sin we could do more than just get mad at ourselves. Joan Murry's falling on an ant bed is not a pattern for skydivers whose chutes won't open. However, David's example gives us a pattern to move from sin and into God's victory.

Now what?

This narrative presents a path that David took when confronted by his sin. It is not a series of magic words or steps that guarantees God will forgive and restore. David's actions are fueled by a right heart. It is a pattern, not an exact recipe to follow. When confronted by Joab before the sin, he did not turn away. Then, after the sin, he is confronted by God directly. The author is setting up a question in our minds: Which way will David turn? There is a moment for each of us when God shows us our sin. It is a pivot point. Which way will we turn?

It was just a few weeks into the new pastorate. I felt strongly that if the church were to grow there needed to be some changes in direction. At staff meeting with associate pastors Bob, Bill, and Mary, I presented my plan, only to have strong resistance. In my insecurity and sin, I got defensive and pulled rank. I told them that we were going to move in that direction because I was the senior pastor. I don't remember my exact words, but I clearly remember the expressions on their faces of shock and disappointment. Their faces were just a hint of what I was feeling from God's Spirit. I was struck by God. What would I do? Get mad? Be hurt and withdraw? I had just closed the door on a unified team. By God's empowerment in spite of my stupid pride, I stopped, and right then apologized. I asked for their forgiveness, I was wrong. Again, God worked, and they forgave me.

How do we respond when God strikes us and shows us our sin? This was the first step in David moving from his sin to God's victory. Here are the key points in David's journey:

- I have sinned (21:8)
- Fully trusted God, not man (21:13)
- Was transparent with leaders (21:16)
- Took responsibility (21:17)
- Obeyed God's direction (21:19)
- Owned his sin (21:24)

These movements in David's journey to victory are fairly easy to see in the text, with the exception of the last one. When David says that he will not offer to God that which cost him nothing, he is not trying to impress God with his sacrifice. This is not David offering reparations to God. He is owning his sin. He was the one coming to YHWH, not Ornan. He is accepting God's discipline, which is costly.

This outline of David's journey can be a pattern for us. The details will vary with the person and the sin. The general flow is trust, repentance, and obedience. And just as David's journey is a pattern, so is God's victory. The marriage may not be saved, the team may not come back together, the student may still fail. But God will bring his victory and bring good even when we have shut the door because of our sin.

Creativity in Presentation

When preaching about sin and repentance, it is important for us to use ourselves as examples. Of course, there are sins that should not be mentioned in a public setting, so discretion is vital. Nonetheless, when we admit our own sin, our listeners more easily identify with us. Presenting a weakness helps break down the barriers that we each have about our own sin. Thus, I presented one of my own past sins above. The preaching/teaching of this passage will be more effective if a personal sin and repentance is presented.

This narrative must be presented as a full story before application can begin. It might be that the overall story is summarized at the beginning, and then as the story details are presented the application is made. If this plan is used, it is important that each point is clearly tied into the overall movement of sin to victory.

If one is comfortable with applying the specific steps that David went through, then the application can be made as the story is told. If one prefers to use a more general progression of faith that leads to repentance and obedience, then the whole story can be told in detail, followed by the application. And because the theme of God moving us from sin to victory is wonderfully illustrated by the gospel, it would fit well in the beginning or at the end. Here is one possible structure:

- Summarize the whole story
- Present the story and applications
  - David sins (21:1–6)
  - God strikes David (21:7)
  - Moving to victory (21:8–30)
    - I have sinned (21:8)
    - Fully trust God, not man (21:13)
    - Be appropriately transparent (21:16)
    - Take responsibility (21:17)
    - Obey God's direction (21:19)
    - Own our sin (21:24)
  - God's victory (22:1)

DISCUSSION QUESTIONS

1. What reactions do we have when we realize that we have sinned?

2. What consequences have you seen come from sin?

3. What feelings may come when we know that a closed door is due to our own sin?

4. What part of David's path to God's victory seems the hardest? Why?

5. When have you seen a door open, even though it was closed by sin?

1 Chronicles 22:2–19

EXEGETICAL IDEA
Following the pattern of Moses and Joshua, David prepared for God's task of building the temple and charged Solomon and the people to obey YHWH's instructions to succeed in finishing the task.

THEOLOGICAL FOCUS
Carrying out God's will calls for a community of devoted followers empowered by God.

PREACHING IDEA
Be a part of God's big plan.

PREACHING POINTERS
God was inviting those in David and Solomon's time, and then those after the exile, to be a part of something bigger than themselves—that is, to be a part of building his temple. The temple was to give light to the nations, to make his glory known, to be a place of prayer and worship, and to show that forgiveness comes through sacrifice. The temple is gone, and now God is inviting us to be a part of a new building—not one constructed of rocks but one fashioned with living stones. Not a physical building, but a breathing building: the church. While there are numerous differences between the temple and Christ's church, the purpose is still the same. God's plan of dwelling in and working through the church calls for a community of people who are committed to the task, devoted to him, and empowered by him. Each of us is invited to play a part in God's big plan of working through the church to show his love for the world.

DAVID PREPARES FOR THE TEMPLE (22:2–19)

LITERARY STRUCTURE AND THEMES (22:2–19)

Once David identifies the site for YHWH's temple, the rest of the account of David's reign recounts his preparations for building the temple. This passage is organized around the three ways in which David prepares for the temple: (1) David gathers human and material resources, (2) David charges Solomon to build the temple, and (3) David charges Israel's leaders to help Solomon build the temple. David speaks in each section (first to himself, then Solomon, then the leaders).

Several features bind these sections together. For instance, when addressing both Solomon and the leaders, David first refers to what YHWH has done (22:6–10, 17–18) to motivate a call for action (22:11–16, 19). Furthermore, the beginning of the section corresponds to the end: the text describes the laborers and the materials for the temple (22:2–4), and later David describes the materials and the laborers for the temple (22:14–16a). The passage uses the technique of *inclusio* to mark out when David admonishes Solomon to build the temple by including the phrase "May YHWH be with you" at the beginning and the end (22:11, 16). Finally, each section concludes with a call to action (David to prepare, 22:5; Solomon to rise and act, 22:16; the leaders to rise and build, 22:19).

Beyond these techniques, the text holds together as a transition, looking back at David's reign and looking forward to Solomon's reign. The Chronicler shows how David prepares to build the temple (e.g., by transferring the ark to Jerusalem, establishing the Levitical musical service, and securing Israel's full possession of the land). The Chronicler emphasizes how Solomon will fulfill David's preparations by building the temple and enjoying Israel's peace. This transition resembles the transition from Moses to Joshua, and the text closely resembles the charge to Joshua to finish the work that Moses began (see Deut. 31:23; Josh. 1:6, 9). Altogether, the unit shows that, following the pattern of Moses and Joshua, David prepared for God's task of building the temple and charged Solomon and the people to finish the task.

- **David Gathers Resources for the Temple (22:2–5)**
- **David Charges Solomon to Build the Temple (22:6–16)**
  - *David Addresses His Past Desire and YHWH's Past Promise (22:6–10)*
  - *David Admonishes Solomon to Complete What David Started (22:11–16)*
- **David Charges Leaders to Help Build the Temple (22:17–19)**

EXPOSITION (22:2–19)

When the Babylonians conquered Judah, they disrupted several institutions that marked Judah as a nation. Among the most prominent were the monarchy and the temple. The first readers did not experience a restoration of the Davidic monarchy, but they had a rebuilt temple. Chronicles points to the significance of the temple and Israel's worship as a people. At the same time, neither the monarchy nor the temple was fundamental to Israel, since neither institution accompanied the formation of the people as a nation. One of the Chronicler's concerns is to show that despite the disruption of the exile, the

Jerusalem temple fits into YHWH's plan for Israel.

In the current passage, the Chronicler addresses this concern by describing the transition from David's reign to Solomon's reign based on the transition from Moses to Joshua. In this way, the Chronicler shows that the temple and the monarchy continue the line of YHWH's activity with Israel, going back to Moses and Joshua. In other words, the monarchy and the temple are not deviations from YHWH's plan for his people but an important institution by which Israel can unite as a people to worship YHWH according to the law of Moses. As a result, in this passage, following the pattern of Moses and Joshua, David prepares for building the temple and charges Solomon and Israel's leaders to finish the task.

David Gathers Resources for the Temple (22:2–5)

After David identifies the temple site, he demonstrates his devotion to YHWH by gathering vast quantities of human and material resources for building a great temple for YHWH.

22:2. As a sign of David's devotion to YHWH, once he recognizes the temple site he immediately starts preparing what is needed to build the temple. He begins by assembling a large workforce to carry out the strenuous physical labor of collecting and preparing the materials needed to build the temple, represented by the basic building material of stone. This workforce consisted of resident aliens, that is, foreign persons who lived in Israel. The Chronicler elsewhere states that only foreigners performed the strenuous labor of collecting materials for the temple building (2 Chron. 2:2 [HB 1], 17 [HB 16]; 8:7–9). Despite their foreign status, Deuteronomy calls for their protection, while 2 Chronicles 30:25 records that they participate in the celebration of the Passover.

> **"Land of Israel"**
> The expression "land of Israel" in Chronicles is likely intended as a general geographic reference to the area that the Israelites inhabit rather than a specifically defined territory within a set border (R. Klein 2006, 432; Knoppers 2004, 770).

22:3–4. Shifting from the labor force, the Chronicler describes the materials David prepares for building the temple. The text emphasizes the quantity and quality of the materials. To indicate the quantity, the Chronicler uses a figure of speech stating that the metals are without weighing and the wood is without number; that is, the quantities are so large that it would be too difficult to weigh or count them. To indicate the quality of the materials, the Chronicler focuses on the wood. Cedarwood is an exquisite material, explicitly mentioned as a building material for palaces (David's, 2 Sam. 7:2 // 1 Chron. 17:1; Solomon's, 1 Kings 7:2–12). Furthermore, the Sidonians and Tyrians who are gathering the wood have a reputation for being competent and proficient at the task (for Sidonians, see 1 Kings 5:6; for Tyrians, see 2 Chron. 2:8 [HB 7]). Finally, although building accounts mention bronze (e.g., in the temple, the sea, pillars) or cedarwood (see above), iron does not occur in either of these contexts. Perhaps for this reason the Chronicler includes the specific uses for the iron.

22:5. At this point the Chronicler provides the practical reason for David to gather such human and material resources. He does so by reporting David's inner dialogue (indicated by the fact that David is not talking to anyone else, similar to 22:1). David's thoughts reveal two practical reasons for his preparation: (1) Solomon is young and inexperienced, and (2) the temple must be impressive (which Chronicles consistently describes using the language of greatness, e.g., 1 Chron. 29:1; 2 Chron. 2:5 [HB 4], 9 [HB 8]). By referring to Solomon's lack of experience, the text implies that Solomon will build the temple soon after he becomes king, rather than delaying until he has more experience. Furthermore, even if Solomon were an experienced ruler, the task of building this temple requires more than one person, even a king. It requires a whole nation, along with help from others (e.g., Huram-abi, 2 Chron. 2:13–14 [HB 12–13]; Japhet 1993, 395).

"Inexperienced Young Man"

On occasion, Chronicles records an expression that may seem out of place: it records the expression "inexperienced young man" to describe a new king. For instance, when Abijah describes Rehoboam just as he ascends the throne, he describes him as an "inexperienced young man" (נַעַר וְרַךְ־לֵבָב), even though Rehoboam is forty years old when he becomes king. In this case, rather than focusing on the age of the new king, the expression indicates the vulnerability of the new king as he leaves his father's mentoring and guidance (Leeb 2000, 94–95). The same is likely true concerning Solomon. David describes Solomon as "an inexperienced young man" (1 Chron. 22:5) even though it seems quite likely that Solomon was fully grown.

The temple clearly should be an impressive structure. David calls it exceedingly great, built to be famous and beautiful. The temple should be splendid—that is, it should be a beautiful place that attracts admiration, even the admiration of other nations. This language points to YHWH's desire for Israel as his people. Other passages (Deut. 26:19; Jer. 13:11; 33:9) describe the ideal Israel using the same language: famous and beautiful. As a splendid structure for YHWH, the temple is a material expression of what YHWH intends for his people. Furthermore, as a temple for YHWH, the temple's splendor points to YHWH's splendor. International recognition and admiration for the temple open up international recognition and admiration for Israel and for YHWH, the God of Israel (Lynch 2014b, 108).

For the first readers living within a relatively unimportant province of the Persian Empire, international recognition was not likely to take place for military, political, or economic reasons. By focusing on the temple, the people might attract international attention that could result in others recognizing YHWH as truly God (cf. 2 Chron. 6:32–33; Lynch 2014b, 108).

Finally, this verse serves two roles from a narrative perspective. First, it demonstrates that David follows up on his commitment to prepare. Since the passage has already recorded that David has gathered resources for building the temple, his statement immediately rings true. Second, since the text mentions that David prepares such materials before his death, it marks this period as a transition from David's reign to Solomon's reign. Therefore, from here on out, the Chronicler presents David's activity as preparing for Solomon's reign and his building the temple. Even though David is not allowed to build a temple for YHWH, David prepares vast resources to help his son Solomon build a great temple for YHWH.

David Charges Solomon to Build the Temple (22:6–16)

David charges Solomon to obey YHWH's instructions so that Solomon may fulfill David's desire to build a temple for YHWH in Jerusalem. David explains that even though he desired to build a temple for YHWH, YHWH promised that a Davidic son would do so instead. David then blesses Solomon, requesting that YHWH grant Solomon what he needs to build the temple. Finally, David charges Solomon to obey YHWH's instructions laid out in the law of Moses and to build the temple.

David Addresses His Past Desire and YHWH's Past Promise (22:6–10)

David explains why Solomon will build a temple for YHWH, even though David desired to do so and is now preparing resources for the task.

22:6. As David prepares resources for building a temple for YHWH, he also prepares Solomon, the temple builder. At this point the narrative shifts from David's self-talk to his charge for Solomon to build YHWH a temple. The following verses provide the content of David's charge.

22:7–8. David begins by explaining why he doesn't build the temple for YHWH. He states that he previously desired to build the temple (1 Chron. 17:2); however, YHWH instructed him specifically that he would not. YHWH does not condemn David's desire to build a temple; in fact, Chronicles later records that YHWH affirms David's desire (2 Chron. 6:7–8).

YHWH's House and YHWH's Word

David desires to build YHWH "a house" (rather than "the house"), recognizing YHWH's residence elsewhere in Israel's history (e.g., Bethel, Gen. 28). This statement points to a balancing act taking place throughout Chronicles: the Jerusalem temple is greatly important, but it is not fundamental to who YHWH is or who Israel is. However, 1 Chronicles 22:8 records YHWH's word to David: David may not build the temple. It is important that the text uses the phrase "the word of YHWH" because it makes clear that this prohibition is based directly on YHWH's revelation. The phrase "word of YHWH" occurs frequently to introduce prophetic oracles. More than likely, the "word of YHWH" in this verse refers to the revelation Nathan delivered to David in 1 Chronicles 17. I base this conclusion, in part, on the use of the preposition used with the phrase (עָלַי). Although translations render the phrase "to me," more commonly it indicates either "against" or "concerning." I translate the phrase as "concerning me [David]." At the same time, the text does not directly cite Nathan. It leaves open the idea that David himself receives this revelation directly; thus, David looks more like a prophet. Later, David will claim more explicitly that he receives divine revelation (1 Chron. 28:3, 6; see also Schniedewind 1995, 198–200).

TRANSLATION ANALYSIS:
Translations approach the phrase to describe David's desire to build a temple in various ways. Some (e.g., CSB, ESV, NIV) translate the phrase along the lines of "it was in my heart," while other translations render it as "intended" (NASB) or "wanted" (NET, NLT, NRSV). The phrase carries the sense of thinking, planning, and intending (e.g., Deut. 15:9; Josh. 14:7; 2 Chron. 9:1; 24:4; 29:10). In this case, the text is communicating more than that David simply thought about building a temple, as though it were a random idea, but that he intended to build it.

Furthermore, YHWH does not reject David entirely, only as the temple builder, since David has "spilled much blood and waged great wars" (22:8). Earlier in Chronicles David wages war according to YHWH's instructions (e.g., 1 Chron. 14:10–17), and YHWH himself fights on behalf of David and all Israel (e.g., 1 Chron. 18:6, 13), so this comment does not condemn David for waging war. The significance of spilling blood and waging war for temple building is likely twofold. First, it shows that David's reign is not characterized by the rest that Deuteronomy 12:8–12 indicates will precede YHWH's choosing a place for Israel's ritual worship (Braun 1976, 583–84). Second, it likely indicates that David's activity in war has rendered him "ritually unfit to build the Temple of YHWH [*sic*]" (Knoppers 2004, 775). As a result, even though David desires to build a temple and makes extensive preparations to do so, YHWH assigns the task to David's son Solomon.

Pouring Out Blood

The imagery of pouring out blood occurs in various contexts in the Old Testament. Most often the imagery describes pouring out the blood of an animal for sacrifice or eating within the context of ritual purity (e.g., Lev. 4:7; 17:13). The imagery also applies to killing another person within the context of nonmilitary conflict (e.g., Gen. 9:6; 37:22; 1 Sam. 25:31). In Numbers 35:33, both contexts occur as the shedding of blood leads to pollution of the land. Although David is unlikely referring to this verse directly in any way, the verse reveals a connection between pollution and bloodshed that may form the backdrop to the reason David may not build the temple.

22:9–10. Even though YHWH does not allow David to build the temple, YHWH provides a way to build the temple "through David," that is, through one of David's sons. The text signifies the importance of this Davidic son in three ways. First, YHWH proclaims this son's birth using language found elsewhere, to indicate that YHWH will fulfill his plan and purpose (e.g., Samson's birth, Judg. 13:3–7; Josiah's birth, 1 Kings 13:2; Immanuel's birth, Isa. 7:14). Second, the text provides a wordplay on Solomon's name. His name (שְׁלֹמֹה) relates to peace (שָׁלוֹם), one of the conditions necessary for constructing the temple (see below). Third, YHWH declares that this Davidic son will also be YHWH's son. As Eugene Merrill puts it, Solomon "will be God's special son, that is, one adopted to fulfill a divine role and destiny" (2015, 267).

Beyond signifying Solomon's importance, the text describes the conditions of Solomon's future reign. Especially important is the theme of rest. As stated above, based on Deuteronomy 12:8–12, rest is a condition for YHWH's choosing a site to place his name, that is, a place for him to dwell among his people and receive their sacrifices. The Chronicler elaborates on the theme in various ways. Using the language of Deuteronomy 12:10, YHWH declares he will give rest to Solomon from all his enemies; that is, other nations will not threaten Israel. Furthermore, YHWH will provide peace and quiet for all Israel during Solomon's reign. The overall image depicts Israel as a stable, peaceful nation settled in its land without fear of internal or external turmoil.

These verses also relate the essential connection between Solomon and these conditions. Not only does Israel experience rest, peace, and quiet, but Solomon himself is a man of rest. The description contrasts sharply to David, who has spilled much blood and waged great wars. As a result, the text highlights that Solomon is the temple-builder, whose royal authority over Israel will remain into the distant future.

Highlighting Solomon

When one compares 22:10 to the parallel passage (1 Chron. 17:13), one finds changes in word order. The changes emphasize Solomon as the one who will be the temple-builder and the son of YHWH. R. Klein notes that "the effect of this change is to put more emphasis on Solomon's sonship than on Yahweh [*sic*] as the divine parent and so exalt him as the equal to David" (2006, 438).

David Admonishes Solomon to Complete What David Started (22:11–16)

David admonishes Solomon to build the temple by requesting that YHWH empower Solomon for the task, by exhorting Solomon to obey YHWH's instructions, and by pointing to the preparations David has already made.

David to Solomon and Moses to Joshua

As David's speech shifts from what has been said to what should be done, it closely resembles another significant moment in Israel's history: the transition from Moses to Joshua. In both cases a speech marks the transition from one leader to another. Both speeches share common elements and phrases. The elements consist of (1) encouragement, (2) description of the task, and (3) assurance of divine aid, although the elements do not occur in the same order in both accounts (Knoppers 2004, 785; Lohfink 1962, 32–44; McCarthy 1971, 31–37; Williamson 1982, 155). The shared phrases include "be strong and courageous," "be careful to do," "do not be afraid or dismayed," and others. The similar language also points to similar circumstances. Most importantly, in both cases the first leader begins a task that YHWH does not allow him to finish; instead, the second leader must finish the task.

The connections between David-Solomon and Moses-Joshua relate to the Chronicler's purposes. First, he intends to show that building the Jerusalem temple is a part of YHWH's plan for Israel. The temple is not David's innovation; it fits into what YHWH was doing even before the monarchy. The Jerusalem temple is an important part of YHWH's plan for Israel, but it is not the only place where YHWH has dwelled (see comments on 22:5). Second, these similarities bind the reigns of David and Solomon together (Williamson 1976, 356–57). This link helps alleviate some of the tension created by David's being a good king, but not able to build temple. His reign flows naturally into Solomon's and reflects Moses's situation with Joshua.

22:11. Although speaking to Solomon, David really begins by requesting that YHWH help Solomon. David accomplishes this purpose by blessing Solomon ("May YHWH be with you"). This blessing requests that YHWH's beneficial presence be with Solomon, so that Solomon may succeed in building the temple. Solomon needs YHWH's help because the task is so overwhelming (see above). Furthermore, David shows that building the temple is ultimately a divine task when he alludes to what YHWH has promised: YHWH is the one who promised that Solomon would build the temple; he is also the one who will help Solomon succeed (for the divine origin of the temple, see Lynch 2014b, 110–14).

22:12. To complete the task, Solomon will need insight and understanding far beyond his capacity as a young, inexperienced man (22:5). David requests that YHWH will provide such understanding. However, David does not describe the result of such understanding as building the temple, but obeying YHWH's law. This surprising fact implies that successfully building the temple requires obeying YHWH's law. At the same time, YHWH may provide Solomon insight and understanding (which he does; see 2 Chron. 2:12 [HB 11]) so that Solomon may obey.

> **What YHWH Provides and Expects**
> Other passages in Chronicles also address this combination of what YHWH provides and what he requires. For instance, 2 Chronicles 30:12 recounts how Judah observed the Passover obediently as "the hand of God was upon Judah to give them one heart." These and similar passages show that the "Israelites have a sacred obligation to obey their God. But divine gifts, in turn, help Israelites honor their commitments to the deity" (Knoppers 2004, 776–77).

22:13. Here David shifts from what YHWH may provide for Solomon to what YHWH requires of Solomon. Returning to the theme of obedience mentioned in 22:12, the text makes explicit that success requires obedience. In this context, success is specifically success in building the temple, while obedience entails keeping the stipulations of the law of Moses. In Chronicles, these stipulations are primarily the laws regarding proper worship (e.g., 1 Chron. 16:40; 2 Chron. 7:19; 33:8; 34:31–33). This requirement plays off the language of YHWH's promise to Solomon: in 22:12 YHWH will give Solomon charge over Israel (*piel* צוה and עַל־יִשְׂרָאֵל) and require that Solomon keep the law commanded to Israel (*piel* צוה and עַל־יִשְׂרָאֵל). In this way the text indicates that to succeed, Solomon is primarily obligated to obey Mosaic law, especially regarding Israel's ritual worship.

To encourage Solomon to obey, David calls on him to be strong, courageous, and unafraid. This language closely resembles that of Joshua's installation (see excursus "David to Solomon and Moses to Joshua" above). The language applies to military conflicts, indicating that obeying the law is as serious a matter as facing an enemy in battle. However, neither physical strength nor military power will secure success, "but spiritual fortitude is necessary for the success of Joshua and Solomon" (Knoppers 2004, 777). This point runs throughout the books of Joshua and Chronicles (e.g., 2 Chron. 20:15–22).

22:14. The text returns to the theme at the beginning of the narrative unit: David's preparations for building the temple. David points out his own efforts to secure such great quantities of materials and laborers. David denies himself many spoils of war to dedicate them to building the temple (see also Ps. 132:1–5; Knoppers 2004, 777). His efforts pay off because the specific quantities of gold and silver he mentions far outnumber quantities mentioned elsewhere in Chronicles, while other materials are so numerous that they cannot be weighed (22:3). Despite these large quantities, the temple is so great that Solomon will still need to add to them. Chronicles records later that Solomon does add to these materials for the temple (e.g., 2 Chron. 2:8–9 [HB 7–8]), presenting Solomon as the one who completes what David begins.

TRANSLATION ANALYSIS:
Translations render the first phrase of this verse (בְעָנְיִי) in various ways. Many translations (e.g., CSB, ESV, NASB, NIV, NRSV) use the language of pain (e.g., "with great pains"). Other translations, trying to take into greater account the context, focus on the effort involved (e.g., "I have made every effort" NET; "I have worked hard" NLT). In this case the phrase does not communicate a sense of pain or necessarily effort, but a sense of denial, or as Knoppers puts it, "a self-imposed restraint" (Knoppers 2004, 768). For this reason, a suitable translation might be "with discipline" or "by denying myself."

22:15–16. David further points out the laborers he has prepared for Solomon. These laborers include those who collect the materials, those who shape them, and artisans skilled in making items of various materials. David has provided the type of laborers needed to build the temple.

Solomon will add his own craftsmen and request a master craftsman from Tyre to join these artisans in building the temple (and the palace). Although Solomon will still need to add to these resources, David's preparations should encourage Solomon to build the temple as soon as possible since so many resources are already available.

As a result, David calls Solomon to action. To motivate this action, David requests that YHWH be with Solomon. In 22:11, David has already made the same request, creating an *inclusio* marking 22:11–16 as a literary unit and drawing attention to the fact that Solomon requires YHWH's aid to build the temple. This request for YHWH's aid also provides a contrast to David. When David first proposed to build YHWH a temple, Nathan encouraged David to act (עֲשֵׂה) because God was with him. This repeated phrasing helps draw together the reigns of David and Solomon and sharpens the contrast between David who desires to build the temple and Solomon who fulfills the desire to build it. One sees a similar contrast between Moses who leads the people to the edge of the land and Joshua who leads the people to take possession of it (see excursus "David to Solomon and Moses to Joshua," above). In the end, Solomon will succeed in building the temple.

David Charges Leaders to Help Build the Temple (22:17–19)
Since YHWH has given Israel complete possession of the land, David charges Israel's leaders to help Solomon build the temple.

22:17–18. David makes his final preparations of the chapter by encouraging Israel's leaders to help Solomon build the temple. David prompts the leaders to recognize YHWH's beneficial presence with them by asking a rhetorical question ("Is not YHWH your God with you?"). David proceeds to show them the evidence for YHWH's presence: YHWH has defeated Israel's enemies and given them rest in their land. This rest recalls the future rest promised to Solomon (22:9) and is a present reality only at the end of David's life.

The language describing this rest also points to the period of Joshua. The expression that the land is subdued before YHWH and his people Israel draws on Numbers 32:22, 29, and Joshua 18:1. These passages refer to the conquest during the days of Joshua. By incorporating the language here, the text implies that even though Israel occupied the land before the monarchy, Israel's full possession of the land does not take place until the final stages of David's life. Since YHWH has brought about Israel's full possession of the land, David argues that YHWH is with Israel.

22:19. Since YHWH is with Israel, David encourages the leaders to commit themselves to seek YHWH. The expression of giving heart and soul to something carries the sense of attempting to do something or committing oneself to do something (e.g., 2 Chron. 11:16; Eccl. 1:13, 17; 8:9, 16; 9:1). The language of seeking YHWH occurs frequently in Chronicles, often with overtones of participating properly in the ritual worship directed toward YHWH (see sidebar "Seeking YHWH"). David calls them to perform a concrete sign of their devotion: building the temple. The text describes this temple as a sanctuary to house the ark and other sacred items as well as a house built for YHWH's name. The temple is to be a sacred structure at a sacred location containing sacred items for YHWH's name, that is, for his glory.

By including David's address to Israel's leaders, the Chronicler reiterates a point made earlier in the chapter: building the temple is an immense task that will require all Israel, not just its king. This point would be especially significant for the first readers of Chronicles. Many from Israel were scattered among other nations while a few returned to the land and Jerusalem. Even so, the temple in Jerusalem was to be a source of blessing for all YHWH's people. The

Chronicler envisions all Israel working together to build, support, and maintain the temple and its ritual worship. The temple would serve as a visible sign of YHWH's presence, encouraging others to worship him (see above on 22:5).

Just as Solomon and the leaders needed YHWH's beneficial presence, the first readers also did. David's words to Solomon requesting YHWH's help ("May YHWH be with you") point forward to the final words of Chronicles ("YHWH his God be with him and let him go up," 2 Chron. 36:23). This final affirmation points to the hope of a future Davidic king (see commentary on 2 Chron. 36:23), but also encourages the postexilic community to maintain the temple as part of YHWH's restoring the people to their land.

THEOLOGICAL FOCUS
Carrying out God's will calls for a community of devoted followers empowered by God.

This passage contains several elements foreign to the experience of most contemporary readers: an ancient king, a fledgling dynasty, a national temple, and so on. However, beyond these elements, this passage addresses significant theological themes helpful for the contemporary setting. One theme especially prominent in this passage is God's will.

One way the passage addresses God's will is by portraying David and Solomon in terms similar to Moses and Joshua. These similarities demonstrate that God has an intended plan that he is working out throughout Israel's history. In this case, that intended plan involves preparing the legitimate means for God to dwell among his people in a way they will understand in their context. As a result, God secures what is needed to construct a temple in Jerusalem.

Also, like Moses and Joshua, David and Solomon play different roles in accomplishing God's plan. At first, it is surprising that even though David desires to build the temple, God refuses to let him. In the context, building the temple is certainly a good thing to do, but God has a different role for David in his plan. Rather than building the temple, David secures peace for Israel through military victory and administrative skill. As the passage points out, this role suits David because he is a military leader (22:8). In contrast, God chooses Solomon to be the temple-builder. Since God has planned for temple construction to occur during a time of peaceful rest, Solomon suits this role because he is a man of rest (22:9). In this way, both kings play necessary roles in bringing about the temple construction. Furthermore, God's chosen roles for both kings suit them well.

These preceding observations point to God's planning in accomplishing his will, but the passage also points to human participation in God's will. First, the entire chapter reveals that all Israel must participate in building the temple because it is such an immense task. Even though Solomon is God's chosen temple-builder, Solomon cannot accomplish the task alone. This point seems rather obvious when it comes to the physical labor of constructing a temple (it is hard just to imagine a single person carrying all the materials needed), but this point is not limited to the physical labor. Building the temple will require a lot from the people. In fact, the task is too big even for all Israel. God must be present with them to empower them to finish the work. As a result, to see it to completion, Solomon needs the community, empowered by God, working to the goal.

Although God does not require believers to construct a physical temple, God's plan of dwelling with people does not change. The NT points to a spiritual building made up of believers who offer up spiritual sacrifices (1 Peter 2:5) and, as a group, display the manifold wisdom of God (Eph. 2:19–3:12). Constructing such a spiritual building to offer sacrifices, and displaying the wisdom of God while doing it, requires the community of believers working together.

Second, the chapter points to the role that devotion to God plays. David shows his devotion by assembling workers and materials needed for the temple. Even though David's gifts come at his personal expense, he gladly gives them because they honor YHWH. An offering like David's points to the type of devotion that falls within God's will. At the same time, David encourages Solomon's devotion by praying that God will grant Solomon wisdom to obey God's commands. David recognizes that this type of obedience requires spiritual courage and strength. Solomon's obedience to God's commands points to another type of devotion that falls within God's will.

The theme of God's will throughout this passage draws numerous theological threads together. On the one hand, God has an intentional plan running through history, in which he chooses certain people for certain tasks at certain times. On the other hand, people may participate in God's plan through their devotion to him. He empowers them in their work and brings about their success as a community. As a result, he is worshipped.

PREACHING AND TEACHING STRATEGIES

Exegetical and Theological Synthesis

God's plan has always been that he would be known and worshipped throughout all the nations. Israel was to build a temple that would help facilitate that in a physical sense. The temple was also the central place of worship for Israel, so that YHWH would be more fully known within Israel. The first readers were to continue with this plan of God's by rebuilding the temple. What a task. They needed to acquire the resources, but even more, they needed motivation. Encouragement came through the Chronicler recounting David's preparation for the building and his charges to the builders. Three times, David gives a charge to build the temple. The first is *about* Solomon, the second is *to* Solomon, and the last is to the leaders. Though each charge is unique, three actions emerge: commitment to the specific task, devotion to YHWH, and a trusting dependence upon YHWH to work.

God's plan is still that he would be known and worshipped throughout the world. The church is now the primary means of spreading that good news. God's purpose hasn't changed. God is now working through the church to reach the nations, and the same three directives still apply: commitment to the task of spreading the good news through the church, devotion to God, and utter dependence upon him. It is important to notice the NT emphasis upon Christ building the church. Just as Israel could not build the temple without YHWH's direct help, so too the church is built by God.

Preaching Idea
Be a part of God's big plan.

Contemporary Connections

What does it mean?
When a teenager sits at the computer and plays hours on end of what my wife calls "killing dots"—what keeps them gaming? Instant gratification? That is part of it, but there is also a sense of being a part of something bigger than themselves, albeit purely fictional. When a well-motivated young person joins the military or the Peace Corps or volunteers for Habitat for Humanity, there is a desire to make a difference in the world. When we see that our individual efforts in some small way accomplish a bigger-than-us goal, it brings great satisfaction. God hardwired us with a heart that yearns to accomplish something significant.

What could be more helpful to the world than helping people get in touch with the one who made them and sustains them? The building of the temple, either Solomon's or the postexilic second temple, was purposed to do just that. Its splendor was to give us humans, who depend so much on our senses, a physical building of splendor to help us know God's

splendor. It was to be for all nations to see. The temple was also a place for Israel and for all who feared God to worship him. It was a central place to grow in one's understanding of God. By faith in him, expressed in sacrifices, one could be forgiven and experience the security and joy of being known by him.

The problem comes when an event is over, or we can no longer be a part of the organization, or when we see that what we thought was something worthwhile seems to make little difference. The play that took so many hours of rehearsals and productions has its last showing. Great memories are shared at that last cast party, but there is an unspoken emptiness. The growing and building of a winning team that finally wins that ultimate crucial final game brings a long-awaited euphoria. But this joy is only a memory that with time grows more and more distant. God not only offers us a place in his eternal kingdom, he invites us to be a part of building it.

This passage gives us something that is bigger than ourselves of which we can be a part—and through it, God guides us as to how to be a part of it.

Is it true?
Let's step back into ancient Israel and see how it is true that being involved in something beyond ourselves is in each of our hearts.

From his teenage years until his mid-twenties, a young man worked with his father cutting stones out of the quarry. He then went to serve in David's army to help subdue the nations around them. As the battles grew less and stability came to the nation, he returned to the quarry, got married, and began to build a life. Life was getting better and better. The nation was unified. His income was such that he could build an addition to his father's house and start his own family. Life was good, but it was much the same every day: cut blocks of stone out of a mountain to be used in someone's building. As peace came to the nation, so did more orders for stone. The routine of life was settling in upon him. This rut changed when a messenger from King David arrived, asking him to report to the palace. After cleaning up and putting on the right clothes, he reported. He had to wait outside the king's throne room until he was called, which allowed him a moment to try to pull his thoughts together. "What would the king want from me?" As he stepped into the king's presence, he was relieved that David greeted him warmly and began to recount battles in which they had fought side by side. The king had not forgotten him. Then the king turned the conversation to matters at hand. "You were summoned here today to ask you be part of a huge undertaking. We will need more blocks than any building you have even seen, cut to exact specifications, and cut from the finest of stone. I would like for you to oversee this crucial project. I have always had a deep desire to build a temple for Elohim, but he told me that I was not to build it. Instead, I was to prepare what was needed to build the temple. My question to you: Would you oversee the cutting of stones for Elohim's temple? Before you answer, if you choose to be a part you will need to enlist many others to help. And you will need to commit to finish the task. Most importantly, you will need to set your mind and heart to seek Elohim."

Stepping back into our century: the surroundings and physical experiences of an ancient Israelite stonecutter's life are very distant from us, but the emotions are very close. The honor of being asked and the excitement of the grandeur of the project ring true in our hearts. We all want to be a part of something bigger than ourselves—something that will last beyond our own lives.

Now what?
God has not called us to cut stones for the temple; he has called us to *be* the stones of a new and different holy temple. As the Lord tells us in Ephesians 2:19–22 and 1 Peter 2:4–5, we are the ones who will display God's splendor.

We are the ones who will by faith depend upon his sacrifice. We are the living stones who will carry his message to the nations. Each believer in Jesus has a part to play in building this eternal building.

The parts today vary from those of ancient times, but the charge from David is still good for us. We need to be committed to the health and growth of God's church, both universal and local. Sometimes the grandeur of the church universal is obscured by the frustrations in a local body. But our commitment must not waver. We must remember that God is building something worldwide, something eternal, something bigger than me and my local church. While loyalty to a local church is good, it must not take the place of loyalty to God. David told the workers to be devoted to YHWH, and out of that would flow the right motivation to build the temple. Likewise, the right attitude toward building a healthy and growing local church is to be devoted to God first. It is hard work to be an involved member of a local church. There are people to teach, children to care for, finances and facilities to manage. David reminds us that we are to depend upon our Lord to empower us.

And we must not forget that we must be willing to work with others. The temple wasn't built by one person; thousands worked on it. The universal church and each local body can't be built by one person; we must work with others in the body. At the same time, working with others means they won't do it just like we would. Other people are sinful and so am I. We must be patient with others and ourselves, as we work together.

Creativity in Presentation
Since the application of this passage comes from a compilation of the three charges that David gives to build the temple, it will probably work best to present the whole story before application. Since it is a relatively short section, the entire passage could be read with comments.

A key in maintaining attention and prompting interaction is to ask the congregation to listen for the common elements in the three charges that David gives. Then, present the common elements that will form the basis for application. We have suggested three requirements that come from the charges, and then a fourth requirement that comes from the observation that it took thousands to build the temple.

A movie clip that could be used to heighten the emotion of wanting to be in something bigger than oneself is from *Rudy*, a 1993 family movie. The story is about a high school student who wants to play football at Notre Dame even though his size, grades, and finances were all against him. There is a three-minute section when Rudy is first denied entrance to Notre Dame, and then when he is accepted, that encapsulates the joy of being a part of something big. Here is one possible structure:

- Tell the story: God's big plan for the temple
  - David gathers resources for the temple (22:2–5)
  - David charges Solomon to build the temple (22:6–16)
    - David addresses his past desire and YHWH's past promise (22:6–10)
    - David admonishes Solomon to complete what David started (22:11–16)
  - David charges the leaders to help build the temple (22:17–19)
- Make the correlation: God's big plan for the temple and the church are the same
  - To show God's glory
  - To tell the nations about him
  - To worship him
  - To present the message of forgiveness through sacrifice
- Apply: Requirements to be a part of God's big plan
  - Commit to the task
  - Devote yourself to God
  - Depend upon God
  - Work with others
- Wouldn't you like to have a part in God's big plan?

DISCUSSION QUESTIONS

1. What was a bigger-than-yourself event or group that you were a part in high school?

2. What major event in history would you have liked to have played a part in?

3. What movie or past sporting event do you wish you could have acted in or played in?

4. What would have been the requirements to have been involved in that event?

5. When is it hard to stay committed to a task bigger than oneself?

6. What motivates us when we are involved in a task or event far bigger than ourselves?

1 Chronicles 23:1–27:34

EXEGETICAL IDEA
During his last days, David promoted the worship of YHWH and the well-being of Israel by meticulously organizing the personnel to serve in the future temple and by securing a peaceful transfer of royal authority to Solomon.

THEOLOGICAL FOCUS
Worshipping YHWH is a serious task of obedience, worthy of meticulous care and consideration, resulting in blessing.

PREACHING IDEA
Meaningful corporate worship begins with meticulous work.

PREACHING POINTERS
Across the centuries, worship in Israel changed: when Israel built a permanent structure instead of a tent, when the temple was destroyed and the Babylonians took Israel into captivity, and when the exiles returned to rebuild the temple. But greater changes were in store. Jesus's death and resurrection changed everything. When we study a passage that lists the personnel for temple worship, we must remember the changes and looks for what has not changed: we still worship the same God. We are still sinful people living in a sinful world. Because of this, we need order and structure to help us as sinners come together and worship our Lord.

This passage doesn't give us direction as to what happens in worship; rather, it shows the importance of order and personnel structure. The Israelites needed meticulous work to have meaningful worship, and we need the same.

ORGANIZING ISRAEL FOR YHWH'S FUTURE TEMPLE AND FUTURE KING (23:1–27:34)

LITERARY STRUCTURE AND THEMES (23:1–27:34)

Following David's private charge to Solomon to build the temple, Chronicles shifts to the last days of David (1 Chron. 23–29). During his last days, David privately enthrones Solomon as king and then organizes the personnel to serve in the temple and in the royal administration. This passage is a collection of lists, generally organized around the number twelve and its multiples, along with commentary. The lists begin with the Levitical personnel. Following a genealogical overview of the Levites (1 Chron. 23:3–32), the lists occur in the sequence from those serving within the innermost regions of the temple to those serving outside Jerusalem: priests, other Levites, musicians, gatekeepers, and officials. Concluding the list with Levites serving outside Jerusalem eases the transition to the political personnel listed in 1 Chronicles 27: the leaders of the military divisions, the leaders of the tribes, administrators of royal assets, and royal advisors (R. Klein 2006, 501). Listing the names of so many of Israel's leaders also builds anticipation for the formal ceremony recorded in 1 Chronicles 28–29, in which all Israel enthrones Solomon as king and prepares to build the temple.

- **Enthroning Solomon and Gathering Personnel (23:1–2)**
- **Levitical Personnel (23:3–26:32)**
  - *Overview of Levites (23:3–32)*
  - *Priests (24:1–19)*
  - *Levites (24:20–31)*
  - *Musicians (25:1–31)*
  - *Gatekeepers (26:1–19)*
  - *Officials (26:20–32)*
- **Political Personnel (27:1–34)**
  - *Military Divisions (27:1–15)*
  - *Tribal Leaders (27:16–24)*
  - *Royal Administrators (27:25–31)*
  - *Royal Advisors (27:32–34)*

EXPOSITION (23:1–27:34)

An important moment for any nation occurs at the transition of political power from one administration to another. The death of a king could easily result in warring factions as different individuals attempt to occupy the empty throne. In Chronicles, the final days of David's reign look forward to the transition of power to the next generation. David puts things in order so that his son Solomon may rule in peace (1 Chron. 22:9).

At the same time, David serves as more than just one king in Israel's history; he is also the founder of a dynasty. These chapters point to David's legacy as a founder, beyond just the realm of his royal administration. They capture part of David's enduring legacy as a worshipper of YHWH. David not only sets up systems for military service, civic leadership, and royal administration, but he also organizes the personnel serving YHWH in the temple: the priests, Levites, musicians, and gatekeepers. As a result, in Israel's following history, even into the postexilic situation, these institutions look back to David as an authority for their legitimate organization. They can do so in part because these chapters preserve the names, roles, and functions of various personnel. In this way, the lists of 1 Chronicles 23–27 as a whole function as a source of authority for postexilic practice. At the same time, they reinforce the picture of

David as a good king, focusing on his efforts to promote the worship of YHWH and secure the well-being of Israel (Wright 1991, 237).

Enthroning Solomon and Gathering Personnel (23:1–2)

Toward the end of David's blessed life, he prepares for his succession by privately enthroning Solomon as king and then gathering Israel's leaders to ensure Solomon's success as the future temple-builder.

23:1. Following David's private charge to Solomon to build the temple (1 Chron. 22:6–16) and to Israel's leaders to support Solomon (1 Chron. 22:17–19), the Chronicler introduces the remainder of his account of David's reign (1 Chron. 23–29). These chapters focus on the preparations that David takes to ensure a smooth, peaceful transition to Solomon's rule, so that Solomon can fulfill his role in building YHWH's temple.

The Chronicler notes that David makes these preparations toward the end of his life. The Chronicler describes David as "old and full of days." This language serves three functions. First, this language points to David as one whom YHWH has blessed, since the same expression occurs elsewhere in the Old Testament to honor Abraham (Gen. 25:8), Isaac (Gen. 35:29), and Job (Job 42:17) at their deaths (Japhet 1993, 411). Second, despite the positive characterization, the language also foreshadows David's death. First Chronicles 29:28 describes David's death using the same language. In other words, the description of David's age functions as bookmarks around the rest of 1 Chronicles. Third, the language focuses the following chapters on the transition to Solomon, as David takes his final measures to prepare Solomon for his reign.

The text states that David makes Solomon king. Since a public ceremony will take place in 1 Chronicles 29, this enthronement appears to be a private ceremony in which David hands over the rule of Israel. This private ceremony follows the private charge to Solomon to build the temple (1 Chron. 22:6–16). Mentioning the enthronement at this point in the narrative characterizes the following activity as part of the transition to Solomon's reign. Furthermore, David is the only king in Chronicles who enthrones his own son. By mentioning this fact, the Chronicler connects the reigns of David and Solomon closely together, emphasizing the stability of the kingdom of all Israel in the transition from David to Solomon.

> #### Enthroned the First Time
> The MT in 1 Chronicles 29:22 indicates that David enthroned Solomon "a second time," thereby presenting this verse as an earlier private ceremony. Without this note, the activity here is more likely a general statement, with the specifics of the activity detailed in the following chapters. Other ANE texts describe a double enthronement, private and then public (see Peterson 2018, 564–73), so such an idea is natural in the context.

23:2. Next, the Chronicler introduces the following lists by describing David's activity. David gathers Israel's leaders, priests, and Levites to assign them various positions and provide them with various instructions. Interestingly, the lists occur in the inverse of their mention here: a list of Levites, priests, and then the leaders.

> #### Two Types of Assembling
> The verb occurring here אסף ("to gather") carries different connotations in Chronicles than the verb קהל ("to gather"; 1 Chron. 28:1). In 28:1 the verb communicates a sense of a national ceremony. Here, the verb refers to gathering a group to provide assignments and instructions for them (see Wright 1991, 230–31).

Levitical Personnel (23:3–26:32)

David demonstrates his devotion to YHWH by meticulously organizing the priests and Levites for proper ritual worship in the future Jerusalem temple and for other service to the rest of Israel.

The rest of chapters 23–26 contain lists of Levitical personnel serving in the ritual worship at the Jerusalem temple and serving as officials within Israel's royal administration. Even though these chapters contain several distinct lists, these lists communicate several points in common. An examination of the lists in general reveals some of the following points.

First, the fact that Chronicles includes these lists points to the meticulous care that David has for the future temple and for the nation Israel. John Sailhamer draws the following analogy: "Like a mother planning the wedding of an only child, David gave every detail his full time and attention" (1983, 57). Although it is unusual in contemporary literature to include detailed lists of this nature, these details reveal the importance of the temple, its worship, and its personnel. One can discern a similar strategy in Ezekiel's detailed description of the temple in Ezekiel 40–48. Furthermore, by recording how David organized the temple personnel in the last days of his reign, these lists present David's legacy in a positive way as he sets up the temple personnel for the future (Wright 1991, 234–37, 241).

Second, the lists show that even as David introduces new patterns into Israel's worship, he does so by building on Israel's tradition. The changes in historical circumstances (i.e., rise of the Davidic monarchy and construction of Jerusalem temple) lead to these innovations, but the innovations are still rooted in Israel's past. For instance, as David creates new administrative structures for the Levites, he organizes them according to their genealogy, drawing on tradition, especially the Pentateuch (Jonker 2013a, 150). Furthermore, one can detect the influence of the Pentateuch in the vocabulary used for census summaries (cf. 1 Chron. 23:24 to Num. 1) and for the descriptions of the duties of the priests and Levites. In the list of priestly duties (1 Chron. 24:19), the Chronicler draws closely from Deuteronomy 10:8. David describes the duties of the Levites based on Numbers 3:5–8; 18:2–7, but he expands their duties because the Levites no longer need to carry the tabernacle and its implements (as set forth in Mosaic law), since Solomon will build the temple in Jerusalem (1 Chron. 23:26). Even the age associated with Levitical service varies according to patterns of the Pentateuch and the changing circumstances of the temple (cf. 1 Chron. 23:3, 24–27). These connections to the Pentateuch indicate David's concern to obey the Mosaic law even as he responds to changing circumstances.

> ### Shifting Ages of Levitical Service
> The shift in age from thirty (1 Chron. 23:3) to twenty (1 Chron. 23:24, 27) results from the shift in the Levites' duties. Numbers 4 indicates that the Levites should be at least thirty years old and that their responsibility is to carry the tabernacle and its implements, including the ark. Since the tabernacle and ark will remain in the future temple in Jerusalem, the age requirement associated with the task of carrying them is no longer needed.

Third, the lists show that the organization of the Levites takes place under proper sources of authority. Not only does David authorize the assignments as king, but Zadok and Ahimelek authorize the assignments as priests. To preserve the integrity of the assignments, the Levitical scribe records the assignments for future generations. Furthermore, by assigning the duties according to lot (as occurs repeatedly), the lists demonstrate that the assignments are impartial, determined by YHWH's will rather than human manipulation. The lists repeatedly record the use of lots and the impartiality demonstrated in using them (priests: 1 Chron. 24:5–6; Levites: 1 Chron. 24:31; musicians: 1 Chron. 25:8; gatekeepers: 1 Chron. 26:13). As a result, the lists represent a legitimate, authorized organization of the personnel carrying out YHWH's ritual worship within the Jerusalem temple.

Fourth, the lists center around the number twelve and its multiples. David assigns twenty-four thousand Levites to oversee care of the sanctuary (1 Chron. 23:4). David organizes the priests into twenty-four divisions (1 Chron. 24:3–4). The musicians consist of 288 serving, that is, twenty-four divisions consisting of twelve musicians each. Although the text does not indicate the theological significance of arranging the personnel around the number twelve, these lists tie the number to the calendar, likely indicating that the priestly divisions reflect something inherent in creation. Furthermore, the consistent use of twelve and its multiples contributes to the picture of order for Israel during the final days of David's reign.

Fifth, the lists concern the Levites, that is, members of the tribe of Levi. The lists clearly demonstrate that the tribe of Levi has been set aside for special service to YHWH, especially service focusing on Israel's worship. As a result, it is no surprise that the list includes the priests. At the same time, Chronicles distinguishes the priests from the Levites, even within the lists themselves (1 Chron. 24:6, 31). In this case, the designation "Levites" refers to a more specific group: those who assist the priests in making offerings and who care for the sanctuary and its implements (1 Chron. 23:28–32). One may refer to this specific group as cultic Levites (Jonker 2013a, 148–49). The lists demonstrate the importance of the tribe of Levi by presenting the following roles its members fulfill in Israel: priests, cultic Levites, musicians, gatekeepers, officials, and judges (see also 1 Chron. 23:4–5).

Overview of Levites (23:3–32)

23:3. This list presents how David organizes the tribe of Levi into divisions to ensure that Israel's ritual worship at the temple occurs properly and consistently. The list of Levitical personnel begins with a census. This census differs from 1 Chronicles 21: it is not a general census to determine military strength but a special census to organize the Levites for ritual worship in the future Jerusalem temple. As a result, this census does not incur YHWH's wrath.

23:13–14. The genealogy of Levi includes Moses and Aaron. Aaron's descendants are distinguished from the rest of the Levitical tribe because they serve as priests. The priests are distinguished to fulfill certain tasks. First, the priests sanctify the implements found in YHWH's sanctuary (see Num. 4:4–15). This task reflects the holiness of the sanctuary, since common, mundane items are not appropriate for use in YHWH's sanctuary. Second, the priests make offerings to YHWH. Third, the priests attend to YHWH by setting out the shewbread and lighting the lamps each day. Fourth, the priests pronounce blessings in YHWH's name. Numbers 6:24–27 records this type of blessing, which results in placing YHWH's name on the people and requesting YHWH's favor upon them. In contrast, even though the list recognizes the special status of Moses as "the man of God," his descendants are not priests, but included among the other Levites.

23:25–26. Following this list of Levites, David reflects on the significance of Jerusalem. He highlights two points. First, YHWH has granted Israel rest from their enemies. Chronicles portrays Israel's rest as a necessary condition for building the temple (1 Chron. 17:9–10). Furthermore, Solomon, the man of rest, rather than David, the man of war, will build the temple (1 Chron. 22:8–9). In David's final days, he points out that YHWH has fulfilled this condition. Second, David mentions that YHWH dwells in Jerusalem forever. As a result, there is no longer a need for the tabernacle and ark to move from place to place. Furthermore, by mentioning Jerusalem as YHWH's dwelling place within the listing of cultic personnel and connecting it to Israel's rest, David depicts the Jerusalem temple as a fundamental institution within Israel's life as YHWH's people (Knoppers 2004, 813).

23:28–32. Considering both Pentateuchal instruction and the building of the temple, David outlines the duties for the Levites. These Levites assist the priests so that Israel can conduct its regular, proper ritual worship. They assist in several ways: (1) in maintaining the temple's courts and chambers, (2) in purifying the holy implements, (3) in securing the proper measures and types of flour products used in offerings, (4) in accompanying the daily offerings with musical praise, (5) in preparing animals for sacrifice, and (6) in attending to whatever needs arise within the temple among the priests as they conduct Israel's ritual worship. By listing how the Levites serve alongside the priests, David tries to ensure Israel's proper worship for generations to come.

Priests (24:1–19)
This passage lists what members make up the priestly divisions (i.e., groups for service) and how, under Davidic and priestly authority, the casting of lots determines the assignment for each division.

24:5. This verse highlights the important role priests play in Israel's worship by referring to them using two unusual expressions: "officers of holiness" and "officers of God." The expressions likely draw on an analogy between the official of the royal court and the officials of the temple court. As a result, the priests are holy officials, that is, dealing with holy (religious) matters. Just as the royal court plays a key role in Israel's well-being, so also does the temple. As result, "the priests share responsibility, together with monarchs and the people themselves, for the fate of the nation" (Knoppers 2004, 833).

TRANSLATION ANALYSIS:
The expressions referring to the priests pose two issues for translators. First, most translators render the phrase שָׂרֵי־קֹדֶשׁ along the lines of "officers of the sanctuary." Such a rendering is possible, although it would be more likely if the second word possessed an article. As it stands without an article, the sense is more likely "officers of holiness," that is, holy officers. Second, the translations generally render the phrase שָׂרֵי הָאֱלֹהִים as "officers of God" (except for NKJV, "officers of the house of God"). The phrase can be superlative ("highest officers"), but in this case, it occurs in apposition to the previous phrase. Therefore, the translation "officers of God" is preferred.

24:19. Priestly service carries significant risk. Failure to act appropriately within the sanctuary can lead to disastrous results (e.g., Nadab and Abihu, 1 Chron. 24:2; cf. Lev. 10:1–2). To avoid such consequences, the priests should follow the instructions of their ancestor Aaron. This comment alludes back in general to instructions regarding priestly procedure, as observed in the Pentateuch.

Levites (24:20–31)
24:20–31. Following the list of priests, the passage returns its focus to the other Levites. The list repeats much of the information from 1 Chronicles 23, but it omits some genealogical lines (most notably Gershon) and extends others by one generation. The reasons for the changes are not clear; however, the theme of the passage is clear: the same authorities and means for determining priestly assignments also determine these Levitical assignments.

Musicians (25:1–31)
This passage lists the Levitical musicians who perform as a part of Israel's ritual worship within the sanctuary and the assignments made for the major musician families (Asaph, Heman, and Jeduthun).

25:1. The passage introduces the musicians by describing their activity as "prophesying" with musical instruments. The text describes the musicians' activity as prophesying for three reasons: (1) Chronicles highlights how Levites fulfill prophetic tasks, especially mediating God's message to his people (e.g., Jahaziel, 2 Chron. 20:14), (2) the Chronicler likely understands the songs of Israel's worship to be divinely inspired (cf. 1 Chron. 16 to Pss. 96, 105, and 106), and (3) these musicians serve within the royal court as advisors (seers) to King David (1 Chron. 25:2, 5–6). Assigning the royal Levitical musicians to an integral part of Israel's ritual worship within the sanctuary is one of David's lasting legacies (2 Chron. 29:25–30; 35:15).

Gatekeepers (26:1–19)

This passage lists the divisions and assignments of those who serve as gatekeepers. Although gatekeepers perform various tasks, their primary function is to serve as a "security force" for the sanctuary, protecting its sanctity (Wright 1990, 69–79). As a result, the list focuses on their competence, especially their military ability.

26:4–8. The text mentions Obed-edom among the gatekeepers. Although the text is not explicit, this Obed-edom is likely the same person who receives the ark after David's first failed attempt to deliver it to Jerusalem (1 Chron. 13:13). When the ark arrives, YHWH blesses the house of Obed-edom (1 Chron. 13:14); 26:5 here specifies YHWH's blessing as numerous children.

Large Families as Blessing

Throughout Chronicles, having many children is a blessing. Two observations are important to recognize. First, the Chronicler is concerned with genealogy and the preservation of the genealogical lines from the past to his present and into the future. Without children, the people of Israel would come to an end. Second, Chronicles emphasizes duties that are passed down genealogically. Therefore, the Chronicler brings out this theme when addressing Levitical singers (Heman, 1 Chron. 25:5), gatekeepers (Obed-edom, 1 Chron. 26:5), and kings (e.g., Rehoboam, 2 Chron. 11:18–23; Abijah, 2 Chron. 13:21; see also R. Klein 2012, 176).

Officials (26:20–32)

This passage lists the roles and responsibilities of Levites who are not assigned directly to work in the ritual service of the sanctuary. They serve as treasurers, officials, and judges.

26:20–28. Several Levites oversee the treasuries of the temple. These treasuries include the regular offerings in the treasuries of the temple (26:20, 22) and exceptional offerings in treasuries of the dedicated gifts (26:20, 26). The dedicated gifts include offerings made from the spoils of war (Merrill 2015, 288 n. 36). The text specifies several who make such offerings, emphasizing that all Israel, past and present, plays a role in constructing and maintaining the temple (Boda 2010a, 200).

26:29–32. Other Levites serve as officials and judges. Although the text does not describe the specific duties of each role, the following is likely: the officials administer the law, while the judges determine whether someone has violated the law and the consequences if one has done so (Merrill 2015, 288 n. 39). Their roles take place outside the temple, addressing both religious and political pursuits of the nation. Including these officials shows that David recognizes that the Levites are significant for the nation beyond just their roles at the temple; even secular affairs benefit from their oversight.

Political Personnel (27:1–34)

During David's last days, he organizes the military, tribal, and royal administrations into an ordered system that will provide a smooth transition to Solomon's reign and serve Israel well into the future.

Two observations regarding the lists in 1 Chronicles 23–26 apply to the lists of personnel in 1 Chronicles 27 as well. First, including the lists points to David's meticulous care in organizing Israel for its future success. These lists demonstrate how David organizes the political personnel to secure Israel's peace, provide tribal leadership, oversee royal assets, and contribute advice. In this way, David creates structures to benefit Israel in the future.

Second, the lists repeatedly build off the number twelve. David assigns twelve military divisions composed of twenty-four thousand, each division serving one month of the year. As before, this number ties the structure to the calendar so that the structure likely reflects something inherent in creation. Furthermore, the consistent use of the number points to the order and symmetry of the administration. At the same time, the number twelve is not the only number to play a role; the number seven also shows up in the list of royal advisors (1 Chron. 27:32–34). This number carries a sense of perfection or completeness, reflecting the calendar week and pointing to something inherent in creation.

Finally, the final chapters of 1 Chronicles demonstrate how David prepares for Solomon's reign and the task of building the temple. David secures the land through many battles so that Solomon may be a man of rest (1 Chron. 22:8–9). David sets aside numerous resources for the building of the temple, even leading all Israel to give generously as well (1 Chron. 22:14–16; 29:3–8). In the previous chapters, David organizes all the Levites for their service around the temple and throughout Israel. In this chapter, David organizes the military and tribal leaders as well as royal administrators and advisors. Because of David's preparation, the kingdom can smoothly transition to Solomon, and Solomon can begin building the temple.

Military Divisions (27:1–15)

This passage lists the twelve leaders of the military divisions, consisting of twenty-four thousand, who rotate in their service to the king one month per year. The list depicts Israel as always prepared for any threat. At the same time, Chronicles has already presented David's reign as a time of military success. As a result, some of the information in this list overlaps with information mentioned previously in Chronicles (e.g., Benaiah; 1 Chron. 11:22–25 // 1 Chron. 27:5–6). However, the list in 1 Chronicles 27 differs from previous lists of David's warriors because this list does not focus on their accomplishments but presents them as part of a larger military structure: a "national institution centered in Jerusalem" (Knoppers 2004, 904).

27:6–7. These verses list Benaiah and Asahel as commanders of two divisions; however, the verses also mention their sons. Asahel dies before David ever rules over all Israel (2 Sam. 2:23); as a result, even though the list honors Asahel as a division commander, his son Zebadiah commands the troops. Since 1 Chronicles 27:6 mentions Benaiah's son Amizabad, the situation may be similar: Benaiah's role is honorary whereas Amizabad commands the troops (Boda 2010a, 204; Japhet 1993, 476).

Tribal Leaders (27:16–24)

This passage lists the tribal leaders of Israel. The list contains thirteen names, each leading the following groups: Reuben, Simeon, Levi, Aaron, Judah, Issachar, Zebulun, Naphtali, Ephraim, half of Manasseh, the other half of Manasseh in Gilead, Benjamin, and Dan. Notably, two tribal names are omitted: Asher and Gad. Their absence is likely intentional; the list intends to present twelve tribal leaders. Omitting these tribes makes sense since Asher and Gad occur last in other lists of Jacob's sons (Gen. 35:26; 1 Chron. 2:2; see Knoppers 2004, 896). The thirteenth name in the list is a result of distinguishing the leader of the Levites from that of the priests (Aaron). By drawing on the tribal structures of Israel, the list portrays how Israel's traditional structure now fits within David's royal administration in an ordered, complete fashion.

27:23–24. Following the listing of tribal leaders, the Chronicler makes a note regarding David's numbering of the people: David does not number those twenty years of age or younger. Numbering those under twenty years old both violates the principle set forth in Mosaic law (Num. 1:3) and casts aspersions on YHWH's promise to bless Abraham with innumerable descendants like the stars of the sky (Gen. 22:17). Even though David does not number those under twenty, counting the people still results in YHWH's wrath. Furthermore, even though Joab starts counting the people, he does not finish. This picture reflects the events in 1 Chronicles 21, but such a connection does not explain why the comment occurs here. Determining the reason for including this comment involves examining the structure of the list of leaders. No numbers accompany the list of tribal leaders; therefore, this comment explains that such numbers do not occur because Joab never completes a full census recorded in the Chronicles of King David, a source no longer available beyond what is recorded in Chronicles itself.

Royal Administrators (27:25–31)

27:25–31. This passage lists the administrators assigned to oversee various royal properties and national assets, emphasizing a sense of order and completeness for the administration of the nation's resources. The list encompasses all Israel, including the royal treasures (most likely in Jerusalem) and those throughout various locations in the land (27:25). The list also encompasses all kinds of agricultural activity (farming, cultivating vineyards, cultivating forests, and animal husbandry). Finally, the list contains twelve names, pointing to the well-organized and complete structure of the royal administration.

Royal Advisors (27:32–34)

27:32–34. This passage lists several members of David's personal advisors, rounding out the picture of David's administration in his last days. Chronicles has already addressed David's

royal court (1 Chron. 18:15–17); however, this list appears to list those with close personal ties to King David, regardless of their formal role in the administration. As a result, the list includes figures with a range of duties: from David's uncle Jonathan, a wise scribe, to Jehiel, who cared for the king's sons (not necessarily limited to his biological offspring; Knoppers 2004, 910–11); to Joab, the commander of the military. Despite the diversity, the number of advisors listed is seven. The number signifies that even though the list contains a range of persons with different roles, they fit into a complete system.

For the first readers, David's organizing Israel's religious and political administration had practical implications for their own practices. First, the lists served as references for determining the roles of inhabitants returning to Yehud, at least at some point in the postexilic period (Ezra 2:59–62). Even though the lists do not extend into the generations of the postexilic community, they did provide historical touchpoints for assigning responsibilities to certain individuals based on their genealogical records. Second, the lists validated the roles and organization of the temple personnel as priests and Levites. As a result, the postexilic community would expect the same roles and organization in the temple of their own time. In this way, not only did the text provide a picture of which families participated in Israel's ritual worship in the past but also what functions those various families fulfilled in the past. Third, the lists authorized these families, their roles, and their organization because the assignments were made by proper authorities: David, Levitical priests, and the will of YHWH (through the casting of lots). As a final consequence of these practical points, the lists encouraged the postexilic community to pay careful attention to the personnel of the temple and their political administration both for YHWH's worship and their own well-being. One important way to show such care was to visit and support the temple with sacrifices and offerings.

THEOLOGICAL FOCUS

Worshipping YHWH is a serious task of obedience, worthy of meticulous care and consideration, resulting in blessing.

Contemporary readers of these lists do not share the same practical concerns from the text as the first readers had: concern for tracing the lineages, assigning the proper priestly and Levitical roles and structures, or supporting the temple through sacrifices and offerings. At the same time, these lists reveal several theological points that are important beyond the concerns of the first readers.

The lists present David as a good king who worships YHWH in such a way that he creates a long-lasting legacy. What appears particularly important is the meticulous care David takes in organizing the worship. Meticulous care for YHWH's worship, not only for the present but even into the future, is a great virtue for anyone serious about worshipping YHWH and continuing that worship beyond the scope of one's place and time. Not only can one ensure that future worship takes place by teaching the truth regarding who God is and what he has done, but also this passage points to David's work in organizing, promoting, and materially supporting that worship into future generations. Although contemporary readers are not kings of ancient Israel, God still opens the doors for some to worship him through carefully planning, organizing, and supporting future worship by planning, organizing, and supporting current ministries.

As these lists say something about David, they also say something about YHWH: YHWH accepts this type of ordered worship. In fact, the text would suggest that YHWH delights in worship that is orderly and harmonious. Paul, speaking about worship in the churches, appears to draw on this same understanding of God's approach to worship when he speaks of God as "not a God of disorder but of peace" (1 Cor. 14:33). The harmonious quality of the worship speaks to the harmonious quality of God.

Looking beyond the nature of worship, the lists point to the result of worship: blessing. The lists focus on the future material blessings of Israel as a nation, particularly the peaceful transition from David to Solomon. At the same time David, from his perspective, would never experience the benefit of his work in preparing the temple and royal administrations; his reward would come beyond his lifetime. Consequently, even beyond the historical situation described and even beyond the context of the first readers, the lists present a pattern of YHWH's activity: he blesses those who worship and obey him. This truth remains into the New Testament era; as Paul says, "So let's not get tired of doing what is good. At just the right time we will reap a harvest of blessing if we don't give up" (Gal. 6:9 NLT).

PREACHING AND TEACHING STRATEGIES

Exegetical and Theological Synthesis

God wanted us to know about the meticulous planning David had initiated in order to provide for the ongoing worship of YHWH. This passage was written to teach the exilic and postexilic communities of Israel, and the church, about the importance of worship. Of course, how we worship has changed dramatically from that of the temple, but the "how" is not the focus of this passage. The Chronicler describes the structure of the personnel of worship and the personnel for sustaining the nation. This is David's organizational chart for worship.

The New Testament clearly commands us to meet together to worship (Eph. 5:19–20; Col. 3:16; Heb. 11:25); the Old Testament commanded the same. Though what happens when we meet is different, it still requires clear and structured organization. Worship has changed, but God has not and neither have we. We still need a structure in which to find the freedom to express God's glory. Our structures for those who lead us in worship and what we do in worship will vary greatly. The common directive from this passage is that corporate worship requires detailed planning. There is a place for purely spontaneous worship, which is wonderful, but this most often occurs in individual worship. If we are to worship corporately there must be structure, or it can't take place. Something as simple as a time and place must be communicated. This passage teaches us that church leaders must do the meticulous work of planning worship services, from defining roles to being prepared to lead. Church members must support the leaders and the structures they implement. When the church gathers to worship there should be adequate preparation and definition of roles so that worship can be experienced by all.

The details of this text paint a clear picture of orderly and structured corporate worship, which results in the blessing of God being glorified. While the details of our worship look different, the theme of the painting is the same: meaningful corporate worship requires meticulous work.

Preaching Idea
Meaningful corporate worship begins with meticulous work.

Contemporary Connections

What does it mean?
If you've been to a formal professional development seminar or the informal weekly Monday morning company staff meeting, you've heard them. They show up with different wording and different pictures on the motivational posters hung in break rooms and classrooms. They read something like: "Good ideas boils down to hard work"; "Opportunity usually comes with hard work so most people miss it"; "Good things don't just happen; they come from hard work." This passage focuses on the hard work of setting up the personnel structure and orderliness of worship. If we were to paraphrase its application it would read something like, "If you want to have wonderful worship, it takes work."

As I write this, I am listening to a grand choral arrangement of the chorus "Our God Reigns." Musical productions such as these of course require rehearsal, but think about what happens even before rehearsals—training, writing, individual practicing, first run-through. If the choir and orchestra are to participate, they must have a clear structure. People don't just show up and say, "Hey let's put together a great chorus of praise to God." It takes a director, section leaders, musical scores given to musicians, and many more details. A clear structure prompts the involvement of each musician. Organizing personnel, planning content, and preparing ahead of time allows for more meaningful music and for more meaningful worship.

Is it true?
God made us to live and work with others. When people come together, great things can be accomplished. I saw this clearly in two very different worlds. In my younger days I worked for an electrical contractor building power lines, the big ones called highlines. An old lineman was complaining about an overzealous foreman who wanted to get everything done ASAP. The old lineman put down his tools and, taking a drink of water in a paper cup, suggested to the foreman, "You need to ease up; highlines aren't built in a day and you can't build them by yourself."

Construction projects have a very rigid organizational chart, including both who does what and how and when it needs to get done. I found the same need for structure in the world of theater. A play is performed only after much work, which comes out a structure of directors, lighting and sound crews, actors, and many other contributors. This is affirmed by the old theater adage, "There are no small parts, only small actors." Successful productions are about *we*, not *me*.

Our corporate worship requires the same preparatory hard work as construction projects and theater performances. The hard work that this passage prompts us to engage in is not about construction or performance; it is about leading the church to worship. Musicians and pastors must give attention to what preparation is required to encourage and engage the church in worship.

Now what?

It was rare, but occasionally a seminary student would come to my preaching class unprepared to preach. Clark was naturally gifted as a speaker, and he knew it. He at least opened the Bible and read from it, but it was clear that he had invested little or nothing in preparation. Since he'd had weeks in which he should have been preparing, there was no excuse. He not only received a low grade, but also received a one-on-one lecture from the professor (me): "Clark, you are a gifted speaker, but never again step into the pulpit the way you did today. God's Word and God's people deserve your hard work to prepare." Fortunately, he received the rebuke with contrition and grace.

Pastors and teachers must prepare the content of sermons and lessons. So too, those responsible for leading worship service must prepare. Of course, this will vary with traditions and the size of the congregation. This preparation is not just with the content and familiarity with the music; there must also be a clear structure of personnel and order. This does not rule out spontaneity prompted by the Spirit or by healthy creativity. That can take place, but in the context of some kind of order. The point is, corporate worship takes planning, so leaders must plan and congregations should expect and respect those plans.

God told the ancient Israelites, and he is telling us, that corporate worship requires us to get organized and stay organized. It takes meticulous work. Run from laziness in preparing for worship. Remember that the work is not to show our excellence but to help the congregation see God's excellence.

Creativity in Presentation

God inspired this list for our benefit. It is not a story and can't be presented as a story. So how does one present a list to benefit those not on the list? The historical setting can help. How this list was communicated or read in David's time is not clear, but somehow this information was communicated to those on the list. To make the importance of this list more apparent to modern listeners, perhaps one could incorporate a current example of a posting of a list of those who made the team, got a part in a play, or some other setting in which people are eager to see who is on the list. Another historical setting is that of the exilic and postexilic communities hearing this list and recognizing their family name or tribe. If appropriate, physical lists could be posted around the pulpit and used as the text is presented.

When it comes to the reading of the text, it would probably be wise to read only representative names from each of the categories articulated by Dr. Williams above. As each category is introduced, an explanation of the duties of that group would allow the congregation to grasp the breadth of David's structure.

When presenting a text such as this the introduction is particularly important, because when listeners see that the text is a long list, the tendency is to not see the relevance. Thus, making the subject clear and articulating the need is most important. Perhaps begin by asking, "We all want to have meaningful worship. What do we need to do to accomplish this? What does God tell us that can help ensure that our worship is not only pleasing to him but beneficial to us?" Help the congregation stay focused by asking them at the beginning of the sermon to think about what God might want us to learn about worship from these lists. As the text is presented, an occasional applicational comment could remind the listeners that there is a fuller application coming.

When the differences between Old and New Testament worship are mentioned, it would be a great time to explain how Jesus's death and resurrection changed everything and how faith in him gives us the most meaningful worship. Here is one possible structure:

- Introduction
  - Need
    - Highlight our desire for the benefit of meaningful worship
  - Subject
    - What can we do to help ensure meaningful worship?
  - Historical setting
    - The temple was about to be built.
    - Who will be doing what?
- Present (selections from) the lists
  - Levitical personnel (23:3–26:32)
    - Levites (23:3–32)
    - Priests (24:1–19)
    - Levites (24:20–31)
    - Musicians (25:1–31)
    - Gatekeepers (26:1–19)
    - Officials (26:20–32)
  - Political Personnel (27:1–34)
    - Military divisions (27:1–15)
    - Tribal leaders (27:16–24)
    - Royal administrators (27:25–31)
    - Royal advisors (27:32–34)
- Application
  - Clear personnel structure
  - Sense of order
  - Provision of support
- Meaningful corporate worship begins with meticulous work.

DISCUSSION QUESTIONS

1. What are the benefits and shortcomings of organizational charts?

2. What are some issues involved in setting up an organizational chart?

3. When we are part of a group working on a project, what do we need to know?

4. What kind of structure have you experienced in a sports team, musical or theater production, work project, etc.?

5. How important was this structure?

6. Why is organizing people hard?

7. Why is organizing people important?

1 Chronicles 28:1–21

EXEGETICAL IDEA
YHWH chose Solomon to lead Israel in following YHWH, especially by building a temple according to a divinely revealed plan that resembled both the tabernacle and the postexilic temple.

THEOLOGICAL FOCUS
God works according to his plan to dwell with his people, to bless those loyal to him.

PREACHING IDEA
God's supreme royalty demands our complete loyalty.

PREACHING POINTERS
This narrative of motivational speeches to build the temple is more than a pep rally for Solomon and Israel. While there are charges to accomplish that task, there is a deeper lesson for us. God's character is revealed through what is said about God's choice and provision. The God-ordained task to build a temple reveals that God desires to dwell with us. As the story is presented, some of God's characteristics emerge. These characteristics are of a perfect king. We might say he alone is supreme royalty. It is his supreme royalty that commands our complete loyalty to him.

YHWH REVEALS THE PLANS FOR THE TEMPLE
(28:1–21)

LITERARY STRUCTURE
AND THEMES (28:1–21)

After David organizes the temple and royal administrations (1 Chron. 23–27), he assembles all Israel's leaders to charge Solomon and the people to build the temple. This charge closely resembles 1 Chronicles 22. Both passages share several themes (e.g., David's desire to build the temple, David's role in waging war, and Solomon as the temple builder) and allude both to YHWH's promise to David in 1 Chronicles 17 and to Joshua's charge to take the land (Deut. 31:23; Josh. 1:6–9). However, the setting for each charge differs. In 1 Chronicles 22 David charges Solomon and Israel's leaders privately in an informal setting; in 1 Chronicles 28 David charges them publicly in a formal, national gathering.

This passage consists of four units. The first unit primarily contains David's address to Israel about building the temple. This speech records David alternating between what YHWH has spoken and what David is speaking. Following this address to Israel, David admonishes Solomon to follow YHWH. This brief charge focuses on devotion to YHWH rather than focusing on the specific task of building the temple. The third unit is a narrative describing the plans for the temple that David gives Solomon. These plans describe elements that allude to the wilderness tabernacle, Solomon's temple, and the postexilic temple. The final unit recounts how David admonishes Solomon to build the temple. David uses language that closely resembles the charge to Joshua (Josh. 1:5–9) and focuses on the help that Solomon will receive from YHWH and all Israel.

Repetition of key terms such as "be strong" (חזק), "seek" (דרש), "choose" (בחר), "build" (בנה), and "house" (בַּיִת) holds the passage together (Japhet 1993, 484). Furthermore, after each major unit (1–8; 11–19), the text records David's charge to Solomon to have courage to act.

- ***David Addresses Israel About Building the Temple (28:1–8)***
- ***David Admonishes Solomon to Follow YHWH (28:9–10)***
- ***David Gives Solomon Plans for the Temple (28:11–19)***
- ***David Admonishes Solomon to Build the Temple (28:20–21)***

EXPOSITION (28:1–21)

Contemporary culture tends to put less value on what is old, including long-standing institutions. Innovation and novelty are generally regarded more highly than tradition and stability. However, in the biblical context, people valued what was old, including traditions and institutions. As a result, while the postexilic community faced several challenges that required innovation and change, they sought what was rooted in the past. This passage focuses on one such institution: the temple in Jerusalem. The postexilic temple was a new building, and locations outside Jerusalem were building temples as well (e.g., Elephantine and Leontopolis). In this passage, the Chronicler looks back to Solomon's temple to demonstrate that it carried forward the traditions of the wilderness tabernacle, rooting the temple in the formative years of Israel as a people. Furthermore, the Chronicler looks to the postexilic Jerusalem temple to show that it carries forward those same traditions and therefore is rooted in this same past. In this past, YHWH established his relationship with Israel as his people. The Chronicler highlights that the temple is part of YHWH's plan for Israel by showing that YHWH chose Solomon to build the Jerusalem temple, that YHWH revealed the plan for this temple to David, and that the temple retains elements of the tabernacle essential for proper worship.

David Addresses Israel About Building the Temple (28:1–8)

David assembles Israel's leaders to assure them that YHWH has chosen Solomon to be king over Israel and to build the temple if he obeys YHWH's commandments; therefore, following Solomon's lead, the people must devote themselves to YHWH by obeying his commands so that they may remain securely in their land.

28:1. Previously in 1 Chronicles 22, David charged Solomon in a private setting to rule over Israel and to build the Jerusalem temple. Now David charges Solomon in a public address before Israel's leaders. David assembles these leaders for a national ceremony to inaugurate Solomon's rule (1 Chron. 29:22–24) and to call Solomon to his appointed task of building the temple.

The listing of leaders recalls 1 Chronicles 27, showing that David's administrative work has prepared the way for Solomon to fulfill his role as king and temple-builder. The makeup of the list points to the Chronicler's reason for including this address. Since the list includes only military and administrative leaders, David is rallying the secular leadership to support the temple's construction and ongoing service. Even though the priests and Levites are present at the speech (see 28:21), the list does not include them because, as temple personnel, their support is assumed. Therefore, David's words intend to encourage the first readers to support the Jerusalem temple in their day (Boda 2010a, 211).

Military and Administrative Posts

The listing of leaders consists of military and administrative positions. It lists military officers (leaders of thousands and hundreds) along with trained warriors. It also lists administrative positions (attendants to the king, stewards over the royal possessions) along with other administrative staff. The word used to describe the staff is traditionally "eunuch," but the translation is debated. For more details on the translation, see Grayson 1995, 89–97; Tadmor 1995, 317–25; Yamauchi 1980, 132–42.

28:2. Once David assembles the leaders, he rises to address them. David encourages those assembled as his brothers and his people to pay attention to his words. David reminds them that he desired to build a temple (for the expression used here, see comments on 1 Chron. 22:7) and even prepared for it (see 1 Chron. 17:1). David wanted to build a permanent structure for the ark to rest.

Significance of Rising to His Feet

David rises to his feet to address the people. This action is appropriate for making a public address (cf. 1 Kings 8:22, 54; 2 Chron. 13:4; Knoppers 2004, 925). Some detect an allusion to Moses, who remained vigorous even as he was approaching his death (e.g., Japhet 1993, 486); however, there is insufficient evidence to suggest such a theme.

The language of rest is an important theme for temple construction in Chronicles; however, here it functions differently. Before this passage, rest for Israel serves as a prerequisite for building the temple (cf. Deut. 12:8–12; 1 Chron. 22:9); however, here the rest applies to the ark, also referred to as God's footstool in this verse. This language of "rest" and "footstool" combines images from other OT passages: Numbers 10:33–36 and Psalm 132:7–8. Numbers 10:33–36 describes how the ark precedes the people as a sign of YHWH as a warrior, leading his people into rest (for use of "rest" here, see R. Klein 2006, 520). Psalm 132:7–8 describes YHWH and the ark coming to a resting place where Israel may worship him. The psalm refers to the ark as a footstool, depicting YHWH as a king who sits on a throne and "rests his feet not on the ground but a splendid footstool" (Merrill 2015, 299). Combining these images summarizes David's reign: YHWH has fought for Israel (e.g., 1 Chron. 18:6, 13), providing them rest from their enemies (1 Chron. 22:17), and upon the building of the temple, he will come to rest like a king upon his throne.

28:3. Despite David's desire to build a temple, YHWH prohibits him from doing so. The text reveals two important points regarding this prohibition. First, David employs the language of direct speech ("God said to me") to show that the prohibition is truly YHWH's will. Furthermore, the language presents David like a prophet, hearing God's word. This presentation continues a trend in the Chronicler's portrayal of David. Beginning in 1 Chronicles 22, the Chronicler portrays David in more prophetic terms. This prophetic picture reaches its most direct expression in 28:19 (see further commentary on 1 Chron. 22:7–8). Second, the prohibition is based on David's role as king within YHWH's plan for Israel. Since David fought many wars against Israel's enemies to secure the land fully, he would not be the temple-builder (regarding securing the land fully, see comments on 1 Chron. 22:17–18). The timing for building the temple was not right (since Israel needed to have rest) and the act of shedding blood in battle left David ritually unclean (see comments for 1 Chron. 22:17–18). In fact, the text characterizes David as a "man of war," a direct contrast to Solomon, the "man of rest" (1 Chron. 22:9). For these reasons, YHWH prohibits David from building a temple.

28:4. Although YHWH prohibits David from building a temple, YHWH does not reject David.

David points out that YHWH has taken pleasure in choosing David as king forever. David describes YHWH's choice in a manner resembling the casting of lots, whereby YHWH narrows his selection from Judah (see 1 Chron. 5:2; cf. Gen. 49:8), to the house of Jesse, and finally to David. This description of YHWH's choice reveals that the choice does not coincide with the natural processes of dynastic succession or the right of the firstborn. Unlike the Persian ruler Darius, who emphasized his royal lineage as a sign of divine choice, David recognizes that his lineage does not secure him the throne (Knoppers 2004, 938–39). YHWH has made him king by acting contrary to normal conventions. YHWH is not bound to such conventions.

> **David as King Forever**
> By describing David as king forever, the Chronicler shows that he considers the promises of Nathan's oracle (1 Chron. 17:7–14) "to be valid in perpetuity" (Knoppers 2004, 927).

28:5. Although YHWH is free to act beyond normal conventions, he is also free to act within them. David announces that YHWH has chosen Solomon to be king. Since Solomon is David's son, YHWH's choice coincides with the conventional means of dynastic succession. However, David also points out that Solomon is one of many sons. Like David, Solomon is not the firstborn; therefore, YHWH's choice runs contrary to the conventional right of the firstborn. Furthermore, David makes a parenthetical comment ("for YHWH has given me many sons") to highlight YHWH's freedom (since there is more than one son) and to recall YHWH's blessing on David (since having many sons is a sign of blessing; see sidebar "Large Families as Blessing"). David presents YHWH's free choice and blessing of David and Solomon as confirmation that YHWH favors the Davidic line.

David further relates the rule of the Davidic line with the kingdom of YHWH. Alluding back to YHWH's promise to David in 1 Chronicles 17:4–14, David states that Solomon will occupy the throne of YHWH's kingdom over Israel. As king, Solomon represents YHWH's rule. The text specifies that this rule is "over Israel," not because YHWH's kingdom is limited to Israel, but Solomon's rule is. YHWH rules over all creation (1 Chron. 16:31–33).

28:6–7. David relays another direct speech from YHWH. Drawing on 1 Chronicles 17:11–14; 22:10, YHWH again employs the language of adoption to describe his relationship with Solomon. This relationship entails YHWH's securing Solomon's throne and Solomon's building the temple and its courtyards. The speech portrays Solomon as a fulfillment of YHWH's promise to David, since Solomon will carry forward the Davidic dynasty and build YHWH's temple in Jerusalem.

Temple Courtyards

Chronicles does not typically mention the courtyards when describing the task of building the temple. However, for most of the first readers, their experience of the temple was almost exclusively limited to the courtyards. Perhaps as a way of addressing these readers, Chronicles mentions them in 28:6 (Japhet 1993, 490).

At the same time, YHWH brings out Solomon's responsibility to obey YHWH's laws to secure Solomon's rule into the future (through a dynasty). This verse raises a significant question for the theology of Chronicles: Is YHWH's promise to David conditional or unconditional? I will not address the question fully here, but I will make four points that I find helpful. First, generally, in Chronicles YHWH's laws refer to stipulations regarding proper worship (e.g., 1 Chron. 16:40; 2 Chron. 7:19; 33:8; 34:31–33). Second, the text demonstrates that Solomon is obeying these laws at the time of David's speech ("as this day"). Third, Chronicles portrays Solomon as an

ideal king and focuses on Solomon and his obedience when addressing the conditions of the covenant (for a detailed discussion of this feature of Chronicles, see Williamson 2004, 176–85). Fourth, Chronicles highlights two truths, unconditional and conditional: (1) Israel is YHWH's people while YHWH is Israel's God, and (2) YHWH rewards obedience while punishing disobedience. YHWH punishes Israel for their disobedience by removing them from their land; however, they remain his people and many return to the land. YHWH's commitment to the Davidic line follows a similar path: YHWH punishes the Davidic line but will one day restore it (for helpful look at conditional and unconditional elements, see Hwang 2017, 239–46).

28:8. After relaying God's message to David, David calls on the people to respond. David tells the people to obey and follow YHWH's commandments (see sidebar "Seeking YHWH"). The text then provides a benefit for Israel's obedience: they will remain in the "good land" in which they now have rest (1 Chron. 22:17–18) and preserve that land from generation to generation as an inheritance. The language of possessing the good land comes from Deuteronomy (see esp. 4:21–22; 6:18) which looks forward to Israel's possessing the land in the conquest. David applies the language of the conquest to his present setting such that possessing the land "is a goal to be achieved in every generation, and observing the commandments provides the means for achieving the goal" (Japhet 2009, 304).

Furthermore, the text shows how the Davidic king parallels Israel as a whole. As David hands over the kingdom to Solomon, so Israel of that generation will hand over the land to the next generation (Knoppers 2004, 928). Furthermore, as Solomon (and future Davidic kings) must obey the law to establish the kingdom, so the people must obey the law to retain the land.

Finally, David marks the significance of Israel's response by calling on two witnesses: (1) all Israel as YHWH's assembly, and (2) YHWH as Israel's God. The language, especially of YHWH's hearing, recalls formal settings of making oaths (e.g., Isa. 5:9; 22:14). Therefore, Israel's response is a solemn duty, and YHWH along with this generation of Israel can testify whether Israel fulfills this duty in the future. Reward or punishment, land or exile, kingdom or service—all these reflect Israel's devotion to YHWH and his commandments.

David Admonishes Solomon to Follow YHWH (28:9–10)

David encourages Solomon as the chosen temple-builder to follow YHWH fully because YHWH rewards obedience but punishes disobedience.

28:9. After addressing the people, David addresses Solomon directly. His words move in two directions. First, they point to the need for Solomon to recognize YHWH as the true king. The text calls on Solomon to know YHWH and serve him. In this context, the word "know" (ידע) reflects covenant contexts in which one party recognizes the other as the lord in the relationship and therefore agrees to follow the lord's covenantal stipulations (Huffmon 1966, 31–33; Knoppers 2004, 929–30). The word "serve" (עבד) confirms this picture (see 1 Chron. 19:19; 2 Chron. 10:4). At the same time, the word "serve" introduces a sense of worship, since the word occurs most often in Chronicles in that capacity. This language indicates that Solomon should not only acknowledge YHWH as his lord but also as his God. As a result, Solomon is to remain fully loyal (the sense of "whole heart and willing mind" [CSB]; 1 Chron. 12:38; 2 Chron. 16:9; 19:9; 25:2) to YHWH, especially since YHWH discerns every person's thoughts, intentions, plans, and the rest, whether good (1 Chron. 29:17) or bad (2 Chron. 24:22).

Discerning Intentions and Thoughts

Although the language recalls the conditions immediately preceding Noah's flood (Gen. 6:5), the language does not necessarily carry negative connotations (see McConville 1986, 105–8).

Second, David's words point to the principle of retribution that governs the relationship between YHWH and Solomon and characterizes the theology of Chronicles. The way YHWH treats Solomon corresponds to the way Solomon treats YHWH. If Solomon seeks YHWH, YHWH will be found. If Solomon abandons YHWH, YHWH will reject him.

28:10. David's words applying the principle of retribution to Solomon raise the possibility that YHWH may reject Solomon; however, David immediately assures Solomon that YHWH has chosen him to build the temple. In other words, YHWH has not rejected Solomon but chosen him. Furthermore, when Solomon seeks YHWH by building the temple, YHWH will be found. The text provides a subtle hint to this fact by referring to Solomon's temple as a sanctuary. The use of "sanctuary" (מִקְדָּשׁ) alludes to the tabernacle where YHWH is found among his people (e.g., Exod. 25:8). In this way, this passage presents one way in which the dynamic of YHWH's choice relates to the principle of retribution. YHWH chooses Solomon to build the temple, and Solomon seeks YHWH by building the temple. Election and retribution coincide. Furthermore, the passage shows that YHWH's choice serves to motivate Solomon to do the task for which YHWH has chosen him: to build the temple.

David Gives Solomon Plans for the Temple (28:11–19)

David delivers Solomon a divinely revealed written plan for the temple in Jerusalem that looks back to the tabernacle and forward to the postexilic temple.

28:11–19. Following David's initial address to the assembly, David hands over a written plan for the temple, its furnishings, and its personnel. In this activity, the text highlights how David resembles Moses. First, the word translated "plan" (תַּבְנִית) occurs for both the tabernacle and the temple. Second, just as Moses received the plan for the tabernacle through divine revelation (Exod. 25:9, 40), the text shows that David receives the plan through divine revelation (1 Chron 28:12, 19). Third, several elements included in the plan correspond to the tabernacle. In this way, David appears as a second Moses, communicating the plan for YHWH's sanctuary, which he receives through divine revelation.

28:11. This verse describes the three main areas of the temple (porch, main building, most holy place) using unconventional language (see R. Klein 2006, 525). Rather than referring to the main building, it refers to some of the various parts, its storehouses and upper and inner chambers. Rather than using the typical expressions of "most holy place" or "inner sanctum," it speaks of the "house of the atonement cover." This unconventional language leads in three directions. The upper and inner chambers relate explicitly to the Solomonic temple, since later in Chronicles the terms apply to the first temple. The expression "house of the atonement cover" points to the tabernacle because the atonement cover repeatedly occurs in contexts regarding the tabernacle but not in contexts regarding the temple (except here). The word translated "storerooms" is a Late Biblical Hebrew term, possibly a Persian loanword (*HALOT* s.v. "גִּנְזָךְ" 199), which does not occur elsewhere in the OT. Its use likely points to a designation used for parts of the second temple. This passage describing the temple plan looks toward these three horizons throughout.

28:12. After addressing the three main areas of the temple, the text moves into more details from what lies around the temple (e.g.,

courtyards) to what lies within the temple (e.g., furnishings). The text points to the comprehensive nature of the plan; however, translations differ regarding what is comprehensive. Many translations (e.g., CSB, ESV, NET, NLT, NRSV) translate the verse so that the plan covers everything David conceives of for the temple. Other translations (e.g., NIV, NKJV) translate the verse so that the plan covers everything David receives by the spirit of God. Although either translation is possible, the text more likely intends to communicate what David receives by revelation rather than what he imagines. As a result, the text also conveys the divine source for the temple plan. Perhaps the text mentions the divine source of the plan because of the differences between Moses's tabernacle plan (as a portable tent) and David's temple plan (as a permanent structure).

TRANSLATION ANALYSIS:
In other similar cases, the Chronicler conveys what a person intends or imagines by using the term "heart" (לֵבָב/לֵב) rather than "spirit/mind" (רוּחַ). For examples, see 1 Chron. 17:2; 22:7; 28:2; 2 Chron. 7:11; 24:4. See also Knoppers 2004, 931; Lynch 2014b, 153–54 n. 72.

28:15–18. The text mentions several specific items among the temple implements. Three things are important to notice about the list. First, many of the items allude to the tabernacle: lampstands, table for the bread of presence, forks, basins, the altar of incense, and the cherubim who cover the ark of the covenant. These similarities lend authority to David's plan and indicate that the temple reflects YHWH's past relationship with Israel.

Second, despite the similarities, these items also differ from the tabernacle account. As an example, David's plan includes several tables of gold and silver rather than just one gold table for the bread of presence. This type of difference shows that not only is there continuity between the tabernacle and temple, but there is also discontinuity. This discontinuity reflects the changes in the type of sanctuary, a transportable tent versus a stationary structure. Furthermore, the text mentions the cherubim as a chariot covering and overshadowing the ark (for significance of this description, see comments on 2 Chron. 5:8). Nowhere else in the OT are the cherubim referred to as a chariot. However, several passages present the cherubim like a throne (2 Sam. 6:2 // 1 Chron. 13:6; Pss. 80:1; 99:1) while others mention that YHWH flies upon a cherub (2 Sam. 22:11 // Ps. 18:10 [HB 11]). Furthermore, Ezekiel 10:1 speaks of something like a throne appearing above the cherubim and their wheels (Knoppers 2004, 934). The text integrates these biblical descriptions, showing that David's plan reflects a wider biblical picture.

Third, some of the items do not correspond to the tabernacle or the account of Solomon's temple. Most likely they point to the second temple context and nomenclature. For instance, the term translated "bowls" (כְּפוֹרִים) only occurs in late writings (e.g., Ezra 1:10; 8:27); therefore, its use most likely corresponds to the use and language of the second temple.

This list of items exhibits the continuity and discontinuity among the tabernacle, first temple, and second temple. This depiction of continuity and discontinuity assures the first readers that the second temple in Jerusalem corresponds to YHWH's sanctuary in the past (tabernacle and first temple) even if there are elements of the second temple that directly correspond to neither past sanctuary.

28:19. This unit closes with a statement describing the plan that David gives Solomon. First, the plan is written. Moses only saw the pattern for the tabernacle; he did not receive it in writing (Exod. 25:9, 40). The fact that the temple plan is written has several implications, but most importantly David can transmit a written plan to Solomon accurately since David himself will not build the temple. Even though the plan

is written, its sense may still not be obvious. For this reason, the text states that YHWH gives David insight to understand the written plan. Both having a written record and understanding it properly were significant issues for the first readers, especially when dealing with authoritative documents such as the law (see Neh. 8:7–8) and the prophetic books (see Dan. 9; Knoppers 2004, 935).

Second, David receives the plan through divine revelation. The text speaks of YHWH's hand being upon David. This idiom may convey YHWH's favor with someone (e.g., Ezra 1:3); however, here it more likely conveys prophetic activity (see 2 Kings 3:15; Ezek. 1:3; 3:14, 22; 37:1; 40:1). In this way the text intensifies its presentation of David as a prophetic figure, who receives divine revelation and passes it along (see commentary on 1 Chron. 22:7–8).

Third, the plan is comprehensive. It entails everything that David receives through divine revelation, including all the necessary details of the temple structure, personnel, and furnishings. Solomon only needs to follow the instructions given to him.

David Admonishes Solomon to Build the Temple (28:20–21)
Drawing on the charge to Joshua to conquer the land, David charges Solomon to build the temple and points to the help Solomon will receive from YHWH, the priests and Levites, the willing craftsmen, the leaders, and the people.

28:20–21. After David delivers the written plan for the temple, he charges Solomon to build it. David's charge to Solomon closely resembles the charge to Joshua to take the land (Josh. 1:5–9; see chart below and comments on 1 Chron. 22:11–16). This charge highlights further the picture of David as a second Moses, as seen in 28:11–19. The charge further brings temple-building into the center of attention for Solomon's reign, and indicates its significance for YHWH's relationship with Israel.

Verbal Similarities Between Charges to Joshua and Solomon	
Joshua 1:9 (1:5d inserted) ESV	**1 Chronicles 28:20 ESV**
"Have I not commanded you? *Be strong and courageous. Do not be frightened, and do not be dismayed, for the* LORD *your God is with you* [I will not leave you or forsake you] wherever you go."	Then David said to Solomon his son, "*Be strong and courageous* and do it. *Do not be afraid and do not be dismayed, for the* LORD *God, even my God, is with you. He will not leave you or forsake you,* until all the work for the service of the house of the LORD is finished."

Following David's commands to build, David provides reasons for Solomon to act. First, following the pattern of Joshua's charge, David assures Solomon that YHWH will be present to help Solomon in the task. The text states that YHWH will be present with Solomon until construction of the temple is over. The text does not intend to communicate that YHWH will withdraw his presence once the construction is complete. The text is only stating that Solomon does not need to worry that YHWH will withdraw his presence while Solomon performs the difficult task of building the temple. What lies beyond building the temple is not in view in David's words.

Second, David points to the help of the priests and Levites. Their work is essential for constructing and maintaining the temple as YHWH's sanctuary, since YHWH has consecrated them alone for specific ritual worship practices. For this reason, they are present to perform all the service of the temple.

Third, David encourages Solomon that there will be willing craftsmen to fulfill every kind of work needed for building the temple. Like YHWH, these craftsmen are with Solomon in the task of building the temple. The language to describe these craftsmen ("willing" and "wise") alludes to the tabernacle account as well (Exod. 28:3; 31:3–6; 35:21–35). Furthermore, the use of "willing" looks forward to the generous offering of the people in 1 Chronicles 29.

Fourth, David assures Solomon that all Israel, its leaders and people, are available to do as Solomon commands. The task of building the temple is too great for a single king or just a segment of the nation, such as the priests and Levites; instead, building a temple for YHWH will require the whole nation (see Japhet 1993, 395). David shows Solomon that all Israel stands behind him in the task of building. Furthermore, with divine aid the task will certainly succeed.

For the first readers, David's charge would also resonate as a charge for them, not to build a temple in Jerusalem but to support it. The text shows that the Jerusalem temple (both preexilic and postexilic) properly carries forward the function of the tabernacle as YHWH's sanctuary. As a result, even for those far from Jerusalem, the Jerusalem temple deserves the people's support as the legitimate site for Israel's ritual worship.

Furthermore, all Israel is needed to support the temple, just as all Israel was needed to build it. Even though political leaders (e.g., Zerubbabel, Nehemiah) and religious leaders (e.g., Jeshua, Ezra) played an essential role in building and maintaining the temple and its service, the consistent service of the temple required all Israel. The postexilic community sometimes neglected their support of the temple and its personnel, such that some left the temple to work fields to support themselves (Neh. 13:10–12). To those neglecting the temple, David's charge would serve as a powerful word to change their ways and renew their support. In this way, Israel could work together in its proper worship of YHWH.

THEOLOGICAL FOCUS

God works according to his plan to dwell with his people to bless those loyal to him.

As mentioned in the exposition, this passage repeatedly addresses three horizons of Israel's history: the Mosaic age, the First Temple period, and the Second Temple period. Including allusions and references to these three horizons reinforced for the first readers that the Jerusalem temple, even after its reconstruction in the postexilic period, was the legitimate place to conduct Israel's ritual worship (making of sacrifices, celebrating of festivals, lighting of lamps, burning of incense, etc.). This point held practical significance for them as they would travel to Jerusalem and support the temple service even as they waited for another Davidic king to arise. In the contemporary context, this point does not hold the same practical significance; however, it does carry theological significance in understanding God's work.

The correspondences between the three horizons of Israel's history (Mosaic age, First Temple period, and Second Temple period) point to three aspects of God's character. First, as the Chronicler intends to communicate, these correspondences reveal that God has been working throughout the history of his people according to his intentional design. These correspondences are not just random similar occurrences through time but take place through God's design. God directs his people's history according to his own plan.

Second, these correspondences reveal that when it comes to his people, God prioritizes dwelling with them. Through the various stages of Israel's history, God prepares a way to dwell among his people. Even though the means for his dwelling changes based on the historical circumstances (e.g., tabernacle or temple), the priority of dwelling remains the same.

Furthermore, God's dwelling with the people opens a channel between God and his people, in which God blesses them while they praise him. As a result, God prioritizes dwelling with his people so that he may bless them and so that they may praise him.

Third, these correspondences point to God's faithful commitment to his people. Pointing to the second temple recalls the fact that the first temple was destroyed. God acted justly by punishing Israel when they forsook him. Despite Israel's failure, God did not abandon his people forever. Although many individuals suffered the consequences of Israel's sin, God did not abandon the nation. One can see his faithfulness when taking the long view.

These aspects of God's character still apply today. First, although the NT emphasizes that God has extended his plan beyond just Israel's worship, God still has a plan regarding worship and has been working to bring it about (e.g., Rom. 8:28–32). Second, God still chooses to dwell among his people, individually and corporately. No longer is a tent or temple required since in the Holy Spirit, Christ may dwell in believers' hearts through faith (Eph. 3:17). God's presence through the Holy Spirit characterizes God's work among his contemporary people and secures unimaginable blessings for them. Third, God is still faithful. For this reason, Paul can be confident that what God began in the Philippian church he would finish (Phil. 1:6). Sometimes, as with Israel, one can only see God's faithfulness when taking the long view; however, regardless of how long it takes, God will not abandon his own. He will not forsake his own but lead them into everlasting blessings.

A final point regarding God's plan in this passage: The passage focuses on the chosen temple-builder. As part of God's plan, Solomon will build the first temple in Jerusalem and lead Israel in worshipping YHWH there. God chose Solomon for the task, and David prayed that God would strengthen Solomon to fulfill it. The first readers had no one like

Solomon in their day. They were living under Persian rule without a king of their own, much less a Davidic king. As a result, they were waiting for another Davidic king to come along. The gospel of John identifies this picture of a Davidic king coming to build or rebuild the temple with Jesus, because Jesus rises from the dead (John 2:19–22). The picture of Solomon in Chronicles anticipates Jesus as the coming Davidic king who will lead God's people to worship God in spirit and truth. The correspondences point to the important role of the Davidic king in God's plan.

PREACHING AND TEACHING STRATEGIES

Exegetical and Theological Synthesis

God's Word is rich in application, not only from the specific and direct messages but also in the messages that are implied and come through a broader view of a passage. Dr. Williams gives us this broader view as he shows how this passage gives us a better understanding of God's character. The postexilic community read this account of the building of the first temple and heard the connections to the tabernacle and allusions to the very temple they were trying to build. God could have directed the Chronicler to pedantically spell out the connections and dissimilarities of the three worship buildings and how these display his character. However, the stronger way to let a message sink in is to let the readers or listeners discover the implications for themselves. When we look at this passage, God's sovereign plans are clear. His desire to dwell with Israel (and us) brings us affirmation, and his faithfulness ensures that his plans and his dwelling with us can be accomplished.

David's exhortation to the people, followed by his public charge to Solomon, makes clear that God's character is not only being presented, but that our response to his character is mandated. We are to obey, seek after, have a whole heart, a willing heart. Simply put, we are to be loyal to YHWH. This admonishment is given in the context of witnesses. It is serious business. God graciously gives us a directive as he presents his character, which is a great foundation and motivation to be loyal to him.

Preaching Idea

God's supreme royalty demands our complete loyalty.

Contemporary Connections

What does it mean?

Loyalty seemed to be more common in a bygone generation: my father worked for a local power company for forty years; my uncle worked at steel plant for thirty years; an aunt worked at the same hospital where she graduated from nursing school for fifty years. I know of very few employees who have stayed with a company for that many years. I remember people being loyal to a brand of coffee or food product line. Perhaps loyalty was abandoned because of dishonesty or failure to keep promises in those in whom the loyalty was placed. Our culture seems to be losing loyalty to loyalty. Perhaps it is because loyalty has no foundation.

My college roommate Jack and I were spending a few days at a cabin out in a forest. We planned to hike, build fires, and hang out. We stopped at a small country grocery store to get our supplies. Jack was about to buy butter but couldn't decide what kind to get since he had never bought butter before. As he pondered the various brands and kinds, a lady was also looking at the selections. He asked her, "What kind do you think is best?" Picking up a popular brand she responded, "Oh this kind. I always get it." Then he asked, "Have you tried these other brands?" She said no. Her loyalty had no foundation. Her reason was based upon what she had always done. Certainly, there is nothing wrong in her being loyal to a brand of butter. Obviously, if pushed, the metaphor breaks down because we aren't tasting and choosing between gods. The point is God doesn't want our loyalty to him to be lacking a foundation.

God gives us a foundation for our loyalty. He presents his character not only in this pericope, but throughout Scripture. There is no one like our God; no one else has the plans set for us. He wants to be next to us, to dwell with us. He is faithful to his word. When we seek him, we will find him. Our loyalty is to someone who loves us and wants to dwell with us. Our loyalty is not misplaced; it has the solid foundation of his revealed character.

Is it true?

The postexilic community was undergoing constant change. They were back in their homeland, and yet only those over seventy-five remembered seeing this land. It was all new to almost all the returning exiles. And as more returned, there was a constant change in who was in the land. New houses had to be built. Fields that were fallow for seventy years had to be plowed. The temple had to be rebuilt. With all these changes, decisions had to be made about how new these things would be. Did the architecture of Babylon and Persia affect how they would build? Were there new kinds of crops to plant? Would the diet they had in exile be the standard, or would they return to what their grandparents ate? What would change and what would be the same? What about the worship of YHWH? Chronicles does not specifically direct them to build a new temple, but their prophets clearly commanded them to do so, Haggai being the most direct. The Chronicler makes clear that there is a connection between the three worship structures; the new temple would be patterned after Solomon's, which was patterned after the tabernacle. But there would be differences. The structure and its furnishings simply could not be as extravagant, though it would still be an impressive structure. This passage directs the first readers to never change their loyalty to YHWH. His unchanging character displayed in this passage is the basis for an unchanging loyalty.

As those who live in a culture of change, we need to never change our loyalty to God. We might change our phones, our banks, our internet provider, our address, our jobs, our leaders, but we must never change our loyalty to God.

Now what?

What does loyalty look like? We think of a cowboy and his horse. The cowboy is in trouble, and a mere whistle brings the horse to the rescue. Or we think of the loyalty of a dog that is lost for a year and finally makes it home. But what does loyalty look like in people?

There is a built-in problem with loyalty to others like us. We all fail, and loyalty will be disappointed: the team will have a string of losing seasons, the employer will go bankrupt, the car will break, the spouse will lie, the church will split. There are different levels of loyalty. Loyalty to a spouse is different from loyalty to an employer. Loyalty to a sports team is different from loyalty to an accountability group. And loyalty to God is different and above all of these. Because of who he is, our loyalty must be deeper and more comprehensive.

Sociologists have examined what they term "emotional labor." When a profession requires that an employee appear pleasant and concerned, it requires emotional work. The flight attendant must be considerate and friendly, even though he is having a terrible day and the passenger is rude. The emotion of caring must be there. This emotional labor is divided into two types: surface acting and deep acting (Frederick, Thai, and Dunbar 2021). The surface acting is simply putting on the smile and doing what the employer expects. That server behind the counter at your local chicken sandwich place smiles and says, "My pleasure," when inside they are hurting and don't really care. Perhaps they would rather throw the sandwich down on the counter and say, "There is your stupid sandwich. And the ketchup and other sauces are over there, stupid." But as long as they keep acting like they care about the customer, they have a job—in fact, that *is* their job. In contrast, deep acting is changing the inner motivation so that care is coming from the heart. Both require emotional labor.

God doesn't want surface acting; he wants a whole heart. But that doesn't mean that we are always happy and smiling. Sometimes following him and obeying him is hard and involves pain and sacrifice. But loyalty from the heart remains because it is a response to his character.

Creativity in Presentation

This section does not have an obvious conflict or engaging plotline other than the progression of the charges. So, it is particularly important to give the listeners a reason to listen. One way to help them is to suggest that they listen not only to the details of the story but for what it says about God's character. This is not always easy, so give them the first characteristic as an example and ask them to listen for others.

After presenting the story, show the broader implications of this pericope that teaches us about God's character that Dr. Williams articulates. I suggest highlighting an exemplary verse(s) for the charge, and then presenting each characteristic. Try to word the characteristics in such a way to lead to application. This can be done by first stating the charge to be loyal to God, followed by presenting the characteristics as reasons why we should be loyal.

The second characteristic is a logical place to present the gospel. Jesus opened a whole new level of God dwelling with us. His death and resurrection give us permanent access to his presence. A magnificent temple doesn't have to be built to enjoy his presence. Simple faith in Jesus's work on our behalf builds a personal relationship with this same magnificent God. Here is one possible structure:

- Introduction
  - Need and struggle for loyalty
- Present story
- Present the charge and characteristics
  - Why should they heed this command to be loyal to YHWH? (28:8)
  - We should be loyal to God because he is the one who has the plan (28:6–7)
    - To bless and discipline
  - We should be loyal to God because he wants to dwell with us (28:19)
    - For us, it is deeply personal and through Jesus
  - We should be loyal to God because he is faithful (28:20)
    - We can fully trust him
- The supreme royalty of God commands our loyalty to him. Royalty demands loyalty.

DISCUSSION QUESTIONS

1. What does being loyal look like?

2. What are some good things about being loyal?

3. What are some dangers in being loyal?

4. How do you choose to whom or to what you will be loyal?

5. How do the following characteristics of God prompt loyalty to him?
    - His sovereignty: he has a good plan
    - His desire to dwell with us: he loves us
    - His faithfulness: he will provide

6. Of these three characteristics, which helps you the most in your loyalty to him? Why?

1 Chronicles 29:1–30

EXEGETICAL IDEA
The end of David's reign presented an ideal picture of all Israel: devoted to YHWH as the everlasting, universal ruler, generously supporting the temple, and experiencing a stable transition from one of YHWH's chosen kings to another.

THEOLOGICAL FOCUS
As the everlasting, universal ruler, God deserves people's full devotion and brings peace for his people.

PREACHING IDEA
As you put your hand to the task, keep your heart on the Lord.

PREACHING POINTERS
One of the great blessings of technology is that how-to videos are available for just about everything. This passage presents the key element in every task that our Lord puts in front of us. Some tasks like those that the Israelites faced are particularly hard. While working hard, having a team, and planning well are all important, it was not the focus of David or of the Israelites. Their focus was not on giving to build the temple and transitioning to a new king; instead, their focus was devotion to the Lord.

DAVID'S FAREWELL (29:1–30)

LITERARY STRUCTURE AND THEMES (29:1–30)

This passage continues the national assembly that David gathers to prepare Solomon and the people to build the temple (1 Chron. 28). It incorporates several themes present in 1 Chronicles 22 and 28, including allusions to the tabernacle account and the Moses-Joshua transition.

At the same time, the passage holds together as a distinct unit. It consists of five parts: two speeches by David, the people's responses to each speech, and a conclusion to the account of David's reign. In the first speech, David addresses Israel about his own preparations for the temple. The people respond by giving generously themselves. In the second speech, David blesses YHWH as the universal, eternal ruler who accepts gifts made with pure motives. The people respond by blessing YHWH and anointing Solomon king over Israel. This alternating pattern between David's speeches and the people's responses creates cohesion. Furthermore, the text provides an *inclusio*, by mentioning the term "citadel" (בִּירָה) in 29:1 and 19.

Structurally, this passage also relates to larger parts of Chronicles. The words of praise in 1 Chronicles 16:8–36 provide the prelude for the section of David's reign that addresses his concern for building YHWH a temple. The text marks the close of this section when David blesses YHWH (29:10–19). The text also marks off the entire account of David's reign by referring to David as "David the son of Jesse" on two occasions: at the beginning of David's reign (1 Chron. 10:14) and the conclusion to David's reign (29:26).

- *David Addresses Israel About Temple Preparations (29:1–5)*
- *Israel Responds by Giving Generously (29:6–9)*
- *David Blesses YHWH (29:10–19)*
- *Israel Responds and Anoints Solomon King (29:20–25)*
- *Conclusion to David's Reign (29:26–30)*

EXPOSITION (29:1–30)

Having a temple in the ancient world required a significant investment. Not only did building a temple demand sizable material, agricultural, and human resources, maintaining a temple demanded these types of resources on an ongoing basis. The postexilic community repeatedly struggled to make this investment in the temple, demonstrated by delaying its building (e.g., Hag. 1:2) or failing to support its personnel (e.g., Neh. 13:10–12). In this context, the Chronicler describes the end of David's reign to demonstrate how Israel prepares to build the first temple for YHWH. The text points out how Israel's devotion to YHWH as the divine ruler leads to a willing, generous offering for the temple and to a united, stable transition in Israel's leadership.

David Addresses Israel About Temple Preparations (29:1–5)

Since building a temple for YHWH is such a big task, David calls all Israel to follow his example by devoting themselves to YHWH through giving generously to the temple.

29:1. David begins his next address to all Israel by inviting them to help build the temple. David provides two reasons that their help is needed. First, Solomon is young and inexperienced. On his own, Solomon is not up to the task. Even though YHWH has chosen Solomon as the one to build the temple (cf. 1 Chron. 28:5), YHWH has not chosen him because he has already proven himself as an experienced king. Only later, when the temple-building is imminent, does YHWH provide Solomon the wisdom and skill needed to build the temple (see 2 Chron. 1:11–12).

Second, building the temple is a big task. On his own, even the most astute, experienced king is not up to the task. The task YHWH has chosen Solomon to complete is such a big task because it involves building something for YHWH rather than for humans. In this case, the text uses a word that is not usually associated with a temple. The word בִּירָה, translated "palace" (e.g., ESV, NET), "temple" (e.g., CSB, NASB, NLT, NRSV), or "palatial structure" (NIV), most often refers to the citadel of Susa, a capital during the Persian Empire. By using this term, the text presents YHWH as king, ruling from the temple, his palace.

Difficult Task of Building the Temple
In Nehemiah 2:8, the term בִּירָה refers to a larger structure associated with the temple, apparently consisting of more than one building. This sense of the word may reinforce the picture that the task of building is so difficult (Knoppers 2004, 944, 950).

29:2. David earlier acknowledged to himself both these concerns regarding the temple project (1 Chron. 22:5), and responded by setting aside materials from the royal treasuries for the temple building. He calls the people's attention to these provisions. He points out that he has provided as much as possible, including all kinds of materials needed to build and decorate the temple. Beyond the materials listed previously (gold, silver, bronze, iron, and wood; see 1 Chron. 22:14), David includes precious stones, a material also mentioned in the tabernacle account. For instance, 29:2 lists onyx or carnelian (שֹׁהַם) and stones of installation (מִלֻּאִים). These

terms occur repeatedly in the tabernacle account (Exod. 25:7; 28:9, 20; 29:3, 5, 13, 27; 35:9, 27). As a result, this language draws a connection between the tabernacle and the temple, a theme seen throughout the reigns of David and Solomon. Furthermore, mentioning these materials points to the splendor and grandeur of YHWH's temple.

29:3–4. Despite all the materials that David has provided from the royal treasuries, David desires to give more. Because of his willing care for YHWH's temple, David goes beyond those provisions to give from his personal resources. What he gives includes large quantities of high-grade gold and silver. The gold is from Ophir (cf. 2 Chron. 8:18; 9:10); the silver is refined (see comments on 1 Chron. 28:18). Even though these quantities are still quite large, they are much less than the quantities provided from the royal treasures (1 Chron. 22:14: one hundred thousand kikkars of gold and one million kikkars of silver). It makes sense that David's contribution is much less, since it comes only from his personal wealth. With these materials, the craftsmen can adorn the walls and produce the various items for use in the temple.

TRANSLATION ANALYSIS:
The text describes David's relationship to the temple with רצה, translated either as his "delight" (CSB, NASB) or "devotion" (ESV, NIV, NLT, NRSV). Knoppers points out, "In a late legal context, the locution can denote free volition" (2004, 950). As a result, I have described the expression as "willing care," in order to convey both devotion and volition.

29:5. What David has given, both from the royal treasuries and his personal resources, is a vast quantity of materials. However, for the temple it is not enough. David has already pointed out two reasons for this conclusion: (1) Solomon is young and inexperienced, so he needs as much help as possible, and (2) the temple is for YHWH, so the project is too big for any individual. For these reasons and based on David's example of willing concern for the temple, David asks all Israel to give to the temple project out of their personal resources.

At the same time, this text recounts more than a capital fundraising program. It reflects the spiritual condition of the people. When David invites the people to contribute to the temple, he includes the idiom of filling one's hand, often translated with language of consecrating oneself (see CSB, ESV, NIV, NKJV, NRSV). Elsewhere in the Old Testament, this idiom applies to consecrating someone for priestly service (e.g., Exod. 28:41; 29:9; Lev. 8:33; Num. 3:3). Since the temple is the holy house (1 Chron. 29:3) to be built for YHWH (29:1), David communicates that contributing to the temple both demonstrates the people's commitment to YHWH and indicates that they are set apart for YHWH's service.

Set Apart for YHWH's Service

The expression that many translations render as "consecrate" (e.g., CSB, ESV, NASB, NIV, NKJV, NRSV) elsewhere in the Old Testament refers to consecrating priests (e.g., Exod. 28:41; 29:9; Lev. 8:33). Since Chronicles applies the language of priestly consecration, Japhet wonders if the Chronicler is attempting to present Israel in terms of Exodus 19:6 as "a kingdom of priests" (1993, 508). Whether the text alludes to Exodus 19 or not, the Chronicler certainly presents this moment as a highpoint of Israel's devotion to YHWH within Israel's history.

Israel Responds by Giving Generously (29:6–9)

Israel expresses its devotion to YHWH by giving willingly and generously to YHWH's temple.

29:6–8. Israel responds to David's invitation by giving generously for the temple.

Although the text does not mention all Israel, it presents all Israel by listing various types of leaders. This list alludes to 1 Chronicles 28:1, condensing that list while still encompassing tribal, military, and administrative leaders. Furthermore, what and how much they give indicates their generosity. They give precious materials of gold, silver, bronze, iron, and precious stones; the recorded quantities even exceed what David has just given. Finally, they give all these materials for the "service of the house of God," that is, to the temple construction.

Use of Darics

First Chronicles 29:7 lists two separate quantities of gold: talents and darics. The use of daric is likely an attempt to update the text to correspond to the Persian period since the daric as coinage did not exist until that time. One may compare the mention of the daric to "the attempts of some modern Bible translations to give up-to-date equivalents when rendering sums of money" (Williamson 1982, 184).

Levites as Treasurers

The text mentions that the people offer the materials for the temple treasury, supervised by Jehiel. Mentioning Jehiel creates a reference to previous material in Chronicles (1 Chron. 23:8), confirming that a Levite is overseeing the temple treasuries (1 Chron. 26:21–22).

29:9. The text relates this picture of Israel's gift by comparing it to others. First, the text shows how all Israel resembles David. As David gives beyond what is expected, the people give beyond what is expected. As David gives various precious stones, the people give precious stones. As David rejoices over their giving, the people rejoice. Therefore, the Chronicler's positive picture of David and his devotion to YHWH also reflects the positive picture of Israel during his reign.

Relation of King to People

Throughout Chronicles, the picture of the people's conduct reflects the picture of the king's conduct. For instance, during Amaziah's reign, the Chronicler points out that Amaziah sets up idols of Edomite gods and then worships them (2 Chron. 25:14–15). When his punishment comes, the text states that the people have worshipped the Edomite gods (2 Chron. 25:20), drawing a close connection between the conduct of the king and the conduct of the people. This same connection applies in a positive sense as well (see reigns of David, Solomon, Hezekiah, Josiah, etc.). See also Ben Zvi (2006a, 167–68), who presents further examples and exceptions to this theme throughout Chronicles.

Second, the text shows how the people reflect the generation building the tabernacle. As mentioned already, some of the precious stones that David contributes allude to the materials in the tabernacle (see comments for 29:2). Here the text alludes to the tabernacle by describing the voluntary offerings made for the work of the sanctuary. Looking at Exodus 35:29 reveals such similarities: "All the Israelite men and women who were willing brought to the LORD freewill offerings for all the work [of the tabernacle] the LORD through Moses had commanded them to do" (NIV). In both cases, the people give generously for YHWH's sanctuary. However, the passage reveals differences. For instance, the people giving for the temple exceed those giving for the tabernacle by giving joyfully, even without a command to do so (see Exod. 35:4–5).

Recording the details of such a gift of all these materials from all Israel for the temple construction intends to leave an impression on the reader; however, the Chronicler moves even beyond this incredible gift to the attitude of those giving it. Israel gives willingly, joyfully, and without reservation. The text emphasizes this point through various word choices. First, the text speaks of the people "offering freely." This word carries the connotation of doing something that is not required or expected (e.g., Ezra 3:5). Second, the text describes the people as rejoicing (see "Cult" section in the introduction, for the importance of joy in Chronicles). In this context, not only does the word carry connotations of joyful emotions, but it also carries a connotation of willingness; that is, the people feel no external demand or threat to give but do so freely. Third, the text describes the people as giving with a "whole heart." This expression here conveys a sense of their full commitment to give (as demonstrated by 2 Chron. 16:9; 19:9; 25:2). They give without any doubt or reservation. Generosity, joy, and full commitment—these three characterize Israel's response. Furthermore, these concepts recur in Chronicles at important moments of Israel's commitment to YHWH. For this reason, Roddy Braun states, "Taken together, these three concepts epitomize the Chronicler's understanding of the faithful response of God's people—generosity and joy flowing from a fully committed heart" (1986, 280).

The nature of the people's offering and the attitude with which they give it marks this moment as a high point of Israel's devotion to YHWH.

David Blesses YHWH (29:10–19)

In response to Israel's giving, David publicly blesses YHWH, pointing out YHWH's greatness, Israel's weakness, and the need for YHWH to empower Israel and its king to remain faithful to their God.

29:10. In response to Israel's giving, David blesses YHWH before all the people, that is, David praises YHWH for who he is and what he does (regarding the translation of "blessing" *piel* ברך as "praise," see comments on 2 Chron. 20:26). This verse identifies YHWH as the God of the patriarch

Israel (i.e., Jacob). Although such an identity appeals to the past, David recognizes that YHWH remains the same since YHWH should be praised "from everlasting to everlasting" (NIV).

Israel as Father

The text is ambiguous whether "our father" modifies YHWH or Israel. The phrase most likely modifies Israel for the following reasons: (1) 29:20 describes YHWH as "God of their fathers," providing a parallel to David's blessing, (2) Chronicles does not describe YHWH as father elsewhere; and (3) the rest of the blessing does not present YHWH as father but as king.

29:11–13. As David lays out his reasons for praising YHWH, he picks up on an important image: David describes YHWH as a powerful king who has the rightful claim to all things. Not only do these verses explicitly point to YHWH as king (e.g., use of "kingdom" and "ruler"), but the listing of what belongs to YHWH (i.e., strength, splendor, majesty, wealth, glory, etc.) characterizes kings in other passages (e.g., Num. 24:7; 1 Chron. 29:25, 30; Esther 1:4).

The image of YHWH as king communicates YHWH's power and authority. The text strengthens this image by stringing together words to describe YHWH's power and splendor. Moreover, the text emphasizes the comprehensive nature of YHWH's rule by repeating the word "all" several times. The text is communicating that no earthly mortal or heavenly being supersedes YHWH's ability or authority. This point is important in the final days of David's life. A king's death can lead to instability and disorder as the kingdom transitions to another king. As David prepares to transfer the kingdom to Solomon, YHWH remains the true king. Furthermore, as the divine king, YHWH has the power to continue David's dynasty and strengthen Solomon as king (which he does, 29:25).

For the first readers, this point would hit home. Even as they found themselves struggling in their homeland under foreign rule, YHWH remains the true king. Practically for them, this image encouraged them to give generously and willingly to the Jerusalem temple, since it was YHWH's temple. YHWH deserves more than one can imagine and can support his people, since he is able "to magnify and give strength to all" (29:12 NET).

29:14–15. After praising YHWH as the universal, eternal ruler, David points out the weakness and frailty of the people of Israel, including himself. He turns his focus to the immediate context of Israel's generous offering. Rather than boasting at the generous contribution made for YHWH's temple, David responds in humility.

David asks a rhetorical question pointing out the people's inability to make such a gift to YHWH (see sidebar "Use of Rhetorical Questions"). He responds that YHWH has rightful claim to everything. What Israel possesses is something YHWH has given them; therefore, Israel can only give YHWH what YHWH has given. As a result, Israel cannot boast about its generous offering.

Next, David turns to the status of the people of Israel in the land. David refers to the people of Israel as aliens and residents (for discussion of the status of resident aliens, see comments on 1 Chron. 22:2). This statement is surprising, since much of the latter part of 1 Chronicles has been related to Israel being planted in the land as YHWH gives them rest from all their enemies (1 Chron. 17:9–10; 18:1–20:8; 22:18). However, David is not describing Israel at the political level; the statement relates to YHWH's everlasting claim on the land and Israel's contingent status before him (see esp. Lev. 25:23; Ps. 39:13). Since David is approaching the end of his life, the statement paints the people of Israel (David included) as those who briefly reside in YHWH's land before inevitably passing away.

Metaphor of Life as Shadow

The metaphor of life as a shadow intends to indicate the brevity of life, not the vanity or senselessness of life, as one might find in passages in Ecclesiastes (e.g., Eccl. 1:2). For other instances of the metaphor of life as a shadow, see Ps. 144:4; Eccl. 6:12.

TRANSLATION ANALYSIS:

Translations vary in rendering the final phrase of 29:15. Some translations (e.g., CSB, NIV, NRSV) render the phrase as "without hope." Although the word hope often carries an emotional connotation, in this case, the phrase most likely relates to the chances of changing the mortal status of humankind. As David approaches his final days, he recognizes the brevity of his life and his inability to change that brevity. This observation strengthens the contrast between the eternal king YHWH and the short-lived King David.

The text describes Israel as aliens and residents just like their ancestors. This statement would carry special significance for the first readers in their situation, whether speaking of those who returned to the land (Yehud) or those who remained scattered among the other nations. Both groups, to differing degrees, lived distinctly from those in their surroundings. Both groups faced threats of various kinds. However, recalling Israel's ancestors points to YHWH's faithfulness to Israel because, even though Israel's ancestors were aliens, YHWH protected them and sustained them, despite the oppositions they faced (see 1 Chron. 16:19–22). Eventually, YHWH planted them in the land, provided a king like David, enabled Israel to build a temple in Jerusalem, and gave them rest from all their enemies. The first readers could have confidence that just as YHWH protected their ancestors, he would protect them as well.

29:16. David returns to the point that YHWH owns everything and that whatever Israel has to give to YHWH, they first received from YHWH. However, as he makes the same point, he relates it more explicitly to the occasion. He specifies that Israel has given the offering to build YHWH's temple. Furthermore, the offering itself represents a great deal of wealth. David is pointing out Israel's proper behavior toward YHWH. If these statements occurred in a different setting, they might sound like boasting through false humility (e.g., Luke 18:11–12). However, here these statements demonstrate Israel's devotion to YHWH while still presenting them with sincere humility. In light of YHWH's possessions, his universal rule, and his eternality, Israel has nothing to offer except for the willingness to offer back what properly belongs to YHWH (Muffs 1979, 92).

29:17. As David points out Israel's giving, he acknowledges that YHWH sees beyond the external act to the inner motivation. YHWH accepts upright actions with upright motives. David affirms that he has given to the temple with integrity in his motives. He implies the same for the people, since the people have given to the temple with joy.

Matters of the Heart

The text uses the language of YHWH's "testing the heart" (בֹּחֵן לֵבָב). This language is like 1 Chron. 28:9 in which YHWH "seeks all hearts" (דּוֹרֵשׁ כָּל־לְבָבוֹת). In that context, the text articulates the principle of retribution: "If you seek him [YHWH], he will be found by you, but if you forsake him, he will reject you forever." Furthermore, the text provides a pun between what YHWH examines and how David has given. YHWH examines the "heart" (לֵבָב) and accepts uprightness (מֵישָׁרִים), while David has given "with uprightness of heart" (בְּיֹשֶׁר לְבָבִי).

TRANSLATION ANALYSIS:

Some translations (e.g., NASB, NET, NIV, NKJV) indicate that David looks upon the people with joy. The word order of the verse supports this

224

type of translation. However, when looking at the context, it is more likely that David is attempting to say something about Israel's motives, which he cannot know directly. As a result, he points to the joy as a sign of their motives (see, e.g., CSB, ESV, NLT, NRSV).

29:18. For David, this event marks a high point for Israel as they demonstrate their devotion to YHWH by willingly giving to build YHWH's temple. As a result, David requests that YHWH will preserve Israel's motivations of devotion exhibited through their giving. David's statement is important for two reasons. First, it shows that to have this type of commitment, Israel requires YHWH's help, a theme that recurs in Chronicles (cf. 1 Chron. 22:12; 2 Chron. 30:12). Second, it shows that Israel's highpoint of commitment occurs in the context of building the temple. Put another way, the text indicates that Israel's spiritual condition can be measured by their willingness to support YHWH's temple.

29:19. After making a request for Israel, David makes a similar request for his son Solomon. David asks YHWH to give Solomon a "whole heart," reflecting the full commitment that the people have shown as they have given to the temple (29:9). This full commitment involves fulfilling two responsibilities. First, Solomon must obey YHWH's commandments, testimonies, and statutes. This combination of terms points to the Mosaic law where these words occur repeatedly to describe the laws YHWH gave to Moses (see esp. Deut. 6:17). Second, Solomon must build YHWH's temple. David (along with all Israel) has made virtually every preparation for building the temple, but the task for completing the project falls to Solomon. The reigns of these two kings are tightly connected as David prepares for building the temple and Solomon carries it out.

For the first readers, David's request for Israel's devotion would have a bittersweet taste. On the one hand, they had seen their ancestors abandon YHWH, and as a result their ancestors suffered the destruction of Judah and exile. On the other hand, the request provides hope that YHWH may keep the Chronicler's generation devoted. For the Chronicler, this devotion resembled that of David's day: willing, generous giving for the support of the temple. Proper support of the temple made possible proper worship of YHWH according to Mosaic law. Furthermore, the Chronicler is calling for the people to offer proper support and worship with pure motives, without reservation or under compulsion.

In this section, David praises YHWH for his greatness while recognizing Israel's weakness and their need for YHWH to keep them faithful to their God.

Israel Responds and Anoints Solomon King (29:20–25)

The kingdom transitions smoothly from David to Solomon as Israel responds to David by making Solomon king and pledging allegiance to him while YHWH responds by magnifying Solomon as YHWH's chosen king over Israel.

29:20. As Israel follows David's example of giving to the temple, they follow his example of praising YHWH. Along with their praise, they bow down to show reverence to YHWH and King David. Their bowing before YHWH reflects the image of YHWH as ruler, emphasized in David's blessing (29:11–13). It may seem surprising that the text includes the king as well. However, other passages report people bowing to show such respect to a king (e.g., 1 Chron. 21:21; 2 Chron. 24:17) even though no other passage in Chronicles records someone bowing in respect to both YHWH and king. In this case the passage most likely includes both YHWH and king to indicate "that the king is the custodian of Yahweh's kingship and prostration before the king implies reverence for the Lord" (Jonker 2013a, 163). This relationship between YHWH and the king informs this section, as seen below.

29:21–22. Looking back to YHWH's kindness in their offering for the temple, Israel celebrates with sacrifices. These sacrifices are made on behalf of all Israel, picking up on a theme running throughout David's reign and showing Israel's unanimous devotion to YHWH and allegiance to the king. Their celebration extends for another day, demonstrating their joy in the occasion and anticipating other celebrations recorded in Chronicles, such as the dedication of the temple (2 Chron. 7:8–10; see also 2 Chron. 30:23). Furthermore, these sacrifices lead to all Israel eating and drinking together, suggesting that the sacrifices are peace offerings. These offerings celebrate the "oneness and commonality" shared among YHWH and all Israel (Merrill 2015, 307–8). Such eating and drinking together resembles other important moments in Israel's history such as the crowning of David (1 Chron. 12:38–40 [HB 39–41]), the giving of the law at Mount Sinai (Exod. 24:11), and the reading of the law for the postexilic community (Neh. 8:10). This image of Israel confirms that this event is a high point in David's reign and, more widely, a high point in Israel's relationship to YHWH.

At the same time, the celebration not only looks back to the offering but looks forward to the transition of the kingdom from David to Solomon. During the celebration, Israel makes Solomon king. Since David is still alive, the text clarifies that the people anoint Solomon as the king designate (נָגִיד), meaning that Solomon will assume full, exclusive rights of the kingdom upon David's death. In 1 Chronicles 23:1 David had already made Solomon king; however, as a national public event, this installation differs from that private one. Furthermore, this public event includes anointing Zadok as the priest. Including the priest in this passage reflects the authority structure of the postexilic community in which both the Persian political leadership and the priesthood exercise authority over the people. In this way the text addresses the transition of authority within a framework familiar to the first readers.

TRANSLATION ANALYSIS:
Translations indicate that Solomon becomes king "for a second time." This reading follows the MT. Some ancient versions do not include the phrase. The phrase is likely an explanatory comment made to show awareness of 1 Chron. 23:1. Others have argued that the Chronicler records two instances of making Solomon king as a way of magnifying Solomon, based on ANE texts describing the twofold coronation of Esarhaddon (Peterson 2018, 564–73).

29:23–24. The text continues to focus on the transition of the kingdom. The text specifies that Solomon sits on the "throne of YHWH." This statement confirms Solomon's role as the representative of YHWH's rule within Israel, but it also points to the stability to be expected during the transition to Solomon because YHWH himself is the true king (see discussion in Kalimi 2019, 232–35). The emerging picture fulfills this expectation as Solomon prospers, all Israel obeys him, and Israel's leaders pledge allegiance to him. These administrative and military leaders include Solomon's brothers, potential rivals for the throne. This presentation emphasizes the stable and peaceful transition to Solomon's reign and confirms the truthfulness of David's charge to Solomon that all the people are at his disposal (1 Chron. 28:21).

Transition to Solomon's Reign
The Chronicler simplifies the picture of transferring the kingdom from David to Solomon. The picture of the transition in 1 Kings 1–2 presents a much more complicated series of events. The Chronicler's version differs from Kings because the Chronicler emphasizes the stability of the transition from David to Solomon, and presents the reigns of the kings as essentially one unit focused on the nation's proper worship to YHWH and the building of the Jerusalem temple.

29:25. To confirm further the picture of a stable transition, the Chronicler points out the greatness of Solomon's reign. Solomon's regal majesty exceeds all those before him, notably David. Since the context deals with building the temple, Solomon's greatness is tied to his role as temple-builder. Later, the Chronicler mentions that Solomon becomes greater than any king in wisdom, riches, and glory (2 Chron. 1:12). As Knoppers points out, "In the context of the monarchy, the two incomparability formulas (regal majesty; wisdom, wealth, and glory) distinguish Solomon's reign as the highpoint in Israelite history" (2004, 957).

TRANSLATION ANALYSIS:
The expression "before him" may be an idiom to communicate that Solomon exceeds all kings, not just those who preceded him. On the one hand, the expression may be an abbreviated form of the typical comparison formula that compares the king to those who come before and after the king (e.g., 2 Chron. 1:12). On the other hand, the expression may carry the sense of "more than him," resulting in a translation as follows: "He [YHWH] set upon him [Solomon] regal majesty which was not upon any king more than [it was upon] him."

This picture of Solomon draws on other passages. First, it continues the Moses-Joshua allusion running through 1 Chronicles 22, 28–29. Here Solomon resembles Joshua: as the people obeyed Joshua (Deut. 34:9; Josh. 1:17), they obey Solomon (1 Chron. 29:23); and as YHWH magnified Joshua before Israel (Josh. 3:7; 4:14), YHWH exalts Solomon (1 Chron. 29:25; 2 Chron. 1:1). For the significance of this allusion, see commentary on 1 Chronicles 22 and 28. Second, the picture of Solomon draws on the picture of YHWH. David's blessing points out that YHWH possesses, among other things, majesty (הַהוֹד) and the kingdom (הַמַּמְלָכָה). YHWH grants Solomon regal majesty (הוֹד מַלְכוּת), reflecting YHWH's own majesty.

Furthermore, David's blessing affirms that YHWH has freedom to exalt anyone. YHWH exalts Solomon. Solomon sits on the throne of YHWH. In this way, the Chronicler sets up the expectation that Solomon's reign will reflect YHWH's reign.

Conclusion to David's Reign (29:26–30)

The conclusion to David's reign emphasizes the blessings he enjoyed as a faithful king and points to the prophets who deliver YHWH's word directing David's life.

29:26–28. The account of David's reign closes by recording elements that become typical at the end of the accounts of future kings. The conclusion reports the length of his reign, his death, burial, successor, and other sources pertaining to his reign.

When compared to the reigns of other kings recorded in Chronicles, the end of David's reign confirms the picture of David as a faithful king. First, David reigns over all Israel. For Chronicles, Israel is ideally a unified Israel. Second, he reigns for a long time (forty years). Third, he dies at an old age, resembling other important figures in OT history such as Abraham (Gen. 25:8), Isaac (Gen. 35:29), Gideon (Judg. 8:32), and Job (Job 42:17). Fourth, David possesses wealth and glory, like other good kings in Chronicles (Solomon, 2 Chron. 1:12; Jehoshaphat, 2 Chron. 17:5; Hezekiah, 2 Chron. 32:27).

29:29–30. Chronicles lists other sources for learning about David's reign. These sources are prophetic records, derived from the three figures who explicitly deliver YHWH's word regarding significant events of David's life: Samuel addresses David's crowning as king (1 Chron. 11:3); Nathan addresses David's desire to build a temple (1 Chron. 17:3); and Gad addresses David's census and discovery of the temple site (1 Chron. 21:9). Furthermore, their records indicate the influential role

David plays as a strong king ("his reign and his strength"). His royal strength affects not only Israel but the neighboring nations, likely referring to David's victories over those nations (see esp. 1 Chron. 18–20).

Prophetic Activity Under David

The text refers to these prophetic figures using different designations: seer, prophet, and visionary. These designations overlap considerably. What is significant is that each describes someone as a messenger of the divine word. The inclusion of all three designations may highlight that David's reign experiences "the entire range of prophetic activity" (R. Klein 2006, 544). For a summary regarding the overlap and distinction among these designations, see Schniedewind 1995, 53–54.

THEOLOGICAL FOCUS

As the everlasting, universal ruler, God deserves people's full devotion and brings peace for his people.

This passage records how David leads Israel to provide an incredible offering for building YHWH's temple in Jerusalem. Understanding the nature of this gift is important for understanding the significance of the passage. However, the gift seems to be the wrong place to start. The better place to start is with the passage's portrayal of authority, especially YHWH's authority. YHWH's authority makes sense of the entire chapter.

The passage presents YHWH as an everlasting, universal king. To speak of YHWH as king is to speak metaphorically, comparing YHWH's character and activity to ancient kings. Therefore, as a king, YHWH possesses authority, land, splendor, honor, victory, wealth, and other desirable attributes. Furthermore, YHWH exceeds other kings because his domain is heaven and earth, his authority absolute, and his insight penetrating the intentions of others. Furthermore, YHWH directs human history as demonstrated by similarities in Israel's worship through its history from Moses to David, from

tabernacle to temple. The similarities reveal YHWH's design in the history of Israel's worship. The image of YHWH as king intends to inspire wholehearted devotion to him.

Interestingly, the Davidic king also receives honor in this passage. He represents YHWH's rule over Israel. The Davidic king occupies the throne of YHWH (29:23) and receives the people's reverence alongside YHWH (29:20). Even though this special relationship between YHWH and the king is limited primarily to religious and political qualities, this picture of the Davidic king points forward to the future Davidic king, the messiah. His kingdom will encompass more than religious or political concerns; his rule will be spiritual and cosmic. Furthermore, he will deserve the same honor and reverence shown to YHWH in this passage. In other words, this passage points in the direction of Christian worship: acknowledging God the Father and God the Son as worthy of the same devotion, honor, and reverence.

Having looked at YHWH's authority and its relation to the Davidic king, a closer look at Israel's offering is in order. As mentioned, understanding the nature of the offering helps understand the significance of the passage. The passage emphasizes three points. First, it emphasizes the greatness of YHWH and the frailty of humanity. Even though Israel makes an enormous contribution to build the temple, it is not because YHWH is weak or impoverished. Instead, everything that Israel gives, YHWH has already given. As a result, not only does YHWH deserve such an offering, but he also enables it. Therefore, anyone making an offering has no room to boast. God provides the ability to give the gift; therefore, the proper response is gratitude, not pride.

Second, the passage emphasizes Israel's true devotion to YHWH. David and Israel demonstrate their devotion by giving YHWH enormous resources willingly, joyfully, and without hesitation. Their attitude appears to be true devotion, and indeed David recognizes that it must be true devotion because YHWH can discern people's intents and motivations. At the same time, David recognizes that Israel's devotion to YHWH is a testament of YHWH's working among his people to hold them to himself (29:18–19).

Moving to the contemporary situation: even though New Testament believers do not offer resources for a temple building, they often give to support other congregations or missionary efforts. Paul suggests that believers should offer these gifts with the same attitude as Israel: willingly and without hesitation as cheerful givers (2 Cor. 9:7). Therefore, Israel's attitude in offering serves as a model for any follower of the Lord. One cannot fake such an attitude because YHWH can discern people's intents and motivations (consider Ananias and Sapphira, Acts 5:1–10). Not only does YHWH discern the heart, but he also works to hold and sanctify his own to the end (1 Cor. 1:8–9; 1 Thess. 5:24–25).

Finally, this passage shows the fruit of David and all Israel's efforts to prepare for building the temple. In this case, the apparent fruit is a peaceful transition from the reign of David to Solomon. For New Testament believers, peace is still a reward for devotion to God, even though such peace does not have in view military or political peace. Regarding an inner peace, Paul prays, "May the Lord of peace Himself give you peace always in every way. The Lord be with all of you" (2 Thess. 3:16 CSB). As the sovereign Lord is present with his people, he gives them peace.

PREACHING AND TEACHING STRATEGIES

Exegetical and Theological Synthesis

Jesus does not call his followers to an easy life. We are called to love, to forgive, to teach, to make disciples, and many other very demanding tasks. There were two specific tasks that the Israelites faced in the mid-tenth century B.C.: raising provisions to build the temple

and transitioning to a new king. The attitude that David demonstrated and led Israel to have serves as an example for the spirit and motivation that we should have when facing any task the Father puts in front of us. It is interesting that two of the most volatile times in the life of a church are building projects and transition of staff. The first readers of this passage faced building another temple and adjusting to a new kind of government. Thus, while we can apply the thrust of this passage to those times, devotion to God should be our focus for accomplishing any task.

Preaching Idea

As you put your hand to the task, keep your heart on the Lord.

Contemporary Connections

What does it mean?

Why the ruins of ancient civilizations attract tourists is a bit of a mystery. Whether it is the easy-to-reach Roman ruins in Italy or the very remote Machu Picchu in Peru, millions of visitors roam through broken-down walls, gaze at a statue that had to be reassembled, study artists' recreation of what the great city looked like. One can even don a visor and have a 3-D virtual tour of what the great civilization looked like. Why are these crumbling rocks so fascinating to us? They are a reminder to us that even our greatest cities and civilizations are not eternal. Do we visit the cities that died because they somehow remind us that we too will die? Are they warnings against pride? If they remind us of death and dying, it seems odd that they remain tourist attractions. Carl Sandburg captures this mysterious emotion in his "Four Preludes on Playthings of the Wind":

> It has happened before.
> Strong men put up a city and got
> a nation together,
> And paid singers to sing and women

to warble: We are the greatest city,
the greatest nation,
nothing like us ever was.

And while the singers sang
and the strong men listened
and paid the singers well
and felt good about it all,
there were rats and lizards who listened
. . . and the only listeners left now
. . .are . . .the rats . . . and the lizards. (https://poets.org/poem/
four-preludes-playthings-wind)

We don't know what ruins Sandburg had in mind, but this poem could have been written by the first readers of this passage. The temple that David resourced and Solomon built was destroyed roughly four hundred years later. The destruction was so complete that there weren't even ruins to tour. So why would the writer give such focused attention to this building? He doesn't. Though the passage talks much about the temple, his focus is on the eternal God. For these first readers the place where God was worshipped was only a memory, but the person who was worshipped was still alive and still reigning.

It is only natural for us humans to focus on the tangible and physical structures. After all, we see them as our creations, the work of our hands. We can touch them; we can admire the handiwork and beauty. This passage teaches us that we are to look to the one who will never be torn down. We are to be devoted to the one who can't be destroyed. Our devotion is to the eternal universal ruler.

Is it true?

My first reaction to this passage was to be cautious lest we make this into a template for a capital fund drive for a new church building. I could just see banners reading "Give Like David Gave" or "If Israel Could Do It, So Can We." While it is not the intent of these efforts, they can still come across in such a way that the joy that David

and Israel experienced is absent. Unfortunately, these events often create an atmosphere of guilt and emotional pressure. This is not what we see in this passage, but often it is how people can feel about giving to the church.

I still remember a message from Leviticus that Don Sunukjian preached in seminary chapel. He presented the giving of the tithe as a joyful offering to the Lord. He then described his joy at writing out his check (that is what we used to transfer money years ago) for his regular offering for an amount greater than he ever thought he could give. I recently experienced this joy when I reflected that my regular monthly giving was double the monthly salary of my first church staff position. To be sure that salary was almost fifty years ago, but the point is that we can rejoice at how much the Lord provides for us to give. The key is the devotion to our great Lord who enables us to give generously to his work. We can give like David gave, with a joyful heart, committed to the Lord.

Now what?

After the giving is noted and celebrated, David offers a grand description of our Lord (29:10–13) which is the heart of this passage. He wonderfully expresses that God is the eternal and universal ruler of all creation. Remember this praise is in the middle of accomplishing a great task. A pastor or teacher can follow this example. Devotion to God should be expressed and encouraged through praise of God's characteristics. This could be done through public prayer as David did. It can be done in everyday conversation: just talk about our great Lord and his amazing salvation through Jesus. And of course, music is a grand and effective way of keeping our focus on our great Lord. David kept his focus on God while accomplishing very difficult tasks. This example is not only a pattern for leaders. The praise of our great Lord should be a part of lives as well as part of accomplishing a task.

After the praise to the eternal and universal ruler, it only follows that David expresses his humility. Not by saying that he was humble but by expressing that all he has and all he has done was because of God's provision. He further shows his humility by referring to himself and Israel as sojourners who are only here for a short time. He realizes, as we should, that our role in God's larger plan is very small. To stay focused on our devotion to the Lord we must be humble.

David then reinforces that when we are involved in accomplishing a task for God's work, uprightness must always be remembered. We sometimes get so committed to getting something done that we forget obedience. We want to see the church grow, but we shouldn't use manipulative marketing techniques to get more people in the building. One area that is particularly vulnerable to losing focus is the use of multimedia. As the use of this wonderful tool becomes more accessible, remembering uprightness is of particular importance. A full-length film that experienced good success even in the non-church world was *Fireproof*. The producers were very careful to be upright in all they did. Kirk Cameron experienced this when he auditioned for the lead role:

> They even had a spiritual interview with me! It kind of went like this: "Hey Kirk, is there anything going on in your life, personally, that might cause God to remove his hand of blessing from this project? We don't want any hypocrites. So, if you're involved in any drug or alcohol problems, or you're sleeping around or have issues with some morality, we'd like you to tell us so we can move on and find a different actor." (https://www.patheos.com/blogs/filmchat/2008/09/interview-kirk-cameron.html)

Creativity in Presentation

This passage teaches something that is counterintuitive to most of us. We want to focus on a task rather than on our devotion to the Lord. Thus, it requires a strategic approach. The introduction could be something like this:

As followers of Jesus we all have difficult tasks (give examples). So how do we accomplish these? We roll up our sleeves and get to work. For sure, but there is more to it than this. We need to carefully plan out the steps necessary to accomplish the task. Yes, planning is important, but there is still more. In the passage today we are going to find the most important part of accomplishing a difficult task.

It is important to bring up these mental barriers to the thrust of the passage. There probably are other barriers that come to your mind that are particular to your situation. That should be addressed in the introduction or somewhere in the sermon/lesson.

An inductive approach could help the congregation accept the thrust of the passage. Ask them to look for the true focus of David and Israel as they accomplished two great tasks. The answer to this doesn't emerge until the middle-to-end of the sermon. Here is one possible structure:

- Present the text
- Explain the text
  - Israel successfully completed two potentially divisive tasks
    - Gave generously with a joyful heart (29:1–8)
    - Transition to Solomon as king went smoothly with stability (29:21–30)
  - Israel was at its peak of devotion to YHWH
    - David's devotion (29:10–19)
    - Israel's devotion (29:9, 20)
- Apply the text
  - As God's people, we face difficult tasks
  - As God's people, our devotion to God must be our focus
  - As you put your hand to the task, keep your heart on the Lord

DISCUSSION QUESTIONS

1. Why does a farmer need to focus on the end of the row when he plows a field?

2. What happens if a sports team focuses on winning the first quarter but forgets about winning the game?

3. What is it about focusing on what is only in front of us that is so appealing?

4. What does devotion to the Lord look like?

5. What are some ways to ensure devotion to the Lord while working at a task?

6. What are the benefits of focusing on our devotion to the Lord while working at a task?

7. What are the dangers of focusing only on a task and not our devotion to the Lord?

REIGN OF SOLOMON
(2 CHRONICLES 1:1–9:31)

In many ways, the reign of Solomon represents a climax in Chronicles. Unlike Kings, Chronicles does not point out Solomon's faults. Instead, Chronicles presents the reign of Solomon as the fulfillment of the work that David prepared for building the temple. Solomon builds the temple of YHWH in Jerusalem according to the specifications handed to him. His great wisdom becomes a key attribute that allows him to build such a great temple as the one in Jerusalem. His great wealth provides the resources to construct a splendid temple to YHWH. Chronicles focuses on Solomon as the temple builder, the one who fulfills the work that his father began.

Solomon's reign also represents a time of Israel's peace and security. Unlike David, Solomon does not need to fight the Philistines or oppose invading armies. The kings of other nations recognize Solomon's wisdom and grant him authority because of it. Furthermore, the peace and security accompany vast wealth that YHWH provides. These conditions and Solomon's wisdom attract rulers from other nations such as the king of Tyre and the queen of Sheba. These foreign rulers praise YHWH because of what they observe during Solomon's reign.

The reign of Solomon represents a picture of Israel as the Chronicler hoped it would one day be. All Israel gathers in Jerusalem to worship YHWH according to stipulations of Moses and the instructions of David. The Davidic king devotes himself to the Jerusalem temple and its required personnel and materials. The king rules with wisdom, justice, and righteousness. Israel as a nation experiences peace and security while gaining great amounts of wealth and even attracting international renown. Furthermore, all these conditions lead to Israel worshipping YHWH and the nations worshipping YHWH as well.

2 Chronicles 1:1–17

EXEGETICAL IDEA
Because of YHWH's promise to David, YHWH prepared Solomon, who was a true worshipper, to build the temple.

THEOLOGICAL FOCUS
According to his plan, YHWH blesses those who truly worship him in order to enable them to worship him more.

PREACHING IDEA
When our worship controls our requests, his provision is realized.

PREACHING POINTERS
Second Chronicles begins with a most encouraging event. The postexilic Jews were trying to rebuild a land that was neglected and a nation that had been destroyed. While they faced a national crisis, the individual tasks of starting again in an unfamiliar land must have compounded that crisis. They needed encouragement. They needed to know that God was faithful and that he would provide what they needed to accomplish his will. This passage shows us that YHWH is faithful and, by Solomon's example, gives us a directive to experience that faithfulness. Solomon placed a priority on worship. His worship of God enabled him to realize the amazing blessing of God that was beyond what he could ask or think.

While our crises may be different from the ancient Israelites, we are still asking the same questions and wrestling with the same challenges. How can the church continue her mission in such a difficult time? How can I, as an individual follower of YHWH, continue my mission? Will God provide? Yes, of course, we say, but our feelings may not agree. This passage helps us see that a faithful God will provide what is needed to accomplish his will in our lives.

WORSHIP, WISDOM, AND WEALTH AT THE BEGINNING OF SOLOMON'S REIGN (1:1–17)

LITERARY STRUCTURE AND THEMES (1:1–17)

It is fitting that 2 Chronicles begins at this point in the narrative. A major transition takes place as the narrative shifts from David to Solomon. The transition from David to Solomon is more than just a political event; it also marks a transition in Israel's worship because Solomon will build the temple. Even though to this point Chronicles has demonstrated how David lays the groundwork for building a temple, Chronicles now shifts to show how Solomon carries out building the temple.

Even though previous passages record Solomon's accession to the throne, 2 Chronicles 1 actually begins the account of Solomon's reign. This initial chapter shows how YHWH prepares Solomon, who is a true worshipper, to build the temple. The chapter focuses on the character of both YHWH and Solomon. The chapter consists of three parts. In the beginning of this chapter, Solomon proves to be faithful to YHWH by leading all Israel to worship in the proper way at the proper place in Gibeon. At the center of the chapter lies the conversation that takes place between YHWH and Solomon as YHWH appears to Solomon at night. Because YHWH has blessed Israel as he promised, Solomon asks for wisdom to govern YHWH's people successfully. Because Solomon prays for such wisdom, YHWH chooses to give him wealth, riches, and glory as well. The final section provides another example of YHWH's faithfulness. By recording the number of Solomon's horses and the abundance of rare materials during Solomon's reign, these verses show that YHWH has fulfilled his promise to grant Solomon great wealth.

Importantly for the rest of Solomon's reign, both his wisdom and his wealth prepare him to build the temple.

- *Solomon and All Israel Worship at Gibeon (1:1–6)*
- *Solomon Asks YHWH for Wisdom (1:7–13)*
- *Solomon Acquires Great Wealth (1:14–17)*

EXPOSITION (1:1–17)

In the ancient Near Eastern world, temples often connected kings to the deities they worshipped. Both the king and the deity held obligations to one another. The deity (or group of deities) was responsible for placing a devout king on the throne. The king was responsible for building and preserving a temple (or temples) for this deity (or group of deities). If the king maintained worship of the deity through the temple(s), then as a reward the deity promised that the king would have a long, prosperous reign, leading to a stable dynasty. Chronicles describes Solomon's reign within this context.

In Chronicles the beginning of a king's reign often sets the tone for his whole reign. In Solomon's case, the Chronicler records Solomon's first action as worshipping YHWH and asking for his help. Because of these early actions YHWH grants Solomon great wisdom and wealth. Solomon needs this wisdom and wealth to fulfill the task that YHWH has chosen him to do: to build the temple. The Chronicler shows that not only has YHWH chosen Solomon to build the temple for YHWH's name, but that

Solomon also worships YHWH properly, qualifying him to build the temple.

Solomon and All Israel Worship at Gibeon (1:1–6)

At the beginning of his reign, Solomon leads all Israel to worship YHWH properly at the sanctuary at Gibeon.

1:1. The Chronicler introduces Solomon's reign by stating that Solomon consolidates the kingdom under his royal authority (*hithpael* חזק). The Chronicler implies that Solomon can accomplish this result because of YHWH: YHWH is with Solomon and magnifies him as king. Earlier in Chronicles, David twice prays that YHWH will be with Solomon (1 Chron. 22:11, 16) and once assures Solomon that YHWH is with him (1 Chron. 28:20). David also blesses YHWH as the one able to magnify a person (1 Chron. 29:12). By alluding back to David's words, the Chronicler shows that YHWH is behind Solomon's success and that he is already fulfilling David's prayers for Solomon. In this way, the stage is set for YHWH to bring about more of what David has requested and more of what YHWH has promised, in particular, raising up David's son to build a temple (1 Chron. 17:12).

When a King Consolidates Power

When the text uses *hithpael* חזק to indicate that a king consolidates his power over the nation, this expression carries neither positive nor negative connotations. To illustrate, Jehoram consolidates his power by killing his brothers (2 Chron. 21:4), but Solomon consolidates power as part of the legitimate transition of the throne from his father, affirmed by popular support. In Solomon's case, it is clearly a positive situation since YHWH is with him and makes him great. This expression applies to other kings in Chronicles as well (e.g., Rehoboam, 2 Chron. 12:13; Jehoshaphat, 2 Chron. 17:1).

1:2–6. After the introductory statement, the Chronicler describes how Solomon brings representatives from all Israel to worship with him at Gibeon. Several important themes emerge from this account. First, even though the Chronicler does not state when this activity takes place, by putting this narrative at the very beginning of Solomon's reign the Chronicler presents this activity as of first importance for Solomon. In other words, as soon as Solomon becomes king he leads Israel to worship YHWH. This point emphasizes Solomon's own devotion to YHWH, following in the footsteps of his father David.

Starting Off Right

On several occasions, the Chronicler structures his account of a king's reign to highlight that the king focuses on YHWH's worship early in his reign. For instance, David attempts to transfer the ark immediately upon the transfer of the kingdom to him (cf. 1 Chron. 11–13). Josiah also begins his reform in Judah when he turns twenty, following the discovery of the law book. On occasion, the Chronicler explicitly assigns activity associated with worshipping YHWH at the beginning of a king's reign: Hezekiah's reform begins "in the first year of his reign, in the first month." (2 Chron. 29:3). Cyrus also issues his declaration in the first year of his reign (2 Chron. 36:22). For further information, see Cogan 1985, 201–7.

Second, this event is a large public time of worship for all Israel. The Chronicler repeatedly emphasizes the role of all the people in various aspects of Israel's life. The Chronicler lists the various leaders who represent all Israel. As R. Klein states, "The listing of officials in this verse seems to be the Chronicler's effort to give concrete substance to the concept of all Israel, that will be important in the following verses" (2012, 21). The phrase "all Israel" occurs repeatedly in Chronicles. Here, all Israel is involved in worshipping YHWH at the beginning of Solomon's reign. Not only does the narrative present a picture of a unified Israel, led by

Solomon, worshipping YHWH together, but it also sets the stage for building the temple. The temple is not just Solomon's temple; it reflects all Israel's devotion to YHWH (see sidebar "Relation of King to People").

Third, the narrative goes out of its way to show that when Solomon worships YHWH at Gibeon, he is worshipping YHWH properly. At first glance, Solomon's activity looks questionable because he is going to a high place, a term associated with pagan worship throughout Kings and Chronicles. However, Chronicles points out that Gibeon is a legitimate site to worship YHWH because it contains the tent of meeting and the bronze altar, both of which trace back to Moses.

TRANSLATION ANALYSIS:
The text is ambiguous regarding the designation of the tent (אֹהֶל מוֹעֵד הָאֱלֹהִים). The ESV attempts to preserve the ambiguity with the awkward phrasing "the tent of meeting of God." Other translations interpret הָאֱלֹהִים as describing the tent, therefore, translating the phrase as "God's tent of meeting" (CSB, NASB, NIV, NRSV). Others interpret הָאֱלֹהִים as describing the meeting, therefore, translating the phrase as "the tent where they met God" (NET) or "the tabernacle of meeting with God" (NKJV). In context, the latter is preferable because here YHWH meets with Solomon that night (1:7).

High Places in Chronicles

The word "high place" (בָּמָה) occurs more than twenty times in association with pagan worship in Kings. It designates a location where acts of ritual worship take place (e.g., sacrificing animals). Worshipping at high places is one of the reasons YHWH judges the northern kingdom by exile (2 Kings 17:9, 11). In Chronicles, following Solomon's reign, the word "high place" occurs fifteen times. Each time the word refers to a site of pagan worship with one exception: 2 Chron. 33:17. In this passage, following Manasseh's repentance, the people worship at the high places, but they only worship YHWH.

Furthermore, to emphasize their legitimacy, the Chronicler refers to Moses more specifically as "the servant of YHWH." Gibeon is a legitimate site for worship even though the ark of the covenant is not located there. The Chronicler reminds the reader why the ark is not located at Gibeon by referring back to David's reign. During that time, the people delivered the ark to Jerusalem; David set up a tent to house it (1 Chron. 15:1, 3) and stationed musicians there to worship YHWH through music (1 Chron. 16:4–6, 37–38) but not sacrifice (1 Chron. 16:39–40). To worship through sacrifice, David had stationed priests at the high place at Gibeon. Therefore, Solomon's sacrifice at Gibeon worships YHWH in a legitimate way at a legitimate site.

TRANSLATION ANALYSIS:
In this verse, one could understand the text to say that Solomon occupies the role of the priest by ascending the altar and making offerings. Chronicles records how Uzziah attempts to act as a priest by offering incense in the temple; YHWH punishes him immediately (2 Chron. 26:16–20). For this reason, the Chronicler most likely does not intend to portray Solomon as ascending the altar as a priest. The OT often speaks of a king making offerings; however, the sense is most likely commanding such offerings, not acting as the priest. Rather than speaking of Solomon as ascending the altar to make the offerings himself, this verse offers two other options: either the sentence has a start and restart (e.g., "Solomon offered sacrifices . . . he offered a thousand burnt offerings," CSB) or the preposition עַל carries the sense of "to" rather than "upon" (e.g., ESV, NASB, NET, NIV, NLT).

Fourth, not only is Solomon's worship legitimate, but it is also tied into the history of YHWH's relationship with Israel. When Solomon builds the temple, he introduces an important new element in the worship of YHWH. However, this new element does not appear out of thin air; it builds on Israel's previous history. The narrative specifically alludes to people (Moses and Bezalel, the temple craftsman) and equipment (tent of meeting and bronze altar) from Israel's history as the people of YHWH. It looks back to the time when Israel wandered in the wilderness and connects their worship in the portable tent with their worship in the permanent temple. Besides lending credibility to the temple, this connection has two additional effects: (1) it shows how YHWH and his demands for worship remain consistent through differing historical circumstances, and (2) it associates the building of the permanent temple with the permanent possession of the land promised to Israel.

For the first readers, both effects would be significant. As the postexilic community sought to reestablish proper worship, this text encouraged them to look to the models of their history, especially Moses. Repeatedly, Chronicles promotes the significance of the law of Moses for Israel's worship (e.g., 1 Chron. 15:15; 2 Chron. 8:13; 24:6; 35:6). For the struggling postexilic community, the text also encouraged them both in their present and for their future. In their present, this community could promote and maintain the temple in Jerusalem as a sign that YHWH has returned them to their land, even if YHWH has not yet fulfilled all his promises to Israel. For their future, they could look for the Davidic king who will come to secure their position in the land and build the temple to YHWH. This future will be much greater than their present circumstances and bring in the fulfillment of all YHWH has promised.

Fifth, the account draws a close connection between David and Solomon. The Chronicler refers to Solomon as "son of David." Solomon acts in a way similar to David by assembling leaders from all Israel (1 Chron. 28:1), even though the vocabulary to describe each event differs. Furthermore, at the beginning of David's reign, the Chronicler uses the word דרשׁ ("seek, attend to") to describe how David and

the assembly attend to the ark by bringing it to Jerusalem (1 Chron. 13:3). The Chronicler uses the same word (דרשׁ) to describe how Solomon and the assembly attend to the bronze altar by sacrificing a thousand offerings upon it. These similarities connect the reigns of the two kings, providing continuity from David to Solomon.

TRANSLATION ANALYSIS:
The verb דרשׁ occurs with a pronoun as its direct object. The antecedent of this pronoun is ambiguous: it may refer to the bronze altar or to YHWH. If the pronoun refers to the altar, then one should render the verb as "care for, attend to," in line with other passages where the verb דרשׁ has an object as its direct object (cf. Deut. 11:12; Prov. 31:13; Ezek. 34:8, 11). If the pronoun refers to God, then one should render the verb along the lines of "seek, inquire of." The same ambiguity here lies in other passages as well (1 Chron. 13:3; 15:13). Some translations render all three passages consistently as referring to God, therefore translating each along the lines of inquiring of God (CSB, NET). Most translations do not render all three passages the same way. Beyond the translation of these particular verses, it is important to note that the Chronicler is drawing a connection between David and Solomon through the use of the word דרשׁ in 1 Chronicles 13:3 and here in 2 Chronicles 1:5. Here in 2 Chronicles 1:5, the pronoun seems more likely to refer to YHWH since YHWH responds to Solomon that night by asking Solomon what he wants from YHWH. YHWH's question makes good sense if Solomon went with the people to the altar to ask YHWH for guidance at the beginning of Solomon's reign.

This narrative unit presents a positive portrait of Solomon, all Israel, and YHWH. Solomon and all Israel appear devoted to YHWH and worshipping him appropriately. YHWH has already begun answering prayers made by David and fulfilling promises made to David. On the one hand, this portrait depicts a God worthy of a temple to be built; on the other hand, it depicts a king and a people qualified to build it. In this way, these verses lead up to Solomon's building the temple.

Solomon Asks YHWH for Wisdom (1:7–13)

When YHWH appears to Solomon, Solomon requests wisdom; YHWH promises him wisdom and so much more.

1:7–8. After Solomon offers a thousand sacrifices upon the bronze altar, YHWH appears to him at night. In 2 Chronicles 7:12 YHWH appears to Solomon again at night, after Solomon has finished building the temple. The two passages relate to one another. Here YHWH appears in order to ask what Solomon desires; in 2 Chronicles 7:12 YHWH appears in order to assure Solomon that YHWH has heard his prayer and chosen the temple as a "house of sacrifice." These two passages create bookends to mark off the temple-building account. As a result, what Chronicles records of Solomon's reign from here through 2 Chronicles 7:12 should be understood in light of Solomon's temple-building.

Furthermore, the language of YHWH appearing (*niphal* ראה) to someone occurs in one other passage in Chronicles: 2 Chronicles 3:1. The verse states that YHWH appeared to David at Mount Moriah, the site for the temple. Here again, YHWH's appearance relates directly to building the temple (in David's case, to selecting the temple's site). By including this language, the Chronicler strengthens the picture of continuity from David (who prepares building the temple) to Solomon (who builds the temple), while demonstrating that YHWH approves the Jerusalem temple as a legitimate innovation in Israel's worship.

1:7–10. While YHWH appears to Solomon, the two have a conversation. YHWH begins the conversation by asking Solomon what he would like YHWH to give him. When Solomon responds, he raises several important points for understanding this passage and its significance. First, Solomon's response reveals YHWH's faithfulness to David. Solomon does not respond to YHWH immediately with a request; instead, he begins by praising YHWH and giving him thanks for what he has already done. Solomon emphasizes YHWH's faithfulness to David by recalling that YHWH has made Solomon king over Israel, fulfilling his promise that David would have a son to reign on Israel's throne (1 Chron. 17:10–14).

Second, at the same time, Solomon's response reveals that YHWH has not finished fulfilling his promises. Solomon requests that YHWH will fulfill what he has promised to David ("may your promise . . . be realized," NET). Even though YHWH has been faithful to fulfill his promise, the promise still requires more. It requires that David's lineage remains on the throne and that one of David's sons builds the temple. Solomon's request for wisdom helps bring about both aspects of the promise: as Solomon rules well, he and his descendants are more likely to reign; and as he possesses wisdom, he is equipped to build the temple (cf. 2 Chron. 2:7, 12–14). The passage presents YHWH as the one who is faithful to his promises. It presents Solomon as an appropriate instrument for continuing to fulfill those promises.

TRANSLATION ANALYSIS:
Solomon specifies the nature of his requested wisdom in terms of leading the people rather than deciding legal cases (see ESV, NASB, NIV, NLT, NRSV). The significance of this observation is that it shifts the emphasis away from Solomon and his cunning and toward YHWH's promises to David (Japhet 1993, 531). In other words, in the first part of Solomon's reign, the Chronicler is not interested in Solomon's wisdom for its own sake as he will be in the latter part of Solomon's reign. Instead, he is interested in Solomon's wisdom and wealth in so far as they enable him to build the temple.

Third, Solomon's response reveals YHWH's faithfulness to the patriarchs. Solomon alludes to what YHWH has promised the patriarchs by describing Israel as a people "as numerous as the dust of the earth" (1:9). This phrase occurs in Genesis where YHWH reiterates his promise to Abraham (Gen. 13:16) and to Jacob (Gen. 28:14). By stating that Israel is a great people, Solomon acknowledges that YHWH has already fulfilled part of what he has promised the patriarchs.

Fourth, the allusion to the patriarchal promises reveals interconnections among events in Israel's history. As the Chronicler begins his account of Solomon's building the temple as a fulfillment of what YHWH has promised to David, he also shows how the building of the temple relates to and builds on the promises to the patriarchs. In this way, YHWH's activity with Israel and his word to Israel provide the glue that holds Israel's history together. Furthermore, by drawing on the promises to the patriarchs and to David, the narrative elevates the significance of the temple as a part of fulfilling YHWH's promises to his people. For the Chronicler the temple is of first importance and a symbol that YHWH fulfills (at least partly) his promises to Israel.

1:11–12. When YHWH answers Solomon, he affirms Solomon's request and commends him for requesting wisdom rather than other royal pursuits (wealth, glory, vengeance, etc.). Since Solomon makes such a commendable request for wisdom, YHWH promises to give Solomon not only what he requests but also some things he did not request: wealth and glory. In fact, YHWH promises to give him more wealth and glory than any other king before or after him.

Solomon's Wealth

Even though the context suggests that this promise refers to any preceding or following king of Israel, the language itself does not limit the promise to Israelite kings. In other words, Solomon may not only represent the wealthiest king of Israel, but the wealthiest king anywhere.

The language of YHWH's response distinguishes between two groups of gifts: (1) YHWH has already given Solomon wisdom and knowledge, and (2) he will give Solomon wealth and glory. Perhaps since Solomon already possesses such wisdom, the Chronicler does not include a demonstration of Solomon's wisdom within the temple-building account (cf. 1 Kings 3:16–28 where immediately following Solomon's request for wisdom, the narrative demonstrates his wisdom in the judicial case involving the two harlots). At the same time, the Chronicler does prove that YHWH gives Solomon incomparable wealth (see below). What is important to remember in this context is that Solomon's wisdom, wealth, and glory are gifts from YHWH that prepare Solomon to build the temple.

TRANSLATION ANALYSIS:
Translations differ slightly in rendering the tense of the two occurrences of the verb "to give" (נתן). Most translations render the second occurrence with a future tense since the Hebrew verb is imperfect/*yiqtol*. Translations vary more widely on the first occurrence. Many render it as present tense (e.g., CSB, ESV, NET, NKJV, NRSV); some, past tense (e.g., NASB); others, future (NIV, NLT). Grammatically, the first occurrence is a *qal* passive ptc. (נָתוּן). As a participle, the form does not contain specific time information; however, based on the Greek translation and the parallel in 1 Kings 3:12, one should most likely understand the verb as something that has already taken place.

1:13. This section closes by recounting that Solomon returns to Jerusalem and rules over Israel. This is the second time that Chronicles has stated specifically that Solomon rules over Israel (cf. 1 Chron. 29:28). Its mention has two effects within the narrative: (1) it strengthens the impression that Solomon's worship at Gibeon was of first importance to him, and (2) it shows that YHWH's gifts of wisdom, wealth, and glory are prerequisites for Solomon to rule over Israel and to build the temple.

Solomon Has Great Wealth (1:14–17)

YHWH begins to follow through on his promise by providing Solomon with great wealth.

1:14–17. The Chronicler turns his attention from YHWH's appearance at Gibeon to Solomon's wealth. It is interesting to note that these verses (except for 1:17) occur again later in the account of Solomon's reign (2 Chron. 9:25–27). Since they occur again elsewhere, a close look at their context becomes even more significant for determining how they function. In this case, these verses serve two primary functions: (1) to confirm that YHWH gives Solomon the wealth he has just promised, and (2) to show that Solomon has sufficient wealth to build a magnificent temple for YHWH (cf. 2 Chron. 2:5 [HB 4]).

Beyond these two primary functions, the text also raises other points regarding Solomon and his wealth. First, Solomon's accumulation of chariots contrasts sharply with David (see Japhet 1993, 533). David does not use many chariots; when he defeats Hadadezer, he seizes a thousand chariots, but leaves only a hundred for his own use (1 Chron. 18:4). In contrast, Solomon amasses fourteen hundred chariots. Even though, as noted above, the Chronicler emphasizes the continuity between David and Solomon, he also points out matters where they differ. In this case, the difference points to ways that Solomon surpasses David. As YHWH has promised, Solomon's wealth will exceed all other kings, including David. Even though the Chronicler shows that David and Solomon share a desire for YHWH's temple, David can only prepare for it; Solomon builds it.

Second, the text connects Solomon's wealth with horse trading. Before and after the expression of Solomon's wealth in terms of silver, gold, and cedar, the Chronicler addresses Solomon's horses. It presents Solomon's amassing of horses as part of his attempt to fortify Israel. Furthermore, it presents Solomon's servants as significant players in the horse trade among Israel's neighbors (1:16–17). This latter point may not only illustrate Solomon's wealth but may also help explain partly how he receives such wealth: through horse trading. The mention of the king's traders at least presents Israel as having international influence (cf. Isa. 23:2, 8; Ezek. 27).

Describing Solomon's Wealth

The Chronicler uses metaphorical language to communicate how much wealth comes to Israel under Solomon's rule. He compares the quantity of wealth with two materials ubiquitous in ancient Israel: rocks and sycamore trees. It is not clear if the Chronicler intends one to think of these as building materials or as individual items, since Solomon uses such rare materials in building the temple and his palace.

The circumstances of the first readers differed sharply from those describing Solomon's reign. The postexilic community was struggling to survive as a relatively insignificant region under foreign imperial rule. They were not experiencing the vast wealth or international influence that characterizes Solomon's reign. Still, the promise to Solomon and YHWH's fulfilling of the promise must have offered hope to the struggling community. Just as YHWH gave Solomon great wealth to build the temple, YHWH may choose again to give such wealth for the building and maintenance of the Jerusalem temple. This picture of Solomon points to the hope that a future son of David will arise—one who will fulfill all YHWH's promises to the patriarchs and David.

THEOLOGICAL FOCUS

According to his plan, YHWH blesses those who truly worship him in order to enable them to worship him more.

This passage focuses on YHWH's faithfulness. From the text's point of view, YHWH has been faithful, will be faithful, and is being faithful to his promises. YHWH has been faithful to David by establishing David's son as king over Israel. YHWH has been faithful to the patriarchs by making Israel a great nation. YHWH will be faithful again to David by providing Solomon the skill required to rule over this great nation. YHWH is being faithful to Solomon by granting Solomon great wealth, even the resources required to build a great temple for YHWH. The way that the text presents YHWH as faithful addresses both YHWH's character and his ability, since YHWH not only intends to follow through on his promises (his character) but has the power to fulfill them (his ability). Whether YHWH makes those promises in the near or ancient past, he remembers them and, according to his plan and timing, he acts on them. He is faithful.

Alongside faithful YHWH, the text also presents Solomon as faithful. Solomon is faithful to worship YHWH properly. Solomon leads all Israel to the legitimate place for making sacrifices. Solomon does not seek YHWH through a medium as Saul did (1 Chron. 10:13) but seeks YHWH properly. He does not handle the ark of the covenant inappropriately as David first did (1 Chron. 13), but he sacrifices to YHWH in the proper place. Furthermore, he leads all Israel in making a thousand offerings. In this way, Solomon proves to be a faithful follower of YHWH.

Solomon's significance in this passage is twofold. On the one hand, Solomon is the model for the Davidic king: he leads Israel to worship YHWH properly and prays for what he needs to rule Israel well. This picture of a faithful Davidide anticipates another faithful Davidide who will be like Solomon as depicted in this passage. This faithful Davidic descendant, Jesus, will lead not only Israel but all people to worship YHWH properly and possesses the wisdom and power necessary to rule well not only over Israel but all nations.

On the other hand, Solomon is a model for a follower of YHWH. From the start of his reign, he leads others to worship YHWH properly, according to his historical circumstances (i.e., at the tent of meeting at Gibeon). He offers numerous sacrifices to YHWH. He humbly prays for YHWH to give him what he needs. Proper worship and humble requests are an example for anyone following YHWH, whether in the Old or New Testament era.

Finally, the interaction between YHWH and Solomon reveals something about how YHWH works. Although YHWH can accomplish his promises through any means he wishes, in this case (and in many others) YHWH uses a faithful worshipper. As a result, not only does YHWH fulfill what he has promised, but the worshipper also experiences great blessing. In Solomon's case, YHWH proves to be even more than faithful when he grants Solomon much beyond what Solomon requests. At the same time, the further blessing enables Solomon to fulfill YHWH's plan for the magnificent temple that Solomon would build in Jerusalem. YHWH provides everything that is needed to build such a magnificent temple, both as a fulfillment of promises made long ago and as a response to Solomon's proper request for wisdom. The NT picks up on such a pattern in Ephesians 3:20–21: "Now to him who by the power that is working within us is able to do far beyond all that we ask or think, to him be the glory in the church and in Christ Jesus to all generations, forever and ever. Amen" (NET).

PREACHING AND TEACHING STRATEGIES

Exegetical and Theological Synthesis

This passage helps us understand the relationship of worship, prayer, and God's provision. When we properly worship, our prayers are affected so that our requests are in line with God's sovereign provision.

The narrative begins with emphasis upon Solomon's proper worship and his leading the nation to do the same. In this context of worship God appears to him and invites him to "Ask what I will give you." At first it seems like God is simply asking, "What would you like?" But the phrasing puts emphasis upon what God will give, not upon what Solomon wants. It is as if God is saying, "Ask for what I already planned to give you." God is not giving Solomon a winning lottery ticket so that he can have anything he wants. Rather, God is saying to him, now that you have properly worshipped, your heart is ready to ask for what I want to give you.

When our supplications come out of worship, they become in line with what God has planned to give us. If one takes away God's sovereign knowledge and plan, then it sounds like a father who only gives to his children when they ask for what he has already planned to give them. We must not impose our human limitations and sin-affected motives upon God. We must not think that God is playing a game with us by telling us to keep asking until we ask for the right thing. This view is a misunderstanding of the purpose of prayer and brings God down into human limitations.

Prayer doesn't change a faithful God; it changes unfaithful sinners. In this case, worship changed Solomon. His prayer was a continuation of his worship. God was not so surprised at Solomon's selfless request that he decided to give Solomon even more. This was God's plan for provision to accomplish his will. God brought Solomon into his plan through Solomon's worship. When our hearts are made right through right worship, God faithfully provides for us so that we can worship him even more by accomplishing his will. For Solomon this was building the temple.

Preaching Idea

When our worship controls our requests, God's provision is realized.

Contemporary Connections

What does it mean?

I had never driven a BMW, but the rental car company was offering a special deal; I could rent a BMW for the same price as a Hyundai. Sitting down on the leather seat, I pressed the controls to adjust the seat to just the right setting. Knowing that I only had to have the fob in the car to start it, I pressed the button mark "start." Nothing happened. I checked to be sure it was in park, or maybe it was to supposed to be in neutral: nothing. After what seemed like hours of embarrassed frustration I went back inside and asked, "How do I start this thing?" I was told that I must step on the brake while pushing the button. Ah, success! Often there is a line of progress or a sequence that must be followed if we want to accomplish our goals. When I understood the process of how that luxury car worked, I was able to enjoy the provision.

Those Israelites fresh back from exile were some of the first to read or hear this story of Solomon's request. They were rebuilding everything: the walls, the temple, and their lives. They had many goals to accomplish, but finding the resources for this rebuilding must have overwhelmed them. Israel had few natural resources, and what was there had been neglected for seventy years. It would be easy for them to doubt God's provision, even though he had just miraculously brought them back to the land. Perhaps they would gain some understanding about God's provision as they read or heard of God's abundant blessing for Solomon. If God provided for Solomon, perhaps he would provide for them.

The passage does end with God's abundant provision of material wealth and military might that enabled Solomon to build a temple for YHWH and then protect that temple. But the writer took pains to not only show God's provision but the process of his providing. What leads up to God's provision is crucial in understanding how and what he provides. Solomon's first act was to worship and then to lead his people to worship in the proper way. When our worship is a priority and done properly, it affects our requests and our view of God's provision.

Is it true?

Wendy was struggling to like living with her husband Brad. They had been married for six months, enough time for the two different ways of keeping house and personal habits to create conflict and disappointment. Marriage was supposed to be a delight, but Brad's leaving wet towels on the floor and her always being just a little late were eating away at their liking each other and even loving each other. Wendy knew that she was to pray for her husband—and as she prayed for him, she discovered something: when she took time and effort to truly pray for Brad (more than just mentioning his name) it was as if God was giving her a fresh love for him. She discovered what Solomon experienced: out of her worship of God came his provision. She found that she loved Brad most when she prayed for him.

Now what?

Our requests come out of our hearts; so, to have right requests, we need to have right hearts. True worship requires a heart of humility and submissiveness to our loving and sovereign Lord. We can't hold on to a self-centered request when our hearts are centered on our Savior, on the Lord of all. When we bow our knees before a faithful God, it affects what we ask to be put in our sinful hands.

Rather than focusing on the provision of God, we should focus on the character of God who is faithful to provide. Solomon did not have his request directly answered. He only asked for wisdom; God had greater plans for him. God has greater plans for us. We must focus on the worship of a God who is faithful. His provision is not only enough but more than enough to accomplish his will.

The postexilic Israelites were wondering if God would once again provide Israel with a strong king to lead the nation and a place of worship that would bring YHWH glory. Though they could not see it, God's provision for them would come. Ultimately it would not be through a king who was only strong, but through a king who would be the Savior (Luke 2:11; 1 John 4:14)—and through a building not made with hands but made by the Spirit, not made with rocks but with living stones (I Peter 2:5). His provision for a dwelling place is far beyond a temple; it is the church, a body of people to proclaim his glory (Eph. 2:19–22).

Creativity in Presentation

Often the request that Solomon makes for wisdom is highlighted, but this is not the main focus of this text. Care should be given to the show that Solomon's priority was worship, and that he followed God's guidelines for that worship. The three parts of the passage can be approached with variety in presentation. The first (1:1–6) is a third-person description of the time of worship. The second section (1:7–13) is a dialogue between God and Solomon and should be presented almost as a drama, in keeping with the text. The last portion (1:14–17) requires additional explanation and modern equivalents to let the congregation sense the abundance of material and military provision. Amassing fourteen hundred chariots was a massive display of military might. Rather than present the three sections in the same way, the preacher/teacher will do well to let the variety of the text affect the presentation. The first section is descriptive of an event. The second is a dialogue and the last section requires modern-day equivalents. Here is one possible structure:

- Solomon and all Israel worship at Gibeon (2 Chron. 1:1–6)
  - Make worship our priority.
- Solomon asks YHWH for wisdom (2 Chron. 1:7–13)
  - Let our worship affect our requests.
- Solomon acquires great wealth (2 Chron. 1:14–17)
  - Continue to worship as God provides.

DISCUSSION QUESTIONS

1. What have you requested of God in the past that you are grateful that he did not grant?

2. What are some ways that you have seen God provide so that his will could be accomplished?

3. How does bowing before God in worship affect our requests of him?

4. What has God already provided for us? Did we deserve these things?

5. What must happen in our hearts in order for us to truly worship?

2 Chronicles 2:1 (HB 1:18)–5:1

EXEGETICAL IDEA
As a part of God's plan, God's chosen, wise king Solomon built a great temple to worship the great God YHWH.

THEOLOGICAL FOCUS
As God, YHWH deserves the best in worship. He works in history according to his plan to enable his people to worship him appropriately in their context.

PREACHING IDEA
Worship of our great God deserves our best.

PREACHING POINTERS
The postexilic Jews had to rebuild the temple. How would they do it? Solomon had great resources that had been accumulated by his father David. These Jews had next to nothing. The land and resources were devastated. They were moving back after seventy years of exile. Why did God give them this account of the first temple being so elaborate and extravagant? Certainly, they could not duplicate what Solomon did. Putting ourselves in their shoes not only helps us see how they would apply these chapters, but also gives us a direction as to how this pericope should change our lives. As they heard about Solomon's heart to build a great house for the name of YHWH, hopefully they would want the same heart. This is not a passage about external gifts to God; this is about our working to have great worship because we worship the great God.

SOLOMON BUILDS THE TEMPLE (2:1 [HB 1:18]–5:1)

LITERARY STRUCTURE AND THEMES (2:1 [HB 1:18]–5:1)

This passage starts a significant part of Solomon's reign, that which is devoted to building the temple. Verse 2:1 [HB 1:18] records that Solomon intends to build a temple for YHWH and a palace for himself. This introduction to the building has three passages that close it: 2 Chronicles 5:1; 7:11; and 8:16. Each closing statement expands the activity associated with building the temple. For instance, 5:1 concludes the section that describes making the temple structure and furnishings. The section closing at 7:11 describes depositing the ark in the temple and the various activities associated with dedicating the temple.

This passage in particular falls into three sections. The first section describes Solomon's efforts to secure the labor and materials needed for building the temple. This section contains an *inclusio*, beginning and ending with the same information regarding the number of laborers Solomon assigns to the construction work. The second section describes the temple structure with some of its significant ornamentation, such as the cherubim in the most holy place and the pillars standing at the entrance of the temple. The section begins by stating when and where Solomon builds the temple. This information shows how the temple relates to Israel's previous history. The third section describes the temple furnishings such as tables, lampstands, and basins. Among the details, the passage as a whole emphasizes two points: (1) the temple is an impressive structure with exquisite ornamentation and furnishings, and (2) the temple appears as a stationary counterpart to the wilderness tabernacle.

- *Solomon Secures Labor and Materials for Building the Temple (2:1–18 [HB 1:18–2:17])*
- *The Temple and Its Ornamentation (3:1–17)*
- *The Temple Furnishings (4:1–5:1)*

EXPOSITION (2:1 [HB 1:18]–5:1)

In the ancient Near Eastern world, temples served important functions. The people believed that a temple housed whatever deity to which the temple was dedicated. From this temple the deity supposedly ruled over and protected the land. A temple also served as a center for worship, both secret worship (performed by priests and other cultic servants) as well as public worship, since worshippers of the deity would visit to offer sacrifices and perform other religious duties.

The Jerusalem temple functions in similar ways for ancient Israel. However, this temple differs from others because YHWH is not like the other nations' gods, which are simply worthless idols (cf. 1 Chron. 16:26). In this passage the Chronicler points out how the temple, as an exquisite structure constructed for the worship of YHWH, reflects who YHWH is.

Solomon Secures Labor and Materials for Building the Temple (2:1–18 [HB 1:18–2:17])

This section describes how Solomon prepares to build the temple by gathering thousands of laborers within Israel, hiring the most skillful workers from outside Israel, and purchasing the most exquisite wooden building materials.

2:1–5 (HB 1:18–2:4). Once Solomon decides to build the temple, he reaches out to the king of Tyre Huram (spelled Hiram in Kings) to help with the project. When Solomon contacts Huram, he not only requests labor and materials but also explains why building such an impressive temple is an important task. First, Solomon states that the temple is a house for YHWH's name. Since the temple is a house for YHWH's name, YHWH is uniquely present at the temple. One way this uniqueness reveals itself is by making the temple and its various implements holy. In this context, for the temple and its implements to be holy means that they are separated from ordinary things and the rest of mundane life. Since they are no longer ordinary items, they should be treated differently and never used outside the temple.

Second, Solomon presents the temple as the focal point for Israel's worship of YHWH, especially its formal, cultic worship. Such formal worship consists of burning incense, providing for the showbread, making morning and evening offerings, and making offerings for other religiously significant days (e.g., Sabbaths and festival days).

Legal Requirements in Worship

The Chronicler provides this list as a summary for what the law requires in worship. The elements correspond to commands given regarding the tabernacle: burning incense, Exodus 30:7–8; displaying showbread, Exodus 25:30; offerings for morning, evening, and festival days, Numbers 28–29. These practices become a standard for assessing the people's devotion to YHWH (2 Chron. 13:11).

Third, Solomon states that the temple should reflect the grandeur of YHWH. Solomon reasons that since YHWH is great, even greater than all the other gods, his temple must be great. In other words, as a "house" (בַּיִת) for YHWH, it should reflect some aspect of YHWH's nature, in this case his greatness (Lynch 2014b, esp. 102–5).

When referring to YHWH, "greatness" likely conveys the sense of his power and royal dignity. When referring to the temple, the word more likely carries the sense of splendor, impressiveness, or exquisiteness. For these reasons, Solomon intends to build an impressive temple for YHWH.

2:6 (HB 5). Even while the text presents the reasons to build such a temple, it alludes to some of the temple's limitations. First, it shows that even though YHWH may be uniquely present in the temple, he is not confined to it. Solomon asks rhetorically how the temple can hold YHWH when even the farthest expanses of the sky cannot contain YHWH.

TRANSLATION ANALYSIS:
Two issues arise translating this verse. First, most translations render the expression הַשָּׁמַיִם וּשְׁמֵי הַשָּׁמַיִם as "heaven(s) even the highest heaven(s)" (CSB, ESV, NASB, NIV, NRSV). This translation suggests to some readers the spiritual realm. In fact, several passages point to הַשָּׁמַיִם ("heaven") as the dwelling place of YHWH (e.g., Deut. 26:15; Pss. 11:4; 115:3; 2 Chron. 6:21). At the same time, the image that the Chronicler portrays is not a distinction between the physical and spiritual, for he speaks of "heavens of heaven" containing YHWH. For this reason, I think it is better to translate the expression as "the farthest expanses of the sky"—as the widest, farthest possible extent that one would regularly encounter in the ancient world. In this way, the text focuses on the immensity of YHWH; that is, he cannot be contained or limited. Second, the translations render the final phrase of 2 Chronicles 2:6 (HB 5) differently. Some translations render it with a more precise sense of "burning incense" (CSB, NASB). In this case, the term more likely carries a more general sense of "making offerings/sacrifices" (ESV, NET, NIV, NKJV, NLT, NRSV). The *hiphil* קטר carries this generic sense elsewhere in Chronicles, e.g., 1 Chron. 6:34; 29:11; 32:12.

The text implies, of course, that the temple cannot hold YHWH, but his special presence in the temple relates to the temple as a center of ritual worship—that is, a place for making sacrifices.

Second, even though the temple serves as a center for ritual worship, the worship itself is a perpetual obligation for Israel, even without a temple. The fact that Solomon encounters YHWH at Gibeon and makes sacrifices to YHWH there already shows that the temple is not necessary for Israel to worship YHWH (1 Chron. 1:1–6). Third, YHWH is greater than all gods regardless of whether Israel has a temple or not. When Solomon argues that the temple should be great because YHWH is great, he does not imply the inverse: that YHWH is great because the temple is great. Even if the temple falls into disuse, disrepair, or even destruction, YHWH does not change.

YHWH's Superiority

Comparing YHWH to other gods is one way the OT describes YHWH's superiority. Chronicles also states that YHWH is the only god (1 Chron. 17:20). Taken together, these statements communicate YHWH's unique superiority over everything else (Lynch 2014a, 47–68, esp. 52–56).

At this point, Solomon's message to Huram strikes a balance between showing that the Jerusalem temple is important for Israel and revealing that it is not necessary for Israel or YHWH. In the Persian context of the first readers, this balance would be important to keep in mind, as Israel's history proves that Israel did not always maintain this balance between the temple's importance and its limitations. On one hand, during the days of Jeremiah, many in Jerusalem believed that YHWH would not destroy the Jerusalem temple despite their wicked behavior (cf. Jer. 7:14). On the other hand, during the days of Haggai and Zechariah, the postexilic community delayed rebuilding the temple at all. Chronicles reminds the postexilic community

that the temple is important to promote proper worship of YHWH, but it is not a magical charm to protect them even if they abandon YHWH.

This part of Solomon's message alludes to another important point regarding the temple. When Solomon questions who can even build a temple for YHWH, he raises the question whether a human being—in particular, himself—is able to build a temple for YHWH at all (see sidebar "Use of Rhetorical Questions"). Even before this section, the Chronicler has shown how YHWH himself has been involved in building the temple. YHWH provides David with the pattern for the temple building and administration (1 Chron. 28:11–19). David acknowledges that all the resources he and the people give for building the temple come from YHWH himself (1 Chron. 29:14–16). Furthermore, YHWH provides Solomon with the wisdom and wealth required to build the temple. Again, the Chronicler strikes a balance between the divine origin of the Jerusalem temple and its human construction.

2:7–10 (HB 6–9). The rest of Solomon's message to Huram turns from the nature of the temple to the preparations for building it. Exemplifying Solomon's desire for a great temple, Solomon asks Huram for an expert craftsman, expert woodcutters, and large quantities of exquisite woods. Both the quality and quantity of these craftsmen and materials reveal how impressive Solomon intends YHWH's temple to be. Furthermore, the vast quantities of supplies that Solomon agrees to spend for Huram's workers and materials recalls the vast wealth that God promised and gave Solomon (cf. 2 Chron. 1:12–17).

2:11–12 (HB 10–11). Next, the Chronicler records how Huram responds to Solomon. First, Huram states explicitly that YHWH shows his love for his people Israel by making Solomon king. The statement implies even more. Regarding Solomon, it implies that Solomon as king benefits Israel as a whole. As Boda states, "Although this [statement] affirms Solomon, it reminds the reader that the Davidic dynasty was ultimately a benefit for the people of Israel—that is, the covenant with David was not merely about the royal house but was also about the nation as a whole in keeping with the Abrahamic and Sinai covenants of earlier generations" (2010a, 241).

Even though Solomon's rule provides other benefits for Israel (cf. 2 Chron. 9:8), given the context, the benefit in view is likely Solomon's building the temple. Regarding YHWH, the statement implies that YHWH is carrying through on his commitment to David, that is, his commitment to build David's house by setting one of his sons on the throne (1 Chron. 17:10–11). Within the Persian context of the first readers, Huram's statement overall points to a hope that a Davidic king will arise to build YHWH's house again as a blessing to all Israel.

Second, Huram states that YHWH made the sky and land. This comment builds on Solomon's claim that YHWH is greater than all other gods. First Chronicles 16:25–26 connects YHWH's creative activity with his superiority over other gods, who are worthless idols. By making a similar claim here, the text reveals an aspect of YHWH's greatness over other gods: YHWH alone made all things.

Third, Huram states that YHWH gave David a wise son, possessing insight and understanding, who will build a palace and a temple. This statement shows that YHWH is further carrying through on his commitment to David, in this case, his commitment to enable one of David's sons to build the temple (1 Chron. 17:12). Furthermore, the statement reveals that YHWH has answered David's request that YHWH grant Solomon insight and understanding (1 Chron. 22:12). Since Huram is a foreign king, his statements exemplify the kind of international acclaim that YHWH deserves as a great God who fulfills his commitments to Israel and David (Lynch 2014b, 105–8).

2:13–14 (HB 12–13). After Huram speaks of YHWH and Solomon, he turns to what he is sending Solomon. He starts by describing the master craftsman who will assist Solomon in building the temple. Huram emphasizes the skill of the craftsman, his ability to work with every type of material and create any type of conceivable design. The impressive temple that Solomon will build requires such a skilled craftsman. The phrase describing the craftsman as wise and possessing understanding closely parallels the phrase describing Solomon in the previous verse.

TRANSLATION ANALYSIS:
The traditional translation of the phrase אֶת־הַשָּׁמַיִם וְאֶת־הָאָרֶץ is "heaven(s) and earth" (cf. CSB, ESV, NASB, NIV, NKJV, NLT, NRSV). Although this translation is serviceable, it often conveys modern images of the planet whirling through space. The perspective within biblical Hebrew is on the ground: the sky seen above and land seen below (cf. NET). At the same time, the expression in this context is a figure of speech called a merism, in which two contrasting terms represent a whole entity. "Sky" as that which is above human beings, and "earth" as that which is below human beings, represents the entirety of the created world.

TRANSLATION ANALYSIS:
Generally, translations capture the sense of the phrase describing the craftsman (אִישׁ־חָכָם יוֹדֵעַ בִּינָה) quite well. What is in view is Huram-abi's skill and competence as a craftsman. Some translations capture this sense by using only terms commonly associated with craftsmanship (NET "skilled and capable man"; NIV "man of great skill"; NLT "extremely talented"). Other translations also include "understanding" to render the Hebrew יוֹדֵעַ בִּינָה. One should note that the phrase is not intended to communicate understanding in a general sense, but specifically in the context of his craftsmanship. For this reason, one may even translate the phrase as "know-how."

Furthermore, it corresponds closely to Solomon's request for such a craftsman (2 Chron. 2:7 [HB 6]) and recalls David's request that YHWH grant Solomon such wisdom (1 Chron. 22:12). These connections show that the craftsman is a suitable counterpart to Solomon for building the temple.

The description of the craftsman also reveals several subtle connections to the craftsmen who built the tabernacle, especially Oholiab (see Exod. 31:2–6; 35:31–35). The temple craftsman's name is Huram-abi. The text traces his lineage to the tribe of Dan while describing his competence to work with any type of material to create any type of design. Exodus mentions two craftsmen in particular who build the tabernacle: Bezalel and Oholiab. Bezalel comes from the tribe of Judah; Oholiab, from Dan. Both craftsmen are competent to work with virtually every type of material to create any type of design.

Three specific elements connect the temple craftsman Huram-abi to the tabernacle craftsman Oholiab: (1) the craftsman's name, (2) the craftsman's lineage, and (3) the craftsman's competence. This connection between Huram-abi and Oholiab falls in line with other connections between Solomon's temple and the wilderness tabernacle, including connections between Solomon and the tabernacle craftsman Bezalel.

Comparison to 1 Kings

Each of these elements appears to be an intentional sign connecting the two craftsmen together because each differs from the parallel account in 1 Kings 7:13–14. Concerning the first element, although the –ab/i element occurs in many names, its significance here is that the craftsman is also known simply as Huram/Hiram, both in Chronicles and in Kings (1 Kings 7:13, 40, 45; 2 Chron. 4:11). Concerning the second element, Huram-abi's connection to the tribe of Dan stands out because 1 Kings 7:14 connects him to the tribe of Naphtali. Concerning the third element,

---

1 Kings 7:14 only mentions the craftsman's competence with bronze; it does not mention any other materials. Furthermore, the expanded list closely resembles the list describing Oholiab's competence, with some linguistic updating. For more information regarding the connection between Solomon and Bezalel, see Dillard 1981, 296–99; 1987, 4–5.

2:15–16 (HB 14–15). Huram finishes his correspondence with Solomon by addressing some of the details regarding payment and shipment of the materials. Huram agrees to Solomon's terms for paying the workers who gather the materials. Furthermore, he describes how his workers will transport the cut wood over water so that Solomon's workers can pick it up at Joppa and transport it from there to Jerusalem.

2:17–18 (HB 16–17). This section closes by returning to the subject that started it: Solomon's labor force. The verses record that Solomon counts the number of resident aliens living in Israel and then divides them into different categories: those who transport the materials (seventy thousand), those who cut stone to use for building (eighty thousand), and those who ensure the work is done (thirty-six hundred). The verses allude to a census that David took earlier. This census is not likely the census described in 1 Chronicles 21; instead, it is more likely what is described in 1 Chronicles 22:2. In that verse, David issues a command to gather all the resident aliens in Israel, and then assigns at least some of them the task of cutting stone to use in building the temple. David issues the command as part of his plan to prepare everything needed to build the temple. In this way, the Chronicler portrays Solomon as carrying out what his father David prepared.

The Temple and Its Ornamentation (3:1–17)

This section describes the main structures of the temple that Solomon builds to honor YHWH.

3:1. The text now shifts from preparation to construction of the temple. The account begins by emphasizing where Solomon builds the temple. The text identifies the location in several ways: at Jerusalem, on Mount Moriah, where YHWH appeared to David, the place David prepared as the temple site, and the threshing floor of Ornan (spelled Araunah in Samuel). These geographical identifications link the temple building with two individuals significant to Israel as a people and nation. The first is David, mentioned explicitly in the verse. Identifying the location with Jerusalem points to YHWH's choice of the city and his choice of David as king over his people (2 Chron. 6:6). Identifying the location with the threshing floor of Ornan recalls David's census and the sacrifices made at the altar purchased by David to restrain the angel of YHWH's destructive activity (1 Chron. 21:15–28). Identifying the location with the place David prepared for building the temple recalls his words concerning the threshing floor of Ornan and the labor and materials David set aside for the temple building (in particular, 1 Chron. 22:1–5).

Identifying the location with Mount Moriah recalls a second significant individual: Abraham. Moriah occurs elsewhere in the OT only in Genesis 22, the story known as the *Aqedah* or the Binding of Isaac. The text recounts that Abraham ascended the mountain to sacrifice his son, but at the last moment the angel of the YHWH stopped him and provided a ram for sacrifice instead. When the text mentions Mount Moriah, it connects this story of sacrifice and deliverance with Solomon's temple. Furthermore, as Boda points out, Abraham's story resembles David's sacrifice at Ornan's threshing floor: "In both the Davidic tradition of 1 Chronicles 21 (paralleled in 2 Sam 24) and the Abrahamic tradition of Genesis 22, the angel of the Lord appears and stops the destruction of human life and instructs an individual to offer an animal sacrifice in place of the human life" (Boda 2010a, 246). In this way, as the text begins to describe the temple, it relates the temple both to David and Abraham. These connections point to the significance of the temple as a "house of sacrifice" (cf. 2 Chron. 2:5; 7:12).

3:2–17. Throughout this section, the Chronicler continues to show how the temple relates to other moments in Israel's history. In particular, the description presents several similarities between the temple and the wilderness tabernacle. One may notice the following similarities between the two: (1) the overall layout of both structures with courtyard, holy place, and most holy place; (2) the two cherubim placed within the most holy place (cf. Exod. 25:18; 2 Chron. 3:10); and (3) the colorful veil at the entry of the most holy place (cf. Exod. 26:31; 36:35; 2 Chron. 3:14).

Cherubim in Temple and Tabernacle

The presence of the cherubim reflects the tabernacle; however, the facing of the cherubim differs. In Exodus, the cherubim face each other upon the ark; in Chronicles, as in Kings, the cherubim face the front of the holy of holies. The text provides no reason for this difference.

Therefore, as this passage describes the temple building, it alludes to the gamut of YHWH's previous history with Israel: from the father Abraham, to the lawgiver Moses, to the king David, and finally to the temple-builder Solomon. These connections demonstrate that the temple is not a new idea pulled out of thin air, but a continuation of YHWH's activity extending from Abraham through Moses through David to Solomon. The text validates the Jerusalem temple as the place for sacrifice and the counterpart to the Mosaic tabernacle by showing that it is a part of YHWH's plan, extending through Israel's history.

The description of the temple emphasizes another theme introduced in 2 Chronicles 2: the temple is an impressive structure. First, the text notes the exquisite construction materials used for the building. These materials include the cypress wood used to overlay the main room (2:5), the precious stones used to beautify the temple (2:6), and the gold of varying quality covering so much of the temple (2:4–10). Regarding the gold, it is not only the quality of gold but also the quantity of gold that demonstrates the exquisiteness of the temple. For the most holy place alone Solomon used six hundred talents. Such an amount is extraordinarily large but corresponds to the amount David paid for the temple site (1 Chron. 21:25). In other words, it is not a price too high for YHWH's temple.

Second, the description includes exquisite images such as cherubim, palm trees, and pomegranates. These images point to a garden paradise setting. As Merrill states, "The whole [temple] is reminiscent of a paradisiacal, Edenic world, a reminder of the perfection of God's pristine creation in which he had placed man as a setting for fellowship and worship" (2015, 333). The materials and images create an exquisite structure that reflects YHWH's grandeur.

As a final concern, this section demonstrates that the temple really is for YHWH. Although we do not know the precise differences among the terms used to describe the varying qualities of gold, the description seems to indicate that the quality of gold increases as one moves from the entryway of the temple into the most holy place. When one considers that human access becomes more restricted closer to the most holy place, this point becomes increasingly significant since YHWH, with few exceptions, is the only one present with these exquisite materials and designs. In this way the temple really is for YHWH and not people.

3:3, 10–13, 17. Before leaving this section, we must address three architectural elements that apparently symbolize something regarding the nature of the temple, although the text does not explicitly clarify the symbolism: the foundations, the cherubim statues, and the pillars Jachim and Boaz. Mentioning the foundations

(3:3) likely symbolizes the enduring nature of the temple, since firm foundations lead to a permanent structure. Mentioning the cherubim statues within the holy place (3:10–13) is more difficult to determine. Most likely the statues symbolize divine protection for the sanctity of the most holy place (like the cherubim stationed east of Eden; Gen. 3:24). They also serve as a reminder of YHWH's royal authority since 1 Chronicles 28:18 refers to the cherubim as the chariot covering the ark. Finally, the appearance, function, location, and symbolism of the pillars Jachim and Boaz remain quite enigmatic (3:17). Their material and dimensions signify strength, endurance, power, value, and proximity to YHWH's presence where ritual worship activities occur (Prokop 2020, 90–95). Although the meaning of the names remains somewhat speculative (even through textual transmission), they likely either symbolize the endurance and strength of YHWH's royal power or recall proper names associated with the establishment of the Davidic dynasty (Prokop 2020, 95–99). Their location in front of the temple likely symbolizes a gateway between the holy realm of the temple and the mundane world, and thereby YHWH's enduring authority both in the divine and earthly realms (Merrill 2015, 335; for political concerns of pillars and their location, see Meyers 1983, 170–78).

The Temple Furnishings (4:1–5:1)

This section describes the furnishings that Solomon builds for the temple as a place to honor YHWH through Israel's ritual worship.

4:1–5:1. The remainder of the temple's description focuses on the temple's furnishings. Some of the emphases from the previous sections carry over into this section. The description continues to show how the temple reflects the tabernacle. One can discern the similarities in the furnishings themselves: for example, a bronze altar, a table for displaying the showbread, a large basin, and a lampstand (even if the temple contains a greater number of tables and lampstands).

Table(s) for Showbread

It is not clear whether the tables mentioned in 4:8 are intended for the showbread or not. Second Chronicles 4:19 suggests that they are, but elsewhere Chronicles only refers to a table of showbread (2 Chron. 13:11; 29:18). From a literary standpoint, the ambiguity may result from combining the description of the temple and tabernacle in various passages.

Furthermore, these furnishings serve the same purpose. For instance, in both the tabernacle and temple, the priests use the basin (called "the sea" in the temple) for washing themselves (Exod. 30:18–21; 2 Chron. 4:6). Solomon constructs the lampstands in particular "according to their specification" (2 Chron. 4:7). The specification in view is most likely what the law prescribes regarding worship in the tabernacle. By showing that the lampstands conform to the specifications of the tabernacle, the text further identifies the temple with the tabernacle.

This section also continues to portray Solomon as carrying out what David prepared. For instance, the final verse of the account (2 Chron. 5:1) provides the clearest example of this activity: Solomon brings into the temple all the gold, silver, and implements that David dedicated to YHWH (see esp. 1 Chron. 18:10–11). This final verse does not address the bronze that makes up several items in the temple (see esp. 2 Chron. 4:12–16); instead, the account addresses the bronze when it states that Solomon used so much bronze that it could not be measured. This amount of bronze alludes back to the very large (לְרֹב מְאֹד) amount of bronze that David took from Hadadezer; the text even specifies that Solomon used this bronze to make the bronze furnishings of the temple (1 Chron. 18:8).

A further emphasis of this section concerns the materials used for the furnishings.

The description lists two main categories of items: items made with gold and items made with bronze. This distinction in material corresponds to other distinctions in the account as well. For instance, the gold items belong in the holy place while the bronze items remain outside it. Furthermore, the account assigns the bronze materials specifically to the craftsman Huram-abi (4:16), while it assigns the gold items specifically to Solomon (4:19–22). In this way the material represents the relative proximity to the most sacred space and the relative priority of Solomon and Huram-abi (similar to Bezalel and Oholiab) in the temple construction.

Solomon and Huram-abi

At the same time, the account, especially in the first half, leaves unclear who specifically makes what. For most of the account, the text implies that Solomon makes the items; however, the text mentions that Huram-abi finishes all the work that Solomon assigned to him (4:11). Solomon is responsible for all the work on the temple; at the same time, Huram-abi and the other craftsmen likely perform the actual work itself. The account maintains two concerns: (1) to demonstrate that Solomon is the temple builder, and (2) to show that Huram-abi is the temple craftsman. The ambiguity results from balancing these two concerns with one another.

Boda characterizes the distinctions as follows: "The distinction between 'bronze' and 'gold' not only symbolizes the distinction between regions of sacred space and relative proximity to the manifest presence of the Lord but also the distinction between Solomon and Huram-abi. Solomon as the lead craftsman was associated with the gold items, while Huram-abi was his assistant and worked in bronze" (2010a, 250).

As pointed out earlier, the temple (its structure, its ornamentation, and its furnishings) resembles the tabernacle in numerous ways. However, the temple also differs from the tabernacle in numerous ways. To name a few examples: the temple contains the large pillars absent from the tabernacle, the temple's bronze altar is considerably larger than the tabernacle's, and the temple contains several lampstands rather than just one. The text does not specify why these changes occur. However, Chronicles does indicate an important difference between the tabernacle and the temple: the tabernacle is portable, while the temple is stationary (1 Chron. 17:5–6). Many of the differences between the tabernacle and temple occur because the temple is a permanent structure: the large pillars, the large altar, the larger number of furnishings, to name a few. This point is important to notice because it gives some insight for how the Chronicler understands the role of the past. For the temple, the past provides a pattern to be followed; however, he recognizes that the pattern may shift based on changing circumstances. Most often in Chronicles, a king will authorize such changes. This observation points to the importance of the Davidic monarchy for Israel's worship. The first readers did not have such a king, but the text points to a hope for such a king in the future.

Royal Changes

The following are examples of a king authorizing changes: (1) David introduces music in worship, (2) David categorizes the priests and Levites, (3) Hezekiah postpones the Passover for all Israel until the second month, and (4) Josiah assigns the role of the Levites during the Passover.

Beyond these emphases, this section contains several items whose significance and function are not explicitly stated in the text nor are apparent from context. For instance, one cannot discern the precise purpose for some of the pots, basins, tables, and lampstands from the text itself. Most likely these items have a practical purpose for those

serving in the temple (e.g., the lampstands provide light for the priests, since the holy place would be quite dark) and some type of symbolic significance. For one item, the text specifies its practical purpose but does not provide any clues for its symbolic significance: the bronze basin or sea. The text states that the priests use this basin to wash; however, the text describes its ornamentation in detail. The significance of this ornamentation remains enigmatic. Despite the likely symbolic significance of these implements (see Levenson 1985, 120–21), for the Chronicler their importance is related solely to worship. The Chronicler only mentions the basins, tables, and lampstands elsewhere in relation to Israel's obligation to worship YHWH properly (see Williams 2019, 89–94).

The Sea and Its Ornamentation

The following are possibilities regarding the significance of the sea and its ornamentation. The basin may recall the primordial sea from which dry land emerged (Gen. 1:6) or the rivers that flowed from Eden to water the ground (Gen. 2:10–11). Perhaps associated with this sea (especially given its location), Ezekiel 47:1–12 describes a flow of water proceeding from the temple and providing life everywhere it goes (Hahn 2012, 118). Furthermore, "in Egyptian and Canaanite tradition, cult basins (the 'bronze sea,' cauldron carts) and plant and animal symbolism (lotus, pomegranate, palmettos, bull images, etc.) point to the cosmological, creation-maintaining function of the sanctuary" (Keel and Schroer 2015, 67).

Within the context of the first readers, this account of the temple's construction encourages them to recognize that YHWH has been faithful to his people. Throughout their history, he has provided a means to sacrifice to him and experience his presence. The line that extends from Abraham to Moses to David to Solomon points to the significance of the temple. In fact, for the first readers this account affirms the legitimacy and priority of the temple in Jerusalem. In this period other temples existed. The Chronicler shows that the Jerusalem temple is the place that YHWH set aside as the place of sacrifice even from the time of Abraham, the place that followed the pattern of the Mosaic tabernacle, and the place that David acquired to build an altar of sacrifice. Even though the first readers were under Persian rule, they could see YHWH's faithfulness to his people in the building of the second temple. Their responsibility was to support the Jerusalem temple through contributions and sacrifices, and to celebrate YHWH's festivals there with proper music and offerings. In other words, Jerusalem, not some other place, should stand as the heart of their ritual worship.

THEOLOGICAL FOCUS

As God, YHWH deserves the best in worship. He works in history according to his plan, to enable his people to worship him appropriately in their context.

At first glance, this passage appears to deal with an institution that is far removed from contemporary Christianity: a temple, a physical structure built to house a deity and his attendants while blessing the region around it. Such a situation contrasts sharply with the NT where the temple is no longer a physical structure but a body (John 2:19–21; 1 Cor. 6:19) or a congregation (Eph. 2:21), and worship is no longer tied to a special place (John 4:21). At the same time, Solomon recognizes that the temple cannot contain God and therefore limit him to a particular place. Although the passage does not speak of the temple in the same terms as the NT, it does present several points important for proper worship.

First, the worship of God forms a thread that stretches through Israel's history. From the nation's ancestor Abraham, through Moses, to David, and then Solomon, God orchestrates a plan for his people to worship him properly while he pours out his blessings on them and their land. This plan speaks to God's foresight, power, faithfulness, and purpose. The site testifies to God's steady mercy through the generations, since from the Temple Mount God held back Abraham's hand from striking Isaac, and later the destroying angel's hand from striking Jerusalem. The site testifies to God's benevolence through history as he promises Abraham a great nation, a secure land, prosperity, and international acclaim, and as he provides those benefits for Israel when they faithfully follow him (2 Chron. 9, 14, 18, 26, 32). The site testifies to his presence, since he dwelled among the people in the wilderness tabernacle and remains with them in the Jerusalem temple. This passage shows God's consistent character through Israel's history.

Second, God deserves the best we have to offer. Although Chronicles presents the temple as an impressive structure from the outside, the most valuable construction material belongs to the innermost, darkest, most private parts of the temple. Virtually no human saw them or enjoyed them. They were set aside only for God. Solomon sets aside all these materials and organizes all the labor because it is appropriate to Israel's ancient setting; the temple was the place where God dwelled in a special way. God's worth demanded such exquisite craftmanship as appropriate for that day and age. Within a NT context, God's worth remains the same, even though what we have to offer may have changed.

Furthermore, the splendor of the Jerusalem temple encouraged the first readers to recognize the importance of the second temple and to support the ritual worship that took place there. Although the NT does not point to supporting the Jerusalem temple in the same way, it does point to supporting and promoting proper worship. Often, this support takes the form of providing aid for congregations in need (e.g., Rom. 15:26) and supporting the activities of missionaries (e.g., Phil. 4:15–18).

Third, the way we worship God communicates who we think he is. In the passage, Solomon recognizes that the temple should reflect something of God's nature. For this reason, Solomon builds an exquisite temple because YHWH is truly God. Such a building—with its structures, furnishings, and implements—represents God's character in a manner appropriate and understandable in that day and age. On the one hand, the temple represented a change in Israel's worship from a mobile tabernacle to a permanent temple. On the other hand, certain precedents from the older forms of tabernacle worship translated into the newer forms of temple worship.

In a somewhat similar way, even though historical circumstances changed and because of the life, death, and resurrection of Jesus certain forms of worship changed (e.g., sacrifice, Heb. 10:1–18), the NT still draws on precedents from the OT when discussing the believer's body and the believers' congregation as a temple. For instance, the New Testament focuses on the principle of holiness. The temple in the OT was holy because God is holy. New Testament authors argue similarly that the believer and the community of believers should be holy because God is holy (Rom. 12:1; Heb. 10:19–25; 2 Peter 1:15–16; 2:5). In both cases, holy worship reflects a holy God.

PREACHING AND TEACHING STRATEGIES

Exegetical and Theological Synthesis

As the postexilic Jews looked at where the first temple stood and heard this account of its beauty, perhaps they were reminded of the national sins of idolatry that had led to its destruction. And this comparison also showed them that as wonderful as that first temple was, it was not what should be worshipped. Before the exile Jeremiah spoke harshly against those that thought the temple would save them (Jer. 7:4). YHWH alone was to be worshipped, not other gods or a building. So, as they built the second temple, they needed to keep in mind that while they didn't have the gold that was dedicated to YHWH in the past, they could have hearts that were devoted to YHWH. The best was not the gold, but the undivided hearts.

This was true for Solomon. One must not think about his building the temple as an elaborate gift given to God to appease him. By using the best materials and human resources, Solomon made a statement about what he thought about YHWH. Simply put, Solomon thought God was great and he wanted to display that greatness in the house that he built for YHWH's name. Solomon wanted his worship of the great God to be great. By using the best Solomon made it clear to those around him and to the nation that YHWH was the best, the greatest. More than a great building, it was most important that Solomon believed and felt that YHWH was the great God.

As we move into applying this passage, we see that the cross fulfilled the sacrificial purpose of the temple, and that the resurrected Christ working through his church and his believers is meant to display the greatness of God. Our belief that God is truly great should affect how we function within the church and with his people. Just as Solomon wanted his worship to be the priority, so we should strive to make our worship the priority, both corporately and privately. The inner heart of the temple was most beautiful, and Israel's inner heart needed to be the most worshipful. Our personal worship should have the attention that the inner parts of the temple had. But just as Israel was not to worship a building, we must not worship the church or the worship that occurs in the church. Our hearts are to be devoted to our great Lord; out of that comes great worship. Great worship comes out of great devotion.

Preaching Idea

Worship of our great God deserves our best.

Contemporary Connections

Is it true?

It was two days before the wedding, and the bride was in tears—not because of second thoughts, nor because a family member couldn't come to the wedding. Her meltdown came because the printed napkins for the reception were not correct. They misspelled her new last name, and it was her fault. How could she possibly misspell her groom's last name? To be fair, her fiancé's European last name had more unpronounced letters than pronounced ones. Fortunately, the printers came through and made the corrections, and the wedding was a success.

The details of a wedding are important. From that first "save the date" card with the carefully chosen colors to the groom's boutonniere that has same color theme, there is great care in the details. The list of details for a wedding seems endless: shower decorations, bridal luncheon, dresses, ties for the men, table decorations, food, pictures of parents, music. . . . To be sure, there are varying degrees of how much goes into a wedding, but at some level the details are always important. One couple only had a simple courthouse ceremony, but they wanted to get married at 11:00 on November 11 in 2011.

This attention to detail and giving our best effort can be seen in other areas. A hunting trip or fishing weekend begins weeks before with the sighting-in of the gun, or the purchase of a new lure. The family gathering on July Fourth lasts only for an afternoon, but the preparation began weeks before. The attention to details and the preparation makes the day special.

There is not a one-to-one comparison of weddings and weekly corporate worship. Hopefully the wedding is a one-time event, and hopefully our worship is weekly. The elaborate planning and carrying out of those plans display how important it is to us. Perhaps the great efforts we put into a wedding, vacation, or family reunion can be a standard to measure how much effort we put toward worship.

What does it mean?

"Give of Your Best to the Master" is an old hymn I remember singing back in the 1960s. It always struck me as a little off. What if I can't give my best? Should I then not give anything? Is it OK to give our average? Does God want *only* our best? These questions indicate that there is a misunderstanding in what this text teaches us about *the best* being offered to God. Clearly Solomon is using the best materials and the best personnel, and he is even building the temple in the best place. The best and greatest expresses not his wealth but his great desire that worship of YHWH is to be the greatest and the best. Having the best worship begins by having the best heart. Do we desire that our worship be great? Perhaps before we think about giving God the best, we should examine our hearts.

The weekly nature of our worship can reduce it to a meaningless routine, like our driving to work each day and hearing the same radio program, at the same time, at the same intersection. Just as preparation and the attention to detail makes the difference in other events, our worship can become greater when we give attention to details, being careful not to let our main focus ever shift from God. We could cover our pulpits with gold, but that wouldn't disguise a divided heart.

To be fair to Howard B. Grose, the writer of the old hymn above, he closes with these lines:

Give Him your heart's adoration;
Give Him the best that you have.

That is the best that we can and should offer to God: our heart's devotion. This is emphasized by the writer when he includes the details of the letter sent to Huram. In 2 Chronicles 2:4–6 we see Solomon's heart.

Now what?

Most churches give detailed attention to the celebrating of the Lord's Table or communion. Why not give this same attention to other areas? It could be something as simple as washing the car on Saturday for the ride to worship on Sunday. Or, as once done in another time, have Sunday-go-to-meeting clothes. In our current church culture of informal attire, the details of our clothes for worship will be different, but clothing can still be special. Perhaps decide the day before what you'll wear. It's not a wow wardrobe for others to see, but the attention given to God to prepare to worship him. How many people see the bride's shoes? But they are carefully chosen.

It is not the amount of gold leaf or exotic wood paneling, but the amount of attention given to God and the preparation to worship him. Attention to details in worship can and will vary greatly. An established city Presbyterian church in an affluent neighborhood receives the offering with a military formality, while a rural Baptist church takes up the offering amid handshakes and short greetings. Either can be done with no intentionality or purpose, or can be done as an expression of what that church thinks is the best for the worship of God. The preparation of the music, the order, those helping guests find their seats and receive the offering—all these details can be attended to with special care. The purpose is to show that God is great.

Personal worship can also be given the best. A designated place and time for us to focus our attention on our great God can help. Newer homes have elaborate media centers with surround-sound and multiple screens. Perhaps thought should be given to a place for personal worship: a back porch, a special chair in a quiet corner. Again, it is not the externals that are most important, but that our internal hearts are being expressed by the externals. Solomon put great effort into the externals; perhaps these should have more attention in our personal worship.

Creativity in Presentation

It would be hard to not present the whole text in a unit, since the text describes a building that is being constructed. We naturally want to get the whole picture. This pericope can be presented with an inductive/deductive structure. Present the story of the text, then the idea for the sermon could come in the middle of the sermon/lesson, followed by the application. To help present the text, a computer-generated walk-through could be helpful. One good walk-through graphic presentation of Solomon's temple is "Solomon's Temple Explained." One version of this presentation can currently be found at https://www.youtube.com/watch?v=y2tha7ogpec; a simple internet search will provide other several access options. I found that watching the presentation at double speed made it more useful, and could enhance viewers' grasping of what Solomon was building.

The introduction to the video would be a great place to present the gospel, by explaining the restricted access to the inner portions of the temple. Our faith in Christ allows us in. This virtual journey through the temple could be enhanced with a well-crafted monologue, beginning something like, "Walk with us through this temple that is described here. We step through the gate of the outer wall, and there in front of us is a pure white building with golden doors and two massive bronze pillars beside them—like two trees, so large that you couldn't reach around the trunk. Over on the left is what looks like a massive grill." Then in the application portion of the sermon/lesson, use the same genre of presentation for the application. "Let's walk together as we prepare for worship. It is Saturday night. Though we attended a dinner party, we let the host know ahead of time that we had to leave by 9:00. Sunday morning comes, and as we get in the car we pause and ask the Lord to help us worship Him. We play some worship music on the way, to help create a worship mindset."

While there is a place for multimedia, we must not forget how the first readers heard this. They had only heard about this structure; they had no video. Therefore, the teacher/preacher must not feel that a video presentation is necessary. The beauty and grandeur of the first temple, however it is presented, should lead us to hearts that desire great worship of our great God. Here is one suggested outline:

- Solomon builds the temple
  - Solomon secures labor and materials for building the temple (2 Chron. 2:1–18 [HB 1:18–2:17])
    - Highlight 2:4–6 [HB 3–5], because it shows us Solomon's heart
  - Solomon constructs the temple and its ornamentation (2 Chron. 3:1–17)
  - Solomon constructs the temple furnishings (2 Chron. 4:1–5:1)
- Present graphic or video, and monologue (if used)
- Sermon Idea: Worship of our great God deserves our best.
  - Perhaps revisit 2:4–6 (HB 3–5)
- Application
  - Suggestions for great corporate worship
  - Suggestions for great individual worship

DISCUSSION QUESTIONS

1. Why do most churches give special attention to the details of communion and baptism?

2. How does attention to detail enhance an event, like a wedding?

3. What are some dangers of focusing too much on the details of an event?

4. How was God's greatness displayed in the temple?

5. What are some ways God's greatness can be displayed in our worship?

2 Chronicles 5:2–14

EXEGETICAL IDEA
The Jerusalem temple took over the role of the tabernacle, both as the center of all Israel's ritual worship and as the seat of YHWH's unique presence, when Israel transferred the ark according to Mosaic legislation and fulfilled the work David began.

THEOLOGICAL FOCUS
God always wants to dwell with his people and enjoy their worship.

PREACHING IDEA
When we need to feel God's presence, it is time to worship.

PREACHING POINTERS
With the advance of technology aimed at individual use, we have become more emotionally isolated. We were created with a need to be with others and with God. Though it is expressed in various ways, we all desire God's presence. This passage is about God letting Israel, and us, know that he is with us. While we should not expect another cloud, we can look for a renewed awareness of God's presence. The text shows us that Israel's proper worship led up to the cloud filling the temple. That proper worship included sacrifice, a focus on God's written covenant, and majestic music. The result was, and can be, a special awareness of God's presence.

SOLOMON TRANSFERS THE ARK INTO THE TEMPLE (5:2–14)

LITERARY STRUCTURE AND THEMES (5:2–14)

Once Solomon completed the temple structure and its furnishings, he gathered all Israel together to bring the ark into the temple, following the example of David his father. David had moved the ark into a tent in Jerusalem, but now Solomon brings the ark to its permanent resting place in the temple. Most of the narrative describes how the Levites carry the ark to the temple so that the priests can deposit the ark in the temple. Many narrative details point back to the Mosaic law, to the wilderness tabernacle, and to David's example. The temple houses the wilderness tabernacle and takes over its role as the center of Israel's ritual worship and the seat of YHWH's unique presence in Israel. To confirm this role, a cloud manifesting YHWH's glory fills the temple.

- **Solomon Gathers Israel (5:2–3)**
- **Levites and Priests Deposit the Ark in the Temple (5:4–10)**
- **The Cloud of YHWH's Glory Fills the Temple (5:11–14)**

EXPOSITION (5:2–14)

In the ancient Near East, temples served as earthly residences for deities. For this reason, the temples of this region and period consistently would have held some type of "cult image, most often an ornate statue, in the most secluded area of the entire [temple] compound" (Hundley 2013, 134). In some way, the deity would be present in the image. However, following Mosaic law, Chronicles demonstrates that YHWH is not like other gods since they are idols, the work of human hands (see 2 Chron. 32:19). At the same time, Solomon's temple does provide a permanent place for Israel to serve YHWH through its priests and Levites, and to meet YHWH in worship through its offerings and music. Since the ark is a symbol of YHWH's special presence within the temple, Solomon transfers it to the most holy place within the temple as soon as he completes the temple building. In this way, Solomon's activity resembles other ancient Near Eastern expressions of worship. However, the ark is not an idol. It is not an image, nor is it a vessel to contain YHWH. Instead, it symbolizes YHWH's presence by pointing to the relationship between YHWH and Israel, represented by the tablets contained within the ark (5:10). Against this backdrop, the Chronicler describes how Solomon brings the ark to the temple and reflects on how the temple functions as YHWH's residence.

Solomon Gathers Israel (5:2–3)

Just as his father David did, Solomon assembles the leaders of the people to celebrate the procession of the ark from one place to another.

5:2–3. Previously, David moved the ark into a tent that he set up for it in Jerusalem. Now Solomon moves the ark to its permanent resting place within the temple. In this way the Chronicler continues a theme developed throughout the early part of Solomon's reign: Solomon fulfills what David begins. The language confirms that this connection between Solomon's transferring the ark and David's is intentional since the statements share noticeable features of vocabulary and word order.

This verse states the purpose for gathering the leaders together. Virtually all translations render the purpose as "to bring up" (לְהַעֲלוֹת) the ark. In this case the verb signifies that all Israel is involved in transferring the ark in some way. The NET attempts to clarify how all Israel is involved by translating the purpose in the following way: "so they could witness the transferal of the ark."

Similarities Transferring the Ark

Chronicles records three occasions when Israel transfers the ark. To transfer the ark, the king gathers all Israel. The cases share similar language.

So David assembled all Israel, from the Shihor of Egypt to the entrance of Hamath, to bring the ark of God from Kiriath-jearim. (1 Chron. 13:5 CSB)	וַיַּקְהֵל דָּוִיד אֶת־כָּל־יִשְׂרָאֵל מִן־שִׁיחוֹר מִצְרַיִם וְעַד־לְבוֹא חֲמָת לְהָבִיא אֶת־ אֲרוֹן הָאֱלֹהִים מִקִּרְיַת יְעָרִים:
David assembled all Israel at Jerusalem to bring the ark of the LORD to the place he had prepared for it. (1 Chron. 15:3 CSB)	וַיַּקְהֵל דָּוִיד אֶת־כָּל־יִשְׂרָאֵל אֶל־יְרוּשָׁ־ לָ͏ִם לְהַעֲלוֹת אֶת־אֲרוֹן יְהוָה אֶל־מְקוֹמוֹ אֲשֶׁר־הֵכִין לוֹ:
At that time Solomon assembled at Jerusalem the elders of Israel—all the tribal heads, the ancestral chiefs of the Israelites—in order to bring the ark of the covenant of the LORD up from the city of David, that is, Zion. (2 Chron. 5:2 CSB)	אָז יַקְהֵיל שְׁלֹמֹה אֶת־זִקְנֵי יִשְׂרָאֵל וְאֶת־ כָּל־רָאשֵׁי הַמַּטּוֹת נְשִׂיאֵי הָאָבוֹת לִבְנֵי יִשְׂרָאֵל אֶל־יְרוּשָׁלָ͏ִם לְהַעֲלוֹת אֶת־אֲרוֹן בְּרִית־יְהוָה מֵעִיר דָּוִיד הִיא צִיּוֹן:

Admittedly, the passages are not exactly the same in each case. The differences demonstrate that the texts intend to recall distinct historical events. The similarities indicate that these historical events are not isolated but fall into a pattern.

5:2. When Solomon assembles the people, he calls for the leaders of Israel. The leaders consist of Israel's elders and tribal leaders, including leaders of individual family units. The text does not highlight administrative or military leaders (cf. 1 Chron. 28:1); instead, it uses familial or genealogical categories. This language makes sense within Chronicles, both as a way of alluding to the picture of Israel found within the opening genealogies (De Vries 1989, 255) and as a way of reflecting Israel's leadership during the wilderness journey (cf. Num. 7:2). Most importantly, these leaders represent all Israel, since 5:3 states that all Israel joins Solomon in Jerusalem. The text confirms that transferring the ark is not only a royal concern but a concern for all the people.

When Solomon assembles the people, the ark of the covenant is in a tent David prepared for it within Zion, also known as the city of David (1 Chron. 11:5, 7). Although the text here distinguishes the temple from Zion, other passages—especially poetic and prophetic texts—associate Zion with the temple so closely that Zion becomes a way of designating the temple area and/or Jerusalem in general (e.g., Pss. 9:12; 74:2; 146:10; Isa. 8:18; 10:12; Amos 1:2; Mic. 4:7). Mentioning Zion here alludes back to David's capture of the stronghold (1 Chron. 11:4–7) and the preparations he made for the temple construction. In other words, the mention of Zion provides another indication that Solomon fulfills what David begins.

Designations for the Ark

Chronicles refers to this same box with a number of designations: "the ark" (1 Chron. 6:16; 13:9–10, 13; 15:23–24, 27; 16:37; 2 Chron. 5:4–6, 8–10; 6:11), "ark of our God" (e.g., 1 Chron. 13:3), "ark of God" (e.g., 1 Chron. 13:5–7, 12, 14; 15:1–2, 15, 24; 16:1; 2 Chron. 1:4), "ark of YHWH" (e.g., 1 Chron. 15:2–3, 12, 14; 16:4; 2 Chron. 8:11), "ark of the covenant of YHWH" (1 Chron. 15:25–26, 28–29; 16:37; 17:1; 22:19; 28:2, 18; 2 Chron. 5:2, 7), "ark of the covenant of God" (1 Chron. 16:6), "ark of your strength" (2 Chron. 6:41), "holy ark" (2 Chron. 35:3).

5:3. The text states that all Israel assembles to Solomon during the seventh month "at the time of the festival" (בֶּחָג). The identity of this festival is unclear. The most common interpretation is to identify this festival with the Festival of Booths (סֻכּוֹת), scheduled for the fifteenth day according to the Pentateuch (e.g., Lev. 23:34). The Festival of Booths lasts seven days, with an assembly on the eighth day. Second Chronicles 7:9–10 states that after Israel celebrated the dedication of the altar seven days and the festival seven days, Solomon sent everyone home on the twenty-third

day of the month. If these verses mean that the total celebration took place over fourteen days, then the festival designated at the transfer of the ark cannot be the Festival of Booths, since moving the ark takes place before dedicating the altar. An alternative interpretation identifies the festival with the Day of Atonement (Boda 2010a, 271). In this case, the people assemble ahead of time for the Day of Atonement, scheduled for the tenth day, and transfer the ark before the Day of Atonement takes place. A final alternative interpretation identifies the festival as a unique event celebrating the transfer of the ark (*HALOT* s.v. "חַג" 289–90). In this case, the celebration is not directly connected to any festival mentioned in the Pentateuch.

Regardless of whether one identifies the festival with the Festival of Booths, the Festival of Booths is clearly in view within the larger narrative. Comparing the transfer of the ark to the Festival of Booths provides an interesting contrast. During the Festival of Booths, the people set up temporary shelters to commemorate how YHWH led Israel from Egypt to the land of Canaan, moving from place to place, but now that the ark rests in the temple, YHWH no longer dwells in a portable tent (Merrill 2015, 341).

Levites and Priests Deposit the Ark in the Temple (5:4–10)

The priests and Levites transfer the ark and the tabernacle into the temple while all Israel celebrates.

5:4–7. Once all Israel, represented by its leaders, arrives in Jerusalem, the Levites pick up the ark to carry it to its permanent resting place in the temple. By specifically mentioning the Levites here, the text shows that the same lesson David had to learn to transfer the ark (see 1 Chron. 13, 15), Solomon has learned as well. At the same time, mentioning only the Levites creates a bit of tension through the narrative because although the Mosaic law assigns the Levites the duty to carry the ark, they do not have access to the most holy place where the ark belongs. Likely for this reason, the verses as a whole present a picture in which both the priests and the Levites are responsible for moving the ark but in different ways. Numbers 4:1–33 lays out how priests and Levites should work together to transfer the ark, the tabernacle, and all its implements. The verses show that the Levites have the job of carrying the items, while the priests supervise and prepare the items so that the Levites do not see or touch the sacred objects directly. The Chronicler describes the ark's transfer in line with these instructions. To start, the Levites pick up the ark to carry it. At the end, the priests bring the ark into the most holy place to deposit it there. In the middle, the Chronicler states that the priests and Levites bring up the ark and other sacred items. It seems the Chronicler intends this final comment in a general sense (see 5:2, where the same verb applies to all Israel's leaders). As a result, the Chronicler shows how the process follows Mosaic law for both the priests and the Levites.

TRANSLATION ANALYSIS:
Translations render the final subject of the verse differently. Some render it as a compound subject "the priests and Levites" (CSB, NET, NKJV, NLT, NRSV); others render the subject as "the Levitical priests" (ESV, NASB, NIV). The different translations result from a textual variant. Both 1 Kings 8:4 and the versions of Chronicles read "the priests and Levites." MT Chronicles reads "Levitical priests." The difference in Hebrew is one consonant (ו), so one can easily imagine a copyist accidentally either inserting the consonant or omitting it; therefore, other factors are more important for rendering a decision. Although the Chronicler almost always distinguishes the priests from the Levites, on occasion he does not (2 Chron. 23:18; 30:27); therefore, this argument regarding distinction should not play a significant role in rendering a decision. Given the number of manuscripts and traditions that read "the priests and Levites," I have used that reading in the text. See also sidebar "Priests and Levites" at 2 Chronicles 13:9–10.

5:5. Even though the narrative focuses on the ark, it includes a significant comment regarding the tent of meeting and its implements. At this time Israel contains two tents significant for their worship: (1) the tent David set up for the ark, and (2) the tent/tabernacle Moses set up in the wilderness. David's tent is in Jerusalem and houses the regular daily musical performance of Asaph's division of musicians along with priestly trumpeters (1 Chron. 16:4–6, 37–38). The wilderness tabernacle is located at Gibeon and includes the altar for sacrifice. At Gibeon the priests perform the regular sacrifices, and Heman's and Jeduthun's divisions of musicians accompany the sacrifices with praises to YHWH (1 Chron. 16:39–42). Although one might expect the text to address David's tent since it houses the ark, in Chronicles, as elsewhere, the "tent of meeting" refers to the wilderness tabernacle (see 2 Chron. 1:3–6).

Mentioning that the priests and Levites bring up the tent of meeting as well as the ark is significant for two reasons. First, since the ark and the tent reside in different locations with different components of Israel's ritual worship, moving both the ark and the tent into the temple unifies worship within the temple. This point demonstrates that the Jerusalem temple houses all that Israel needs for proper ritual worship—a point made repeatedly through Chronicles.

Second, moving the tent of meeting to the temple depicts the temple as replacing or subsuming the wilderness tabernacle. Since the tabernacle is the legitimate place for sacrifice (see 1 Chron. 16:39–40; 2 Chron. 1:3–6), taking it over demonstrates the legitimacy of the Jerusalem temple as a "house of sacrifice" (2 Chron. 7:12). Even though Mosaic law does not mention a temple, this text presents the Jerusalem temple as a legitimate place for fulfilling the ritual worship requirements of the law. This activity also presents the temple as a part of YHWH's plan. As mentioned elsewhere (see particularly sections on 2 Chron. 1–4), the Chronicler situates the temple within YHWH's historical activity with Israel. He does not present it as something emerging from thin air, but a culmination of YHWH's activity from Abraham through Solomon.

From Tabernacle to Temple

Since the tabernacle is a mobile sanctuary, one may interpret the temple as its stationary replacement. With a permanent place prepared for YHWH's presence, a mobile sanctuary is no longer needed. In fact, Chronicles does not use the expression "tent of meeting" after 2 Chronicles 5:5. However, the picture in Chronicles is a little more complex. Although Chronicles does not mention the tent of meeting, 2 Chronicles 29:6 speaks of the "tabernacle" (מִשְׁכָּן) and 2 Chronicles 24:6 speaks of a "tent of testimony" (אֹהֶל הָעֵדוּת); both refer to the temple. It seems more likely that this language figuratively describes the temple subsuming the tabernacle; however, one may interpret the language literally so that the tent is set up within the most holy place (see Friedman 1980, 241–48).

5:6. The text provides few details regarding what takes place during the procession of the ark, especially regarding the king and the people. The text only states that they perform sacrifices ahead of the ark as it moves toward the temple. This activity resembles how David and the people worship as the ark proceeds to Jerusalem (1 Chron. 15:26); however, in the case of Solomon and the people, the sacrifices were too numerous to even count. This comparison between the two events continues the theme of Solomon fulfilling the work David begins.

5:7–8. When the procession finishes, the priests set the ark in its designated place under the cherubim within the most holy place. The text elaborates on some features of the ark within the inner sanctuary. First, it communicates how the ark sits in relation to the cherubim and provides some hints for their function there. The cherubim's wings spread out and cover the ark, likely

protecting the ark as a sacred object and perhaps also concealing it as an object dangerous to humans (see 1 Chron. 13:10–12; also Merrill 2015, 341).

Covering and Protecting the Ark

In 5:8, the word used to describe how the cherubim's wings relate to the ark is *piel* כסה, usually translated "to cover." The parallel in 1 Kings 8:8 is סכך, translated as "to cover, overshadow." The difference between the two words is switching the first and second consonants. Since Chronicles also uses the term סכך elsewhere to describe how the cherubim relate to the ark (1 Chron. 28:18), its use here is likely the same. In Ezekiel 28:14, 16 the term סכך describes a cherub apparently assigned the task of protecting. In the case of the ark, the cherubim's wings may have a dual function: to protect the temple's sanctity and to conceal YHWH's appearance so that it does not harm those who approach it (e.g., Lev. 10:1–2; 1 Chron. 13:10–12).

5:9. Second, the text mentions the poles to carry the ark. Retaining the poles seems unnecessary, since the ark is now placed in its permanent position. Perhaps retaining the poles intends to fulfill Exodus 25:15, which commands Israel not to remove the poles from the ark (Japhet 1993, 578). Furthermore, the cherubim's wings cover the ark and the poles. If the wings represent protection, then their wings would deter anyone from moving the ark. At the same time, the text highlights how the poles extend quite a bit beyond the ark itself. In this way the ark retains some of its character as a portable object, even though it will now remain stationary in the temple.

5:10. Third, the text describes what the ark holds. In the ancient Near East, other gods are present with the people through idols of various kinds. However, as a symbol of YHWH's presence, the ark is an empty box. It only contains the two tablets YHWH gave to Moses at Horeb (also known as Mount Sinai). The presence of the tablets is a reminder that YHWH is present through his Word and not his image (see Deut. 4:5–15).

What the Ark Contains

The OT associates two other items with the ark of the covenant: a jar of manna (Exod. 16:33) and Aaron's budding rod (Num. 17:10). In neither OT passage is it clear that these items were placed in the ark; however, Hebrews 9:4 states that the ark held these items as well as the tablets. Hebrews is also looking back to the wilderness tabernacle and not the temple itself.

The Cloud of YHWH's Glory Fills the Temple (5:11–14)

YHWH fills the temple with his overwhelming glory as the priests and Levites worship through music.

5:11–14. After the priests place the ark within the most holy place, YHWH signifies both his approval and his presence by filling the temple building with a cloud of his glory. Even though it is difficult to determine how the various statements of 5:11–14 relate to one another, the timing of YHWH's filling the temple is still clear: YHWH fills the temple with his glory after the priests have left the building and once the musicians have begun their musical worship service. Since the cloud of YHWH's glory is such a forbidding, dreadful presence, preventing the priests from even entering the temple, it makes sense that it does not appear until the priests leave. The timing of the music is not quite as clear. One could argue that the Chronicler presents the music—in particular, the refrain ("YHWH is good, his loyal love endures forever," 5:13)—as evoking YHWH's presence in the cloud (Kleinig 1993, 165–66). More likely the Chronicler shows how depositing the ark in the temple unifies and completes the full priestly and Levitical worship service with all the Levitical musicians (Asaph, Heman, Jeduthun, their

sons, and relatives) as well as a full complement of priestly trumpeters. In other words, the cloud fills the temple once the ark, the tent of meeting, and its furnishings are brought together in one place and all the priests and Levites, from both Jerusalem and Gibeon, come together to fulfill their ritual worship duties.

TRANSLATION ANALYSIS:
The greatest challenge to translating these verses is determining how the clauses relate to one another, since there are some parenthetical statements and temporal markers. Second Chronicles 5:11 begins with a temporal marker (most often translated "when"). The next clause does not complete the sentence; instead, it forms a parenthetical statement. Based on the verb forms, I would argue that 5:12 continues the parenthetical statement, but the beginning of 5:13 completes the sentence. As a result, when the priests left the holy place, it was the responsibility of the musicians to play their music together to praise YHWH and give him thanks. The rest of 5:13 then introduces two more temporal clauses ("as the sound of their music arose" and "when they praised YHWH"). Second Chronicles 5:13 closes with the clause that completes the sentence: "the temple, that is, the temple of YHWH, was filled with a cloud."

For this significant event, the text emphasizes that all the priests and musicians participate. Second Chronicles 5:11 mentions that all the priests sanctify themselves regardless of division. The priestly divisions determine which group of priests serves at a particular time, since normally not all the priests serve at once. However, on this occasion, all the priests prepare to serve by sanctifying themselves. Second Chronicles 5:12 also points out that all the Levitical musicians—that is, all the male relatives from Asaph, Heman, and Jeduthun—also participate in the celebration. Finally, the 120 priestly trumpeters, probably representing the twenty-four priestly divisions, participate along with the Levitical musicians. Again, the fullness of the celebration points to the Jerusalem temple as the proper center for all Israel's unified worship of YHWH.

5:13b–14. The cloud's filling the temple is not a large public display for the people as a whole. It only involves the temple building, not the larger complex, and therefore only affects those who have close access to the temple: priests and Levites. The emphasis here involves one important aspect of the Jerusalem temple's role: it serves as YHWH's house—that is, the focal point of his unique, hidden presence in Israel. The priests and Levites minister to YHWH hidden from public sight by burning the incense, caring for the lampstands, setting out the showbread, and so on (see 2 Chron. 2:4 [HB 3]; 13:11). They also make music to praise and give thanks to YHWH. However, the public sacrifices are not in view in this context. YHWH approves the temple as a place of sacrifice as the king and people make countless offerings (2 Chron. 7:1–4). In that context YHWH publicly displays his glory as fire falls on the altar.

The glory cloud appears as a theophany, an intense momentary visible presentation of YHWH's unique presence. This theophany's intensity lets up at some point so that the priests can return to the temple's inner chambers and resume their duties. At the same time, the cloud represents YHWH's continual intense, even dangerous, presence within the temple. Leviticus 16:2 warns Aaron and his descendants not to enter the most holy place as they wish, for they may die, as YHWH reveals himself in the cloud. In this way, following the example of several theophanies in which YHWH promises his continual presence (Fretheim 1984, 98; Greene 2018, 774–75), the Chronicler presents this moment of YHWH's intense manifestation while also alluding to YHWH's continual, only slightly less intense, presence in the temple.

> ### YHWH's Continual Presence
> Chronicles records another incident in the temple that confirms YHWH's intense, dangerous presence in the temple: the account of Uzziah's skin disease (2 Chron. 26:16–21). During the account Uzziah enters the temple to burn incense when a defiling skin disease suddenly breaks out upon his forehead. As a result, he must leave the temple immediately and may not return during the rest of his life.

The event of the cloud filling the temple resembles another event in Israel's history: the completion of the wilderness tabernacle. When Moses completed setting up the tabernacle, the glory of YHWH filled the tent so that Moses could no longer enter (Exod. 40:33–35). In a similar way the cloud of YHWH's glory fills the temple and prevents the priests from performing their duties. The Chronicler shows again how the temple replaces or subsumes the wilderness tabernacle as the place for the priests and Levites to fulfill their duties of service to YHWH.

TRANSLATION ANALYSIS:
Some translations render the verse in such a way that implies that the priests could not continue their duties (CSB, NKJV, NLT). Other translations render the Hebrew more formally as "could not stand" (ESV, NASB, NRSV); however, in English, this expression carries the connotation of extreme displeasure, as though the cloud made it so uncomfortable for the priests to fulfill their duties that they chose to stop. In this context, the text more likely simply indicates that the cloud prevented the priests from fulfilling their duties. For this reason, a translation that conveys this sense (e.g., NET, NIV) is preferable.

In some important ways the differences between the events described in this narrative and the context of the first readers resembles the differences between those same events and the contemporary context. For the first readers the ark was long gone; the tent of meeting and its implements were no longer around; no cloud of YHWH's glory descended upon the temple; no Davidic king occupied Israel's throne; the people of Israel were scattered among various nations. As a result, the first readers could not relive this experience in their own day. At the same time, their context did overlap with the events described in some important ways. The first readers did have a temple in Jerusalem. They did have priests and Levites set aside to serve YHWH in ritual worship by maintaining the Jerusalem temple and performing the musical service. They also had YHWH's promise to be with them. As a result, the first readers could take comfort in YHWH's presence among them, especially as they worshipped YHWH according to the law of Moses, just as Solomon did in bringing up the ark to Jerusalem.

THEOLOGICAL FOCUS

God always wants to dwell with his people and enjoy their worship.

Ancient Near Eastern religions involved numerous physical objects believed to embody and/or represent various divine beings. Most of these objects were idols, that is, images of deities of one sort or another. Worshipping the idol was worshipping the deity. Furthermore, the idol's presence represented the deity's presence. In contrast, Mosaic law did not allow the use of images to represent or symbolize God. The true God has no idol.

The lack of any idol raises the following question: How could Israel recognize God's presence among them? The ark of the covenant serves as one way in which God shows his presence among the people. However, unlike the religions of the ancient Near East, the ark is not an idol but a nearly empty box. There is no image of God portrayed on the box or found within it. The lack of an image demonstrates that the God of Israel is not like the gods of the other nations because they are useless idols made by human hands (1 Chron. 16:26; 2 Chron. 32:19).

Instead of an image, the box contains the tablets of divine law. The tablets point to the covenantal relationship between God and his people. As a result, God's relationship with his people is not mediated through an idol but through the covenant established with them at Sinai. During the reign of Solomon, the ark serves as an important link to the period of the wilderness, in which God made himself known to Israel through his covenant with them at Sinai. However, the evidence available suggests that the ark did not survive into the postexilic period. Although the postexilic community did not have the ark, they did have a temple. This temple would serve as the link between the postexilic community and the generations of Israel that preceded them, even into the wilderness period.

As a symbol of God's presence among his people, the Jerusalem temple serves as something of a paradox. On the one hand, the temple is a place from which God is present with his people. On the other hand, the temple is a place that keeps people at a distance from God. The temple functions both to bring God near and keep him away. Because God's presence will overwhelm any human being, the temple provides a means for God's people to experience his presence without dying. God is present but veiled in certain ways.

During Jesus's earthly ministry, the function of the temple shifts to Jesus in certain aspects. The divine Word becomes flesh and dwells among human beings, revealing God even though no one has seen God (John 1:14–18). Although Jesus reveals God, his earthly presence only reveals his divine nature in a veiled manner. Only during his transfiguration does Jesus pull back the veil, so to speak, to reveal his divine nature in greater measure. Jesus's transfiguration not only serves as a confirmation of his divine nature during his earthly ministry, but it also looks forward to a time when God will finally judge the world and glorify his saints so that they may experience and enjoy his presence fully.

This passage points to God's work throughout history. It points to the deep connections between God's presence among his people during the wilderness period, the Solomonic period, and the postexilic period. The NT picks up on these deep connections to show how God's new work in Jesus and the church relates to God's past work. Furthermore, it points to the hope that someday God's glory, which has only been observed in part, will be experienced fully (Rev. 21:11, 23).

PREACHING AND TEACHING STRATEGIES

Exegetical and Theological Synthesis

After great effort was put into proper worship and celebrating the arrival of the ark of the covenant, a cloud filled the temple to let the priests know—and through them, to let Israel know—that God was with them. Jesus stated often, and left this world, with these last words: "I am with you always." We were created with a desire to be with others, which is a reflection of a deeper desire to be with God and him with us. This unique experience and its record are one way that the Israelites knew that God was with them. This written record is for us as well and is sufficient for us to know that God is with us. However, the knowledge of God being with the Israelites was greatly enhanced in this experience. We can't re-create the experience, but we can experience an enhanced awareness of God's presence. The sacrifices, the proper handling of the ark that held the covenant, and the majestic music led up to the cloud filling the temple. This is not a formula that guarantees an awareness of God's presence, but it does teach us that proper worship enhances our awareness of his presence.

Preaching Idea

When we need to feel God's presence, it is time to worship.

Contemporary Connections

Is it true?

The three-year-old had difficulty going to sleep unless a parent was in the room. So for weeks the parents took turns sitting on the floor, in the dark, in the midst of picture books, surrounded by toys with batteries and frayed stuffed animals. When the child's breathing finally slowed, sounding like he was asleep, the stealth exit was attempted. Crawling as quietly as possible, careful not to squash a squeaking duck or bump a battery-powered police car, the parent carefully moved toward the door, only to be stopped by, "Daddy, are you there?" "Yes, son I'm still here."

We want to know if God is with us. If we could see the cloud filling the temple, as the Israelite priests did, then we would know that he is with us. But we were not there and the only cloud we experience in our churches might be from a fog machine during a children's program. But remember, those reading this account for the first time didn't see the cloud; they had only heard about it. Even those who lived under Solomon's rule did not see the cloud. Only the priests saw it, for the cloud was in the temple. Just like the Israelites, each of us still wants to know, "Daddy, are you still there?" While God doesn't give us a cloud, he gives us a clear record of that event—not just a legend or myth but a written record of the sign of his presence.

God gives us his story and through it says to us, "This is how you know I am with you. I came and filled that temple as a cloud." The cloud came in the midst of proper worship. God's physical metaphor told them, and tells us, that a cloud can't be captured and exiled to Babylon. A cloud can't be pinned down. A cloud invades all the areas of a room or a life.

While it is hard to point and say "there it is," a cloud's presence is undeniable.

What does it mean?

The music was almost too loud, but the retired preacher wanted to experience this new innovative church that met in a converted grocery store building. The songs sung, while recently written, spoke the truth that transcends time. The lighting was dim, but the focus of the morning was clearly on the light of Scripture. Christ, his sacrifice, and his resurrection were at the heart of even the warm welcome. The pastor, in the contemporary evangelical clerical uniform of blue jeans, untucked collared shirt, and black glasses, presented the truth of God's covenant with clarity and relevancy. The retired pastor was delighted with the proper worship of this innovative church: the sacrificial and victorious work of Jesus was highlighted, the truth of God's written Word was presented, and proper God-honoring music was sung. However, it wasn't until the closing that he felt the presence of God. After the sermon, this church took time for the parents to bring their children into the worship center so they could worship together as a family. A mom who had sat by herself during worship left and came back with her seven-year-old daughter. The daughter stood just in front of the mom, facing forward. The mom hands rested on the pony-tailed girl's shoulders in a soft embrace. As they both sang of God's power and presence, the little girl occasionally looked back and up at her mom as if to ask, "Are you there, mom?" It was then that the presence of God flooded over this retired pastor like a cloud.

When we worship in the proper way, remembering that God's presence came to the first temple in a cloud and to the second temple in the person of Jesus, God renews our awareness that he is always with us. When we ask, "God, are you there?," through the record of this event, and through the work of Jesus, he says to us, "Yes, my child I am."

Now what?

When is it that you fear being alone? Some will quickly say, "I don't want to die alone." Some have a fear of being alone on a daily, moment-by-moment basis, perhaps because they had an experience in which they were abandoned as a child. When we experience grief, it is comforting to have people around us—not to say the right words, but just to be with us. When a thunderstorm hits with the deafening claps of thunder a child may run to the parents because they don't want to be alone. The feeling of being alone can take place in the midst of a crowd, or a family, or a marriage, or a church due to a secret struggle within. Two people can be alone in a marriage that on the surface seems perfect, but is filled with two cold, stubbornly independent people, with their address being the only thing they have in common.

So, what do we do when we need to sense God's presence? We do what the Israelites were doing: worship. When we give attention to private and public worship, our awareness of God's presence is enhanced. The cloud didn't bring God's presence; the cloud only showed them the reality that God was already with them. So too God's presence is always with us, through the sacrifice of Jesus for us. Focusing upon God's written covenant to us, and adding proper music, can help us sense his presence.

This threefold pattern of worship can be reflected in our worship. Our trust is in the sacrificial work of Jesus and his resurrection. We should properly handle the old and new covenant, his written Word to us. And, in an appropriate way, our music should reflect the majesty of God. In our time, the expression of these three elements varies greatly across the numerous cultures that span the globe. No matter where we are, when we need to feel his presence, it is time to worship.

Creativity in Presentation

This passage is filled with excitement and celebration, and that can and should be reflected in the sermon/lesson. It could be helpful to compare this celebration to a celebration familiar to the listeners: football games, holiday celebrations, weddings, graduations, or something as simple as the unhindered joy of grandchildren running to greet their grandparents. The aim is to bring something to mind that helps re-create the emotion of the ark coming to the newly finished temple. God presents his story with a plot that rises to the climax at the end.

As the text is presented, try to build excitement in each element of the story. One possibility is to present the story from the perspective of a priest who was in the heart of the activities. This could be done in a first-person narrative type of format or, as the text is read, insert what a priest might be thinking. The advantage of either of these formats is the background of why this event is so special, which can be added along with the priest's growing anticipation. For example, the priest shares that he had never seen the ark; he had only been told about it. Now it was to be moved. The crowds and the number of sacrifices was more than he had ever seen; it was good that the new altar was so large. The climax of the cloud filling the temple can be maximized by the priest remembering accounts of how the cloud filled the tabernacle in the wilderness. Using this device, whether presenting the event as a priest or presenting it with insights that could have come from a priest who witnessed the event, will aid in recreating the celebratory nature of this text. Here is one possible structure:

- Present the text
  - Solomon gathers Israel (5:2–3)
  - Levites and priests deposit the ark in the temple (5:4–10)
  - Cloud of YHWH's glory fills the temple (5:11–14)
- Application
  - Times when we want to experience God's presence
  - Proper worship enhances our awareness of God's presence

DISCUSSION QUESTIONS

1. What about a cloud made it an effective way for God to reveal his presence?

2. How do you think the music affected those gathered at the dedication of Solomon's temple?

3. How does music affect our worship?

4. How has the presence of someone affected you at a time of crisis or celebration?

5. What were the specific actions of those participating? How did those actions affect them?

6. How does your behavior change when you are in the presence of certain people?

2 Chronicles 6:1–42

EXEGETICAL IDEA
The temple was important because it was a worthy place for YHWH to dwell in hiddenness, because it fulfilled part of YHWH's promise to David, and because it would become a place for prayer.

THEOLOGICAL FOCUS
God is present and transcendent, faithful to his promises, and attentive to those who pray to him.

PREACHING IDEA
Yes, God does hear our prayers.

PREACHING POINTERS
Remember the old mobile phone commercials that featured the phrase, "Can you hear me now?" Mobile phone coverage has greatly improved, but we still experience disruption in our phone service. When driving through a hilly or rural area, we might have to ask, "Did you hear me?" This episode in the life of Israel teaches us that we don't have to ask that of God. His character and love for us leads us to pray—and he is attentive to our prayers. In the communication of law-enforcement officers in TV series, we often hear, "Copy that." The phrase means that a person not only heard what you said but that they have also understood it. In a sense, when we pray, God says, "Copy that"—not in the sense that he is taking orders from us, but that he truly hears us and is attentive to our need.

SOLOMON'S PRAYER OF DEDICATION (6:1–42)

LITERARY STRUCTURE AND THEMES (6:1–42)

After Israel deposits the ark in the temple, YHWH fills the temple with his glory. In this passage Solomon takes the lead role. He responds to the temple in several ways. First, he celebrates the temple as YHWH's residence. Solomon points out that even though YHWH dwells in a special way in the splendid Jerusalem temple, he is still hidden. Second, Solomon turns to Israel, blesses them, and reminds them how YHWH fulfilled his promise to David by making Solomon king and temple-builder. Third, Solomon kneels on a platform before all Israel to pray to YHWH. He begins his prayer by requesting YHWH to fulfill his promise to David, just as he did when addressing the people. Second Chronicles 6:12–13 seems to interrupt the flow of Solomon's discussion, but they separate two parallel sections: one moves from past to present (6:4–11), while the other moves from present to future (6:14–17).

After Solomon finishes reflecting on the promises to David, he prays that the temple will be a house of prayer. After a comment on the nature of YHWH's presence in the temple, he describes seven scenarios in which Israel should pray to YHWH. With few exceptions, the scenarios share the following pattern: (1) situation, (2) cause, (3) repentance and/or prayer, (4) place, (5) supplication, and (6) request that YHWH act or forgive (Knoppers 1995, 236–37). Finally, Solomon closes by requesting that YHWH will inhabit the temple, bless his people, and grant Solomon's request. Solomon's response in this chapter shows how important the temple is—because it is a place worthy for YHWH to dwell in hiddenness, because it fulfills part of YHWH's

promise to David, and because it could become a place for prayer.

- **Solomon Celebrates the Temple as YHWH's Residence (6:1–2)**
- **Solomon Reminds the People How YHWH Fulfilled the Promise to David (6:3–11)**
- **Solomon Requests YHWH to Continue to Fulfill the Promise to David (6:12–17)**
- **Solomon Prays That the Temple Will Be a House of Prayer (6:18–42)**

EXPOSITION (6:1–42)

In the ancient Near East, people held temples in high regard. Often a king built a temple for a deity whom he believed to have secured the throne for him. He believed that, as a result, the deity would dwell within the temple and provide protection and prosperity. Since the deity inhabited the temple in some way, people could seek the deity's favor there as well. At the same time, the deity remained hidden within the restricted areas of the temple. Against this background, Solomon responds to YHWH's special presence within the temple. In some ways, his response coincides with the culture. Solomon recognizes that YHWH dwells in the temple, but in a hidden manner. He recognizes YHWH's role in establishing him as king and requests that YHWH will secure his dynasty after him. He encourages the people to pray at or toward the temple to seek YHWH's favor in different situations.

However, because of who YHWH is, Solomon downplays the temple as a divine residence. He focuses on YHWH's immensity, extending far beyond the temple. He repeatedly calls heaven the place of YHWH's dwelling, while the temple is the object of YHWH's special attention. In the end, the chapter shows how important the temple is as a place worthy of YHWH's special presence, as a fulfillment of YHWH's promise to David, and as a place for prayer.

Solomon Celebrates the Temple as YHWH's Residence (6:1–2)

After YHWH fills the temple with the glorious cloud, Solomon celebrates that he has built a splendid temple for YHWH and that YHWH has chosen to inhabit it.

6:1. After Solomon deposits the ark in the temple and YHWH affirms his action by filling the temple with a glorious cloud, Solomon responds by acknowledging the temple as a divine residence. Here, he briefly addresses the nature of the temple as YHWH's residence. First, YHWH's presence is always veiled. Solomon states that YHWH chooses to dwell in a "dark cloud" (עֲרָפֶל). This term occurs in contexts of theophany throughout the OT, most notably the theophany at Sinai (Exod. 20:21; Deut. 4:11; 5:22). Here, the term also connects this "dark cloud" with the "cloud" (עָנָן) that overshadows the temple (2 Chron. 5:14). Leviticus 16:2 warns the priests not to enter the holy place as they please because they may die, since within the holy place YHWH reveals himself in the "cloud" (עָנָן). In this way, the Chronicler has accomplished several purposes through this brief comment. He has connected Israel's previous theophanies to the temple as the focus of YHWH's dwelling among his people. He has also explained some of the hidden, secretive, restricted nature of the temple. At the temple, YHWH can "safely" dwell among his people without his glory overwhelming them.

TRANSLATION ANALYSIS:
Translations generally render the word אמר with some form of "said." The sense of the verb in this context appears to be closer to "plans, intends, chooses." Similar usages, especially with an infinitive, occur elsewhere in Chronicles (e.g., 2 Chron. 28:10). See also *HALOT* s.v. "אמר" 65–67.

6:2. Second, Solomon has constructed a lofty, exalted temple for YHWH. The nature of the temple corresponds to the nature of YHWH. As Solomon has already expressed in his plans to construct the temple, he intended to build a great temple for YHWH because YHWH is a great God. Solomon's comment here helps clarify the meaning of that great temple: it is a lofty, splendid temple for YHWH (see comments on 2 Chron. 2:1–18 [HB 1:18–2:17]).

Third, the temple is YHWH's place of residence. The expression "place of dwelling" (מָכוֹן שֶׁבֶת) draws connections in two directions. First, it looks back to Moses's song in celebration of the exodus from Egypt. Exodus 15:17 speaks of YHWH's (then) future activity of planting his people and establishing a "place of dwelling" (מָכוֹן שֶׁבֶת), identified as YHWH's sanctuary. This connection shows that by building this extravagant temple Solomon not only fulfills his own previous purposes (2 Chron. 2:4–5 [HB 5–6]), nor just the promises made to David (6:4–11), but also a plan begun in Israel's exodus from Egypt. Second, the expression looks to passages that speak of YHWH's royal throne. Psalm 97:2 describes YHWH as king: cloud (עָנָן) and dark cloud (עֲרָפֶל) surround him while righteousness and justice form the foundation (מָכוֹן) of his throne. Therefore, when the text speaks of YHWH's dwelling in the temple, it implies more precisely his sitting on his throne.

Solomon Reminds the People How YHWH Fulfilled the Promise to David (6:3–11)

Solomon blesses the people by reminding them of YHWH's promise to David, and how YHWH has fulfilled it through Solomon.

6:3–6. After Solomon initially responds to YHWH's glory filling the temple (6:1–2), he faces the people to address them. The narrative describes a solemn scene: Solomon blesses all Israel as they stand. The text does not record what Solomon says as he blesses the people (the speech of 6:4–11 blesses YHWH, not the people).

Blessing Through Israel's History

Solomon's blessing resembles other moments in Israel's history. For instance, David blessed the people after he successfully delivered the ark to Jerusalem (1 Chron. 16:2). The text also does not record what David said in that blessing. Further back, Moses blessed the people when they completed the tabernacle, all its furnishings, and its implements (Exod. 39:43). Again, the text does not record what Moses said. In this way, Solomon's activity falls in line with Israel's previous history. The activity also focuses attention on the close connection between David and Solomon.

Even though the text does not record what Solomon says as he blesses all Israel, it does record what he says as he addresses them. Solomon blesses YHWH as the one who has made a promise to David and fulfilled it through Solomon (6:4). Solomon focuses on YHWH's past and present activity with David and Solomon. He captures the essence of YHWH's promise to David by speaking of YHWH's choice of Jerusalem and David. Before David, YHWH did not choose a specific city to house a temple, nor did he choose a specific person to rule over all Israel.

TRANSLATION ANALYSIS:
The text uses the expression דִּבֶּר בְּפִיו ("spoke with his mouth"). This phrase may carry the connotation of speaking "directly" (CSB); however, especially in this case, it more likely carries the connotation of making a promise or oath. It strengthens the notion that YHWH has fulfilled what he obligated himself to do (see Jer. 44:25).

Characterizing YHWH's Promise

The language appears as a direct speech from YHWH; however, no other passage in the OT records this specific statement to David. For this reason, the text most likely intends the statement to be a faithful characterization of what YHWH promised to David rather than a direct quotation of an extrabiblical oracle or prophetic utterance.

The language of this passage is to some degree hyperbolic, since it overlooks previous sanctuaries (e.g., Shiloh) and previous rulers (e.g., Saul). At the same time, their exclusion makes good sense in context: once built, the Jerusalem temple is the only legitimate sanctuary (e.g., 2 Chron. 29:6), and once the kingdom is transferred to David the Davidic line is the only legitimate dynasty (e.g., 2 Chron. 13:5).

David as Head of a Dynasty

Apparently, the significance of choosing David as "ruler" (נָגִיד) is making him the head of a dynasty. Even though in other contexts the word may refer simply to one in a role of authority, such as a king, here it points beyond just David to his descendants. Therefore, the text would exclude Saul, since his entire house died with him (1 Chron. 10:6).

Not only does the language exclude any predecessors, but it also connects YHWH's choice of Jerusalem as the site for the temple with YHWH's choice of David as ruler. Partly for this reason, the Chronicler records that immediately after Israel coronates David, he captures Jerusalem. Furthermore, this theme recurs in Chronicles as the Chronicler demonstrates that how a king treats the temple determines the king's fate (e.g., Ahaz, 2 Chron. 28; and Hezekiah, 2 Chron. 29–32). Solomon's speech confirms this connection by mentioning right after YHWH affirms his choice of Jerusalem and David that David wants to build a temple.

6:7–10. These verses reflect on YHWH's choice of Jerusalem as the temple site and David as the head of a dynasty. Unlike Saul (1 Chron. 13:3), David follows YHWH by caring for the ark and wanting to build a temple. Furthermore, Chronicles mentions on multiple occasions that David wants to build a temple (1 Chron. 17:2; 22:7; 28:2). David's desire corresponds with YHWH's choice to establish his dynasty and strengthens the picture of David as the one to initiate building the temple. However, even though David does well to initiate building the temple, YHWH does not allow David to finish it. Instead, one of David's sons will build the temple. Since David does not build the temple, but one of David's sons does, the verses present both parts of YHWH's promise coming to pass at the same time: (1) YHWH fulfills his promise to give David a dynasty and not just a kingdom, and (2) Jerusalem becomes the site for the temple. Solomon sees YHWH fulfilling his promise in this moment because Solomon's rule means that David has a dynasty and because Solomon has constructed the temple for YHWH in Jerusalem.

David and Abraham

The language to describe David's biological son likely draws an allusion to Genesis 35:11. In that passage YHWH promises Abraham that kings will be among his biological descendants. The allusion's significance at this point is twofold: (1) it presents the Davidic dynasty as at least a partial fulfillment of this promise to Abraham, and (2) it draws a parallel between Abraham and David, since neither one of them saw YHWH fulfill his promises to them.

6:11. Solomon finishes his comments by pointing out that he has moved the ark within the temple. This comment regarding the ark is important because the temple itself does not fulfill its purpose as a place for YHWH's residence until the ark of the covenant rests within it. The comment is also important because it

shows another way that Solomon completes what David began in bringing the ark of the covenant to its permanent resting place within the Jerusalem temple.

Covenant of the Present, Not Just the Past

This passage refers to the ark as "the ark of the covenant that YHWH made with the sons of Israel." Because of this specific language, H. G. M. Williamson argues that the Chronicler is pointing more to the covenant now in effect, not just a covenant of the past made with the fathers (1982, 216). This designation of the ark also foreshadows the mention of covenant in following verses.

Solomon Requests YHWH to Continue to Fulfill the Promise to David (6:12–17)

Solomon praises YHWH for his faithfulness and power to fulfill what he has promised to David and calls on YHWH to continue to fulfill his promises in establishing David's dynasty.

6:12–13. Since Solomon continues into this section to speak about YHWH's promise to David and its fulfillment, it is somewhat surprising that the text describes Solomon's posture and position at this time, appearing to interrupt the flow of Solomon's words. However, the comments regarding Solomon's posture here point to prayer: (1) he spreads his hands toward the sky, and (2) he kneels. Previously, Solomon had turned to the people to address them as they stood before him. Therefore, the text draws a distinction between what Solomon has been saying to the people and what he now begins to say. In the previous section, Solomon delivered a speech to Israel, focusing on the past up to the present. In the current section, Solomon prays to YHWH, focusing on the present into the future.

The Function of Passage's Interruption

Both sections (6:4–11 and 14–17) share a similar structure: (1) praise to YHWH for his faithfulness, (2) a statement that YHWH has fulfilled with his hands what he promised with his mouth (6:4 and 15), and (3) further elaboration on the Davidic promise. Second Chronicles 6:12–13 make this parallel structure possible and sharpen the distinction between Solomon's address to the people and Solomon's prayer to YHWH.

Not only do these verses mark a transition in the text, but they also say something about Solomon. First, the verses explain Solomon's position in relation to the temple. Second Chronicles 6:12 states that Solomon stands before the altar, but 6:13 clarifies that Solomon stands upon a platform he constructed in the larger courtyard where the people have access. Solomon's position on the platform places him above the people even as they stand (6:4); however, his posture of kneeling shows that he is subordinate to YHWH. Both points—the exaltation of the king over the people and the subordination of the king to YHWH—recur frequently in Chronicles (Lynch 2014b, 242–43). Chronicles even picks up on this pattern when it mentions that good kings have a place designated within the temple for them to stand before the people as they make a covenant with the people before YHWH (e.g., Joash, 2 Chron. 23:13; Josiah, 2 Chron. 34:31).

6:14. When Solomon prays, he begins by praising YHWH. He shows how YHWH is unique. He emphasizes two characteristics of YHWH: (1) YHWH is God, and (2) YHWH is faithful. The language is somewhat ambiguous about how YHWH is unique in these characteristics. First, one may interpret the statement to mean that there is not a god in heaven or on earth who is like YHWH, because he is faithful. In this case YHWH is unique as a faithful God. One may also interpret the statement to mean that YHWH is unique because he is God both in heaven and on earth; furthermore, he is faithful. His faithfulness is part of his character as God,

but what makes him unique is that he is God of heaven and earth. In light of other passages in Chronicles, the latter is more probable.

Second, one may interpret the nature of YHWH's faithfulness in different ways. The text explicitly speaks of YHWH's faithfulness in terms of covenant loyalty. One may interpret this covenant loyalty as YHWH's commitment to his people. The verse indicates that YHWH shows this commitment to those who wholeheartedly obey him. This interpretation implies that YHWH may not be faithful if Israel is disobedient. However, one may also interpret covenant loyalty in the sense of YHWH carrying through on what he obligates himself to do in his covenant with Israel. The implication of this interpretation would be that YHWH faithfully blesses those who obey as he has committed himself to do in his covenant (see Lev. 26:1–13; Deut. 28:1–14). The fact that other biblical authors use the phrase to begin confessing sins to YHWH (Neh. 1:5–11; Dan. 9:4–19; Harris , Archer, and Waltke 305–7) supports the latter interpretation. For Israel during and after exile, this characteristic of YHWH provided comfort and a rationale for confessing sins to YHWH and asking YHWH to restore his people.

TRANSLATION ANALYSIS:
Three significant issues confront the translator of this verse. First, one must determine the nature of the verse's message regarding other gods. English translations point to an interpretation of this verse as a statement meaning that there is no god who is like YHWH because they render the first part of the verse as "there is no god like you in heaven or on earth." This translation is possible and follows the accents of MT. The accents reflect a Jewish reading of the verse at least since the medieval period. At the same time, the accents are not always a reliable guide. In this case it is also possible to translate the text as "there is none like you, God in heaven and on earth." This latter interpretation aligns more closely to other passages

in Chronicles, (e.g., 1 Chron. 16:25–26; 17:20). Second, translations must determine how to render the phrase שֹׁמֵר הַבְּרִית וְהַחֶסֶד. Some treat each term separately (ESV, NKJV, NLT); however, the two nouns likely form a hendiadys in which the two words work together to represent one combined sense rather than two separate senses. One may see this interpretation in translations such as "keeping his gracious covenant" (CSB) or "maintain[ing] covenant loyalty" (NET).

Third, the Hebrew phrase הַהֹלְכִים לְפָנֶיךָ בְּכָל־לִבָּם ("those who walk before you with all their heart," ESV) requires further clarification. Second Chronicles 6:16 demonstrates the sense of this phrase. It compares David's walking before YHWH with walking in YHWH's law. To walk in the law carries the sense of obeying the law. Therefore, the phrase signifies obeying YHWH's law wholeheartedly (cf. NET).

6:15–17. Solomon reiterates what he said previously (6:4): YHWH has fulfilled what he promised to David. However, Solomon orients his remarks differently: rather than focusing on the past, he draws attention to how YHWH has fulfilled his promise in the present. Since YHWH has fulfilled his promise, Solomon requests YHWH to fulfill his promise to David. At first, these two points appear to contradict each other and raise the following question: If YHWH has fulfilled his promise to David, then why does he still need to fulfill his promise to David? Two observations help answer the question. First, what YHWH says to David is a promise and not a prediction. A prediction is a statement about what will happen in the future. Generally, the one making the prediction has no control over the outcome. In contrast, a promise is a commitment regarding the future. The one making the promise has at least some control over the outcome. In this case YHWH's promise is a commitment to regard Jerusalem as his place of residence and

to keep one of David's descendants on the throne. In this way YHWH has fulfilled his promise and yet may fulfill it in the future.

Second, the nature of YHWH's commitment also requires something from David's descendants. Chronicles demonstrates how YHWH makes the promise to David, in part, as a response to David's desire to honor YHWH by building a temple. YHWH honors that commitment as David's descendants demonstrate the same type of devotion. In this case that devotion appears as obedience to YHWH's law. Since YHWH punishes the kings for their disobedience, his punishment opens up opportunities for him to renew his promise by returning a Davidic descendant to the throne (e.g., Athaliah and Joash, 2 Chron. 22–23). Third, part of the message of Chronicles is that the Davidic promise both has been fulfilled and still awaits to be fulfilled. When the book ends, neither the temple nor the Davidic dynasty remains. However, the book closes with a call for someone to go up to rebuild the temple. Such a call opens the door for a Davidic descendant to rise up who will again build a temple as the place for YHWH's residence.

> ### Let YHWH's Word Come True
> The language of 6:17 "let your word . . . come true" (NIV) occurs in other passages in Chronicles. David makes the same request in 1 Chronicles 17:23 as he awaits the fulfillment of both temple and dynasty. Solomon previously has made the same request after he rose to the throne (2 Chron. 1:9). The repetition of the request shows both how YHWH has already been faithful in fulfilling his promise during the life of Solomon and how he may still fulfill the promise among the future descendants of David.

Solomon Prays That the Temple Will Be a Place of Prayer (6:18–42)

Solomon asks for YHWH to pay special attention to the temple as a place of prayer by describing several scenarios in which YHWH upholds justice or extends forgiveness.

6:18. This section shifts the focus from the Davidic promise to the temple as a place of prayer. The section begins with general comments regarding the nature of the temple and how it relates to prayer. Two important points emerge from these comments: (1) the temple does not hold YHWH, but (2) YHWH may still pay it special attention. The first sentence of the section is a rhetorical question whether YHWH will live on earth with humanity. The expected answer is clearly no. The point of this comment is that YHWH is not like other gods, mere idols that are made from earthly materials and dwell in earthly places (see 1 Chron. 16:25–26; 2 Chron. 32:19); instead, YHWH inhabits the heavenly realm. Solomon acknowledges that this temple cannot hold YHWH, since heaven, even the highest heaven, cannot contain him. At this point Solomon is drawing a contrast between YHWH's presence at the temple and his presence in heaven.

Balanced Presentation of the Temple

Chronicles repeatedly aims to create a balance regarding the nature of the temple, especially when recounting Solomon's reign. For instance, in 6:18–39 the text distinguishes the earthly temple from the heavenly realm; however, earlier in the chapter (6:2), the nearly identical phrase to describe heaven as the "place of dwelling" (מכון שבת) describes the temple. In this way, the temple is both distinct from the heavenly realm but also seems to coincide with it in some way. See further comments regarding 2 Chronicles 2:3–7 (HB 2–6).

When it comes to prayer, Solomon emphasizes YHWH's presence in heaven. Even though YHWH is not present at this earthly temple in the same way he is in heaven, Solomon requests that YHWH will pay special attention to the temple as a place of prayer. There is a certain irony in Solomon's request: at the temple Solomon asks that YHWH will answer his prayer, yet his prayer is that YHWH will answer prayers at, or at least directed to, the temple. If YHWH accepts Solomon and his prayer, it opens the door for YHWH to accept those after Solomon and their prayers. The language in 6:19–21 reflects this connection, since the word "servant" (עֶבֶד) refers to Solomon in 6:19, to others in 6:20, and perhaps to either in 6:21.

6:19–21. Solomon makes two requests as consequences of YHWH's special attention to the temple: (1) that YHWH will hear those prayers made at the temple or directed toward the temple, and (2) that YHWH will respond to those prayers by forgiving. The text reiterates that YHWH dwells in heaven and yet emphasizes that YHWH hears prayers by repeating the verb "to hear" (שמע) four times. This type of hearing means more than simply YHWH perceiving a prayer—it means that YHWH responds favorably to it. The specific response that Solomon requests is that YHWH forgive those who pray.

6:22–39. Since Solomon requests that YHWH give special attention to the temple, he then provides seven model scenarios in which people pray. With few exceptions, the models share the following pattern: (1) situation, (2) cause, (3) repentance and/or prayer, (4) place, (5) supplication, and (6) request that YHWH act or forgive (Knoppers 1995, 236–37). These models build on Solomon's general request. For instance, the models explicitly portray the people praying at or toward the temple (6:24, 26, 29, 32, 33, 38). They use the language of hearing from heaven (6:23, 25, 27, 30, 33, 35, 39). Furthermore, they repeatedly request that YHWH will respond to the different prayers by forgiving (6:25, 27, 30, 39).

6:22–23. The first model scenario follows the pattern except it omits the repentance and/or prayer (#3). The situation involves two parties in which one appears to have wronged the other. The scenario most likely portrays the accuser requiring the accused to swear an oath of innocence at the temple's altar. Solomon requests that YHWH ensure that if innocent the accused is cleared, and if guilty the accused is punished corresponding to the consequences of the offense. Since most of these models request that YHWH forgive, it is significant that the first requests that YHWH uphold justice, even between fellow members of Israel.

TRANSLATION ANALYSIS:
Many translations render the initial clause as though one person has wronged another (e.g., "If a man sins against his neighbor," CSB, ESV); however, the point of the verses is to determine whether or not a person has wronged another. A translation such as "When someone is accused of sinning against his neighbor" (NET) is preferable.

Relation to Pentateuch
The scenario appears to be similar to that described in Exodus 22:7–12 (HB 6–11), even though little vocabulary is shared between the two passages. The passage in Exodus 22 has informed the interpretation of this passage in Chronicles. Furthermore, 2 Chronicles 6:23 uses the expression לָתֵת דַּרְכּוֹ בְּרֹאשׁוֹ to describe the punishment for the one who is guilty. In this case the expression not only means that the guilty should be punished, but that the punishment is appropriate for the offense. In Numbers 5:7 the expression describes making restitution for whatever wrong a person has committed against another (see also Judg. 9:57; 1 Sam. 25:39; 1 Kings 2:32, 44; Neh. 3:36; Joel 4:4).

6:24–25. The second scenario moves from sin against a neighbor to sin against YHWH. This scenario follows the pattern described above. The situation is Israel's defeat by a military opponent because Israel has sinned. Because of the situation, Israel returns to YHWH, praises YHWH by acknowledging that he is right to punish them, and prays to YHWH at the temple. Solomon requests that upon Israel's actions, YHWH will hear their prayers, forgive their sins, and return them to the land that YHWH gave them.

TRANSLATION ANALYSIS:
Translations render the phrase וְהוֹדוּ אֶת־שְׁמֶךָ in 6:24 and 26 in different ways. In Chronicles the phrase occurs often in the context of praise. In this context, it likely carries a sense of praise, that is, acknowledging YHWH's authority and his right to punish his people (cf. Japhet 1993, 595; R. Klein 2012, 93). This explanation combines the sense of many translations, such as "praise" (CSB, NIV), "acknowledge" (ESV, NLT), and "confess" (NASB, NKJV, NRSV).

The Land to Them and Their Fathers
In this case the text describes the land more specifically as the land that YHWH "gave them and their fathers" (6:25). This language differs from similar passages that speak of YHWH giving the land to the fathers (e.g., 6:31, 38) because the land is given to "them." In this case *them* refers to the contemporary people who are praying, likely intended by the Chronicler to relate this scenario and Israel's response to the scenario more directly to his postexilic audience. In this way Israel not only has a historical claim to the land but a current claim to the land as YHWH's gift at that moment.

6:26–27. The third scenario describes the situation as drought because Israel has sinned. Although many elements look the same as the second scenario, Solomon adds an additional element to YHWH's response. The further result is that YHWH will teach Israel how they should live, implying how they should live to avoid such disaster in the future.

6:28–31. The fourth scenario generally follows the pattern above; however, it addresses the elements differently. Some of the significant changes are as follows. First, rather than listing one situation (#1), it lists a whole range of situations. Second, it modifies the prayer element (#3). It focuses on both individuals and all the people of Israel, balancing between these situations as community disasters (for which all Israel prays) and individual hardships (for which the individual prays). It also portrays the posture of prayer, drawing a parallel between Solomon who is praying with his hands extended to the sky and these future supplicants. Third, it elaborates on YHWH's forgiveness and action (#6). Picking up on the balance between the individual and all the people, rather than just dealing with forgiveness, Solomon requests that YHWH respond to individuals within Israel based on each person's choices (see Ezekiel 9:4–10 for a related situation dealing with the fate of the righteous and wicked during a disaster on an entire city or nation). This statement upholds YHWH's justice in two ways: (1) he treats individuals according to their choices, and (2) he alone discerns their actual intentions. This scenario also adds another element to the pattern. As the result of YHWH's forgiveness and justice, Israel will worship YHWH properly by obeying him as they remain in the land YHWH gave them. These modifications invite the readers to emulate Solomon by worshipping YHWH and praying to YHWH at the temple.

TRANSLATION ANALYSIS:
This verse speaks of fearing or revering *YHWH.* Most translations render the word ירא as "fear" (CSB, ESV, NASB, NIV, NLT, NRSV). Translating this word depends, to some degree, on translating the following phrase לָלֶכֶת בִּדְרָכֶיךָ "to walk in your ways." The idiom "to walk in YHWH's ways" communicates compliance to YHWH's standards or obedience to his laws. If one understands this phrase as a purpose or result of fear, then "fear" may be the best translation. Such a translation communicates that YHWH's

forgiveness and justice might frighten the people into obeying YHWH. One might soften the picture of fear by translating the word as "revere, regard with awe." In this case, such reverence motivates obedience. However, one may understand the verse differently. First, the word translated "fear" occurs in contexts where it carries the sense of worship (cf. Jonah 1:9). In this case, the second phrase does not likely indicate a purpose or result but a means. In other words, the people worship YHWH by obeying him (cf. NET). This interpretation fits the context well and foreshadows well how the foreigner learns to fear YHWH, that is, worship him as Israel does (6:33).

6:32–33. The fifth scenario expands the temple's influence by talking about a foreigner who comes to pray at the temple. This scenario focuses on YHWH as God beyond Israel. One can perceive this emphasis in three ways: (1) the specific identity of the one praying, (2) the motivation for the prayer, and (3) the consequence of the prayer. First, regarding the person's identity, the person is a foreigner, a non-Israelite living in a foreign land, someone who would be unfamiliar with Israel's way of life (or its God) under normal circumstances. However, second, this foreigner journeys to the temple to pray, motivated by YHWH's international fame. YHWH is famous as a powerful deliverer: his "mighty hand" and "outstretched arm" are symbols of his great strength and allude to YHWH's delivering Israel from Egypt (see Deut. 4:34; 5:15; 7:19; 9:29; 26:8). Third, as a consequence of the prayer, Solomon asks that YHWH fulfill what the foreigner requests so that all people may know who YHWH is and worship him as Israel does and so that they may recognize that the temple is called by YHWH's name; that is, it is YHWH's temple. Therefore, YHWH and his temple will enjoy international acclaim—a theme occurring elsewhere (e.g., 2 Chron. 2; also Lynch 2014b, 105–8).

TRANSLATION ANALYSIS:
These verses raise two considerations for translation. First, 6:32 refers to YHWH's "great name" (CSB, ESV, NASB, NIV, NKJV, NLT, NRSV). The expression here likely carries two connotations: (1) that YHWH is famous and (2) that he has an honorable reputation. A translation such as "great reputation" (NET) can preserve both connotations. Second, for 6:33, translations differ concerning what all the peoples will do. Some translations render this part of the verse as "may know your name and fear you" (ESV, NASB, NIV, NKJV, NRSV). I understand the phrase to mean that the peoples will acknowledge YHWH according to his fame as the powerful, delivering God and therefore show him devotion and honor. See also the translation analysis on 6:31 above.

6:34–35. The sixth scenario addresses military conflicts that YHWH directs Israel to fight. The scenario follows the same pattern as the others; however, it expands the place and modifies the request for YHWH to act. The text implies that whoever is praying is not in Jerusalem but on the battlefront, since the place the prayer is directed to is not only the temple but also the city Jerusalem. Solomon then requests YHWH to act by upholding their cause, here referring to granting them victory.

6:36–39. The seventh scenario forms the climax of the scenarios by expanding several elements of the pattern. First, it describes the situation (#1) specifically in terms of defeat and deportation. The language applies to the Babylonian exile; however, it may apply to other circumstances recorded in Chronicles as well (e.g., 2 Chron. 30:9). Second, it expands the cause (#2) to make explicit that Israel's sin provokes YHWH's anger that leads to their defeat. It further sets the expectation that this situation will happen, since everyone sins. Third, it expands the repentance and/or prayer (#3) in three ways: (1) it describes Israel as recognizing their circumstances; (2) it provides the words for the

prayer for repentance; and (3) it emphasizes their repentance and prayer by mentioning both twice. These expansions emphasize that the people acknowledge the seriousness of their sin and repent with sincerity. Fourth, it expands the place (#4) to include the temple, Jerusalem, and all the land, confirming that YHWH will hear prayer no matter how far away it happens. Fifth, it expands the request for YHWH to respond by adding the phrase "uphold their cause," mentioned in the previous scenario. Here, the phrase refers generally to working for their benefit, likely in the sense of returning them to the land. The scenario clearly points to exile and serves as a model for those after Judah's downfall such as Daniel (Dan. 9:4–19, esp. 9:5) and others (e.g., Neh. 1:5–11; 9:2–37; Ps. 106).

TRANSLATION ANALYSIS:
Translating the beginning of this verse poses a challenge because of the idiom "to turn to one's heart." Some translations render the idiom as a change of devotion or affection (ESV, NIV); however, in other contexts, the idiom is associated with perception and recognition rather than devotion or affection. For instance, in Isaiah 44:19 the idiom describes those who create idols as never stopping to think about what they are doing. Perhaps for this reason, a few translations render the idiom as "coming to one's senses" (CSB, NET, NRSV), since Isaiah presents idolatry as absurdity; however, other contexts do not carry such negative connotations (cf. Deut. 4:39; 30:1). I prefer to render the idiom without such negative connotations, something like "recognizing their circumstances."

6:40. Following the seven model scenarios, the prayer concludes with a request regarding the temple and the Davidic king. An ambiguity runs through 6:40–42: whether these statements are intended as requests for that moment or for all time. For instance, this verse returns to Solomon's initial request that YHWH will pay special attention to the temple in order to respond "to the prayer of this place." This prayer could refer just to Solomon's present prayer or to future prayers. Both are possible, and in some sense both are in view, since Solomon's present prayer is a request that YHWH respond to future prayers.

6:41. Even though the beginning of this verse connects more closely to the specific circumstance of YHWH accompanying the ark in ascending to his/its resting place within the temple, the latter parts are ambiguous as they speak of "salvation" and "goodness." One may understand this request as a general request in abstract terms: that the priests may represent YHWH's deliverance at any time and that the people may rejoice in whatever goodness they experience from YHWH. The text also applies to the situation at hand: as YHWH fills the temple, the priests experience victory and those loyal to YHWH rejoice at his indwelling.

6:42. Solomon finishes his prayer by asking that YHWH not reject his anointed but remember the loyal commitment of David. If one understands the request in a general sense, then the verse calls for YHWH's present and future commitment to the Davidic line. If one understands the request in this specific situation, then Solomon asks that YHWH will accept his request either because of YHWH's faithful commitment to David (as shown previously in the prayer) or because of David's faithful commitment to YHWH (as shown previously in the prayer).

TRANSLATION ANALYSIS:
Two issues arise from the translations. First, translations differ regarding the singular or plural of "anointed." They differ because the textual witnesses vary on this point. The primary Hebrew text reads plural: "anointed ones" (NET). Other Hebrew manuscripts, other ancient translations, and Psalm 132:10 read the singular: "anointed one" (CSB, ESV, NIV, NLT, NRSV). Some translations render the word as just "anointed" so that one cannot tell if it is singular or plural in English (NASB, NKJV). The evidence suggests that the singular is correct. Second, the verse uses the idiom "to turn the face of someone." In certain contexts, this idiom carries the sense of rejecting someone (CSB, NET, NIV, NLT, NRSV). However, the idiom occurs often in contexts in which someone is making a request. In these contexts, the sense of the idiom is "to refuse the request." If this verse concerns Solomon's immediate request at the temple, then a better translation would read, "YHWH God, do not refuse the request of your anointed."

To understand the significance of the ambiguity, one should note that 6:41–42 borrows from Psalm 132. Psalm 132 recounts how David labors to take care of the ark, how as a result YHWH makes a promise to David, how YHWH chooses the temple, and then how he spreads his blessing from it. The phrases picked up by Chronicles occur twice in the psalm: the first time looking to the past, and the second time looking to the future. In other words, David's faithful deeds and YHWH's ascending to the temple in the past become the model for YHWH's future blessings through the temple. Solomon's request is likely to be understood primarily as applying to his present situation. However, following the same strategy as Psalm 132, it sets the stage for a future recurrence.

For the first readers of Chronicles, this connection between the past and the future is what provided hope. As they read about YHWH filling the temple, they could expect that YHWH will fill the temple again. At the same time, during the postexilic period, there was no Davidic king to pronounce a blessing and a prayer for YHWH's special attention to the temple. There also was no account of YHWH indwelling the second temple as he indwelled Solomon's temple. In their circumstances, this prayer reflected partly what they had seen. They had a temple, Jerusalem, and the land, where they could pray with confidence that YHWH would direct his special attention to such a place. At the same time, they lacked a Davidic king for whom they waited.

THEOLOGICAL FOCUS

God is present and transcendent, faithful to his promises, and attentive to those who pray to him.

When Solomon finishes building the temple, God fulfills his promise to David regarding a dynasty and a future temple-builder. At the same time, the temple construction does not exhaust the promises to David. Instead, as Solomon recognizes, God must continue to work to fulfill the promises. At the end of Chronicles, these promises appear to be in jeopardy: the Davidic line has been removed and the temple destroyed. However, just as God was faithful to David through Solomon's building the temple, the people could expect that he would be faithful again.

Generations after the downfall of the Davidic line, the NT writers recognize that Jesus fulfills these promises as well. Matthew introduces his gospel by designating Jesus as the son of David (1:1). Paul identifies his gospel message as the good news regarding Jesus, son of David, declared son of God by the resurrection from the dead (Rom. 1:1–4). Furthermore, John points to Jesus as the one who will rebuild the temple in three days (John 2:19–20). As these writers recognize, God demonstrates his faithfulness to fulfill his promises through Jesus. At the same time, God's promises have not been exhausted. The final defeat of God's enemies and the universal recognition of his rule still awaits. However, just as God has been faithful in the past through Jesus, he will be faithful in the future.

An aspect of God's faithfulness is his presence among his people. This passage focuses on the role that the temple plays revealing God's presence. The passage strikes a fine balance. On the one hand, God is too immense to be contained. On the other hand, God dwells in the temple on earth while he also dwells in heaven. The temple functions like a connection point between heaven and earth, even though neither can confine God. The temple points to God as both present and transcendent. This concern for the intersection of heaven and earth extends beyond the OT. The message that the kingdom of heaven is near points to the intersection of heaven and earth in the coming of Jesus (Matt. 3:2; 4:17). Jesus's incarnation (from heaven to earth) and his ascension (from earth to heaven) further confirm the point. Furthermore, this concern extends into the future. Revelation speaks of future glorification in terms of the new Jerusalem descending from heaven. At that time, God will dwell fully with his people (Rev. 21:2–27). The temple in Jerusalem foreshadows this final reality.

Besides viewing the temple as a place of God's presence, this chapter focuses on the temple as a place of prayer. Much of this chapter recounts Solomon's prayer to dedicate the temple as a place of prayer. His prayer reveals important characteristics about God. First, the prayer demonstrates that unlike the idols that other nations worship, God sees and hears. If God were just an idol, then praying to him would be useless. Second, the prayer reveals that God has the power to help. God can maintain the cause of those who pray or carry out what they ask (6:33, 35, 39). Third, the prayer reveals how God relates to sin. On the one hand, God upholds justice, judging individuals by their works (6:23, 30). On the other hand, God exercises mercy, forgiving individuals who confess their wrongdoing and call to him for mercy. These characteristics of God are not limited to his presence in the temple nor to the time of the OT. The NT affirms that God continues to hear prayers (1 Peter 3:12), to have the power to help (Acts

8:15–17; 12:3–17; James 5:13–16), and to forgive those who confess their sin and cry out for mercy (Luke 18:10–14; 1 John 1:9). This pattern characterizes God's activity in the OT, NT, and beyond.

PREACHING AND TEACHING STRATEGIES

Exegetical and Theological Synthesis
The character of God revealed in this passage leads us to prayer. He is present. This was indicated by the cloud filling the temple. Solomon affirmed this in his opening praise, and then later in the fullness of time God's presence was made even more evident with the incarnation. Prayer is linked to God's presence. If God were not present, he would not be there to listen. Yet he is also transcendent or far above and outside of the event, which Solomon affirms in his public prayer.

If God were not transcendent, he could well be part of the problem about which we pray. Solomon's prayer also affirms God's faithfulness to keep his promises. When we need help, we go to someone who has proven their trustworthiness. It only follows that after Solomon presents God's character through his prayer, that he gives these sample prayers.

The requests for forgiveness that Solomon includes in these exemplary prayers give us another reason to pray. It is not only God's about character; he desires a relationship with us. Thus, forgiveness is an important part of each of these prayers. Forgiveness enables a relationship between the holy God and his sinful people. This relationship allows us to experience his attentiveness. Without forgiveness we may logically know that he is aware of our prayers, but when we have a relationship with him we know that he truly hears our prayers. This passage is a call to prayer based upon who God is, and upon his desire for us to have

a relationship with him. God is present and transcendent, faithful to his promises, and attentive to those who pray to him.

Preaching Idea
Yes, God does hear our prayers.

Contemporary Connections

What does it mean?
In the preaching classroom, I emphasize that broad general applications become more powerful and effective when they are more pointed and specific. To illustrate this I suggest that preachers often leave a congregation with the application: "We need to pray more." Well, this passage is teaching that very thing: we need to pray more. But it also adds *why* we should pray: because of God's character. And the request for forgiveness leads us to a relationship with God in our prayers. The examples give us specific situations that teach us that God wants us to be specific in our prayers. Not that generalities are wrong, but these examples speak in very concrete terms. Solomon could have just given us a broad general example: "When times are tough, pray and God will answer." Rather, he gives us seven different occasions.

The seven examples were, of course, not an exhaustive list of times to pray. Rather, they give us a guide as to how we can pray. The six parts of the prayers cited by Dr. Williams can be summarized into three general moves that could be more transferable to any situation:

> Why we need help: (1) situation, (2) cause
> Our submission to his help: (3) repentance and/or prayer
> Our crying out for help: (4) place, (5) supplication, (6) request that YHWH act or forgive

As this passage sets an example of how to pray, Solomon's lifting of his hands merits comment. It should be noted that in the Old Testament the lifting of hands is most often used at a time of great need rather than in a time of joyful praise. While the practice can be a helpful physical expression of the heart, it should not become a forced practice (for a more in-depth consideration, see Pearson 2013).

Is it true?

She let the bananas and peaches get way too ripe before throwing them away. That's what brought the annoying gnats. It wasn't as bad as the plague of the gnats that the Egyptians suffered, but when they buzzed around her eyes she knew she needed to take action. Though she was past eighty-five, she took care of her problems herself, mostly. But this time she knew she needed some help. To whom would she turn? Her son-in-law? No, he was too involved with his law practice. An exterminator? No, too expensive, and besides she didn't like the idea of her whole house being filled with pesticide. To whom would she turn?

After remembering how to spell gnats with a "g," she typed in *getting rid of gnats*. Up came a video for a homemade gnat-catcher. Her granddaughter happened to stop by while she was looking at the video. Using some tape, a cup, paper cut to make a funnel, a little red-wine vinegar, and soap, her craft-oriented granddaughter made a gnat trap for her Mimi. Her gnat problem was in the process of being solved, but even more significantly, she got to spend time with her precious granddaughter.

As the warmer weather of spring came in, so did the pressure to get the taxes done. For years the engineer had always figured out his own tax return. But this year was different: he had started a consulting business, sold a house, was renting another, and had started working on another graduate degree. Two hours into the pages of governmental directions of, "If box 16 is more than box 17 go to page 58, unless your income is less than it was the previous year and . . ." he decided he needed help. To whom could he turn? A childhood friend came to mind who was a CPA, so the call was made. Box 16 was filled in correctly—but even better, an old friendship was rekindled.

To whom do we go when we need help? We need a source who is present and yet outside of our problem (transcendent), who can be trusted (faithful), is attentive to us in our need, and is forgiving of our errors. Solomon's prayer makes it clear that God is all of these and more. It is not just that God fits the bill and we should turn to him for help as a good source for help; he wants a relationship with us. When we are helped by someone, it changes our attitude toward them.

Now what?

We hear the invitation to pray and to enjoy a relationship with God, but we have some reservations. How do you talk with a being who is so different and otherworldly? Is he really listening? God gave the Israelites a temple to help them know that he was listening. Perhaps our understanding of God doesn't require a place as it did for the Israelites, but we still have a hesitancy to pray. Did God allow something in your life that hurt you deeply? Frankly, you are mad at him, and you aren't about to talk to him. Several of the situations Solomon mentions are crises when his people were far from him. So, pray even if you are mad at God. Even when we are in the bitter consequences of sin, God invites us to enter into prayer with him. The first situation Solomon mentions is perhaps the most common: a conflict with others.

These exemplary situations show us that no matter what is going on in our lives, we are to pray—and that, no matter what is going on in our lives, God wants a relationship with us. Though the passage doesn't explicitly mention it, the basis for this relationship is faith in God. For the first readers, it centered on sacrificial temple worship; for Christians it centers around the sacrifice of Christ. The first readers were told to pray toward the temple; we are to pray not *toward* Christ, but *because* of Christ's work and through his intercession.

Creativity in Presentation

This passage should not be presented without some type of outlet for prayer as part of the sermon or lesson. God's invitation to pray should lead us to pray not only in our daily lives but even at the moment of preaching. Before the service or lesson is over, some kind of opportunity for individuals to pray should be given. It could be an altar call, stations for prayer in different places in the room, or even asking people to form groups of three or four. There are numerous ways to provide people with an appropriate structure for the immediate application of this passage. Here is one possible structure:

- Pray because of God's character (6:1–17).
- Pray with this example in mind (6:18–42).
- Pray—lead the congregation in a time of prayer.

DISCUSSION QUESTIONS

1. When have you cried out for help from God?

2. Of the seven different situations described in 6:22–39, which do you identify with most and why?

3. How have you been helped by someone you didn't know? How did you feel about that person after they helped you?

4. When have you needed help and didn't ask, but wish you had?

5. Are you quick to ask for help or slow? Why?

6. How does asking for help enhance a relationship?

2 Chronicles 7:1–22

EXEGETICAL IDEA
YHWH and all Israel affirmed the Jerusalem temple as the focal point for Israel's ritual worship, a place for Israel to turn for YHWH's help as long as they turned to YHWH alone.

THEOLOGICAL FOCUS
All true worship is directed to God alone as part of a relationship in which he blesses obedience and disciplines disobedience.

PREACHING IDEA
Our relationship with God is to be enjoyed, not endured.

PREACHING POINTERS
It is a clear theme throughout the Bible: we enjoy God's blessings through obedience, and we endure God's discipline when we disobey. This passage gives us a foundation for our obedience when we face a struggle. The grand celebration of God showing his coming to dwell in the temple, along with the sacrifices and feasting, gave the Israelites a wonderful experience of God's presence. This public mountaintop experience is followed by a private session in which the king is warned about the consequences of disobedience. These two events almost seem in opposition, but linking them together shows us the uniqueness of this passage. The celebration and the memory of it hopefully motivated Israel to obey God's laws. In our own lives, the memory of a special experience of God's presence can prompt us and help us to obey.

YHWH, SOLOMON, AND ISRAEL AFFIRM
THE JERUSALEM TEMPLE (7:1–22)

LITERARY STRUCTURE
AND THEMES (7:1–22)

This passage consists of two sections. The first begins once Solomon finishes his prayer (2 Chron. 6). YHWH responds by sending fire from the sky to consume the offerings on the altar. This demonstration of YHWH's approval leads Solomon and Israel to dedicate the temple in Jerusalem to YHWH. They dedicate the temple by offering unfathomable numbers of sacrifices. After the dedication, all Israel together observes the Feast of Booths in Jerusalem. Once the observance concludes, Solomon dismisses all the people to their homes. The text associates this activity with Solomon completing all his building projects for his palace and the temple, linking back to 2 Chronicles 1:18. This link creates a frame around the temple construction account.

The second part of the passage begins once Solomon finishes building the temple. YHWH affirms the temple to Solomon by appearing to him at night. YHWH tells Solomon that he has heard Solomon's prayer and granted his request. YHWH affirms the temple as a place for sacrifice, prayer, and his special presence. YHWH emphasizes the effect that Israel's conduct has for the Davidic dynasty and the Jerusalem temple. To summarize, obedience leads to blessing and disobedience leads to destruction. At the same time, humble repentance leads to YHWH restoring conditions to the way he intended.

- *YHWH, Solomon, and Israel Dedicate the Temple in Jerusalem (7:1–11)*
- *YHWH Affirms the Temple to Solomon at Night (7:12–22)*

EXPOSITION (7:1–22)

Temples in the ancient world served as residences for deities. As such, they became focal points for divine-human interaction. The interaction took place both in secret where priests performed their duties in the temple's isolated chambers and in the open where the people called on the deity, most often for help, through various rituals (festivals, sacrifices, prayers, etc.). Second Chronicles 5–7 shows how the Jerusalem temple truly becomes a temple: YHWH inhabits, in some special way, its inner chambers (2 Chron. 5), he hears the prayers directed toward it (2 Chron. 6), and he accepts the sacrifices made on its altar (2 Chron. 7). This chapter shows that the Jerusalem temple is the focal point of Israel's ritual worship (festivals, sacrifices, and prayer), as both YHWH and the people recognize it as YHWH's temple. As a result, it is also the place for Israel to seek YHWH's help—as long as they turn to him alone.

YHWH, Solomon, and Israel Dedicate the Temple in Jerusalem (7:1–11)

YHWH, Solomon, and Israel dedicate the temple as a place of sacrifice and feasting: YHWH brings fire from the sky, while Solomon and all Israel make sacrifices and observe a religious feast.

7:1–3. When Solomon finishes his prayer in 2 Chronicles 6, fire descends from the sky to consume the offerings upon the altar while YHWH's glory continues to fill the temple. These two elements, glory and fire, show how significant this scene is within Israel's history. First, YHWH's glory connects this scene to

2 Chronicles 5 and other passages in the OT (see comments on 2 Chron. 5). After the priests deposit the ark in the temple, YHWH responds by filling the temple with his glory expressed as a cloud (2 Chron. 5:13–14). After Solomon prays, YHWH responds by continuing to fill the temple with his glory, this time accompanied by fire. At first, the cloud only fills the temple building proper. The glory fills the areas where the priests perform their ritual service, so the priests cannot perform such service while the cloud remains (2 Chron. 5:14). The text seems to present the glory remaining within the temple while Solomon prays. Then, the glory not only fills the temple proper but appears upon the temple structure so that everyone present can see it. The glory appears alongside the fire that descends from the sky.

People in the Outer Court

The text mentions that the people bow their faces upon the הָרִצְפָּה ("pavement"). Ezekiel 40:17–18; 42:3 associates this term with the outer court. Therefore, the people are standing in the outer court, outside the restricted areas of the temple.

Second, the fire descending from the sky connects this scene to other scenes in the OT. The most important connections are to David and the tabernacle. First, when David offers a sacrifice upon the altar built at Ornan's threshing floor, YHWH responds by sending fire from the sky to consume the offering (1 Chron. 21:26). As a result, David recognizes that this location is the site for the future temple with its altar (1 Chron. 22:1). Therefore, when YHWH responds to Solomon's prayer by sending fire from the sky, he confirms both his choice of the Davidic heir Solomon and his choice of this place for the temple. Second, when Moses and Aaron perform the rites to set aside Aaron and his descendants as Israel's priests, fire falls from the sky and consumes the offering (Lev. 9:23–24). In both cases, the people see the glory and respond by falling on their faces. These connections strengthen

the link between the temple and the tabernacle to show that YHWH approves the temple just as he approved the tabernacle. The connections to both David and the tabernacle confirm that YHWH approves the temple in Jerusalem.

Regarding the elements of glory and fire, another narrative combines these elements: YHWH's appearance at Sinai. Exodus 24:17 describes both elements on Mount Sinai, just before Moses enters the cloud. This verse immediately precedes the instructions for the tabernacle. However, several contrasts to the temple dedication occur. First, Moses enters the cloud, whereas no one enters the cloud during the dedication. Second, the people respond differently. In Exodus, the people have already stepped back from the mountain because they are afraid of YHWH (Exod. 20:18), and they are about to commit idolatry with the golden calf (Exod. 32). Both responses form a stark contrast to Chronicles. In Chronicles, the people respond by bowing their faces to the ground and worshipping YHWH, confessing that "he is good, and his loyal love endures forever." As Japhet says regarding the people in Chronicles, "Their reaction illustrates in the best way their profound experience of and absolute trust in God's presence" (1993, 610).

7:4–7. After fire descends from the sky and YHWH's glory appears to the people, Solomon and the people make sacrifices to YHWH to dedicate the temple. The narrative highlights some points regarding this dedication. First, the narrative points out the enormous extent of participation in the sacrifices. It begins by recording the quantity of sacrifices that Solomon makes. The number far exceeds any other offering recorded in Chronicles, confirming the picture of Solomon's tremendous wealth. (Josiah offers thirty thousand sheep and three thousand bulls [2 Chron. 35:7], while David and the people sacrifice one thousand bulls, one thousand rams, and one thousand lambs [1 Chron. 29:21]). Because the quantity is so large, the altar cannot contain all the different kinds of offerings being made. Furthermore, the text points out that Solomon does not act alone, but all the people participate in dedicating the temple.

Jerusalem as the Place for All Offerings

The text mentions different types of offerings (burnt offerings, meal offerings, and the fat portions of the peace offerings), probably as a sign that the Jerusalem temple is where all these offerings should take place.

Second, the narrative points out the role that music plays in the dedication. By mentioning music, the narrative draws connections in several directions in Chronicles. When the musicians praise YHWH by confessing that "his loyal love endures forever" (לְעוֹלָם חַסְדּוֹ), they respond the same way as they responded to the fire descending from the sky. In this way, their confession marks both affirmations to the temple: YHWH's and the people's. By mentioning the instruments that David made, the text alludes to the role that David plays in creating the instruments (1 Chron. 23:5) as well as organizing the Levitical musicians (see 1 Chron. 25). By mentioning the music alongside the sacrifices, the text associates music with making sacrifices, a point that recurs throughout Chronicles (e.g., 2 Chron. 23:18; 29:27–28; 30:21; 35:15).

Organizing Levitical Musicians

A peculiar phrase in 7:6, בְּהַלֵּל דָּוִיד בְּיָדָם ("when David praised through/by them"), resembles another passage in which David appoints the musicians. In 1 Chronicles 16:7, David arranges for praising YHWH through the Levitical musicians. Here also, the Levitical musicians continue the role of praising YHWH just as David had arranged (see Kleinig 1993, 92).

Third, the narrative points out how the people observed the sanctity of the temple area. Solomon respects the sanctity of the sanctuary by consecrating the courtyard to

accommodate all the offerings being sacrificed. Also, the positions of the various groups reflect a concern for the sanctity of the temple. All Israel remains in the outer courtyard (see 7:3) when the fire descends from the sky. The priests remain in their designated places according to their duties. The Levitical singers also remain with their musical instruments so that the priestly trumpeters can stand opposite them. These details, although accomplishing other purposes as well, depict the sanctity of the temple and those who approach it.

Posts and Responsibilities

Second Chronicles 7:6 describes the priests "at their posts" (עַל־מִשְׁמְרוֹתָם). The term מִשְׁמֶרֶת ("post") here likely indicates where the priests stand according to their assigned responsibility. In 2 Chronicles 35:2, Josiah assigns the priests their responsibilities for the Passover observance and encourages them to fulfill those responsibilities.

7:8–10. Up to this point, the dedication has focused on sacrifice: YHWH has approved the altar as a place of sacrifice, and the people have approved the temple by making sacrifices. Now the narrative shifts from sacrifice to the feast. The feast is one of the pilgrimage feasts in which Israel must travel to the place that YHWH chooses to observe it (see Lev. 23; Deut. 16). By connecting the temple dedication to the feast, the text confirms that the destination for the feast is now the temple in Jerusalem. As a result, within 2 Chronicles 5–7, the Chronicler demonstrates that the temple is the center of Israel's ritual worship: the temple is the place for the ark (2 Chron. 5), the place for prayer (2 Chron. 6), the place for sacrifice (2 Chron. 7:1–7), and the place for observing the feasts (2 Chron. 7:8–10).

TRANSLATION ANALYSIS:
Translating the Hebrew term חַג poses a couple of challenges. Several translations (e.g., ESV, NASB, NKJV) use the English word "feast," but

in contemporary American English, the term feast is most often associated with a large or extravagant meal. One could translate the term as "observance," although an observance carries different connotations. Instead, the Hebrew term likely communicates the idea of a time set apart for some type of significant religious observance. The word "holiday" (that is, a holy day) could capture such a sense; unfortunately, "holiday" in English is more associated with a day off from work than a day set aside for a particular observance.

In context, identifying the feast is not difficult. The text provides some details about the timing of the feast. Since the text specifies that the feast takes place in the seventh month, that the people hold a sacred assembly on the eighth day of observing the feast, and that Solomon dismisses the people on the twenty-third of the month (so that the feast began on the fifteenth), the Feast of Booths is the logical choice.

Coordinating the Feasts

The law of Moses specifies that the Feast of Booths begins on the fifteenth day of the seventh month (Lev. 23:34; Num. 29:12; Deut. 16:13). The feast lasts seven days and then concludes on the eighth day with a sacred assembly (Lev. 23:36; Num. 29:35).

Although the text provides clear clues that the feast in view here is the Feast of Booths, it is not as clear how the events recorded in 2 Chronicles 5–7 correlate with the dedication of the temple and the observance of the Feast of Booths. See commentary on 2 Chronicles 5 for more information.

Identifying the feast is not the main reason for including details about the feast's timing; the text provides these details to show that Solomon and the people observe the feast as the law requires. The text shows that even though

Mosaic law does not explicitly speak of a temple, Solomon's temple in Jerusalem does not contradict Mosaic law; Israel can still follow the law, even with the temple.

Beyond the details of timing, the text provides geographical details. The text specifies that Israel observes the feast, from Lebo-hamath to the Brook of Egypt. These geographical features mark the northern and southern boundaries of Israel's land respectively (for the River of Egypt as the southern boundary, see Num. 34:5; Josh. 15:4; for Lebo-hamath as the northern boundary, see Num. 34:8; Josh. 13:5; Ezek. 48:1).

TRANSLATION ANALYSIS:
This verse contains place information that translations treat differently, in particular the Hebrew phrase לְבוֹא חֲמָת. Many translations (ESV, NET, NIV, NLT, NRSV) treat the entire phrase as the name of a town. Others treat the first element (לְבוֹא) as a common noun, therefore translating it as "entry" (CSB, NASB, NKJV). Even though the first element can function as a common noun (e.g., 1 Chron. 5:9), since it occurs with חֲמָת so frequently as a fixed phrase (e.g., Num. 13:21; 34:8; Josh. 13:5; Judg. 3:3; 2 Kings 14:25; Ezek. 47:15; 48:1), it is more likely a part of the town's name.

The significance of these details extends in several directions. First, they indicate that all Israel to its fullest extent participates in the temple dedication. By showing that all Israel participates, the text reinforces the importance of the Jerusalem temple for all Israel and not just the king, priests, or some other subset of Israel. Second, the details connect the land under Solomon's rule to the land David secures for Israel. When David defeated Hadadezer, he extended the territory of Israel as far as Hamath (1 Chron. 18:3). Solomon continues to rule over all this territory. Third, the details indicate that building the temple completes the work that David began. Just as David assembled all Israel from its northern to southern borders to bring up the ark (1 Chron. 13:5), with Solomon all Israel observes the feast concluding the dedication of the temple. Fourth, the details present all Israel as obeying the Mosaic law. The law requires Israel to go to the place YHWH chooses (Deut. 16:16), so Israel's presence at the feast indicates that they are obeying YHWH's command at this point. The temple construction account emphasizes that Solomon and the people obey. This emphasis accomplishes two purposes: (1) it confirms YHWH's choice of Solomon as the temple-builder, and (2) it presents the temple itself as a benefit that YHWH provides for the people as a reward for their obedience.

Dedicating Temple and Altar

Second Chronicles 7 refers to the dedication ceremony as both a dedication of the temple (7:5) and a dedication of the altar (7:9). By focusing on the altar specifically, the text affirms the temple as a place for sacrifice, a point made repeatedly in the temple narrative of Chronicles.

7:10. This verse recounts that Solomon dismisses all the people after they observe the Feast of Booths. As they return home, the people feel good and are happy because of what YHWH has done. The text characterizes what YHWH has done as something good (הַטּוֹבָה), but it does not specify what this good is. Although one can interpret this "good" (הַטּוֹבָה) in a general sense, the "good" appears to be more specific to the context. The people are happy for two primary reasons: (1) YHWH has approved the temple, demonstrated by his glory filling the temple and the fire from the sky consuming the offerings on the altar, and (2) YHWH has fulfilled his promise to David by placing Solomon on Israel's throne and allowing him to build the temple (see, e.g., 1 Chron. 17; 2 Chron. 6:4–10). Notably, the text points out that this activity benefits David, Solomon, and all the

people. The text recognizes that the temple is important for all Israel, not just the king.

TRANSLATION ANALYSIS:
Second Chronicles 7:10 describes the people as returning to their tents. In this case, this expression communicates that they returned home. It does not emphasize the type of dwelling where the people lived. One can see a similar usage in 2 Chronicles 10:16. Furthermore, the verse describes the people using the expression טוֹבֵי לֵב ("good of heart"). Most often the phrase describes someone who has been drinking alcohol (Judg. 16:25; 2 Sam. 13:28; Esther 1:10). However, the expression occurs in Deuteronomy 28:47 alongside the word שִׂמְחָה ("joy") to describe the way Israel should serve YHWH. In this context alcohol is not in view; instead, the passage speaks of the gratitude that Israel should have because YHWH provides "an abundance of everything." An English expression that might convey the full range of these usages is the expression "feeling good" (see "in good spirits," NRSV).

7:11. This section concludes by stating that Solomon finishes building the temple and his palace. This verse looks back to 2 Chronicles 2:1 (HB 1:18), in which Solomon decides to build both the temple and his palace, as well as 2 Chronicles 2:12 (HB 11), in which Huram characterizes Solomon as David's wise son who will build both the temple and palace. This verse confirms that Solomon completes what he begins. Furthermore, it elaborates on the building by stating that Solomon succeeds in all his plans for the temple and palace. Throughout Chronicles, when people obey YHWH, success follows (2 Chron. 14:6; 20:20; 26:5; 31:21; 32:30). The verse affirms Solomon as the temple-builder. YHWH chose Solomon to build the temple and commanded him to obey (1 Chron. 28:5–10); now Solomon fulfills YHWH's purpose, demonstrating that he obeys YHWH's command.

Solomon's Success

Second Chronicles 7:11 contains an ambiguity regarding Solomon's success. The text uses a unique expression in the Hebrew Bible: it speaks of Solomon succeeding in everything that "came upon Solomon's heart" (כָּל־הַבָּא עַל־לֵב שְׁלֹמֹה). Generally, interpreters understand this expression to convey a sense of planning. Therefore, Solomon succeeds in all he plans to do. However, one might interpret the expression to indicate that something was demanded of Solomon. As Williamson notes, "This is added by the Chronicler in order to note the fulfillment of the conditions laid on Solomon by David which would lead to the establishment of the dynasty" (1982, 224). Although such a point fits well in Chronicles, other similar expressions to the one here suggest that the former interpretation is the more likely (see 2 Chron. 24:4; 29:10; Neh. 3:38; Esther 7:5; Dan. 1:8).

YHWH Affirms the Temple to Solomon at Night (7:12–22)

YHWH appears to Solomon at night to affirm that he accepts the Jerusalem temple as a place for sacrifice and for prayer, as long as Israel and its king obey YHWH.

7:12. Following the comment that Solomon successfully completes the temple and palace, the text recounts how YHWH appears to Solomon at night. At the beginning of Solomon's reign, YHWH appeared to him at night (2 Chron. 1:7). At that time, YHWH allowed Solomon to make a request. Solomon requested wisdom, and YHWH granted it to him along with great wealth. Solomon needed both wisdom and wealth to build the splendid temple that Chronicles recounts. Now that the temple is finished, YHWH appears to Solomon again. These two appearances form bookends around the temple construction narrative. They demonstrate that the temple construction is a project in which YHWH is involved from start to finish.

In other words, it is a divine project rather than merely a human one.

When YHWH appears this second time, he again grants Solomon what he has requested. The request in view is presumably Solomon's prayer in 2 Chronicles 6, since what YHWH says alludes back to chapter 6 in multiple ways (see below). However, how YHWH responds in 7:12 does not correspond to what Solomon prays. In 2 Chronicles 6 Solomon prays that YHWH will pay attention to the temple as a place for prayer; YHWH responds that he has chosen this place as a house for sacrifice. In the larger context of Chronicles, YHWH's response makes complete sense. When Solomon proposes to build the temple, he points out that making sacrifices to YHWH is part of Israel's perpetual responsibility (2 Chron. 2:4 [HB 3]) and acknowledges that the temple cannot contain YHWH but only serves as a place for sacrifice for him (2 Chron. 2:6 [HB 5]). Furthermore, 7:1–3 illustrates that YHWH accepts the temple as a place for sacrifice, since the fire descends from the sky and consumes the offering.

Allusion to Deuteronomy

In the beginning of YHWH's response, he refers to "this place" as the place he has chosen. This expression alludes to the language of Deuteronomy that anticipates a place that YHWH will choose to be the center of Israel's worship (e.g., Deut. 12:5, 11, 14, 18, 21, 26; 14:23–25; 15:20; 16:2, 6, 7, 11, 15, 16; 17:8, 10; 18:6; 26:2; 31:11). As one moves through YHWH's address to Solomon, one can see that the phrase creates the same openness at the beginning of the speech, but that openness is narrowed down to the temple by the end of it.

Despite these connections to the larger context, why does the text introduce sacrifice as a response to Solomon's prayer? First, prayer and sacrifice probably should not be separated too sharply. Isaiah 56:7 speaks of the temple as a house of prayer and then describes it as the place where the nations make sacrifices. Second, the temple as a place for prayer and for sacrifice brings together two strands of the temple construction account. On the one hand, the account emphasizes sacrifice (see above). On the other hand, the account emphasizes prayer (see 2 Chron. 6). The text already suggests that these two should be combined: these themes emerge when Solomon considers the limits of the temple. Since the temple cannot contain YHWH, it can only serve as a place to make sacrifices (2 Chron. 2:6 [HB 5]), or as a place where YHWH directs his attention so that he can answer prayers (2 Chron. 6:18–20). Combining both themes elevates the importance of the temple while also recalling its limitations. Third, YHWH later makes clear that the temple will be a place for prayer because he explicitly states that he will direct his attention to it as Solomon has requested (7:15; see 6:40).

7:13–14. After YHWH affirms that the temple will be a place for sacrifice, he seems to sidestep the temple altogether. Like 7:12, these verses allude to Solomon's prayer by presenting a series of calamities that resemble those outlined in 2 Chronicles 6:26, 28. In 2 Chronicles 6, Solomon requests that if the people will pray toward the temple and repent, that YHWH will hear their request from heaven and forgive them. However, surprisingly, these verses do not mention the temple at all, even though they mention similar calamities (drought, insect infestation, and pestilence) and similar responses (prayer, repentance, YHWH's hearing from heaven, and forgiving). Furthermore, these verses do not mention sacrifice, even though YHWH has just affirmed the temple as the place for sacrifice. Not mentioning the temple or sacrifices communicates something significant about the intended purpose of these verses: these verses apply even when Israel is without a land, king, or temple. R. Klein points out that

"these are calamities that could typically affect postexilic Judah and that the Chronicler omits the references from chap. 6 to war, defeat, or exile" (2012, 111).

7:14. This verse provides a model that Chronicles applies repeatedly. The verse contains several elements. First, it identifies those who respond to the calamities of 7:13 as people who bear YHWH's name. The expression of bearing one's name carries a connotation of ownership, just as it does in 2 Chronicles 6:33 (see comment there). In context, YHWH's people is Israel.

Second, the verse identifies the people's actions. They include humbling themselves, praying, asking for YHWH's favor, and rejecting their wicked activities. These actions go together; they are not isolated or separated from one another. They represent what the people should do and how they should do it. For this reason, Chronicles elsewhere can draw from this model without including all the elements (e.g., 2 Chron. 33:12–13).

TRANSLATION ANALYSIS
This verse uses the expression of seeking *YHWH*'s face (וִיבַקְשׁוּ פָנַי). Most translations (e.g., CSB, ESV, NASB, NIV, NKJV, NLT, NRSV) simply render the expression as "seek my face." In the Hebrew OT, the expression occurs in contexts in which someone calls upon another for some type of benefit (e.g., 2 Sam. 21:1; Prov. 29:26). For this reason, some translations (e.g., NET) translate the expression as "seek to please me."

Turning from Wicked Ways
The notion of turning from someone's wicked ways requires some clarification. The expression doesn't exactly mean to stop doing such things for a moment. At the same time, the expression indicates more than just acknowledging that such activities are wrong. The expression indicates an attitude that rejects them and a commitment to avoid doing them in the future.

Third, the verse identifies YHWH's response: he will hear from heaven, forgive their sin, and heal their land. The first two elements are typical of Solomon's prayer (e.g., 2 Chron. 6:21, 25, 27, 30, 39); the third element is something new. The term "to heal" occurs often elsewhere in the OT in the context of forgiveness; for instance, in 2 Chronicles 30:20 the term describes that YHWH forgives the people. In this context, the term appears to communicate more than just forgiveness, since 7:13 describes calamities that would ruin the land (even speaking of the grasshoppers as "eating the land"). Therefore, healing the land entails both restoring the people to a proper relationship with YHWH and restoring the land to its proper, fertile function (i.e., *shalom* שָׁלוֹם in Hebrew, see de Moor 1976, 336; Hasel 1983, 201–2; Taylor 2011, 150–54).

The model this verse presents is important for understanding the message of Chronicles. A significant theme of Chronicles is retribution: the principle that YHWH rewards obedience and punishes disobedience. This verse qualifies the principle of retribution. YHWH still punishes disobedience (see 7:13); however, 7:14 shows that there is still hope for the disobedient. If they approach YHWH with the proper attitude and reject their disobedient activities, then YHWH will restore them (see "Covenant" section in the introduction).

7:15–16. The text returns to Solomon's request to make the temple a place for prayer. YHWH affirms that he will give special attention to the temple so that he may answer prayers. Furthermore, he grants Solomon's request using the same wording as 2 Chronicles 6:40. He continues by pulling together several strands from the temple construction account. YHWH shows that the temple fulfills what Solomon intended. In 2 Chronicles 2:4 (HB 3), Solomon states that he intends to build the temple for YHWH's name and to consecrate it for activities that priests perform to serve YHWH. Now YHWH confirms that the temple fulfills this purpose and even

goes beyond it, since YHWH himself has consecrated the temple for his presence. Furthermore, YHWH adds that he will keep his eyes and his heart at the temple. The image of YHWH's eyes being at the temple draws on the previous verse as a way of affirming that he will pay it special attention. In this context, the image of YHWH's "heart" (לֵב) being at the temple most likely indicates the same: YHWH will pay attention to the temple. Adding even more weight to his statement, YHWH states that his name, eyes, and heart will remain in the temple perpetually. In this way, YHWH affirms the abiding importance of the temple but does not limit himself to it. These verses reiterate a point made throughout the temple construction: YHWH is present at the temple but not in a way that restricts him, especially to the earthly realm.

Meaning of "Heart"

The word translated "heart" (לֵב) has a wide range of connotations in Hebrew (see *HALOT* s.v. "לֵב" 513–15). In English, "heart" relates more often to emotions. Although לֵב can be related to emotions, often it is not. In 7:11, the text describes Solomon as succeeding in everything coming upon his heart, that is, everything that he planned. Just as Solomon directed his attention to the temple as a place for sacrifice and prayer, now YHWH promises to direct his attention to the temple as a place for sacrifice and prayer.

7:17–18. After YHWH affirms the temple, he shifts from the temple to the conduct of the people. The text builds off the theme of retribution found throughout Chronicles. It presents the positive side and the negative side of retribution. The positive side concerns the Davidic dynasty, while the negative side concerns the people as a whole. It describes what Solomon, and by extension his successors, must do for the dynasty to endure uninterrupted: to walk before YHWH as David did, to do what YHWH has commanded, and to observe YHWH's statutes and judgments. If the Davidic king obeys, then

YHWH will reward the obedience by ensuring that a descendant of David will rule over Israel.

Not Cutting Off the Dynasty

Second Chronicles 7:18 speaks of the dynasty enduring with the image of cutting off (*niphal* כרת) a king from Israel's throne. I will make two observations regarding this language. First, Chronicles uses the same root (כרת) to speak of his commitment to David as a covenantal commitment (7:18). Just as YHWH cut a covenant with David, so he will ensure that a Davidic heir is not cut off. Second, it is important to notice that the language in the text remains open. It communicates clearly that the Davidic line will face punishment if the members continue in disobedience; however, the language does not require that the dynasty end forever. Instead, the language allows for a period in which there is no Davidic ruler on the throne; however, the dynasty itself could still be restored at another time.

These verses draw on other passages to make their point. Second Chronicles 7:17 alludes to Solomon's prayer, where Solomon uses the language of walking as David did in order to ensure that the dynasty endures (2 Chron. 6:16). Second Chronicles 7:18 alludes to Micah 5:2 (HB 1), which speaks of Bethlehem as the place where "the ruler of Israel" will emerge. These allusions highlight the significant roles that Solomon and the temple play in relation to the Davidic dynasty in Chronicles. Solomon partially fulfills what YHWH promises to David, but even in the elements that remain unfulfilled (e.g., uninterrupted endurance of dynasty), he provides a model for kings to follow just as he follows his father, David.

7:19–22. In contrast, on the negative side of retribution, the text describes the punishment for Israel if they disobey YHWH. The text summarizes Israel's possible disobedience as abandoning YHWH's laws, that is, abandoning YHWH (7:22) and worshipping other gods.

These two issues, obedience to Mosaic law and worshipping YHWH alone, are the criteria used repeatedly in Chronicles to evaluate Israel and their kings.

Vocabulary for False Worship

The standard vocabulary for worship deserves a closer look. The translations fall into two patterns: "worship" and "serve" (CSB, ESV, KJV, NKJV, NRSV) or "bow down" and "worship" (NIV, NLT). In both cases, the term חוה connotes the honor that Manasseh grants the host of heaven. The term often occurs to indicate one person bowing to honor another (e.g., Gen. 23:7, 12; 24:52; Exod. 11:8; 1 Sam. 20:41), although it may also indicate worship activity in general with or without bowing (Gen. 22:5; 24:26, 48; Exod. 4:31). The second term (עבד) connotes the activity performed because of one's devotion or obligation to another.

The consequences for such disobedience are severe: YHWH will exile the people from the land and reject the temple he has consecrated. The language here resembles Deuteronomy 29:24–28 (HB 23–27); however, in Deuteronomy YHWH uproots the people from the land and casts them into another land. Here, YHWH uproots the people, but he casts the temple away rather than the people. The imagery works much better with the people than with the temple; however, this dissonance is most likely intentional. The temple construction account recounts that Solomon builds the temple to be splendid (2 Chron. 2:5 [HB 4]) and acknowledges that it is splendid once he completes it (2 Chron. 6:2). Now, YHWH has just consecrated the temple to be a place for his presence, for sacrifice, and for prayer. YHWH's possible rejection of this splendid temple is significant in that it shows that the temple is not necessary for YHWH. Losing the temple does not threaten YHWH even though it is a tremendous loss for the people (see 7:10). Therefore, these verses confirm a theme running throughout the temple construction account: the temple is important for Israel as the focal point of Israel's worship of YHWH, but it is not necessary.

TRANSLATION ANALYSIS:
This verse describes *YHWH* as "casting out" (*hiphil* שׁלך) the temple from his presence (see ESV, NASB, NKJV, NRSV). This expression carries a sense of rejection or abandonment (see NET, NIV, NLT); that is, YHWH no longer regards the temple with his favor (see, e.g., 1 Kings 14:9; 2 Kings 13:23).

In describing Israel's disobedience and punishment, one matter is not addressed: the Davidic dynasty. Admittedly, 7:17–18 encourages Solomon (and by extension, his successors) to remain faithful to YHWH; however, when the text turns to the consequences for disobedience, "although the full horrors of loss of national sovereignty and of exile are listed, there is no hint that this will entail the dynastic promise losing its validity" (Williamson 1982, 227). In this way, the text holds out hope for a future Davidic king, even if there is a period of exile and destruction.

The first readers faced a difficult situation in the land. Some of the people had returned. However, many promises about better days had not been fulfilled. They faced considerable hardships. Despite these hardships, Chronicles points to the Jerusalem temple as a source for blessing as the people look for YHWH to inhabit it again, as they make sacrifices there and as they pray at and toward the temple. Although other Jewish temples existed, the Jerusalem temple alone becomes part of the people's hope in YHWH. Although this temple is not necessary, the people could expect that worshipping YHWH alone properly at the Jerusalem temple would be a critical part of YHWH's restoration of Israel. At the same time, whenever Israel faced a disaster such as drought or pestilence, they could humbly pray to YHWH and he would restore them, with or without the temple. Israel's actions would lead to consequences, good or bad. For the first readers, the text calls on them to continue to obey the Mosaic law and worship YHWH exclusively at the Jerusalem temple, while also holding out hope that if they failed to do so, their sin would not be the end of the story. YHWH would still hear and restore those who humbly sought him.

THEOLOGICAL FOCUS

All true worship is directed to God alone as part of a relationship in which he blesses obedience and disciplines disobedience.

The book of Chronicles centers around the Jerusalem temple. The structure of the book revolves around building the temple: the account of David's reign points forward to it; the account of Solomon's reign revolves around it; the accounts of later kings point back to it. The Jerusalem temple obviously plays an important role in the book. This passage helps explain that importance. First, because God chooses to dwell in the Jerusalem temple, it becomes the focal point of Israel's ritual worship: their sacrifices, their prayers, and their feasts. To enjoy God's blessings, Israel draws as close to him as possible through their sacrifices, prayers, and feasts. Therefore, God's special presence grants the Jerusalem temple its importance. Second, not only is the Jerusalem temple the focal point of Israel's worship, but it is also the exclusive place to offer sacrifices, direct one's prayers, and observe the feasts. Proper ritual worship takes place at the temple in Jerusalem alone. The Jerusalem temple as the only legitimate place for such activity points to YHWH as the only legitimate God.

The NT shifts its focus from the Jerusalem temple. Jesus is the reason for the shift in focus. As mentioned above, God's presence in the Jerusalem temple grants its significance. At the same time, in the temple God dwells in a partial, veiled sense, since no one may be in his direct presence. In contrast, in Jesus all the fullness of God dwells in bodily form (Col. 1:19; 2:9). As a result, Jesus supersedes the Jerusalem temple as he fills out what is only partially experienced in the temple (see Hoskins 2007, 194–201). As a result, Christian worship focuses on Jesus.

Also, like the Jerusalem temple, Jesus is exclusive. On the one hand, this exclusivity points to one way to approach God. Access to God and his blessings only comes through Jesus. Jesus claims, "No one comes to the Father except through me" (John 14:6). Peter and John declare that God's blessing of salvation comes only through Jesus and no one else (Acts 4:12). On the other hand, this exclusivity points to one God. God's dwelling in Jesus reinforces that there is only one legitimate God. Jesus affirms that the Father and he are one, such that one who has seen Jesus has seen the Father (John 10:30; 14:6–11). There is one God and one mediator between God and humanity: Jesus (1 Tim. 2:5). As a result, God alone deserves all worship, to the Father, through the Son, in the Holy Spirit.

Not only does God deserve worship, but he also desires it. God is jealous in the sense that he does not share honor or allegiance with anyone or anything else (e.g., Exod. 20:5; 34:14; Deut. 4:24; 1 Cor. 10:21–22; James 4:4–5). Viewing worship as an expression of honor and allegiance points to the relationship between God and the worshipper. God desires this relationship and provides benefits for those who relate to him through worship. Chronicles shows how the directives of Moses and David guide Israel's worship as sources of authority. Remaining faithful to God entails following those directives. As a result, God blesses obeying those directives while he punishes disobeying them.

The NT points to an authority beyond Moses or David. Jesus's directives guide Christian worship as the source of authority. In the Great Commission, Jesus instructs his disciples to teach their disciples to obey all that he has commanded them (Matt. 28:20). Paul understands his obligation under the law of Christ (1 Cor. 9:21). Therefore, obeying Jesus is an expression of allegiance to God. As a result, rejecting or disobeying Jesus has dire consequences (Heb. 2:2–3). In contrast, for those who follow Jesus, God has secured spiritual blessings in the heavenly places (Eph. 1:3) and continues to provide blessings in this age and the age to come (John 10:10).

PREACHING AND TEACHING STRATEGIES

Exegetical and Theological Synthesis

God gave the postexilic Israelites a reminder that in their history there was a grand beginning: the spectacular worship when the temple was dedicated. The joyful celebration of the beginning of temple worship was the foundation for God's warnings, like the favorite uncle saying to the groom, "You need to know that the work is just beginning. Your marriage can be endured or enjoyed. If you love your wife and put her first you will find joy, but if you put yourself first and don't love her more than you love yourself, your marriage will be something to endure." The well-meaning uncle spoke truth, but he needed to give a caveat: the bride will need to do her part as well, and if she doesn't then likewise it is enduring and not enjoying.

But unlike a new bride or groom, God always keeps his covenant. This amazing experience at the dedication is very similar to the Exodus fire-and-glory episode, which should have reminded the Israelites that God keeps his word. As we read this account and visualize the fire and the glory, the sacrifices, the music, and the feasting, it might prompt a memory of one special worship experience of our own.

Preaching Idea

Our relationship with God is to be enjoyed, not endured.

Contemporary Connections

What does it mean?

Being raised and primarily ministering in the South, an open-house celebration for a graduate from high school was a foreign concept to me. The very first week we began the new ministry in Michigan we were invited to several open houses for graduates. Not knowing the importance of them, we didn't go to any of them. Apologies were made, and fortunately the church understood the mistake—and the following year we attended all of them. While each graduate was special and celebrated as an individual, the trappings were the same for all of them: tables of food, pictures of the graduate in elementary school, a trophy or ribbon from a sporting event, and a t-shirt of the college or branch of the military that awaited in the graduate's future. All this went together to celebrate the completion of this milestone. It was a joyful time. Hopefully, that joyful open house would lead to an enjoyable college or military experience. The graduation celebration was a foundation for making good choices in that student's next chapter.

There are other grand and wonderful beginnings: weddings, convocations at the beginning of a school year, retirement parties that rejoice not only in the past but in the new beginning, and birthday parties celebrating the completion of one year and stepping into the next. A joyful experience can be helpful to remember when life gets difficult. Remembering the joy of a wedding should prompt a couple to keep their vows when the joy fades.

The worship of Israel could not have been more joyful and grand, for they were celebrating YHWH's presence and his approval of the temple. This setting of celebration is where God spoke to Solomon in very clear terms that to obey was to experience blessing, but to disobey was to feel his discipline. Through Solomon Israel was given the choice to enjoy or endure a relationship with YHWH. The joy of the celebration was a taste of what the future relationship could be like. Not every day would be celebratory, but every day could be joyful.

Is it true?

We may not experience the fire and glory, but God seems to give each of his children some kind of unforgettable experience of his presence. Notice that this event was filled with sacrifices seemingly beyond count. Just as sacrifice was central to Israel experiencing the presence of God, so too it is with us. Whether it is the first time or a time later in our walk with him, our encounter with God's presence is not based upon unnumbered sacrifices but based upon one perfect sacrifice.

Often, we experience God's presence at a corporate worship service. I remember singing in choir an uplifting arrangement of the old hymn "When I Survey the Wondrous Cross." Much like the Israelites' musical worship, the music enhanced the worship. As I sang this new arrangement of this grand old hymn, God used the crescendo in the music to highlight the words, "Demands my soul, my life, my all." I can still feel the rejoicing and happiness in my heart that came as I sang those words with a deep conviction to keep them.

Hopefully each member of God's family has, in some way, had a moment that could parallel the experience of those at the temple dedication. It could have been a private moment of prayer when it seemed like God was sitting in the room, or the overwhelming feeling of the grandness of his creation at the Grand Canyon or looking at a spectacular sunset. Not only do we sense his presence at joyful times, but also during times of grief. I am always amazed at the sacredness of the moment when a saint passes into heaven.

Those moments of sensing the palpable presence of the Lord should remind us that, through faith in Jesus, we have a relationship with God. We always will. Whether we are enjoying that relationship or enduring, it comes back to our obedience.

Now what?

Israel, both the nation and the person, always struggled with obedience, thus the name Israel. When we think about the postexilic Israelites reading this account of God being so very real to their ancestors, we would hope that it would motivate them to obey and to exclusively worship YHWH. Did it?

It would be wise to reflect on the moments in our own lives when God's presence was so very real: a baptism, a new ministry assignment, a baby dedication, and others as mentioned above. How does it affect our obedience and worship? We can rejoice and thank him for those moments and let those times of intimacy with him lead to an eagerness to worship and obey. It is like he gives us a taste of what obedience and worship can bring. And the sweetness of that moment should also serve as a warning. Obedience brings delight; disobedience brings discipline. We should let the joy of obedience warn us of the consequences of sin. As a new pastor officially begins to serve and hears the affirmations and prayers, he must take it as a warning to never seek to be served. As a new couple enjoys the supporting applause as they are introduced for the first time as husband and wife, the delight of that moment should be a warning that a successful marriage takes hard work.

We can't fabricate these high moments of worship; they are God's special gifts. The Israelites seem to have wasted the gift of his presence, for only a few years after this the nation turned to the worship of other gods. How could they, after such an amazing time of worship? How can we disobey after our own amazing times of worship?

Creativity in Presentation

This passage has a built-in tension. How do these two parts fit together? The first part occurs during the day; it is a public setting and is celebratory, resulting in happiness of heart within the nation. The second part is at night. The setting is a private audience that Solomon has with YHWH. The tone is somber, due to the warnings that God lays out. This section ends not with the nation rejoicing but with the prospect of other nations calling attention to Israel's sin. To highlight the two settings, different parts of the podium could be used. The first section can perhaps be read in front of the pulpit area, emphasizing the grand celebration (7:1–11). The second could be toward the back or off to the side, heightening the solitude of God's encounter with Solomon and the sense of retribution (7:12–22). Then as a third section of the sermon, the parallels and differences and application can be articulated from the pulpit or center stage. This then leads to the application: our special times of worship should result in our enjoying our relationship with the Lord in obedience, rather than enduring it in his discipline. Here is one possible structure:

- Present the story
  - YHWH, Solomon, and Israel dedicate the temple (7:1–11)
  - YHWH affirms the temple to Solomon at night (7:12–22)
- Explain and apply the idea
  - Our relationship with God is to be enjoyed, not endured.

DISCUSSION QUESTIONS

1. List the actions of God at this special time of worship. Which ones do you think stood out the most in Israel's memory? Which ones would stand out the most in your memory?

2. How do past pleasant experiences motivate us in the present?

3. When have you felt the presence of the Lord in a special way? How can that affect our lives today?

4. God's timing is always perfect. Why do you think he gave these warnings to the king for those specific times?

5. God's methods are also perfect. Why do you think he gave these warnings to the king, and not directly to the people?

2 Chronicles 8:1–16

EXEGETICAL IDEA
Solomon built up Israel as a consequence of building the temple and prepared the temple for its continual use in worship according to Mosaic and Davidic authority.

THEOLOGICAL FOCUS
Worshipping God builds up the community when conducted properly.

PREACHING IDEA
To grow spiritually, invest in good habits of worship.

PREACHING POINTERS
Sometimes the most important events in life are the moment-by-moment activities. A marriage is built not so much on the big events, but through the daily forgiveness and acts of love that are offered each day. Growing in our walk with the Lord has the mountaintop experiences, which need to be there, but the spiritual growth is a matter of an ongoing routine of daily practices of the spiritual disciplines. This passage presents some very normal activities. Solomon does his job as king to lead the nation in continual, ongoing worship. He does this by securing the nation and making provision for worship. These very normal activities of the king give us the assurance that great good comes out of normal, ongoing, routine habits of worship.

SOLOMON COMPLETES BUILDING
THE TEMPLE (8:1–16)

LITERARY STRUCTURE
AND THEMES (8:1–16)

After the Chronicler records that YHWH appears to Solomon to inform him that YHWH has heard his prayer and accepted the temple, the Chronicler turns to Solomon's building activities elsewhere in Israel. Solomon fortifies the far northern boundary of Israel, extending the work that David began there. He continues fortifying other areas to defend the land. This section associates building the temple and palace with building up the rest of Israel. In this way, the Chronicler implies that building the temple benefits all Israel.

The Chronicler then records Solomon's labor force to explain how he can carry out such extensive activity. Solomon conscripts the descendants of the peoples who inhabited the land before Israel took possession of it. This slave labor force carries out Solomon's building projects. In contrast, Solomon does not conscript any Israelites for his building projects; instead, he assigns them tasks as military personnel to supervise these projects.

The narrative shifts to show how Solomon provides for Israel's continual worship at the temple. This section covers three distinct items. First, it records that Solomon transfers Pharaoh's daughter to outside the city of David because he is concerned for the sanctity associated with the ark. Second, it recounts that Solomon makes some offerings, initiating Israel's sacrificial worship according to Mosaic law and fulfilling part of the temple's purpose. Third, it narrates that Solomon follows David's instructions when he appoints the priests, Levitical musicians, and gatekeepers for service at the temple.

This section closes with a summary statement of the temple's completion, thus bringing the larger temple construction account to a close. This verse helps connect Solomon's building activities throughout Israel with his building the temple and palace.

- ***Solomon's Building Activities (8:1–6)***
- ***Solomon's Labor Force (8:7–10)***
- ***Solomon Provides for Israel's Worship (8:11–15)***
- ***Summary Statement of the Temple's Completion (8:16)***

EXPOSITION (8:1–16)

In the ancient world, people understood temples to be sources of blessing because the deity would reside there. Since the king was responsible for building the temple, he would receive special divine blessings, particularly the promise of continued rule over the land (Kapelrud 1963, 56–62). However, the divine blessings extended beyond just the king; the deity's presence in the temple secured fertility and protection throughout the land. To maintain this blessing, the people would need to ensure that the deity remained at the temple. Therefore, special provisions were made to ensure the sanctity of the temple area, to provide regular offerings to the deity, and to organize personnel consecrated to attend to the deity. In this larger ancient context, this passage shows how Solomon's building activity extends to other parts of Israel and how he provides for Israel's continual worship to YHWH.

Solomon's Building Activities (8:1–6)

After completing the building of the temple and palace, Solomon builds up the rest of Israel by fortifying strategic cities.

8:1. This section begins by looking back to the building of the temple and palace. As elsewhere (e.g., 2 Chron. 2:1 [HB 1:18], 12 [HB 11]; 7:11), it connects the temple and palace together. In this case, it states that building the temple and palace took twenty years, half of the time of Solomon's reign. After Solomon completes building the temple and palace, he builds up Israel in various ways. Since the Chronicler states that Solomon's building up of Israel takes place after he completes the temple and palace, the Chronicler implies that this activity is a result of the temple and palace construction. Solomon as the temple-builder also builds up Israel (see 2 Chron. 2:11 [HB 10]; 9:8).

Length of Construction

Chronicles does not state how long each construction project took; however, 1 Kings 7:1 states that Solomon took thirteen years to build the palace. The text does not explain why building the palace took nearly twice as long as building the temple. Perhaps taking longer to build the palace betrays Solomon's lack of wholehearted devotion to YHWH (see Gunn and Fewell, 1993, 168). Josephus suggests that the palace took nearly twice as long to build because Solomon was not as motivated to build it as the temple (*Antiquities* 8.130). Whatever the reason, since the Chronicler only mentions building the palace but does not include any account of it, the Chronicler simply records that the time to build both took twenty years (cf. 1 Kings 9:10).

8:2. This section shows several ways in which Solomon builds up Israel. First, Solomon settles the Israelites into towns that King Huram gives to him. Chronicles earlier records that Huram has provided Solomon with materials and expertise to build the temple and palace (see 2 Chron.

2:1–15). Here, Chronicles does not explain why Huram gives these cities to Solomon; the focus lies on Solomon's settling Israelites into the new cities. This activity is a sign of God's blessing over Solomon and Israel, in contrast to other passages where Israel loses cities because of disobedience (e.g., 1 Chron. 10:7; 2 Chron. 28:18).

Comparing Kings to Chronicles

When one compares 2 Chronicles 8:2 to 1 Kings 9:11, one finds a different picture. In 1 Kings 9:11, Solomon gives Huram twenty cities that, upon inspection, are not acceptable to Huram. At first glance, the two accounts appear contradictory; however, Merrill notes that neither account should be judged wrong nor should they be thought irreconcilable to each othe. One may reconcile the accounts in several ways. For instance, one may infer that the kings made an equal exchange of cities but each account only preserves one side of the exchange (e.g., Kitchen 2003, 113–14), or that Huram returned the cities to Solomon after he inspected them (e.g., Merrill 2015, 363). In any case, the image in Chronicles is consistent with the way that Chronicles portrays the relationship between Solomon and Huram: Huram appears to be the less important party (see, e.g., the use of "my lord" אֲדֹנִי in 2 Chronicles 2:15 (HB 14); see Knoppers 2015, 51–70). For this reason, it is not surprising that the different books address the information about cities in different ways.

8:3–4. Second, Solomon expands his border to the north. Solomon gains control of Hamath-zobah by fighting against it. The image of Solomon as a fighting king occurs only here in Chronicles. In other passages, the Chronicler presents Solomon as a man of peace (see 1 Chron. 22:9). Including this information here likely draws a parallel to David, who defeated Hadadezer, king of Zobah (1 Chron. 18:3). Second Chronicles 8:4 presents Solomon again as a builder, this time building up Tadmor and storage cities he set up in Hamath. These verses present Solomon as establishing and extending what David has done earlier in relation to the region north of Israel.

Tadmor

Tadmor, identified with the city later known as Palmyra, is located beyond the usual boundaries of Israel, being northeast of Damascus.

8:5–6. Third, Solomon builds up and fortifies cities elsewhere in his kingdom. Solomon fortifies Upper and Lower Beth Horon. Chronicles describes how Solomon fortifies the cities: he builds walls, gates, and bars, standard elements for fortifying cities in those days (see Deut. 3:5; 2 Chron. 14:7). These two cities lie northwest of Jerusalem, on the border between the tribal allotments for Benjamin and Ephraim (see Josh. 16:3–5; 18:13–14) along a significant route from the Valley of Aijalon to Jerusalem (Dillard 1987, 65). The text then mentions specifically another city that Solomon builds up: Baalath. The specific form identifies a city within the tribal allotment of Dan (Josh. 19:44); however, the form may be a variant of Baalah. Most likely, the text here refers to the city Baalah, also known as Kiriath-jearim, located not too far from Upper and Lower Beth Horon. As Raymond Dillard points out, "Kiriath-jearim was along the second route into the central Benjamin plateau; the mention of Kiriath-jearim alongside the Beth Horons would then refer to fortification of both routes up from the valley of Aijalon [toward Jerusalem]" (1987, 65).

Identity of Baalath

Baalath may refer to other locations as well. It is possible that it refers to Baalah, located in the tribal allotment of Simeon according to Joshua 15:29 (see Japhet 1993, 623). It is also possible that it refers to a city named Baalath-beer, within Simeon's tribal allotment according to Joshua 19:8 (see R. Klein 2012, 122, for further information).

Beyond Solomon's activity building up specific fortified cities, Solomon sets up cities to store military supplies and equipment. The text emphasizes that Solomon builds up what belongs to him as king: an unspecified number of sites for the storage of general supplies useful in times of military conflict (such as food and weapons) as well as all the cities that Solomon prepared to store horses and chariots. This type of military preparation characterizes how YHWH rewards obedience throughout Chronicles and recalls the beginning of Solomon's reign, when the Chronicler demonstrates how YHWH prepares Solomon to be able to build the temple (see 2 Chron. 1:14–17 and the commentary on those verses).

This section concludes with a note that Solomon builds up everything that he desires to build up. The text emphasizes the extent of his activity by describing it as taking place "in Jerusalem, in Lebanon, and throughout his entire kingdom." Furthermore, this note sounds similar to 2 Chronicles 7:11, which records that Solomon successfully completed everything that he desired to do with the temple and palace. This similar language draws another connection between building the temple and palace and building up Israel. Perhaps this connection helps explain why this information occurs within the larger temple construction narrative (cf. 8:16).

Solomon's Labor Force (8:7–10)

Solomon establishes a large manual labor force of non-Israelites supervised by Israelites.

8:7–8. Following the account of Solomon's building activity beyond the temple and palace, the text turns to the labor force used to accomplish this activity. The text records that Solomon conscripts the descendants of those nations that occupied the land of Canaan before the sons of Israel took possession of it during the days of Joshua. The Chronicler draws on a standard list of nations commonly found in the Pentateuch (although in the Pentateuch, the list often includes Canaanites, e.g., Exod. 3:8, 17; 23:23; 33:2; 34:11; Deut. 20:17). In most of the passages in which this list of nations occurs, YHWH instructs the sons of Israel to destroy them because of their detestable practices (e.g., Deut. 20:17–18). Second Chronicles 8:8 recalls that the sons of Israel did not completely remove the inhabitants of Canaan. Solomon also does not destroy the descendants of these nations; instead, he conscripts them into forced labor for his building projects.

TRANSLATION ANALYSIS:
When Solomon conscripts these people into forced labor, the extent of the labor force is not clear. Chronicles indicates that it includes all (see the use of כֹּל in 8:7) the nations who remained in the land after the conquest; however, Solomon conscripts those from (מִן) their descendants. The use of "from" (מִן) in 8:8 leaves open the possibility that Solomon conscripts some of the descendants from all the nations rather than all the descendants from all the nations (see Japhet 1993, 624).

In the context of the Pentateuch and Joshua, with few exceptions, these peoples make up the enemies of Israel, either because they oppose Israel (e.g., Josh. 11:1–5) or because they lead Israel to engage in practices that YHWH finds detestable (e.g., Judg. 3:5–8). In these ways, they threaten Israel's existence and possession of the land. Solomon's conscripting of these peoples is a picture of Israel overcoming its enemies and exercising continual power over them.

Meaning of "To This Day"
Second Chronicles 8:8 ends with the expression "to this day" (עַד הַיּוֹם הַזֶּה) to describe how long these peoples continued in forced labor; however, during the time of the Chronicler such peoples were not subject to forced labor by Israel. The Chronicler takes this expression over from 1 Kings 9:21, but even during the time in which Kings was composed, this statement would no longer be true. Given how often the phrase occurs in a variety of contexts, the phrase may be an idiom with a sense of "from then on" or something similar (Dillard 1987, 42).

8:9–10. After describing the forced labor Solomon used, the text turns to the role of the Israelites. Two points arise: (1) Solomon does not conscript Israelites to work as slaves, and (2) Israelites still participate in the building projects. First, the text states clearly that Solomon does not force Israelites to work as slaves on his building projects. It is important for the Chronicler to make this point because making Israelites slaves seems to violate Mosaic law. Leviticus 25:39–46 commands Israel not to enslave a fellow Israelite permanently and thereby exercise authority over him in a harsh manner. Therefore, the Chronicler makes this point explicitly.

TRANSLATION ANALYSIS:
The word in this verse translated as "slaves" (עֲבָדִים) carries a wide semantic range. In some contexts, it carries the more general sense of someone under a royal or imperial authority. In these contexts, one might translate the word as "subjects" (e.g., 2 Chron. 10:7; 36:20). In other passages describing Solomon's reign, the word refers to Solomon's attendants, which one may translate as "servants" (e.g., 2 Chron. 9:4). In 8:9, the word occurs in the context of forced labor, so "slaves" is an appropriate translation.

For the second point, the text states that Israelites serve as soldiers and military leaders. The text specifically points out officers over the chariots and the chariot horses. Mentioning chariots connects 8:9 to 8:6 above, in which Solomon builds up cities for the chariots and chariot horses. Second Chronicles 8:10 connects these military personnel to Solomon's building projects more explicitly. This verse suggests that some of these military officers also oversaw, in some way, the building projects for Solomon's fortifications and cities for storing and maintaining military supplies and equipment, such as the cities for the chariots and chariot horses mentioned in 8:6. Second Chronicles 8:10 describes their role as exercising authority (רדה) over "the people." The Chronicler does not intend for "the people" to refer to the people of Israel, but to those conscripted to forced labor (see Lev. 25:39–43, mentioned above).

Solomon Provides for Israel's Worship (8:11–15)

Solomon prepares for Israel's future worship at the Jerusalem temple as he observes the regulations set by Moses and David.

8:11. The text now shifts from Solomon's building projects to Solomon's provision for Israel's continual worship. The text begins by discussing one of Solomon's wives, the daughter of Pharaoh. The Chronicler records that Solomon relocates this wife from the city of David into a house built especially for her. According to the verse, Solomon relocates her because places that the ark enters become holy.

This verse raises several questions. First, how does this verse relate to what precedes and follows it? This verse functions as a transition from Solomon's building projects to his specific provisions for Israel's continual worship. Mentioning the house that Solomon builds (בנה) for Pharaoh's daughter ties it into the sequence of the verb "to build" (בנה) found in 8:1, 2, 4, 5, and 6. In this way it connects to what precedes it. Since it demonstrates Solomon's desire to observe the sanctity around the ark, it points forward to the provisions Solomon makes for proper worship at the temple. In this way it connects to what follows it.

Second, why does the Chronicler mention Pharaoh's daughter specifically? Most likely, to demonstrate Solomon's international influence. Egypt is a powerful nation; by taking a daughter of Pharaoh as a wife, Solomon relates to Egypt as an ally.

Third, why does the sanctity of the city of David require Pharaoh's daughter to leave the area? Williamson represents several commentators when he states, "As a gentile and as a woman she should not be allowed contact with the holy" (1982, 231). However, contrary to Williamson, her identity as a non-Israelite does not appear to be a factor, since Solomon's reason for relocating her says nothing about her ethnicity (see Jonker 2016, 41–47). At the same time, Williamson's point regarding her identity as a woman does appear to be a factor, since Solomon's reason addresses her as a woman.

Although one could argue that simply her identity as a woman requires Solomon to relocate her, other reasons associated with her being a woman are more likely. For instance, as a woman she would be ritually unclean regularly because of menstruation (see Lev. 12:2–8; 15:18–33); therefore, Solomon would be concerned to observe the sanctity of the ark as well as protect his wife. Although her regular uncleanness may be a factor, Solomon addresses her identity beyond just that of a woman: she is specifically Solomon's wife. As Cohen states, "This [fact] implies that Solomon was trying to avoid the pollution which results from the relations between husband and wife" (Cohen 1984–1985, 36; also Exod. 19:15; 1 Sam. 20:26; 21:5–6). In this way Solomon observes the sanctity associated with the ark while protecting both his wife and himself.

In light of the above observations, the Chronicler includes 8:11 as a way of reinforcing Solomon's international influence while showing his concern to observe the sanctity associated with the ark. Not only does observing the ark's sanctity speak to Solomon's devotion to YHWH, but it also protects his wife and himself, since violating the sanctity of the ark can lead to disastrous results (e.g., 1 Chron. 13:9–10).

8:12–13. Following the comments regarding Pharaoh's daughter, the Chronicler recounts sacrifices that Solomon makes. The text refers to an occasion in which Solomon makes offerings, apparently as part of the final preparations for the temple. However, this occasion of making offerings initiates the regular offerings that take place as part of Israel's continual worship at the Jerusalem temple. Three observations from these verses follow. First, the Chronicler portrays Solomon as making these offerings properly. The text makes clear that Solomon does not violate the sanctity of the holy place, since the altar he uses lies in front of the temple building (Williamson 1982, 232). The text also describes the regular daily offerings and offerings for special occasions (Sabbaths, new moons, and annual festivals) as corresponding to Mosaic law.

Ritual Worship in Mosaic Law

When the Chronicler describes the offerings, he appears to have Numbers 28 in mind. The chapter outlines the required offerings for each day, Sabbath, new moon, and festivals. At the same time, he derives his list of three annual festivals from Deuteronomy 16:16. As seen throughout Chronicles, the Chronicler often combines wording from various passages when referring to Mosaic law (see esp. comments on 2 Chron. 35:13).

Second, the Chronicler presents these offerings as fulfilling part of Solomon's purpose for building the temple. In 2 Chronicles 2:4 (HB 3), Solomon plans to build the temple "for offerings for each morning and evening, for the Sabbaths, the new moons, and the appointed festivals of YHWH our God." Here, as the temple construction account closes out, the Chronicler shows that the temple is fulfilling this stated purpose.

Third, these verses affirm that the Jerusalem temple replaces Gibeon as the place for sacrificial worship. In 2 Chronicles 7, YHWH accepts the altar as the place for sacrifice when fire from the sky consumes the offerings there. This passage makes the point again by alluding back to 2 Chronicles 1:6. In 2 Chronicles 1:6 Solomon offers up offerings on the altar at the tent of meeting at Gibeon. Again, Solomon offers up

offerings on the altar, but now the altar is located at the temple in Jerusalem.

8:14–15. Solomon continues with final preparations for the temple's continual worship, appointing the primary personnel performing Israel's ritual worship. In this case, when Solomon appoints these personnel he is really just affirming what David has already done. This passage alludes to David's previous activity (see esp. 1 Chron. 23–26) and characterizes him in a significant way. It appeals to David as an authority by referring to his order (מִשְׁפָּט) and then his commandment (מִצְוָה). It connects that authority to the designation of David as "the man of God." This title often refers generally to a prophetic figure, presenting David as a prophet. In this case it also intends to associate David with Moses (Boda 2010a, 279). Although "servant of YHWH" is a more common title for Moses, "man of God" also occurs, notably twice in Chronicles (1 Chron. 23:14; 2 Chron. 30:16). Furthermore, this verse builds on 1 Chronicles 28:11–13 in which, similar to Moses, David receives the plans for the temple and its organization, records those plans in writing, and transfers them to Solomon. Therefore, the Chronicler is comparing David's authority, revealed in his order and commandment regarding the temple personnel, to Moses's authority, revealed in the law.

The Chronicler views these authorities as complementary. When the text describes the roles of the Levites as "praising" and "ministering before the priests," it draws on both Mosaic and Davidic authority, since David assigns the Levites their musical tasks (see 1 Chron. 16:4), while Moses assigns them the tasks of assisting the priests (see Num. 3:6–9).

Finally, these verses look to another authority: Solomon. The text shows that the people follow Solomon's commands regarding the priests, Levites, and treasuries; however, unlike Moses and David, the text does not refer to Solomon by name but as king. This detail coincides with a picture found throughout

Chronicles. When it comes to Israel's ritual worship, the Chronicler points out three authority figures: "Moses, as the authority for the sacrificial system; David, responsible for clerical reorganization and the introduction of liturgical music; and the reigning king, as *ad hoc* authority in situations requiring intervention, most notably in the time of Hezekiah and Josiah" (Japhet 1993, 628). The text does not present Solomon as an innovator within Israel's worship but as one who faithfully follows Mosaic legislation and finishes the work his father David began.

Levitical Occupations

First Chronicles 23:4–5 lists three occupations for the Levites: (1) officers and judges, (2) gatekeepers, and (3) musicians who praise (הלל). Here in 2 Chronicles 8:14–15, the Chronicler alludes to these three groups: the musicians are the Levites who "praise" (הלל); the gatekeepers are those assigned to each gate; and the officers and judges are those responsible for the treasuries of the temple (cf. 1 Chron. 26:20–28). In this way, the Chronicler mentions all the duties of the Levites associated with the temple and its worship (see Japhet 1993, 629).

Summary Statement of the Temple's Completion (8:16)

The Chronicler records that Solomon completes the building of the temple.

8:16. The final verse of this section closes out the entire temple building account which began in 2 Chronicles 2:1 (HB 1:18). The verse mentions that the temple is finished and mirrors two other statements that the temple is finished (2 Chron. 5:1; 7:11). Each of these verses marks a significant stage in setting up the temple as a place for Israel's worship. Each statement also communicates what the Chronicler associates with temple building. For instance, after describing the temple structure and furnishings, 2 Chronicles 5:1 states that the temple is finished. However, the narrative goes on to describe how

Israel transfers the ark into the temple and how Solomon dedicates the temple through prayer, offerings, and observing the Feast of Booths. Therefore, in one sense the temple is finished in 2 Chronicles 5:1; however, in another sense, it is not finished until 2 Chronicles 7:11. Here also 8:16 shows how building up Israel and preparing for Israel's continual worship at the Jerusalem temple is required for the temple to be finished.

The language of 8:16 highlights three other significant points. First, the language shows that the scope of this statement includes the entire temple-building process, since it refers to laying the temple's foundations. In other ancient Near Eastern temple-building accounts, laying the foundations is the celebrated first step in building the temple (Boda 2006, 226–30; 2010b, 312; Ellis 1968, 5–33). Even though the Chronicler only alludes to laying the foundations elsewhere (2 Chron. 3:3), referring to them here reveals that the entire process of building the temple is in view. Second, the language looks back to 1 Chronicles 28:20, where David charges Solomon to have courage to build the temple because YHWH will be with him until "all the work of the service of YHWH's temple is finished" (Japhet 1993, 629). Solomon fulfills David's charge here. Third, the language alludes to Solomon as the chosen builder. The word translated "is finished" (שלם) is likely intended as a pun on Solomon's name (שלמה). In 1 Chronicles 22:9, the text utilizes a pun to describe Solomon as a man of peace (שלום). These puns demonstrate that God chooses Solomon uniquely to fulfill the task of building the temple, a task that his father David initiates and directs.

For the first readers, the picture of Solomon and his kingdom would be a picture of a long-gone, glorious past for Israel. The first readers were living in relative obscurity, struggling to survive financially within the enormous Persian Empire. At the same time, this picture of the glorious past makes an important connection for them: building (and maintaining) YHWH's temple in Jerusalem leads to building up Israel as a whole. On the one hand, in their context, the first readers would be encouraged to maintain the Jerusalem temple and its ritual worship in accordance with Mosaic and Davidic regulations so that YHWH may again provide them with international influence, economic development, and secure borders. On the other hand, they would also be waiting for another Davidic king, a temple-builder who could usher in another glorious age for Israel.

THEOLOGICAL FOCUS

Worshipping God builds up the community when conducted properly.

During the OT period, the Jerusalem temple plays a key role in mediating the relationship between God and his people. The people bless God as they care for the sacred space, maintain certain rituals, and bring regular offerings, while God blesses the people as he secures their peace, makes their land fruitful, and prospers their work. At the same time, building the Jerusalem temple requires certain conditions, such as fully securing the land, establishing a stable line of rulers, and raising up a chosen builder. In the chapters preceding this passage, God brings about these conditions. This passage shows how the Jerusalem temple benefits all the people, since proper worship takes place there.

During his earthly ministry, Jesus points beyond the Jerusalem temple, promising that because of his obedient life, death, resurrection, and ascension, God will be present in a special way with each believer through his Spirit rather than in a specific geographic location. Consequently, the forms of worship shift, but many principles of OT worship carry over into the NT era.

One principle derived from this passage is that God benefits all his people through an individual that he chooses to fulfill a particular task of worship. Just as God chooses Solomon to build the temple, resulting in blessings for all Israel, so also God chooses individuals to fulfill specific tasks to bless the church. Two NT passages

illustrate this principle well. First, in Ephesians 4:11–13, Paul speaks of the specific roles granted to certain individuals: apostles, prophets, evangelists, and pastor-teachers. He has granted such roles to build up the body of Christ so that God's people may grow to full maturity. Second, when Paul addresses spiritual gifts, he recognizes the contributions of different individuals to sing, teach, offer a revelation, speak in another language, or interpret what is said. Each person has something specific to offer as the congregation gathers to worship. However, Paul emphasizes that what should govern their time of worship is that everything should be done to build up the congregation (1 Cor. 14:26).

Furthermore, this passage emphasizes how Solomon prepares for Israel's worship by following the proper authorities: Moses and David. Following their instructions helps secure Israel's well-being as they worship God properly. As Paul addresses the question of eating meat, he points to a different criterion for evaluating proper conduct together: building up another. As Paul instructs the more mature to be patient with those who are weaker, he encourages them not to please themselves but to please their neighbors so that the mature may build up their neighbors. Paul draws on the example of Jesus as the authority for instructing them in this way (Rom. 15:1–3). In this way, the NT shifts the authorities in worship from Moses and David to Jesus. Furthermore, the authority of Jesus points to setting aside one's desires to benefit others.

The discussion above has focused on this passage from the perspective of the people. The passage also points to the important role that Solomon plays as king. In this role, Solomon anticipates another king who will arise to lead God's people in worship. Furthermore, like those under Solomon, all God's people will benefit under the reign of this coming king. This coming king is Jesus, and those who believe in him share in his benefits. They are made heirs of God and joint heirs with Jesus, sharing in God's glory at the end of this present age (Rom. 8:17).

PREACHING AND TEACHING STRATEGIES

Exegetical and Theological Synthesis

This pericope stands in contrast to the preceding ones. The end of 1 Chronicles through chapter 7 of 2 Chronicles is filled with nationwide celebrations, a new king, a new temple, national choirs and orchestras, and deeply motivational and spiritual addresses from David and Solomon. Second Chronicles 8 is about minor military events, building new fortifications, and ongoing temple worship. The contrast is perhaps similar to our holiday season being followed by January. The six weeks of celebrations starts with Thanksgiving, then we move into the season of Advent, which culminates in Christmas Eve and Christmas Day, finally ending with New Year's Day. Then January comes. Yes, we remember Dr. Martin Luther King Jr. and we should, but the excitement of December gives way to the routine of January. School teachers have expressed to me that from January to spring break is a long stretch of routine, seemingly unexciting teaching. Though this pericope doesn't have the excitement, it still has a message for us.

It is as if the writer is giving us a glimpse into the day-in, day-out routine of living in Israel. The king was leading well and, most importantly, worship of YHWH was ongoing. It must not be overlooked that all these somewhat normal activities were done properly, that is, in line with God's order. There is great benefit in establishing and being consistent in routines.

It is easy to understand how temple worship, sabbath after sabbath, festival after festival, sacrifice after sacrifice was probably seen as just a routine. But these routines of normal life in Israel were creating a mindset that directed them toward YHWH. Solomon, as a good king, provided what was needed for proper worship and led the nation to follow God's commands to sacrifice in a routine, habitual, yet meaningful way. The benefit was in how the routine would shape the thinking of Israel.

As we consider how to apply the teaching of this passage, we know that the coming of Jesus changed the manner and the content of routines of worship. Our weekly gatherings to worship, our consistent reading of the Word, and our daily prayers before meals are routines that can have amazing results as they shape our thinking.

Preaching Idea

To grow spiritually, invest in good habits of worship.

Contemporary Connections

What does it mean?

Often routines can seem meaningless, and surely there are those that are just routines. However, other routines can be very meaningful. This is easily seen when it comes to our bodies. For more than twenty years I have to stretch my back muscles every morning. Week after week, month after month, I stretch. When I keep up this routine, my back is fine. If I stop because of a change in schedule, perhaps a vacation or guests in our home, the pain in my back returns, and I am reminded that the routine stretching has a great effect on my back, even though when I was faithful to the routine I didn't see its value.

This passage shows that routines and practices ordained by God need to be followed. Christ's coming certainly changed the elements of our routines from those of Israel, and caution must be exercised because the routines are not an end in themselves. In the first century, the Pharisees had added so many detailed rules that the focus shifted from God to the rules. They seemed to worship the routines. Across the last two centuries Christian routines for worship both private and corporate have been developed, often referred to as spiritual disciplines. Some that we recognize are prayer, reading of Scripture, regular corporate worship, and service to others. Richard Foster (1988) and Donald Whitney (2014) are two such authors who have recently written on these proven practices.

313

Another element in the text is that Solomon was leading the nation to worship, and that David had prepared resources so that worship could take place. It is the responsibility of pastors and other leaders to provide resources for worship and spiritual growth. The church that I am a part of currently has a structure for small groups. I might set it up differently if I were the leader of that ministry, but I chose to willingly follow the structure that is presented to me and am blessed by their leading.

Is it true?

Just as Solomon's activities in this chapter were routine but important, so too something as simple as our saying a prayer of thanks before a meal can have a very positive effect on our thinking. If done with proper respect that is due our Lord when we speak to him, it is a reminder that provision comes from him and that we are dependent beings. Setting aside a day to worship highlights the importance of connecting with God and with other believers. The songs we sing over and over again, the prayers that we always pray, baptisms, participating at the Lord's Table—all these practices that we repeat so often affect our thinking.

Sometimes prayer can be just a way to gather everyone together before we start to eat, like a starting gun to signal that it is OK to start eating. But, if done with proper respect and genuine thanksgiving for God's provision, this can become part of our instinctive reaction, so much so that when we have been in a situation where prayer is not offered before a meal, our instinct is to pray silently. It is as if we can't eat a meal without praying first. Is it a habit? Yes it is, and a good one.

James K. A. Smith articulates how routine affects our thinking:

> Our desires are caught more than taught. All kinds of cultural rhythms and routines are in fact, rituals that function as pedagogies of desire precisely because they tacitly and covertly train us to love a certain version of the kingdom, they teach us to long for some rendition of the good life. They aren't just something we do: they do something to us. (2016, 21–22)

Now what?

When we speak of routines, there is a great spectrum of how people function with them. There are some who love rigid routines and thrive in them. Others see the need for routines but like flexibility. When it comes to meals, my New England relatives were on the rigid end of the spectrum. Their weekly menu didn't change from week to week. Monday was spaghetti, Tuesday meatloaf, and so on. Every week was the same. Others would quickly reject that rigidity as being terribly boring. They would rather have a menu that is creative and always changing, with different ethnic dishes and a great variety of tastes. But for both, there is the same routine of eating. When we come to exhorting our people to have spiritual disciplines and routines, we must remember that there can be flexibility in what these may look like. However, each of us as followers of Jesus must follow the teaching of this passage and develop some of the ongoing normal habits of worship and following our Lord. Below is a list of possible routines or spiritual habits to start or further develop; it is not an exhaustive list, only a catalyst to help us make changes:

- Make a voiced prayer before a meal standard practice.
- Set and keep a specific time each day for prayer and reading of Scripture.
- Set and keep a certain amount of time that you will read and pray.
- Make a plan to increase giving.
- Read a book that will help you grow in your love toward God.
- Read a book that will help you love your family more.
- Enroll in a Bible study class.

- Join a small discipleship group.
- Fast one meal a week, or from technology.
- Serve your local church in some way, either monthly or weekly.
- Give an offering in some regular pattern.
- Develop a friendship with someone outside the faith.

As leaders, pastors and teachers need to provide resources to help the saints practice these good disciplines, such as suggesting books, offering classes, initiating mentoring, and setting up systems that connect people with each other.

Creativity in Presentation

The difficulty in presenting the application of this passage is helping people see that little habits are of great importance. In the front matter of his book mentioned above, Smith (2016, vii) quotes Winnie the Pooh: "Sometimes the smallest things take up the most room in your heart." These seemingly small routine spiritual habits of worship can make a huge difference over time.

Presenting the concept of a spectrum can be very helpful in applying this to both new believers and seasoned saints. One might use the front of the speaking area, remembering to present from right to left so that the congregation will see it from left to right. Using prayer as an example, begin by stepping to the far right, where you could start the spectrum by pointing out that some only pray occasionally. Then move slightly toward the right, establishing another point on the spectrum, you might say that some pray a short sentence prayer. Again, moving further to your left creating another point on the spectrum you describe a more extended prayer. This continues as you create a spectrum from just barely praying at all to one who would spend a day in prayer. The purpose of the spectrum is not to compare oneself with others, but rather to compare where you are in reference to where you have been. Encourage everyone to move up the spectrum and take steps to better their prayer lives.

Since the thrust of this text becomes clearer when it is seen in context of the preceding chapters, it might be helpful to remind or summarize the celebratory events that lead up to this chapter, so that the contrast of this chapter can be more easily seen.

Here is one suggested structure:

- Review the celebration of the temple dedication (6:1–7:22)
- Present the text
  - Solomon's building activities (8:1–6)
  - Solomon's labor force (8:7–10)
  - Solomon provides for Israel's worship (8:11–15)
  - Summary statement of the temple's completion (8:16)
- Explain the text: worshipping God builds up the community when conducted properly
- Apply the text: to grow spiritually, invest in good habits of worship

DISCUSSION QUESTIONS

1. What are some routines or habits that have helped you?

2. Why do we sometimes resist routines?

3. What routines or habits are essential for sustaining physical life? Spiritual life?

4. What is a spiritual discipline that is easy for you to do on a regular basis? What spiritual discipline is hard for you?

5. What helps you start a routine?

2 Chronicles 8:17–9:31

EXEGETICAL IDEA
Other nations acknowledged YHWH's rule and love for Israel when YHWH gave Solomon what he promised: wisdom and wealth beyond compare.

THEOLOGICAL FOCUS
God demonstrates what he is like when he faithfully fulfills his promises to his people.

PREACHING IDEA
The Lord has, and will, provide with extravagant abundance.

PREACHING POINTERS
Solomon's wealth and wisdom are presented here in such a way that it is almost surreal, even more so to modern readers. Just one of the two hundred gold decorative shields would be worth around $300,000 today. These abundant blessings that the writer is asking us to remember are based upon God being the source and God keeping his promises. And it is this same foundation of God's character that allowed Israel, and allows us, to look for a better future. God is not leading us to live in the past, but through an affirming picture of the past he is leading us to trust in him for a better future. This future will be with extravagant abundance—not necessarily in terms of gold, silver, and human wisdom, but with what he knows is the very best.

SOLOMON'S WISDOM AND WEALTH (8:17–9:31)

LITERARY STRUCTURE AND THEMES (8:17–9:31)

After closing the full temple construction account, the Chronicler focuses on the greatness of Solomon's reign, especially in relation to other kings. Comments regarding the maritime activities of Solomon and Huram mark the major divisions within the unit (8:17–18; 9:10–11, 21). Furthermore, mentioning Huram draws connections back to the beginning of Solomon's reign (see 2 Chron. 2). The mention of Solomon's horses and horse trade confirms this concern to draw the reign of Solomon to a close by alluding back to the beginning (forming a partially concentric structure, see Dillard 1987, 5–7).

The chapter switches between the centripetal and centrifugal forces of Solomon's kingdom (see Boda 2010a, 282). The interactions between Solomon, Huram, and the queen of Sheba illustrate these forces. On the one hand, Solomon's joint maritime ventures with Huram (8:17–18) represent occasions for Solomon to increase his kingdom by going out. He goes to other lands (e.g., Ezion-geber and Elath in Edom). He sends ships along with Huram to distant, exotic locations (e.g., Ophir). From such ventures he brings back tremendous wealth and rare materials. On the other hand, the visit from the queen of Sheba represents the draw that Solomon exerts on other nations. The queen comes from a distant land, bringing a large entourage and fine gifts because she has heard of Solomon's wisdom. This movement in and out characterizes this entire narrative section.

Following Solomon's interactions with these specific kings, the text mentions Solomon's great wealth, especially in terms of the gold he receives. With the vast amount he receives, he creates several products that illustrate his great wealth. Furthermore, Solomon's great wealth contributes to his international greatness. The text draws a picture of kings continually coming into Jerusalem to hear Solomon's wisdom and to honor him and his achievements.

Finally, the text provides a conclusion to Solomon's reign by recording other sources regarding his reign, its length and extent, as well as the notice of his death, burial, and successor.

- ***Solomon, Huram, and the Queen of Sheba (8:17–9:12)***
- ***Solomon's Great Wealth (9:13–21)***
- ***Solomon's International Greatness (9:22–28)***
- ***Conclusion of Solomon's Reign (9:29–31)***

EXPOSITION (8:17–9:31)

Up to this point, the Chronicler has focused on Solomon's task of building the temple. However, this unit focuses on Solomon's greatness, especially his wisdom and wealth. At first, focusing on one man's wisdom and wealth may seem out of place. However, kings in the ancient Near Eastern world occupied special roles, even in relation to the divine realm. Some kings even claimed to be divine, either in life or death; however, most saw themselves as intermediaries between the gods and humans (for short summary of this issue, see N. Fox 2018, 475–76). Chronicles certainly does not claim divinity for Israel's kings; however, Chronicles does show a close relationship between YHWH and Israel's kings. In this context, the Chronicler shows that in a limited way, Solomon as the royal temple-builder reflects the characteristics of YHWH. Therefore, Solomon's greatness exhibits YHWH's greatness.

Solomon, Huram, and the Queen of Sheba (8:17–9:12)

Because of YHWH's gifts, Solomon enjoys international wealth and fame, as demonstrated in his interactions with the king of Tyre and the queen of Sheba.

8:17–18. The narrative section begins by recounting how Solomon continues to interact with Huram, king of Tyre. Chronicles has explored their interaction throughout Solomon's reign (2 Chron. 2:3–16 [HB 2–15]; 8:2), portraying the two kings as allies. In these verses, Solomon goes south to Ezion-geber and Elath in Edom, located on the Gulf of Aqaba. From this location, Huram provides ships and skilled sailors to accompany Solomon's servants in traveling to Ophir to return vast amounts of gold from there (about two-thirds of Solomon's income for a year; see 2 Chron. 9:13). As Solomon and Huram send out ships to distant places, they bring back wealth, particularly to Solomon. This activity highlights the extent of Solomon's influence and wealth.

Solomon's Relation to Huram

The Chronicler portrays the two kings Solomon and Huram as cooperating with one another, although there are some hints that Solomon holds a higher status, even from Huram's point of view (see 2 Chron. 2:14, use of אֲדֹנִי "my lord"; see also Knoppers 2015, 51–70).

9:1. The narrative next shifts to the queen of Sheba. Because of what the queen has heard about Solomon, she travels to Jerusalem with her large entourage and other signs of great wealth to test Solomon with various riddles. This verse raises three important points. First, the text indicates that Solomon's fame has traveled quite far and that what people are saying about him is so unbelievable that the queen visits Solomon herself. The text emphasizes this type of international fame throughout the rest of the chapter as well. Second, the queen arrives

with great wealth. By including a description of her wealth, the text anticipates the gifts that she will offer Solomon later (9:9), thereby elevating Solomon's status. Third, the queen seeks to test Solomon by asking him riddles or other kinds of challenging questions. In the OT the ability to solve riddles comes with wisdom (Prov. 1:6). Therefore, by asking Solomon whatever riddles or other challenging questions the queen can think of, she tests Solomon's wisdom.

Sheba

The location of Sheba is uncertain. The most likely possibility is that it refers to the southern Arabian Peninsula, perhaps the lands inhabited by the Sabeans. Regardless of its specific location, the Bible presents it as a land far from Israel (cf. Ps. 72:10). See further R. Klein 2012, 136.

TRANSLATION ANALYSIS:
Two issues arise in translating this verse. First, English translations render the Hebrew חִידוֹת as "difficult or challenging questions." In some contexts, the Hebrew term clearly refers to a riddle (see Judg. 14:12–19). In this case, the word likely carries a similar sense to a riddle, that is, an enigmatic question that requires cleverness or ingenuity to solve. However, in English, the word "riddle" usually carries a connotation of humor or games. The Hebrew word does not carry such a connotation. Second, translations treat the final expression differently. Some translations (e.g., NASB, NKJV) render the expression as "all that was in/on her heart"; however, "heart" in English most often carries connotations of emotions. Emotions are not in view in the context. Other translations (e.g., CSV, ESV, NET, NIV, NLT, NRSV) render the phrase "everything/all on her mind"; however, in English this expression often carries connotations of concerns or problems occupying someone's thoughts. In this context, the expression relates to the queen's attempt to test Solomon's wisdom. For this reason, I would translate the expression as "everything she can think of," that

is, every riddle or challenging question she can think of to stump Solomon.

9:2–4. When the queen tests Solomon, he passes. First, Solomon demonstrates his unbelievable wisdom by explaining everything the queen asks him. In fact, the text emphasizes the extent of Solomon's wisdom since nothing is too hard for him to explain. Second, Solomon demonstrates his unbelievable achievements through his palace, his provisions, his personnel (their service and their apparel), and his procession up to the temple. Solomon's wisdom and works fill the queen with such wonder that she cannot breathe.

TRANSLATION ANALYSIS:
Two issues arise in this verse. First, translations differ regarding the final item that the queen observes: either burnt offerings (e.g., CSB, ESV, NET, NIV, NLT, NRSV) or "ascent/stairway" (KJV, NASB). The difference occurs because of challenges deciphering the reading of MT. Since the immediate context focuses on the splendor of Solomon's court, I have translated the expression as "ascent"; that is, the queen saw Solomon's grand procession from his palace to the temple. Second, translations treat the expression at the end in different ways. The translations tend to focus either on her spirit/breath (CSB, ESV, KJV, NASB, NRSV) or on her emotional state (NET, NIV, NLT). Even though the queen is amazed in this context, the expression occurs in Joshua 5:1 to describe the terror that fills the nations when they hear that YHWH has dried up the waters to let Israel cross over. I would translate the expression as "she could not breathe" to preserve the figure of speech regarding her breath, while using an expression that would fit a context of either amazement or fear.

9:5–6. The queen confirms that Solomon has passed her test. Her response brings up matters significant for this unit. First, it emphasizes that Solomon's wisdom and achievements are incredible—that is, one can hardly believe they are real. The queen admits that she could not believe what she had heard about Solomon; however, after seeing the proof of Solomon's wisdom through his ability to answer her questions and his tremendous achievements, she recognizes not only that Solomon is as great as what she heard but that he even exceeds all her expectations. One can hardly imagine a way in which these verses could present a more astounding picture of Solomon.

TRANSLATION ANALYSIS:
The end of this verse explains the topic of what the queen heard about Solomon. Translations differ regarding that report. Some translations (e.g., CSB, ESV, NET) interpret the text to say that the report is limited to Solomon's wisdom and his wise words. Others (e.g., NIV, NLT, NRSV) translate the word "your words" (דְּבָרֶיךָ) to refer to more than what Solomon says, but also what he accomplishes. Since the queen has just observed Solomon's wisdom and his accomplishments, the latter interpretation is more likely.

9:7–8. Second, her response connects Solomon's greatness to the welfare of Israel. The connection begins with those in Solomon's court. The queen points out how fortunate those who attend to Solomon must be, since they regularly hear his words of wisdom. The benefits of Solomon as king extend to Israel as a whole (see Merrill 2015, 370). The queen explains that YHWH has made Solomon king because YHWH loves Israel. Furthermore, since Solomon lives up to the moral ideal of carrying out "justice and righteousness" (Japhet 1993, 673), YHWH will establish the nation forever, an expression alluding back to YHWH's promises to David (1 Chron. 17:7–14).

TRANSLATION ANALYSIS:
The beginning of this verse presents two challenges to the translator. First, there is a text-critical issue. Some English translations (e.g., ESV)

follow some ancient translations that read "wives, women" instead of "men," although most English translations follow MT "men." Second, the proper translation of אֲנָשֶׁיךָ ("your men") in this context is not apparent. The word could refer more generally to the people of Israel, although given the context of those who appear regularly before the king such an interpretation seems unlikely. Instead, in this case, "your men" most likely is a term used alongside servants of a king, so that the two nouns refer to one group within the royal court rather than two separate groups (cf. 1 Kings 1:9). A translation such as "your attendants" (NET) captures this sense well.

Similarity to Huram

Huram makes a similar statement that YHWH has made Solomon king because of YHWH's love for Israel (2 Chron. 2:11 [HB 10]). In fact, Huram and the queen of Sheba share other similarities in Chronicles: (1) both are foreign monarchs, (2) both speak about YHWH like an Israelite would, and (3) both bless YHWH for making Solomon king over Israel (see Ben Zvi 2006a, 275–76).

Third, her response connects Solomon's greatness to YHWH's greatness. The text shows that observing Solomon's incredible wisdom and achievements leads the queen to praise YHWH for making Solomon king. In other words, seeing Solomon's greatness leads to praising YHWH. Furthermore, the text acknowledges that when Solomon sits on the throne over Israel, it is not really his throne. The throne belongs to YHWH, and Solomon serves as king on behalf of YHWH. Therefore, when Solomon's kingdom is great, YHWH's kingdom is great. In this way, the queen's response points to an important point underlying the entire narrative unit: Solomon as king reflects YHWH as king. For this reason, Solomon should carry out justice and righteousness to reflect how YHWH carries out justice and righteousness (e.g., Jer. 9:24 [HB 23]).

9:9. Following the queen's verbal response, she offers Solomon gifts from the wealth that she brought with her. The text points out the quantity and quality of what she gives, particularly the quality of spices. Like many other items throughout this chapter, these spices are incomparable. The fact that the queen gives Solomon gifts, much less such great gifts as these, further elevates Solomon's status and foreshadows what rulers of other lands will do (9:23–24).

9:10–11. These verses describe how Solomon's maritime activities with Huram create even more wealth and accomplishments. These verses perform three functions. First, the verses create an *inclusio* around the account of the queen's visit, since the text returns to the same fleet that brought back gold from Ophir (2 Chron. 8:18). This *inclusio* highlights the significance of the queen's visit, especially her recognition of Solomon's (and thereby YHWH's) greatness. Second, these verses interrupt the account of the queen's visit. Perhaps this interruption occurs because 9:9 mentions gold and precious stones among the queen's gifts. The mention of these materials prompts the comment regarding the fleet returning gold and precious stones, along with algumwood. Mentioning algumwood then prompts the comment regarding how Solomon uses the wood. The first use concerns the entryways to the temple and the palace. For the second use, Solomon has stringed instruments constructed of incomparable quality ("Nothing like them had been seen in Judah"). These comments further build up the picture of Solomon's greatness.

Algumwood

The identity of algumwood is not certain. Traditionally, it has been understood to be sandalwood; however, it is most likely not sandalwood. Instead, the current evidence suggests that it may be some type of cypress. Regardless its specific identification, it was clearly a rare, expensive wood.

Third, these comments allude back to Solomon's earlier dealings with Huram. In 2 Chronicles 2:8 [HB 7], Solomon requests algumwood as a material for building the temple and palace. This verse demonstrates that Huram has delivered on the deal. In this way, these verses also connect the beginning of Solomon's reign to the end.

9:12. Following the interruption concerning Solomon and Huram's fleet, the narrative returns to the queen of Sheba. Solomon shows great hospitality, giving the queen whatever she desires, even beyond the gifts she has given to him. Just as Solomon has explained every matter the queen could think of, Solomon now gives the queen every desire that she requests. After they exchange their gifts, the queen returns home with her entourage.

Solomon's Great Wealth (9:13–21)
As YHWH promised, Solomon possesses tremendous wealth, as demonstrated by what Solomon brings in and what he produces.

9:13–14. The narrative now moves to describing Solomon's tremendous wealth, particularly in gold. The section begins by stating how much gold Solomon receives in a year (666 talents). The amount is amazing; however, it is not out of step either with the rest of Chronicles or with other ancient Near Eastern accounts (see 1 Chron. 22:14; 29:4; Millard 1989, 20–34). At the same time, this amount does not include any gold Solomon acquires from traders and merchants or from rulers of groups in Arabia or other foreign officials.

9:15–16. Solomon uses this amazing amount of gold for several items. First, Solomon makes shields from hammered gold. He creates two sizes: two hundred large shields and three hundred small shields. The text does not state the function of these shields; however, they most likely serve ornamental purposes rather than military ones. Solomon deposits the shields in the House of the Lebanon Forest, a large building within the palace complex described in 1 Kings 7:2–5. Furthermore, 2 Chronicles 12:9–11 records that after Shishak takes Solomon's shields, Rehoboam replaces them with bronze shields that the royal guard uses. These shields likely fulfill the same function. Regardless of their specific use, they are an impressive display.

9:17–19. Second, Solomon makes an extravagant throne. The text conveys this sense of extravagance in many ways. The throne is large and consists of ivory and pure gold, both exquisite materials. The throne sits higher than ground level, with a series of steps leading to it. Atop the steps, there is a gold footstool attached to the throne. The throne itself contains armrests with a lion statue perched next to each armrest. Statues of lions also stand at each end of the steps, flanking whoever approaches the throne. Since lions in the OT appear as animals who are courageous (e.g., 2 Sam. 17:10), dangerous (e.g., Gen. 49:9; Ps. 17:12), and honorable (e.g., Eccl. 9:4), their presence around the throne likely intends to evoke a sense of fear and wonder. Finally, the text records that this throne is incomparable.

Solomon's Throne
Other thrones in the ancient world resemble features of this throne (see esp. Metzger 1985, 298–308). However, the point of the text is not that this throne's design is unique, but that no other kingdom (at least at that time) possessed a throne as extravagant as this one.

9:20. Third, Solomon makes household items from gold. The text points out that Solomon made even the mundane serving utensils within the palace, particularly in the House of the Lebanon Forest, from pure gold. Often, at least a portion of these items would be made from silver; however, Solomon's wealth is so great that silver is not valuable.

9:21. The text then describes another one of Solomon's maritime activities with Huram. Several items regarding the description of this activity deserve attention. First, the text describes Solomon's fleet as either ships going to Tarshish or ships of Tarshish. More than likely, a "ship of Tarshish" designates a type of ship, that is, a merchant ship capable of traveling long distances, rather than a destination. Since the text describes the ships as "going to Tarshish," many interpret the text to say that Solomon's fleet heads to Tarshish. However, the items that the fleet returns suggest that the fleet does not travel across the Mediterranean but somewhere in Africa. Within the OT, Tarshish occurs as a destination as far out as one can imagine (Ps. 72:10; Jonah 1:3). Perhaps, for this reason, the description of the ships as "going to Tarshish" either refers to ships capable of traveling to Tarshish, that is, as far away as possible, or that Tarshish itself has become a figure of speech for a remote, faraway location.

Ships of Tarshish

As evidence that the text may refer to ships capable of traveling to Tarshish, one can find a similar use of the participle elsewhere in Chronicles. For instance, several passages (e.g., 1 Chron. 5:18; 7:11; 12:33–37 [HB 34–38]) describe men who are "capable of fighting in battle" (יֹצְאֵי צָבָא). As far as Tarshish as a figure of speech for a remote, faraway land, one might draw an analogy to the European or American use of Timbuktu. Timbuktu (an older spelling) is an actual location; however, it is also a figure of speech for a remote, faraway land (see also Dillard 1987, 73).

Second, Solomon's fleet returns periodically (once every three years). This delay in returning its cargo points to the extreme distance that the fleet must travel. In other words, the text emphasizes that Solomon's maritime activity stretches to faraway lands. Third, when the fleet returns, it brings items such as ivory, apes, and other primates, along with the precious metals of gold and silver. These items are valuable (gold and silver) and/or exotic (ivory, apes, and other primates). This list of items bolsters the picture that Solomon's maritime activity stretches to distant, and even exotic, locations.

TRANSLATION ANALYSIS:
The meaning of the term תֻּכִּיִּים is unclear. Older translations render the word as "peacock," but comparative studies suggest the term refers to a type of primate (see Noonan 2020, 119).

Faraway Lands

This comment regarding Tarshish provides a certain balance to the chapter. At the beginning, the queen of Sheba travels from Sheba to Jerusalem with many goods. Here, Solomon travels from Jerusalem to Tarshish to secure goods. Both Sheba and Tarshish represent locations of the greatest distance from Jerusalem (see Ps. 72:10).

Solomon's International Greatness (9:22–28)

As YHWH promised, Solomon's wealth and wisdom exceed other kings, so that Solomon exerts influence throughout the region and becomes a model for an ideal king.

9:22. This section emphasizes the extent of Solomon's greatness in relation to other nations. It begins by stating that Solomon's wealth and wisdom exceeds those of all other rulers. This comment is significant in Chronicles for two reasons. First, it implies that worshipping YHWH properly—particularly in this case, building YHWH's temple—leads to a king's greatness. The distribution of the word "wealth" (עֹשֶׁר) in Chronicles confirms this point: David (1 Chron. 29:28), Jehoshaphat (2 Chron. 17:5; 18:1), and Hezekiah (2 Chron. 32:27) all ensure that the people worship YHWH properly, and all possess wealth. Second, the comment confirms that YHWH fulfills what he promises to

Solomon. At the beginning of Solomon's reign, he requests wisdom from YHWH (2 Chron. 1:10). YHWH responds by promising not only that Solomon will have wisdom but also wealth, and that his wisdom and wealth will exceed other kings (2 Chron. 1:11–12). The rest of the chapter illustrates this incomparable wisdom and wealth in detail.

9:23–24. The Chronicler illustrates Solomon's greatness in comparison to other rulers by recording that rulers from all over the world visit Solomon to observe his wisdom and offer him gifts. This text alludes to the visit from the queen of Sheba since she also visits Solomon to observe his wisdom and offer him gifts. That specific occasion with her is here applied generally to all other rulers. This picture of kings streaming into Jerusalem to gain an audience with Solomon points to Solomon's international fame, especially for his wisdom. At this point the text notes that Solomon's wisdom is a gift from YHWH. This comment likely points to both the source and quality of Solomon's wisdom. This wisdom comes from YHWH, as promised (2 Chron. 1:11–12), but it also resembles divine wisdom since it appears inexhaustible (9:2). For this reason, Solomon as king reflects YHWH as king (see comments on 9:8 above). Therefore, extolling Solomon's wisdom also extols YHWH's wisdom.

Kings Seeking Solomon's Face

Second Chronicles 9:23 describes various kings "seeking Solomon's face" (מְבַקְשִׁים אֶת־פְּנֵי שְׁלֹמֹה). The expression of seeking one's face usually refers to seeking YHWH's face or his favor; however, it also occurs in relation to rulers (e.g., Esther 4:8; Prov. 29:26). In these contexts, the expression relates less to the king's presence or even his favor, but rather to an opportunity to speak to the king and hear him respond.

As a means of honoring Solomon for his wisdom and recognizing his authority, the kings bring Solomon gifts. Solomon receives these gifts year after year. Unlike the exotic items brought in by Solomon's ships, these gifts are valuable but more commonplace: gold and silver articles, clothing, perfume, spices, horses, and donkeys.

9:25. Solomon also possesses many horses and chariots, as demonstrated by how many stalls for horses and chariots and how many horsemen Solomon has. The verse feels out of place in this location, since the next verse returns to Solomon's relationship with other kings. Perhaps the mention of horses in 9:24 prompts the insertion of this comment here (see discussion above regarding 9:10–11). The large numbers of horses and chariots point to Solomon's wealth and reinforce the picture of his fortifying his land (see 2 Chron. 8:1–6).

TRANSLATION ANALYSIS:
The traditional translation for the word אֲרָיוֹת is "stalls." The word may also refer to teams of animals rather than just stalls (see Davies 1989, 25–38). Since there is insufficient evidence to decide one way or the other, I have used the traditional translation.

9:26. The account returns to Solomon's relationship to other kings, stating that Solomon rules over the kings from the Euphrates River to Philistine territory to the border of Egypt. The Euphrates River and the border of Egypt represent the northern and southern boundaries of Solomon's territory. Furthermore, these boundaries point to the ideal extent of the land promised to Abraham (cf. Gen. 15:18) and established by David (see 1 Chron. 18:3 for the Euphrates River and 1 Chron. 13:5 for the border of Egypt). This verse helps establish Solomon's reign as nearly fulfilling the ideal picture for Israel; however, here the picture is incomplete, explicitly excluding the Philistine territory from Solomon's reach.

9:27–28. The last verses of this section repeat statements from the beginning of Solomon's reign (see 2 Chron. 1:15–17). They repeat that during Solomon's reign, rare, expensive materials (silver and cedarwood) were so abundant they were as common as ordinary rocks and trees.

Silver and Gold

In 2 Chronicles 1:15 gold also occurs alongside silver as rare materials that Solomon makes commonplace. In this case, the text may only mention silver, since previously in the context (9:20) silver is already regarded as a common material.

They also summarize Solomon's horse-trading activities by simply stating that Solomon receives horses from Egypt and everywhere else. Repeating these statements from the beginning of Solomon's reign has an interesting effect. On the one hand, when these statements occur before Solomon builds the temple, they show that Solomon has sufficient wealth to build a splendid temple (see commentary on 2 Chron. 1:14–17). On the other hand, when these statements occur after Solomon has built the temple, they appear as a reward for Solomon's role in building the temple. In this case, Solomon's wealth is both a requirement and a reward for building the temple. Tensions of this sort occur often in Chronicles, creating a sense of proportion in the Chronicler's theological message (Ben Zvi 2006a, 160–73).

Conclusion of Solomon's Reign (9:29–31)

The Chronicler provides a typical conclusion to Solomon's reign, citing prophetic sources and recounting his death and burial.

9:29–31. The account of Solomon's reign closes with the common formulas that conclude the accounts of those kings after Solomon with few exceptions. Two noteworthy points emerge. First, the conclusion draws a connection between David and Solomon. Just as David ruled forty years (1 Chron. 29:27), so does Solomon. Just as David ruled over all Israel (1 Chron. 29:26), so does Solomon. Just as the text cites three prophetic sources for David's reign (1 Chron. 29:29), so with Solomon, and Nathan the prophet occurs in both lists (Williamson 1982, 237). Finally, unlike other kings neither David nor Solomon is buried "with his fathers," although admittedly "neither king had more than one generation before him" (R. Klein 2012, 149). These connections reinforce what has been observed throughout the account of Solomon's reign. The Chronicler joins David and Solomon so that David is the one who prepares to build the temple while Solomon is the one who carries it out.

Second, the text lists three prophetic sources for Solomon's reign. The use of prophetic sources is consistent throughout Chronicles and provides some insight regarding the nature of prophecy as properly interpreting what has happened (for fuller discussion, see Schniedewind 1995, 209–30). These sources also point to affairs only alluded to in Chronicles. For instance, the text mentions the prophecy of Ahijah and the visions of Iddo concerning Jeroboam, the son of Nebat. First Kings 11:29–39 records Ahijah's prophecy that the kingdom shall divide in two because of Solomon's idolatrous actions at the end of his life, while 2 Chronicles 10:15 only alludes back to the prophecy. Furthermore Jeroboam, the son of Nebat, becomes the first ruler of the divided nation. Even though the Chronicler does not include these accounts, his source citations suggest he knows of them and is willing to refer his readers to sources regarding them. The Chronicler is not attempting to "whitewash" Solomon; instead, he intends to show the positive effects of Solomon's desire and success in building the Jerusalem temple. His present narrative accomplishes this goal quite well.

As the Chronicler brings the account of Solomon's reign to a close, two points deserve further comment. First, Solomon reflects YHWH. Solomon serves as YHWH's king who sits on YHWH's throne (9:8). Therefore, Solomon's authority over the kings of other nations points to YHWH's authority over all nations (notice the occurrence of מוֹשֵׁל in 9:26 and 1 Chron. 29:12). Solomon's wisdom reflects YHWH's wisdom, especially since YHWH grants Solomon such wisdom (2 Chron. 9:23). Solomon's tremendous wealth points to YHWH as the source of wealth (notice the occurrence of עֹשֶׁר in 9:22 and 1 Chron. 29:12). In this way, the Chronicler shows how Solomon's reign manifests YHWH's reign: it possesses royal supremacy, wealth, wisdom, and a unified Israel (see "all Israel" in 2 Chron. 9:30; Lynch 2014b, 234–43).

Second, related to the first point, the picture of Israel under Solomon's rule is virtually ideal. Although the Chronicler is aware of Solomon's faults (see comments on 9:29 above), he emphasizes the rewards that Solomon (and all Israel) experiences for building the temple to worship YHWH properly. As a result, Israel is united together in worshipping YHWH at the Jerusalem temple, following the regulations of Moses and David, experiencing the blessings of wealth, international fame, and living securely in the land promised to them.

For the first readers, this picture of Solomon's entire reign, and especially in this narrative unit, has several implications for their situation. Living under Persian rule, in a time of relative obscurity and economic insignificance, the readers would find this text as holding out hope for Israel in different ways. On the one hand, the text holds out hope for a situation drastically different than their own. This future hope includes the return of a Davidic heir to Israel's throne. Like Solomon, this king would be responsible for ensuring Israel's proper worship at the Jerusalem temple according to the regulations of Moses and David. At the same time, this king would reflect YHWH's greatness over all the nations.

On the other hand, the text presents hope within the community's circumstances. Since YHWH is the true king over everything, his rule continues even when there is not a Davidic king on the throne. Instead, the community can look to the temple and Israel's unified worship there as a way to reflect YHWH's greatness over all nations. As a result, at some point the community can expect YHWH to reward them in similar ways: with some prosperity, peace, and even prominence.

THEOLOGICAL FOCUS

God demonstrates what he is like when he faithfully fulfills his promises to his people.

Solomon appears to be the star of the show in this passage. However, an interesting feature of this passage is that even though it is devoted to exalting Solomon's wisdom, wealth, achievements, and authority, Solomon himself is quite passive. God is the real mover behind Solomon's success. As a result, Solomon's authority points to God's authority; Solomon's achievements points to God's achievements; Solomon's wealth points to God's wealth; and Solomon's wisdom points to God's wisdom. Therefore, through Solomon God demonstrates what he is like: wise and wealthy, powerful and authoritative.

God demonstrates these aspects by fulfilling the promises he makes. He fulfills the promise to Solomon to grant him wealth and wisdom. He fulfills the promise to David to establish his dynasty and provide peace during Solomon's reign. He fulfills the promise to Abraham by extending the boundaries of Israel's authority from the Euphrates to Egypt. As God fulfills these promises, he demonstrates the qualities of a king, and others recognize it as well.

In looking toward the NT, first it is important to recognize that Solomon was a past king of Israel. He was important in the past for his role in confirming the Davidic dynasty and building the temple in Jerusalem. At the same time, he is important for the future as a model of an ideal king. Solomon and the conditions that accompanied his reign point to the hope for the postexilic community. The New Testament indicates that Jesus is this ideal king, and like a king is worthy to receive power, wealth, wisdom, might, glory, honor, and blessing (Rev. 5:12). At the same time, Jesus exceeds Solomon (Matt. 12:42 // Luke 11:31) because unlike Solomon, Jesus is God.

Furthermore, the NT points to Jesus as fulfilling God's promises. As Jesus fulfills the promises, God demonstrates what he is like, and others acknowledge who he is. In Philippians 2:5–11 and 1 Corinthians 15:24–28, Paul describes how all will confess Jesus as Lord when he is highly exalted, subjecting all things under himself so that God the Father may be glorified. As God ultimately fulfills the promises he makes, he will demonstrate the qualities of a king and receive praise and glory for it.

On the one hand, God has already fulfilled his promises. In certain aspects, Jesus already reigns as king, has already defeated death, has already put an end to sin, and has already brought in everlasting righteousness, as demonstrated through his resurrection and imparting of the Holy Spirit. On the other hand, in other aspects, these promises remain to be fulfilled. There will be a day in which all recognize Jesus as king, death no longer exists, sin passes away, and all things are made right. As God's people wait for that day, they reflect God's supreme authority as they confidently and obediently worship him alone, not held captive through fear by the spiritual forces that oppose them. They reflect God's multifaceted wisdom when, as Jews and Gentiles together, they worship God, having access to the Father through the Son in the Spirit.

Although this passage does not speak of God's ultimate fulfillment of all his promises in such detail, it anticipates the picture by looking back to Solomon's reign. It reminds readers of any age of the goodness of God's promises and the assured hope that he will bring them to pass in his time.

PREACHING AND TEACHING STRATEGIES

Exegetical and Theological Synthesis

"The good old days . . ."—often when people say this, they are remembering the past through eyes that only see the positive and overlook the negative. While we must not write out from our memory the mistakes and sins of the past, there is something hopeful about remembering the past with a positive fondness. We might think of high school days with affirming emotions: football games, band performances, one-act plays, being with friends, and of course, that favorite song. It is not that we pretend that the pains of the past didn't exist, but at that moment of remembrance we are looking at the past in order to have hope for the future. We had good times in the past; perhaps we can have some good times again. We hope for a future that is as good as our selective painting of those past memories. It seems this is part of what the writer is doing in this passage.

Solomon is presented not only as a good king but an amazing king who is wealthy and wise beyond imagination. Perhaps in the future Israel could have a king as wonderful as this selective memory of Solomon. The writer admits that there is more to the story, but his purpose is to remember these very positive parts to Solomon's reign. There is a hope for a better future based upon the (albeit selective) memory of the past.

The picture of Solomon's wisdom and wealth points us to God. The writer makes it clear through the visiting dignitary, the queen of Sheba, that Solomon's abundance comes from God. She further articulates that this extravagance is a sign of God's blessing on the nation.

These great abundant blessings are presented in such a way as to tie them to the promises that God made to Solomon at the beginning of his reign. He and the nation are blessed because God keeps his promises. It needs to be remembered that the Chronicler's positive portrayal of Solomon includes his obedience. Not that he was perfect, but the writer is linking enjoyment of blessings to obedience. As Israel remembered the past, they could have hope for the future.

Preaching Idea

The Lord has, and will, provide with extravagant abundance.

Contemporary Connections

What does it mean?

Think about the images that are most often seen on the weekly news. By far most are of violent weather, terrible vehicle crashes, a family mourning over a loss, and other painful catastrophic events. These are the images that flood newscasts. They do try to end with a sixty-second encouraging story, but the dominant image that the news paints is a dismal picture of our world. It is hard for us to visualize a world that is greatly blessed when we are flooded with pictures of disaster and failure. Perhaps that is why we like the sports section. But even that is a mixed blessing—because half the teams win and half the teams lose. We need a way to see a different picture.

The Chronicler gives us a different visual. While the writer did not paint a literal painting of the blessings of Solomon, he does create a mental picture filled with a degree of longing. His words prompt an image of a time of great blessing, and along with the image comes emotion, not just of nostalgia but of hope. His directive for us is not to paint a positive picture of our past as he does of Solomon; rather, he is directing us to trust the same God who blessed Solomon with such extravagance. If God did that for Solomon, what will he do today?

The exilic community needed hope—not to expect these exact blessings, but to hope and trust in the God who provides. He provided for Solomon; he will provide for them. And, he will provide for us. God wants us to know that he is fully capable of blessing us in such a way that it will amaze all who see it. Since he is faithful and capable, we need to trust and obey him.

Is it true?

God will bless, but we are not to focus on the blessing; we are to focus on the giver of the blessing. The full story of Solomon's great blessings is that he died and left them all behind. The postexilic community knew well that his great wealth was gone. Much of it went to Babylon, where some of the exiles might have seen it. Physical blessing will not last. So, the focus is on the one who provides the blessings. He will keep his promises. We can trust him.

Trusting people to keep their promises is hard. In our world people intentionally lie. The complexity of modern life with multiple communication channels, and complex systems, makes it easy to lie. The mechanic says the $2,000 car repair is essential. Is it really? The HVAC repair company, after a four-week delay, continues to say, "Our supplier doesn't have the part yet." Did it not come in, or did someone forget to order it? We easily doubt what another says to be the whole truth, because we have done the same thing to cover our own mistakes. We live in a world of liars, and each of us is guilty.

But we can trust God. He told Solomon that he would bless him, and God was true to his promise. He can be trusted.

Now what?

Because of our great Lord, we can exchange the image of a dismal world to one of great blessing, and choose to trust the God who will provide. This is God's version of the power of positive thinking, with an important change in the object. This passage helps us see that the power in not our thinking but in our Lord—positive thinking, yes, but positive thinking about our Lord and how he blesses. The object of our positive thinking is not to be on the blessing, but on the one who gives it.

When the picture of the world is filled with stories about leaders with moral failures, hurricanes, floods, and pandemics, we can trust in our Lord who provided beyond imagination for Solomon. A better world is coming. When our own personal world is filled with unemployment, financial challenges, sickness, death, abuse, and mistreatment, we can look to our God who will give us a better life. In fact, an eternal life is promised. Remembering God's blessing of Israel through Solomon's wealth and wisdom gives us a sure hope that our Lord will bless us with even more through our grand and glorious, perfect and eternal, soon and coming, savior and king: Jesus.

So, what does it look like to wait and hope for the future? Again, the picture of Solomon helps us. In Chronicles, his obedience is highlighted. Not that Solomon didn't sin grievously, but the writer is showing us that obedience is the key to enjoying God's current and future blessings. This obedience, like the wealth and wisdom, comes from a relationship with him. He gave wealth and wisdom to Solomon, and he gives us the power to obey and enjoy his blessings. We are not to do it on our own.

This picture of God's blessings gives us hope for the future and motivation to obey him today.

Creativity in Presentation

It is challenging to tell the story about the wealth of someone who lived three thousand years ago. What makes it even more challenging is identifying with what is described. The amounts of gold and silver are such that even if we convert Solomon's wealth into modern terms, it is so vast that it remains surrealistic. The writer is trying to paint a picture of God's abundant extravagant blessing. Strive to illustrate with extravagances that will help your listeners sense the awe: a car or pickup truck, perhaps a house, or job, or vacation. Don't forget the generational differences: perfect high school or retirement plan.

Another option is to reminisce about a memory and present it with all the positives.

Even as I wrote this, I called a childhood friend who deals in precious metals to find out how much six hundred shekels of gold would be worth today. After he gave me the factual info, we began to relive some childhood events: hunting snakes with our bows, sleeping in a tent in the backyard, catching crawdads (crawfish), playing stickball in the street. We painted a memory of a perfect childhood filled with abundance. Somehow even the trouble we got into was painted with a brush of joy. This phone call for information turned into an affirming remembrance of an extravagant childhood friendship and gives me hope that God is blessing and will bless with an even more extravagant friendship—with him.

It seems that the thrust of this passage is not so much to help us understand the fine points of Solomon's wealth or wisdom. Rather, God's aim is to create an emotional response so that in our minds we would say, "Wow!" Here is one possible structure:

- Modern picture(s) of extravagant abundance
- Solomon's blessings are extravagant abundance
  - ○ Solomon, Huram, and the queen of Sheba (8:17–9:12)
  - ○ Solomon's great wealth (9:13–21)
  - ○ Solomon's international greatness (9:22–28)
  - ○ Conclusion to Solomon's reign (9:29–31)
- The foundation and source of the extravagant abundance is God
  - ○ God is the source (9:8, 23)
  - ○ God keeps his promises (2 Chron 1:11–12)
- God's extravagant abundance is best seen in Jesus's gift of life
  - ○ Abundant life (John 10:10)
  - ○ Eternal life (John 3:16)
- Trust the Lord who has and will provide with extravagant abundance

DISCUSSION QUESTIONS

1. Pick one of the following and then describe what yours would look like:
   ◦ luxurious house
   ◦ perfect hunting trip
   ◦ ideal high school experience
   ◦ best-ever job
   ◦ retirement plan that beats all plans

2. Describe one of your favorite memories of Christmas. How could it have been even better?

3. Why do we call memories that are favorable "the good old days"?

4. Why do we sometimes paint a positive picture of the past?

5. How might a positive picture of the past affect how we think about the future?

REIGNS OF JUDAH'S KINGS
(2 CHRONICLES 10:1–36:23)

Following the reign of Solomon, the political situation of Israel changes significantly. The tribes divide into two separate political states: Israel and Judah. In Kings, one feels this separation acutely because Kings alternates its accounts between kings from Israel and kings from Judah. In Chronicles, this separation of political states does not affect the narrative much because the book only follows the reigns of the kings of Judah. The kings of Israel enter the narrative only when they encounter Judah. Chronicles maintains its focus on the Davidic dynasty even after most tribes rebel against that dynasty and form their own political state. At the same time, Chronicles still treats the members of the other tribes as part of the same people. They are still Israel in an ethnic sense.

Probably more than anywhere else in Chronicles, the reigns of Judah's kings illustrate the principle of immediate retribution. As the narrative moves from one king to the next, each king experiences either reward for obedience or punishment for disobedience. Like the rest of Chronicles, obedience involves proper worship of YHWH. The narratives often reveal the concern for proper worship in two ways: (1) keeping the Law of Moses and/or (2) maintaining the Jerusalem temple. Despite the pattern of retribution within each king's reign, the narrative also presents a downward direction to Judah's worship. In the end, Judah drifts far from the days of David and Solomon. As a result, YHWH removes the people through exile and destroys Jerusalem with its palace and temple. However, the last word is not destruction or exile. The last word is a word of hope as YHWH raises up Cyrus so that the people may return to the land and rebuild the Jerusalem temple.

2 Chronicles 10:1–19

EXEGETICAL IDEA
Through the interactions of Rehoboam, his counselors, Jeroboam, and Israel, YHWH fulfilled his prophetic word to separate Israel into two kingdoms.

THEOLOGICAL FOCUS
God ultimately works through all circumstances to accomplish his plan.

PREACHING IDEA
God doesn't need a backup plan; he only has Plan A.

PREACHING POINTERS
As I write this, Great Britain is mourning the death of Queen Elizabeth II. She completed her reign, and her son Charles is now on the throne. She will be missed. One of the talking points of newscasters is how this will change the plans of the monarchy. What will be King Charles's emphasis? (If there is a current transfer of power that is well known by your listeners, use that instead.)

This passage gives us great comfort by assuring us that YHWH's plans and emphasis will never change, and every circumstance will be used by him to further his plan. When we look at blunders and sins in our own lives, in the lives of those around us, and in our world, God's sovereignty can comfort us, guide us, and lead us to worship him.

THE KINGDOM DIVIDES (10:1–19)

LITERARY STRUCTURE AND THEMES (10:1–19)

Most of this passage involves the dialogues between Rehoboam and others. The shift in dialogue partners marks the structure for much of the passage. At the center of the dialogues lies the contrast between two groups of counselors. This focal point contrasts Solomon and Rehoboam, the wise and the foolish.

After Solomon dies, Israel meets Solomon's son Rehoboam at Shechem to recognize him officially as king. Jeroboam, one of Solomon's rebel officials, leads the group meeting with the king to let Rehoboam know that they expect him to reduce the hard work assigned to them by his father. Rehoboam seeks counsel concerning how to answer. First he visits the older men who served Solomon; they advise him to respond favorably to the people's demands. Then he visits the younger men who serve him and who grew up with him. They advise him to respond harshly to the people's demands. Rehoboam accepts the younger group's advice and responds harshly to all Israel. In response, all Israel does not recognize Rehoboam's authority. When Rehoboam sends a representative to restore the relationship, Israel stones the man to death and Rehoboam flees to Jerusalem. In this way, Israel rebels against Rehoboam and forms its own political state.

- *Israel Meets Rehoboam at Shechem (10:1–5)*
- *Rehoboam Seeks Counsel (10:6–11)*
- *Rehoboam Responds to Israel (10:12–15)*
- *Israel Rebels Against Rehoboam (10:16–19)*

EXPOSITION (10:1–19)

Transitioning from one king to another was hazardous business in the ancient world. Because the king held so much individual power, a nation could experience drastic changes, from domestic policies to international relations. As a result, the transition could open doors to influence the new king and reform previous policies. In Rehoboam's case, Israel attempts to exercise such influence. In the end, the new king missteps, and Israel rebels.

Behind this narrative lie several unexpected twists and unexplained events. These features make it difficult to get a clear sense of the reasons for the division of the kingdom into Israel and Judah. Apparently, the Chronicler is not interested in providing the rationale for each person's decisions. Instead, the Chronicler comments that YHWH sets this turn of events into motion to fulfill what he said through the prophet Ahijah. Whatever the individual reasoning of Rehoboam, Jeroboam, or the rest of Israel, YHWH is ultimately the one guiding the events according to his plan (see Ben Zvi 2006a, 123–25). This narrative shows how all Israel, united under David and Solomon, becomes Judah under the Davidic king and Israel under another king.

Israel Meets Rehoboam at Shechem (10:1–5)

Israel meets with Rehoboam at Shechem to demand lighter work before agreeing to make him king.

10:1. The Chronicler begins the narrative by setting the stage. He introduces Shechem as the city where the narrative takes place. Shechem is a northern city where several important political and religious events have taken place. In the context of this narrative, two of those events deserve specific mention because they relate to the identity of Israel and their relation to royal power. First, Shechem is the place where Jacob's daughter Dinah was raped. In the aftermath of that event, Shechem proposes to become unified with Jacob's sons as one people (Gen. 34:16). However, the sons of Israel deceitfully attack the city, kill its men, and plunder it. Second, the citizens of Shechem follow Abimelek as an illegitimate king because he is their relative (Judg. 9:1–6). However, Abimelek kills his brothers, and ultimately Abimelek and all Shechem suffer punishment for what they do (Judg. 9:7–57). Both cases raise the question of identity (as a people and as relatives) and bring about negative consequences. The Chronicler is not likely alluding specifically to either one of these cases; however, mentioning Shechem as the place where the narrative takes place at least casts a possible shadow over the events (cf. the Babylonian Talmud, which states that this location is predestined for misfortune, b. Sanhedrin 102a). Since not all events that take place at Shechem are negative, it remains to be seen in the narrative whether this possible shadow falls on the upcoming events.

Events at Shechem

The following is a sample of what takes place at Shechem: YHWH appears to Abraham (Gen. 12:6–7), Jacob builds an altar (Gen. 33:18–20), Joshua makes a covenant with the people (Josh. 24:25), and the people bury Joseph's bones (Josh. 24:32).

10:1–2. Next, the Chronicler introduces the characters. First, Rehoboam is Solomon's son (2 Chron. 9:31). At this point, the Chronicler says virtually nothing more than that Rehoboam is Solomon's son and successor. Second, all Israel gathers at Shechem to recognize Rehoboam as king. Up to this point in Chronicles,

the phrase "all Israel" carries the sense of all the tribes stemming from Jacob's sons (see 1 Chron. 12:24–38 for the Chronicler's complete listing). However, there are some clues that this sense may have changed. One clue is that Rehoboam must go to Shechem to be recognized as king, rather than remain in Jerusalem. Another clue is the mention of the third character: Jeroboam. To this point the Chronicler has not mentioned Jeroboam at all. Here the Chronicler reports that he fled to Egypt because of Solomon. Once he hears that Solomon has died, he returns to Israel. In Chronicles, this activity raises suspicions concerning Jeroboam, because there is no stated reason in Chronicles for this type of activity. These three characters—all Israel, Rehoboam, and Jeroboam—are at the heart of the narrative.

Jeroboam Returns

The narrative does not specify what Jeroboam heard. Two possibilities are most likely: Jeroboam heard either that Solomon died, or that Israel was meeting with Rehoboam at Shechem. The former option makes the most logical sense, since then Jeroboam would have time to return to Israel from Egypt to be present at the meeting from its start. To read the text this way, one can take 2 Chronicles 9:31 as describing what he heard, skipping over 2 Chronicles 10:1, or one can emend the text to include the phrase "that Solomon died" (cf. BHS).

10:3–5. The reason all Israel comes to Shechem is to recognize Rehoboam officially as king. However, before they take this action, Jeroboam and all Israel meet with Rehoboam to communicate what they expect from him before declaring him king. Their expectation is simple: before they pledge their loyalty to him, they want Rehoboam to reduce the hard work placed upon them by his father. Even though the request is simple, the way in which it relates to the rest of Chronicles is more complicated. Chronicles consistently presents Solomon in a positive light. Furthermore, 2 Chronicles 8:9 specifically states that Solomon did not force Israelites to be slaves for his construction projects. However, Israel's statement suggests that Solomon somehow had conscripted Israelites for some type of hard labor.

Three considerations may help relieve this tension. First, the Chronicler does not have to present a perfect picture of Solomon to present a positive picture of Solomon (Jeon 2013, 27). The Chronicler shows that Solomon qualifies as the temple-builder, and YHWH blesses him both to build the temple and as a result of building the temple. However, the Chronicler does not need to purge everything that might reflect negatively in some way on Solomon. Even Solomon himself confesses that everyone sins (2 Chron. 6:36).

Second, the nature of Israel's "hard labor" and "heavy yoke" is unclear. It appears to be associated with Solomon's forced labor (מַס) because Rehoboam sends the official over the forced labor after Israel refuses to make Rehoboam king (10:18). However, when Chronicles describes the forced labor as those who are not of Israel, it states that Israelites do not serve as slaves for Solomon's work of fortifying various cities but that they must serve as military officers assigned as sentries to watch over the people (2 Chron. 8:2–10). The Chronicler would be consistent if he is referring not to this comment regarding fortifying cities but some other task(s) Solomon required of Israel.

Israelites in Solomon's Labor

The text in 2 Chronicles 8:9 states that Solomon did not make the Israelites slaves for his work (לִמְלַאכְתּוֹ). Although one can interpret this comment as referring to all of Solomon's work, the comment itself occurs within the context of fortifying various cities. In fact, because Solomon is fortifying these cities, he decides to appoint the Israelites as sentries and guards at these locations.

Third, Israel's perspective appears distorted given the narrative in Chronicles (see Japhet 1993, 653; R. Klein 2012, 158). Chronicles does not present the idea that Solomon grows rich on the backs of Israelite workers. Instead, Solomon's reign is a blessing to Israel (2 Chron. 9:8) and his wealth and fame are the result of YHWH's blessing (2 Chron. 1:12). In other words, even though the Chronicler may be presenting Israel's legitimate complaint regarding their compulsory labor, the complaint appears out of proportion compared to their joy in crowning Solomon king (1 Chron. 29:22) and dedicating the temple (2 Chron. 7:10) and their prosperity and peace under Solomon's rule. In other words, their complaints seem exaggerated because Solomon's reign is so positive. Even though these three points do not completely remove any tension in the narrative, they provide ways for holding the picture together in a coherent way.

Jeroboam and Israel use serious vocabulary to describe the work assigned to them: a heavy yoke (עֹל כָּבֵד) and hard service (עֲבֹדָה קָשָׁה). The yoke likely symbolizes the king's dominating authority (e.g., Lev. 26:13; Isa. 47:6; Jer. 27:8). By describing it as heavy, the people convey that the king has placed many difficult demands upon them. The hard service likely refers more specifically to some type of conscripted labor, since Exodus describes the slave work in Egypt as hard service (Exod. 1:14; 6:9). Israel communicates that they have grown tired of Solomon's rule and his requirements for their work. Ironically, if Rehoboam lightens Israel's "service" (עֲבֹדָה), then they will serve (עבד) him. In other words, they will loyally submit to his rule. Therefore, Israel makes two points: (1) they demand he lighten his burden on them, and (2) if he does so, they will submit to his rule. The encounter finishes when Rehoboam tells them to return in three days for his answer and the people leave as he instructs them.

Rehoboam Seeks Counsel (10:6–11)

Rehoboam seeks counsel from two groups who offer opposite opinions: one wise and one foolish.

10:6–11. After the people leave, Rehoboam seeks advice concerning how to respond to the people. The Chronicler describes two groups who advise him. The first group consists of older men who served Solomon while he was still alive. Although the text refers to these men as "elders" (זְקֵנִים), here it probably does not refer to their official role as elder but to their age. The second group consists of younger men who grew up with Rehoboam and currently serve him in some official capacity. The text contrasts the two groups both in terms of age and association (Solomon vs. Rehoboam), to hint that the advice of the first group (older and associated with Solomon) is superior to the advice of the second group (younger and associated with Rehoboam).

Role and Identity of Advisors

It is unclear how these two groups function within Rehoboam's administration. It appears the Chronicler is focusing on their age rather than their official capacity, since they seem to have held the same official capacity—except that the older group is no longer serving because Solomon has died. Furthermore, since the narrative makes the point that the older counselors gave Rehoboam sound advice while the younger gave him disastrous advice, the issue of age is more important than their official capacity.

Regarding their identities, the older group are at least former officials who had served Solomon. The younger group may well be Rehoboam's half-brothers. There are two reasons for thinking that such may be the case. First, a king's sons often serve in some capacity to secure and administer the kingdom (2 Chron. 11:22–23; 21:3). Second, the text states that these young counselors grew up with Rehoboam (see Malamat 1963, 248–50; 1965, 45–46, 54–55). Although there is insufficient evidence to demonstrate that this phrase requires that all these men be related, it is certainly consistent with it.

10:7. The dialogues between Rehoboam and the two groups reveal subtle clues concerning each one's interpretation of the situation. When Rehoboam approaches the older men, he is looking for how they would handle the situation. The older men only cite the end of Israel's request ("we will serve you") to advise Rehoboam to respond positively so that Israel will be his loyal subjects. The older advisors see Israel's request as a commitment to follow Rehoboam's rule, even if their commitment is conditional.

TRANSLATION ANALYSIS:

Translations render the phrase דְּבָרִים טוֹבִים in different ways. Many translations (ESV, NASB, NKJV, NRSV) render the phrase quite generically as "good words." Others attempt to translate the sense of טוֹב more specifically as "kind" (CSB) or "cordial" (NET). In this context, טוֹב likely has treaty or covenant overtones. Therefore, to speak "good words" means to make a legal arrangement that benefits the northern tribes (cf. Weinfeld 1982, 42–53).

10:8–11. The Chronicler points out that Rehoboam rejects the advice of the older men and turns to his younger advisors. Since he has rejected this first advice, he asks the younger men for advice in a different way. First, he reveals that he plans on taking their advice by including them in the response ("What do you advise we say in response?"). Second, he cites only Israel's demand ("Lighten the yoke your father put on us"), not their (conditional) pledge of commitment. At this point, apparently following Rehoboam's lead, the young men interpret Israel's demand as questioning his royal authority. For this reason, they give him a speech to deliver. The speech has three points, each one contrasting Rehoboam to his father. The first point contrasts Rehoboam's "little finger" to his father's waist. The exact comparison is unclear, although its intended meaning is clear: Rehoboam is much tougher than his father. The second point contrasts his father's heavy yoke to Rehoboam's heavier yoke. In other words, if Israel thought Solomon required a lot as king, Rehoboam will require even more. The third point contrasts his father's punishment with whips to Rehoboam's punishment with scorpions. Here, the word "scorpions" (עַקְרַבִּים) carries a metaphorical sense, since the end of a scorpion's tail delivers stinging pain. Each point of their speech presents Rehoboam as harsher than his father. Since the young men interpret Israel's demand as questioning royal power, they advise him to respond with even more power.

Rehoboam's Strength

Interpreters understand the comparison in different ways. Japhet argues that the sense of the saying is as follows: what Solomon must gird up for, Rehoboam can lift with his little finger (1993, 655). Other interpreters understand the "little finger" (קָטָנִי) as a euphemism for the male reproductive organ, such that Rehoboam exhibits far more virility than his father. Rehoboam leaves out the first point of the young men's speech, contrasting Rehoboam's "little finger" to his father's "waist." If this expression is a crude remark, then it makes sense that he omits it from his official response.

Rehoboam Responds to Israel (10:12–15)

Rehoboam follows foolish advice and rejects Israel's proposal; God uses Rehoboam's actions to fulfill his prophetic word.

10:12–15. After Rehoboam consults with his advisors, he meets Jeroboam and all Israel to respond to their request. The Chronicler makes several important points regarding this meeting. First, he points out that Rehoboam rejects the older men's advice and answers Israel harshly. He follows the advice of the younger men, quoting most of what they proposed. Second,

the Chronicler summarizes Rehoboam's response as "not listen[ing] to the people." Rehoboam has heard what the people requested and even sought advice from two groups of advisors. In fact, when Rehoboam seeks the older men's advice, it is not clear what course Rehoboam will take. However, as pointed out, after they give their advice, Rehoboam seems to have made up his mind to some degree. As the narrative progresses, it becomes clearer and clearer that Rehoboam is choosing to reject Israel's request. When the Chronicler speaks of Rehoboam not listening to Israel, he means more specifically that Rehoboam does not grant their request. Third, the Chronicler explains that Rehoboam's response fits into YHWH's plan. Even though the Chronicler presents Rehoboam as having a clear choice between two options, he shows that Rehoboam's choice ultimately fulfills what YHWH had already spoken through the prophet Ahijah.

The Chronicler characterizes Rehoboam as harsh and foolish. Rehoboam resembles the Pharaoh of the exodus. In fact, several elements of the narrative recall the exodus account (for details, see Hahn 2012, 145–47). For instance, Israel now complains of its "hard labor" (10:4) just as Israel then complained of its "hard labor" (Exod. 1:14; 6:9). Just as Rehoboam threatens to make Israel's labor harder, Pharaoh had ordered that Israel's labor be harder (Exod. 5:5–8). Just as Rehoboam refuses to listen to the people because of YHWH's plan, so also Pharaoh refused to listen to the people according to YHWH's plan (Exod. 7:4, 13, 22–23; 8:11, 15; 9:12; 11:9). Within the narrative of 2 Chronicles 10, one should not make too much of the comparison to the exodus Pharaoh (Berner 2011, 211–40). For instance, the Chronicler does not interpret these events as a "new exodus" for the northern tribes, because their rebellion against Rehoboam leads to idolatry and apostasy without reconciliation (2 Chron. 11:13–15; 13:4–9).

Based on 2 Chronicles 10:15 and the larger narrative context describing Rehoboam, the Chronicler compares him to Pharaoh to show how YHWH is working to fulfill his plan in both cases.

10:15. The Chronicler refers to Ahijah's prophecy, but Chronicles does not record this prophecy. Although the Chronicler may have several reasons for omitting this information, including Ahijah's prophecy would affect the Chronicler's overall presentation of Solomon. Since the Chronicler is interested in presenting Solomon as the temple-builder—and in large part for this reason, as a model king—including Ahijah's prophecy in the text of Chronicles would obscure this point. However, the Chronicler still alludes to the prophecy because he can point out that YHWH directs Rehoboam's response without placing blame for all these events on Solomon.

Israel Rebels Against Rehoboam (10:16–19)
In response to Rehoboam, the northern tribes rebel against the house of David.

10:16–19. Once Israel realizes that Rehoboam rejects their request, they reject his rule. The Chronicler casts a negative light on the northern tribes as they do so. Their cry for the men of Israel to return to their tents echoes what Sheba says when David returns to Jerusalem after Absalom's death (2 Sam. 20:1). Second Samuel describes Sheba as a scoundrel (אִישׁ בְּלִיַּעַל), so this connection is hardly flattering. In contrast, the last phrase of Israel's cry ("David, look after your own house"), which has no parallel to Sheba's statement, suggests that Israel recognizes that Rehoboam may legitimately be king—just not over them.

However, when Rehoboam sends Hadoram to them, they stone him to death, with the result that Rehoboam runs for his life. Moreover, the Chronicler describes Israel's action as rebellion. The verb "to rebel" (פשׁע) almost always carries negative connotations, describing activities that do not recognize legitimate authority, such as revolt or criminal activity (*HALOT* s.v. "פשׁע" 981). The Chronicler reports that Israel as a political entity never places itself under Davidic rule again.

Similarities to Sheba
Israel's cry closely resembles Sheba's statement against David, except for the addition of the last clause. The similarities, as shown below, speak to the Chronicler's characterization of Israel.

2 Chronicles 10:16	2 Samuel 20:1
מַה־לָּנוּ חֵלֶק בְּדָוִיד	אֵין־לָנוּ חֵלֶק בְּדָוִד
We have no portion with David	We have no portion with David
וְלֹא־נַחֲלָה בְּבֶן־יִשַׁי	וְלֹא נַחֲלָה־לָנוּ בְּבֶן־יִשַׁי
and no inheritance with the son of Jesse.	and no inheritance with the son of Jesse.
אִישׁ לְאֹהָלֶיךָ יִשְׂרָאֵל	אִישׁ לְאֹהָלָיו יִשְׂרָאֵל
Israel, everyone to your tents.	Israel, everyone to his tents.
עַתָּה רְאֵה בֵיתְךָ דָּוִיד	
Now, David, tend to your own house.	

10:16. The Chronicler records how Israel answers Rehoboam by focusing on the distance between the southern tribes and all the northern tribes. Their answer contrasts sharply with their declaration when they made David king; at that time, they declared that David was "flesh and bone" (1 Chron. 11:1). In other words, he is one of them, not an outsider. Furthermore, 1 Chronicles 11–12 shows how all Israel pledges their loyalty to David when they come together to make him king. In contrast, when Jeroboam and "all Israel" come together to make Rehoboam king, they reject his rule.

Israel's Former Loyalty

First Chronicles 12 recounts how all the tribes of Israel loyally follow David as he is becoming king. In the middle of this section, the spirit inspires a soldier to announce allegiance to David. He begins by saying, "We are yours, David! We are with you, son of Jesse!" (1 Chron. 12:18 [HB 19]). The words "David" and "son of Jesse" occur also in Israel's response to Rehoboam. However, in this case, the point is the opposite: Israel declares that they are no longer loyal to the Davidic house, since they do not share in each other's interests.

TRANSLATION ANALYSIS:
Israel responds to Rehoboam with a question in Hebrew; however, in this context, the text is not presenting a real question. Although many translations retain the form of a question (CSB, ESV, NASB, NIV, NRSV), the statement functions as an emphatic negative in this case. In other words, the text is indicating that Israel has no portion with David (see the parallel expression in 2 Sam. 20:1). Although translating it as a question can still serve this function, its function becomes clearer by translating it as a negative statement (NET, NLT).

10:17. Despite the rebellion of the northern tribes, the Chronicler confirms that Rehoboam does rule over the southern kingdom. Even

though YHWH orchestrates the kingdom's division, the Davidic house still retains power over Judah and those who live in its land (e.g., the cities of Judah). The kingdom's division does not nullify YHWH's promises to David and Solomon, even if at that time it restricts them to the southern tribes.

Sons of Israel in Judah

The text states that Rehoboam rules over the "sons of Israel living in the cities of Judah." The phrase is ambiguous. On one hand, it may refer to the Judahites, in which case the Chronicler is saying that even though the northern tribes rejected Rehoboam as king, the southern tribes did not. On the other hand, "sons of Israel" often refers to those from the northern tribes (cf. 10:18). In this case, the Chronicler would be pointing out that not all northerners rebelled against Rehoboam because some of them remained in the cities of Judah. Within Chronicles, this latter interpretation makes sense because the Chronicler shows that at different times northerners choose to live in Judah (e.g., 2 Chron. 11:13–14; 15:9). However, the former interpretation is more likely for the following reasons: (1) the Chronicler uses "sons of Israel" and "all Israel" to refer to the southern kingdom in this context (2 Chron. 11:3), and (2) this is the only verse in this narrative that affirms that Rehoboam rules over Judah. If this verse refers to the northerners who live in Judah, then the Chronicler would nowhere affirm that Rehoboam rules over Judah itself.

The division of the tribes into two kingdoms is a significant event in Chronicles. Despite this fact, the Chronicler leaves several ambiguities in the text. For instance, he is not clear on how much one can blame Rehoboam or Jeroboam (along with Israel) for dividing the kingdom. The Chronicler presents a negative picture of both sides. Rehoboam looks like a pharaoh who tries to tighten his grip on the people by increasing their hard labor and rebuffing their requests harshly. He also looks naïve and foolish because he does not take the advice of the older men who served under Solomon. On the other hand, Jeroboam, along with Israel, looks like the scoundrel Sheba, a man who does not even recognize David's authority (for further contrasts between Rehoboam and David, see Levin 2017, 12). Israel kills one of the king's officials and endangers the king himself. It appears both sides share the blame.

However, there is another character to consider. He appears only once in the entire chapter, and yet he plays the most significant part. The Chronicler makes it clear that YHWH lies behind the events of this chapter. Specifically, he directs Rehoboam's response to the people. He does so to fulfill what he has said through his prophet. Ultimately, YHWH works through the interactions of Rehoboam, his counselors, Jeroboam, and Israel to accomplish his plans and fulfill what he has spoken.

For the first readers, this narrative might provide some comfort when asking: Why are things the way they are? Why are so many of Israel still scattered among the nations instead of living in the land? Why are the north and south still separated into different districts (Samaria and Yehud)? Why do those who have remained in the land continue to struggle with those returning from Babylonian captivity (see Ezra and Nehemiah)? Why does Yehud remain a relatively insignificant district with little prosperity and development (see Haggai and Zechariah)? In other passages, the Chronicler emphasizes that human disobedience leads to unwanted results. However, in this narrative, he is making a different point. Even though human actors play a significant role in shaping the first readers' circumstances, ultimately YHWH is directing the events, even if they lead to unwanted results. The reasons or even the purpose for these circumstances may not be clear, but the Chronicler still encourages them to be confident that YHWH is in control and directing events to fulfill what he has spoken through his prophets. In the Chronicler's terms, these promises point to a united people of YHWH inhabiting the land he promised, ruled by a Davidic king, worshipping rightly at his temple in Jerusalem.

The narrative also addresses the relationship between the northern and southern tribes for the first readers, who await a future day when YHWH will unite all his people. Even though the Chronicler repeatedly presents all the tribes of Israel as "brothers" (אַחִים), during this narrative Israel no longer identifies with the house of David, at least politically. For the first readers, the fact that all the tribes are brothers even when they are separated politically encourages those from the northern tribes to join with Judah (during their time Persian Yehud) even though the north is still politically distinct. For the Chronicler writing to those first readers, joining with Judah primarily means worshipping YHWH according to the Mosaic law at the Jerusalem temple (e.g., 2 Chron. 35:18).

THEOLOGICAL FOCUS

God works through whatever circumstances to ultimately accomplish his plan.

Focusing on the Chronicler's presentation of the main actors (Rehoboam and Jeroboam) helps uncover the theological focus of this passage. Both Rehoboam and Jeroboam appear in an ambiguous light. On the one hand, the Chronicler shows Rehoboam to be foolish and even harsh. On the other hand, at this point the Chronicler does not present him as one who forsakes God or breaks covenant with him. Instead, Rehoboam appears to be out of his league when attempting to assume his role as king, since he meets with Israel on their turf at Shechem (Frisch 2011, 38–41) and does not realize the power of the opposition against him. Furthermore, God is bringing these events together to fulfill his word. For this reason, Rehoboam is swept up in these circumstances and to a degree carried along by them. Therefore, he appears as both a little bit of a villain and a little bit of a victim (see title of Knoppers 1990).

Phases of Rehoboam's Reign

Like other kings in Chronicles, Rehoboam's reign consists of (at least) two phases. Second Chronicles 11 presents Rehoboam in a good light. He obeys the warning of the prophet and experiences several of YHWH's blessings such as fortifying cities, gaining the allegiance of the priests and Levites, marrying wives, and having many children. Only in 2 Chronicles 12 does the Chronicler mention that Rehoboam forsakes the law of YHWH. Therefore, 2 Chronicles 10 most likely belongs to the good phase of Rehoboam's reign. This point supports the claim that the blame for the kingdom's division should not fall entirely on Rehoboam, and certainly not because of some specific act of disobedience (Knoppers 1990, 432–37).

Characterization of Jeroboam

Even though the Chronicler presents Jeroboam in an ambiguous light here, especially since Israel seems to be the main actor and not Jeroboam himself, in other passages the Chronicler presents him specifically in a more negative light. In 2 Chronicles 13:4–7 Abijah describes Jeroboam as one who rebels against Solomon, gathers a group of scoundrels (similar to Sheba, they are described as "sons of worthlessness" בְּנֵי בְלִיַּעַל), and takes advantage of an inexperienced Rehoboam in order to rebel against Davidic rule. How Abijah reflects on these events recounted in 2 Chronicles 10 also shows how the Chronicler explains these events in complex, sophisticated ways.

Jeroboam also appears in an ambiguous light. In the beginning of 2 Chronicles 10, Jeroboam does not take the initiative to confront Rehoboam. Instead, Israel calls him to appear before the king. Furthermore, the narrative confirms that Israel's concern about the Davidic king treating them harshly is justified, since Rehoboam responds so harshly. Furthermore, one can understand how Jeroboam and all Israel respond when Rehoboam threatens them with harsher treatment, especially when, as the Chronicler points out, God has already said in Ahijah's prophecy that Israel will become a separate kingdom with Jeroboam as its king. At the same time, Chronicles does not legitimize Jeroboam's role as king. He does not include any mention of the peoples making him king, as in the parallel of 1 Kings 12:20 (Frisch 2000, 21–22). Furthermore, the end of the narrative characterizes Jeroboam and Israel as rebels, associating them with the scoundrel (אִישׁ בְּלִיַּעַל) Sheba, and recording how they stoned one man to death and threatened the Davidic king's life. Jeroboam also appears as a bit of a villain and a bit of a victim.

Therefore, the Chronicler's understanding of the events is more complex and sophisticated than simply blaming Rehoboam, Jeroboam, or even God. Instead, the Chronicler shows that various factors play into this set of historical events. However, whatever the role or even amount of blame Rehoboam or Jeroboam has, God is directing these events to a result that fulfills what he has said. Our text does not explain why God brings about these events. His reasons are hidden and unknown.

Even though Chronicles does not specify God's reasons for Israel's division, Chronicles often speaks to God's character. Israel's repeated refrain captures the Chronicler's picture of God's character well: "He is good, for his loyal love endures forever" (e.g., 1 Chron. 16:34, 41; 2 Chron. 5:13; 7:3, 6; 20:21). Since God is good and maintains his love for his people, one can trust that he is accomplishing his purposes, regardless of the situation. God truly is actively working to bring about what is good for his people (Rom. 8:28).

For the first readers, God's plan likely seemed strange and counterintuitive, since a politically divided Israel hardly seems to fit into Israel's hope or God's plan. However, God works in strange and counterintuitive ways. Certainly, there is no greater example of God's strange and counterintuitive ways than the person and work of Christ. As Luke records, the disciples headed to Emmaus did not know how to make sense of the life, death, burial, and resurrection of Jesus as a part of God's plan (Luke 24:13–25). Although the disciples could not make sense of what was happening, Jesus showed them that the events corresponded to what God had said in Scripture. Through Christ God demonstrates that he works through whatever circumstances to accomplish his plan.

PREACHING AND TEACHING STRATEGIES

Exegetical and Theological Synthesis

One of the broadest and most frequent themes of Scripture, and certainly of 1 and 2 Chronicles, is that YHWH is in control. This passage focuses on that truth. He is in control and has a plan, even when the national situation is complex and discouraging. Rehoboam and Jeroboam are both the good guy and the bad guy. They each acted unwisely, and yet they both seemed to have logical reasons for their actions. Both made foolish or unwise decisions: to rebel against the chosen king, to unwisely levy heavy taxes as a form of punishment. They were each a mixture of reason and stupidity. The Chronicler could well be describing some of the leading politicians in our current century. It seems that candidates are either nice guys with poor policies or mean guys with more traditional policies.

The ninth-century-B.C. mess that is seen in this chapter could reflect the situation that the first readers faced hundreds of years later. They had to rebuild a nation while under foreign rule. They worshipped in the temple but without the holy vessels—the most important being the ark of the covenant, which should have been in the central place of the temple, the holy of holies. Some people in their nation hadn't even been born there; some had. Some of the first readers were still in exile, hundreds of miles from the homeland of Israel. The writer says it only once and doesn't take much space to say it (10:15), but the message is clear: God's plan is not ruined by the political mess caused by Jeroboam and Rehoboam. Though in Chronicles God doesn't make clear the reason or the purpose, it is still his plan.

Since God is on still on his throne, he works through even the most frustrating circumstances to accomplish his plan. We have hope that the mess in our world or in our lives can and will be used by him. God ultimately works through whatever circumstances to accomplish his plan; therefore, we can trust him even when it seems like his plans have failed. If God can use the foolishness of Jeroboam and Rehoboam to bring about his plan, then the chaos that we bring into our own lives because of our foolishness can still be used by our great God. Only God can take our sin and use it in his plan. What a great God to take the sins of the world and use them as part of his plan: to give us salvation through Jesus. Who else could do this?

Preaching Idea

God doesn't need a backup plan; he only has Plan A.

Contemporary Connections

What does it mean?

To say that God works through every circumstance should affect us. Yet often, the power that this knowledge could have in our lives is hindered by the frequency of hearing it or by an academic discussion of how God's sovereignty might violate human free will. We need to hear afresh that God's plan will never fail.

We struggle with human leaders because they are limited; they all make mistakes. Every leader would say that their plans are good. Even the vilest dictator promises good times. Apparently, Rehoboam and Jeroboam both had a plan for what they thought was good. What leader would stand and say, "I have a plan to destroy this nation, this city, this business, this family"? When foolish people are on the throne and their selfish desires go unchecked, then distress, hardship, uncertainty, and worse come to the people.

But let's not judge too quickly. How do you and I handle our own plans? We also struggle with sin and foolishness. We might make plans for good, but our plans quickly change and often fail. Just like a dictator we plan for good, but none of our plans are perfect. We must not view God's plans like we do our own. God is on the throne, and he is never foolish; he is always wise. And in his wisdom, he somehow works even through the foolishness and sinfulness of each of us.

As we look at our world, our nation, our church, or our families, there are probably some areas that are causing us distress or disappointment: the aggression of one nation upon another, the policies of a political leader whom we didn't vote for, church leaders who are acting like children, a family member who once followed the Lord but has since walked away from him, the loss of a job, or debt that is out of control. In all these areas and any others that one can think of, God's plan is still at work. These difficulties will somehow be used in his plan.

Is it true?

If God can use the disastrous actions of Jeroboam and Rehoboam in his plan, then he can work with the messes that I have made in life. We all will make messes, sometimes because of sinful, rebellious, self-centered decisions. We see that God used the foolishness of Jeroboam and Rehoboam to accomplish his plan, and we can discover the principle that God works through whatever circumstances to ultimately accomplish his plan. But can he do this through a divorce, through a pastor failing morally, or the suicide of a teenager? Yes, he can. This passage doesn't seek to answer the problem of why God allows tragedies like this; it simply teaches that he will use all circumstances to accomplish

his plan, even the harsh events that are a part of living in this sinful world. Sometimes it is hard to see how he does this and often we can't see his hand at all.

I know of some marital strife that God used to help someone see their need to trust Christ. Sometimes a sinful habit can lead a person to commit a terrible act that shocks them. God can use that shock as a wake-up call that leads them to get help in breaking the habit. He uses all circumstances: a flat tire, a lost set of keys, a word spoken in anger, a sickness, even a pandemic. When the COVID pandemic hit, many churches stopped meeting. God prompted a woman to start a "social distancing" prayer meeting at the end of her driveway. The neighbors came, and to this date are still coming every Sunday night for a time of prayer, even though the fears of COVID have passed.

When we start with our plan A, it always seems to morph into plan B, and then C, and so on. Our plans are in a constant state of flux. God only has plan A. He somehow brings all things into his plan.

Now what?

In God's economy there is no waste. He takes every circumstance and uses it to further his plan. This can have a wonderful effect upon our view of the past. We often beat ourselves up over past mistakes and past sins. Thinking about these past blunders does not bring us comfort, but knowing that God can use even these blunders to advance his plan can be encouraging. After confessing our sin and restoring our relationship to the Father, we can rest and even rejoice that our great God wastes nothing. Even our most disheartening sins do not disrupt God's plan. Knowing he uses every circumstance to accomplish his plan can abate our frustration with the blunders and sins of others. Their mistakes and rebellion will not stop God's plan.

When circumstances in our life are disappointing, confusing, and even harsh, we

343

tend to focus on those events. To some degree they need our attention, but we need to add something to our view. We need to see that no matter how unsettling, how unfair, how shameful the circumstance, our Lord's plan is not ruined. He does not say, "Sorry, but I need to change the plan." We need to remember that God is on his throne and his plan will be accomplished. Comfort and rest can come when we include his sovereign rule in the focus of our thoughts.

Since our Lord is so amazing, who can take every circumstance and use it for his glory and plan, how can we not worship him? An American proverb says, "When the going gets tough, the tough get going." Let us say, "When the going gets tough, the tough get worshipping."

Creativity in Presentation

Present the story, emphasizing the complexity of the characters being both the victim and the villain, pointing out how their actions had disastrous effect on both Israel and themselves. The aim is to present a set of circumstances that are disappointing, tragic, complicated, and so on. The key verse about God's plan (v. 15) is not to be emphasized at this point. It should be read, but almost skipped over.

The next move is to present several contemporary situations: starting with a national scene, moving to a more local situation, and ending with the description of everyday life. This move from the general to the specific will help listeners be open to look at their own lives. Try to draw from real situations, but change them enough to protect confidentiality. The aim is to create a picture of circumstances in life that are disappointing and frustrating. Strive to re-create the emotion that the Israelites had under Jeroboam and Rehoboam.

The third move is to go back and highlight verse 15. Show how this verse leads us to the principle: God ultimately works through whatever circumstances to accomplish his plan. Reinforce the truth of this idea. The most outstanding example of how God uses every circumstance in his plan is in his using the sinful and grievous actions of the Romans and Jews during Christ's crucifixion to bring about his plan. This can also wonderfully lead into a gospel presentation and invitation to come to faith and trust in Christ. Here is one possible structure:

- Present the text
  - Israel meets Rehoboam at Shechem (10:1–5)
  - Rehoboam seeks counsel (10:6–11)
  - Rehoboam responds to Israel (10:12–15)
  - Israel rebels against Rehoboam (10:16–19)
- Explain the principle (10:15)
- Apply the principle

DISCUSSION QUESTIONS

1. What kind of events bring on a sense of hopelessness?
   ◦ National
   ◦ In the church
   ◦ In our homes

2. Share a disappointment from your past (that can be appropriately shared) that you saw God turn into something good.

3. God uses all circumstances to accomplish his plan. How does this change the way you look at the past? the present? the future?

4. Since God uses the blunders of others in his plan, how could this change your attitude toward others when they blunder?

5. How does God only having a plan A make you feel about him?

2 Chronicles 11:1–12:16

EXEGETICAL IDEA
When Rehoboam listened to YHWH's word, YHWH responded favorably, but when he forsook YHWH, YHWH responded with judgment.

THEOLOGICAL FOCUS
Responding to God's revelation shapes the course of human lives: accepting it leads to blessing, but rejecting it leads to disaster.

PREACHING IDEA
Obey God's Word, not to get (receive) good but because he is good.

PREACHING POINTERS
At first glance Rehoboam is a picture of each of us. Just like him, I obey; I disobey; I listen to God; I don't listen. In many ways we are like him, but he is described as evil. So, in my sympathetic identification with this very human king, how do I escape this negative and condemning description? I don't want to be called evil. The Chronicler gives the reason for the description of evil: Rehoboam did not set his heart to seek YHWH. This passage is a call to worship our great Lord. This less-than-desirable king leaves us wanting a king who has a heart of obedience and submission. Jesus is our obedient king who submitted to the Father and gives us the foundational sacrifice for our worship.

REHOBOAM'S REIGN OVER JUDAH—YHWH'S FAITHFULNESS EXPRESSED (11:1–12:16)

LITERARY STRUCTURE AND THEMES (11:1–12:16)

After the kingdom's division, YHWH's word through the prophet Shemaiah shapes the rest of Rehoboam's reign. His first word warns Rehoboam and Judah that they should not attempt to bring Israel back under Rehoboam's rule by attacking Israel. Rehoboam and Judah obey the prophet. Consequently, YHWH rewards them by fortifying many cities; by relocating priests, Levites, and others from the northern tribes to strengthen Judah and Rehoboam; and by increasing Rehoboam's family through many wives, sons, and daughters.

YHWH's second word through Shemaiah condemns Rehoboam and Judah for forsaking YHWH. Because they disobey YHWH, YHWH punishes them as the Egyptian king Shishak attacks various fortified cities in Judah, threatening Jerusalem itself. As a result, Rehoboam and Judah accept that Shemaiah has told them the truth. They humble themselves, confessing their guilt and affirming YHWH's justice to punish them. In response, YHWH sends his third word through Shemaiah. In this case, YHWH tells them that because they humbled themselves, he will relent from punishing them fully. YHWH still punishes them, but the punishment does not last long and is not as severe as it could have been. The passage ends with a conclusion to Rehoboam's reign.

- ***Rehoboam and Judah Obey the Prophet and YHWH Rewards (11:1–23)***
- ***Rehoboam and Judah Forsake YHWH and YHWH Punishes (12:1–5)***
- ***Rehoboam and Judah Humble Themselves and YHWH Relents (12:6–12)***
- ***Conclusion of Rehoboam's Reign (12:13–16)***

EXPOSITION (11:1–12:16)

Prophets served important functions in the ancient Near Eastern world. For instance, prophets provided advice for all kinds of people, from kings to common citizens. Generally, people sought out prophets because they believed the prophets had insight into affairs past, present, and future. In Israel's case, true prophets spoke YHWH's word. Therefore, the people had to take seriously whatever the prophet spoke as YHWH's word, for YHWH would hold anyone accountable for ignoring the prophet's word (Deut. 18:19). During this part of Rehoboam's reign, the prophet's word shapes the entire passage. When Rehoboam listens to the prophet's word, YHWH responds favorably; but when he forsakes YHWH's instruction, YHWH punishes him.

Rehoboam and Judah Obey the Prophet and YHWH Rewards (11:1–23)

Because Rehoboam obeys the prophet Shemaiah, YHWH blesses him by strengthening the nation through fortifications, immigration, and descendants.

11:1–2. The narrative of Rehoboam's reign after the kingdom divides begins with an important prophetic word. Just after Rehoboam assembles an army of 180,000 to bring the separated northern tribes back under his rule, YHWH sends a prophet named Shemaiah to warn Rehoboam and his people and to explain the situation.

Troop Numbers in Judah

The Chronicler provides specific troop numbers for several kings of Judah (David, Rehoboam, Abijah, Asa, Jehoshaphat, Amaziah, and Uzziah). For their historical contexts, these numbers represent improbably large forces. Although scholars have proposed several ways of interpreting these texts, "the best solution seems to be that the large numbers in such cases (almost always in military contexts) are deliberate exaggerations or hyperbole designed to glorify Yahweh and his mighty hosts" (Merrill 2015, 120; for fuller treatment, see Fouts 1997, 377–87). Enumerating troop sizes with such large numbers occurs commonly in the ANE (e.g., for Assyrian inscriptions, see Fouts 1994, 205–11).

Beyond the intention to glorify YHWH, the numbers reveal another consideration in the Chronicler's message. Since the first king with troop numbers (David) has well over a million troops and the last king with troop numbers (Uzziah) has around three hundred thousand, it appears that the Chronicler intends to show a decline in the size of troops from the high point under David to his own time (Ben Zvi 2008, 76–77). Furthermore, if one looks at the number of troops for Rehoboam, Abijah, Asa, and Jehoshaphat, one will notice that the number of troops increases. In fact, Jehoshaphat's troops constitute the sum of Judah's preceding kings Rehoboam, Abijah, and Asa, indicating that Judah's army grows through the reigns of good kings (see N. Klein 2017, 6–13). In this way, the details of the text reinforce a common theme in Chronicles: YHWH rewards obedience and punishes disobedience.

11:3. As YHWH introduces what the prophet should say, YHWH refers to Rehoboam and the people in a way that highlights important themes in this narrative. First, he refers to Rehoboam as the son of Solomon, the king of Judah. Despite the kingdom's division in 2 Chronicles 10, YHWH still preserves his promise to David and Solomon by keeping a Davidide on the throne (e.g., 1 Chron. 17:10–14; 2 Chron. 7:18). An important theme of 2 Chronicles 11 is that Rehoboam remains king over Judah and strengthens his power as king. Second, YHWH refers to the southern kingdom as all Israel in Judah and Benjamin. This designation serves a significant role in Chronicles by highlighting the relationship between Israel and Judah as kingdoms. Even though they are two kingdoms, they constitute one people: Israel. They are brothers (אַחִים), sharing the same forefathers (אָבוֹת) and the same God.

11:4. When the prophet speaks to Rehoboam and his people, he warns them to abandon their plan to restore the kingdom. He warns them not to attack Israel but to return home. Then he explains the situation so that they will know why they should leave things as they are: YHWH has brought about the kingdom's division. If Rehoboam and his people fight to restore the northern tribes to the kingdom, then they will be opposing the work of YHWH.

Rehoboam and the people obey what the prophet says and abandon their plan. Unlike Israel, who initiates a rebellion against Rehoboam by returning to their tents, Judah maintains peace by returning to their homes. This act of obedience sets the stage for the rest of the chapter. Because Rehoboam and the people obey the prophet's warning, YHWH rewards them greatly.

11:5–12. Rehoboam fortifies several cities to secure his hold on the kingdom and promote stability within it. The Chronicler consistently uses building accounts, especially building fortifications, as a sign of YHWH's blessing (e.g., 1 Chron. 11:8; 2 Chron. 8:2–6; 14:5–6; 17:12; 26:9; 27:3–4; 33:14). The Chronicler lists fifteen cities without an overall discernible pattern. Even though these cities are in the eastern, southern, and western parts of the tribal territory of Judah, the Chronicler describes them as the fortified cities in Judah and Benjamin. He likely includes Benjamin as a way of recalling that the southern kingdom Judah consists of the two tribes of Judah and Benjamin. Besides building up the fortifications of these cities, Rehoboam also provides leadership and supplies (both of food and weapons) for each city. As a result, Rehoboam firmly establishes his royal authority over Judah and Benjamin.

Lack of Northern Fortifications

Rehoboam does not fortify cities in the northern part of his kingdom. One can guess Rehoboam's reasons for leaving out this part: perhaps hostilities with Israel to the north prevented him from fortifying cities in that region; or perhaps he thought he might regain control of Israel at another time, so that eventually fortifications in the northern part of Judah would lose their strategic usefulness. Regardless of Rehoboam's intentions, the Chronicler does not give any clues regarding its importance for his understanding of Rehoboam's reign.

11:13–15. As Rehoboam strengthens his position in Judah, he finds a group of supporters from the north. Even though YHWH has brought about the kingdom's division, Israel's new king Jeroboam begins leading his people away from YHWH by making several changes to Israel's worship. He changes the personnel of worship, the places of worship, and the objects of worship. The Chronicler first states that Jeroboam prohibits the priests and Levites from serving as priests of YHWH because he appoints his own priests. Furthermore, these new priests serve at various illicit worship sites, high places (בָּמוֹת). Finally, they worship idols of goats and calves. Each of these changes violates YHWH's word regarding true worship. YHWH said that the

sons of Aaron are his appointed priests (e.g., 2 Chron. 26:18), that the other Levites are their assistants (e.g., 2 Chron. 13:10), that the temple in Jerusalem is the place of sacrifice and worship (e.g., 2 Chron. 7:12), and that Israel should worship YHWH alone without any idols (e.g., 1 Chron. 16:25–26).

TRANSLATION ANALYSIS:
The Hebrew word occurring here (שְׂעִירִים) refers to some form of illicit object of worship. These idols most likely either were images of goats or beings possessing features of goats and humans. They occur rarely in the Old Testament (Lev. 17:7, Isa. 13:21; 34:14; perhaps 2 Kings 23:8) and their nature is not entirely clear. The verses in Isaiah may simply refer to wild animals. Some translations (e.g., NASB) render the word as "satyrs," but such a translation is anachronistic, since satyrs are specifically characters within Greek and Roman mythology of a later period. Other translations (CSB, NRSV) render the word as "goat-demons"; however, their identity as demons is not clear. Therefore, in this case, it seems most prudent to translate them as goat idols (ESV, NET, NIV, NLT). The passages in Leviticus and here in Chronicles clearly condemn worshipping them.

Calves as Idols

The Chronicler specifies that Jeroboam made the calves. This observation ties into a theme in Chronicles: YHWH is not human-made, but idols are (cf. esp. 2 Chron. 32:19). As a result, any attempt to worship an object, whether intended to represent YHWH or not, is not worshipping YHWH. Chronicles systematically avoids signs of syncretism (Japhet 2009, 169–70; Lynch 2014b, 75–78).

11:16–17. As a result of Rehoboam's obedience and Jeroboam's disobedience, a group of those from Israel who remain faithful to YHWH, including the priests and Levites, return to Judah. The scene emphasizes that even though Israel and Judah are now two kingdoms, the people are still related to one another. What they share most importantly is that YHWH is their God. The Chronicler calls YHWH "the God of Israel" and "the God of their fathers." This point is particularly important because Jeroboam is leading Israel as a nation away from YHWH. However, within this apostate nation Israel, some people remain determined to follow YHWH. The Chronicler illustrates how they follow YHWH by focusing on one of his recurring themes: worship. He recounts that they return to Jerusalem to make sacrifices to YHWH. By sacrificing at the temple, they prove their loyalty to him, since they acknowledge that YHWH has chosen the temple as the place for sacrifice (2 Chron. 7:12). The Chronicler summarizes their actions as "walking in the ways of David and Solomon." By mentioning David and Solomon, the Chronicler ties together two themes. First, the Chronicler points to Israel and Judah's common heritage since both kings ruled all the tribes of Israel. Second, the Chronicler points to Jerusalem as the proper place of worship since both kings focused on building YHWH's temple.

Because the priests, Levites, and others from Israel return to Judah to worship YHWH properly, in contrast to Israel, Judah grows stronger and Rehoboam's royal power and prestige increase. The Chronicler indicates that YHWH lies behind this increase in strength, because he relates it directly to their obedience—that is, walking in the way of David and Solomon. Even though he does not specify here in what ways the kingdom and Rehoboam grow stronger, he illustrates it in the surrounding verses. In the preceding verses (11:5–12), he shows that the kingdom grows stronger through the various fortifications built. In the following verses (11:18–23), the Chronicler shows that Rehoboam grows stronger as his family increases in number. At the same time, here in the middle of the narrative unit, he foreshadows a coming disaster because he states that their obedience lasts for three years. The Chronicler often foreshadows a coming change in events by including chronological details such as this one (e.g., the reign of Asa; 2 Chron. 14:1; 15:19; 16:1, 12).

TRANSLATION ANALYSIS:
This verse describes how those coming from the northern tribes affect Rehoboam. The Hebrew term is וַיְאַמְּצוּ. Translations render this word differently. Many translations (CSB, NASB, NIV, NLT) read "supported." This translation introduces some ambiguity, since it may mean that they sided with Rehoboam as opposed to siding with Jeroboam or that they helped him out. Given the context of the verse, the latter seems more likely. For this reason, translations that read "made secure, made strong" (ESV, NRSV) capture this sense well.

11:18–23. Despite the hint that change is coming, the Chronicler continues by showing how YHWH blesses Rehoboam by increasing his family. Rehoboam marries several women, becomes the father of several children, and prepares for their future. The text states that Rehoboam has eighteen wives and sixty concubines; however, it mentions only two wives in particular: Mahalath and Maacah. These wives fall within David's family tree. Mahalath is Rehoboam's first wife, usually a prominent position among the other wives, and Maacah is Rehoboam's most-loved wife. Although both wives give birth to sons, Rehoboam chooses to designate Maacah's firstborn as the royal heir. Furthermore, he provides for many of his other twenty-seven sons by distributing them among his fortified cities and ensuring they have what is required for the next generation: wives and sufficient supplies. These activities help secure the king's power and authority over Judah, for himself and his future generations.

Maacah's Lineage

There is some question regarding Maacah's lineage. Here in 2 Chronicles 11:20 the text reads "Absalom," David's son. First Kings 15:2, 10 record his name as Abishalom. These two forms are most likely variants of the same name. Furthermore, Maacah is most likely not Absalom's daughter, but granddaughter (see comments regarding 2 Chron. 13:2). Furthermore, in the ancient Near Eastern world, it was common for kings to marry relatives to limit and preserve the royal bloodline.

Rehoboam and Judah Forsake YHWH and YHWH Punishes (12:1–5)

Rehoboam and Judah forsake YHWH's instruction, so he sends the Egyptian king Shishak to punish them.

12:1–2. Because YHWH blesses Judah and Rehoboam, Judah becomes secure under Rehoboam's rule and Rehoboam secures himself as a strong ruler. From this position Rehoboam and all Israel (in this case, referring to Judah) abandon YHWH's law and act unfaithfully (מעל) toward him (see sidebar "Unfaithfulness Against YHWH"). Usually in Chronicles, these verbs designate improper worship. Since the text provides no more details, they most likely carry a generic sense of disobeying YHWH. The Chronicler is not concerned with the specifics of the violations. Instead, he points them out to show that YHWH punishes Judah for disobeying him.

12:3–4. YHWH punishes Judah when the Egyptian Pharaoh Shishak (also known as Shoshenq) comes against Judah. Shishak leads a large, international force to attack Judah, composed of twelve hundred chariots, sixty thousand horsemen, and innumerable other warriors, including warriors from the Libyans, Sukkites, and Cushites. These details paint the picture of an unstoppable force. They capture several fortifications, undoing the blessings recorded

in the previous chapter both by capturing the fortifications and by threatening Rehoboam's sons whom he has just stationed among those fortifications. Many of Judah's officers flee from Shishak by going to Jerusalem. Shishak's army then follows, stopping at Jerusalem.

Threat to Rehoboam's Sons

By mentioning that Rehoboam appoints his sons to the fortified cities so close to Shishak's capture of those cities, the Chronicler makes a connection between the two. At the same time, he mentions that Judah's officials, likely including many of Rehoboam's sons, seek refuge in Jerusalem (12:5). Therefore, even though the Chronicler does not specify whether Shishak's troops directly threaten, capture, or kill any of Rehoboam's sons, he portrays Shishak's invasion as a serious threat to them. However, he presents Jerusalem as a refuge, linking their future fate with Jerusalem's. If Jerusalem is spared, then it seems they will be also. This observation is significant for two reasons: (1) it shows that even though Judah's disobedience brings about punishment that undoes YHWH's previous blessings, it does not undo them completely, and (2) it opens the door to repentance and deliverance, since the invading army stops before Jerusalem, where the people have taken refuge.

12:5. As Shishak's unstoppable force threatens Jerusalem, the prophet Shemaiah again communicates YHWH's word to Rehoboam and Judah's officers, and interprets the situation for Rehoboam and Judah. The message is simple: they have abandoned (עזב) YHWH, so YHWH has abandoned (עזב) them to Shishak. Even though the same word occurs in both places, they communicate something slightly different each time. Judah abandons YHWH by disobeying him, while YHWH abandons Judah by punishing them. In other words, when Judah abandons YHWH, they fail to honor their relationship with YHWH; however, when YHWH abandons Judah, he is honoring his relationship with Judah because he is doing as he has repeatedly promised (e.g., 1 Chron. 28:9; 2 Chron. 7:19–22; 15:2).

The Language of Forsaking

This connection between forsaking YHWH and YHWH forsaking occurs again in Chronicles, once as a warning (2 Chron. 15:2) and once as a sign of punishment (2 Chron. 24:20). It also occurs in a slightly modified form as a warning to Solomon (1 Chron. 28:9).

Rehoboam and Judah Humble Themselves and YHWH Relents (12:6–12)

Following Shishak's attack on Judah, Rehoboam listens to the prophet's words, resulting in YHWH relenting from total disaster.

12:6. Unlike Shemaiah's first encounter, this time the prophet does not tell Judah what they should do. He only explains what is really going on: YHWH is punishing them for their disobedience. Nonetheless, Rehoboam and Judah's officers know how to respond. They receive YHWH's simple message with a simple reply: YHWH is right. By making this claim, they are not presenting some theoretical fact but confessing their guilt and admitting that YHWH is justified in punishing them in this way. The Chronicler characterizes this activity as "humbling themselves" (*niphal* כנע), indicating that their actions correspond to 2 Chronicles 7:14. Furthermore, their actions exemplify how others respond to the conditions after Jerusalem's fall. For instance, as Daniel reflects on Jerusalem's fate, he also declares that YHWH is right for punishing them because they did not obey what he commanded (Dan. 9:14; see also Ezra 9:15; Neh. 9:33). However, in this case, Judah responds before a foreign invader destroys Jerusalem. As a result, YHWH relents from destroying Jerusalem completely.

Officers of Judah and Israel

In 2 Chronicles 12:5, the text refers to the leaders according to a geographical perspective as "the officers of Judah." In 2 Chronicles 12:6, the text refers to the same group as "the officers of Israel" according to their "role as representatives of their people" (Japhet 1993, 679).

12:7–8. For a third time, YHWH communicates through Shemaiah, but this time he communicates his decision to spare Jerusalem from destruction. Even though YHWH promises that he will deliver them soon rather than destroy them completely, Judah still suffers further consequences for their disobedience. YHWH summarizes these consequences as becoming Shishak's servants, and explains that this punishment serves the purpose of teaching Judah how serving YHWH compares to serving foreign kings. In this case, "service" (עֲבוֹדָה) refers to the conditions (favorable or unfavorable) that result from submitting to someone, whether YHWH or foreign kings. The text implies that serving YHWH is better than serving foreign kings. The rest of the narrative confirms this implication by showing that serving Shishak results in Judah losing its wealth. In contrast, serving YHWH results in significant benefits, including strengthening both king and kingdom (see 2 Chron. 11:17).

TRANSLATION ANALYSIS:
In 12:7, the expression כִּמְעַט is ambiguous, either meaning "a little bit" or "soon." Many translations (CSB, ESV, NASB, NKJV, NRSV) render the expression in the sense of "a little bit." This translation implies that YHWH's punishment is severe, but that YHWH relents a bit from it. Other translations (NET, NIV, NLT) render the expression in the sense of "soon." This translation implies that YHWH's punishment will not last long. In this case, the latter translation seems to fit the context best. Shishak does empty the treasuries of Jerusalem, but then nothing else is said concerning further attacks or

signs of punishment. The latter part of 12:8 reads as follows: וְיֵדְעוּ עֲבוֹדָתִי וַעֲבוֹדַת מַמְלְכוֹת הָאֲרָצוֹת. Most translations render this clause in some way to indicate that the text implies that Judah will know that YHWH's service differs from that of foreign nations (e.g., "they may learn the difference between serving me and serving the kings of other lands" NIV). ESV translates the clause simply as follows: "that they may know my service and the service of the kingdoms of the countries." However, the point of the statement is not that Judah will learn how to serve YHWH and the other nations at the same time, but that they will learn the difference between the two.

12:9. After YHWH tells Rehoboam and Judah's leaders that they will become Shishak's servants, the text illustrates what it means for them to be his servants: Shishak attacks Jerusalem and plunders the city of its wealth. Like others who break through Jerusalem's defenses (e.g., Joash in 2 Chron. 25:24; Nebuchadnezzar in 2 Chron. 36:18), he empties out the royal and temple treasuries. To communicate how thoroughly Shishak plunders Jerusalem, the text says that Shishak took everything (אֶת־הַכֹּל לָקָח). In fact, Shishak goes beyond everything in the treasuries by taking the gold shields that Solomon made.

The way the Chronicler describes these events resembles the way he describes the Babylonian attack on Jerusalem (2 Chron. 36:17–20). In both texts, Judah becomes the servants of the attacking king. Both kings also remove everything from Jerusalem, including the royal and temple treasuries. Despite the similarities, the two texts differ in significant ways. The Chronicler records Shishak's attack on Jerusalem as less severe than Nebuchadnezzar's. Shishak does not kill anyone, but Nebuchadnezzar kills many; Shishak does not take the temple's equipment, but Nebuchadnezzar takes all of it; Shishak does not destroy anything, but Nebuchadnezzar destroys Jerusalem's wall, its fortifications, its palace, and its temple.

The similarities and differences between the accounts demonstrate an important point for the Chronicler. In each case, the Chronicler records that YHWH warns Judah's leaders that disaster is coming. In Shishak's case, Rehoboam and Judah's leaders humble themselves and accept the prophet's warning; however, in Nebuchadnezzar's case, Zedekiah and Judah's leaders do not humble themselves and reject the prophets' warnings (2 Chron. 36:12, 15–16). These two activities tie into recurring themes in Chronicles: YHWH responds to those who humble themselves (see 2 Chron. 7:14) and those who submit to prophetic warnings (following Deut. 18:19). The fact that Shishak's attack is less severe than Nebuchadnezzar's demonstrates how YHWH responds to humility and submission.

These events demonstrate another important point. They show how seriously YHWH responds when his people abandon him by disobeying his law and being unfaithful. Up to this point in Chronicles, the Chronicler has focused on the righteous reigns of David and Solomon. He even refers to both kings positively during Rehoboam's reign (2 Chron. 11:17). However, immediately following the reigns of the two righteous kings, the similarities between the two attacks on Jerusalem suggest that YHWH almost destroys Judah and Jerusalem because of their disobedience. The Chronicler points out that Judah's past obedience does not ensure their future blessing, nor does their past disobedience ensure their future destruction. Their actions and their reactions in relation to YHWH's past word (his law) or his present word (his prophetic warning) shape how YHWH acts and reacts to them.

For the first readers, the comparison and contrast of these attacks on Jerusalem would relate well to their situation. First, even in the less-than-ideal conditions in which they lived, this text in Chronicles encourages them to recognize their past guilt, humble themselves, and lean on YHWH to bring about blessings. More specifically, the first readers would have recognized that they would need to humble themselves, repent from their past evil deeds, and submit to YHWH's word to restore Israel fully and prepare for YHWH to fulfill his promises (e.g., Neh. 9:5–37; Dan. 9:4–19). At the same time, this text encourages them to obey YHWH's word because even if they experience YHWH's blessing at any moment, their disobedience can undo those blessings. As an example, even when the temple again stands in Jerusalem, the Chronicler encourages them to remain faithful to YHWH, or they may again provoke YHWH to destroy it. They cannot lean on the righteous actions of the previous generation(s) to secure the temple's future; they must obey him also.

12:10–11. A result of Shishak's attack is that he takes Solomon's gold shields. Since he takes them, Rehoboam replaces them with bronze ones. The Chronicler includes these details to illustrate both YHWH's punishment and mercy. For instance, the Chronicler indicates the material of these shields as a way of illustrating a contrast between the reigns of Solomon and Rehoboam: Solomon was prosperous, being able to make his shields of gold (2 Chron. 9:15–16), but Rehoboam is not because Shishak has just raided his treasuries as part of YHWH's punishment. At the same time, Rehoboam is free to replace these shields (carrying on the tradition of Solomon) and even assign them to officers of his royal guard so that they may carry them any time he visits the temple. The bronze shields symbolize both YHWH's punishment (Shishak's raiding Jerusalem) and his mercy (Rehoboam remains king and replaces the shields).

Role of Shields in Joash's Enthronement

This detail in the narrative may anticipate the role that such equipment plays in the coup against Athaliah (cf. 2 Chron. 23:9). Since the royal guard carries these shields, they are somehow associated with Rehoboam's role as king. During the coup against Athaliah, the people arm themselves with David's dedicated military equipment to secure Joash as king.

12:12. In fact, the Chronicler summarizes this section along these lines, drawing attention to YHWH's punishing anger but also his decision not to destroy Rehoboam completely (12:12). Furthermore, after focusing on Rehoboam, he includes a comment about all of Judah: there were some good things in Judah. Most likely, these good things refer to good conditions. Again, this statement reveals that even though YHWH has punished Judah through Shishak, he relents so that even though conditions are not as good as they were, they are still good because of YHWH's mercy. For the first readers, this comment about conditions under foreign powers might have encouraged them that conditions may also be good as they are subject to the Persian Empire (Schweitzer 2016, 93).

TRANSLATION ANALYSIS:
The final expression in 12:12 reads:
וְגַם בִּיהוּדָה הָיָה דְּבָרִים טוֹבִים. This expression resembles 2 Chronicles 19:3, where Jehu confronts Jehoshaphat for allying with Ahab, but still finds "some good" (דְּבָרִים טוֹבִים) in Jehoshaphat for removing the Asherah poles and choosing to worship YHWH. However, in this case, the "good things" appear to be the result of YHWH's choosing not to destroy Rehoboam completely. Therefore, the statement is a qualified positive outcome of the events of chapter 12. Most translations (CSB, ESV, NASB, NKJV, NRSV) focus on the good conditions; however, NET expresses the full sense clearly ("Judah experienced some good things"). Other translations leave the sense ambiguous, e.g., "there was some good in Judah" (NIV) and "there were still some good things in the land of Judah" (NLT).

Conclusion of Rehoboam's Reign (12:13–16)

This section includes the conclusion formula for Rehoboam's reign and characterizes Rehoboam's action as wicked because he does not determine to follow YHWH.

12:13. The conclusion to Rehoboam's reign begins with information that most often occurs at the beginning of a king's reign: (1) a statement that the king secures his authority over the kingdom (e.g., 2 Chron. 1:1; 17:1; 21:4; 25:3), (2) his age when he becomes king, (3) how long he reigns, (4) where he reigns, (5) his mother's name, and (6) how he measures up in YHWH's estimation. Postponing these elements, especially the note about establishing his authority, to the end of Rehoboam's reign has two effects: (1) it reflects the kingdom's division, since Rehoboam does not establish his royal authority over all Israel at the beginning of his reign, and (2) it creates a connection back to 2 Chronicles 12:1, where Rehoboam and Judah forsake YHWH's law as Rehoboam establishes his royal authority. This connection naturally segues to the statement that Rehoboam did what is evil (12:14).

Also, the conclusion focuses on Jerusalem as the place where YHWH has chosen to put his name. This notice occurs elsewhere in Chronicles (e.g., 2 Chron. 6:6; 33:4, 7) but not in the context of an introduction or conclusion. It makes sense that it occurs here because Rehoboam's reign threatens Jerusalem itself, highlighting the significant impact one king and/or one generation can have (R. Klein 2012, 188). The disobedience of Rehoboam and his generation almost brings total destruction to YHWH's chosen city.

12:14. The Chronicler summarizes Rehoboam's reign by saying that he does what is evil because he does not firmly commit himself to following YHWH. It is too simplistic to interpret this comment to mean that the Chronicler considers Rehoboam to be a *bad* king. The Chronicler's characterization of Rehoboam is more complex than simply *good* or *bad*. Beginning in 2 Chronicles 10, Rehoboam is an ambiguous character. His brash behavior contributes to some extent to the kingdom's division; however, he is not solely to blame (see commentary on 2 Chron.

10). Even though he forsakes YHWH's law, he also responds properly by humbling himself to Shemaiah's prophetic warning on two separate occasions.

Despite this ambiguous picture, in this context the Chronicler's evaluation most likely focuses on Rehoboam as a worshipper of YHWH. Already in 2 Chronicles 12:1 the Chronicler characterizes Rehoboam and Judah generically as forsaking YHWH's law and transgressing against him (מעל). Even though these verbs appear generic in that context, in Chronicles they often indicate cultic violations or illicit worship practices (see above). Furthermore, Rehoboam does what is evil because he does not commit himself to following YHWH. The phrase "committing himself to follow YHWH" (הֵכִין לִבּוֹ לִדְרוֹשׁ אֶת־יְהוָה) occurs in other contexts in which it is directly related to worship. In 2 Chronicles 19:3 the seer Jehu condemns Jehoshaphat for allying himself with Ahab yet finds some good in Jehoshaphat because he has removed the Asherah poles and committed himself to follow YHWH. In 2 Chronicles 20:33, the people allow the high places to remain because they did not commit themselves to follow YHWH. In 2 Chronicles 30:19 Hezekiah prays for those who have committed themselves to follow YHWH by celebrating the Passover even though they were unclean. Each of these instances call attention to the intention to worship YHWH alone. Even though the Chronicler does not assess every king according to this same standard (e.g., the Chronicler characterizes Amaziah as doing what is upright even though he worships Edomite gods; 2 Chron. 25:2, 14), with Rehoboam the text implies that Rehoboam does what is evil—that is, he does not worship YHWH properly in some way.

TRANSLATION ANALYSIS:

The expression in 12:14 reads as follows: כִּי לֹא הֵכִין לִבּוֹ לִדְרוֹשׁ אֶת־יְהוָה. To interpret the expression properly, one must recognize that לֵב ("heart") often refers to the will and intentions of a person. Most of the translations render לֵב as "heart," intending to draw on this metaphorical sense of the word. NET translates the expression without the metaphor: "he was not determined to follow the LORD." Although most other translations capture this sense metaphorically, this translation clearly communicates that Rehoboam's wrong actions result from his commitments and his intentions.

12:15–16. Following his theological assessment of Rehoboam's reign, the Chronicler turns to the typical conclusion formula. He cites his sources, recounts Rehoboam's death and burial, and then identifies the next king. Most of these elements are typical; however, two features deserve further comment. First, the Chronicler refers to two prophetic sources: the records of Shemaiah the prophet and the genealogical records of Iddo the seer (probably the information regarding Rehoboam's wives and sons found in 2 Chron. 11:18–23). During Rehoboam's reign, Shemaiah shows up on two occasions, and each time he informs Rehoboam and Judah what is really happening. Since Shemaiah accurately and authoritatively informs those in the narrative, his source serves as a trustworthy and authoritative guide to Rehoboam's reign. This authority also extends to Iddo as a seer. In fact, Chronicles repeatedly refers to prophetic sources in the conclusions of kings' reigns as authoritative sources to reveal what really happened (see "Genre" section in the introduction).

Second, the conclusion refers to the continual conflict between Rehoboam and Jeroboam. This comment clears up a possible misconception of Rehoboam's reign. Since, following Shemaiah's warning, Rehoboam does not attack Israel to return it to his control, one may assume that the two nations did not war at all against one another. This comment at the end of Rehoboam's reign proves otherwise; hostilities between the two kingdoms continue throughout Rehoboam's reign. Unlike the days of David and Solomon, all of Israel are separated, divided, and hostile toward one another.

This account of Rehoboam's reign addresses the first readers of Chronicles in a couple of ways. First, during those days, the tribes of Israel had become scattered throughout the ancient Near East. Furthermore, hostility at times characterized the relationship between them. Also, around this time Jews were building other temples (e.g., at Elephantine) as places of worship. The Chronicler's account of Rehoboam's reign encourages everyone from YHWH's people to join to worship YHWH alone at the place he has designated: the Jerusalem temple. Second, for those living in a time after Jerusalem's destruction, still under the rule of foreign kings, this account presents a model for the people to confess their guilt and acknowledge YHWH's justice, so that their conditions may change and their punishment end soon. Third, Rehoboam's reign reveals how quickly the fate of a nation can change. Immediately following the blessed reigns of David and Solomon, the city and temple they prepared and constructed stands on the edge of destruction because of Rehoboam and Judah's disobedience. This fact would serve as a strong warning against disobeying YHWH's law and forsaking him.

THEOLOGICAL FOCUS
Responding to God's revelation shapes the course of human lives: accepting it leads to blessing, but rejecting it leads to disaster.

God's revelation, delivered by the prophet Shemaiah, shapes the course of this passage. The prophet speaks God's words to set the passage into motion, and continues to speak at each major turning point. These words correspond to the reality of the situation and either set events in motion or explain the events already set in motion. At the same time, how Rehoboam responds to the prophecy affects these events. When Rehoboam obeys the prophet's command at the beginning of the passage, God rewards him. When Rehoboam forsakes God, the prophet condemns Rehoboam and explains that his disaster is a result of forsaking God. When Rehoboam responds by humbling himself, the prophet comforts Rehoboam that all is not lost. The prophetic word directs Rehoboam's actions and clarifies his circumstances. The passage reveals a dynamic interchange between God's word and human response that reveals the power of God's revelation and the importance of responding properly to it.

Furthermore, the portrait of the prophet's words and Rehoboam's response speaks to the character of God. Every time the prophet speaks, he shows that God responds to Rehoboam as God has promised: he rewards obedience and punishes disobedience. As a result, the passage presents a view of God in which he is active and responsive while also unchanging and faithful. Jonah presents a similar picture. After God relents from destroying Nineveh, Jonah becomes upset because he knew that God would act this way since God is "gracious and compassionate . . . slow to anger and abounding in mercy, and one who relents concerning threatened judgment" (Jonah 4:2 NET). This picture of a faithful, active God runs throughout the Bible.

This passage raises another important point regarding God's response to Rehoboam. After Rehoboam forsakes God, God brings judgment in the form of a foreign invasion. The text suggests that this invasion could have fully destroyed Judah (2 Chron. 12:12). However, when Rehoboam humbles himself, God mitigates the punishment so that Jerusalem survives. God's relenting of the total devastation is an aspect of his mercy and corresponds to what he has promised earlier (2 Chron. 7:14). At the same time, the passage does not minimize the seriousness of sin. Without sidebar or fine print, the prophet condemns Rehoboam's activity in forsaking God. Furthermore, God does not remove the punishment altogether. Rehoboam's sin still has consequences, even long-lasting consequences (2 Chron. 2:9–11; see also the example of David's census, 1 Chron. 21:8–14).

However, the prophet declares that God transforms the punishment into an opportunity to teach Judah about the benefits of serving God as king. In contrast to the harsh treatment by other nations' kings, God's rule over Judah results in "good things" (2 Chron. 12:12). The passage points to God's ability to transform suffering into something beneficial.

Thankfully, the generation of Rehoboam recognizes the authority and truthfulness of God's revelation spoken by the prophet Shemaiah. When they forsake God, that single generation puts Judah at risk of total devastation, despite the praiseworthy accomplishments of David and Solomon. This risk to Judah highlights how seriously God takes sin, especially the sin of not worshipping and following him. At the same time, God's response to their humility highlights his faithful mercy as he mitigates the punishment and transforms it into an opportunity for their benefit. God still takes sin seriously and even transforms suffering into an opportunity for benefit (Heb. 12:4–11).

PREACHING AND TEACHING STRATEGIES

Exegetical and Theological Synthesis

There is a difference between obeying God to get him to be good to us and obeying him because he is good. That second type of obedience comes out of setting our hearts to seek the Lord. This difference is important when applied to the reign of Rehoboam. The Chronicler says that Rehoboam did evil. Notice why he has this negative description: not because he disobeyed, though he did, but rather because he did not set his heart to seek the Lord (12:14). In other words, he did evil in that he did not worship YHWH. When Rehoboam listened to YHWH's word, YHWH responded favorably, but when Rehoboam forsook YHWH, he responded with judgment. At times Rehoboam obeyed God, but other times he did not. Is he evil because the bad outweighed the good? If that is true, we all would have this negative description. We can't judge a person's heart, but God gives us this description of Rehoboam's heart. Rehoboam did some good and some bad, but most importantly he was not a worshipper in his heart.

Listening to God's revelation is more than just doing what he says. It is setting one's heart to seek him, that is, to have a lifestyle and habits of seeking him. This is worship. If you worship the Lord, you will listen to him. This passage teaches us that when we obey God we enjoy his blessings, and when we disobey him we are judged—and that true obedience comes not from a heart that obeys to get good from God, but out of a heart that worships the God who is good.

Preaching Idea
Obey God's Word, not to get (receive) good but because he is good.

Contemporary Connections

What does it mean?
As we begin this pericope and see Rehoboam leading Judah to fight against Israel, we can't help but shake our heads and say, "Come on Rehoboam, do you always have to act so foolishly?" But then the word of the Lord comes to him, and he listens and obeys. And so goes the rest of his reign. We are never quite sure how he will respond to God, but we are sure how God will respond to him. When he obeys, the blessings of YHWH are his to enjoy. We need to be careful to view God's response to Rehoboam as God being faithful. There is a level of reciprocity, but it is not an emotional, unplanned reaction.

When clear and important instructions given by a foreman, supervisor, or even a parent are ignored, the reaction is often an unplanned, angry emotion. I can still hear my dad's voice, "If I told you once, I've told you fourteen times." I never understood the "fourteen times," but I understood the message. When the coach huddles the players on the sidelines, gives the team the next play, and then watches a player

run the wrong pattern in the play that was just discussed, resulting in the other team getting the ball, the coach throws his clipboard on the ground, rips off his headset, then grabs the face mask of the disobedient player and screams in his face. Only a few of us have experienced being a head coach of a football team but we all have experienced this kind of emotional reaction to being ignored. This is not how God responds. God is sovereign and his response is always in keeping with his faithfulness. He will always do what he promised.

God's promises to discipline a disobedient king and nation came through Moses, and through a promise to David and again to Solomon. Rehoboam had it written down and had it passed down from his father and grandfather. He well knew that if he disobeyed, discipline would follow.

So too with us: if we disobey our Lord, he will discipline us. We must not think that because we are followers of Jesus, God will not discipline us. Proverbs 3:11–12 and Hebrews 12:5–8 make it clear: God disciplines those he loves. But even when we disobey, we should still be worshippers, confessing our sin and running to the faithful God who shows us mercy and yet loves us enough to let us experience the consequences.

Is it true?
There is an Old Testament activity that is central to YHWH worship that is missing from this passage: sacrifice. We have Rehoboam's vacillating between disobedience and obedience. We even see him repenting and calling YHWH righteous. He listens at times and humbles himself, but there seems to be no record of him offering a sacrifice or leading the nation to do the same. The Chronicler mentions those in Israel who did desire to worship YHWH (11:16), which highlights that there is no record of Rehoboam being a worshipper. Dr. Williams pointed out that Rehoboam doing evil is reference to a lack of proper worship of YHWH. Combining this

observation with the clear statement that he did not set his heart to seek YHWH shows us that he was not a worshipper of YHWH. His obedience was not from the heart of a worshipper. Apparently, he obeyed to get good results.

Why do we obey and listen to the Lord? Are we making an investment from which we expect a good return? We should worship God because he *is* good, not to *receive* good. God does reward those who seek him, and he blesses us with good things in abundance, but we can't contract with God to get a high percentage interest on our investment of obedience. Rehoboam seems to listen and obey without a heart of worship.

Now what?

Motives are hard to examine. Paul suggests that he doubts his own motives when he tells us that he does not judge himself (1 Cor. 4:3–4). Often, we don't know why we do something. For years I never realized that a large portion of my motivation to pastor, preach, parent, and love my wife was so that people would tell me that I was good at those tasks. That wasn't all my motivation, but it was far more than I should have been comfortable with. I still struggle with motivation in my obedience to God. Even as I write this, I trust the Father to remind me that this is for the better proclamation of his Word, not for my profit or for respect from others.

The path to right motives comes from Rehoboam's negative example. While at times he did listen to YHWH and affirmed that YHWH is righteous, he was not a worshipper of YHWH. This should lead us to a reflective posture. Am I regularly, both privately and corporately, worshipping our Lord? In worship our heart's motivation and desire is more important than the outward signs. But measuring our heart's motivation is quite difficult. It requires a teachable spirit and the Spirit's examination. However, we can measure some outward signs.

Weekly gathering with fellow believers to worship through song, prayer, and listening to the Word preached does not guarantee a heart

that is striving to seek the Lord, but they are specific actions that can be measured. Taking time to privately read Scripture, pray, and reflect on God's presence and direction in our lives is something that we either do or not do. Praying as a family, reading the Word to our children, and giving financially as God directs are outward acts that do not guarantee the right inner motives, but the outward actions of the body can help inner motives of the heart. Our acts of worship are empty if there is not a heart that submits to God, has respect for God, and is delighted in God. And these attitudes of the heart can be reinforced by the actions of the body.

Just as Rehoboam had some activities without the right heart, these acts of worship could be just as empty. If Rehoboam had employed some of the proper worship that God had ordained—sacrifice in the temple being the most obvious—perhaps it would have helped his heart.

Creativity in Presentation

The structure of this passage lends itself to an inductive approach. The commentary on Rehoboam's life being evil occurs at the end. Thus, one could begin by asking listeners how they would rate or evaluate Rehoboam. As the text is presented, the question can be kept in front of the congregation by asking at the end of each section, "Is he a good king or evil king?" or "How would you rate him?" Then, after the first three sections are covered the last section is presented, which states that he was evil because he was not a worshipper of YHWH. This leads into the application.

The application could lean more toward the importance of corporate worship, helping us keep our hearts set on seeking the Lord. Or there could be an emphasis on private or family worship or worship through a lifestyle of obedience. Another approach would be to speak to each of these areas. With any or all of these there is a great opportunity to show how trust in Christ is the foundation for all worship. With Rehoboam, the sacrifices that he should have offered were foreshadows of Christ's substitutionary death for us. The teaching/preaching of this passage could lead into celebrating of the Lord's Table, as an act of worship to help keep our focus on God's sacrificial love for us. Here is one possible structure:

- Present the story—Is Rehoboam a good king or an evil one?
  - Rehoboam and Judah obey the prophet and YHWH rewards (11:1–23)
  - Rehoboam and Judah forsake YHWH and YHWH punishes (12:1–5)
  - Rehoboam and Judah humble themselves and YHWH relents (12:6–12)
- Present the Chronicler's commentary (12:13–16)
- Explain the principle or main thrust
  - Obey God's Word, not to get (receive) good but because he is good
- Application: How is our worship?

DISCUSSION QUESTIONS

1. List some of the good that Rehoboam accomplished.

2. List some of the right responses that Rehoboam displayed.

3. What reason does the Chronicler give for describing Rehoboam as evil?

4. How would Rehoboam's life have been different if his heart had been set on seeking God?

5. How would our lives be different if our hearts were set on seeking the Lord?

6. What does it look like to have one's heart set on seeking the Lord?

7. How can outward acts affect inner motives?

2 Chronicles 13:1–14:1a (HB 13:23a)

EXEGETICAL IDEA
YHWH strengthened Judah for legitimately worshipping and exclusively trusting him, while he brought disaster on Israel for forsaking him.

THEOLOGICAL FOCUS
God strengthens those who worship and trust him alone, but he opposes those who forsake him and trust others.

PREACHING IDEA
Face battles by seeking the face of God.

PREACHING POINTERS
We live in a world that is filled with opposition to God's kingdom and will. Broadly speaking, we see culture moving away from biblical morality. The mindset is becoming more and more materialistic. Crime seems to be on the rise. Our governmental leaders seem to be more and more hostile toward each other. And the opposition to God's kingdom is also within each of us. The Chronicler gives us a guide as to how to face the battle that comes to us. Abijah faced opposition to God's rule and will with worship. This passage is important for us in a world filled with opposition to God and his kingdom. The way to face battles is to seek the face of God.

REIGN OF ABIJAH—WHEN PROPER WORSHIP LED TO VICTORY (13:1–14:1a [HB 13:23a])

LITERARY STRUCTURE AND THEMES (13:1–14:1a [HB 13:23a])

The passage begins with an introduction, providing some details for Abijah as king, and highlighting that Abijah of Judah and Jeroboam of Israel are waging war against one another. The war provides an appropriate backdrop to the rest of the account, since the account primarily consists of a series of contrasts between Judah and Israel. The contrasts begin as soon as Abijah confronts Israel. His confrontation takes two forms: a military attack and a verbal warning. Abijah's speech focuses on several contrasts between Judah and Israel, especially in terms of their worship. Following Abijah's speech, the series of contrasts continues as the passage recounts how YHWH wins the battle. These contrasts bring attention to the results of the battle: Judah grows stronger while Israel grows weaker. The passages end with a brief conclusion to Abijah's reign, including typical information regarding the sources of his account and the information of his death and burial.

Abijah is the first king to begin his reign after Israel and Judah separate into distinct kingdoms. Even though the Chronicler has described how the separation took place during Rehoboam's reign, during Abijah's reign he provides the clearest comments regarding the nature of these two kingdoms. Because Judah worships YHWH exclusively and properly—that is, with the proper personnel, implements, and practices—YHWH is with them. However, because Israel worships idols and rejects YHWH's chosen worship, they oppose YHWH. As a result, YHWH strengthens Judah but brings disaster on Israel.

- *Introduction of Abijah's Reign (13:1–2)*
- *Abijah Confronts Israel (13:3–12)*
- *YHWH Wins the Battle (13:13–19)*
- *Conclusion of Abijah's Reign (13:20–14:1 [HB 13:23a])*

EXPOSITION (13:1–14:1a [HB 13:23a])

Within the ancient Near Eastern world, there were numerous gods. This statement is intended in two senses. First, virtually every nation believed in a deity that possessed a special relationship with that nation and no other. Since there were numerous nations, there were numerous gods. Second, the people saw their national deity as one member of a larger group of major and minor divine figures. As a result, a significant question in the ancient Near Eastern world would be the question of whom one worshipped. However, this question was not the only significant one. Another would be the question of how one worshipped. The personnel, practices, place, and objects used in worship were all important for determining whether one's worship was proper or not. Within this context, the Chronicler shows that during the reign of Abijah, YHWH blesses Judah because they worship him exclusively and properly, but YHWH brings disaster to Israel because they reject him in their worship.

Introduction of Abijah's Reign (13:1–2)

The beginning of Abijah's reign introduces the king and sets the stage for the upcoming conflict between the apparently weaker Abijah (and Judah) and the apparently stronger Jeroboam (and Israel).

13:1–2. The introduction to Abijah's reign provides a clue to what drives the Chronicler's account of Abijah's reign: the relationship between Judah and Israel. Two specific points of information in the introduction are important for setting the stage for the rest of the narrative. First, the Chronicler synchronizes the reign of Judah's king Abijah with Israel's king Jeroboam. Abijah ascends Judah's throne after Jeroboam has ruled for eighteen years over Israel, which he led to separate from the Davidic monarchy (see 2 Chron. 10). Jeroboam has not only established a separate kingdom, but also a lengthy rule over it; in contrast, Abijah only rules for three years. Jeroboam should have had an upper hand. Second, the Chronicler states that Jeroboam and Abijah wage war against each other. This military conflict forms the backdrop for both kings' reigns.

Abijah vs. Abijam

Kings records the king's name as Abijam. One may account for the two names in different ways: (1) since the two names are so similar in Hebrew, they may be the result of orthographic differences; (2) one might be his birth name while the other might be his regnal name; (3) since Abijah translates as "My father is Yah(weh)" and Abijam translates as "My father is Yam [Sea]," Abijah may occur in Chronicles to match the Chronicler's positive picture of Abijah with an appropriate name; or (4) the Chronicler may be contrasting Jeroboam's son Abijah, who dies because of Jeroboam's sins (1 Kings 4:1–17), with Rehoboam's son Abijah, who lives and rules in his father's place (Amar 2017, 16). Any of these alternatives is possible and they may even overlap, so determining which is more probable is difficult (Dillard 1987, 101). Regardless of how the two names arose, the name Abijah fits this narrative in Chronicles well.

Abijah Confronts Israel (13:3–12)

As Judah and Israel meet each other in battle, Abijah calls out Israel for forsaking the Davidic dynasty and for forsaking YHWH through their false worship, and confirms that YHWH is on Judah's side because they are worshiping him properly.

13:3. Against this backdrop, Abijah and Jeroboam muster their troops to face each other in battle. Even though each king possesses a force of equally well-trained soldiers, Jeroboam possesses twice as many as Abijah (see excursus "Troop Numbers in Judah"). Jeroboam, the established king of Israel, appears to have the upper hand.

13:4–7. However, before the battle commences, Abijah addresses the army prepared to fight against him. He calls out to Jeroboam and all Israel and warns them not to attack. In his speech he draws three contrasts and concludes with a warning. First, he draws a contrast between Judah as a legitimate kingdom and Israel as an illegitimate one. Judah is a legitimate kingdom because YHWH has granted the kingdom to David and his descendants with a permanent covenant. The text describes the covenant as a "covenant of salt" (בְּרִית מֶלַח). The imagery appears to focus on the characteristic of salt to preserve. Numbers 18:19 describes a "covenant of salt" as "perpetual, eternal" (עוֹלָם). However, Israel is an illegitimate kingdom for several reasons: (1) Jeroboam himself is a rebellious servant of a legitimate king (Solomon), (2) he establishes his kingdom with several worthless scoundrels (as Abimelech did in Judges 9:4), and (3) he seizes his opportunity to rebel against the legitimate king Rehoboam while Rehoboam is still just an inexperienced young man (וּרְחַבְעָם הָיָה נַעַר וְרַךְ־לֵבָב; see sidebar "Inexperienced Young Man").

TRANSLATION ANALYSIS:

Two phrases describe the men who join Jeroboam when he rebels against Rehoboam: אֲנָשִׁים רֵקִים and בְּנֵי בְלִיַּעַל. The translations differ in their specific wording; however, most of them capture the essential sense of each phrase. Both phrases address the concept of uselessness or worthlessness. The first phrase describes those whom Abimelech hired to help him become king by killing all his brothers (Judg. 9:4–6). They were unprincipled and reckless. NET captures this sense best by translating it as "lawless." The second phrase reiterates this point; it describes several individuals, including the following: the men of Gibeah who abuse a Levite's concubine all night (Judg. 19:22; 20:13), the fool Nabal who rejects David's kindness (1 Sam. 25:17), and the false witness hired to take Naboth's field from him (1 Kings 21:10, 13). Both phrases carry negative connotations. For this reason, the word "scoundrels," occurring in many of the translations, works well. The overall presentation is a group of people who contribute nothing to society and should never be trusted because they are always looking for trouble.

Characterization of Jeroboam

This picture of Jeroboam's rebellion creates some tension with the earlier picture during Rehoboam's reign. The tension results from the two points of view and their purposes. During Rehoboam's reign, the Chronicler shows that the formation of Israel as a nation was part of YHWH's plan to fulfill the word of Ahijah to Jeroboam (this prophecy does not occur in Chronicles, but in 1 Kings 11:29–39). However, here the Chronicler shows the other side of the coin. God uses the results of Jeroboam's actions to fulfill the prophet's words; however, Jeroboam is still liable for the actions themselves. Abijah points out the rebellious nature of Jeroboam's actions and draws the conclusion that they undermine the legitimacy of his kingdom. The two accounts describing how Israel becomes a distinct nation must strike a balance between two facts for Chronicles: (1) Israel as a nation is the result of YHWH's will, and (2) it is also the result of a rebellion against YHWH's appointed kings. This balance results in a characterization of Jeroboam that grows more negative as one proceeds through the narrative

(Amar 2017, 22–23). For an interpretation of this passage characterizing Rehoboam poorly, see Cudworth 2014, 519–21, and Williamson 1977, 111–13.

13:8. Second, Abijah contrasts the power of each nation. Abijah portrays Judah as representing YHWH's kingdom ruled by the Davidic dynasty. Therefore, opposing Judah constitutes opposing YHWH's rule. The power behind Judah is truly YHWH's power. In contrast, when Abijah looks at Israel's power, he points out that Jeroboam's army consists of vast numbers of troops (הָמוֹן רָב) and possesses the golden calves that Jeroboam made for Israel to serve as their god(s). Even though the Chronicler does not report the details of Jeroboam's making these golden calves, he seems to refer to the same golden calves that 1 Kings 12:26–29 describes. Jeroboam has made these calves for Israel to worship. In 2 Chronicles 11:15 the Chronicler associates them with other pagan objects: שְׂעִירִים, translated as idols, satyrs, goat demons, or the like (*HALOT* s.v. "שָׂעִיר" 1341–42; see Translation Analysis for 2 Chron. 11:15). The Chronicler condemns making and worshipping such objects; however, Israel apparently views them as a source of power, helping them secure a military victory. Israel has a superior number of troops—and, from their perspective, the support of their pagan idols. On the other hand, Judah has YHWH as their true king and the Davidic dynasty as his representatives. Abijah's words set the stage for a showdown between YHWH and the pagan idols with their vast number of soldiers.

13:9–11. Third, Abijah contrasts how each nation relates to YHWH. To summarize, Israel has forsaken (עזב) YHWH, but Judah has not. Abijah focuses on the worship of each nation. Israel has forsaken YHWH in the following ways: (1) Jeroboam forces the sons of Aaron and the rest of the Levites to leave because he rejects them as the worship personnel in Israel, (2) he instead allows anyone with an adequate offering to become a priest, and (3) these new priests serve something that is "not god" (לֹא אֱלֹהִים), that is, the golden calves. The text makes clear that Jeroboam's calves, whether intended to represent YHWH or some other deity, are not divine. As idols, they are like other gods found in Chronicles: nothing more than the products of human work (2 Chron. 32:19) and useless (see comments on 1 Chron. 16:26). As a result, Jeroboam, whatever his intentions, has forsaken YHWH because he worships improperly: he uses idols, he rejects God's appointed priesthood, and he appoints a priesthood to whoever purchases it.

Offerings for a Priest

Exodus 29:1 describes the offering to be made when a priest is consecrated: one young bull and two rams. Jeroboam requires a larger amount, and Abijah's language suggests that the person who wants to become a priest must bring the offering himself. Exodus 29:1 does not suggest that the priest is responsible for providing the offering. For this reason, Abijah is communicating that Jeroboam is selling the priesthood in Israel.

In contrast, Judah has not forsaken YHWH. They have the proper worship personnel: the sons of Aaron and the Levites. Their personnel carry out worship in the proper way with the proper implements according the law of Moses: they make offerings to YHWH every morning and evening (as prescribed in Exod. 29:38–41; 30:7–8), they ensure the bread of presence is placed properly on the table (as prescribed in Lev. 24:5–9), and they oversee the burning of the lamps of the golden lampstand (as prescribed in Lev. 24:2–4). In summary, they are fulfilling YHWH's requirements (מִשְׁמֶרֶת יְהוָה) in maintaining YHWH's holy space (see Num. 3:7–8, 25–36; 4:27–32; 18:3–8, where this same vocabulary occurs regarding care for the tabernacle and its implements). Furthermore, before Solomon builds the temple, he indicates that the temple will be the place where YHWH's people can fulfill these requirements as part of their perpetual obligation (2 Chron. 2:4 [HB 3]). In the days of Abijah, Judah fulfills this obligation through its worship at the Jerusalem temple, the place appointed for this purpose.

Priests and Levites

In 2 Chronicles 13:9–10 there is some ambiguity regarding the relationship between priests, sons of Aaron, and Levites. Usually, the Chronicler clearly distinguishes the priests from the Levites. He uses the term "priest" in a specific way to refer to cult officials who exclusively perform certain activities prescribed by Moses and David. They descend from one branch of the Levitical tribe, the specific line of Aaron. On the other hand, Levites are their helpers and descend from the other lines of the Levitical tribe. In these verses, the Chronicler may be using the term "priest" more broadly to refer to any consecrated cult official. The ambiguity lies in two similar phrases. A look at 13:9 will illustrate the ambiguity. Second Chronicles 13:9 contains the phrase "priests of YHWH, sons of Aaron[, ?] and the Levites" (אֶת־כֹּהֲנֵי יְהוָה אֶת־בְּנֵי אַהֲרֹן וְהַלְוִיִּם). The question is whether both the sons of Aaron and the Levites constitute the priests of YHWH (in English this would appear as "priests of YHWH, the sons of Aaron and the Levites"), or whether only the sons of Aaron constitute the priests of YHWH (in English "priests of YHWH, sons of Aaron, and the Levites"). If one focuses on the book, then it is more likely that the priests and Levites are distinguished here as they are elsewhere. If one focuses on the immediate context, then it is more likely they are identified together as priests because Abijah is contrasting Israel's priests (not priests and assistants) with Judah's priests. Ultimately, the ambiguity cannot be resolved with much confidence.

13:12. Following these three contrasts, Abijah states a final warning for all Israel: they should not fight against YHWH because they will not win. Abijah's warning boils the conflict down to its essentials. Even though it appears to be a military campaign against another nation, the battle is actually about conflicting visions of worship. Judah worships YHWH, following Mosaic law with proper personnel, proper objects, and proper practices at the proper place. Israel worships idols, rejecting Mosaic law with its proper personnel, proper objects, proper practices, and proper place. As a result, YHWH stands on Judah's side as God (הָאֱלֹהִים) and as their leader with a group of trumpet-blowing priests while "not gods" (i.e., the calves) stand on Israel's side with a multitude of soldiers. If Israel chooses to fight with their large army and golden calves, they fight against YHWH. Abijah warns Israel that no matter the apparent odds, every fight against YHWH loses.

YHWH Wins the Battle (13:13–19)

Despite the apparent advantages that Israel holds, YHWH defeats Israel and secures Judah's victory because Judah relies on YHWH.

13:13. Israel does not listen to Abijah's warning. Instead, Jeroboam continues with his plan to attack. With his large number of troops, he employs an effective military tactic: he divides his forces and attacks Judah's forces on two fronts. At this point Israel has every seeming advantage over Judah: they have a long-reigning king leading them, they have double the number of soldiers, they have their golden calves with them, and now they have Judah surrounded.

13:14–15. Despite Israel's numerous advantages, they are no match for YHWH. When Judah's army realizes that it is surrounded, the soldiers do not respond with some military strategy. Instead, they cry out to YHWH. The priests blow on their trumpets and the soldiers shout. Then YHWH defeats Israel's army. Just as Abijah warned, the fight was really against YHWH, and YHWH has won the fight. The Chronicler does not mention any military means for this victory. He does not present the

battle as a struggle. The showdown between YHWH and Israel's golden calves is no contest. YHWH proves himself to be strong enough to overcome his enemy, despite their numerous apparent advantages.

> **Role of Shouting in Combat**
> The way in which Judah calls out to YHWH is that the priests blow on the trumpets and the soldiers shout. At the same time this activity is military in nature. For example, when Gideon and his small force engage the Midianites, they blow the trumpets and shout the battle cry "For the sword of YHWH and Gideon" (Judg. 7:19–21). Blowing the trumpets and shouting usually inspires the warriors to fight, but here in Chronicles, Judah doesn't fight—YHWH does.

13:16–19. After the Chronicler's initial comment that YHWH defeats Israel, he shifts the focus back to Abijah and the rest of Judah. His description of the battle emphasizes that YHWH has fought the battle, but Judah experiences the victory. The Chronicler makes this point by recording several results of the battle. He records that Israel flees from Judah, Judah defeats Israel soundly as five hundred thousand of Israel's troops fall in combat, and Judah captures several cities as Israel withdraws. Abijah captures the cities Bethel, Jeshanah, and Ephron, along with the villages near them. The Chronicler summarizes the results of the battle in 13:18 as he contrasts the fate of Israel to the fate of Judah: Israel loses while Judah wins.

TRANSLATION ANALYSIS:
One of the challenges of translating this verse is determining how to treat the relationship between Israel and Judah and the verbs associated with them. The sentence appears to be carefully worded to avoid saying directly that Judah defeats Israel. This point likely results from the observation that YHWH actually fights the battle. Instead, the verse speaks about Israel and then Judah separately. In context, the best translation

of the verb describing Israel (וַיִּכָּנְעוּ) is probably "was defeated" (NET), while the best translation for the verb describing Judah is "was victorious" (NIV) or "succeeded" (CSB). The idea is that Israel loses while Judah wins; however, it is not because Judah directly defeats Israel. YHWH does that.

Significance of Bethel

Of the cities Judah captures, Bethel is most prominent. The Chronicler may mention it here because Abijah has mentioned the golden calves that Jeroboam made. Even though Chronicles does not specifically identify Bethel as one of the sites where Jeroboam set up the golden calves, he likely assumes the reader will know this fact. The fact that Abijah captures Bethel adds insult to injury regarding the powerlessness of the calves. Not only are they unable to deliver Israel from Judah, but they are even unable to protect one of the cities where they stand.

For the Chronicler, Israel loses, and Judah wins because Judah trusts (נִשְׁעֲנוּ) YHWH. Although one may say that Judah trusts YHWH in general, this verb here refers specifically to their trust in YHWH to win the battle. In fact, this passage anticipates the next time that Judah will face a large army. In 2 Chronicles 14:10, Asa prays to YHWH, confessing that Judah trusts (נִשְׁעֲנוּ) YHWH to win the battle. YHWH wins that battle for Judah, also against the odds. In this case, it appears that the Chronicler is focusing on the power of YHWH to deliver from a military threat. For the book's first readers, who held relatively little power or influence within a large and powerful empire, such a message would lead to a confidence that YHWH can win a battle against all odds, even when the human means for doing so are unknown or lacking.

Conclusion of Abijah's Reign (13:20–14:1a [HB 13:23a])

The closing comments regarding Abijah's reign show that Jeroboam (and Israel) grows weaker while Abijah (and Judah) grows stronger.

13:20–21. Following the aftermath of the battle, the Chronicler provides a summary of the remaining days of Jeroboam and Abijah. Just as the fates of Israel and Judah contrast sharply in the battle, so also Abijah and Jeroboam contrast sharply in their remaining days. Jeroboam never regains his power while Abijah is still alive. Eventually, however, YHWH brings about his death. In contrast, Abijah increases his power during the rest of his life. The Chronicler provides a tangible example of his increasing power by listing the number of wives and children that Abijah gains (see sidebar "Large Families as Blessing").

For the book's first readers, the contrast between Jeroboam and Abijah would remind them that YHWH defeats those who forsake him, but he strengthens those who do not. More specifically, Jeroboam rebels against his master, makes the golden calves, and rejects YHWH's appointed priests. Therefore, Jeroboam's fate warns them against insurrection against Davidic authority and worshiping in illegitimate settings with illegitimate gods and priests. On the other hand, Abijah supports YHWH's priests and their work in the temple and trusts YHWH to deliver him in military conflict. Abijah's fate encourages the first readers to support the priests and Levites whom YHWH has ordained and to trust in his deliverance rather than some other means.

13:22–14:1a (HB 13:23a). The closing words of Abijah's reign follow the typical pattern for closing a king's reign: a source citation for finding further information, a notice of the king's death and his burial, and a statement naming the next king.

THEOLOGICAL FOCUS

God strengthens those who worship and trust him alone, but he opposes those who forsake him and trust others.

In many ways, the battle between Abijah and Jeroboam reveals contrasting visions of worship. On the one hand, Abijah (and Judah) worships God properly by following the instructions for worship as laid out in Mosaic law. These instructions focus on the proper personnel (i.e., priests and Levites), the proper objects (e.g., bread of presence and golden lampstand), and the proper practices (e.g., offerings morning and evening). On the other hand, Jeroboam (and Israel) worships improperly by violating Mosaic law. He appoints illegitimate personnel (i.e., anyone who purchases the priesthood), uses illegitimate objects (i.e., the golden calves), and follows illegitimate practices (i.e., carrying idols into battle). The passage aims to contrast sharply these two visions of worship.

Theologically, this contrast reveals two points regarding worship. First, worship should correspond to the nature of God. Chronicles repeatedly shows how idols as human-made objects are useless. An idol cannot see, hear, taste, smell, touch, move, and so on. As a result, an idol is not like God. Therefore, worshipping an idol is not worshipping God (see Lynch 2014b, 76–78, for how Chronicles develops this point). Proper worship reflects God's nature. Second, worship should correspond to God's instructions. Mosaic law communicates God's specific instructions regarding the priesthood and the Levitical assistants. When Jeroboam appoints anyone with the right payment as a priest, he violates God's specific instructions so that he may follow the customs of the nations around him. He allows the culture to dictate the form of worship rather than God's instructions. This temptation to allow culture to dictate worship continues. The book of Hebrews addresses some of the changes in worship practices because of Jesus's sacrifice (e.g., Heb. 9:1–10:18), showing that animal sacrifices are no longer necessary. Furthermore, Hebrews continues by providing instructions regarding worship together (Heb. 10:19–25). Although some of the specific practices may change, the principle of worshipping according to God's nature and God's Word never changes.

The battle between Abijah and Jeroboam illustrates that the real contest is not a physical one but a spiritual one. Although the two armies face each other in combat, their strength and tactics do not determine the outcome. The contest is really between Judah's God and Israel's "no gods." In fact, virtually every battle in Chronicles is really a divine matter more than a human one, even though human beings may fight one another. At the same time, the apostle Paul picks up on this theme in describing the struggle that Christian churches face: "For our struggle is not against flesh and blood, but against the rulers, against the powers, against the world rulers of this darkness, against the spiritual forces of evil in the heavens" (Eph. 6:12 NET). In this way, these historical battles take on theological significance and point to the unseen forces operating behind this seen world.

The battle between Abijah and Jeroboam illustrates another important theological truth: God can win the victory regardless of the odds. As mentioned, this passage presents a contest between Judah and Israel, between God and "no gods" (i.e., the golden calves). From a practical perspective, Israel has every advantage: a larger army, a tactical ambush, and a more seasoned king. From a religious perspective, Israel also has their gods with them in battle. Apparently, Israel believes that such idols will bring them power. However, despite Israel's advantages and beliefs, God wins. Jesus displays this same power through his resurrection from the dead and his ascension into heaven (1 Cor. 15:20–28; 1 Peter 3:21–22). Furthermore, at the end of all things, God will establish his power and strength as he finally and fully defeats all his enemies. The passage illustrates that no power, practical or religious, can stand against God.

PREACHING AND TEACHING STRATEGIES

Exegetical and Theological Synthesis

This passage brings into focus the relationship of worship to fighting a battle. Abijah had to battle Jeroboam, who wanted to overthrow the southern kingdom. Abijah's battle was for more than the protection of his own throne. The battle was about God's kingdom. Jeroboam was striving to take down God's appointed king and do away with the worship of YHWH. Even in our day we face ideas that erode our worship of God and people who lead us to go against his revealed will. This battle is not only external; we also face this same battle within ourselves.

The other theme in this passage is correct worship. Abijah leads Judah to rightly worship YHWH: in the right place, with the right leadership, and the right practices. We know that these are right because they are in keeping with God's character and revealed will. Abijah's worship even extends into the battle itself, which demands that we wrestle with the relationship of worship to the battles in our lives. Right worship puts us into a position to enjoy the blessing of the all-powerful God, who always wins. Abijah went into battle with the foundation of worship. When we worship correctly, our trust is enhanced because we are more aware of our Lord's character and will. He is all-powerful and nothing can stand against him. The best way to face battles is to seek the face of God.

Preaching Idea

Face battles by seeking the face of God.

Contemporary Connections

What does it mean?

At the 2005 Kenyon College graduation ceremonies the speaker, David Foster Wallace, said that everyone worships something or someone—and it will eat you alive. You don't have a choice about worship; the only choice you have is what you worship. He went on to list the objects of worship referring to JC and YHWH, other religious figures, materialism, beauty, and intellect (https://www.youtube.com/watch?v=-AK87zdMzRI). Three years later, he took his own life because of depression. He rightly described that we all search for something to worship, but tragically he could not find something or someone to worship that could give him peace. Perhaps what he worshipped did just what he said it would do—"eat you alive." In stark contrast is the God that Abijah worships: the God of Abraham, Isaac, and Jacob. The God who became man and dwelt among us. He does not eat us alive; rather, he gives us life.

Whom we worship affects how we live. In the case of Abijah, it affected how he fought a battle against those who sought to rebel against God's revealed will and God's character. Jeroboam created what he would worship, hoping his gods would grant him success, but these false gods created by man could not deliver. The making of golden calves to worship is foreign to our culture, but creating our own gods is still done today; David Foster Wallace listed some of them. It is strange that people worship and submit to their own creation. This passage tells us that YHWH is the only one to worship. He is not our creation, and the worship of him will bring great benefits and victory. Of course, we need to be careful that we remember that it is *his* victory that *we* share in, not our self-centered victory that he shares in.

Is it true?

When it comes to treasures, Jesus told us that where our treasure is, our hearts will be also (Matt. 6:21). When we put money, effort, and time (our treasures) into something, our hearts will follow. In a similar way, what we worship will control our lives. When the legendary Elvis Presley died back in the 1970s

I was serving as a youth pastor. One of our young ladies, who was a loyal and somewhat fanatic fan of Elvis, all but demanded that we hold a special memorial service to honor the king of rock and roll. What never occurred to me or any of the other pastors seemed only fitting to her. I suppose she had pictures of him on her wall, listened to his music, read books and magazines about him. Her worship affected her life.

Our worship of God should affect how we live and think. If we are reading his Word, praying, and being around his people on a regular and frequent basis it will change us. When we gather and sing "How Great Thou Art," we have those words in our minds and the tune in our hearts. Furthermore, we have the memory and affirmation of many others singing alongside us. It was not only our voice that sang these words of that proven hymn: "And when I think that God, His Son not sparing, sent Him to die, I scarce can take it in." Dozens, perhaps thousands, sang it as well. Those voices of our brothers and sisters in Christ echo in our minds and reenforce our knowledge and trust of our great God. Now, it needs to be said that these acts of worship must be done in such a way that God's character and order are honored. That will look different in different cultures.

Now what?

What battle are you facing, in which God's character or revealed will is being challenged? In might be a school system that teaches that gender is unrelated to biology; an employer that encourages dishonesty; a state that votes to legalize the killing of those still in the womb; being faithful to a job that right now is boring and seems to have no path for advancement; trusting God's good hand in the face of a chronic illness that keeps you from experiencing the most basic joys of life such as walking, seeing, eating, being with people; or battling the powerful draw of internet sites that are clearly against God and his work. Where is your battle?

The best way to face these battles is to seek the face of God through worship. For those who cannot attend corporate worship, technology can't bring the people into a hospital room but it can bring in a live worship service.

Abijah described Judah's worship as following YHWH's guidelines. It seems that the evangelical church community is struggling to find guidelines for corporate worship. The New Testament does not give detailed instructions, and the specific guidelines of Old Testament worship were centered around sacrifice—thus, when Jesus offered the ultimate sacrifice for all our sins, worship practices were dramatically changed. But *whom* we worship has not changed. He still should be worshipped with proper personnel and correct theology. Worship practices and styles vary greatly, but we must still seek to focus on our great God in a way that pleases him. In his book *Worship Matters*, Bob Kauflin gives us many good thoughts and guidelines for our worship today. He cautions us to be careful of a "concert mentality" in which "worship sets" are performed (2008, 59).

Creativity in Presentation

This passage has two major parts: Abijah's speech and the battle. The first part could be delivered as a speech. After introducing the passage and the thrust of the message, one could take on the role of Abijah or perhaps of Ezra reading the speech to his first hearers. The congregation could be asked to imagine they were with the northern tribes to whom Abijah spoke. It could be memorized or read. The important element is to present it as though it were being spoken. By setting the scene, you could bring in many details not in the text to add a sense of reality. But the actual speech would be word-for-word from the text. As always, our imagination, while helpful, is not the source of our teaching—only the text is. Either before or after presenting the speech, highlight the teaching points of the speech, then move into the description of the battle and the results. The application follows the presentation of the full story. Here is one possible structure:

- Introduction: battles we face
- Present the text
  - Introduction (13:1–2)
  - Abijah confronts Israel (13:3–12)
  - YHWH wins the battle (13:13–19)
  - Conclusion (13:20–14:1 [HB 13:23a])
- Apply the text: the best way to face battles is to seek the face of God.

DISCUSSION QUESTIONS

1. How does physically attending a sporting event affect you when your team wins?

2. How does attending a graduation ceremony of a son or daughter affect you?

3. Would these events be the same if only three people attended? Why or why not?

4. How do corporate experiences affect us as individuals?

5. How does our corporate worship affect us?

6. How does individual reading of the Word and prayer affect us?

2 Chronicles 14:1b (HB 13:23b)–16:14

EXEGETICAL IDEA
When Asa relied on YHWH, YHWH blessed him; but when he did not, YHWH punished him.

THEOLOGICAL FOCUS
Relying on God is always right and shapes the future of one's life.

PREACHING IDEA
Don't end up an independent, grumpy old person.

PREACHING POINTERS
The essence of the message of the whole Bible is that we must depend upon God for the forgiveness of sin, through the work of Jesus on our behalf. Our salvation is completely dependent upon him and his work. This concept of dependence should continue throughout our lives, not just when we come to faith. This passage teaches us the importance of remaining dependent upon God throughout our whole lives. Asa starts out relying upon God, but ends up living independently from God. He starts out well but ends up an independent, and probably grumpy, old man.

REIGN OF ASA—IMPORTANCE OF RELYING ON YHWH (14:1b [HB 13:23b]–16:14)

LITERARY STRUCTURE AND THEMES (14:1b [HB 13:23b]–16:14)

Asa's reign neatly divides into two periods: a period of obedience and a period of disobedience. Two words tie together both parts of his reign: "seeking" (דרשׁ) and "relying" (*niphal* שׁען). During the first part of his reign, Asa seeks YHWH by removing pagan worship and committing Judah to worship YHWH alone. Asa relies on YHWH to deliver the nation when a large Cushite army invades the land. As a result of Asa's seeking and relying on YHWH, YHWH blesses him, especially with peace. In fact, peace frames this part of Asa's reign. Peace occurs at the beginning (14:1 [HB 13:23]), at the end (15:19), and in the middle (14:5–6 [HB 4–5]; 15:15).

During the second part of his reign, Asa does not rely on YHWH when the northern kingdom of Israel attacks. Instead, he uses some political maneuvering to stop the attack, forming an alliance with Aram. As a result, the rest of Asa's reign features military conflict rather than peace. Furthermore, Asa becomes ill with a severe disease; however, even then he does not seek (דרשׁ) YHWH but the doctors.

One further feature contrasts the first part of Asa's reign to the second: his response to a prophetic word. In the first part, when Asa returns from victory over the Cushite army, Azariah delivers a prophetic warning to encourage Asa to seek YHWH. As a result, Asa makes a covenant with all Judah to seek YHWH alone. In the second part, after Asa removes the threat of Israel's attack, Hanani confronts Asa for not relying on YHWH. As a result, Asa becomes angry, imprisons Hanani, and mistreats the people. Asa's response to the prophetic word reinforces the picture of Asa's seeking and relying on YHWH or not.

Asa's reign illustrates how YHWH treats Judah's kings when they seek and rely upon him and how he treats them when they do not. The way YHWH treats Asa is part of a pattern for the way he treats other kings as well: YHWH rewards dependent obedience but punishes independent disobedience.

- *Asa Relies on YHWH (14:1b [HB 13:23b]–15:19)*
- *Asa Does Not Rely on YHWH (16:1–19)*

EXPOSITION (14:1b [HB 13:23b]–16:14)

The saying goes, "There are no atheists in foxholes." Although the terrifying, life-or-death nature of war often drives soldiers to look beyond themselves to something spiritual, most contemporary Western culture does not view religious faith as a key factor for deciding the outcome of a battle. However, those living in the ancient Near Eastern world apparently viewed religious faith and practice as essential for securing victory. Kings, priests, and prophets would perform various rituals to gain divine favor so that their god(s) might strengthen them to win the victory (for examples, see Schmitt 2014, 149–61; Trimm 2017, 567–88).

Against this backdrop, the Chronicler presents a somewhat different picture. Even though he records Asa's devotion to YHWH and response to military encounters, the Chronicler focuses on YHWH's power to provide peace or create conflict despite human actions taken. In

Asa's first military encounter, the Chronicler records no rituals and no military preparations, only Asa's cry to YHWH for help and Judah's gathering of the spoils of victory. Because Asa relies on YHWH, YHWH defeats the opposing army and grants Judah peace. In Asa's second military encounter, the Chronicler records Asa's political maneuvering to solve the conflict himself. His maneuvering seems to work. However, because Asa does not rely on YHWH, YHWH promises that Judah will experience constant military conflict. In the end, when Asa relies on YHWH, YHWH blesses him with peace, but when he does not rely on YHWH, YHWH punishes him.

Asa Relies on YHWH (14:1b [HB 13:23b]–15:19)

In the first part of Asa's reign, YHWH rewards Asa with peace because he removes pagan worship, relies on YHWH in the face of a military invasion, and makes a covenant with the people to follow YHWH.

14:1b–5a (HB 13:23b–14:4a). The Chronicler introduces Asa as a king who does what is good and upright. To prove the point, the Chronicler shows how Asa tries to remove illicit worship and promote proper worship in Judah. He does so by destroying objects used in such worship and commanding the people to seek YHWH alone. The Chronicler begins by showing the extent of the objects Asa destroys, including the altars, high places, pillars, and Asherah poles (הָאֲשֵׁרִים, see sidebar "Asherah"). When Asa destroys these objects, he obeys nearly verbatim the commands of Deuteronomy 7:5. As he follows these commands, he also tells his people to do the same. He calls on Judah to seek YHWH (and here the implication is to seek YHWH only) and obey the law and commandments. Here, to seek YHWH is a way of speaking of being a worshipper or follower of YHWH. The law and commandments here is likely a generic designation for obeying whatever YHWH communicates.

This would include the law of Moses, especially since Deuteronomy 7:5 is in view in the context. Furthermore, the Chronicler shows the geographical extent of Asa's activity by highlighting that Asa destroyed the high places and shrines (הַחַמָּנִים, see sidebar "Structures for Illicit Objects") throughout Judah.

Obeying Deuteronomy 7:5

One can see that the Chronicler intends to show that Asa is obeying the commands of Deuteronomy 7:5 by the close verbal correlation between it and 2 Chronicles 14:3–5a. Sometimes, English translation can hide the closer verbal correspondences. Nonetheless, for instance, in this case both verses speak of smashing (*piel* שׁבר) pillars (מַצֵּבֹת) and cutting down (*piel* גדע) Asherah poles (הָאֲשֵׁרִים).

The structure of these verses is as follows:

A   Asa destroys pagan objects.
  B   Asa commands the people to seek YHWH and obey his law.
A′   Asa again destroys pagan objects.

This concentric structure points to the center of these actions: to seek YHWH and obey his law. Asa's first righteous activity involves establishing proper worship, that is, worshipping YHWH exclusively without illicit objects or sites.

14:5b–8 (HB 14:4b–7). The account turns from Asa's activity to its results. Asa's concern for proper worship leads to YHWH's blessings. The Chronicler points out three ways in which YHWH blesses Asa and Judah: (1) Judah has peace, (2) Judah builds and fortifies several cities, and (3) Asa raises up a well-trained army (גִּבּוֹרֵי חָיִל) with many troops (see excursus "Troop Numbers in Judah"). Judah's peace primarily entails the lack of conflict—that is, the king and the nation are free from external hostility and internal unrest. The fortified cities and large, well-equipped army portray a secure, formidable nation (even though YHWH decides the outcome of any battle regardless of fortification or military strength).

Dialogue Elaborates Narrative as One Event
In this case, the Chronicler employs dialogue to further elaborate a point made in the narrative. In 14:6 (HB 5) the narrative reads that Asa built some fortified cities. Second Chronicles 14:7 (HB 6) records Asa's encouragement to fortify the cities. The latter dialogue is an elaboration of the former narrative. In other words, these are not two separate episodes but a single one.

14:7 (HB 6). At the center of these verses, Asa encourages the people to fortify their cities. In his encouragement, he states that the land still lies before them. This expression shows that Judah has possession of the land as a reward for their obedience. By including the expression here, the Chronicler foreshadows the upcoming Cushite invasion (see R. Klein 2012, 216). Furthermore, Asa makes the following points: (1) Judah has the land because they seek YHWH, (2) Judah has peace because they seek YHWH, and (3) they should fortify the cities because they have the land and peace. In this way, the text makes more explicit the connection between Asa's obedience and the nation's conditions.

14:9 (HB 8). Following a long period of peace that YHWH has given, the narrative takes a surprising turn: a large army invades Judah. The narrative gives no indication why this invasion takes place; however, it does not appear to be punishment for any wrongdoing (see Japhet 2009, 153). Instead, as it turns out, the invasion becomes an opportunity for Asa and Judah to rely on YHWH.

14:9–11 (HB 8–10). The Chronicler sets the stage for the invasion. On one side, the large Cushite army, composed of a million soldiers along with three hundred chariots, advances upon Judah's fortified city of Mareshah. Asa prepares his much smaller force (580,000 soldiers compared to one million, and no chariots) to meet the invading army in a valley near Mareshah. As the two armies face one another, Asa calls out to YHWH to help Judah win the battle. He clearly professes that YHWH is the only one who is powerful enough to help Judah, that they are relying (*niphal* שׁען) on him, and that YHWH is their God. To emphasize YHWH's power, the text sharply contrasts YHWH to the invaders. YHWH is אֱלֹהִים ("God"), a term often associated with strength (regarding the use in Chronicles, see Williams 2019, 85–86), but the invaders are אֱנוֹשׁ ("human"), a word likely playing on the notion of weakness (see *HALOT* s.v. "אנשׁ" 73; see Waltke 2007, 133). Also, to emphasize that Judah trusts in YHWH, Asa states that Judah "comes against this multitude in your [YHWH's] name." David uses the same expression when he faces Goliath in battle (1 Sam. 17:45). The Chronicler depicts this battle as a contest between YHWH and the invaders, between the truly strong and the weak, much like David and Goliath.

14:12–15 (HB 11–14). It comes as no surprise that after Asa cries for help and professes that YHWH is Judah's God, YHWH defeats the invading army. At this point, the Chronicler gives no military details of the battle or Judah's role in it. YHWH defeats the enemy when Judah calls out for help. Only during the aftermath of the conflict does Judah's army come into view. They pursue the fleeing Cushites, attack their cities and herdsmen, and carry away a large quantity of spoils. However, even in these activities YHWH is the primary actor (Japhet 2009, 100–101). YHWH and his army (in this case, Judah) defeat the Cushites so thoroughly that they can no longer recover, and it is YHWH's terror that allows Judah to defeat the cities around Gerar. The Chronicler describes the battle in a way that emphasizes that YHWH can prevail over an enemy regardless of the odds, that he responds to those who call and rely on him for help, and that when he defeats the enemy those who come in his name and rely on him for victory enjoy the spoils.

Asa's battle against Zerah closely resembles Abijah's battle against Jeroboam (2 Chron. 13). Several textual elements connect these battles. First, both Asa and Abijah face a much larger army (in both cases referred to as a crowd [הָמוֹן]) with other tactical advantages. Jeroboam attacks Abijah on two fronts (2 Chron. 13:13) while Zerah brings chariots (2 Chron. 14:9 [HB 8]). Second, both kings speak before the battle begins. Abijah proclaims that YHWH is Judah's God and they have not forsaken him (2 Chron. 13:10). Asa proclaims that YHWH is Judah's God and they come in his name (2 Chron. 14:11 [HB 10]). Third, both cry out to YHWH for help (Abijah: 2 Chron. 13:14; Asa: 2 Chron. 14:11 [HB 10]). Fourth, both kings rely (*niphal* שׁען) on YHWH (Abijah: 2 Chron. 13:18; Asa: 2 Chron. 14:11 [HB 10]). Fifth, immediately after each king cries out, YHWH defeats (נגף) the enemy (Abijah: 2 Chron. 13:15; Asa: 2 Chron. 14:12 [HB 11]). Sixth, after YHWH defeats the enemy, Judah pursues them and conquers cities along the way (Abijah: 2 Chron. 13:19; Asa: 2 Chron. 14:14–16 [HB 13–15]).

The parallel accounts highlight two of the Chronicler's central themes. First, they serve as illustrations of what happens when Judah relies on YHWH. Second, they highlight the importance of proper worship. Both kings profess that YHWH is their God, and the Chronicler highlights Judah's proper worship before each battle (Abijah: 2 Chron. 13:10–12; Asa: 2 Chron. 14:3–5 [HB 2–4]). These points would resonate with the first readers because they faced temptations to worship other gods who promised to give them peace, health, and wealth. They also faced the temptation to neglect YHWH's temple in Jerusalem. For instance, they might allow the temple to fall into disuse and disrepair, or fail to provide adequate acceptable sacrifices to help maintain the priests and Levites (cf. Neh. 13:4–13; Mal. 1:6–14; 3:8–11). These parallel battle scenes address both temptations and encourage the readers to rely on YHWH alone and to worship him properly.

15:1–7. As Asa and his troops return to Jerusalem, an otherwise unknown person named Azariah meets them with a divinely inspired message. Azariah challenges Judah to continue to seek YHWH and not abandon him. The message begins and ends with the central points: (1) YHWH treats Judah the way that Judah treats him, and (2) Judah should keep following YHWH because he will reward such activity. These two points summarize well the principle of retribution: YHWH rewards those who trust and obey him faithfully, and he punishes those who abandon and disobey him.

> **Divine Inspiration to Speak YHWH's Word**
> The Chronicler describes how God inspires the message by stating that the Spirit of God came upon him. Similar expressions elsewhere in Chronicles indicate when a person other than a prophet delivers a prophetic message: 1 Chronicles 12:19 speaks of Amasai, a captain of the thirty; 2 Chronicles 20:14 speaks of Jahaziel, a Levite; 2 Chronicles 24:20 speaks of Zechariah, son of the priest Jehoiada. This usage raises the question whether Azariah is a prophet or not. Answering the question requires addressing three pieces of evidence. First, he is not identified as a prophet initially. The first verse only refers to him as Azariah son of Oded. Second, his father's name Oded is associated with a prophet during the time of Ahaz; however, such clearly cannot be Azariah's father, since the prophet Oded who prophesies during Ahaz's reign lives much later than Azariah. Therefore, this Oded is otherwise unknown in the Hebrew Bible. Third, 15:8 contains a complicated textual situation. MT reads as follows, "As Asa heard the words and the prophecy." If such is the case, then Azariah is not identified as a prophet, only someone temporarily inspired to give a prophetic message.

15:3–6. In the middle of the message, Azariah describes Israel when it has "no true God, no teaching priest, and no law." A closer look at these elements should prove profitable. First, the expression "true God" (אֱלֹהִים אֱמֶת or אֱלֹהֵי אֱמֶת) occurs only here and in Jeremiah 10:10. The context of Jeremiah 10:10 helps clarify the sense of the phrase because of its context. YHWH is declared to be "the true God, the living God, and eternal King." In this case, the expression communicates that YHWH is the only one who really lives up to the idea of God. Therefore, the Chronicler is stating that during the period described, Israel did not worship YHWH, the only one who truly embodies all that the word "god" entails. Second, the "teaching priest" (כֹּהֵן מוֹרֶה) likely recalls passages such as Leviticus 10:11 and 2 Kings 12:3. In Leviticus 10:11 YHWH assigns the priests the responsibility of teaching the Mosaic law. In 2 Kings 12:3 Jehoiada instructs Joash with the result that Joash does what is right in YHWH's estimation. The Chronicler is describing a time in which Israel did not have a priest who fulfilled the responsibility to instruct the people in the law. Third, since Israel did not have a priest to teach the law, Israel did not live by it. The Chronicler describes a time in which Israel was virtually unaware of YHWH's instructions handed down by Moses.

Without these three, Israel lives in a time of constant conflict and turmoil. However, even during this time, when Israel seeks YHWH he is found by them and, by implication, helps them. The situation described resembles the period of the judges in which Israel suffered through constant conflict, but when they turned to YHWH he raised up a judge and delivered them. At the same time, the first readers would likely recognize the situation as one like their own. The temple with its worship is not everything that it should be. They face conflict, turmoil, and insecurity. At the same time, they can have hope that if they seek YHWH, they will find him (see Deut.

4:30). To remedy the situation, Judah should seek the true God (not false gods), maintain a teaching priest, and live by God's instruction.

15:8–18. When Azariah finishes speaking, Asa immediately obeys. The opening and closing of the section recounts specific acts of seeking YHWH (see sidebar "Seeking YHWH" for more details regarding this expression). In both places, the first act consists of rejecting false worship, while the second act consists of promoting proper worship. In the opening Asa rejects false worship by removing the pagan idols from all the territory he ruled, that is, Judah, Benjamin, and the cities in the hill country of Ephraim (see 14:5 [HB 4] where only Judah is mentioned). In the closing he does so by destroying the image of Asherah that his grandmother Maacah made before he removed her from serving as queen mother. In the opening Asa promotes proper worship by restoring YHWH's altar, preparing it to receive the sacrifice of hundreds of oxen and thousands of sheep that Judah brought back from their victory against the Cushites. In the closing he promotes proper worship by depositing in YHWH's temple some of the silver, gold, and other items which his father and he took in battle.

The Role of Queen Mother

The term usually translated "queen mother" (גְּבִירָה) apparently refers to an official position held by a female close to the king. Since the person may not be the king's mother, the translation "Great Lady" may be more appropriate (Bowen 2001, 618). The OT provides few details to determine the responsibilities of this role although ANE parallels may provide some insight (Sosik 2009, 11–12).

15:9–15. At the heart of this section describing his obedience, Asa makes a covenant with the people to seek YHWH alone and to punish anyone who does not. The Chronicler sets up the making of the covenant by describing Asa as gathering the people to Jerusalem, not only from Judah and Benjamin but also several people from the northern tribes (Ephraim, Manasseh, and Simeon) who migrated to Judah because they observed that YHWH was with Asa. Once the people assemble, they make many sacrifices from the animals captured following their victory over the Cushites. Next, they make a simple covenant: they will seek YHWH and put to death anyone who does not seek him. Drawing on language from Deuteronomy (see esp. Deut. 4:29 and its context), this covenant commits the people in Judah to worship YHWH exclusively. The Chronicler points out that all the people respond by celebrating with a lot of noise from shouts and trumpet blasts because they are excited to make this type of commitment to YHWH. As seen throughout Asa's reign, YHWH responds by providing peace.

Including Northern Tribes with Asa

By including these northern tribes, the Chronicler draws out three points. First, the Chronicler shows that some northerners continued to worship YHWH properly even when Israel itself fell into idolatry (cf. other northerner emigrations: 2 Chron. 11:13–14; 30:11). Second, the Chronicler confirms Asa's devotion to YHWH, since Azariah declared that YHWH will be with him as long as he is with YHWH (2 Chron. 15:2). Third, the Chronicler confirms that YHWH rewards Asa's obedience. Immediately, following his obedience, the Chronicler shows that YHWH's presence is evident, even to those living in Israel.

The covenant corresponds closely to Azariah's warning to Asa. Azariah tells Asa that if Judah seeks YHWH, he will be found (15:2), and in the covenant Judah seeks YHWH and he is found (15:15). At the same time, Azariah describes a time of trouble that results because Israel does not have a true God, a teaching priest, or law. Asa's covenant deals with the first of these conditions: Judah makes a covenant to worship YHWH, the true God,

exclusively. However, the Chronicler does not mention any efforts under Asa to address the lack of a teaching priest or law. These efforts await the reign of Asa's son Jehoshaphat (2 Chron. 17:7–9). Therefore, even though Asa and Judah make such a covenant, they do not fully address the conditions that lead to troubled times like those Azariah describes (2 Chron. 15:3–6).

15:17–18. The closing verses of this section provide an ambiguous picture of Asa and foreshadow his coming troubles. Two points are clearest. First, the Chronicler mentions that no one has removed the high places from Israel, yet Asa is still faithful "all his days" (כָּל־יָמָיו). Even though these high places are generally located in Israel, their presence still creates an ambiguous picture. Second, the section closes with a note that Judah experiences no more war until the thirty-fifth year of Asa's reign. Such a statement at least suggests that some significant event will take place at that time. However, it does not hint at Asa's reactions to such an event. The reader must continue on to find that information.

TRANSLATION ANALYSIS:

Two issues arise in translating this verse. First, one must address the sense of the expression that "Asa's heart was complete" (לְבַב־אָסָא הָיָה שָׁלֵם). In the context of Chronicles, this expression describes the extent of a person's devotion. For example, the Chronicler describes Amaziah as a king who did what was right but not with a whole heart. Given the ambiguous picture of Amaziah's obedience, the expression means that he obeyed, but inconsistently or incompletely. In the case of Asa, his devotion to YHWH has been complete and consistent. Second, one must address the sense of the expression "all his days" (כָּל־יָמָיו). Although this phrase can indicate every day of a person's life from birth to death, such a reading is unlikely here. More likely, it refers to his lifetime up to this point in the narrative. In other words, the Chronicler emphasizes Asa's consistent, clear obedience up to this point in his life. To put these expressions together, one might summarize by stating that Asa remained completely devoted to YHWH each and every day of his life up to this point.

Asa Does Not Rely on YHWH (16:1–19)

In the second part of Asa's reign, Asa does not rely on YHWH in the face of foreign aggression or severe disease, so YHWH punishes.

16:1–6. After Asa experiences a long period of peace, Israel's king Baasha starts a war with him. To gain a strategic military advantage and restrict Judah's movement beyond its borders, Baasha fortifies Ramah. The Chronicler leaves out all other details about the military conflict. He moves directly to Asa's response. Instead of gathering his troops, encouraging them to follow YHWH, and crying out for YHWH's help as he had done before, Asa opens the royal treasuries and raids the temple's treasuries to buy some help from Ben-hadad, the king of Aram. Asa speaks of a covenant between Ben-hadad and himself before requesting that Ben-hadad break his covenant with Baasha by attacking some of Israel's cities. Asa reasons that once Ben-hadad attacks Baasha, then Baasha will have to abandon the fortification of Ramah. His plan works: Ben-hadad attacks some Israelite cities, Baasha withdraws from Ramah, and Asa tears down the fortifications of Ramah to fortify his cities of Geba and Mizpah.

Use of Treaty Language

There is no evidence that Asa's father and Ben-hadad's father formed a covenant with one another. The syntax of the MT does not indicate that Asa requests to make a covenant, but that there already is a covenant between Aram and Judah. The language is most likely diplomatic and figurative.

Up to this point, the Chronicler provides no assessment regarding Asa's plan, except that it appears to have worked. However,

despite the successful outcome of the plan, there are signs of trouble. First, Asa raids the temple's treasuries to accomplish his plan. Only three verses earlier (15:18) he deposits the spoils of war as consecrated items in the temple. Now he robs its treasuries. Second, he relies on another covenant. Only a few verses earlier Asa makes a covenant with the people to seek YHWH (15:12), but now YHWH does not enter the picture. Instead, Asa relies on another covenant to relieve the military pressure against him.

16:7–8. When it appears that Asa's plan has worked, the seer Hanani confronts him. Hanani's speech offers some direct contrasts to Asa's earlier reign. First, Hanani refers to the Cushite attack when Asa relied (*niphal* שׁען) on YHWH and YHWH defeated the two attacking nations (even though the narrative only mentions Cush, Hanani fills in more detail by including Libya). However, in this case, Asa relies (*niphal* שׁען) on Ben-hadad. If Asa relied on YHWH, YHWH would have defeated Israel and even the king of Aram.

Israel and Aram as Enemies

The Chronicler likely intends to regard both Israel and Aram as enemies. Even though only Israel is presented as an enemy in the narrative, the situation would be similar to the Cushites and Libyans mentioned earlier in the narrative. Originally, the narrative only mentions Cush; however, Hanani fills in more detail by including Libya. In this case, the narrative first only mentions Israel as an enemy, but Hanani fills in more detail by painting Aram as an enemy also. See R. Klein 2012, 240 n. 25.

16:9. Second, Hanani points out that YHWH is constantly looking for people who have their whole heart devoted to him (לֵבָב שָׁלֵם) so that he may empower (לְהִתְחַזֵּק) them. Earlier (15:8) Asa takes courage (הִתְחַזַּק) to obey Azariah's words. Asa also has a whole heart (לֵבָב שָׁלֵם) devoted to YHWH (15:17). However, now because Asa relies on Ben-hadad instead of YHWH, neither can be said of him. Finally, Asa previously experienced long periods of peace without war. Now, he will experience war rather than peace.

16:10. Asa's reaction to Hanani's words confirms his change of heart. Rather than obeying as he did when Azariah spoke (15:8), he becomes angry with Hanani, imprisons him, and then mistreats some of the people. In Chronicles, when a king responds in anger to someone confronting him with his sin, misfortune follows (e.g., Uzziah's skin disease, 2 Chron. 26:19). Furthermore, the Chronicler does not specify why Azariah imprisons Hanani or mistreats some of the people, but Asa's actions clearly portray him in a negative light.

16:11–14. The Chronicler closes out Asa's reign with a picture that reinforces Asa's failure, even if with some qualification. At the end of Asa's life, he develops a serious disease in his feet. Even during the disease, he does not turn to YHWH. He pursues his own solutions in the form of ancient physicians (as he did when Israel was fortifying Ramah) rather than seeking YHWH's help. The Chronicler implies that Asa's foot disease is a result of his failure to rely on YHWH. At the same time, the picture regarding the final days of Asa is not so simple. When Asa dies, he is still buried with his fathers in the city of David, and apparently the people honor him with spices and a large fire. In contrast, when Jehoram, a clearly wicked king, dies, the people do not regret his death or honor him with a fire; and even though he is buried in the city of David, he is not buried in the royal tombs (2 Chron. 21:19–20). Nonetheless, even these apparent positive elements are ambiguous because Asa himself prepared both his tomb and the spices that filled it. It appears the Chronicler intends to show that Asa's life ended negatively, but that his end could have been worse.

> **Ancient Physicians**
>
> Like contemporary physicians, ancient physicians attempted to remove or at least control harmful symptoms that the patient or others could observe. Although ancient physicians could consider environmental factors to play a role in developing or healing diseases, they generally considered supernatural forces to be at work. As a result, these physicians used treatments that do not clearly distinguish between magic and medicine (see an excellent summary of ancient medicine in Zucconi 2019, ch. 1). Although the text does not address the details of what the physicians did or how he relied on them rather than YHWH, it states that in this case Asa did not seek YHWH but other means to deliver him from his disease.

The first readers of Chronicles would have observed the contrast between the first and last parts of Asa's reign. As a small province within the Persian Empire, they might be tempted to engage in political maneuvers to ease their tough conditions. One can easily imagine that some Jews during this period attempted to secure positions within the Persian administration to manipulate circumstances for their own benefit. Within Persian Yehud, the Persian administration and Jerusalem temple would require significant resources to maintain and garner significant value for the community. Efforts to increase political power sometimes shifted resources away from the temple and its personnel as well as compromising the temple's sanctity (e.g., Neh. 13:4–11). The picture of Asa encourages the people to look to YHWH and his temple to sustain them rather than leaning of the workings of the political administration.

THEOLOGICAL FOCUS

Relying on God is always right and shapes the future of one's life.

In many ways, what this passage recounts looks quite different than the experiences of contemporary readers. Asa was an ancient king, a descendant of David, a political authority, and a religious leader. His concerns, as revealed in the passage, involved maintaining peace, building fortifications, organizing an army, promoting religious commitment, and responding to military aggression. Despite the differences in experiences, his reign reveals several theological principles of lasting importance.

First, Asa's life reveals the sharp contrast between relying on God and not relying on God. The first part of Asa's life represents an ideal reign for ancient kings: peace from external threats, stability without internal unrest, firm possession of the lands under his authority, and religious devotion among the people. Even when the Cushite army endangers this picture, God quickly defeats the invaders and prospers the nation through the spoils of battle. In contrast, the second part of Asa's life represents the opposite. Rather than peace, there is war and disease. Asa's circumstances change when he no longer relies on God.

Elsewhere, the Bible commonly speaks of this same type of reliance with different vocabulary such as "believing" or "trusting." Jesus presents belief in God or trusting God as the difference between life and death (e.g., John 3:16, 36; 5:24; 6:40, 47; 11:25–26). Paul summarizes the conversion of the Ephesians as a journey from death to life by grace through faith (Eph. 2:1–10). Furthermore, the opposite is never right. Unbelief prevents the exodus generation of Israel, including Moses and Aaron, from entering the Promised Land (Num. 14:11; 20:12; Heb. 3:7–19). Jesus condemns those who rely on themselves to be righteous (Luke 18:9–14). These few examples only scratch the surface of the Bible's presentation. A more exhaustive look would reveal that whenever the Bible speaks of faith, belief, trust, or relying on God, such conduct is always pleasing to God, while unbelief and self-reliance are never pleasing to him. Furthermore, believing God or not, trusting God or not, relying on God or not affects the person's circumstances, in the present and in the future.

Second, the picture of Asa's life (and death) ties into the Chronicler's theme of retribution; that is, God rewards obedience but punishes disobedience. Most often Chronicles presents obedience or disobedience in terms of worshiping YHWH properly or not, determined by Mosaic law or Davidic instruction. In Asa's case, the account presents Asa's measures to worship, but it also presents his obedience in terms of relying on God. Obedience is not simply a matter of instituting the proper ritual practices but relying on God (see, e.g., 1 Sam. 15:22; Isa. 1:11–15).

The principle of retribution is not mechanical. The Chronicler shows that God blesses Asa for his obedience and punishes him for his disobedience. However, the picture is a bit more complicated. For instance, during the period of Asa's obedience a larger foreign army attacks Judah. Such an attack is not a punishment, as it usually is in Chronicles, but an opportunity for Asa to rely on God. Even in Asa's death, the picture of God's reward or punishment is not obvious. Theologically, this point qualifies the principle of retribution. It is true that God rewards obedience and punishes disobedience; however, this truth does not mean that every bad situation is God's punishment, or that every good situation is God's blessing. As with Asa, sometimes what appears to be bad (Cushite attack) turns out to be good, and what appears to be good (stopping the building of Ramah) turns out to be bad. There is no better example of this principle than Jesus. It is hard to imagine a worse circumstance than Jesus's betrayal, arrest, trial, and crucifixion. However, his suffering becomes the opportunity for resurrection and establishing God's rule over sin, death, and hell. As a result, relying on God, regardless of the situation, is always right and, at least in the end, leads to eternal rewards.

PREACHING AND TEACHING STRATEGIES

Exegetical and Theological Synthesis

This passage teaches us that we need to keep relying upon God and never stop relying upon him. But isn't self-dependence an admired trait? When self-dependence means that an individual takes initiative and completes tasks for which they are responsible, it is a positive characteristic. But when this self-initiative becomes independence from God, the results are disastrous. In both the first part of his reign and the last Asa took initiative, but in the latter his initiative turned into independence from God. When he stopped relying upon YHWH and relied upon others, he experienced the disciplining hand of a loving God. It was not that he looked to others in some way for help and guidance. Rather, the text points out that in the last part of his reign he did not rely upon God.

Upon whom do we depend? We have many relationships in our lives that require a level of dependence. Employers tell us when to come to work and what we are to accomplish. The government tells us how fast we can drive, or even if we can drive. Family traditions often dictate how we celebrate holidays. In each of these situations, we choose to submit our will to the will of another. We rely upon our employer, our government, our family heritage to guide us in life. We are not unaccustomed to relying upon someone. At certain times we should rely upon others, but at all times we should rely upon God.

Preaching Idea

Don't end up an independent, grumpy old person.

Contemporary Connections

What does it mean?

Whom or what we depend upon shows up in our daily lives. A person changes eating habits to comply with a diet that they are depending upon to lose weight. A young person may aggressively study, depending upon those practices to gain acceptance into a school. Someone with chronic health issues may look closely at the ingredients in food they consume, depending on natural ingredients to improve health. So, what does depending upon God change in our lives? What does relying upon God look like? This passage gives us a picture of what relying upon God always looks like, and what independence from him looks like. We have two clear pictures.

The first picture is the early part of Asa's reign when he was clearly dependent upon YHWH. This is seen in his making reforms in worship, his depending upon YHWH in the threat of the Cushites, his responding to God's Word from a prophet, and his even properly rejecting his mother's pagan influence. He worshipped, he obeyed, he relied upon YHWH. The thinking that led to these actions is articulated in his prayer (14:11):

- Right view of God—No one is like YHWH; he alone can be fully trusted.
- Right view of himself—I am weak; I can't win.
- Right view of the task—It is God's assignment.
- Right view of the results—God's victory

The second picture shows a different Asa, selling articles that were set aside for worship to hire a king who does not worship YHWH to help with national defense. Asa rejects the words of YHWH through a prophet and does not seek YHWH's healing when illness strikes. The attitude that governed these actions is stated for us in the brief description in 16:7: "He did not rely upon the YHWH his God."

Is it true?

In thinking about being dependent upon God we must not see that always relying upon him takes away self-initiative and responsibility.

Novels and movies about the Old West are a perennial favorite in the United States. The usual plot involves a man who is a rugged individual who alone, against all odds, takes the initiative and in the end, wins the day. Other genres celebrate the same individual resolve to do what is right in the face of all odds. Numerous superhero movies and comic books celebrate this self-dependence. Though at times the hero does depend upon others, there is a moment when he/she must prevail based upon a strong self-will.

This admired trait of the triumph of self can be seen even in the music industry. In a National Public Radio program, Walter Ray Watson and Daoud Tyler-Ameen comment on the song "My Way":

> It's hard to imagine two occasions more different than the inaugural ball for President Trump and the funeral for a murdered rapper Nipsey Hussle, but they have at least one thing in common: The same song was played at both. It's a song that has come to represent a particular idea of American individualism, and in some ways feels even more relevant today than when it was recorded in 1968 by Frank Sinatra. (https://www.npr.org/2019/11/19/774805536)

Often this song can be held up as describing the type of independence from God that Asa displayed in his later years. While it could apply to that, in a different context where belief in God is not the norm and standing up for the gospel is persecuted, this song could speak of that individual who did it his way by following God in the face of great opposition. One thinks of Elijah on Mount Carmel. To say that we rely upon or depend upon God does not take away individual responsibility and courage. Numerous times in Scripture we are exhorted to be strong and take courage. The message of Asa's life is not the absence of initiative; it is constant dependence upon God. It is taking the initiative to depend upon God. It is almost a contradiction: one takes the initiative to submit to God. We are actively being passive to God's will.

Now what?

Dependence upon God is a heart issue. As part of the rebuke to Asa he is told, "For the eyes of the LORD move to and fro throughout the earth that He may strongly support those whose heart is completely His" (2 Chron. 16:9 NASB 1995). In our sinful way we all like to think of ourselves as that lone cowboy or superheroine taking on challenges and winning the victory all by ourselves. There is nothing wrong in wanting to be victorious and successful in facing a challenge, nor is there anything wrong in a strong motivation to fulfill our responsibility. Each day we step into a real world that attacks us with temptations of lust, greed, pride, hate, and other forms of ungodliness. At times, we fail and might want to give in, but God is showing us that our guidance and strength come from him. We rely upon God to empower us; we depend upon the guidance from his Word to govern what we do. We trust his Spirit to superintend the attitudes we have. We choose to make God's way our way.

Creativity in Presentation

These three chapters need to be summarized in such a way that they give the congregation a way to identify with Asa's actions. We have little in common with the actions of an ancient king. So, try to find some common structure from our lives that could serve as a grid on which to present and evaluate Asa's actions. One such structure could be one person's journey through education: his first acts are at elementary school, later years are at high school, then he finally he goes to college. At each point we can give our student a grade: he starts off great, all A's, until he gets to college, then flunks out. Another structure could be a career path where the individual sees good success, keeps getting raises, but then is a failure as retirement approaches. Or use a simpler example, such as baking a cake. Things start well. The amount of flour, eggs, sugar, and other ingredients are mixed according to the recipe, but the baker doesn't depend upon the recipe in the end and lets the cake burn.

Then, using the same metaphorical structure, paint a picture of a person who walks in dependence upon God, only to forsake him in the end. This leads to the question: How can we always depend upon God? By having the right heart (14:11) and not the wrong one (16:7). Here is one possible structure:

- Present the text using a metaphorical structure
  - Asa's progression through school
    - His A+ years (14:1–15:19)
    - His F years (16:1–19)
- Present a modern equivalent of Asa
  - Relied upon God
  - Lived independently from God
- How to always depend on God
  - Have the right heart (14:11)
  - Reject the independent heart (16:7)

DISCUSSION QUESTIONS

1. List Asa's actions. Give each of these actions a grade.

2. How would you describe a heart that is completely God's?

3. What does it look like to depend upon a person, an employer, a government, a family tradition?

4. How does dependence affect actions?

5. What causes one to depend upon someone else?

6. How does recognizing our sin affect us?

7. Share when you first started depending upon God for the forgiveness of sin.

2 Chronicles 17:1–19:3

EXEGETICAL IDEA
Jehoshaphat's sincere commitment to worship YHWH properly reduced the impact of his objectionable action to ally himself with Ahab.

THEOLOGICAL FOCUS
God blesses those who follow him exclusively and protects them from the fate of the wicked.

PREACHING IDEA
Since God is the source of our blessings, only worship him.

PREACHING POINTERS
This stage of Jehoshaphat's reign illustrates how YHWH rewards Jehoshaphat in his obedience and even mitigates his punishment for a foolish alliance. It teaches us to enjoy the blessings that come from fully embracing the worship of God through faith in his merciful sacrifice and to not seek blessings though an alliance with those who do not worship him. Since God is the source of our blessings, we only and always worship him.

REIGN OF JEHOSHAPHAT—SINCERE WORSHIP
BUT A FOOLISH ALLIANCE (17:1–19:3)

LITERARY STRUCTURE
AND THEMES (17:1–19:3)

The Chronicler's account of Jehoshaphat's reign consists of two major stages: 2 Chronicles 17:1–19:3 and 19:4–21:1. Both stages contain many of the same elements: (1) both begin by describing how Jehoshaphat obediently worships YHWH, (2) both describe a military conflict, (3) both involve an alliance with an Israelite king that ends in failure, and (4) both record that a prophet condemns the alliance. Both parts of Jehoshaphat's reign demonstrate his sincere devotion to worshipping YHWH but also his foolish alliances with the wicked kings of the northern kingdom Israel.

In the first stage (2 Chron. 17:1–19:3), when Jehoshaphat ascends the throne of Judah, he determines to seek YHWH properly and exclusively. At the center of the chapter (17:6–9), Jehoshaphat removes sites of illicit worship and appoints teachers to instruct Judah in the law (for a view of the chapter as a concentric structure, see Knoppers 1991, 505). As a result, YHWH is with him and blesses him in many ways: with wealth, influence, and military strength. Despite Jehoshaphat's decision to worship YHWH, he makes an alliance with Ahab, the wicked king of Israel. As part of this alliance, Ahab entices Jehoshaphat into attacking Ramoth-gilead. Despite the warning of Micaiah, a true prophet of YHWH, Ahab and Jehoshaphat proceed with the attack. During the battle, even though the Arameans surround Jehoshaphat, he survives the attack because YHWH delivers him. Ahab dies because a "random" arrow strikes him between the pieces of his armor, leading to his death. In the aftermath of the attack, when Jehoshaphat returns to Jerusalem, a prophet confronts him for allying with Ahab, but still commends him for destroying foreign objects of worship. This stage of Jehoshaphat's reign illustrates how YHWH rewards Jehoshaphat for his obedience and even mitigates his punishment for a foolish alliance.

- ***Jehoshaphat Seeks YHWH and YHWH Is with Him (17:1–19)***
- ***Ahab Entices Jehoshaphat into Attacking Ramoth-gilead (18:1–27)***
- ***The Battle at Ramoth-gilead and Its Aftermath (18:28–19:3)***

EXPOSITION (17:1–19:3)

Proverbs 12:26 reads, "The righteous choose their friends carefully, but the way of the wicked leads them astray" (NIV). Often, parents have offered such advice to their children, especially teenagers. However, this advice is not limited to teenagers or even just personal friends. In the ancient Near East, kings were responsible for managing international affairs, including forming any alliances. Marriage served as one means for forming and solidifying such alliances. Through marriage, the peoples became intermingled in ways that could affect all types of policies. In Jehoshaphat's case, his marriage alliance to wicked Ahab, king of Israel, diverted his own desire to seek YHWH as he became entangled in Israel's ambitions and plans. Ahab's ambitions led to his death and Jehoshaphat's near-death. However, despite Jehoshaphat's foolish alliance with Ahab, YHWH still delivered Jehoshaphat from destruction because he sought YHWH.

Jehoshaphat Seeks YHWH and YHWH Is with Him (17:1–19)

Jehoshaphat commits himself to seek YHWH by removing illicit worship and appointing teachers of the law; as a result, YHWH blesses him with military strength, wealth, and peace.

17:1–2. The Chronicler begins Jehoshaphat's reign in a way similar to the reigns of other kings, most notably Solomon. When Jehoshaphat succeeds his father as king, he begins his reign by securing his royal authority over the nation. He does so by placing troops in strategic locations throughout Judah, including the cities that his father Asa had captured from the northern kingdom. Mentioning Asa at this point helps draw a connection between the two kings.

TRANSLATION ANALYSIS:
The expression describing Jehoshaphat's activity (וַיִּתְחַזֵּק עַל־יִשְׂרָאֵל) is ambiguous for two reasons. First, the word יִשְׂרָאֵל "Israel" may refer to a political entity (northern kingdom) or to an ethnic group (Israel as a people, composed of those from both kingdoms). Second, the verb (hithpael חזק) with the preposition עַל may carry the sense either of establishing a stable rule within one's own area of authority or of strengthening one's position against someone else. Several translations (CSB, ESV, NIV, NKJV, NLT, NRSV) interpret Israel as referring to the northern kingdom; therefore, they translate the expression in the sense of Jehoshaphat strengthening his position against Israel. However, based on the use of the expression elsewhere in Chronicles (esp. 2 Chron. 1:1), it more likely communicates that Jehoshaphat is securing his rule over all the region for which he is king. Therefore, Israel is an ethnic designation here rather than a political one. The Chronicler uses Israel here because Jehoshaphat's domain now includes those cities that his father Asa captured from Israel. Translations that preserve this sense of the text include NASB, NET, and JPS Tanakh.

17:3. The Chronicler strengthens this connection between Asa and Jehoshaphat in two ways: (1) he states that YHWH is with Jehoshaphat, a remark he makes concerning Asa (2 Chron. 15:9), and (2) he compares Jehoshaphat's obedience to his father's obedience in the beginning of his reign. These connections are explicit hints that the Chronicler's account of Asa has influenced his account of Jehoshaphat.

TRANSLATION ANALYSIS:
Translations render 17:3 differently primarily because of a question raised in the transmission of the text. MT reads הָלַךְ בְּדַרְכֵי דָּוִיד אָבִיו הָרִאשֹׁנִים ("he walked in the first ways of his father David"). On the other hand, a few Hebrew mss. and LXX do not include the reading "David." The most straightforward way to understand the function of הָרִאשֹׁנִים is as an adjective modifying בְּדַרְכֵי, that is, as "the first ways of." If one follows MT, then these would be the first ways of David. However, the Chronicler does not present David's reign as having a first "good" stage and a later "bad" stage. In contrast, he does present Asa's reign in such a way. A couple of translations avoid this issue by translating הָרִאשֹׁנִים adverbially ("in the beginning"), indicating that Jehoshaphat's reign has an earlier "good" period followed by a later "bad" period. However, the Chronicler's picture of Jehoshaphat's reign does not break down this way. It seems more likely that since David is such a common standard for comparison with other kings, a scribe inserted David's name rather than omitting it. Therefore, on this issue, the translations that more likely preserve the original text omit David (e.g., NLT, NRSV).

Connections Between Asa and Jehoshaphat

A number of similarities connect the two kings: (1) both kings have periods of obedience and blessing followed by a foreign alliance and punishment, (2) both remove the high places (2 Chron. 14:2–5; 17:6) and also don't (2 Chron. 15:17; 20:33), and (3) YHWH is with both kings (2 Chron. 15:9; 17:3) and places his fear upon other nations (2 Chron. 14:14 [HB 13]; 17:10; 20:29; see Dillard 1987, 129). Theologically, this comparison would be significant for first readers because it shows that YHWH has consistently rewarded (in similar ways) obedience (in similar terms) generation after generation.

17:4–5. After these introductory comments, the Chronicler reveals how Jehoshaphat follows in his father's footsteps: He worships YHWH exclusively and properly. The text shows that Jehoshaphat worships YHWH exclusively by stating that he does not worship the Baals. Even though Chronicles does not mention Baal worship of any kind before Jehoshaphat, Chronicles mentions it several times after his reign, most often associated with Israel's worship practice (cf. reign of Athaliah, daughter of Ahab, 2 Chron. 23:17; 24:7; reign of Ahaz, 2 Chron. 28:2). Furthermore, the text shows that Jehoshaphat worships YHWH properly by mentioning that he walked in YHWH's commandments.

Responding to Jehoshaphat's obedience, YHWH rewards him by securing the kingdom under Jehoshaphat's rule. This statement may seem redundant since 17:1 has stated that Jehoshaphat secured his authority over the kingdom; however, the statement is important because it makes clear that YHWH is really the one behind securing the kingdom and that securing the kingdom is part of YHWH's reward for Jehoshaphat's obedience. Furthermore, YHWH's blessing leads to more blessing, since as a result of Judah's loyalty to Jehoshaphat, the people give him voluntary gifts, contributing to his wealth and prestige.

Jehoshaphat's Blessing

YHWH blesses other obedient kings with wealth and honor (עֹשֶׁר־וְכָבוֹד; David, 1 Chron. 29:28; Solomon, 2 Chron. 9:22; Hezekiah 2 Chron. 32:27), but Jehoshaphat is the only king in Chronicles to receive voluntary gifts from his own people (except perhaps Hezekiah in 2 Chron. 32:23). This similarity and difference demonstrate that for the

kings of Judah, YHWH consistently rewards obedience in similar, although not always identical, ways.

17:6. Wealth and prestige do not come without temptation. Kings Uzziah and Hezekiah both become arrogant by exalting their hearts (גָּבַהּ לֵב; Uzziah, 2 Chron. 26:16; Hezekiah, 2 Chron. 32:23–25). Jehoshaphat also exalts his heart (וַיִּגְבַּהּ לִבּוֹ); however, surprisingly, he does so in a good way. He does not take pride in himself, but in the ways of YHWH. This attitude leads him to remove more illicit forms of worship: the high places and the Asherah poles (see sidebar "Asherah").

17:7–9. After only a short time into Jehoshaphat's reign (in contexts dealing with time, the number three carries connotations of a short period; Cogan 1985, 207), he sends throughout Judah a group of officials, Levites, and priests to teach YHWH's law. Technically, the text does not specify what these royal representatives are to teach; however, since they take YHWH's law with them, they most likely are teaching this law. Jehoshaphat's concern to know and teach the law reminds one of the royal requirements established in Deuteronomy 17:18–19. It also resembles Ezra's teaching mission (esp. Ezra 7:10) since Ezra teaches the people YHWH's commandments upon the authority both of YHWH's law and the king's law (Ezra 7:25–26; Japhet 1993, 749). For the first readers, Jehoshaphat's mission would serve as an encouragement to learn YHWH's law since Jehoshaphat's (and thereby Judah's) success comes from his obedience to YHWH's commandments. Furthermore, by including the officials, Levites, and priests in the teaching task, the Chronicler affirms the legitimacy of these groups in teaching the law, at least for Jehoshaphat's reign. This affirmation suggests that the first readers should also recognize the legitimacy of such groups in their own time (cf. Ezra 7:25; Neh. 8:7–8).

17:10–11. Because of Jehoshaphat's obedience, YHWH blesses him not only with security within his own kingdom, but also peace among the neighboring kingdoms. YHWH brings about this peace by making these surrounding nations afraid of him. The fear of YHWH is not the typical wisdom expression יִרְאַת יְהוָה, but the expression פַּחַד יְהוָה. This latter expression has a more limited semantic range and here carries the sense of "terror, dread." The neighboring nations do not attack Jehoshaphat because they are afraid of what YHWH will do to them if they do so. As a result of this fear, the Philistines and Arabs, two of Judah's common enemies (e.g., 2 Chron. 21:16; 26:7), also send Jehoshaphat tribute: unspecified gifts, a great deal of money, and livestock.

> ### Terror of YHWH
> The Chronicler refers to the terror (פַּחַד) of YHWH on a few occasions. Sometimes, this terror serves as a deterrent as it does here in 2 Chronicles 17:10 (cf. 2 Chron. 20:29 as well). For instance, in 2 Chronicles 19:7 the terror of YHWH should prevent judges from acting unjustly. On other occasions, this terror brings about Judah's military victory (2 Chron. 14:13).

17:12–13. Because YHWH continues to bless Jehoshaphat, he continues to grow stronger. The Chronicler now illustrates that strength by describing Jehoshaphat's military preparations. The Chronicler has already touched on this theme in the first verses describing Jehoshaphat's reign; there he mentions the troops Jehoshaphat places in all the fortified cities and the sentries he sends throughout Judah. Here he first addresses the preparations for supplying his troops throughout Judah and then the troops that he places in Jerusalem. By returning to this theme and filling out the description started earlier, he ties the verses of chapter 17 together as a distinct unit.

As the Chronicler describes Jehoshaphat's military preparations, he moves from Judah as a whole to Jerusalem. Throughout Judah Jehoshaphat builds structures to defend his land (בִּירָנִיּוֹת "fortresses") and to supply his troops (עָרֵי מִסְכְּנוֹת "storage cities") and then provides a large quantity of supplies among its cities. In Jerusalem, Jehoshaphat stations several competent military commanders who oversee large numbers of warriors.

TRANSLATION ANALYSIS:
In this case, the word מְלָאכָה is ambiguous. Some translations (e.g., CSB, NRSV) interpret the word as referring to building projects; however, because of the concern for military preparation and the mention of storage cities in the immediate context, it seems more likely, following other translations (e.g., ESV, NASB, NET, NIV, NLT), that the word refers to goods or supplies such as food, drink, and livestock (cf. Gen. 33:14; 1 Sam. 15:9).

17:14–19. Jehoshaphat organizes this military force in a way similar to other kings: by their ancestral houses within the tribes Judah and Benjamin (cf. 2 Chron. 26:12–13). The Chronicler lists several commanders for both Judah and Benjamin along with the number of troops under their command. This force is quite large, twice the size of Asa's army, and equal to the sum of Judah's preceding kings (N. Klein 2017, 6–13; see also excursus "Troop Numbers in Judah"). The organization and size of Jehoshaphat's force indicates YHWH's blessing on him.

> ### Amasiah, the Volunteer
> Among the listing of commanders, one stands out: Amasiah, son of Zichri (2 Chron. 17:16). The Chronicler describes this commander as one who volunteered to YHWH (הַמִּתְנַדֵּב לַיהוָה). The significance of this phrase is unclear. The comment may reflect the idea that volunteering to serve in Jehoshaphat's army is also in some sense volunteering to serve YHWH. On occasion in Chronicles, the Chronicler identifies Judah as the kingdom of YHWH and resisting Judah as

resisting YHWH (cf. 2 Chron. 13:8–12). Although this understanding may be correct, it is better not to make too much of this phrase since it does not have much of an interpretive context around it.

For the first readers, this stage of Jehoshaphat's reign provides another example to encourage them to follow YHWH because he blesses obedience. In this narrative, the focus for following YHWH lies in two areas: (1) worshipping YHWH properly and exclusively, and (2) learning and teaching the law. Many of those returning from exile did not know the law and would find it challenging to learn on their own either because they did not have access to it, could not read, or did not understand Hebrew. In this situation, the Chronicler promotes an active teaching mission by authorized teachers, in order for the people to know the law so that they may worship YHWH properly by obeying it and therefore remain in the land.

Ahab Entices Jehoshaphat into Attacking Ramoth-gilead (18:1–27)

Ahab entices Jehoshaphat to join him in attacking Ramoth-gilead both through prophetic assurances and despite a prophetic warning.

18:1–27. During the next part of his reign, Jehoshaphat becomes a secondary player in the narrative. The focus shifts to Ahab, the king of Israel, after Jehoshaphat makes a marriage alliance with Ahab. In light of the alliance, Ahab convinces Jehoshaphat to join him in attacking Ramoth-gilead; however, Jehoshaphat first wants to find out what YHWH has to say about this attack. After Ahab's prophets encourage him to go ahead because he will win, a prophet of YHWH named Micaiah warns Ahab that he will die if he proceeds. Despite the warning, Ahab and Jehoshaphat proceed with the attack. YHWH miraculously rescues Jehoshaphat from certain death while a random arrow leads to Ahab's demise. After Ahab dies, Jehoshaphat returns to Jerusalem where a prophet condemns

his alliance with Ahab, but still commends him for his obedient worship to YHWH.

Result of Marriage Alliance
Jehoshaphat forms the alliance by marrying his son Jehoram to Ahab's daughter Athaliah. This marriage leads Judah to act like Israel in false worship and other types of evil. At the center of this evil activity is Athaliah, whose influence has serious consequences for Judah, almost leading to the complete destruction of the Davidic dynasty (cf. 2 Chron. 21–23).

18:1. This next stage of Jehoshaphat's reign begins with a comment regarding Jehoshaphat's great wealth and prestige. The comment repeats verbatim what the Chronicler has stated in 2 Chronicles 17:5; however, what follows this second time is quite different. As mentioned above, wealth and prestige often lead to pride and a downfall in Chronicles (e.g., Uzziah [2 Chron. 26:16] and Hezekiah [2 Chron. 32:25]); however, in the early part of Jehoshaphat's reign, they lead to his pride in YHWH. Now, in the second stage of his reign, his wealth and prestige lead to his alliance with Ahab. YHWH does not approve of such an alliance, as demonstrated by the prophet's condemnation later in the narrative (2 Chron. 19:2). The Chronicler subtly implies that Jehoshaphat's pride leads to the alliance.

18:2–3. As a result of this alliance, Ahab convinces Jehoshaphat to join him in attacking Ramoth-gilead. Ahab offers many sacrifices on Jehoshaphat's behalf, apparently, to honor Jehoshaphat and the royal entourage accompanying him. The plan is effective because Jehoshaphat responds by affirming unity between the kings and their people and by agreeing to support Ahab in battle. The response draws a contrast to what the Chronicler has described of Jehoshaphat's reign to this point. The Chronicler has emphasized that YHWH secures Jehoshaphat's rule distinctly over Judah (2 Chron. 17:5), but now Jehoshaphat seems to blur the lines between Judah and Israel. Furthermore, YHWH has prevented other nations from attacking Judah, but now Jehoshaphat joins with another nation in order to attack. Finally, YHWH has been with Jehoshaphat because he is not like Israel (2 Chron. 17:3–4), but now Jehoshaphat promises to be with Israel even though YHWH is not with them (2 Chron. 25:7). These features of Jehoshaphat's response point to his folly in joining Ahab.

TRANSLATION ANALYSIS:
Jehoshaphat's response to Ahab's request to join him in attacking Ramoth-gilead uses expressions that are not easy to translate, although their function in the context seems clear. Many translations suggest a comparison between the kings and people by translating the expression כָּמוֹנִי כָמוֹךָ וּכְעַמְּךָ עַמִּי as "I am as you are, my people as your people" (CSB, ESV, NASB); however, the expression conveys more than the similarity between the two kings and nations. It carries a sense of unity. Furthermore, in this case, עַם carries the more specific sense of "army" rather than just the general sense of "people." NLT captures both senses well when it translates the expression as "You and I are as one, and my troops are your troops." NET captures the function of Jehoshaphat's response well although it does not convey the sense of unity as explicitly; it reads, "I will support you; my army is at your disposal."

18:4–6. Before Jehoshaphat sets off with Ahab for battle, he requests to hear a prophetic word from YHWH concerning the plan. When Ahab calls his four hundred prophets, they all assure him that God (הָאֱלֹהִים) will give him the victory. This large number of prophets reminds one of the 450 prophets of Baal, four hundred prophets of Asherah, or one hundred prophets of YHWH recorded during Ahab's reign (1 Kings 18:4, 19), but their origin is unstated. One would expect them to be prophets of YHWH, since Jehoshaphat specifically requests a word from YHWH. Even though they initially speak of

God (הָאֱלֹהִים), they later speak specifically in YHWH's name. Regardless of their origin and for whatever reason, Jehoshaphat distrusts their prophecy and asks if there is another prophet.

TRANSLATION ANALYSIS:
Translations interpret Jehoshaphat's question in two different ways. On one hand, some translations (e.g., CSB, NIV, NKJV, NLT) interpret the text as a question of whether there is a prophet of YHWH left at all in Israel. This interpretation implies that Jehoshaphat does not recognize Ahab's four hundred prophets as prophets of YHWH. On the other hand, some translations (e.g., ESV, NRSV) interpret the question as a request for another prophet of YHWH. Within the context, the latter seems more likely because the text does not speak clearly on the origin of the prophets and Jehoshaphat requests to hear from YHWH.

Distrusting Prophecy
The Chronicler does not give any hints regarding Jehoshaphat's reason for distrusting the prophets; therefore, from a narrative point of view it matters little. From a historical point of view, commentators suggest three possible reasons: (1) all the prophets saying exactly the same thing is suspect from the start (e.g., Japhet 1993, 759), (2) the ambiguous origin of these prophets calls into question their authority (e.g., Merrill 2015, 420), or (3) Ahab's prophets work for him so they are not "neutral witnesses" (R. Klein 2012, 262).

18:7–8. At this point, the Chronicler briefly introduces the prophet Micaiah in contrast to the other prophets. He is the "one man" in contrast to the "four hundred men" to inquire of YHWH. He is also the prophet who always predicts Ahab's failure, in contrast to the others who unanimously predict his success. Even though both qualities characterize true prophets elsewhere in the OT (e.g., Jer. 29:24–32), Ahab hates Micaiah and does not bring him out with the other prophets. Despite Ahab's hate for Micaiah, Jehoshaphat's response to Ahab prompts him to bring Micaiah now.

TRANSLATION ANALYSIS:

On the surface, Jehoshaphat's response is straightforward: "Do not let the king say such." However, the function of the response is less straightforward. One could interpret the expression to mean that a king should not speak in such a manner, presumably about hating a prophet. The following translations seem to imply such a translation: CSB, NET, NIV, NLT. However, one may interpret the expression to demonstrate Jehoshaphat's disbelief. An English equivalent would be "say it isn't so" or "that can't be true." Second Samuel 13:32 records an instance in which David is commanded not to "say" (אמר) something because it is not true. In this case, Jehoshaphat would be responding to the comment that Micaiah always predicts failure. To paraphrase, Jehoshaphat is saying, "Surely he doesn't prophesy your failure all the time." Understanding Jehoshaphat's response this way seems to make more sense of Ahab's later reaction to Micaiah's prophecy.

18:9–11. So, the stage is set to hear from a true prophet; however, the narrative does not shift to Micaiah just yet. Instead, the Chronicler returns to the scene of Ahab's prophets. There, Ahab and Jehoshaphat sit on their thrones wearing their royal attire in the place where legal judgments are made. These details emphasize the kings' royal authority and judicial responsibility. As they sit, the prophets carry out their prophetic activities in front of the kings to make their case. The text highlights one prophet in particular: Zedekiah son of Chenaanah. As part of his case, he compares Ahab to a mighty bull and fashions iron horns to symbolize his power. He repeats that Ahab should attack Ramoth-gilead. All of Ahab's other prophets still agree.

> **Threshing Floors and Entryways**
>
> The text mentions both the threshing floor and the entry of the gate of the city. Each of these locations serves as a place for making judgments; therefore, including both emphasizes the legal authority for the king presiding there (Matthews 1987, 30–31).

18:12–17. As Ahab's prophets make their case, the narrative returns to Micaiah. Ahab's messenger informs Micaiah of the current state of things: all the prophets have predicted Ahab's success. As a result, he should do the same. The messenger's statement comes across as a threat; however, Micaiah responds as a true prophet should. He promises that he will only say what YHWH says. Surprisingly then, when Ahab asks him whether to go to battle, Micaiah essentially repeats what all the other prophets have said. Micaiah seems to lie to Ahab and contradict what he has just told the messenger. Ahab challenges Micaiah to tell him the truth in YHWH's name. Micaiah responds with an ambiguous oracle in which Israel is scattered without a leader (a negative situation) but returns home in peace (a positive situation). Ahab recognizes that the prophecy predicts disaster for him specifically and tells Jehoshaphat as much. Micaiah responds with a vision that helps explain the entire narrative episode.

18:18–22. The vision Micaiah sees reveals the reality behind the scene and helps explain many of the narrative's features. Micaiah sees what takes place in heaven, within YHWH's council. Three important points emerge from Micaiah's vision. First, YHWH is the real king with real power. Although Ahab and Jehoshaphat sit on their thrones and consult their prophets, YHWH sits on his throne and consults with the host of heaven. Just as Zedekiah steps forward to answer Ahab's inquiry whether to attack Ramoth-gilead, a spirit steps forward to answer YHWH's inquiry how to judge Ahab. This contrast reveals YHWH as the real king. Second,

YHWH has decided to judge Ahab. YHWH declares that the judgment will take place since Ahab will attack Ramoth-gilead. The question remaining is how this attack will take place. This question leads to the third point: because of the council, the prophets will lead Ahab to battle against Ramoth-gilead by giving him a false prediction. A spirit within the council plans on becoming a deceiving spirit to the prophets; that is, this spirit will inspire Ahab's prophets to give this false prediction.

TRANSLATION ANALYSIS:
The Hebrew term often translated as "deceiving" (שֶׁקֶר) has a wide semantic range, from an intentional, malicious act of misrepresentation to a failure to follow through on a commitment or commandment. In the context of Micaiah's vision, the term suggests the sense of trickery or misdirection (cf. Prov. 20:17).

Divine Council

A few passages in the Old Testament allude to a divine council in which spiritual beings assemble around YHWH who sits as the head of the council. Job 1–2 presents this council as a meeting of the "sons of God" (בְּנֵי הָאֱלֹהִים) who report their current activities to YHWH, much as a royal official would report to the king. This passage in Chronicles presents the council as the place by which YHWH makes his plan known, determines how to carry it out, and dispatches a member of the council to accomplish it (see Heiser 2015).

18:23–27. When Micaiah finishes describing his vision, Zedekiah hits him in the face as part of a challenge to Micaiah's claim to have spoken for YHWH. However, Micaiah defends his claim by looking to the future when Zedekiah will hide because his prophecy has failed. Furthermore, Ahab sides with his prophets and so imprisons Micaiah under harsh conditions. Before Ahab's servants carry Micaiah away, he offers one last piece of evidence: if Ahab returns safely from battle, then he has prophesied falsely.

TRANSLATION ANALYSIS:
Translations treat Zedekiah's challenge to Micaiah in different ways. Some translations (CSB, ESV, NET, NIV, NRSV) interpret the question as asking the path the spirit would take to move from Zedekiah to Micaiah. The implication of the question is that there is no discernible path for the spirit to take. It is unlikely that Zedekiah asks the question because he wants information about the spirit's movements. Therefore, some translations (NASB, NLT) translate the question more directly as a challenge to Micaiah's claim to speak for YHWH.

This episode raises several theological and historical questions. For instance: Why does Micaiah seem to lie to Ahab the first time? Who or what is the deceiving spirit? Is YHWH deliberately deceiving Ahab? Although many of these questions are important, rather than focusing on historical and theological questions the following comments attempt to explain what the Chronicler is doing with this narrative. First, in the larger context of Jehoshaphat's reign, the Chronicler is contrasting the fate of Ahab, the false worshipper, with the fate of Jehoshaphat, the true worshipper. Neither Ahab nor Jehoshaphat is a neutral party in the narrative. What happens to each is based on his previous choices.

Second, the Chronicler presents YHWH as mirroring Ahab's activity in various ways. One can see this feature in the two council settings and the various parallels between them (Ahab with the prophets/YHWH with the host of heaven). This feature helps explain why the Chronicler includes the comment that the spirit within the council becomes a deceiving spirit in the mouths of Ahab's prophets. In this case, one may think of this spirit as a spirit of trickery or misdirection. After Micaiah's prophecy, Ahab disguises himself as he goes into battle. The disguise is Ahab's attempt to escape YHWH's judgment by using trickery. In a similar way, YHWH's plan uses trickery in order to judge Ahab.

Third, when Micaiah announces Ahab's judgment, following the pattern within Chronicles, he also implicitly warns him to repent. This pattern in Chronicles helps put the false prophecies in context. Even though the false prophecies are part of YHWH's plan to judge Ahab, the fact that Micaiah, a prophet of YHWH, announces that these prophecies are part of his plan to judge Ahab accomplishes two purposes: (1) it explains why Micaiah is predicting disaster while the other prophets are predicting success, and (2) it unveils this trickery so that Ahab can see things for what they really are and repent (Miller 2014, 45–58; Moberly 2003, 1–23; Tiemeyer 2005, 339–41).

Fourth, the Chronicler does not present Ahab as an unsuspecting victim. Even though Jehoshaphat doubts the prophecies of Ahab's prophets at first, Ahab discerns when Micaiah does not speak the truth in YHWH's name. Ahab can see what is happening even before Micaiah reveals the scene from heaven; he chooses to reject Micaiah's prophecy and continue with his own plan.

The Battle at Ramoth-gilead and Its Aftermath (18:28–19:3)

Despite Ahab's attempts to circumvent Micaiah's prophecy, wicked Ahab dies despite the odds while Jehoshaphat narrowly escapes despite the odds.

18:28–30. Despite Micaiah's warning, Ahab and Jehoshaphat continue with the plan to attack Ramoth-gilead. The Chronicler tells the story to show the advantages Ahab has to survive the battle in contrast to the disadvantages Jehoshaphat has. Ahab prepares for the battle by disguising himself and convincing Jehoshaphat to wear his royal attire. The disguise is Ahab's attempt to get around YHWH's judgment. The logic seems to be that if Ahab cannot be recognized, then he cannot be judged. However, the Chronicler presents the disguise as even more effective than anticipated because Aram's king commands his chariot commanders to focus solely on fighting Ahab (18:30). How fortunate it appears that Ahab has disguised himself. However, the disguise puts Jehoshaphat at greater risk.

18:31–33. Ahab's disguise seems to work. Aram's chariot commanders do not attack Ahab, but mistakenly pursue Jehoshaphat. As they approach to attack him, Jehoshaphat cries out to YHWH, who rescues him by drawing them away (18:31). Second Chronicles 18:32 may seem unnecessary because it only states that the chariot commanders stop attacking Jehoshaphat because they recognize that he is not the king of Israel. However, the statement shows more directly that Ahab's disguise, which has appeared as an effective trick for the present battle, is beginning to fail. In fact, the next statement shows that it fails totally. The disguise is powerless against a random arrow. An archer shoots the arrow without targeting someone specifically and "by chance" hits Ahab between his armor pieces, fatally injuring him. Such a shot is highly unlikely, but the improbability is the point of the text. Despite Ahab's planning and preparation to get around YHWH's judgment, even when the odds are stacked in his favor, so to speak, he cannot escape.

TRANSLATION ANALYSIS:

The Hebrew text describes the archer as shooting his bow לְתֻמּוֹ. Many translations (ESV, NASB, NET, NIV, NKJV, cf. NLT) render the expression as "at random." This rendering works well as long as one does not interpret it to mean that the soldier unintentionally or accidentally shot his arrow. Because of this ambiguity, CSB offers a better translation: "without special aim." The archer fired without targeting a specific person, just targeting the crowd of enemy soldiers.

YHWH vs. Ahab

This passage presents another contrast between Ahab and YHWH. Ahab convinced (סות) Jehoshaphat to attack Ramoth-gilead; YHWH led the chariot commanders away (סות) to help Jehoshaphat. Ahab's action almost leads to Jehoshaphat's death, while YHWH's action saves his life.

18:34. The Chronicler shows that even after Ahab is seriously wounded, he still makes his final stand, literally. He requests that his chariot driver remove him from the front line of battle; however, he does not withdraw completely. The Chronicler highlights that Ahab props himself up in his chariot so that he may stand against the Arameans as the battle rages on. Ahab does not retreat; even while seriously injured, he does not turn away from his plan to fight against Ramoth-gilead. And then, at the end of the day, he dies. His death confirms Micaiah's prophecy and illustrates the disastrous fate of the false worshipper who attempts to get around YHWH's judgment rather than changing his ways.

19:1. Although Ahab dies in the battle, Jehoshaphat returns to Jerusalem safely. Jehoshaphat's safe arrival rounds out the Chronicler's contrast between the fates of Ahab and Jehoshaphat. Even though they are allies and both participate in the battle despite YHWH's warning, Ahab dies despite the odds while Jehoshaphat returns safely despite the odds.

However, the Chronicler does not allow the reader to think that Jehoshaphat's alliance with Ahab is proper.

19:2. The Chronicler records that the prophet Jehu confronts Jehoshaphat for the alliance. He starts by describing what Jehoshaphat has done: he has helped the wicked and loved those who hate YHWH. The expressions are ways of referring to the alliance. By making the alliance, Jehoshaphat "loves" (אהב) Ahab. In this context, the verb אהב primarily carries the sense of Jehoshaphat's accepting Ahab as an ally and committing himself to the alliance. Part of this commitment is to help Ahab as an ally during war. At the same time, the prophet implies that Ahab "hates" YHWH. In this context, hating YHWH involves being disloyal to him and rejecting him as God.

TRANSLATION ANALYSIS:

When the word שׂנא occurs in covenant or treaty contexts, it carries the sense of disloyalty or rejection rather than strong emotional connotations like the English word "hate" (see Shepherd 2016, 94–102). Therefore, even though most translations (CSB, ESV, NASB, NIV, NLT, NRSV) render the word as "hate," NET's translation "oppose" gets closer to the sense of the Hebrew in this context.

After Jehu describes what Jehoshaphat has done, he explains the consequence. Because of the alliance, Jehoshaphat experiences YHWH's wrath. It is not clear what this wrath entails. Generally, experiencing YHWH's wrath refers to experiencing some form of judgment (e.g., 1 Chron. 27:24; 2 Chron. 29:8). However, in this context, YHWH does not appear to judge Jehoshaphat. Perhaps YHWH's judgment refers back to the previous battle, but the Chronicler does not record who won the conflict, only that Ahab dies and Jehoshaphat returns safely. Therefore, it seems most likely in this case that YHWH's wrath does not include judgment, only his anger. As a result, there is time for Jehoshaphat to change the state of affairs.

Opportunities for Kings

Hezekiah experiences something similar to Jehoshaphat (2 Chron. 32:25–26). As a result of his pride, he experiences YHWH's wrath. However, he humbles himself so that YHWH's wrath (apparently in the sense of his judgment) does not come to Hezekiah or Judah while Hezekiah is alive.

19:3. Even though YHWH is angry with Jehoshaphat, the prophet commends Jehoshaphat's previous activity in removing illicit worship from Judah and determining to follow YHWH. The prophet's words to Jehoshaphat bring the entire narrative into focus. It alludes back to how Jehoshaphat has worshipped YHWH properly and exclusively by removing foreign gods and their symbols of worship from Judah. It also sets up the contrast between wicked Ahab, who has rejected YHWH, and Jehoshaphat, who has sought YHWH. Furthermore, it shows that even though Jehoshaphat's alliance with Ahab is wrong, YHWH still spares him because of his commitment to true worship.

TRANSLATION ANALYSIS:
The Hebrew text reads אֲבָל דְּבָרִים טוֹבִים נִמְצְאוּ עִמָּךְ. Many translations (CSB, ESV, NASB, NIV, NLT, NRSV) render the phrase something similar to "some good is found in you." These translations may imply that there is something inherently good about Jehoshaphat; however, the expression concerns Jehoshaphat's actions and decisions, that is, the activity of removing the Asherah poles and deciding to worship YHWH only. For this reason, NET captures the sense of the Hebrew more clearly: "you have done some good things."

For the first readers, this stage of Jehoshaphat's reign provides some measure of encouragement and warning. The Chronicler has repeatedly emphasized the principle that YHWH rewards obedience and punishes disobedience. With Jehoshaphat, this principle receives some clarification because Jehoshaphat's past obedience in worshipping YHWH mitigated the consequences of his alliance with Ahab. YHWH was angry with Jehoshaphat, but he still rescued him. In this case, YHWH responded to Jehoshaphat's wrong with mercy. Although the Chronicler shows that one cannot presume that past obedience will alleviate future judgment (e.g., Josiah, 2 Chron. 35:21–24), at least on this occasion YHWH chose to do so.

This narrative also serves as a warning. For the small, powerless group returning from exile, there were opportunities to rely on political arrangements with their neighbors (e.g., Ezra 4:1–3). The Chronicler indicates that these arrangements threaten the community and should be avoided, so that the community will rely on YHWH alone (Knoppers 1996, 623–26).

THEOLOGICAL FOCUS

God blesses those who follow him exclusively, and protects them from the fate of the wicked.

Repeatedly, Chronicles addresses the principle of retribution: God rewards obedience and punishes disobedience. The first part of Jehoshaphat's reign illustrates this principle using language and examples occurring in the reigns of previous good kings. Like preceding kings, Jehoshaphat seeks God and removes illicit worship from Judah. Like David, Solomon, Abijah, and Asa before him, Jehoshaphat worships God exclusively. As a result, God rewards him with the typical blessings for Judah's kings: wealth, influence, military strength, and peace. The first part of Jehoshaphat's reign reiterates the principle of retribution using typical images.

At the same time, the passage offers some distinct insights into the principle of retribution. First, this passage presents Jehoshaphat as obeying God when he appoints teachers to instruct the people throughout Judah in the law. Elsewhere, kings have explicitly acted in accordance with the law (e.g., David, 1 Chron. 16:40) or commanded the people to obey the law (e.g., Asa, 2 Chron. 14:4); but organizing officials, accompanied by priests and Levites, to teach the law to all the people is a new development. By including this activity, the Chronicler points to the role that the law has in preserving his people. As one looks to the contemporary situation, this principle remains valid, although some of the details have shifted. For instance, rather than focusing exclusively on the law, one can speak more generally of God's revelation in Scripture. Teaching God's Word remains an essential activity for preserving his people.

Second, this passage reveals the danger of associating with the wicked. When Jehoshaphat forms an alliance with Ahab, he continues to worship God exclusively. However, the alliance, established through marriage, creates a tight bond between Judah and Israel. The prophet Jehu condemns this alliance as helping the wicked and loving someone who hates God. The Bible reveals a concern for this type of close association in other passages as well. For instance, Psalm 1:1 speaks of the righteous one who avoids close association with the wicked. Paul speaks of this principle when he warns the Corinthians not to be "unequally yoked with unbelievers" (2 Cor. 6:14 ESV). These types of close associations often lead to some disaster or threat, as they did for Jehoshaphat.

Third, this passage reveals that God brings about reward or punishment regardless of how people may scheme to avoid their expected fate. This point comes through clearly in the contrast between Ahab and Jehoshaphat. Ahab attempts to work around his fate by disguising himself in battle. At the same time, Jehoshaphat appears to fall haplessly into a trap as the opposing armies surround him. Despite these circumstances, Ahab dies while Jehoshaphat survives. The wicked Ahab cannot avoid the prophesied punishment; at the same time, God delivers his follower Jehoshaphat just in time. Even though in the middle of the battle it appears that justice has been inverted, in the end God preserves Jehoshaphat and punishes Ahab. Such a pattern is typical of God's work as revealed in the crucifixion and throughout the book of Revelation.

PREACHING AND TEACHING STRATEGIES

Exegetical and Theological Synthesis

The concept of reward and retribution is clearly seen in this passage. The two main characters both experience reward and retribution but in very different ways, based upon whom they worship. Jehoshaphat, who faithfully worships YHWH, enjoys abundant blessings and tastes retribution when he is disciplined for his foolish alliances. Ahab who is described as "hating" YHWH, may have some degree of material wealth but experiences the ultimate retribution of death.

Jehoshaphat is a faithful follower of YHWH and has embraced the gospel that was revealed to Old Testament saints. Though he is not perfect, he is described as setting his heart to seek YHWH (19:3) and taking pride in the ways of YHWH (17:6). He only worshipped YHWH and worshipped him in the proper way.

Jehoshaphat worshipped through faith just as we worship. The object of his faith was in the mercy of God expressed through the sacrificial system. Our faith is in the same mercy expressed through the work of our savior, Jesus. We, with Jehoshaphat are followers of God. But we must not see our obedience and commitment to God as earning his reward so that he is obligated to us. Our obedience puts us into a position to enjoy the blessings that he wants to shower upon us. Our disobedience moves us away from his blessings and brings punishment, with the purpose of bringing us back to him.

Preaching Idea

Since God is the source of our blessings, only worship him.

Contemporary Connections

What does it mean?

We can't help but delight in Jehoshaphat's obedience and blessing. The Chronicler not only tells us of his commitment, but he also shows us through Jehoshaphat's action. God has blessed us, and when we walk with him, we can experience these blessings.

Rewards are part of everyone's experience. Even the most basic act of eating rewards us by taking away our hunger. Parents reward children, teachers reward students, and employers reward employees. It is part of how God hardwired us. It only follows that God rewards those who worship him and are committed to his ways. The motivation for obedience could be as basic as seeking the reward, but there is a higher and better view of rewards. Most often, the rewards that we offer to each other are very specific. The parent offers five dollars if the child completes her chores, the class gets an extra fifteen minutes at recess if they all turn in their homework on time, or the thousand-dollar bonus is offered to employees who start ten new accounts. God's rewards are not dangled in front of us as a carrot. In Jehoshaphat's case, he was rewarded in a way appropriate for the king of God's people; his wealth and well-being were a blessing to the kingdom. The blessings God grants to us will be what is best for us and will advance his purposes. God is not teaching us that our rewards will be the same as Jehoshaphat's, but that the end result will be the same: we will be blessed, and God's purposes will be fulfilled.

The list of rewards that parents, teachers, and employers offer is not limited to a specific reward, though it is offered in that way. When a child finishes his chores, he is learning a work ethic; when the class together turns in homework on time, they are learning the importance of meeting deadlines; when the employee brings in new accounts, she is helping secure the company's ability to employ them. These kinds of rewards are hard to codify. God's rewards are even harder to measure. God doesn't limit his rewards to five dollars or more recess time or even one thousand dollars. His rewards are far greater.

Is it true?

The Bible clearly teaches that we do not earn our salvation; it is a free gift from God through Jesus, prompted by the Holy Spirit. Eternal life is not paid to us as a result of enough obedience. So too, God's rewards for obedience are not earned; rather, they are enjoyed when we obey. Salvation is offered as a free gift; our receiving it by faith puts us in a position to experience and enjoy this amazing reward. Without faith in Jesus the reward remains apart from us. So too with any reward from God. We must not ever think that we put God into a position from which he must pay us for our obedience.

We need to be careful when we move from Jehoshaphat's experience to ours. All worship of God is grounded in his grace experienced through faith. We have that in common with Jehoshaphat and all Old Testament saints, but our corporate acts of worship vary greatly from theirs. It is even hard for us to visualize worshipping by leading a lamb to the temple, seeing it killed in front of our eyes, and then burning all or a portion of it. Of course, this was only a portion of the worship, but it was central. They worshipped YHWH because of the grace he provided through his guidelines for their system of worship, and through faith they trusted that he would forgive and bless them. The sacrificial death and resurrection of Jesus is the fulfillment of this system. We no longer offer a lamb, because the *Lamb* was offered for us. Thus, our corporate worship of God is so very different than Jehoshaphat's.

Yet we have much in common. The Old Testaments saints were expected to daily follow the commands of YHWH and we are as well. And there is another sacrifice besides the sacrifice of Jesus. God, through the apostle Paul, calls us to offer ourselves as a living sacrifice

(Rom. 12). Simply put, God calls us to give up our sinful wills and submit to his. Jehoshaphat worshipped daily through obedience, and it is the same for us.

To worship God begins with trusting Jesus's sacrificial death for us and our worship continues when we offer ourselves as a living sacrifice and enjoy the newness of a resurrected life.

Now what?

Well, it sounds like exactly what a preacher would say—we need to worship God through obedience. Of course, this is true, but there is a nuance to this call of obedience. It is in the face of two specific temptations. The first challenge to obedience is the great successes that Jehoshaphat experienced. The implication that Dr. Williams pointed out is that the military and economic success of the king could have set him up for a prideful response of self-affirmation. When we look at the blessings of God and think we have earned them, we shift the source of blessing from God to ourselves. Instead of enjoying the blessing itself, we begin to take pleasure in thinking that it is our obedience and hard work that is the source—which leads to thinking that we can acquire more blessings through our will. We must always remember that blessings are God's gift, and that he is the source. Moses warned God's people: "Otherwise, you may say in your heart, 'My power and the strength of my hand made me this wealth'" (Deut. 8:17 NASB).

In our worship, we are to be diligent in our grateful dependence upon God for all his blessings and to acknowledge that he is the source. When we access our bank statement, we could either be discouraged that we don't have more money or be amazed at how much the Lord has given us. When we achieve a financial goal of paying off a loan or saving a certain amount, we should worship by giving thanks to our Lord who empowered us. At graduations, weddings, births—times when it is easier to see God's blessings—we should worship him as the source.

The success that Jehoshaphat struggled with perhaps led to the second more obvious challenge. In the atmosphere of success, one could easily think that blessings are earned. Jehoshaphat apparently sought to be blessed by an alliance with Ahab. When our mindset believes that we are the one who brings about blessings, we can easily look for other sources from which we can earn additional blessings. Our worship of God should guard us from looking to sources of blessing that he has cautioned us against. Alliances are not wrong unless they are with those who are opposed to the very thing we hold most dear.

We are not tempted to have political alliances as Jehoshaphat was. Our temptation to form dangerous alliances is more subtle. We are flooded with a hurricane of persuasive messages that ask us to align ourselves with their mindset. Advertisers, entertainers, employers, political leaders, even news reporters all send messages that invite us to align ourselves with them: "Buy this car and you will feel like you can go anywhere you want." "If you want to be respected, be like the lead character in this movie." "If you want security, commit your whole life to this company." "Trust this political philosophy for personal security." Each, in their own way, is asking us to think as they do. We need to remember why Jehoshaphat's alliance with Ahab was wrong: Ahab was not a worshipper of YHWH. When the voices come, we need to ask, "Whom do they worship?" Since God is the source of our blessings, only worship him.

Creativity in Presentation

This passage has three distinct parts, each of which needs to be presented:

- Jehoshaphat seeks YHWH and YHWH is with him (17:1–19)
- Ahab entices Jehoshaphat into attacking Ramoth-gilead (18:1–27)
- The battle at Ramoth-gilead and its aftermath (18:28–19:3)

The first and last scenes could be retold or simply read well. The middle episode is particularly dramatic and could be retold in a more artistic tone. Help the congregation see the scene by using some simple props, such as chairs to represent the two thrones. Place these on either side of the pulpit. When drawing the conclusion that there was another unseen throne in the room—that of YHWH—step into the pulpit or center area. God has given us this highly dramatic scene between these two contrasting kings, so give attention to the drama as you present it. As the story is told, be sure to contrast that Ahab doesn't worship YHWH while Jehoshaphat does. After the three scenes are presented, draw the application: seek blessings from God, not from a foolish alliance—which means that we worship God who blesses, rather than seeking blessings from those who don't worship him. Here is one possible structure:

- Present the text
  - Jehoshaphat seeks YHWH and YHWH is with him (17:1–19)
  - Ahab entices Jehoshaphat into attacking Ramoth-gilead (18:1–27)
  - The battle at Ramoth-gilead and its aftermath (18:28–19:3)
- Apply the text
  - Since God is the source of our blessings, only worship him.

DISCUSSION QUESTIONS

1. Make a list of how God blessed Jehoshaphat.

2. Make a list of how God blessed Judah through Jehoshaphat.

3. What are ways that Jehoshaphat could have thought about these blessings?

4. Why is it easy to not include God in our celebrations of our accomplishments?

5. What pressures might have caused Jehoshaphat to form an alliance with Ahab?

6. What is necessary in order to have an alliance?

7. How can an alliance affect each of its members?

2 Chronicles 19:4–21:1

EXEGETICAL IDEA
Even Jehoshaphat's righteous reforms and trust in YHWH in the face of battle could not eliminate the disastrous consequences of his alliance with a wicked nation.

THEOLOGICAL FOCUS
Justice and victory belong to God; therefore, trusting him only leads to blessing.

PREACHING IDEA
We can trust our powerful and just God.

PREACHING POINTERS
This story is astonishing. A nation goes to battle—with the choir leading the way. God, in his surprising ways, brings about victory by causing the enemies to turn upon each other. What a grand victory! Surely, we can trust our all-powerful Lord. However, this unusual victory is in the context of more normal activities: the setting up of a justice system and the disobedience of a king. The theme that is more subtle, which comes out in the fuller narrative, is that of God's justice. We can trust him because of his power and his justice. He can be trusted that he *can* and *will* do what is right.

REIGN OF JEHOSHAPHAT—TESTING JEHOSHAPHAT'S TRUST (19:4–21:1)

LITERARY STRUCTURE AND THEMES (19:4–21:1)

These chapters constitute the second part of Jehoshaphat's reign. This second part has a parallel structure with the first. First, both parts recount Jehoshaphat's righteous reforms in which he organizes officials to warn the people regarding YHWH's law. Second, both parts report a military conflict, but in this case, Judah faces an invasion by a three-nation alliance. Third, both parts conclude with a prophet condemning Jehoshaphat's alliance with an Israelite king.

Despite the parallel structure, the two parts differ considerably in how they present the military conflict. In the first part, the military conflict illustrates Jehoshaphat's alliance with Ahab. The conflict casts a negative light on Jehoshaphat. However, in the second part, the military conflict becomes an occasion for Jehoshaphat, and all Judah with him, to seek, trust, and worship YHWH. The conflict and Judah's response to it present Jehoshaphat quite positively. Only at the conclusion of Jehoshaphat's reign does the Chronicler include a negative note about his allying with the northern kingdom and its negative results. Even though Jehoshaphat worships YHWH and trusts him in times of distress, he cannot avoid the disastrous consequences of making an alliance with Israel's wicked king.

- *Jehoshaphat's Righteous Reforms (19:4–11)*
- *Judah Faces an Invasion (20:1–30)*
- *Conclusion of Jehoshaphat's Reign (20:31–21:1)*

EXPOSITION (19:4–21:1)

Those living in the ancient Near Eastern world understood spiritual forces to be operating in virtually every area of their lives. From agriculture to weather, from politics to warfare, spiritual beings shaped and even dictated the course of events on earth. During the second part of Jehoshaphat's rule, the Chronicler emphasizes the determinative role that God plays in justice, in battle, and in foreign alliances. In justice, the Chronicler emphasizes God's justice and highlights the role that priests and Levites play in carrying out this justice. In battle, the Chronicler highlights the role that priests and Levites play as the people watch God secure the victory. In foreign alliances, Jehoshaphat learns again that creating alliances with those who oppose YHWH only leads to failure. As a result, even though Jehoshaphat enacts righteous reforms and trusts YHWH in the face of an invasion, he still suffers the consequences of trusting a foreign alliance at the end of his life.

Jehoshaphat's Righteous Reforms (19:4–11)
Jehoshaphat returns the people to YHWH by setting up judges entrusted with administering YHWH's justice throughout the land.

19:4. The previous section of Jehoshaphat's reign concludes with a prophet's warning. Even though the prophet commends Jehoshaphat for removing Asherah poles and seeking YHWH, he condemns Jehoshaphat for allying himself with Ahab and claims that YHWH is angry with him. Following the prophet's warning, the Chronicler records that Jehoshaphat went throughout his territory to restore the people back to YHWH (2 Chron. 19:4). Elsewhere, YHWH's prophets warn the people to bring them back to YHWH (e.g., 2 Chron. 24:19; Neh. 9:26); for this reason, the Chronicler portrays Jehoshaphat doing the work of a prophet. The comment creates a link between Jehoshaphat and the prophet Jehu who warns him: just as Jehu warns the king so that he will return to YHWH in full devotion, so Jehoshaphat warns the people so that they will return to YHWH in full devotion.

Jehoshaphat's Territory

The Chronicler represents the extent of Jehoshaphat's activity by including Beersheba (a sign of the southernmost part of Judah) and the hill country of Ephraim (a sign of the northernmost part of Judah). The hill country of Ephraim is also the region that his father Asa previously captured. The implication is that Jehoshaphat went throughout all the territory under his rule, including territory formerly belonging to the northern kingdom of Israel.

19:5. The Chronicler illustrates one way in which Jehoshaphat returns the people to YHWH: Jehoshaphat appoints judges to serve in Judah's fortified cities and other judges to serve in Jerusalem. Three Pentateuchal passages serve as models for these two groups: Deuteronomy 16:18–20; 17:8–13; and Exodus 18:13–26. Based on Deuteronomy 16, the judges in the fortified cities serve as local judges. They are responsible for promoting justice in their region by making decisions that are impartial and fair. Based on Deuteronomy 17 and Exodus 18, the judges in Jerusalem apparently serve as experts who are responsible for discerning YHWH's will in difficult cases. For this reason and in line with Deuteronomy 17:9, this latter group of judges specifically includes Levites and priests (2 Chron. 17:8)—those who, in the first part of Jehoshaphat's reign (17:7–9), teach YHWH's law throughout Judah.

Pentateuchal Passages Regarding Judges

The following table lists passages that inform the presentation of 2 Chronicles 19:5–10. Specific parallel expressions appear underlined.

Deut. 16:18–20
[18] Appoint judges and officials for your tribes in all your towns the Lord your God is giving you. They are to judge the people with righteous judgment. [19] Do not deny justice or show partiality to anyone. Do not accept a bribe, for it blinds the eyes of the wise and twists the words of the righteous. [20] Pursue justice and justice alone, so that you will live and possess the land the Lord your God is giving you.

Deut. 17:8–10
[8] If a case is too difficult for you—concerning bloodshed, lawsuits, or assaults—cases disputed at your city gates, then go up to the place the Lord your God chooses. [9] You are to go to the Levitical priests and to the judge who presides at that time. Ask, and they will give you a verdict in the case. [10] You must abide by the verdict they give you at the place the Lord chooses. Be careful to do exactly as they instruct you.

Exod. 18:20
[20] Instruct ["warn," hiphil זהר] them about the statutes and laws, and teach them the way to live and what they must do. [21] But you should select from all the people able men, God-fearing, trustworthy, and hating dishonest profit. Place them over the people as commanders of thousands, hundreds, fifties, and tens. [22] They should judge the people at all times. Then they can bring you every major case but judge every minor case themselves. In this way you will lighten your load, and they will bear it with you.

19:6–7. One can perceive the spiritual significance of appointing these judges by looking at Jehoshaphat's words to them. First, to the judges serving in Judah's fortified cities, Jehoshaphat warns them to be careful about the decisions they make. Drawing on the vocabulary and overall theme of Deuteronomy 16:18–20, Jehoshaphat explains why they must be careful: (1) they are responsible to YHWH for their decisions, not to other people (including the king), (2) YHWH will know the decisions they make because he will be present when they make their decisions, and (3) YHWH himself is just because he does not show partiality or accept bribes. For these reasons, they should be afraid of YHWH, implying that YHWH will punish them if they make an unjust decision.

Partiality Forbidden in Law

The Mosaic law repeatedly forbids showing partiality (Lev. 19:15; Deut. 1:17; 10:17; 16:19) or taking bribes (Exod. 23:8; Deut. 10:17; 16:19). Jehoshaphat's statement draws on the vocabulary and reasoning of a few verses from Deuteronomy in particular. For instance, he draws on Deuteronomy 1:17 to remind the judges not to be afraid of people because judgment belongs to YHWH. He also combines the language describing YHWH in Deuteronomy 10:17 ("does not show partiality and does not take a bribe" לֹא־יִשָּׂא פָנִים וְלֹא יִקַּח שֹׁחַד) with the command to judges recorded in Deuteronomy 16:19 ("do not show partiality and do not take a bribe" לֹא תַכִּיר פָּנִים וְלֹא־תִקַּח שֹׁחַד). The Chronicler often alludes to the Mosaic law by combining similar elements from different passages.

19:8–10. Second, to the judges in Jerusalem, Jehoshaphat draws on Deuteronomy 17 and Exodus 18 to warn them. As before, he commands them to carry out their duty impartially and fairly—that is, with fear of YHWH, faithfully, and wholeheartedly. However, with this second group of judges, he emphasizes that if the judges fail to do their task, not only will they suffer consequences but the people will be guilty before YHWH and provoke him to anger. Furthermore, the task for these judges involves more than just deciding disputes between parties; it involves

warning the people regarding what YHWH has said in various laws, commandments, statutes, and judgments. For these reasons, their task as judges takes on a spiritual dimension, with serious consequences for the whole nation.

TRANSLATION ANALYSIS:
Several translations (e.g., CSB, ESV, NASB, NET, NIV, NKJ, NLT) render Jehoshaphat's command as "warn" (*hiphil* זהר); however, a small number (e.g., NRSV) render the word as "teach." The translation "teach" likely results from the parallel text of Exodus 18:20. In that context, *hiphil* זהר is followed by *hiphil* ידע. Since ידע focuses on knowledge, one can interpret זהר primarily in terms of imparting knowledge, that is, teaching. However, *hiphil* זהר occurs several times in the watchman passages of Ezekiel 3 and 33. In these contexts, the word carries the connotations of warning, not just instructing or teaching. Furthermore, the idea of warning also fits well in the context of Exodus 18:20. For this reason, the translation "warn" is preferred.

Use of Pentateuchal Language

Jehoshaphat's words in 2 Chronicles 19:10 combine and modify elements from Deuteronomy 17:8 and Exodus 18:20. When Jehoshaphat instructs them to warn or teach the people, he uses the word זהר, which occurs in the Pentateuch only in Exodus 18:20. Deuteronomy 17:8 contains a listing of various types of disputes. The Chronicler takes up the listing; however, he only keeps the first type of dispute and then modifies the listing to contain different types of instructions found in Mosaic law. Furthermore, his concern that the people will be found guilty before YHWH reflects the concern that the people follow the judges' verdict or suffer serious consequences (Deut. 17:10–12).

Jehoshaphat's warning to these judges also plays an interesting role in the larger context of Jehoshaphat's reign. Jehoshaphat commands the judges to perform for the people the same task that the prophet Jehu performed for him: to give a warning so that, by stopping the prohibited activity, YHWH's wrath may be avoided. Since appointing these judges is part of Jehoshaphat's response to the prophet's warning, it is fitting that he commands them to provide the same opportunity for others in Judah.

19:11. Finally, Jehoshaphat points out specific posts among these judges. He distinguishes between two individuals who supervise two types of cases: the chief priest, who supervises cases pertaining to YHWH, and a high official of Judah, who oversees cases pertaining to the king. Although one might be tempted to describe the first group as religious and the second as secular, it is more likely that the Chronicler intends to distinguish between cases involving cultic matters and cases involving noncultic matters (McKenzie 2004, 294). For both types of cases, the Levites serve as administrative officials. Likely, Jehoshaphat intends this administrative structure to promote justice in his kingdom and limit the ever-present danger of corruption (as seen in Jehoshaphat's final words to the judges: "May YHWH be with those who do what is good," 19:11b).

Jehoshaphat's Role in Judging

It is interesting that Jehoshaphat plays no direct role in making judicial decisions himself. He creates this system, but once it is in place these judges have the responsibility to decide all the cases. This aspect of Jehoshaphat's reign contrasts sharply with other kings (e.g., 1 Sam. 8:5; 2 Sam. 8:15; 1 Kings 3:16–28). See R. Klein 2012, 276–77. In this way, this narrative may have provided the first readers with a better model for administrating justice than other narratives, since the first readers did not live under a Davidic king's rule.

For the first readers, this account would carry several implications. First, it addresses two temptations that would be present under imperial rule: (1) to revolt against the foreign

judicial authority, or (2) for those Jews able to serve as local authorities, to abuse their power for personal gain. Second, since the first readers had to navigate how to rebuild and reinstitute temple worship, questions regarding how to proceed would certainly arise. The text points to the priests, supported by the Levites, as judges in such issues. Third, it models how the priests should employ Mosaic law to ensure that the people do not become guilty before YHWH. Just as the text cites, combines, and applies Mosaic legislation, the priests should also ensure that the people know the law so that they may avoid disobeying YHWH.

Judah Faces an Invasion (20:1–30)
When Jehoshaphat leads Judah to trust YHWH to fight a large attacking alliance, YHWH wins the victory and blesses Judah.

20:1–2. Sometime after Jehoshaphat appoints the judges, an alliance of Ammonites, Moabites, and Meunites invades his territory. The Chronicler describes these forces as a "vast multitude," approaching from Edom and already crossing the Dead Sea into Judah's territory at En Gedi, a town within Judah's allotment (see Josh. 15:62). Although the Chronicler does not report the number of warriors in this invading force, he clearly presents the force as quite large. Jehoshaphat's father Asa faced a "vast multitude," a force almost twice as large as his own (2 Chron. 14:8). Here also, the phrase indicates an overwhelming attacking force.

TRANSLATION ANALYSIS:
Some translations (NASB, NKJV) preserve MT's reading "Syria," that is, Aram (אֲרָם); however, the rest of the narrative repeatedly refers to Mount Seir and alludes to passages dealing with Edom. For this reason, it is more likely that MT represents an unintentional copyist mistake, interchanging ר for ד. The more likely reading is "Edom" (אֱדוֹם). Furthermore, most translations list the third group as the Meunites (מְעוּנִים). The

NKJV, following the MT, reads "Ammonites" (הָעַמּוֹנִים); however, the MT reading is the result of a transposition of two consonants מ and ע.

Meunites

The terms for the third foreign ally change during the course of the narrative. The narrative introduces them as the Meunites. Identifying the Meunites is not an easy task; however, the evidence here suggests that they are a group, probably nomadic or seminomadic, who lives in and/or around the land of Edom at the time of this battle (cf. Merrill 2015, 427 n. 72). The narrative later refers to them as those from "Mount Seir," an alternative name for Edom.

20:3–6. This invading force frightens Jehoshaphat. While afraid, he commits himself to seeking YHWH. He calls upon all Judah to fast. In response, individuals from all Judah's cities gather to join the king in seeking YHWH at the temple. As Judah gathers together in the temple, Jehoshaphat stands before the assembly and begins to pray. He begins with an affirmation of who YHWH is, what he is like, and what he has done in relation to Israel. He emphasizes two points: (1) YHWH has universal ruling authority, and (2) as Israel's God YHWH has given them the land. Both points motivate his prayer. Because YHWH has universal ruling authority, he has the right and power to resolve the situation. Jehoshaphat portrays this universal rule by describing YHWH as a king (or perhaps better, an emperor). He rules from heaven over all nations (including the Moabites, Ammonites, and Meunites) and as a powerful king, no one has the power to stand against him. At the same time, because YHWH has handed over the land to Israel, Jehoshaphat appeals to him to defend Israel's right to the land he gave them.

20:7–9. Next, Jehoshaphat describes how Israel has responded to YHWH—in particular, his giving them the land. Even Israel's response to YHWH motivates Jehoshaphat to pray because

Israel has built a temple for YHWH and at that time YHWH said that the temple would be a place for Israel to come so that YHWH might hear them in times of crisis. Using general rather than specific language, he alludes to what Solomon prayed when he dedicated the temple (2 Chron. 6). Jehoshaphat is showing how he (and all Judah with him) is following the model outlined in Solomon's prayer. Therefore, YHWH should hear his cry for help and intervene on his behalf.

There are several interesting points to raise concerning Jehoshaphat's prayer at this point. First, the prayer walks a fine line when describing YHWH's presence. On the one hand, YHWH is in heaven. On the other hand, YHWH is present in the temple. At the same time, YHWH's presence extends beyond both, since neither place can contain him (see 2 Chron. 2:6 [HB 5]). Still, his presence in heaven illustrates his sovereign rule over all nations. His presence in the temple illustrates his relationship with his people because there he receives and accepts worship and sacrifices, and there he hears and answers prayer. This prayer illustrates how Chronicles struggles to capture the nature of YHWH's presence in the world: he is both far away in heaven and close at hand in the temple (for further reflections on YHWH's presence as close and far, see Wright 2003, 240–67).

Second, the language further generalizes the situation of Solomon's temple building. Jehoshaphat does not mention Solomon, but all Israel. He does not cite Solomon's specific words, but several general terms referring to disasters and crises. This general language shows that the principles underlying Solomon's prayer may apply to different historical circumstances. Jehoshaphat's confidence that Solomon's prayer may apply to different circumstances partly motivates him to pray to YHWH and call for help.

20:10–11. Next, Jehoshaphat describes the problem he is facing. He sets the stage by describing how Israel treated those from Ammon, Moab, and Edom/Mount Seir in the past, specifically as Israel was making the journey from Egypt to the promised land. He alludes to Deuteronomy 2 (especially 2:5, 9, and 19) to describe how YHWH allotted land for Moab, Ammon, and Edom with the result that YHWH did not allow Israel to invade them. However, against this backdrop, these people are repaying Israel by trying to drive Israel out of its land. Jehoshaphat is making the point that this invasion is unjust. Not only is it unjust because it repays Israel's kindness with cruelty, but it also violates how YHWH has assigned the nations their lands, in this case, how YHWH has assigned Israel its land. Jehoshaphat highlights this latter claim by referring to the land as YHWH's possession which he gave to Israel to be their possession.

20:12. Having demonstrated that the invaders are acting unjustly, Jehoshaphat calls on YHWH to act justly by punishing the invaders. Furthermore, he contrasts the helplessness of Judah before the powerful enemy approaching them. Finally, he admits that Judah does not know what to do; however, they are looking to YHWH for help. The picture of Judah here contrasts sharply with the picture of YHWH at the beginning of Jehoshaphat's prayer: Judah is without power and plan, but YHWH is full of power and rules over all nations. In fact, the entire prayer plays off such contrasts; as Japhet states, "The prayer is in fact built on antithesis: powerful and treacherous invaders against a powerless and righteous Israel; helpless humans pleading with an omnipotent Lord" (1993, 788; for importance of this theme in Chronicles, see Plöger 2000, 45).

20:13–14. The Chronicler records two responses to Jehoshaphat's prayer. First, all Judah, including their most vulnerable (women, infants, and children), responds to Jehoshaphat's prayer by standing with him in the temple,

affirming what the king has prayed (R. Klein 2012, 288). Second, YHWH responds to Jehoshaphat's prayer by setting his spirit upon Jahaziel, one of the Levites, a son of Asaph, to deliver an answer to Jehoshaphat's prayer.

Jahaziel as Prophetic Figure
Jahaziel appears as a prophetic figure here. First, he is a son of Asaph, a temple singer. Elsewhere the Chronicler portrays the temple singers, including Asaph, as those who prophesy (see 1 Chron. 25:1–3). Second, when Jahaziel uses the expression "Thus says YHWH," he indicates that he is speaking as a messenger of one with higher authority. In the OT, this expression occurs often in prophetic speech, where the prophets deliver YHWH's message.

20:15–17. YHWH's answer precisely corresponds to Jehoshaphat's need. Considering Jehoshaphat's fear (20:3), YHWH encourages him not to be afraid. Considering Jehoshaphat's powerlessness, YHWH reminds him that this is YHWH's fight, and YHWH will win this battle. Considering Jehoshaphat's uncertainty about what to do, YHWH provides specific instructions to follow (for details, see Japhet 1993, 793). These instructions boil down to two actions: (1) go to a place designated by YHWH, and (2) watch as YHWH wins the battle. Finally, YHWH assures Jehoshaphat that he will be with him. If Jehoshaphat will follow these instructions, YHWH guarantees victory.

Slope of Ziz
The text speaks of the slope of Ziz, east of the wilderness of Jeruel. The precise location is unknown; however, 20:20 implies that it is near Tekoa.

20:18–19. Jehoshaphat and all the people respond to YHWH's word of affirmation by worshipping YHWH. The people bow down while some of the Levites stand, presumably to praise YHWH through music and song. In this way, the Chronicler presents a picture of how YHWH's people respond properly to YHWH's word of deliverance.

Bowing in Submission, Standing in Praise

The actions of bowing and standing recur in this narrative. Earlier, when Jehoshaphat prays to YHWH and all Judah and Jerusalem join him, everyone stands together before YHWH in making their request. Now that YHWH has assured them that he will deliver them, they all bow together before YHWH to worship him for answering their request. Only a group of the Levites behaves differently: rather than bowing, they stand to praise YHWH, presumably through music and song.

20:20. The Chronicler briefly transitions to the next day by showing that Judah obeys Jahaziel's instructions. As the people arrive at their destination, Jehoshaphat encourages them to trust in YHWH and his prophets. These words allude to Isaiah's words to Ahaz, recorded in Isaiah 7:9b ("If you do not believe, you will not be secure"). Isaiah speaks these words as Ahaz also faces a threat of attacking forces.

However, Jehoshaphat's words extend beyond the allusion to Isaiah 7:9; they continue by calling for faith in YHWH's prophets as well. This continuation likely alludes to another important OT passage describing YHWH's deliverance: Exodus 14 (Beentjes 1993, 267). Exodus 14 describes how YHWH destroys the attacking Egyptian army by covering them in the waters of the sea. After YHWH destroys the Egyptian army, the text reads, "The people feared YHWH, and they believed in YHWH and in his servant Moses." It is difficult to establish an allusion to Exodus with this evidence alone. However, there are other signs in the context that the Chronicler is alluding to Exodus 14. Jahaziel's words to Judah closely parallel Moses's words to Israel in Exodus 14:13–14, delivered just before they cross the sea. Not only are the words similar, but the narrative structures are also similar:

(1) an enemy attacks, (2) the people lament, (3) a person answers the lament with encouragement and clear directions for what to do, and (4) Israel watches as YHWH defeats the attackers (Beentjes 1993, 265).

Comparing Exodus 14:13–14 to Jahaziel's Words

The following lists the parallel expressions between the two passages by underlining them.

Exod. 14:13–14

[13] But Moses said to the people, "_Don't be afraid. Stand firm_ and_ see the Lord's salvation_ that he will accomplish for you today; for the Egyptians you see today, you will never see again. [14] The Lord will fight for you, and you must be quiet."

2 Chron. 20:15, 17

[15] and he [Jahaziel] said, "Listen carefully, all Judah and you inhabitants of Jerusalem, and King Jehoshaphat. This is what the Lord says: '_Do not be afraid_ or discouraged because of this vast number, for the battle is not yours, but God's. . . . [17] You do not have to fight this battle. Position yourselves, _stand still_, and_ see the salvation of the Lord_. He is with you, Judah and Jerusalem. Do not be afraid or discouraged. Tomorrow, go out to face them, for the Lord is with you.'"

By recalling YHWH's victory recorded in Exodus 14, these words encourage Judah to trust YHWH and his prophets, since YHWH has delivered in the past and so can do it again. Furthermore, these words closely link the prophets' authority with YHWH's authority, just as Exodus 14:13b links Moses's authority with YHWH's. Obeying or ignoring a prophet's warning is obeying or ignoring YHWH's warning. In this case, the word "prophet" designates more than just someone who holds an office of prophet; it refers to one who speaks YHWH's word, just as the Levitical singer

Jahaziel does (20:15–17). Just as Jehoshaphat earlier has listened to the prophet's warning (19:3–4), he calls on the people to do the same.

20:21. After Jehoshaphat speaks these encouraging words, he consults with the people to appoint some musicians to rally the troops by praising YHWH. These musicians are presumably Levites since elsewhere in Chronicles musicians are usually identified as Levites (e.g., 1 Chron. 15:16; 2 Chron. 5:12; 7:6). As the musicians go out before the troops, they shout out a shortened expression of praise found repeatedly in Chronicles: "Give thanks to YHWH because his faithful love endures forever" (see 1 Chron. 16:34, 41; 2 Chron. 5:13; 7:3, 6). This expression of YHWH's faithful character verbally affirms that they are trusting YHWH, just as Jehoshaphat encouraged them to do. Therefore, based on Jehoshaphat's word, one would next expect that the people will be secure and successful (see 20:20), and indeed they are.

TRANSLATION ANALYSIS:
One translation question that arises in 20:21 regards the Levites' praise. The Hebrew text reads וּמְהַלְלִים לְהַדְרַת־קֹדֶשׁ. The phrase contains a certain ambiguity. The word הֲדָרָה carries the sense of "majesty" or "adornment" (cf. *HALOT* s.v. "הֲדָרָה" 240). The expression itself almost always occurs in the context of worshipping YHWH. Some translations render the phrase according to the sense of majesty (CSB, NIV "splendor of his holiness"; NET "his majestic splendor"; NLT, NRSV "his holy splendor"). Some translations render the phrase according to the sense of adornment (ESV, NASB "in holy attire"; NKJV "the beauty of holiness"). In either case, the phrase portrays YHWH as a glorious king before whom the musicians play as part of their service in honoring him.

20:22–23. As the people begin shouting their praises to YHWH, he fights for them. YHWH fights by provoking the attacking forces to fight with each other. To start, the Ammonites and Moabites turn on those from Mount Seir (earlier called the Meunites). Once they destroy the Meunite force, they turn on each other until all three forces are decimated.

Armies Attacking One Another
The text is not exactly clear regarding how YHWH provokes the attacking forces to turn on each other. The Hebrew describes YHWH as setting up מְאָרְבִים (*piel* ptc. masc. plural from אָרב). This form could indicate that he set individuals up in ambush (cf. Judg. 9:25) or the plural might mark the form as abstract (e.g., חַיִּים "life"). If the former is the case, then these may be humans (Japhet 2009, 103) or angelic beings (Rudolph 1955, 261). If an abstract, then the expression just communicates that YHWH attacks them by surprise (see NET "suddenly attacked"). The latter option seems more likely since the Chronicler does not appear to be as interested in how YHWH provokes the forces to turn on each other, only that he successfully does so.

Two verbs that the Chronicler uses to portray the extent of destruction deserve special attention: "to devote to destruction" (*hiphil* חרם) and "to destroy" (*hiphil* שׁמד). Both verbs are associated with the time of the conquest. The root חרם occurs often in Deuteronomy and Joshua to describe how the Israelites were to devote their enemies to complete destruction. The latter verb שׁמד occurs three other times in Chronicles. In each context, the verb alludes back to the time of the conquest. Twice, it refers to the nations who previously occupied Israel (1 Chron. 5:25; 2 Chron. 33:9). Once, in the context of Jehoshaphat's prayer as these attacking forces are coming against him, it describes what YHWH would not allow Israel to do: destroy Ammon, Moab, and those from Mount Seir (2 Chron. 20:10). Now what Israel was not allowed to do to these nations, these nations have done to themselves. However, even though these nations destroy themselves, they only destroy their attacking forces; their national boundaries which YHWH allotted them (that is, their possession; see 20:11) are still intact. In other words, the text reflects a respect for the land YHWH allotted the nations; in this case, it is only when the nations threaten the possession that YHWH has allotted Israel that they suffer destruction.

For the first readers, this example would be a source of hope and comfort. Since the land is still YHWH's possession, the people could expect that YHWH would both bring his people into the land as he had done before and, in light of this particular narrative, defend it if they respond to YHWH the way that Jehoshaphat and the rest of Judah do.

20:24–25. After the attacking forces destroy themselves, the people of Judah look upon the battlefield, only to see that all the invading forces are dead. The narrative shifts to the three significant results of YHWH's deliverance. The first result is that the people gain tremendous wealth because Judah gathers the spoils of the conflict. In fact, the quantity is so great that the people require three days to gather it all. The Chronicler presents these spoils as rewards for Judah's trust in YHWH.

20:26–28. The second result of YHWH's deliverance is that the people celebrate the victory. They initially gather to praise YHWH; therefore, the place where they gather becomes known as the "Valley of Blessing." From this valley, all Judah continues to celebrate as Jehoshaphat leads them back to the temple in Jerusalem. This journey brings the entire narrative back to where it starts: all the people, gathered in Jerusalem, at the temple, with Jehoshaphat leading them. However, in this case rather than fasting and lamenting (see 20:3–13), everyone is celebrating with joyful music. As the Chronicler shows, YHWH reverses the situation by taking this disastrous crisis and making it an occasion for celebration.

TRANSLATION ANALYSIS:

The traditional English gloss for the Hebrew verb piel ברך is "bless." However, the sense of this shifts depending upon the subject and object. When God blesses a person, he bestows upon that person some benefit or special power. However, when a person blesses God, he praises God, usually because God is the source of a benefit or special power. Even though in contemporary English "bless" may carry both senses, "bless" occurs more frequently in the former sense (e.g., God bless America). At the same time, "praise" and "give thanks" occur more frequently for the latter sense. Several translations preserve the English gloss "bless" (e.g., ESV, NASB, NKJV, NRSV); several others render the verb in light of more typical contemporary usage: "praise" and/or "give thanks" (e.g., CSB, NET, NIV, NLT). The challenge for the latter translations is that in the name of this region, the noun form "blessing" (בְּרָכָה) is ambiguous: it may refer to YHWH blessing the people or the people blessing YHWH. Although this verse applies the word "bless" (ברך) to the people blessing YHWH, the context of the narrative shows that both senses of the verb can be in view.

20:29–30. The third result of YHWH's deliverance is that all the surrounding nations become too afraid to attack Judah because they hear how YHWH has fought against Judah's enemies. As a result, Jehoshaphat experiences peace throughout the rest of his reign. This comment about the "dread of God" alludes back to the beginning of Jehoshaphat's reign. In 2 Chronicles 17:10, the "dread of YHWH" deterred nations from attacking Jehoshaphat; however, those verses address nations north, south, and west of Judah. As Japhet says, "Now, after the victory on the eastern frontier, Jehoshaphat's kingdom reaches the blessed state of 'peace' and 'rest round about'—the ideal to which every generation aspires" (1993, 799). In other words, because Judah trusts YHWH, they become an example of the Chronicler's picture of what Israel should be: all the people gathered to praise YHWH in the Jerusalem temple during a period of peace. For the first readers, this picture would again be their goal: to gather all Israel to worship YHWH at the rebuilt temple in Jerusalem, while they experience peace from all their opponents.

Conclusion of Jehoshaphat's Reign (20:31–21:1)

The Chronicler characterizes Jehoshaphat as an upright king but also looks to the coming trouble that an alliance with Israel will bring.

20:31–34. The conclusion to Jehoshaphat's reign raises two important points for the Chronicler. First, the conclusion repeats the theological assessment for Jehoshaphat's reign, commenting that he follows the ways of his father Asa by doing what is upright. Also, like his father Asa (see 2 Chron. 15:17), the people do not follow YHWH exclusively as they still worship at the high places. The Chronicler reiterates that Jehoshaphat is an upright king, even though he is not perfect.

Asa and Jehoshaphat

This same situation applies for Jehoshaphat's father Asa. Even though Asa was upright, the people were not, because they still did not remove the high places (2 Chron. 15:17). For other connections between Asa and Jehoshaphat, see comments regarding 2 Chronicles 17:1–19.

20:35–37. Second, the conclusion includes a small narrative with the following outline: Jehoshaphat forges an alliance with Israel's king Ahaziah, they construct ships together, a prophetic figure condemns the alliance, and the ships are destroyed. The elements of this narrative reflect a similar structure as Jehoshaphat's alliance with Ahab. Again, the upright Jehoshaphat makes an alliance with a wicked Israelite king, ultimately leading to a prophetic condemnation and failure. By closing out

Jehoshaphat's reign in this way, he shows how harmful such an alliance can be even for a king as upright as Jehoshaphat.

In fact, the Chronicler's entire account of Jehoshaphat's reign contrasts Jehoshaphat's faithful devotion to YHWH with his foolish alliance to wicked Israel. In the first part of Jehoshaphat's reign, the Chronicler emphasizes Jehoshaphat's devotion to YHWH. He even shows how this devotion reduces the negative consequences of his alliance with wicked Ahab. In the second half, again the Chronicler emphasizes Jehoshaphat's devotion to YHWH. However, Jehoshaphat's final alliance with wicked Ahaziah casts a negative shadow on his positive actions. In the first part, his devotion saves him from disaster brought about by his alliance, while in the second part his alliance prevents him from having full success.

21:1. Jehoshaphat's reign precedes the reign of his wicked son Jehoram. The Chronicler emphasizes that one reason Jehoram acts wickedly is because his wife is Ahab's daughter Athaliah. The wicked house of Ahab has a tremendous influence on Jehoram (2 Chron. 21:6). Even though Jehoshaphat is an upright king devoted to YHWH, his alliance with Ahab and then Ahaziah paves the road for wicked Israel to steer Judah astray. The Chronicler seems to show that only Jehoshaphat's personal devotion preserved Judah during his reign. For this reason, the Chronicler presents Jehoshaphat's reign in an ambiguous light (see Knoppers 1991, 500–524).

The first readers faced a complex set of possibilities and problems, and this passage seems to address two temptations they faced. The first temptation was turning to other gods, rituals, or religious authorities. The generation of first readers still struggled to rely on YHWH exclusively and worship him according to his ways. The second temptation was turning to other political powers. The postexilic community held little power in a large, powerful empire. As they sought to reconstitute themselves as a people living again in the land of their ancestors, such help from outside groups could greatly benefit them. However, such help would threaten the integrity of the community (see Ezra 4:1–4; Neh. 13:28–31). Jehoshaphat's reign addresses both temptations: he serves as a model to imitate for his devotion to YHWH, but he serves as a model to avoid for his foreign alliances.

THEOLOGICAL FOCUS

Justice and victory belong to God; therefore, trusting him only leads to blessing.

As mentioned above, Jehoshaphat is an ambiguous character in Chronicles. On the one hand, he follows God in righteous reforms and trusts him in the face of an invasion. On the other hand, he entangles himself in alliances with the northern kingdom, which has altogether abandoned YHWH to worship other gods. However, despite the ambiguity of Jehoshaphat, God remains the same, and he deals with his people according to his consistent character.

Throughout this passage God is consistently just. This passage emphasizes God's justice in various ways. First, in the beginning of the passage, God's justice serves as the theme of Jehoshaphat's judicial reform. Jehoshaphat points out that justice belongs to God because he is just, he is present, and he punishes injustice. These qualities of God's justice form a mostly assumed but sometimes stated conviction about the character of God running throughout the Bible. Second, when the three-nation alliance invades Judah, Jehoshaphat cries out to God and relies on God's justice to defend Judah's claim to the land and to repel the invasion. God recognizes the rightness of Jehoshaphat's complaint against these nations; therefore, God defends his people against the injustice and punishes the invaders thoroughly. Third, at the end of the account, God again punishes Jehoshaphat for his alliance with Israel. By punishing Jehoshaphat for this alliance, God proves his consistent character. Just as God punished Jehoshaphat for his alliance

with Ahab (2 Chron. 18), so he punishes his alliance with the sinful King Ahaziah. In these various ways, God proves to be just.

Throughout the passage God is consistently powerful. Again, each of the three main episodes of this passage reveal God's power. First, in the judicial reforms, the text emphasizes that God has the power to punish; for this reason, those who judge should be filled with a fear and terror of God. The fear of punishment should serve as a deterrent against injustice and corruption. Second, during the battle, God shows that he has the power to deliver his people even when his people only stand back and watch. God's power is such that he can take the weapons of his enemies and turn them into weapons against his enemies. Third, in the context of Jehoshaphat's alliance, God frustrates the work of the alliance so that the ships constructed together become useless and never set sail. In each case, God has the power to accomplish his purposes whether protecting his people from injustice, delivering his people from invasion, or rendering useless an inappropriate alliance.

One way God's justice and power come together in this passage is through warning. Warnings frame this passage. At the front, Jehoshaphat responds to the prophetic warning (2 Chron. 19:2–3) by warning the judges to practice justice so that they will warn the people to avoid iniquity (2 Chron. 19:10). At the end of the passage, another prophet warns Jehoshaphat regarding his (second) alliance with wicked Israel. These warnings point to God's justice because they show that God will be angry against sin. They point to God's power because one can be assured that God can carry out the penalty. At the same time, these warnings point beyond God's justice and power to his mercy. The warning serves as an opportunity to repent and mitigate the penalty of sin. Jehoshaphat's reign shifts directions quickly when, following the disastrous defeat at Ramoth-gilead, God again blesses Jehoshaphat greatly because he heeds the prophetic warning—until the last days of his reign. God's justice and power are reassuring qualities for those who are righteous, but terrifying for those who are wicked. However, this just, powerful God is also merciful by repeatedly warning others to repent and responding to them when they do.

Finally, this passage points to the proper human response to God's justice, power, and mercy: trust him alone. In certain ways, Jehoshaphat's reign is a tragedy. He is a righteous king who trusts and follows God at important times. However, the final words spoken concerning him include a prophetic condemnation and the failure of his joint venture with a foreign alliance. The passage raises the question whether a foreign alliance would be acceptable at all. Other kings of Judah have agreements with foreign kings (e.g., Solomon and Huram), so an alliance itself does not appear to be unacceptable.

In this case, the Chronicler appears to have two factors in mind. First, Jehoshaphat makes an alliance with wicked Israel. Israel has abandoned God; therefore, it is not an acceptable alliance at this time. Second, this type of foreign alliance looks to secure Judah's borders rather than trust God. In other words, here the case recalls other instances in Chronicles in which a king relies on some form of military might of his own rather than relying on God (e.g., see 1 Chron. 21; 2 Chron. 14–16). God condemns any attempt to secure Judah's future besides trusting in him. This principle extends beyond Judah as an ancient nation; it also applies to individuals living in the past or the present. One may state the Chronicler's point in the following way: not trusting fully in God means not trusting in God at all.

PREACHING AND TEACHING STRATEGIES

Exegetical and Theological Synthesis
Our Lord is just and powerful. Human authorities can only strive for these two attributes.

Our experience with flawed human authorities causes us to think that God will be like them. People may want to see justice done, but often they lack the power to take the needed action. And the power that we do have is often misguided because we are not always just. Even our best intentions to be just are thwarted because we have limited knowledge and are not in a position to know what is just. Thus, this lack of power and limited ability to be just causes us to withhold our trust in others.

This passage shows us that our Lord is both powerful and just. He can be trusted to be just and do the right thing, and he can be trusted that he *can* and *will* do what is right. Jehoshaphat and Judah see his powerful hand in providing deliverance from enemies, while at the same time bringing about justice that is due to these enemies. The theme of justice is also seen in Jehoshaphat's appointing Levites to exercise judgments in disputes within the nation. And God's power is reaffirmed in his disciplining hand that came against Jehoshaphat in his later days.

The narrative not only affirms that we can trust the just and powerful Lord, but it gives us a picture of what this trust looks like. In prosperity Jehoshaphat acted with integrity to set up a system of judges that promoted justice within the nation. In a time of crisis, trust was expressed in worship. Then, in a negative example, his trust should have been expressed in continued obedience, rather than forming an alliance with evil.

So, our trust in a just and powerful God can be expressed in our living with integrity, worship, and continued obedience.

Preaching Idea
We can trust our powerful and just God.

Contemporary Connections

What does it mean?
Few Christians would argue that God is not powerful and just. Our difficulty in thinking

about what this means is in grasping the extent of his power. Judah saw firsthand the miraculous defeat of her enemies. While we can't fully grasp the extent of his power and justice, we can reflect on power and justice that we can grasp and from that we can at least get a hint of what it means that God is powerful and just.

On November 16, 2022, the first rocket of NASA's Artemis Mission was launched. The payload contained an unmanned solar-powered spacecraft for further exploration of the moon, and is the prototype for a mission to Mars. Watching the rockets fire and lift that massive rocket into space is a testimony to our ability to harness incredible power. We see power displayed in many other ways that are more a part of our daily lives:

- Powerful movies move us emotionally.
- Powerful trucks can drive through mud with a heavy load.
- Powerful sermons touch us spiritually.
- Powerful presentations result in the sale.
- Powerful people make things happen.

We all want to have power. Power simply means that there is an ability to produce an effect. When the electrical power goes out, we are robbed of our ability to do so many things, from cooking to charging our cell phones. From the power to light the smallest flashlight to the majestic and frightening flash of a bolt of lightning, there are limits to power. Even when we envision the massive and seemingly unending power of a massive waterfall like Niagara Falls or Victoria Falls, our concept of power falls far short of God's power. God never has a power failure. God never needs a bigger truck. God never gets tired. There is no end to God's power.

Is it true?

True justice is harder for us to see in this fallen world. What teenager has not, at one time, said, "Life is not fair"? Children who are too young to grasp what justice is are often victims of an unjust system or of self-centered parents. And what adult at one time has not looked at a paycheck or outstanding bill and said, "Life is not fair"? However, occasionally we get a glimpse of true justice: when a teacher admits a test question was unclear and no longer counts it as part of the test; when an employer gives a bonus beyond expectations; when a neighbor not only apologizes for hitting our mailbox, but buys and installs a new and better one. There are moments when the world is fair and just.

And there are the times, due to incomplete knowledge, when we unknowingly are unjust and even cruel. The intent was justice, but the action was injustice. I first heard this story from Charles Swindoll, though I don't know the exact source: As a prank a man was given a fake turkey by his coworkers. The employee thought it was a real turkey. Then on his bus ride home he began talking with a man who was disheartened because he wanted to buy a Thanksgiving meal for his family, but he only had a few dollars, which was utterly insufficient. So the employee, not wanting to take away the man's dignity but wanting to help him, sold his fake turkey to him. Imagine the anger and sense of injustice when the bus rider opened the wrapping, only to discover it was a fake turkey. One of our family sayings, when faced with what appears to be injustice, is "Remember the turkey." We do not know the whole story. A lack of knowledge often causes a judge, jury, employer, foreman, or some other authority to unknowingly dispense injustice. God never has a lack of knowledge. He is always just.

Now what?

Because God is powerful and just, we should fully trust him. The three divisions of this text give us actions to take that are expressions of our trust.

In a time of prosperity Jehoshaphat acts with integrity to set up a government that prompts justice. When we are in a time of prosperity—and other times as well, but particularly when we have material blessings—we need to act with integrity. Do we strive to be explicitly honest in our business dealings? Do we follow through with our promises? When we make mistakes, do we admit the error and then correct it—and if needed, make restitution? If we are going to fully trust a powerful and just God, we need to strive to be just with all the power that we have.

When the crisis came to Judah, Jehoshaphat led the nation to worship. This is not the only action he took. He organized an army and made plans to defend the nation, but worship was highlighted by the Chronicler. Worship of our great God reminds us that he is able to supply our needs and has done so in the past. When the cancer comes, we seek medical care. When the finances dry up, we make changes. When the hard days at work come, we remain faithful to do the work. And all the while, we worship. We gather with other believers to sing of our great God who is all-powerful and just. We spend time alone with him meditating on how he has, across the ages and in our present lives, acted on our behalf.

In our reflecting on his being just, how could we not be aware of our own sin? His justice is not separate from his love and mercy, but our sins must be judged. This should drive us to the power that is in the grace shown to us on the cross. What amazing justice and power! The sins of the world were paid for by Jesus. Justice was done. And through the resurrection, forgiveness and redemption was offered to all. What amazing power!

Creativity in Presentation

Often in presenting a narrative as long as this one, it is wise to summarize portions and read key sections. This narrative is so full of action and stirring prayers that every verse could be read. To help the congregation follow and appreciate each section, explain important but unknown portions of the text before you read. For example, before reading 20:1–4 explain who

the nations are and how close their armies are to Judah. The application of the passage can also be hinted at by pointing out Judah's or Jehoshaphat's action. In this section, one could mention that their reaction is to seek the Lord. It could be argued that this is giving away the punch line; however, this is not the telling of a joke or presenting a mystery novel. It is okay to give the ending ahead of time. In a sense, it is reinforcing the story. We don't mind hearing stories where we already know the ending.

For each section, ask the congregation to notice the power and the justice of God and point out the verses in which we see these. Another tool could be to show pictures of power: waterfalls, an earth-moving dump truck, a chainsaw, a large dog, a snowblower, or lawn mower, and so on. If appropriate, some of these smaller items could be brought into the pulpit. Not that one would start them, but just having them would give something physical that would help visualize power. Each setting would probably have variations that fit that culture and their numerous pictures and videos of power. The Artemis launch mentioned above has numerous videos available; use a search engine to locate these.

Here is one possible structure:

- Present the text
  - Jehoshaphat relied on God's powerful presence as he set up a system of justice (19:4–11).
  - In the face of a crisis Judah worships God, who is just and powerful (20:1–30).
  - Jehoshaphat should have kept obeying the just and powerful God (20:31–21:1).
- Apply the text
  - We can trust our powerful and just God.
    - In prosperity, have integrity
    - In crisis, worship
    - In success, continue obeying

DISCUSSION QUESTIONS

1. When have you used a powerful tool?

2. What dangers come when there is great power?

3. When the electric power goes out, what abilities are lost?

4. How was someone (a teacher, boss, parent, etc.) fair or unfair to you?

5. What makes it hard for us to be fair in our judgments?

6. How is God's power different from ours?

7. How is God's justice different from ours?

8. How does Christ's death and resurrection express God's justice and power?

2 Chronicles 21:2–23:21

EXEGETICAL IDEA

Because Jehoram and Ahaziah followed the wicked ways of Israel, they led the Davidic dynasty to the brink of destruction; however, Jehoiada the priest led the people to restore the Davidic king and proper worship.

THEOLOGICAL FOCUS

Even though sin threatens God's blessing, God remains faithful to his promises.

PREACHING IDEA

The darker the days, the more we need to walk in his light.

PREACHING POINTERS

Each of us has been, or is currently, in a time when God's blessings are hard to see. When the darkness comes, we begin to doubt that he will keep his promises, which can lead us to a lack of trust in his commands. When money is tight, perhaps a little unnoticed and culturally accepted stealing is in order. Adulterous thoughts come easily when a marriage is filled with conflict. When a culture is moving toward immorality, it is hard to resist moving with it. This dramatic story about the near-destruction of the Davidic line teaches us to trust our Lord even when things look very dark.

HOUSE OF AHAB—DAVIDIC DYNASTY SAVED FROM DESTRUCTION (21:2–23:21)

LITERARY STRUCTURE AND THEMES (21:2–23:21)

Following the long reign of Jehoshaphat, Judah enters a time of distress. This passage deals with this time of distress in two stages. During the first stage, the Chronicler shows how the influence of the house of Ahab from the northern kingdom of Israel threatens the survival of the Davidic dynasty in Judah. Following Israel, Judah's rulers promote pagan practices, provoking YHWH's punishment. As a direct threat to the Davidic dynasty, on three occasions all the royal descendants die except for one. When Jehoram begins to reign, he kills all his brothers so that he is the only survivor to lay claim to the throne. As a result of YHWH's punishment, foreign invaders kill all Jehoram's sons except for his youngest, Ahaziah. When Ahaziah reigns, he becomes entangled with Israel so that he dies when judgment comes to the house of Ahab. After Ahaziah dies, his mother Athaliah kills all the Davidic descendants with a claim to the throne—except one who escapes—then she seizes the throne for herself. At the center of the first stage is the constant threat to the survival of the Davidic dynasty.

During the second stage, the Chronicler shows how the high priest Jehoiada leads Judah to restore the Davidic dynasty and proper worship while also putting an end to the house of Ahab. During this stage, the Chronicler focuses on Judah's loyalty to the Davidic king—in this case, Joash, the sole survivor of Athaliah's massacre—and their loyalty to YHWH and his temple. In the end, Judah crowns Joash as king and kills Athaliah, preserving the Davidic dynasty and bringing about YHWH's judgment against the house of Ahab. As a result, even though the house of Ahab leads Judah to follow their wicked ways, bringing the Davidic dynasty to the brink of destruction, through the priest Jehoiada YHWH faithfully preserves the Davidic dynasty and fully punishes the house of Ahab.

- *Wicked Jehoram Reigns (21:2–20)*
- *Weak Ahaziah Reigns (22:1–9)*
- *Athaliah Seizes the Throne (22:10–12)*
- *Jehoiada Restores the Davidic Dynasty and Proper Worship (23:1–21)*

EXPOSITION (21:2–23:21)

Because of technological advancements in transportation and telecommunications, the world seems much smaller now than in the past. What happens in one part of the world can almost immediately have a significant impact on other parts of the world. Although the ancient Near Eastern world was not nearly as small as today's world, those nations still influenced each other in significant ways. Often, a more powerful nation would exert tremendous influence on a weaker neighbor. The most direct means of influence included trade policies, payment of tribute, and military alliances. However, more powerful nations often influenced other nations in more subtle ways as well, especially within the cultural realm. At times, the religious practices of the more powerful nations would influence the practices of the weaker.

During the reign of Jehoshaphat, the larger northern kingdom of Israel begins to influence the smaller Judah in important ways. Israel's ruling dynasty, the house of Ahab, forms close political ties with Judah; but after Jehoshaphat, Israel also influences Judah's worship, inciting the nation to worship gods other than YHWH. As a result, the house of Ahab brings the Davidic dynasty to the brink of destruction. Because of the threat to YHWH's promise to the Davidic dynasty and to the promise of Judah as YHWH's people, YHWH must bring the house of Ahab to an end. These chapters show how Judah's kings Jehoram and Ahaziah follow Israel to the brink of destruction until Jehoiada the priest completes God's judgment against the house of Ahab and restores the Davidic dynasty and proper worship in Jerusalem.

Wicked Jehoram Reigns (21:2–20)

Because Jehoram murders his brothers and leads Judah to worship like the wicked house of Ahab, YHWH punishes Jehoram almost to the point of cutting off the Davidic line.

21:2–4. Before the Chronicler formally introduces Jehoram's reign, he provides a brief look at his family. While his father Jehoshaphat reigns, he distributes his riches among his sons and appoints them to various strategic cities throughout Judah. Such a distribution of wealth and authority among his sons is a wise move to help ensure the continued well-being of the dynasty (cf. 2 Chron. 11:23 where the Chronicler describes Rehoboam's similar activity as "acting wisely" וַיָּבֶן). At the same time Jehoshaphat designates Jehoram, his firstborn, to be the next king. Jehoshaphat's wisdom immediately contrasts with Jehoram's wickedness: as soon as Jehoram, Jehoshaphat's firstborn, becomes recognized as king, he threatens the future of the dynasty by killing all his brothers and some of the kingdom's high-ranking officials. His action is unjustified (2 Chron. 21:13) and sets the tone for the rest of his reign by highlighting his wickedness and the threat that his wickedness poses to the Davidic monarchy.

Names of Jehoshaphat's Son

Among Jehoshaphat's sons, two bear the same name: Azariah. Even though the two forms are not entirely identical (עֲזַרְיָה vs. עֲזַרְיָהוּ), these two forms represent the same name. BHS suggests emending the second occurrence to Uzziah (עֻזִּיָּהוּ), in part, because the Chronicler interchanges the name Uzziah and Azariah in other passages (most notably, the Judahite king named Azariah in Kings is almost always called Uzziah in Chronicles). The two names may have resulted from the fact that each brother had a different mother. David apparently also had two sons with the same name (1 Chron. 3:6, 8; 14:5, 7; cf. R. Klein 2012, 302 n. 20).

21:5–6. After this look at Jehoram's family, the Chronicler provides the typical information introducing a king's reign: the age of his accession, length of his reign, and the theological assessment of the reign. Here, the Chronicler states plainly that Jehoram did what YHWH considers wicked. The focal point of this wicked behavior is the house of Ahab. Jehoram marries Ahab's daughter and follows the practices of the northern kingdom, specifically the house of Ahab. Although the Chronicler does not mention any particular religious activity at this point, one may safely assume that he has in mind the worship of other gods through illicit worship sites and objects (e.g., high places, Asherah poles, altars for Baal).

Wickedness of Israel's Practices

Since the Chronicler does not specify any of Israel's practices or even Jehoram's religious practices, he apparently intends for his readers to recall that Jeroboam worshiped falsely (2 Chron. 11:14–15; 13:8–9) and that Ahab consulted the prophets of other gods and despised YHWH's prophet (2 Chron. 18:5–27). The Chronicler also likely assumes that because of other sources, such as Kings, his reader will at least have an awareness of the wicked behavior of Israel's kings in general and Ahab in particular.

21:7. Immediately after the Chronicler assesses Jehoram's reign, he includes an important parenthetical comment. Despite Jehoram's wicked behavior and the threat to the dynasty that he prompts by killing his brothers, YHWH is unwilling to destroy the Davidic dynasty. YHWH is unwilling to do so because of the covenant he made with David, specifically YHWH's promise to "give him and his sons a lamp for all time" (לָתֵת לוֹ נִיר וּלְבָנָיו כָּל־הַיָּמִים). By giving David and his descendants this נִיר (often translated "lamp"), YHWH ensures that the Davidic dynasty will survive and retain its dominion. This dominion will last "for all time" (כָּל־הַיָּמִים). Since Chronicles records that Babylon conquers Judah and removes any descendant of David from the throne, this phrase apparently does not mean that the Davidic dynasty will retain dominion continuously forever. Instead, it means that despite whatever interruptions may come, ultimately a Davidic descendant will reign as king from Jerusalem. In fact, this promise is tested within the next chapter of Chronicles: Athaliah, who is not a descendant of David, rules over Judah. Despite this interruption, YHWH restores dominion to the Davidic descendant Joash.

TRANSLATION ANALYSIS:
How one interprets the word נִיר affects how one understands the book of Chronicles, especially as it relates to the Chronicler's hope for a future Davidic dynasty. Often, נִיר has been identified with נֵר. In this case, it would refer to a lamp. The "lamp" may refer to the temple. If so, then YHWH did not destroy Jehoram for the sake of the temple, that is, so that the Davidic dynasty could maintain the temple for the time being. If someone else (e.g., another king) could maintain the temple, then the Davidic dynasty would no longer be needed (Riley 1993, 120–21). This interpretation has two problems. First, it is not clear that the lamp refers to the temple. It appears to refer to an enduring dynasty instead (see Shin 2016, 15–21). Second, the word נִיר

more likely carries the sense of "yoke" or "field." The word's sense is extended metaphorically to "dominion" or "domain" (for a helpful summary of issues, see Ben Zvi 1991, 23–30). In this case, the covenant relates specifically to the dynasty's continued rule in the future. Therefore, even if there is a temple without a Davidic king, the covenant with David still applies and waits for its realization.

21:8–11. Next, the Chronicler records that Edom rebels against Jehoram's dominion. Earlier in Chronicles, David subjugates Edom (1 Chron. 18:13). Now, as a counterexample to David, Jehoram's actions lead to Edom successfully rebelling against Judah even though he invades Edom with his troops. Furthermore, Libnah rebels against Jehoram at the same time. His wicked behavior, which the Chronicler describes as "forsaking YHWH, God of his fathers," leads to these rebellions. The Chronicler elaborates on how Jehoram forsakes YHWH: he builds high places, directs Jerusalem into religious harlotry (*hiphil* זנה), and leads Judah away from YHWH. Chronicles shows repeatedly how this type of religious unfaithfulness to YHWH leads to judgment. These rebellions illustrate not only that Jehoram suffers consequences for his evil behavior—in particular, a loss of dominion over certain lands—but also that despite the seriousness of evil behavior, YHWH still does not destroy him or his family.

TRANSLATION ANALYSIS:
Second Chronicles 21:9 defies expectations. Generally, in the context of a battle, the word נכה signals that the subject defeats the object. However, such a reading is quite difficult here because if Jehoram defeats Edom, then it does not explain how Edom is still in rebellion. Translations have generally taken one of three approaches to this tension: (1) they preserve it, (2) they render the word נכה as "attack" or "broke through," implying that even though he was surrounded, he still escaped, or (3) they render the

text as "and Edom defeated him," by emending the text from וַיַּךְ אֶת־אֱדוֹם to וַיַּךְ אֹתוֹ אֱדוֹם.

Religious Harlotry

Several passages in the Hebrew OT use זנה to describe unfaithfulness either to a spouse or to YHWH. In virtually every case in which it refers to unfaithfulness to YHWH, it describes worshipping other gods. Such is the sense here. Furthermore, it occurs alongside the word נדח, here meaning "enticing, tempting." Its use here draws on its use in Deuteronomy 13:11, 14, where it occurs to describe evil people who will tempt Israel away from YHWH to worship other gods.

21:12–15. Because of Jehoram's wicked behavior, Elijah the prophet sends a letter to warn him regarding coming judgment. The letter reveals a few points. First, it contrasts the behavior of Judah's good kings who precede Jehoram (Asa and Jehoshaphat) to the behavior of Israel's wicked kings, especially exemplified in Ahab. Asa and Jehoshaphat, despite their failings, worshipped YHWH alone according to the way YHWH prescribed; Israel's kings do not worship YHWH alone nor according to the way prescribed. Second, the letter communicates how serious Jehoram's wicked behavior is. It characterizes his worship of other gods as religious harlotry and associates it with Israel's kings. Furthermore, it highlights that he has killed his own brothers who are actually better than he is. YHWH forbids both actions. Third, it warns that YHWH will punish Jehoram because of his wicked behavior. YHWH's punishment will be severe, almost destroying Jehoram's wealth, family, and nation. Jehoram himself will suffer a painful condition in his bowels until he dies.

Jehoram's Disease

The text does not provide enough information about Jehoram's condition to make a clinical diagnosis. The Chronicler does not seem to be interested in a diagnosis as much as showing how serious and painful the condition is.

21:16–19a. The Chronicler wastes no time showing that Elijah's warning comes true. YHWH stirs up Judah's enemies, in this case, the Philistines and some of the Arabs to the south. These enemies execute YHWH's judgment by breaching Judah's defenses and capturing the king's wealth, wives, and sons. The text does not mention what ultimately happens to Jehoram's wives, but it does mention that only his youngest son, Ahaziah, survives. Furthermore, YHWH strikes Jehoram with an incurable disease of the bowels. Jehoram receives no relief from this disease until he finally dies an agonizing death, as his bowels come out. In these events the text makes clear that YHWH brings about the judgment as Elijah has prophesied: first by stirring up Judah's enemies, and then by striking Jehoram with a disease. Furthermore, these events lead to a serious threat to the Davidic dynasty: the king himself has died and only one male descendant remains, his youngest son.

21:19b–20. The final remarks concerning Jehoram's life correspond to his character as a king: he dies without a commemorative fire to honor his passing and is buried outside the royal tombs in Jerusalem. Jehoram lives a dishonorable life and dies a dishonorable death. He lives according to the practices of Ahab's house, leading Judah away from YHWH to commit religious harlotry with other gods and killing his brothers when he seizes the throne. His reign seriously threatens the Davidic dynasty, but YHWH still preserves it. However, the dynasty is not out of the woods yet.

Weak Ahaziah Reigns (22:1–9)

Since Ahaziah relies on the counsel of the house of Ahab, when YHWH punishes the house of Ahab the punishment sweeps over Ahaziah as well.

22:1. After Jehoram dies, the inhabitants of Jerusalem crown Ahaziah, Jehoram's youngest son, as king. The Chronicler reminds the reader that the youngest son becomes king because all his older brothers have died at the hands of a raiding party. This raiding party attacked as part of YHWH's judgment against Jehoram (cf. 2 Chron. 21:14, 16–17). Jehoram's judgment and the threat that he has brought on the Davidic dynasty still cast their shadow over Judah during Ahaziah's reign.

Age of Ahaziah
The MT states that Ahaziah's age was forty-two when he ascended the throne. This age is not possible, since Ahaziah would have been older than his father. Therefore, commentators and translators follow the parallel in 2 Kings 8:26, where his age is twenty-two.

22:2–4. The nature of Jehoram's reign continues into Ahaziah's reign. Jehoram rules like the house of Ahab and even becomes related to the house of Ahab by marrying Ahab's daughter Athaliah. Ahab's house has influenced Jehoram, leading to his judgment. This influence becomes even stronger under Ahaziah. He appears quite weak in comparison to Ahab's house, as one can discern from the repeated use of the root יעץ ("to advise") in these verses (Japhet 1993, 821). His mother Athaliah, the descendant of Omri, exerts her influence, but the evil influence extends beyond her as others from the house of Ahab serve as his advisors. Their advice leads him to behave wickedly and ultimately leads to his downfall.

TRANSLATION ANALYSIS:
Translations render the Hebrew בַּת differently. Many (CSB, ESV, NASB, NET, NKJV, NLT, NRSV) render it as "granddaughter" although a few (most notably KJV) render it as "daughter." The word itself most often refers to a daughter; however, it can carry the wider sense of a female descendant. In this case, the text recalls her belonging to the house of Omri (see Japhet 1993, 809; Sweeney 2007, 323).

22:5–9. Because Ahaziah follows the advice of Ahab's house, he joins one of Ahab's descendants, the Israelite king Joram, in a battle against the Arameans at Ramoth-gilead. In this battle, Joram is injured, but he does not die on the battlefield. Instead, he tries to recover in Jezreel. Ahaziah decides to visit him there. During Ahaziah's visit, Jehu, whom YHWH anointed as executioner of Ahab's house, begins his work of destroying it. While doing so, he comes across several of Ahaziah's high-ranking officials and relatives. He kills them and then searches for Ahaziah. Jehu's troops find him hiding in Samaria, return him to Jehu, and then Jehu puts him to death. Even though Ahaziah is related to Ahab, Jehu's troops bury him because they recognize that his ancestor Jehoshaphat worshipped YHWH.

TRANSLATION ANALYSIS:
Translations differ concerning who puts Ahaziah to death. A variant in textual transmission helps explain the differences. BHS preserves a plural form, whereas other Hebrew manuscripts and most versions preserve a singular form. The translations appear to take one of three approaches: (1) follow most textual witnesses and explicitly render Jehu as the subject (NLT), (2) follow BHS and make it the soldiers explicitly or implicitly (CSB, ESV, KJV, NASB, NET), or (3) keep it ambiguous by rendering it in the passive (NIV, NRSV).

By including these events, the Chronicler draws out several points. First, he draws a comparison between Ahab and Joram and between Jehoshaphat and Ahaziah. He does so by alluding to another battle: Ahab, king of Israel, and Jehoshaphat, king of Judah, also joined forces to fight against Aram at Ramoth-gilead. In that battle, Ahab is injured and died later that day from his injuries. However, even though Jehoshaphat received a rebuke for allying with Ahab, he returned home safely without suffering long-term consequences of the battle. Joram is like Ahab in that the battle at Ramoth-gilead precipitates his demise. On the other hand, Ahaziah is unlike Jehoshaphat because the incident also leads to his demise. The Chronicler provides a clue for the different outcomes of the battles by including what Jehu's troops say when they bury him: Jehoshaphat worshiped YHWH; in contrast, Ahaziah did not.

Second, the Chronicler shows how YHWH uses Ahaziah's visit to Joram as the means by which he brings about Ahaziah's downfall (22:7). YHWH already anointed Jehu for the task of destroying Ahab's house. Since Ahaziah is a descendant of Ahab (Ahab was his maternal grandfather) and follows the advice of Ahab's house he, along with his relatives and officials, is swept up into the judgment intended for Ahab's house. The narrative reveals that even though the events may appear to be chance (e.g., Jehu happens upon Ahaziah's servants), in fact YHWH is working to carry out his purpose of ending Ahab's lineage.

Upon Ahaziah's death, no one from his household is able to rule over the kingdom. Since Jehoram killed all his own brothers and a raiding party killed all Ahaziah's brothers, the Davidic dynasty must continue through Ahaziah's household, but there is no one able to rule. The wicked behavior of Jehoram and Ahaziah threatens the continued existence of the Davidic dynasty itself. However, the situation grows even worse.

Athaliah Seizes the Throne (22:10–12)
After Ahaziah's death, his mother Athaliah seizes the throne and removes potential rivals, but a faithful royal daughter saves one of Ahaziah's sons to preserve the Davidic line.

22:10. When Athaliah, Ahab's daughter, finds out that her son Ahaziah has died, she follows the practice of her husband Jehoram by trying to eliminate anyone with a possible claim to the throne. If her plan succeeds, she will wipe out the house of David and escape YHWH's

judgment on the house of Ahab. This plan would nullify what YHWH has said on two occasions: his promise to David of an enduring dynasty and his prophecy to Ahab of an ended dynasty.

Possible Rivals to Athaliah
The Chronicler has emphasized the wide scope of Athaliah's actions with two phrases: (1) "all the royal seed" (כָּל־זֶרַע הַמַּמְלָכָה), meaning any male with a possible hereditary claim to the throne, in particular, the sons of Ahaziah; and (2) "of the house of Judah" (לְבֵית יְהוּדָה), instead of simply "of the house of Ahaziah."

22:11–12. Athaliah's plan to kill all competitors fails. A royal daughter, sister of Ahaziah and wife of the priest Jehoiada, Jehoshabeath (in Kings, spelled Jehosheba, יְהוֹשֶׁבַע) snatches away an infant child of Ahaziah before Athaliah gets her hands on him. She hides him and his caretaker within the temple complex so that Athaliah cannot find him and kill him. The child remains hidden in the temple complex for six years while Athaliah rules over Judah.

Mention of Beds
The text reads that Jehosheba places Joash and the nurse in "a chamber of beds" (בַּחֲדַר הַמִּטּוֹת). Most translations render the phrase "bedroom," although the room may not have housed beds themselves (at least permanent ones), but stored the covers, cloths, and other materials used for beds. Regardless of the room's precise function, the mention of "beds" (sg. מִטָּה) connects the beginning of Joash's life to its end. In the end Joash is killed while in his bed (מִטָּה), because he has killed Jehoiada's son (2 Chron. 24:25).

At this point in the narrative, the situation is unjust. The sole survivor of Ahab's condemned house sits on the throne of Judah, attempting to kill off David's dynasty. However, there is a glimmer of future hope, since the sole survivor of David's promised dynasty remains out of her grasp.

The initial readers of Chronicles lived under foreign rule, yet they knew of YHWH's promises regarding their people, their land, and their king. To some degree, their situation reflected the days in which Athaliah ruled. There was no Davidic king on the throne, and likely they did not know of a specific Davidic descendant who might come to the throne. This passage presents a past situation in which YHWH was able to preserve a Davidic heir even though one was not ruling.

Furthermore, the parenthetical comment regarding Jehoram's reign (2 Chron. 21:7) provides a basis (the covenant with David) for them to expect YHWH to do the same in the future. It shows that despite whatever Jehoram's failing, YHWH still honors his covenant. The postexilic community was likely quite aware of their failings and needed to know that YHWH does not turn his back on his commitment. Furthermore, while living under foreign rule, the community wondered about a future Davidic king (e.g., Hag. 2:20–23) and needed to know that, despite their current circumstances, YHWH still has a plan for the Davidic dynasty. Therefore, they could await a better day when YHWH will bring about what he has promised.

YHWH's providential care for the Davidic dynasty despite its serious sinfulness would shine as a ray of hope for the first readers, those who needed to know that YHWH had not abandoned his people in the past, even when things looked as though they were hanging on only by a thin thread.

Jehoiada Restores the Davidic Dynasty and Proper Worship (23:1–21)

The high priest Jehoiada leads Judah to restore the legitimate Davidic king Joash, to return Judah to worshipping YHWH properly, and to execute Athaliah.

23:1–3. On the brink of destruction, one little hope remains for the Davidic dynasty. Joash, only a child and the only surviving member of the Davidic dynasty, lives within the temple complex, hiding from the destructive despot Athaliah. Jehoiada the high priest and his wife Jehoshabeath have been protecting the boy for six years. Now, Jehoiada makes his move to restore the legitimate Davidic ruler to the throne. He starts by securing the commitment of several of Judah's leaders. The first group consists of five men, described as military leaders. This small group of five then recruits a larger group drawn from the Levites and clan leaders throughout Judah. Jehoiada meets with all these leaders in the temple courts to secure their commitment through a covenant to make Joash king. Once the leaders seal their commitment with a covenant, Jehoiada presents the boy Joash as the one who will rule according to YHWH's promise to David.

> **Character of the Covenant with the King**
> Although the focus of this covenant involves making Joash king, it is likely that the Chronicler has more in mind as well. Since he closely associates wicked rulers with those who encourage worshipping other gods, the commitment to make Joash king would also involve the commitment to worship YHWH (23:16).

Three important features of this narrative emerge quickly. First, the Chronicler demonstrates that the focus of Jehoiada's activity is restoring the Davidic dynasty. Despite whatever other concerns motivated Jehoiada, if any, YHWH's promise to David is the ultimate reason for placing Joash upon the throne. Second, Jehoiada involves the Levites as soon as possible. Since much of Jehoiada's plan takes place in the temple complex, the Chronicler emphasizes that priests and Levites form an essential part of the group to restore Davidic rule and protect the temple's sanctity. Third, the diverse leadership already included (officers of hundreds, Levites, and clan leaders from cities throughout Judah) foreshadows the widespread and popular approval of

Joash's reign. For the Chronicler, restoring the Davidic dynasty is not a secret matter taking place behind closed doors. Instead, it involves all the people publicly participating. These three themes recur throughout this narrative.

23:4–5. Once Jehoiada secures the allegiance of several key leaders for the king, he begins the work of ousting Athaliah. He divides this group of leaders into three groups: (1) a group consisting of priests and Levites coming for duty, who will guard the entrances to the temple, (2) a group who will station themselves in the palace, and (3) a group who will stand guard at the Foundation Gate, perhaps a gate connecting the temple complex to the palace complex. Jehoiada commands anyone else beyond these three groups of leaders to remain in the temple courts.

Gate Connecting Temple and Palace

There are several reasons to think that this gate connected the temple complex and the palace complex. First, when the leaders execute Athaliah, they bring her outside the temple complex to the palace complex. The text describes this entrance using the designation שַׁעַר הַסּוּסִים ("Horse Gate" or "gate for horses"). The Foundation Gate (שַׁעַר הַיְסוֹד) of 23:5 may have originally read "Horse Gate" and changed during scribal transmission, although one cannot be certain. On the other hand, LXX reads "the middle gate," apparently understanding this gate as connecting the temple and palace complexes. Furthermore, it makes sense that the leaders would take Athaliah to a place that they had already secured. Therefore, the Foundation Gate either originally read "Horse Gate" and changed through textual transmission or it is another designation for the gate used by horses mentioned in 23:15. In either case, it appears to connect the temple and palace complexes.

23:6–7. Once Jehoiada divides the leaders into groups, he assigns them their priorities:

(1) protect the sanctity of the temple, and (2) protect the safety of the king. Jehoiada commands the leaders to keep everyone out of the temple building itself except for the priests and Levites. They may enter because they are holy; that is, YHWH has qualified only them to enter the temple. Everyone else must keep YHWH's charge, meaning in this case to respect the sanctity of the temple. Once Jehoiada secures the temple's sanctity, he commands the Levites to protect the king by surrounding him, armed with their weapons, and killing anyone who attempts to enter the temple (apparently to get to the king). Furthermore, this armed guard should stay with the king wherever he goes.

TRANSLATION ANALYSIS:
The text uses the following phrase: בְּבֹאוֹ וּבְצֵאתוֹ. Some translations (ESV, NASB, NKJV) render this phrase more formally as "when he comes in and when he goes out." The phrase is a figure of speech (known as a merism) in which two extremes represent the whole. Therefore, by using the phrase, the Chronicler intends to communicate that these Levites should surround the king wherever he goes and whatever he is doing. Several translations focus on the king's movements, translating the phrase as "wherever he goes" (NET, NIV, NLT), while CSB focuses on the king's activity, translating the phrase as "in all his daily tasks."

YHWH's Charge

By using the phrase מִשְׁמֶרֶת יהוה, the Chronicler alludes to several passages in the Pentateuch and elsewhere in Chronicles regarding the roles and responsibilities of the priests and Levites. One passage appears quite close to the context of this verse: Numbers 18:4. This passage states that the Levites should join the priests in caring for the sanctuary, but that no one else should enter it.

23:8–10. After Jehoiada lays out the plan, the people execute it. The Chronicler draws out two significant points in describing how the people carry out the plan. First, he emphasizes the overwhelming support for the new king. The priests and Levites demonstrate their support when those coming in for their duty join those who are leaving their duty. Also, "all the people" in and around the temple complex form another layer of protection for the king as they line up in a semicircle extending from the southern edge of the temple complex to the northern edge. Second, the Chronicler points out the close connection between the Davidic dynasty and YHWH's temple. When Jehoiada forms this second layer of protection around the king, he distributes weapons that King David donated to YHWH. This comment shows how David's concern for YHWH's house helps secure the future of his own house. It also demonstrates that YHWH's promises to David of building a temple and securing a future dynasty (1 Chron. 17) are not two separate concerns, unrelated to one another. They are connected, even if in ways one may not expect.

Weapons of David
Elsewhere, Chronicles only mentions specifically that David brought several quivers (שְׁלָטִים) back to Jerusalem (1 Chron. 18:7), but 2 Chronicles 23:9 seems to imply that David donated the other weapons as well. These weapons most likely served to commemorate YHWH's victory in past battles, but they could still be used in combat if necessary.

23:11. After everyone is in place according to Jehoiada's instructions, they bring out the legitimate royal heir and make him king through the following steps: (1) they crown him, (2) they give him some symbol of royal authority or obligation, (3) they proclaim him king, (4) they anoint him, and (5) they shout, "Long live the king!" For the most part, the steps represent typical aspects of a king's coronation. Furthermore, the people begin celebrating the king's coronation with music and shouting, while praising the king, most likely in stereotyped language used

for such occasions, such as "Long live the king!" (see Ps. 72). The Chronicler emphasizes the popular support and excitement for the Davidic heir to rule on the throne.

TRANSLATION ANALYSIS:
The precise significance of presenting the king with the testimony (הָעֵדוּת) is unclear because of the specific sense of עֵדוּת (often translated "testimony" or "covenant"). There are basically three approaches to understanding the word. First, one may interpret it by relating it to other parts of the Hebrew Bible, especially the Pentateuch. This approach results in understanding the word as a reference to the Davidic covenant, or to the Mosaic law or a section of it, such as the Ten Commandments or the law of the king (Deut. 17). Second, one may interpret it in light of this disputed coronation. In this case the word would refer to some type of seal or insignia of royal authority. Third, one may interpret it as a sign of the responsibility of the people and the king to one another.

23:12–15. When Athaliah hears the noise of the people celebrating, she goes to the temple courtyard to find that the people are celebrating a new king. The new king Joash stands in a place of royal authority, while all the people celebrate around him with musical instruments and singing. Ironically, she characterizes this coronation as treason, although she had slaughtered every possible legitimate heir to put herself on the throne. She is the obvious traitor. Since the legitimate heir is now king, Athaliah will pay for her treachery; however, Jehoiada does not want bloodshed in the temple, again emphasizing the need to protect the sanctity of the temple. For that reason, he commands the military leaders to remove her from the temple, kill anyone who follows her (apparently to rescue her), and execute her elsewhere. These leaders force her outside the temple and back to the palace complex. As soon as she leaves the temple complex and enters the palace complex through the gate used by horses, the leaders execute her. With this action, the wicked Athaliah, who is an evil counselor, killer of the royal heirs, and usurper of the throne, pays for her sins while the hidden son of David becomes king.

TRANSLATION ANALYSIS:
The text reads וַיָּשִׂימוּ לָהּ יָדַיִם. One may understand this phrase in three ways. The most common interpretation is that they seized her, or in English idiom "laid hands on her." The difficulty for this interpretation is that the next phrase indicates she proceeded on her own rather than being forced. One may interpret the word יָדַיִם as "space" rather than "hands." In this case, the leaders made space or a path for her to leave the temple complex. This translation makes sense in context but depends on interpreting יָדַיִם in a rare sense. Finally, one may interpret the phrase slightly differently by understanding יָדַיִם in the more common sense of strength or power. In this case, the leaders oppose Athaliah, barring her from going any further into the temple. As a result, she goes back to the palace complex. See Dutcher-Walls 1996, 44. The third option balances best the fact that Athaliah moves on her own accord and the fact that this scene involves a violent confrontation between Athaliah and her executioners.

Significance of the King's Column
The Bible does not explicitly mention the significance of the column (or standing place). However, since Athaliah recognizes what is happening, at least in part because Joash stands beside the column, the context indicates that standing in that location represented some type of authority. Furthermore, the Bible provides another example of a king standing specifically in this location: Josiah makes a covenant to follow YHWH (2 Kings 23:3 // 2 Chron. 34:31).

23:16–19. In the case of Joash, restoring the Davidic dynasty also entails restoring proper worship. The Chronicler makes the point clear by showing that immediately following Athaliah's death, Jehoiada, the people, and the king make a covenant together to act in ways loyal to YHWH. This covenant binds together the priest, the king, and all the people in their obligation to worship YHWH exclusively and properly. To demonstrate how they keep this covenant, the Chronicler records the following: (1) how the people remove Baal worship from the land by destroying its images, altars, temple, and priest; (2) how Jehoiada restores proper worship in YHWH's temple by reassigning the priests to their duties as King David had organized them (see 1 Chron. 24:1–19); and (3) how Jehoiada continues to ensure the sanctity of the temple by reassigning gatekeepers to prevent anyone who is ritually unclean from entering. As a result of these actions, Judah worships YHWH exclusively with a priesthood properly organized and a temple properly protected. For the Chronicler, these elements constitute proper worship and demonstrate how Judah acts like YHWH's people.

TRANSLATION ANALYSIS:
Several translations (ESV, HCSB, NASB, NIV, NKJV, NLT, NRSV) render the text as "be the Lord's people" (לִהְיוֹת לְעָם לַיהוָה). The disadvantage of this translation is that it might suggest that they have not been YHWH's people; however, the point of the covenant is not to establish a relationship that did not already exist, but for Judah to act the way YHWH's people should act (for a similar usage, cf. 1 Kings 2:2). Furthermore, at least in this case, what it means to act as YHWH's people is to worship him alone. The NET translation ("be loyal to the LORD") captures this sense well.

Athaliah and Baal Worship
Here, the text implies that Athaliah used her power to promote the worship of Baal, since her death also results in removing Baal worship. Furthermore, she is a member of Ahab's house, closely associated with Baal worship

(1 Kings 16:31). Later in the narrative (2 Chron. 24:7), the Chronicler makes clear that Athaliah played a role in ransacking YHWH's temple to use its resources for Baal worship.

23:20–21. Since Athaliah is dead and proper worship restored, only one thing remains to complete the transition to Joash's rule: sit on the throne. Jehoiada takes the people and their leaders to bring Joash out of the temple and into the palace so that he can sit on the royal throne. Because the Davidic king sits on the throne and Athaliah has been killed, everyone in Judah rejoices and enjoys YHWH's blessing of peace.

Fulfillment of Jehoiada's Plan

At the beginning of this narrative, Jehoiada takes (לקח) five leaders ("officers of hundreds") into an agreement to make Joash king (23:1). At the end of this narrative, Jehoiada again takes (לקח) these leaders ("officers of hundreds") along with many others to place Joash upon the throne. In this way, the Chronicler shows that Jehoiada's purpose has been fulfilled.

The end of 2 Chronicles 23 draws an important storyline in Chronicles to a close. Beginning with Jehoram (but already foreshadowed with Jehoshaphat), the Chronicler points out the devastating connection between David's house and Ahab's house. Jehoram, Ahaziah, and Athaliah represent the disastrous consequences of Ahab's house. Because of their wicked acts, YHWH brings judgment on both houses. YHWH's judgment of these two houses spills over into one another with similar results. For instance, as Jehu executes YHWH's judgment on Ahab's house, he also kills Ahaziah, the only living son of Jehoram. YHWH promises to wipe out Ahab's house, but Athaliah escapes. However, she kills every Davidic heir except one. Her life and reign threaten YHWH's word in two ways: (1) it almost destroys the dynasty YHWH promised to David (1 Chron. 17:10), and (2) it almost negates the judgment YHWH appointed

Jehu to complete (2 Chron. 22:7). However, YHWH stays true to his word, despite the most desperate circumstances. Athaliah dies and with her, Ahab's house. In contrast Joash survives and rules, carrying on the promise YHWH made to David.

For the first readers the reigns of Jehoram, Ahaziah, and Athaliah would coincide in many details with their own days. No Davidic king sits on the throne. False worship—both worshipping foreign gods and worshipping YHWH improperly—occurs on every side. This narrative confirms that in similar circumstances in the past, YHWH restored the Davidic dynasty and proper worship at the temple. Jehoiada's role would encourage the priests that they "have a role to play facilitating and championing the cause of people and king" (Boda 2013, 235). At the same time, they could be confident that YHWH would bring change, because his past actions bring confidence of a future hope.

THEOLOGICAL FOCUS

Even though sin threatens God's blessing, God remains faithful to his promises.

This passage is a story of rescue from near-destruction. Understanding the significance of this story requires a closer look at threatened destruction. This closer look includes an examination of the following: (1) its object, (2) its cause, and (3) its result if not avoided. First, in this case, the object of near-destruction is the Davidic dynasty. Within Chronicles, the Davidic dynasty serves more than just a single family; it is a means to bless Israel (2 Chron. 2:11; 9:8) and to praise YHWH (e.g., David's organizing temple music, Solomon's building the Jerusalem temple). As a result, the threat to the Davidic dynasty is a threat to God's blessing all Israel.

Second, the cause of near-destruction is sin. The passage presents two ways that sin threatens the Davidic dynasty. The first way is murder. Twice in this passage murder becomes the tool to secure the sole claim to the throne of

Judah. These murders leave only one person to carry on the dynasty. The second way is punishment for sin. For Jehoram, God punishes him directly for his sin by sending invaders who kill all his sons (except one) and by sending disease to kill him. For Ahaziah, God punishes the house of Ahab, and because of Ahaziah's close ties to them he becomes swept up in that punishment. Both punishments leave only one surviving Davidic heir.

The passage's description of the sin that nearly brings destruction to the Davidic dynasty points to important theological issues. The presentation points to the seriousness of sin. God takes this sin so seriously that he is willing to bring punishment against it, even though that punishment threatens the Davidic dynasty's survival. The presentation also points to the seriousness of associations. By allying themselves to the house of Ahab, the Davidic kings become entangled in the affairs of Israel. With Jehoshaphat the entanglement is limited to military matters (battle against Ramoth-gilead); however, as is often the case, the entanglement spreads to areas of political maneuvering (e.g., Jehoram's murdering his brothers) and religious practice (e.g., building objects of pagan worship). For this reason, the blessed man does not associate with the wicked (Ps. 1:1), and Paul admonishes the Corinthians not to become partners with unbelievers (2 Cor. 6:14). The subtle influence of associations can lead to disastrous consequences.

Third, the result of the destruction, if not avoided, is the breaking of God's word. On the one hand, if the Davidic dynasty were to come to an end, its destruction would break God's promise to David of an enduring dynasty (see 1 Chron. 17; 2 Chron. 21:7). On the other hand, if the house of Ahab were not to come to an end, its survival would break God's plan to destroy the house of Ahab (2 Chron. 22:7). The rule of Athaliah brings this contrast into sharp focus, since during her reign it appears that the house of Ahab thrives while the house of David disappears into oblivion. Her reign raises doubts about God's power to preserve and his power to punish.

However, in the darkest days, God rescues the Davidic dynasty. God is faithful to both his promise to preserve the house of David and to punish the house of Ahab. In fact, these two sides of God's rescuing the Davidic dynasty characterize God's rescue throughout the Bible. When the Old Testament, especially the prophets, describes God's work of rescuing his people, God restores his people and subdues all his enemies. The apostle Paul points to Jesus as the one who accomplishes both tasks (1 Cor. 15:23–28). In other words, God, past activity in rescuing the Davidic dynasty points to God's future through Jesus in rescuing God's people.

Finally, one can hardly overlook the significance of this threat against the Davidic dynasty and its rescue. The situation extends beyond Judah in the preexilic period. The Davidic promise extends beyond the Chronicler's situation—all the way to Jesus. Since Jesus as Messiah is God's means to bless all creation, the threat to the Davidic dynasty is a threat to God's blessing for all creation. However, God's faithfulness to his promises during the dark days of Jehoram, Ahaziah, and Athaliah points to his faithfulness to his promises in any age.

PREACHING AND TEACHING STRATEGIES

Exegetical and Theological Synthesis

The plot of this pericope is a classic structure of good versus evil, with good prevailing. Evil tries to destroy God's good plan for the Davidic dynasty, through whom the ultimate king and savior would come. God, working through willing servants, saves the line of David. God will always keep his promises in spite of sinful actions.

How will this promise fit into the narrative of our own lives? There is good and evil in us and around us. And we know that God's good shall prevail, but how do we participate in his ongoing work toward his ultimate victory?

When a story is told, the natural response in those listening is to identify with one of the characters in the story. A classic story line is that of a hero or heroine doing the right thing, while powerful evil people try to kill or stop them. We don't consciously say that we want to be like that strong heroic character, but who doesn't want to be the hero? It is part of why that plot is so popular. Right prevails and we empathically feel like we are a part of the victory. That is why we enjoy this kind of story. The key is that we identify with the good guy.

With whom do we identify in this story? Of course, we like to think that we will be like Jehoiada, the priest whom God uses to save the Davidic dynasty. However, when God's blessings are threatened, we need to see that the hero role is not ours; it is God's. He remains faithful to his promises. Hopefully we are in obedience to him, and part of his good hand in bringing good out of evil. But there are other characters in this story. Sometimes we are the nemesis, the bad guy.

We don't like to think about being like Athaliah, but when we decide to live according to our own wants, desires, and rules, we are placing ourselves as the illegitimate sovereign of our lives. We, like Athaliah, try to make ourselves queen or king over our puny little kingdoms of self.

Because of the multiple characters in this narrative, we can choose which character we identify with. Though at times we might be more like a nemesis, we must choose to model ourselves after Jehoiada, and put the right and true king on the throne of our lives.

Preaching Idea

The darker the days, the more we need to walk in his light.

Contemporary Connections

What does it mean?

God will always be true to his word, to his promises. We must be careful that we accurately interpret his promises. One could think the promise regarding the Davidic dynasty is that there would be a Davidic king on the throne at every moment, but as Dr. Williams points out there was not a Davidic king on the throne for six years. God's promise is that ultimately a Davidic descendant will reign as king from Jerusalem. This will happen in the fullest sense through Jesus. That is why his being in the line of David was and is important. This is the encouraging application of this narrative. God will always keep his promises.

We live in a world where many promises are made. The thirty-second story of a lost dog being found while the owner searches in his new truck seems to promise that if we buy that new truck, we will have the same affirming feelings of finding a lost dog. Shampoo is never sold because we see a picture of a woman bending over a sink with wet hair. Rather, we see the promise of clean and dry hair being gently blown by the wind. These commercials imply comforting and beautiful results. But new trucks and pleasant-smelling shampoos don't deliver on the perceived promises.

When God promised to preserve the Davidic dynasty, Israel could have seen this as a promise of prosperity. While prosperity could be a part of his plan, the promise was to lead to trust. He was asking them to trust that the Davidic king was the right king. The first readers, though under Persian rule, were to trust that God would one day provide that king. Today we know who the king is. God calls us to trust that the Davidic king, Jesus, is the only right king over each one of us.

Is it true?

The amount of struggle to believe that God will keep his promises is relative to the perceived power of the evil that is around us. When Athaliah was usurping the throne, it was very hard for the Judahites to believe God's promise that there would always be a Davidic king. While none of us are in the struggle to save the Davidic dynasty, we all have situations in which we feel that God's blessings are threatened:

- Unity in worship is destroyed by resenting a new style of music.
- The security and joy of marriage is replaced with constant conflict.
- The calmness of our nation is in jeopardy because of laws against God's natural design.
- Success in our career is stagnant because of a dishonest and angry employer.
- A good grade is impossible because of a biased teacher.
- A restful retirement evaporates because of unmanageable debts.
- An old friendship is deeply bruised by cruel words.

When blessings are threatened, we need to see that the hero role is not ours; it is God's. Hopefully, we are in obedience to him and part of his good hand in bringing good out of evil. But there are other roles we can play. Sometimes we are the nemesis, the bad guy. Because of our sin nature, our self-centeredness, and our sinful choices, we can be part of the evil battling against God's good. We must ask ourselves, are we part of the threat to God's promised blessings? Perhaps our own sin is trying to destroy God's blessings.

Now what?
Thankfully the triumph of good over evil is not up to us. God will keep his promise to bring good through the Davidic king Jesus. Yet, he gives us the choice as to what role we will play. In the above examples, we can

fuel the fire of evil or we can be a part of the wonderful way that God ultimately prevails. Our role can be that of Jehoiada. Just as he obeyed God in the midst of great struggles and doubt, we too can obey. And this obedience is grounded in trusting that God will keep his promises.

- When unified worship is destroyed by resentment of a new style of music, we can be patient and work to appreciate the new styles, trusting that God is at work in these new styles.
- When the security and joy of marriage is replaced with constant conflict, we can examine our own hearts, confess our own sins of self-centeredness, and trust God to empower us to change.
- When the calm of our nation is in jeopardy because of laws against God's natural design, we can trust God to eventually bring order and to help us to disagree with a loving attitude.
- When success in our career is stagnant because of a dishonest and angry employer, we can trust God to reward those who seek him and do our work as unto him.
- When a good grade is impossible because of a biased teacher, we can trust that God will use even that injustice for our good.
- When a restful retirement evaporates because of unmanageable debts, we can work with a helpful adviser to make new plans, trusting that God's new plan is better.
- When an old friendship is deeply bruised by cruel words, we can lovingly seek to restore the friendship, trusting that God is at work in our friend.

Creativity in Presentation
This passage is a dramatic and complex story. It is a great plot, filled with cliff-hanging turns.

Three times the Davidic dynasty is almost destroyed. But in the end, God is victorious.

Telling this story well will take work. First, give the setting. Be sure to include God's promise to David about his dynasty lasting forever. Second Chronicles 21:1–7 can be told as an introduction to the story, using 21:7 to raise the question the possibility of the Davidic line being destroyed. It is important to articulate the conflict. The rest of the passage can be presented in a story format, reading key verses along the way.

- 21:8–20: Jehoram's evil reign, highlighting 21:17 which states that he lost all his sons except one
- 22:1–9: Present weak Ahaziah's reign, highlighting 22:9 where it seems there was no Davidic descendant remaining.
- 22:10–12: Present Athaliah's seizing of the throne, highlighting 22:11 in which Jehoshabeth rescues the only surviving son of Ahaziah.
- 23:1–21: Present Jehoiada's reforms, his dramatic deposing of Athaliah, and the abbreviated coronation of the seven-year-old Davidic king.

After the story is presented, ask the congregation to consider which character they most identified with. Present the positive example of Jehoiada, but also point out that perhaps at times we are like Athaliah and try to place ourselves on the throne of our lives.

For the last part of the sermon, present how we can keep the rightful king on the throne of our lives:

- Obedience: Jehoram could have trusted God for a secure throne and not murdered his brothers.
- Avoid unholy alliances: Ahaziah listened to his wicked mother, but should have listened to God.
- Worship properly: Jehoiada took necessary drastic measures to put the right

king on the throne and reinstituted proper worship.

DISCUSSION QUESTIONS

1. When we are going through hard times, how are we tempted to sin?

2. Why is it easy to follow the lead of other people, even when they lead us to sin?

3. What makes it easier to turn from God when life is hard?

4. How does godly obedience help during hard times?

5. What effect does corporate worship have on us during hard times?

6. How do we try to set up our own kingdoms and rule over them?

2 Chronicles 24:1–27

EXEGETICAL IDEA
While the priest Jehoiada was alive, he led Joash to obey YHWH by restoring Davidic rule and temple worship; but after Jehoiada died, Joash and Judah forsook YHWH, forgot Jehoiada, and saw their fortunes reversed.

THEOLOGICAL FOCUS
Righteous counsel leads to life, but wicked counsel to forsake God leads to disaster.

PREACHING IDEA
Listen to the one who rewards and judges.

PREACHING POINTERS
Joash's tragic story is a call to obedience in the face of ungodly counsel. Joash displays obedience for us, and the text demonstrates God's blessing of rewards. Even more vivid is the judgment that comes when Joash turns from YHWH and listens to ungodly counsel. Joash listened to a group of Judah's leaders that offered ungodly advice. Ungodly counsel still rings in our ears today. The voices in our culture can often be ungodly. This ungodly counsel can come through cultural traditions, entertainment, and through professionals such as lawyers, accountants, and counselors. It can be heard even from well-meaning family and employers. This passage reaffirms the call to obedience and focuses on the danger of listening to ungodly counsel.

REIGN OF JOASH—THE DIFFERENCE
A PRIEST CAN MAKE (24:1–27)

LITERARY STRUCTURE
AND THEMES (24:1–27)

After the Chronicler's account of restoring the Davidic dynasty to Judah by removing Athaliah and making Joash king, the Chronicler recounts the rest of Joash's reign. This account clearly falls into two parts. The priest Jehoiada marks the transition from one part to the other. During his life, Jehoiada plays an active role in Joash's reign, securing the future of the Davidic dynasty and of temple worship in Jerusalem. As far as the dynasty is concerned, Joash has many children. As far as the temple is concerned, Joash commands the people to repair the temple to restore worship within it.

After Jehoiada's death, Joash's reign takes a turn for the worse as he follows other counselors who lead him to forsake YHWH and forget Jehoiada. When Jehoiada's son Zechariah warns Joash and the people, they conspire to stone him to death at Joash's command. As a result, YHWH punishes Joash. First, a small army of Arameans defeats Judah, wounding Joash. Second, Joash's servants conspire to kill him on his bed. Like the accounts of other kings (e.g., Asa, Amaziah, and Uzziah), the account of Joash consists of a period of obedience followed by a period of disobedience.

The Chronicler describes the latter part of Joash's account with several ironic features that mirror earlier parts of the narrative (see commentary below; for further details, see R. Klein 2000, 126–27). For instance, as mentioned above, the people conspire against Jehoiada's son Zechariah to kill him at Joash's command. Ironically, Joash's servants conspire against Joash to kill him while he attempts to recover

from his wounds. These features connect Joash's enthronement with the rest of his reign. They show how Joash's disobedience leads to the reversal of his fortunes.

- **Reign of Joash During Jehoiada's Life (24:1–14)**
- **Reign of Joash After Jehoiada's Death (24:15–27)**

EXPOSITION (24:1–27)

Different societies hold different social roles in varying degrees of regard, influence, and power. For instance, many in contemporary culture hold entrepreneurs and technology innovators in high regard. As a result, these individuals have a great deal of influence beyond their specific areas of business or innovation (e.g., Bill Gates or Elon Musk). In the ancient Near Eastern world, people generally held religious leaders in high regard. Among these religious leaders, priests played a prominent role. Despite their role being devoted primarily to ritual worship, they often exercised power and influence far beyond a sanctuary or temple. Furthermore, a competent priest could hold considerable sway over a king or other type of political leader. Thankfully, when the Davidic dynasty faced imminent destruction, YHWH prepared the priest Jehoiada to preserve the dynasty and restore proper worship of YHWH. Jehoiada's role extends beyond the removal of Athaliah from the throne; it extends into Joash's reign. The influence of this good priest directs Joash to obey YHWH. However, after Jehoiada's death, Joash listens to other advisors who lead him and Judah to forsake YHWH and forget Jehoiada. As a result, YHWH punishes Joash and the people.

Reign of Joash During Jehoiada's Life (24:1–14)

During the first part of Joash's reign, Joash and Jehoiada restore the Davidic dynasty and temple worship.

24:1–2. The Chronicler introduces Joash's reign with some typical information. He records Joash's age when he becomes king, how long he reigns, his mother's name, and a theological assessment of his reign. Joash is the youngest in Chronicles to become king, and reigns for a long time (forty years). The Chronicler states that Joash does what YHWH considers right, but with one caveat: he does so while Jehoiada is alive. This caveat raises the question at the beginning of Joash's reign whether he will remain faithful to YHWH or not.

24:3. The Chronicler includes a bit of information not typically included when introducing a king's reign. He records that Jehoiada arranges two wives for Joash and that Joash has many sons and daughters. This information is important for two reasons: (1) it shows that YHWH rewards Joash for his obedience (see sidebar "Large Families as Blessing"), and (2) in contrast to Joash's predecessors (Jehoram, Ahaziah, Athaliah), it helps secure the future of the recently restored Davidic dynasty.

24:4–5. After the Chronicler introduces Joash as a king who does what YHWH considers right, he provides an example of what right action Joash takes. At some point in his reign, Joash wants to repair YHWH's temple, so he orders the priests and Levites to travel throughout Judah without delay to collect money for the repairs. However, they don't obey.

24:6. When the king confronts the high priest because the priests and Levites have delayed,

he points out the basis for making this collection: Mosaic law. The text alludes to a tax that Moses requires to maintain the tabernacle, here referred to as the tent of testimony. Exodus 30:12–16 describes this tax: it is a fixed amount (half shekel) collected for each person counted during a census (those over twenty years old) to provide for the upkeep (עבודה) of the tabernacle. The law does not specify how often the tax should be collected, but the Pentateuch apparently only records once that Moses collects this tax to provide the materials for making the tabernacle (Exod. 38:25–26). Joash specifies that the priests and Levites should collect the money each year to repair and maintain the temple (24:5).

The way Joash implements this law from Israel's past preserves the spirit of the law but modifies its details because of his own historical circumstances. In particular, he calls for the upkeep of the temple instead of the tabernacle and specifies that the tax be collected annually. Neither of these interpretive moves is a stretch. In other passages in Chronicles, the Chronicler shows how the temple continues the function of the tabernacle as the place where YHWH dwells and where Israel worships him (see excursus "David to Solomon and Moses to Joshua"). Also, the political structure of Israel/Judah as a kingdom and the permanent nature of the temple as a building would require regular maintenance, even beyond a period of initial repair. This passage provides an example of how Israel has implemented Mosaic law even in changing historical circumstances.

24:7. After Joash provides the basis for collecting the money, he states why the temple needs repair: followers of Athaliah have ransacked the temple, stolen offerings set aside for it, and used those resources to worship the Baals. The text describes Athaliah in a unique way: she is מִרְשַׁעַת, that is, wickedness personified (*HALOT* s.v. "מִרְשַׁעַת" 639). This assessment makes sense in Chronicles, since Athaliah violates both the Davidic dynasty and YHWH's temple, the two focal points of the Chronicler's picture of Israel.

TRANSLATION ANALYSIS:
The Hebrew text reads בְּנֶיהָ. This word could refer to Athaliah's sons; however, all her sons besides Ahaziah died either when the Philistines and Arabs attacked Judah (2 Chron. 21:17) or when Athaliah killed all the possible heirs to the throne following Ahaziah's death (2 Chron. 22:10). This interpretation of בְּנֶיהָ creates quite a bit of tension in the narrative and suggests that this event took place before Athaliah ruled over Judah. One may understand the word to refer to Athaliah's followers or supporters. The word בֵּן would allow for this sense, or one may re-point the text to read as a participle from בנה. In either case, the event would refer to the period of Athaliah's reign and reinforce the connection between her rule and Baal worship.

Furthermore, the comment regarding ransacking the temple emphasizes a recurring theme in Chronicles: worshipping YHWH alongside other gods is not worshipping YHWH at all. For the Chronicler, the only way to worship YHWH is to worship him exclusively. Here, the Chronicler makes this point by showing that since Athaliah worshipped the Baals, her followers virtually put an end to the temple's worship. For this reason, the Chronicler uses the term פרץ ("break through, break into") to describe how Athaliah's followers treat the temple. This term occurs often to speak of destroying and breaching walls (2 Chron. 25:23; 26:6; 32:5). The Chronicler is presenting the temple as a broken-down structure, ransacked—a place where normal activities, including regular offerings, are not possible. For this reason, these repairs signify more than simply patching some holes or replacing some furniture; they signify restarting the temple's proper operation in worshipping

YHWH. This fact is likely another reason to mention Moses's tax: it was collected to build the tabernacle, so it is fitting to use it to (re-) build the temple in a similar way.

24:8–13. After the Chronicler demonstrates the significance of rebuilding the temple, he records how it is done. Moses's tax still provides the means for repairing the temple; however, the king alters his original plan for collecting the funds. Instead of sending the priests and Levites to travel throughout Judah, he orders that a chest be stationed near the entrance of the temple so that the people can deposit the tax as they visit the temple. Once the word gets out that everyone is supposed to bring the tax to the temple, all the people, including the leaders (שָׂרִים), are glad to bring this tax and deposit it into the chest. When the chest fills up, officials from the palace and the temple cooperate to deposit the money and return the chest to its place at the temple. The king and high priest cooperate to distribute the funds to those who perform the work of repairing the temple until it is finished.

How the Chronicler describes this event communicates three important points. First, the Chronicler shows how glad the people are to pay this tax. This type of joy in giving occurs frequently in Chronicles, especially when the money is set aside for the temple and/or its worship (see "Cult" section in the introduction). Furthermore, this joy results in generous contributions. The Chronicler points out that the officials must check the chest daily because the people bring in so much money. For the first readers, the Chronicler's attention on Judah's joy in paying the tax to support the temple would be an encouragement for them to support the temple faithfully and cheerfully, since it needs regular resources to ensure its maintenance and upkeep. Second, since the chest sits at the temple, the people must visit the temple to pay the tax. This point coincides with the Chronicler's emphasis on the temple. It serves as an encouragement for the first readers also to visit the temple in Jerusalem. Third, the Chronicler points out that both royal and temple administrators manage collecting the funds. The Chronicler seems to confirm this type of cooperation between king and priest. For the Chronicler, the situation is best when political power and temple authority mutually support one another to promote YHWH's worship. This comment would encourage any of the first readers with some political power to use it to benefit the temple. However, since a Davidic king is not sitting on the throne during their time, it would also encourage them to wait for a future day when the Davidic king and the priests would work together to worship YHWH.

24:14. The Chronicler makes one final comment to close out his description of the temple repairs. He records that the king allocates the extra resources to make implements used in the regular temple worship, especially the burnt offerings and incense offerings. In the context of Chronicles, producing these implements makes sense, since Athaliah's followers have ransacked the temple. The priests require these implements to restore their regular worship of making sacrifices and burning incense. The Chronicler presents these repairs not only as a construction project but as a necessary step to reinstitute YHWH's regular worship in the temple. The wicked Athaliah disrupted this worship; Joash and Jehoiada restore it.

At the same time, this narrative closes with an unsettling phrase: "all the days of Jehoiada." The Chronicler describes Joash as one who does what YHWH accepts "all the days of Jehoiada." Including this phrase at the end of 24:14 raises doubt that Joash will continue to do what is right in the coming verses.

Use of the Funds

Second Kings 12:13 says that the funds collected went to those performing the repairs rather than for use in making implements. This passage in Chronicles indicates that the funds were used for implements. Since the passage in Kings communicates that the funds designated for repairs were used for that purpose and no other, this passage in Chronicles seems to only speak of funds that remained after all the repair work was finished.

Reign of Joash After Jehoiada's Death (24:15–27)

After Jehoiada's death, Joash listens to wicked counsel, forsakes YHWH, and suffers an ironic fate.

24:15–16. After the Chronicler records that temple worship has resumed, he notes that Jehoiada dies after a long life of 130 years. He is buried like a king in the city of David because he has done what is good in Israel for God and his temple. Jehoiada had helped restore the two most prominent institutions in Chronicles: the Davidic dynasty and temple worship. However, even though the Chronicler points out that Jehoiada is buried like a king, he does not suggest that Jehoiada should replace the king. Part of Jehoiada's honor was restoring Davidic rule, not usurping it. This issue would be important for the first readers, who had a functioning priesthood but no Davidic king. The Chronicler reminds these readers that it is not the priest's job to rule as a king; that job belongs to the line of David.

24:17–19. Following Jehoiada's death, certain Judean officials become Joash's advisors. Much like the advisors for Joash's father Ahaziah, these new advisors lead him on a road to destruction (see 2 Chron. 22:3–5). This road begins by abandoning YHWH's temple and worshipping human-made objects:

Asherah poles and idols (see sidebar "Asherah"). YHWH responds in two predictable ways: (1) he becomes angry because they have neglected his temple (and by implication, his worship), and (2) he sends prophets to call them to repent. Both reactions occur frequently in Chronicles. They form parts of a consistent pattern of YHWH's activity: he rewards obedience and punishes disobedience. Disobedience often brings YHWH's wrath specifically (קצף; 1 Chron. 27:24; 2 Chron. 19:2, 10; 29:6–8; 32:25–26). At the same time, even when his people disobey, he sends his prophets to warn them so that they will return to him (2 Chron. 12:5; 16:7; 19:2; 21:12; 25:7; 36:16; etc.).

By including these general statements regarding Joash's sin and YHWH's response, the Chronicler reinforces the idea that YHWH is faithful and reliable. Even if present circumstances obscure this fact, it remains true. The first readers lived in a time when many did not hold worshipping YHWH and providing for his worship in high esteem (Mal. 1:8–14; 3:14–15). This recurring pattern of YHWH's response reminds them that YHWH rewards obedience and punishes disobedience consistently, reliably, and faithfully, even if one cannot presently see it.

24:20–22. After providing these general statements, the Chronicler provides some specific examples. He begins by showing how YHWH moved Jehoiada's son Zechariah to act like a prophet and warn Judah so that they would repent. Zechariah stands up at a place where he can address the people, apparently in the temple, and declares that YHWH is judging them because they are violating his commandments. The people, following Joash's command, respond by stoning him to death. As Zechariah dies, he appeals to YHWH for retribution. He asks that YHWH take notice of his death and hold the king responsible for it accountable.

> **Zechariah and Moses**
>
> Zechariah warns Judah using the same words with which Moses warned all Israel after they had refused to enter the land but planned on doing so by themselves (Num. 14:41). In both situations, the people did not listen to the prophetic warning and suffered because of it.

Two details regarding Zechariah's death require further attention. First, the people conspire against Zechariah. Athaliah uses this same root to describe Joash's enthronement: קשר. Ironically Zechariah, one of Jehoiada's sons who help enthrone Joash by conspiring against Athaliah (2 Chron. 23:11), becomes a target of a conspiracy because he proclaims YHWH's warning to the people. Second, Zechariah dies in the temple courtyard. When Jehoiada orchestrates overthrowing Athaliah, he takes several precautions not to defile the temple, including removing Athaliah from the courtyard of the temple before executing her. In an ironic reversal, Joash conspires against Jehoiada's innocent son to execute him in the same place his father was not willing to shed Athaliah's guilty blood. The Chronicler points to these ironic elements when he states that Joash does not remember what Jehoiada did for him. These ironic elements highlight the difference in Joash's actions before and after Jehoiada dies.

24:23–24. The final scenes of Joash's reign illustrate how YHWH punishes Joash and Judah for their disobedience and how he avenges Zechariah's death. YHWH sends an army to punish them. The Arameans successfully attack Judah, kill the officials, and plunder cities. These officials are most likely the same officials who have been advising Joash to abandon YHWH and serve other gods. The Chronicler points out their deaths as a way of reinforcing YHWH's retribution.

Furthermore, the Chronicler points out specifically that the Arameans win in battle even though they have a small military force. Joash's ancestors Abijah, Asa, and Jehoshaphat each faced a much larger foreign military force but prevailed because they depended on YHWH, who fought for them. In this case, the situation is reversed: YHWH fights on behalf of the small foreign military force because Judah has abandoned him. The Chronicler summarizes the attack by stating that the Aramean army executed judgment upon Joash (וְאֶת־יוֹאָשׁ עָשׂוּ שְׁפָטִים). This expression most often occurs with YHWH as the agent (e.g., Exod. 6:6; 7:4; 12:12; Ezek. 5:10, 15; 11:9; 25:11; 28:22, 26, etc.); however, here the Arameans are the agent. The Chronicler is more explicitly portraying the Arameans as the instrument to punish Joash.

24:25–26. As another sign of YHWH's judgment, after the Arameans severely injure Joash during the conflict, conspirators kill Joash. Several ironic details regarding Joash's death reveal YHWH's hand orchestrating the events (see R. Klein 2000, 126–27). For instance, the Chronicler points out that Joash's servants conspire against him because he is responsible for Zechariah's death. One can hardly miss the irony that Joash dies in virtually the same way as Zechariah. The Chronicler also sets the stage for Joash's death by stating that the Arameans left (עזב) him because of his wounds. The Chronicler has already explained that Aram defeated Judah because Judah left (עזב) YHWH. Now, initially one would expect a positive outcome from the Arameans' leaving; however, their leaving leads to his death. Furthermore, the Chronicler records that Joash dies upon his bed (מִטָּה)—but when Joash was a boy, Jehoiada's wife Jehoshabeath kept Athaliah from killing him by hiding him in the room of beds (מִטָּה). Joash's burial also contrasts to the burial of Jehoiada, Zechariah's father. Jehoiada is buried with the kings even though he is not a king, but Joash is not buried among the tombs of the kings. Finally, when the Chronicler mentions those who conspired to kill Joash, he may be pointing back to Jehoshaphat's battle against Ammon, Moab,

and Edom. In that battle Jehoshaphat wins the battle even though he has a much smaller military force. In Joash's case he suffers defeat from a smaller military force and dies at the hands of servants with Ammonite and Moabite ancestry. These reversals are not coincidences. They show how YHWH uses various means to punish Joash for worshipping other gods and ignoring, even killing, YHWH's prophets who warn him.

24:27. The Chronicler closes out Joash's reign with an atypical conclusion: he refers to Joash's sons, the oracles directed to him, and his repairing of the temple. The repairing of the temple characterizes the positive phase of Joash's reign when Jehoiada is alive. The oracles characterize the negative phase of his reign after Jehoiada dies. The Chronicler seems to mention Joash's sons for two reasons: (1) as an allusion back to his killing Jehoiada's son Zechariah, and (2) as an assurance that the Davidic dynasty has rebounded from its near-extinction during the days of Jehoram, Ahaziah, and Athaliah. Since Joash's son Amaziah takes the throne despite a conspiracy against Joash, he confirms this assurance regarding the Davidic dynasty. Even while concluding Joash's reign, the Chronicler ties together the health of the Davidic dynasty and the well-being of YHWH's temple. This final point is especially important for the first readers. By linking the dynasty and the temple, the Chronicler encourages these readers to wait for the day when both the king rules on the throne and the priests minister in the temple.

THEOLOGICAL FOCUS

Righteous counsel leads to life, but wicked counsel to forsake God leads to disaster.

The Chronicler's portrait of Joash consists of a positive phase followed by a negative phase. The dividing line between the two phases is the death of Jehoiada. This dividing line points to a central theological theme of the passage: the importance of counsel. As Joash's reign demonstrates, good counsel can protect a king's life, preserve a royal dynasty, and provide benefits for an entire nation. However, his reign also demonstrates that bad counsel can corrupt a good king, conspire against God's spokesperson, condemn a nation to military defeat, and kill a wounded king through conspiracy.

Although the narrative elaborates on the consequences of the counsel that Joash receives during the two phases of his reign, it does not provide the details of the counsel itself. However, the narrative reveals an obvious contrast between the counsel of each phase. The good counsel of Jehoiada the priest leads to restoring the temple so that the people can again worship God properly at the Jerusalem temple. The bad counsel of Joash's advisors leads to forsaking God by worshipping other gods. In other words, worshipping the true God properly is always good counsel, but worshipping false gods is always bad counsel.

This theme of counsel plays a part in the larger theme of retribution running through Chronicles; that is, God rewards obedience but punishes disobedience. This passage highlights this theme through its use of irony (see above). Theologically, the use of irony communicates something about God and something about Joash. Regarding God, the irony shows that God is directing the course of history. Irony suggests that Joash's fall is not a random series of events or just the natural consequences of his actions; irony reveals a plan that ties together the various events of Joash's life. This plan points to God's justice as he rewards obedience and punishes disobedience. Regarding Joash, the irony demonstrates his ingratitude to Jehoiada the priest and, by implication, to God (see R. Klein 2000, 127). Even though Jehoiada preserved Joash's life, restored him to the throne, secured the future of the Davidic dynasty, and repaired the Jerusalem temple, Joash kills Jehoiada's son Zechariah, violating the sanctity of the temple space and bringing God's punishment upon himself. Unfortunately, the Bible consistently shows how people can be ungrateful (e.g., Adam

and Eve, Gen. 3; David, 2 Sam. 11; Hezekiah, 2 Chron. 32:25; the nine lepers, Luke 17:12–19). The use of irony highlights the contrast between God's just treatment of people and people's unjust treatment of God.

Finally, it is important to note that Joash's good counsel comes from a priest. For the first readers, this point would be especially important as they were seeking to determine the voices that would shape their community. The Persian province Yehud would require political leadership; however, this account suggests that such political leadership should not be divorced from spiritual counsel. Looking beyond the situation of the first readers, the passage calls for a combination of political authority and spiritual authority. In Chronicles, these authorities remain distinct; however, moving beyond that historical situation, the New Testament shows how Jesus serves the roles of both authorities: king and priest. In Jesus's life, death, resurrection, and ascension, the Chronicler's hope that God's people would be ruled by king and priest has come in its first stages. Now, like the Chronicler, God's people continue to wait for the coming of Jesus when he will subdue all his enemies, rule over all the nations, and present his people as a sanctified bride, thus fulfilling the roles of king and priest forever.

PREACHING AND TEACHING STRATEGIES

Exegetical and Theological Synthesis

The reign of Joash is particularly tragic. Other kings were just as wicked, but were so throughout their reigns. Joash starts out wonderfully. Apparently, it was because he was following the counsel of Jehoiada. Later in his reign the text explicitly says he listened to wicked counsel (24:17) and abruptly turned away from YHWH.

In the first part of his reign, he is rewarded for his "doing what was right in the sight of the Lord" with family and the joy of rebuilding the temple. He led Judah to give toward the rebuilding of the temple, not only the required amount but even more. Even better, there was joyful generosity in the giving. What a delight to see God's people giving generously to him.

The second part of his reign dramatically shifts when Jehoiada dies. Apparently, Joash's obedience was linked to his following Jehoiada's counsel, because his first act after Jehoiada's death was to listen to wicked counsel. This counsel led to the wicked deeds of serving other gods, murder, and forsaking Jehoiada's counsel. God's judgment followed—a recurring theme in the book. The somewhat unique characteristics of these judgments against Joash are seen in their ironic reversals. It prompts one to see just how powerful our Lord is. He is more than capable to reward and judge. When evil deeds are committed, he uses similar evil deeds against those who committed them. He is so much in control and so just that those who murdered were murdered in a similar way. He is so powerful that he arranged the irony of Joash being saved in a bedroom and then dying in a bed. He blessed Joash by having him anointed as king, but Joash was not buried as a king. We can trust our great and fully capable God.

Sometimes we doubt that God will reward obedience and judge sin. We intellectually know that he rewards and judges, but we can forget just how powerful he is. The way in which he judges Joash reminds us that he is fully capable to discipline and to reward. Our response should be to continue in obedience to him and turn from sin—more specifically, to follow godly counsel and turn away from wicked counsel.

Preaching Idea
Listen to the one who rewards and judges.

Contemporary Connections

What does it mean?
Throughout his writing, the Chronicler has emphasized obedience. This passage reaffirms the call to obedience in the first part of Joash's reign and then focuses that call to obedience in the second part by showing how wicked counsel leads to disastrous disobedience. We are naturally influenced by those around us, because God created us to live in community. Being influenced is unavoidable. However, we can choose not to let ungodly counsel influence us. So, the call is to obey and to heed godly counsel.

Hopefully we want to obey, but all of us experience the temptations that are fueled by unwise counsel. I remember as a child being encouraged by the neighbor kids to steal a five-cent candy bar from a local corner store. As teenagers, perhaps we were encouraged by our peers to be more physical with a boy- or girlfriend than we should have been. When careers came, the disobedience of worshipping a career was taught by employers painting a picture of financial success if the commitment to the company was high enough.

It seems to us that Joash should have seen how wicked the counsel was and continued to follow what Jehoiada had taught him. But the advice to turn away from YHWH could have seemed acceptable because it was not too different from what he saw in his predecessors. Often we are not aware of the evil that lies in the counsel of others.

In our world that sees ever-increasing accessibility to information, one can find someone that will give them the counsel they want rather than what is godly. We can be like the person who keeps asking a question until they find someone who will answer it the way they want.

This passage teaches us to be careful to evaluate the counsel we hear—and when it is contrary to God's will, to not follow it nor even listen to it. This is not to say that all counsel outside of God's written revelation is bad counsel. God has given us good minds and there is much to learn from others, providing it is evaluted by the standard of God's will.

Is it true?

When we listen to bad counsel and take action on it, there is a part of us that wants to pass the blame to those who gave us the counsel. We think it wasn't our fault; they made us do it. Those who gave the counsel were wrong, but our listening to it, heeding it, and acting on it was also wrong.

We often are given wrong counsel, but it doesn't have to result in sinful behavior. We can be given the wrong directions and end up being late to a meeting. We apologize and pass on the blame. "Sorry I am late; I was given the wrong directions." There was not a moral decision involved in receiving this kind of wrong counsel.

The counsel we need to turn from is that which directs us to sin. We know that the sin is wrong but listening to (not just physically hearing) the counsel is also wrong. This kind of listening is embracing and agreeing with the counsel, even though we haven't acted on it. Would that Joash had not listened to the leaders of Judah. But he heard and then embraced their counsel, putting it into disobedient action. Though it is hard to separate, he sinned not only in his actions but by embracing the counsel without evaluating it.

Counsel comes to us in various forms. One form that is often overlooked is that of story. Stories are an effective form of giving counsel because they are indirect persuasion, which adds to their power. We watch a movie that presents a sin in a favorable or at least humorous light, be it drunkenness, adultery, rudeness, or any other type of sin. Often when the action that is sinful is portrayed, the music crescendos and it all seems well and good. If we are not careful, we begin to think that it is acceptable to commit that sin; after all, those in the movie were better for it. We may logically remember that it is sinful, but the danger lies in embracing the positive emotions that accompany that indirect but evil counsel. We begin to feel that the sin is not all that bad. We might even daydream of participating in that sin.

God wants us to obey him and not even listen to wicked counsel.

Now what?

We are called to obey and to avoid ungodly counsel. Both require us to know the will of God. We have no record of Joash consulting or reading the Torah, God's written revelation at that time. But we know it was available to him. In the Torah, God's will was very clear. For us, God's will is even more clear in the collective Old and New testaments. God's Word is the standard for our obedience and for evaluating counsel. Thus, we need to be students of God written revelation to us.

The sharp contrast in Joash's life leads one to think that his obedience was grounded not in his knowledge or submission to the Torah, but in the influence of Jehoiada. We can speculate that if it had been grounded directly in God and his written Word, Joash would not have made the abrupt turn to disobedience. We need to be grounded in God's Word, and we need to see how influential those around us can be. Joash listened to Jehoiada, and Jehoiada listened to God and his Word. We have the Scriptures, but who is our Jehoiada? To what persons or groups do we listen?

God made us to be relational creatures, so we are influenced by those around us. Thus, we need to seek out godly counsel. When we need professional counsel, we should find a lawyer, accountant, counselor, or other professional who has a biblical worldview. Not that a nonbelieving professional couldn't give good advice, but their advice might not follow God's revealed will. Even believing professionals could steer us in a wrong direction, but it is less likely. In all cases, when advice is received it must be evaluated according to God's revealed will.

Most of us do not consult a professional for guidance in everyday life. However, we do have those who influence our daily decisions. Who is it that we pattern our lives after? To what and to whom do we listen? Are we disappointed when a wedding, Christmas gathering, or birthday celebration doesn't live up to the pictures we saw on social media? Do we agree in silence when a respected family member might suggest that we forgo attending an Easter or a Christmas service because it is just too hard to go to church when so much is going on? Do we respectfully reject that counsel?

Rejecting counsel is hard because it most often involves another person. Rejecting the counsel is often seen as rejecting not only the counsel but rejecting the one who offers it. While this is not necessarily true, if pleasing the one offering counsel is our standard, then shouldn't pleasing or displeasing the powerful God give us higher motivation for following him?

Creativity in Presentation

The abrupt and disappointing change in Joash's reign needs to be remembered when presenting this passage. One way to accomplish this is to present the first part of his reign with excitement and encouragement, yet at the same time giving hints that it might not last. In telling the good part of Joash's reign, the presenter could insert the following: "He is doing so well; I hope he continues"; "If he keeps going, he could be as respected as David"; or "He is doing so wonderfully; I'm glad he is not following his father or grandfather." These kinds of statements add a suspense and an unspoken anticipation of a tragic end.

When the second part is presented, there needs to be a sense of tragedy. If we only look at Joash as a bad guy and separate ourselves from him, then we are taking on the role of God. Rather, we need to be sad and disappointed. When I read his story, I can't help but think of friends and fellow pastors who have failed morally. It hurts. There is a loss. So too when Joash turns from the Lord; it should hurt us, disappoint us. Here is one possible structure (using the familiar metaphor of a sports game to help present the structure of the pericope):

- What we are to do: obey. It leads to rewards.
  - Joash's righteous reign (24:1–16) (this could be presented as the first half of a game)
- What we are *not* to do: listen and follow ungodly counsel. It leads to disaster.
  - Joash's unrighteous reign (24:17–22) (this could be presented as the second half)
- Why we should do these: God is more than capable.
  - God's ironic reversals of judgment (24:23–27) (this could be the post-game commentary)
- Listen to God: He is the one who rewards and judges.

DISCUSSION QUESTIONS

1. How was Joash blessed during the first part of his reign?

2. What do you think the leaders of Judah may have said to Joash in 24:17?

3. What may have motivated Joash to follow ungodly counsel?

4. What are obvious sources for advice that we receive?

5. What are some more subtle voices that give advice?

6. How does social media give advice?

7. How are we to evaluate the counsel that we hear?

8. How would you describe the difference between just hearing and listening to counsel?

2 Chronicles 25:1–26:2

EXEGETICAL IDEA

Because Amaziah did not trust YHWH completely and turned away from him, YHWH punished him with defeat and death.

THEOLOGICAL FOCUS

When God's people do not trust him completely and consistently, he disciplines them.

PREACHING IDEA

Partial trust in God leads to self-dependence and God's discipline.

PREACHING POINTERS

The unique element in Amaziah's life is his ambivalence. He is making up his mind to follow YHWH or not. His life is presented in two clearly defined parts: (1) the ambivalent section: whether to fully trust God or not; and then, (2) his descent into trusting only in himself, followed by God's discipline. This serves as a warning to us to not be half-hearted in our commitment to Christ. While Amaziah is a negative example, the writer doesn't leave us there. By mentioning that God has power to help and has "much more to give," the Chronicler gives us hope that we can have a wholehearted commitment to God.

REIGN OF AMAZIAH—HALF-HEARTED DEVOTION FOLLOWED BY FOOLISH IDOLATRY (25:1–26:2)

LITERARY STRUCTURE AND THEMES (25:1–26:2)

Following the reign of Joash, the Chronicler records the reign of his son Amaziah. Like Joash, Amaziah obeys during the first part of his reign and disobeys during the latter part. During the first part, the Chronicler provides an introduction in which he describes Amaziah as obeying YHWH but not wholeheartedly, then describes the period of Amaziah's qualified obedience. Amaziah starts well by following Mosaic law, punishing some conspirators but not their children. Amaziah then prepares for battle against Edom, but hires many Israelite mercenaries to help him. After a prophet confronts him, reminding him that YHWH secures victory, not Israelite mercenaries, Amaziah sends the mercenaries away. As a result, YHWH grants Amaziah victory in a battle over Edom. However, this victory becomes the occasion for Amaziah's apostasy and its results. Inexplicably, Amaziah takes the idols of Edom's gods and worships them. YHWH sends a prophet to confront Amaziah, but Amaziah threatens the prophet. Even so, because of Amaziah's victory over Edom, he challenges Israel to battle. Israel defeats Judah and captures Amaziah. In the conclusion to Amaziah's reign, Amaziah dies by conspiracy because he worshipped other gods, but his failures do not cause failure for his son.

Alongside this twofold structure, the account has an imperfect concentric structure. At the beginning and end of this account, the theme of conspiracy occurs. Then, elements of a foreign war correspond to each other. Finally, in the center of the structure is Amaziah's idolatry and the prophetic warning that he rejects.

This structure highlights that although Amaziah starts well, when he worships other gods YHWH punishes him with military defeat and death by conspiracy.

- ***Introduction of Amaziah's Reign (25:1–2)***
- ***Amaziah's Qualified Obedience (25:3–13)***
- ***Amaziah's Apostasy and Its Results (25:14–25)***
- ***Conclusion of Amaziah's Reign (25:26–26:2)***

EXPOSITION (25:1–26:2)

Prophets in the ancient Near East served significant but varied roles. On the one hand, many prophets helped maintain social order within their communities. Usually, such prophets supported the royal or temple administration and in return were supported by those same institutions. On the other hand, other prophets spoke out for reform, criticizing the political or religious leaders. Sometimes, these leaders would take such prophets seriously, or at least would tolerate such reforming prophets if they did not become too disruptive (see Wilson 1980, 89–134). Amaziah's reign features two prophetic figures. Both prophets rebuke the king on separate occasions. In one case, Amaziah takes the prophet seriously, though not wholeheartedly; in the next, Amaziah does not take the prophet seriously at all. The way Amaziah treats these prophets reflects the way he treats YHWH. Because he does not take the prophets seriously he turns away from YHWH, with the result that YHWH punishes him with defeat and death.

Introduction of Amaziah's Reign (25:1–2)

The Chronicler characterizes Amaziah as doing what is upright during his reign, except that he does not do so wholeheartedly.

25:1–2. The Chronicler begins Amaziah's reign in a typical fashion by mentioning his age when he became king, how long he reigned, and his mother's name. Then, using typical phrasing, the Chronicler states that Amaziah did what was right in YHWH's estimation. However, he adds a qualifier to Amaziah's uprightness: he acts rightly, but "not with his whole heart" (לֹא בְּלֵבָב שָׁלֵם). One may interpret this qualification to mean that like his father Joash, Amaziah obeys YHWH during an initial period of his reign, but then disobeys him later. In fact, Amaziah's reign does take such a path. Amaziah begins by following the law of Moses regarding punishing fathers and sons (Deut. 24:16). However, later he disobeys YHWH by worshiping the Edomite gods, provoking YHWH's wrath and leading to further trouble. Each of these actions introduces a different period in Amaziah's reign. However, the first period is not clearly represented as a time of faithfulness. Even in the first period Amaziah's actions and their results are ambiguous (see commentary below). Therefore, Amaziah's reign is not a simple case of a clearly good king who later falls away, but a complex portrait of a king who does some things right but not consistently or completely.

Amaziah's Qualified Obedience (25:3–13)

Since Amaziah obeys YHWH, although not wholeheartedly, YHWH still grants him victory in his battle against Edom.

25:3–4. As his first act as king, Amaziah executes those who conspired against his father. The verb הרג (translated "killed, executed") does not occur elsewhere during Amaziah's reign; however, it does occur twice during the reign of his father Joash. First, after the priest Jehoiada's son Zechariah delivers a prophetic condemnation

against King Joash, the king becomes angry and kills him (וַיַּהַרְגֻ, 2 Chron. 24:22). Because of this unjust murder, Joash's servants later conspire against him and kill him (וַיַּהַרְגֻהוּ, 2 Chron. 24:25).

Now, Amaziah kills those servants who struck down his father. However, unlike his father, who kills Jehoiada's son unjustly, Amaziah does not kill the conspirators' sons. One can see the contrast between Joash and his son Amaziah at this point.

When Amaziah does not kill the sons of the conspirators, he obeys YHWH's explicit commandment written in Mosaic law (Deut. 24:16). The Chronicler quotes the commandment. Only in this passage does he quote a commandment rather than just citing it as an authority (e.g., 1 Chron. 6:49 [HB 34]; 15:15; 16:40; 2 Chron. 8:13; 23:18; 24:6; 30:16; 31:3; 35:6, 12). By quoting the commandment, the Chronicler emphasizes a theological theme important to his entire work (retribution), but especially important for the reigns of Amaziah, Uzziah, and Jotham. The Chronicler connects each father-and-son pair explicitly to one another and describes their reigns as illustrations of Deuteronomy 24:16 and its related passage in Ezekiel 18. These reigns illustrate that the failure and fate of the father does not determine the fate of the son.

The Fates of Fathers and Sons in Chronicles

The reigns of Amaziah, Uzziah, and Jotham highlight an important theme in Chronicles. For these kings, one can see that the father can bring neither honor nor punishment to the son. Deuteronomy 24:16 makes the point regarding punishment: a son should not die for his father's sins, nor a father die for his son's sins, because each one is held accountable for his own sins. At the start of Amaziah's reign, the Chronicler quotes this passage to affirm Amaziah's decision to spare the sons of those who conspired to kill his father. Ezekiel 18 illustrates the principle with examples. First, a righteous father who has a wicked son: the father lives while the son dies for his sin.

Second, a wicked father who has a righteous son: the father dies for his sins while the son lives. Third, a wicked person turns from his wickedness: his wickedness is forgotten, and he lives. Fourth, a righteous person turns from his righteousness: his righteousness is forgotten, and he dies.

The Chronicler illustrates the principle more subtly. First, he links the son to his father when he evaluates his reign: Uzziah did what was right "like his father Amaziah" (2 Chron. 26:4) and Jotham did what was right "like his father Uzziah except he did not enter the temple" (2 Chron. 27:2). The Chronicler uses these connections to clue the reader in on this larger principle. Second, in the cases of Amaziah and Uzziah, the Chronicler shows how these kings did what was right in the first part of their reigns but fell away at some critical point. In the cases of Amaziah and his father Joash, the Chronicler shows how these kings did what was right in the first part of their reigns but fell away at some critical point. In both cases they did by conspiracy because of their sins. However, even though each was punished, the punishment did not carry over to the son. Third, the Chronicler depicts Jotham as a person who consistently does what is right. YHWH does not punish him. His reign shows that even the pattern that marks the reigns before him, that is, beginning well and finishing poorly, does not apply in every case. Fourth, the Chronicler shows that Jotham as a righteous king has a wicked son Ahaz. Jotham's righteousness does not carry over to Ahaz. YHWH punishes Ahaz for his sins. Finally, the Chronicler emphasizes that Manasseh as a wicked king finally turns to YHWH. His sins are forgotten, and YHWH blesses him greatly. Following Amaziah, the Chronicler presents several historical examples that fulfill the portraits painted by Ezekiel 18. Such a theme makes sense given the Chronicler's postexilic context. The Chronicler shows that despite past failures (like those that led to exile), each person (and generation) has a choice to make, and YHWH will treat each person (and generation) according to those choices. Furthermore, the Chronicler points out many more examples of kings who begin righteously but end wickedly, compared to kings who remain righteous or turn from wickedness to righteousness. Those kings who end badly serve as a warning for each person (and generation) to stay alert (Ben Zvi 2008, 73–74).

25:5. After Amaziah executes those who killed his father, he creates a military force. As seen elsewhere, the creation of such an army is a sign of YHWH's blessing because of the king's obedience. The organization, composition, and size of his military force resembles other good kings (e.g., Jehoshaphat, 2 Chron. 17:14–18; Uzziah, 2 Chron. 26:11–13; partially Asa, 2 Chron. 14:8). Amaziah organizes the troops according to their ancestral houses (לְבֵית־אָבוֹת), under the command of officers, designated as the commanders of thousands and hundreds. He takes a census of adult men (twenty years and older; see sidebar "Adulthood in Ancient Judah") to serve in the army. Through the census he discovers that three hundred thousand men are capable of fighting with standard military equipment, the spear and shield. Even though some of the details differ among the military information of other good kings, the similarities demonstrate that YHWH consistently blesses those kings who obey him.

Composition of Amaziah's Army

For the significance of the army's size, see excursus "Troop Numbers in Judah." In this case, the Chronicler has only presented the number of warriors with spear and shield (Seevers 2013, 49, 58–60). Although the sword is mentioned often in military contexts, Chronicles generally describes the standard military force as bearing the spear and shield. This is especially true for Judah (1 Chron. 12:24 [HB 25]; 2 Chron. 14:8). On the other hand, the bow is associated with Benjamin (1 Chron. 8:40; 12:2; 17:17; 2 Chron. 14:8) and not listed separately here.

25:6. After Amaziah creates his army, he takes a surprising next step: he hires one hundred thousand warriors from Israel. Although the Chronicler does not give a great number of details besides the number and origin of warriors, he does provide the price Amaziah pays. He pays one hundred talents of silver. To understand why the Chronicler included the detail regarding the payment, one must look at the next event in the narrative.

Significance of One Hundred Talents

In Chronicles, one hundred talents corresponds to the amount of tribute Jotham receives from the Ammonites (2 Chron. 27:5), and the amount of silver (plus one talent of gold) that Egypt imposed upon Jehoahaz each year (2 Chron. 36:3). However, Chronicles also records that earlier the Ammonites paid one thousand talents of silver for thirty-two thousand chariots accompanied by a military force to aid them. Therefore, within Chronicles the amount is a sizable burden, but not extraordinary.

25:7. After Amaziah hires the warriors from Israel, a prophetic figure (in this case, entitled "man of God" (אִישׁ הָאֱלֹהִים) warns him not to allow these warriors to join him in battle because YHWH is not with Israel. The phrase "YHWH is not with Israel" (אֵין יְהוָה עִם־יִשְׂרָאֵל) means that YHWH will not help Israel succeed, and more particularly in this context, he will not help them succeed in battle. In contrast, the Chronicler records several times when YHWH is with others to help them succeed in battle, even when the odds of success seem impossible (e.g., 2 Chron. 13:12; 20:17; 32:8). In each case, YHWH helps those who obey him.

If YHWH helps those who obey him, then since he is not with Israel, how is Israel disobeying YHWH? Earlier in Chronicles King Abijah answers the question when he addresses Jeroboam before battle (2 Chron. 13:6–12). He recounts how Jeroboam rebels against the Davidic king Rehoboam, but he continues by reminding Jeroboam that he set up the golden calves as idols and allowed anyone to serve as a priest. As Abijah points out, YHWH is not with Israel because of these improper worship practices; however, since Judah has followed the ritual worship regulations by having a proper priesthood serving YHWH in a proper manner, he is with Judah (2 Chron. 13:8–12). In other words, the Chronicler is not saying that YHWH has universally rejected Israel. If they follow him, he will be with them; if not, then he will not be with them (2 Chron. 15:2; cf. Japhet 1993, 863).

In fact, by referring to the Ephraimites as Israel, the Chronicler helps illustrate the point. First, during Asa's reign, several from Israel, including those from Ephraim, join Asa to devote themselves to YHWH through an oath because they see that YHWH is with Asa (2 Chron. 15:9). Second, the use of the name "Israel" points to the common heritage shared between the northern and southern tribes. Therefore, YHWH is rightfully their God. However, in general, the Ephraimites do not devote themselves to YHWH; therefore, YHWH opposes an alliance with them (Knoppers 2019, 57–58).

25:8. The man of God explains the consequences Amaziah will face if he allows these Israelite warriors to join him: God will make him fall before his enemy. Furthermore, the man of God provides the theological cause for Amaziah's downfall if he continues: YHWH is powerful enough to grant victory or defeat. Given the context, the Chronicler implies that YHWH can grant victory or defeat regardless of either side's military strength or strategy. Other good kings rely on YHWH to fight their impossible battles (e.g., Abijah, 2 Chron. 13:3–18; Asa, 2 Chron. 14:8–13 [HB 7–12]); Jehoshaphat, 2 Chron. 20:1–24; Hezekiah, 2 Chron. 32:1–22), but Amaziah hires these Israelite mercenaries. This theme of relying on YHWH in combat is especially prominent in Chronicles. Amaziah's hiring the Israelites puts a dark blot on an otherwise positive picture.

TRANSLATION ANALYSIS:

Translations treat the first part of 25:8 differently. Even though the overall sense of the verse is clear, translating the verse requires making several exegetical decisions. First, one must determine how to understand כִּי אִם. Most translations treat the phrase as two separate words, resulting in a translation "but if" or "even if" (CSB, NASB, NET, NIV, NKJV, NLT); however, a small number treat it as a single unit translated only "but" or "rather" without a conditional "if" (ESV, NRSV). Second, one must determine whether to follow the consonants of MT. The versions read differently than MT; in particular, they preserve a reading of "with them" (בָּם). Only the NLT seems to take this approach. Third, one must determine to treat the vowel pointing of MT. MT preserves the three verbs in 25:8a as imperfective (בֹּא, עֲשֵׂה, חֲזַק). Some translations render the second and third verbs as imperfective but not the first (CSB, NASB, NKJV). Fourth, one must determine the function of אַתָּה. Most translations render it as the subject or do not render it at all. In contrast, the NRSV renders it as "by yourself." Fifth, one must determine how the clauses 25:8a and 8b fit together. MT preserves the two clauses next to one another without any conjunction. However, many translations require a conjunction to make sense of the verse (e.g., CSB, ESV, NASB, NKJV, NRSV). For NRSV (and perhaps ESV) the conjunction appears to assume that the word לָמָה ("Why?" or "otherwise") has dropped out.

As stated, translating the first part of the verse requires making a few exegetical decisions. The best way to make good sense of MT is to follow the NRSV. If one values the versions more, then it results in the following translation: "If you strengthen your forces with them [Israelite warriors], God will make you fall before the enemy."

25:9. At this point, the narrative returns to the detail regarding Amaziah's payment. When Amaziah asks the man of God what he should do about the payment to the Israelites, he responds by again affirming YHWH's power—this time, his power to grant wealth. Chronicles repeatedly illustrates both sides of YHWH's power since he repeatedly rewards obedience with military victory and wealth. Even though Amaziah wins the battle he is preparing to fight, nowhere in the narrative does YHWH give Amaziah more wealth. However, later in Chronicles, Jotham, Amaziah's grandson, receives the same amount of the payment (one hundred talents of silver) as tribute from the Ammonites. Furthermore, this amount is multiplied by three, since Jotham receives the tribute for three years. Therefore, the Chronicler illustrates in specific detail the man of God's theological assertion that YHWH can give more, even though he does not give Amaziah more. The key difference between Jotham and Amaziah is that Jotham does what is right without qualification, whereas Amaziah does what is right but not with his whole heart.

25:10. After Amaziah hears these statements of YHWH's power and the warning against letting the Israelite warriors join him in battle, he obeys the man of God by sending them away to return to Israel. These Israelite warriors (now referred to as a troop הַגְּדוּד) become very angry as they return home. The Chronicler does not say why they are angry; apparently, this information is not relevant to his point. However, by mentioning their anger and referring to them as a "troop" (גְּדוּד), he foreshadows their actions later in the narrative.

TRANSLATION ANALYSIS:

The term גְּדוּד refers to a small group of warriors. Sometimes the word is used generally for a subdivision within an army. In many contexts, especially in Kings, it carries a more specific sense of a raiding party. In many cases, these raiding parties harass Judah and Israel (e.g., 2 Kings 5:2; 6:23; 13:20; 1 Chron. 12:22; 2 Chron. 22:1). The use of the term in this verse may foreshadow the fact that these same warriors will later raid Judean cities, killing many and seizing a good deal of plunder.

25:11–12. The Chronicler turns his attention from the Israelite warriors to Amaziah's conflict with the Edomites. Amaziah prepares himself for war and leads his army against the Edomites in the Valley of Salt (גֵּיא הַמֶּלַח; a location of David's conflict with the Edomites; 2 Sam. 8:13 LXX; 1 Chron. 18:12; Ps. 60:2). Initially, he kills ten thousand Edomites and captures another ten thousand. Amaziah's army leads the captives to the top of a cliff and hurls the captives to their deaths. To make a couple of subtle points, the Chronicler employs wordplay. First, since the Chronicler refers to the Edomites as the sons of Seir, he creates similar sounds with the numbers of those who die and are captured: ten thousand (בְּנֵי־שֵׂעִיר עֲשֶׂרֶת אֲלָפִים וַעֲשֶׂרֶת אֲלָפִים). The wordplay hints at a natural connection between those of Seir and the ten thousand of those killed and another ten thousand captured (Ben Zvi 2006a, 60–61). Second, the Chronicler takes advantage of the meaning of the word "rock, cliff" (סֶלַע). The word occurs often as a common noun; however, it also occurs as the name of an Edomite fortification evidently built upon some cliffs. In fact, the parallel passage in Kings (2 Kings 14:7) states that Amaziah captured the city Sela and changed its name. The Chronicler clearly uses the word as a common noun. By using this wordplay, the Chronicler shows how (1) the city that the Edomites intended for their protection, Sela (הַסֶּלַע), is powerless before YHWH, and (2) the cliffs (הַסֶּלַע) that led to its name become their means of destruction (Ben Zvi 2006a, 60–61). This account illustrates YHWH's power to prevail in battle, even by dramatic or ironic means (for a closer look at the role irony plays in 2 Chron. 25, see Graham 1993, 85–89).

25:13. However, following this victory, the Chronicler records an incident that complicates the picture: the Israelite troop that Amaziah sent back to Israel raids several Judahite cities, killing thousands and taking spoils. The Chronicler does not indicate the troop's reason for attacking, nor does he seem to provide a theological reason for the attacks. However, the Chronicler may expect the reader to understand this verse based on what follows (see below).

Geographic Overlap Between Judah and Israel
Deciphering the significance of the geographic information is difficult. Samaria is the capital city of Israel, while elsewhere in Chronicles (1 Chron. 6:68 [HB 53]) Beth-horon is a city lying within Ephraim near the border of Judah. Apparently, this Israelite troop returned to Samaria and then began moving down to the border of Judah. Either along the way or perhaps close to the border near Beth-horon, they attacked Judahite cities.

One may also note that the Chronicler refers to the Israelite warriors as "sons of the troop" (בְּנֵי הַגְּדוּד). The word "sons" marks an important theme for the first half of Amaziah's reign, the period of his ambiguous obedience. He begins well by sparing the sons of the conspirators (25:4), but later finds out that YHWH is not with Israel, that is, the sons of Ephraim whom he has hired (25:7). As a result, he leads the sons of Judah (25:12) into battle and prevails over Edom, that is, the sons of Seir (25:11). However, at the same time, the Israelite troop he sent back, that is, the sons of the troop (בְּנֵי הַגְּדוּד, 25:13), raids Judahite cities, killing thousands and taking spoils. By looking at these "sons," one can see the course of the first part of his reign: obedience, warning, obedience, victory, and then unexpected disaster. This course of events shows the ambiguous path and results that characterize even the first part of Amaziah's reign (25:2).

Amaziah's Apostasy and Its Results (25:14–25)
Because Amaziah worships other gods his reign turns toward disaster in which, despite repeated warnings, he suffers defeat in combat.

25:14. After Amaziah defeats the Edomites, he brings their gods back, sets them up, and worships them. The way that the Chronicler describes what Amaziah does depicts the true nature of these gods: they are objects that someone can move and then must set up. In other words, they are merely objects but treated as though they are something different. Furthermore, the Chronicler clarifies what he means by setting them up as gods when he describes what Amaziah does: he treats them as gods when he reverently bows down to them and makes sacrifices to them.

25:15–16. Amaziah's actions immediately provoke YHWH to anger. YHWH responds by sending a prophet who interprets Amaziah's actions correctly. Whatever Amaziah's own motivations, the prophet reveals that Amaziah's actions show he is seeking foreign gods and that these gods can't even help their own people. The king interrupts the prophet to rebuff this interpretation. The king denies the prophet the right to address him in this way. The king warns the prophet that if he continues, he will be struck down. The prophet stops but offers a final judgment to the king.

TRANSLATION ANALYSIS:
How one translates the king's response depends on two factors. First, many MT manuscripts preserve the reading נְתַנּוּךָ ("we set you"). One would likely understand the first-person common plural as a plural of majesty; therefore, the king is speaking of himself, just using the plural form. However, several MT manuscripts as well as the Targum preserve the reading נְתָנוּךָ "they set you; you have been set." This form coincides with the verb in the same verse יַכּוּךָ "you will be struck." The difference between the two readings is a *daghesh*. Since LXX reads δέδωκά "I have set," it seems likely that the reading is נְתָנוּךָ, translated according to its sense; cf. 2 Chron. 10:9; Allen 1974, 2:150.

One may note the contrast between this encounter with a prophet and the earlier encounter with the man of God. When the man of God confronts Amaziah for hiring the Israelite mercenaries, he correctly interprets Amaziah's action, offers a warning, and affirms YHWH's power in battle. Amaziah heeds the warning and sends the Israelite mercenaries away. When the prophet confronts Amaziah for worshipping the Edomite gods, he also correctly interprets Amaziah's action and implicitly affirms YHWH's power in battle; however, in contrast, Amaziah interrupts the prophet, gives him a command, and offers him a warning. The prophet heeds the warning but concludes by saying that YHWH has determined to destroy Amaziah because he is unwilling to follow the prophet's advice. The contrast between these two encounters confirms that Amaziah's reign has taken a turn for the worse.

Other features of the text confirm this turn for the worse. These verses create a parallel between YHWH and the Israelite troop by mentioning their burning anger (25:10 חֳרִי־אָף // 25:15 וַיִּחַר־אָף). The troop's anger leads to an attack on Judahite cities, killing thousands and taking plunder. Their anger, and its consequences, foreshadow YHWH's anger and its consequences, since YHWH's anger leads to an attack on Jerusalem, capturing hostages and taking plunder (25:23–24). In both cases, Amaziah's actions question YHWH's ability. In both cases, Amaziah suffers.

25:17a. After the encounter with the prophet, the narrative shifts to Amaziah's confrontation with the Israelite king Joash. Even though this incident may seem unrelated to the preceding, the Chronicler has skillfully connected the prophet's warning with Amaziah's confrontation with Israel. The Chronicler uses a group of words concerning the theme of counsel (יעץ). The king denies that the prophet is a royal counselor (יוֹעֵץ לַמֶּלֶךְ), but the prophet responds that YHWH has decided (יָעַץ) to destroy Amaziah because he did not listen to the prophet's counsel (עֵצָה). Then Amaziah takes counsel

(וַיִּוָּעֵץ) to confront Israel. The Chronicler's use of "counsel" (יעץ) here foreshadows the disastrous results of the confrontation with Israel and confirms that the outcome is a result of YHWH's decision.

25:17b–19. When Amaziah challenges the Israelite king Joash to battle, Joash responds with a fable (that is, a story with personified animals and/or plants, designed to teach a moral). The fable describes a worthless plant, a thistle, that wants to join the ranks of a stately tree, a cedar, through marriage. As soon as the thistle makes the request, an animal tramples it down. The story's moral is that those who overstep their proper place for greater status are destroyed. The story is not an allegory or parable of the situation, but a reminder to Amaziah that improper ambition leads to danger. Joash confirms this interpretation when he describes Amaziah as seeking glory because he defeated Edom; that is, because Amaziah intends to overstep his place to gain glory, he will be destroyed. As a result, Joash tells Amaziah to stay in his own place; otherwise, he will stir up trouble for himself and his people Judah.

TRANSLATION ANALYSIS:
"Let us see each other's face" (נִתְרָאֶה פָנִים) only occurs in this context. Its occurrence here and in 25:21 suggests that it means "to face each other in battle." However, some scholars have interpreted the phrase without negative connotations, meaning only "let's meet." In this line of interpretation, Amaziah proposes a marriage alliance with Joash, but when the two kings meet, Joash ambushes Amaziah and defeats him. This interpretation does not fit well with the account as it is. The battle does not appear to be an ambush. Furthermore, the interpretation ties the events of the fable too closely with the events of the narrative because nowhere in the narrative outside the fable does Amaziah propose a marriage alliance. In contrast, the fable only intends to illustrate the moral; it is not an allegory of the present situation.

Joash's Fable
Although some interpreters have tried to read the story as an allegory, it breaks down. Even if one relates Judah to the thistle and Israel to the cedar (comparisons that are still problematic), one cannot identify the wild animal in the present context. Furthermore, in the context Amaziah is not requesting a marriage; he is challenging Joash to battle.

25:20. At this point, the narrative shifts its focus from the king's individual disobedience to the people's collective disobedience. In 25:14 Amaziah brings the Edomite gods, sets them up, bows down to them, and sacrifices to them. In 25:15 the prophet says that he has sought the Edomite gods. Now, however, the Chronicler introduces Judah's collective role in the disobedience, explicitly including Judah: "They [Judah] sought the gods of Edom."

Despite the fable's moral and Joash's clear warning, Amaziah continues to follow his plan to challenge Joash. The narrative confirms what the prophet spoke to Amaziah: YHWH has decided to destroy him. The Chronicler states that God orchestrated these events (מֵהָאֱלֹהִים הִיא) to punish Amaziah and Judah for worshipping the Edomite gods (using the verb דרש to describe this action creates symmetry between the prophecy and the narrative). From this point, the narrative demonstrates how YHWH punishes them.

25:21–24. Joash meets Amaziah on the battlefield at Beth-Shemesh, within Judah's territory. The Chronicler summarizes the results of the encounter. First, Judah is defeated (וַיִּנָּגֶף) and retreats, returning home ("each fled to his tent"). Second, Joash captures Amaziah. Third, he assaults Jerusalem, breaking down some of its defenses, specifically a significant length of the city wall. Fourth, he raids the temple's wealth entrusted to Obed-edom and the royal treasury. Fifth, he takes hostages (בְּנֵי הַתַּעֲרֻבוֹת). Finally, he returns to Samaria.

Confusing Names

The names used in this encounter between Judah and Israel may cause confusion. Judah's king is Amaziah. Amaziah's father is Joash; his grandfather is Ahaziah. Israel's king is Joash (the same as the name of Amaziah's father although a different person). His father is Jehoahaz; his grandfather is Jehu. This similarity is enough to invite confusion; however, the situation is a bit more complicated. The names Ahaziah (אֲחַזְיָהוּ) and Jehoahaz (יְהוֹאָחָז) are variant forms of the same name meaning "YHWH seized." Therefore, translations differ regarding the name of Amaziah's grandfather. Some translations (CSB, NASB, NKJV) follow MT here, preserving the spelling Jehoahaz. Others (ESV, NIV, NLT, NRSV) use the more common name for Amaziah's grandfather: Ahaziah.

The way the Chronicler describes the latter part of Amaziah's reign places the king among the worst kings of Israel. When Amaziah sets up the Edomite idols "as gods" (לֵאלֹהִים), he acts like the wicked founder of the northern kingdom, Jeroboam. Jeroboam makes the golden calves "as gods" (לֵאלֹהִים) for Israel. As a result of Jeroboam's forsaking YHWH (2 Chron. 13:11), Judah defeats Israel even though Israel has every military advantage (2 Chron. 13:13–15). The reverse takes place during Amaziah's reign: Israel defeats Judah even though YHWH is not with Israel (25:7). In both cases (and others throughout Chronicles), the Chronicler clearly points out the consequences for worshipping idols, especially foreign idols: disaster.

Mention of Obed-edom

The Chronicler states that Obed-edom (meaning "one who serves Edom") cares for the treasures of YHWH's temple. The mention of Obed-edom here is a stinging irony for Amaziah. Because Amaziah worshipped the gods of Edom, in this sense serving Edom, YHWH brings judgment on him by plundering the wealth under Obed-edom's care (cf. Japhet 1993, 870–71).

Conclusion of Amaziah's Reign (25:26–26:2)

Because Amaziah has worshipped other gods, conspirators will kill him, but his failures do not cause failure for his son.

25:25. In some ways, the conclusion to Amaziah's reign is ambiguous, just like the beginning of his reign. It begins with information occurring rarely in Chronicles: the length of a Judahite king's lifespan compared to the length of an Israelite king's lifespan. The Chronicler's reason for including this information is not evident. He may have included it to imply that Joash kept Amaziah as a captive until the Israelite king died (Dillard 1987, 198–202). Although such a reading is possible, the text states that Joash brought Amaziah to Jerusalem (25:23). Joash may have carried Amaziah back to Samaria after he assaulted Jerusalem, but the text is silent on this point. He may have included it because of his concern for Israel when it relates directly to Judah (Japhet 1993, 871).

One effect of the information is that it clears up the characterization of Israel since it is at times ambiguous in the narrative. In the narrative's beginning, YHWH is not with Israel; therefore, fighting alongside the Israelite mercenaries would lead to defeat. These same mercenaries raid Judahite cities, killing and plundering. However, following this negative portrayal, Israel defeats Judah. Even though the narrative makes it explicit that Judah's defeat is YHWH's punishment, the status of Israel is left open. Since the Israelite king Joash dies much earlier than Amaziah, perhaps the Chronicler intends for this final comment to reveal no real change in Israel's status at this point (Ben Zvi 2008, 82).

25:26–28. The concluding formula consists of typical language with virtually no variation: it includes the "first and last" and cites the Book of the Kings of Judah and Israel. The actual burial notice (25:28b) also uses typical language, with little variation: he was buried with his fathers in the city of David. However, the death notice does not follow a typical pattern.

TRANSLATION ANALYSIS:
Most MT manuscripts read "the city of Judah" (עִיר יְהוּדָה); however, several others along with the versions read "the city of David" (עִיר דָּוִיד). The former reading may have resulted from inserting Judah from the following verse (see R. Klein 2012, 353, 364).

25:27. The Chronicler describes Amaziah's death in a way that draws his reign together and highlights his decision to worship the Edomite gods. The same kind of tragedy that begins his reign also ends his reign: conspiracy. Amaziah responds appropriately to the conspiracy against his father (i.e., he spares the conspirators' sons), but himself dies by conspiracy. The tables have been turned. They turn because Amaziah worships the Edomite gods, described here as turning away from YHWH. Even though Amaziah tries to escape to Lachish, he cannot escape YHWH's plan to destroy him.

> **Amaziah's Relation to Jerusalem**
> There is a certain irony in Amaziah's relation to Jerusalem. Joash captures him outside the city, only to return him to it. Yet his return to Jerusalem actually puts him further in harm's way since a conspiracy forms against him in the city. As a result, he flees the city, resulting in his death outside the city. Finally, horses return him to be buried in the city.

26:1–2. These verses form a postlude to Amaziah's reign. In this postlude the Chronicler presents a peaceful transition from Amaziah to Uzziah, despite the conspiracy. The Chronicler records that "all the people of Judah" enthrone Uzziah as his way of affirming that Amaziah dies because of his unfaithfulness to YHWH rather than social or political reasons. The postlude also presents a final illustration of

Amaziah's failure. After Amaziah dies, his son Uzziah restores the city Eloth (אֵילוֹת, in Kings Elath אֵילַת), located in Edom (2 Chron. 8:17), to Judah's domain. Solomon maintained control of the city; however, Amaziah did not despite his military victories over Edom. Even though this verse points out Amaziah's failure, it also affirms the point that the fate of the fathers does not determine the fate of the sons. Uzziah starts well, but one must wait for the account of his reign in full to see how it turns out.

For the first readers, certain aspects of Amaziah's reign would likely stand out. First, because the first readers were part of the community coming out of exile, the affirmation that the sons may not be punished for the sins of the father and vice versa would be especially comforting. The postexilic community was aware both of their ancestors' sins and the devastating punishment for those sins. However, recognizing that those sins will not seal their fates would provide comfort and encouragement to follow YHWH. Second, the account would encourage the first readers to maintain wholehearted devotion to YHWH. This devotion, in part, would consist of avoiding foreign elements in their worship, taking the prophetic word seriously, and supporting the Jerusalem temple (see Neh. 13). Less than complete devotion to YHWH would threaten the well-being of the community, already a struggling community within a larger imperial context.

THEOLOGICAL FOCUS
When God's people do not trust him completely and consistently, he disciplines them.

Amaziah's reign follows a pattern in Chronicles: a king starts well by seeking God but then forsakes God so that his reign ends badly. In Amaziah's case, a prophet confronts Amaziah during both parts of his reign. The interactions with these prophets point to the central theological issue of the passage: trust. Amaziah does not trust God fully.

The first prophetic figure confronts Amaziah because he has hired Israelite mercenaries to strengthen his army. The prophet warns Amaziah not to let the Israelite mercenaries join him in battle because God is not with them. The prophet reminds him that God determines the outcomes of battle, not military strength. The prophet exposes Amaziah's doubt regarding God's power to fight. Then, Amaziah thinks of the payment he has already made to the mercenaries. The prophet reminds him that God can give far more than what Amaziah is giving up. Here, the prophet exposes Amaziah's doubt regarding God's power to prosper. Despite Amaziah's doubt, he listens to the prophet and dismisses the mercenaries. As a result, God grants him victory in battle.

The doubts about God in the first part of Amaziah's reign grow into rejection of God in the second part of his reign. The second prophetic figure confronts Amaziah because he has worshiped Edomite gods. The prophet again addresses God's power to fight, but inexplicably Amaziah decides to worship gods who cannot fight. Amaziah ignores the prophet's warning and invites a confrontation with Israel, trusting that he now has the strength to defeat them. Unfortunately, Amaziah's earlier doubts about God's power to fight have been twisted into a confidence that he (or others) has the power to fight. However, this confidence is misplaced. Israel attacks Judah, ransacks Jerusalem, and captures Amaziah. Amaziah's incomplete and inconsistent trust in God leads to his downfall.

This observation regarding Amaziah applies beyond his individual circumstances. Although many passages throughout the Bible address the question of belief, trust, and doubt, the letter to the Laodicean church correlates closely in theme to Amaziah's situation. The letter describes how the congregation is inconsistent in its works. Furthermore, the letter points out the Laodiceans' trust in themselves, for they believe they are rich even though they are poor. Therefore, the letter reminds them that Christ rebukes

and disciplines those he loves. Like Amaziah, the Laodiceans face God's discipline if they do not trust him completely and consistently.

Even though Amaziah does not trust God fully, God can be fully trusted. The passage affirms God's power in several ways. The first prophet affirms that God has the power to determine the outcome of any battle, regardless of the degree of military strength on either side. Judah's victory against Edom confirms this point. The first prophet also affirms that God has the power to grant wealth. The reigns following Amaziah confirm this point. The second prophet warns Amaziah that God has determined to destroy the king because he worshipped other gods. God's decision controls the rest of the narrative, even when Amaziah's own pride leads him into a battle that he will not win (25:20). God's power has not diminished since the days of Amaziah; God still rules over heaven and earth (Eph. 1:18–23; Col. 1:15–20). Therefore, all people should fully trust him.

PREACHING AND TEACHING STRATEGIES

Exegetical and Theological Synthesis
Amaziah's partial trust in YHWH is highlighted at the beginning of this narrative. He did right, but not with a whole heart. This lack of total trust in YHWH led to an inexplicable sin. By God's power Amaziah defeats the Edomites and then, rather than giving praise to YHWH for the victory, he bows down to the gods of the Edomites whom he just defeated. When we see this, we can't help but exclaim, "What are you doing? Who just gave you victory? Are you out of your mind?" Apparently, his partial trust in YHWH caused him to think that he, himself, was the power behind the victory. This boasting in his own strength is articulated by Joash, king of the northern kingdom. Amaziah's partial trust in God degenerated into trust in himself. This self-reliance led to his inexplicable sin and even more.

In response, God shows that he is the powerful one by bringing discipline upon Amaziah.

When we only partially trust in God, it means that we are partially trusting in ourselves. We might think, "I will obey God, but I can't fully depend upon him. After all, I have a role to play as well. He does his part and I do mine." When the task is completed, it is easy to forget that God is the source of power and victory. Our boasting about the great work that was accomplished can easily become boasting about *our* work. While God does ask us to be involved in his work, it is still his work. It is accomplished by his power, not ours. This setting aside of trust in God and replacing it with trust in ourselves will bring God's wrath and discipline. When we wholeheartedly trust in God and fully trust him to work, our joy comes in boasting about him. The glory is his.

Preaching Idea

Partial trust in God leads to self-dependence and God's discipline.

Contemporary Connections

What does it mean?

What does half-hearted trust in God look like? Amaziah still did some things right, so where do we see his lack of a wholly committed heart? Of course, we see it in the second part of his reign, but the text says the partial trust was there in the beginning. Perhaps it was in the hasty killing of the servants who killed his father without examining each of them. As king he did right in enlisting an army, but then he hires soldiers from the northern kingdom. After being confronted that this was wrong he sent them back, but worried about the wasting of one hundred talents of silver. So, there are hints of obedience, but he must be coached to obey.

How do we know if the right things we do are not purely surface actions? Are they done without a whole heart? Having a whole heart does not mean perfection. No one can achieve

that. A lack of complete trust is hard to codify because it is a heart issue. The text sees it as a matter of the heart. When we look at our motives and desires, it gives us some indication of how wholeheartedly we are following God.

A college close to me has an amazing school spirit. Their football games are electric, even when they lose. Students are expected to fully participate. There is even a yell practice, where students gather the night before the game to practice the songs and the cheers. If a student doesn't participate wholeheartedly in these events, they are shunned and called "two-percenters." When I resent going to a prayer meeting, or read a verse and give it no more thought than I would to an advertisement adressed to a current resident, or sing through a hymn without ever thinking about what I am singing, perhaps in my lack of wholeheartedness towards God, I am just a two-percenter. Are there times when sin is not turned away from but toyed with and looked at from a distance? An impure thought intrudes our mind, and rather than replace it with pure thoughts we savor it. We let our imagination go down a road that is displeasing to the Father. Undisciplined thoughts can reveal that we do not have a whole heart to trust in God. Another indication of a lack of complete trust could be when we hesitate to obey. We know what God would have us do, but we have to think about it. Do we see worship as something we have to do, or something we get to do?

Is it true?

Two applications of this passage are easy to minimize by thinking that this was Amaziah's problem, but I am not Amaziah.

Partial obedience and half-hearted commitment to the Lord are easy to live with because we think that someday we will get our act together and fully follow the Lord. We are satisfied with some minimal level of commitment to God. We pat ourselves on the back and think that at least we have obeyed at some level. After all, no one is perfect. And we let that be our excuse for doing right without a whole heart. While none of us are perfect, we should at least want to be—not in a prideful, self-affirming way, but because that is what our Father wants for us. It seems that Amaziah was satisfied with a partial commitment to God, and it led him away from YHWH.

God harshly disciplined Amaziah with the humiliation of being conquered by the northern kingdom and then being taken back to Jerusalem by those who conquered him. What shame he must have felt, to be taken back to his capitol city as a captive. Of course we sin, but not like Amaziah; surely God's disciplining hand will not be on us. We must remember the proverb affirmed in Hebrews 11:4–6: God disciplines those he loves.

His disciplining hand will, of course, be appropriate for each person, but it does come. It might be a lack of inner peace or excessive worrying. I will never forget the shame and guilt I heard in the voice of a fellow pastor when he told me that he was stepping down from his church because of immorality. Shame and guilt are part of God's loving hand of discipline. When I reflect on a conversation I had with a friend and realize that I dominated the time with my story and my life and didn't listen enough, there is shame and guilt. When we go to prayer and feel as though God is far away, it might be God's hand of discipline. It would be unproductive to try to articulate other ways that God disciplines us, because it is so tailored to the sin and the person who commits it. But this passage teaches us that it is there. The writer tells us that God has the power to bring down. And that same verse tells that he has the power to help (25:8)—which leads us into the "Now what?" of this passage.

Now what?

The other side of not having a whole heart is how we develop one. Our partial trust is not only sin in itself, but it also leads to other sins. So how do we nurture a heart that is totally his?

Just as one sin can lead to another, one act of obedience can lead to greater obedience. This passage only briefly mentions this positive application, but it is there. The prophet tells Amaziah that God has the power to help and then later tells him that God has much more to give him. Amaziah doesn't cry out for help, nor does he receive the "much more" that God wants to give to him; nonetheless, it had been offered.

For those who have embraced the work of Christ on their behalf, there is great help and so much more to nurture a whole heart. It comes not so much in the big events but in everyday acts of obedience. The consistent life of prayer, worship, abiding in God's Word, and declaring his gospel are daily efforts that change one's heart. Add to this a thought life controlled by the Spirit. These are the activities that will shape a heart. Most important is the power of God's help in all these. Shannon Wexelburg says it well in her song "Whole Heart." There she speaks of a heart that is undivided and totally dependent upon Christ's power to heal and empower us.

Creativity in Presentation

The two-part division of this pericope gives us the foundation for the structure. In telling any story it is good to build tension. In this case the tension is presented for us in 25:2. Amaziah's character is in the balance. Will he continue to do right? Will his heart grow and become wholly for God? Will he fully trust God or descend into trust in himself? Which will win out? The options are presented in 25:8: God can help, or God can bring down. Which will Amaziah choose? A classic movie with a similar theme is *The Empire Strikes Back*, in which the hero is tempted to go over to the dark side. The first part of Amaziah's story should be presented in such a way that the answer is not clear. Then in the second portion, Amaziah's move into trusting in himself instead of YHWH is made clear, along with God's punishment.

While the text is primarily dealing with the negative results of Amaziah's life, which must be covered and applied, it is also appropriate to highlight the positive options that the text presents. God was willing to help and had much more for him. The application of these can be expanded into a discussion of the richness of the life offered to us in Christ. Here is one possible structure:

- We have the option to partially trust or fully lean upon God.
  - Amaziah's life, part one: Trust God fully or self? (25:1–13)
  - Are we partially or fully trusting God?
- We should choose wholehearted trust because it guards us both from self-dependence and from God's discipline.
  - Amaziah's life, part two:
    - His descent into self-trust (25:14–10)
    - God's discipline (25:20–28)
  - We need to heed these warnings.
- We can nurture a whole heart through Christian disciplines.

DISCUSSION QUESTIONS

1. In everyday life, in whom do we place our trust?

2. Is this trust partial or complete?

3. Is there any human we can totally trust?

4. Why do we hesitate to fully trust God?

5. When you trusted Christ for salvation, were you fully trusting him?

6. When have you withheld your full trust in God?

7. When we disobey, what does it say about our level of trust?

2 Chronicles 26:3–27:9

EXEGETICAL IDEA
When Uzziah followed YHWH, YHWH helped him; when Uzziah became arrogant enough to violate YHWH's sanctity, YHWH punished him, but carried on his work through his obedient son Jotham.

THEOLOGICAL FOCUS
Although God may reward past obedience, he still disciplines those who pridefully presume upon his sanctity; however, future obedience may restore such rewards.

PREACHING IDEA
Help from God doesn't mean we can help ourselves.

PREACHING POINTERS
Uzziah should have set his pride aside when he received God's help, but he held onto it. One would think that if you open your hands for God's help you have emptied your hands of pride, but Uzziah held onto his pride. His pride provided a pathway to arrogance. In his arrogance he thought he could violate God's law. When we are given help by God, we can see that gift as a sign that we now have special privileges. It can make us think that since God helped us, we can help ourselves to whatever we want. Uzziah ignored the sanctity of the temple, and, if not careful, we can ignore the sanctity not of a place, but of a relationship. Our faith in Christ's death and resurrection brought us into a sacred relationship with God. How can we cling to prideful disobedience when we embrace the cross?

REIGNS OF UZZIAH AND JOTHAM—REWARDS OF RIGHTEOUSNESS AND PUNISHMENT OF PRIDE
(26:3–27:9)

LITERARY STRUCTURE AND THEMES (26:3–27:9)

This passage records the reigns of two kings, Uzziah and Jotham; however, it consists of three parts. Uzziah's reign falls into two sharply divided periods. During the first period, Uzziah seeks YHWH and succeeds. Most of the text describes how Uzziah succeeds in battle, in building, and in preparing troops and strategic locations. The keyword "help" (עזר) holds the first part of Uzziah's reign together as YHWH helps Uzziah in battle (26:7), Uzziah's army stands ready to help him against any enemy (26:13), and he grows strong because he is helped (26:15). As result of YHWH's help, Uzziah grows wealthy, famous, and influential.

Unfortunately, Uzziah's success leads to his pride. During the second period of his reign, Uzziah transgresses the sanctity of the temple by entering it to burn incense. When Uzziah enters the temple, Azariah (meaning "YHWH has helped") opposes the king and states that his actions will not bring him honor (26:18). The king objects, but as he does, a skin disease appears on his forehead. As Azariah warned, Uzziah suffers from the skin disease that leaves him without honor through the rest of his life and even burial.

The final part of this passage recounts the reign of Uzziah's son Jotham. The Chronicler draws several parallels between Uzziah and Jotham. However, unlike Uzziah, Jotham does not become proud and does not transgress. Instead, Jotham seeks YHWH and succeeds where his father fails. He even extends much of the work that his father did. In this way, even though YHWH punishes Uzziah for arrogantly violating the temple's sanctity, YHWH uses Jotham to carry on the work from Uzziah's success in the first part of his reign.

- ***Uzziah Seeks YHWH and Succeeds (26:3–15)***
- ***Uzziah Transgresses and Suffers (26:16–23)***
- ***Jotham Seeks YHWH and Succeeds (27:1–9)***

EXPOSITION (26:3–27:9)

In many ways, contemporary Western culture tends to be more pragmatic than the ancient Near East. For instance, most people in the ancient Near East regularly recognized places, people, and/or objects as sacred. Violating their sacred status would bring negative consequences. Today, few people seem to regard many places, people, and/or objects as sacred. Furthermore, in the ancient Near East, certain roles were restricted to certain families. A royal family would produce kings, a priestly family would produce priests, and so on. Today, virtually all roles are available to anyone.

This contrast between contemporary and ancient cultures can make the account of Uzziah and Jotham seem strange. Uzziah is a good king who follows YHWH. YHWH rewards him greatly. Then, he tries to do what appears to be a good thing: offer incense. However, his decision oversteps his role by performing a task limited to priests and fails to treat the temple as a sacred place. For this reason, YHWH punishes him. However, his son Jotham, who is also a good king, does not commit the same violations. Therefore, YHWH rewards Jotham, even carrying out the work Uzziah began in the earlier days of his reign.

Uzziah Seeks YHWH and Succeeds (26:3–15)

Because Uzziah seeks YHWH, YHWH helps him to become victorious, wealthy, famous, and influential.

26:3. Even though the Chronicler has already briefly introduced the reader to Uzziah as he closed out the reign of Amaziah (2 Chron. 26:1–2), here he formally introduces Uzziah. He follows his typical convention of introducing the king by stating (1) his age when he became king, (2) how long he ruled, and (3) the name of his mother. Uzziah was fairly young when he began to rule (sixteen), and his reign lasted for a long time (fifty-two years). His mother is unknown except for this verse.

Names of the King

The king bears two names: Uzziah עֻזִּיָּהוּ ("YHWH is my strength") and Azariah עֲזַרְיָהוּ ("YHWH has helped"). Although both names occur in Kings and Chronicles, Kings most often uses the name Azariah while Chronicles most often uses the name Uzziah. Likely the names represent a birth name and a royal name, given upon succession to the throne.

The fact that the priest's name late in the narrative is Azariah may contribute to the Chronicler's choice to use the king's name Uzziah. In other passages he has rendered two individuals with the same name in Kings (Hiram, king of Tyre, 1 Kings 5:7; and Hiram, temple craftsman, 1 Kings 7:13) by distinguishing them (Huram, king of Tyre, and Huram-abi, temple craftsman, 2 Chron. 2:11–13 [HB 10–12]).

26:4–5. Following this information, the Chronicler offers a theological assessment of Uzziah's life. The Chronicler states that Uzziah does what was upright in the eyes of YHWH, and then explains why: he commits himself to seek YHWH. The expression "seek YHWH" (דרשׁ יהוה) occurs frequently in Chronicles to represent a lifestyle of devotion to YHWH (see sidebar "Seeking YHWH"). Since Uzziah devotes himself to YHWH, YHWH makes him successful as a king. Here the Chronicler reinforces a point made throughout Chronicles: YHWH rewards those who devote themselves to him (see "Covenant" section in the introduction).

Despite Uzziah's positive assessment, there are signs of trouble. First, Uzziah does what is upright like his father Amaziah. The Chronicler introduces a bit of tension into the account by comparing Uzziah to Amaziah. Amaziah also did what was upright, although he did not do so wholeheartedly (2 Chron. 25:2). The Chronicler recounts Amaziah's reign as two-sided: it began well, but ended badly. Uzziah's reign follows the same pattern. Second, Uzziah's commitment to seek YHWH has a condition: it takes place while Zechariah teaches him to fear YHWH.

TRANSLATION ANALYSIS:
The construction at the beginning of the verse (ויהי + inf.) occurs infrequently in a context like 26:5. Although many translations render the phrase like a simple past tense (CSB, KJV, NET, NIV, NKJV, NLT), the construction seems to carry a sense of determination or direction with it. For this reason, ESV and NRSV translate the phrase as "he set himself to seek God," with the sense that he committed himself to follow God.

Furthermore, the translations differ regarding Zechariah's description. The issue is text-critical. KJV, NASB, and NKJV accept the MT reading of בִּרְאֹת, an infinitive of ראה. Therefore, they translate the phrase in light of seeing or visions. Most other translations (CSB, ESV,

NET, NIV, NLT, NRSV) accept the reading preserved in most manuscripts and versions: בְּיִרְאַת. Therefore, they translate the phrase as they translate other instances of יִרְאַת יְהוָה, "fear of YHWH/the Lord."

26:6. The account transitions to the signs of Uzziah's success. Like other kings YHWH rewards for upright conduct, Uzziah succeeds in battle, in building, and in preparing troops and strategic locations for battle. Uzziah's success starts with the battles he fights against some of the usual suspects among Israel's enemies. He defeats the Philistines, successfully breaking through the defenses of some towns (Gath, Jabneh, and Ashdod). The Old Testament typically mentions Gath and Ashdod as Philistine cities (cf. Josh. 11:22; 1 Sam. 6:17); however, Jabneh (יַבְנֵה), most likely a city in the same general vicinity, is not a typical Philistine city (cf. Josh 15:11 where it occurs by the name Jabneel [יַבְנְאֵל]). Its mention is unique to Uzziah's reign.

Uzziah's activity against the Philistines compares and contrasts him to other kings in Chronicles. By defeating the Philistines, he becomes like David (1 Chron. 18:1). As David obeys YHWH, YHWH gives him victory over his enemies. By breaking down (פרץ) the walls of Philistine cities, he becomes unlike his father Amaziah. When Amaziah disobeys YHWH by worshipping Edomite idols and begins a conflict with Joash of Israel, Joash breaks down (פרץ) a section of Jerusalem's wall (2 Chron. 25:23). These similarities of Uzziah to David and differences from Amaziah confirm the point that YHWH responds to obedience by granting victory, but to disobedience by bringing defeat.

26:7–8. The Chronicler explicitly makes the point that YHWH grants Uzziah victory over his enemies. The Chronicler states that YHWH helps (עזר) Uzziah. The word עזר functions as a key term for Uzziah's reign.

Here one may note that the king has two names: Uzziah ("YHWH is my strength"), used most often in Chronicles, and Azariah ("YHWH has helped"), used most often in Kings (see "Names of the King" above). Even though the Chronicler uses the name Uzziah, he plays off his other name throughout the account (see comments below).

Among Uzziah's enemies are the Philistines, the Arabs, and the Meunites. On two other occasions the Chronicler relates the Philistines and the Arabs to Judah: as he recounts the tribute that these nations pay to Jehoshaphat (2 Chron. 17:11), and as he describes how God punishes Jehoram by inciting these nations to attack him (2 Chron. 21:16). The contrast between Jehoshaphat and Jehoram highlights two important points: (1) YHWH is God over the nations—that is, his power and plan extend beyond Israel, and (2) he can direct the nations to either reward those who seek him (like Jehoshaphat, 2 Chron. 17:4; or Uzziah, 26:5) or punish those who forsake him (like Jehoram, 2 Chron. 21:10). At the same time, the only other passage in Chronicles to address the Meunites outside of this context (2 Chron. 20:1) confirms a similar point. The best reading of 2 Chronicles 20:1 (see Translation Analysis for 2 Chron. 20:2) records that the Meunites join other nations to fight against Jehoshaphat, but that YHWH defeats them despite their large numbers. YHWH prevails over these nations to reward Jehoshaphat for seeking him. YHWH rewards Uzziah in a similar way for the same reason.

From the military victories recounted, the following picture emerges. First, the Chronicler shows how Uzziah gains wealth. He attacks important Philistine cities, breaking down their walls and plundering the region. Then, the Meunites send him tribute. Between these two statements lies the important theological rationale tying them together: YHWH helps Uzziah both in fighting his enemies and motivating the tribute. Since YHWH helps him defeat his enemies and gain wealth, he becomes a very powerful and influential person. His strength leads to fame throughout the region, especially to the south (such is the implication of the phrase "to the border of Egypt" עַד־לְבוֹא מִצְרָיִם). This section illustrates how YHWH gives Uzziah success because the king seeks him (26:5).

TRANSLATION ANALYSIS:

Even though many translations read "Ammonites," the original reading is most likely "Meunites" for three reasons: (1) LXX preserves the reading "Meunites", (2) the context fits well with Meunites, and (3) the usual phrase for referring to the Ammonites as a nation is בְּנֵי־עַמּוֹן (e.g., 2 Chron. 20:1, 10, 22, 23; 27:5). Furthermore, the reading הָעַמּוֹנִים results from transposing two consonants of the name הַמְּעוּנִים. The same procedure also takes place in 2 Chronicles 20:1 where MT reads, "the Moabites, and the sons of Ammon, and with them some Ammonites."

26:9. The Chronicler continues to show how YHWH makes Uzziah successful by describing Uzziah's building projects. He begins with the fortifications that Uzziah makes to the Jerusalem wall. He fortifies several locations; however, the most important to note is the Corner Gate, because during the reign of Amaziah (Uzziah's father), Israel attacked Jerusalem and tore down four hundred cubits of the wall, ending at the Corner Gate. Uzziah is contrasted to his father at this point: Amaziah saw the wall fall, while Uzziah fortifies it.

26:10. The Chronicler moves to Uzziah's agricultural accomplishments. Because Uzziah possesses a large quantity of livestock, he builds towers primarily to protect the animals and digs wells to provide water for them. He maintains many farmers in the Shephelah and coastal plains, an area likely secured from the Philistines (see 2 Chron. 28:18, which recounts that the Philistines take it back), and several vinedressers in the hills and fertile lands. He

maintains these agricultural workers because he loves the soil (כִּי־אֹהֵב אֲדָמָה הָיָה). This passage is the only place in the Hebrew OT where this expression occurs. Here it refers to his dedication to agriculture. Although Chronicles shows that other kings maintain agriculture (e.g., David, 1 Chron. 27:26–31a; see R. Klein 2012, 374), Uzziah stands out at this point. The main point in this verse is to show that Uzziah succeeds in agriculture not only because he has large quantities of livestock and produce, but also because he is able to do what he desires: care for the land because he loves agriculture.

26:11–15. Continuing to show how YHWH grants Uzziah success, the Chronicler describes how Uzziah organizes and equips his army. He characterizes Uzziah's military force according to the following: (1) a group of professional soldiers ready for war, (2) organized according to the records of the king's officials, (3) led by 2,600 skilled clan leaders, (4) composed of 307,500 skilled warriors who fight well, (5) capable of helping the king against any enemy (לַעְזֹר לַמֶּלֶךְ עַל־הָאוֹיֵב), (6) thoroughly equipped with weapons and armor, and (7) providing devices for Jerusalem's defense.

26:11–13. Uzziah joins other good kings who maintain a large army such as Asa, Jehoshaphat, and Amaziah (see excursus "Troop Numbers in Judah"). Uzziah's large army is YHWH's blessing. It is well organized, functioning under the king's leadership (demonstrated by mentioning the scribe, the officer, and the king's official), within traditional familial relations (רָאשֵׁי הָאָבוֹת). It is capable of helping the king against any enemy. By using the word "help" (עזר), the Chronicler connects YHWH's help for Uzziah against the Philistines, Arabs, and Meunites (26:7) with the army's help against any enemy. YHWH's help may take different forms, such as in this case where it takes the form of a potent military force. Still, in the end, it is YHWH's help and none other.

YHWH Directs History

The Chronicler often shows that YHWH alone directs the course of history. The Chronicler is often silent regarding human motivations for certain actions; rather, YHWH executes the action (sometimes through human agents) in accord with his own plan and purpose. Uzziah's reign confirms the point: YHWH gave Uzziah success by helping him against the Philistines, Arabs, and Meunites. YHWH's purpose directs the activity. The Chronicler does not mention any human means, motivations, or explanations for any of this activity. He is concerned to show what YHWH does (see Japhet 2009, 98–107).

26:14–15a. Uzziah equips his army with weapons, armor, and defensive devices. This list of military equipment is more comprehensive than any other in Chronicles. Uzziah provides the equipment for the entire army. Other kings provide large numbers of equipment (e.g., Asa provides three hundred thousand shields and spears and 280,000 shields and bows), but only Uzziah provides all these items for all the troops. The fact that Uzziah equips so many items to the entire army further confirms his wealth. Furthermore, Uzziah provides devices for defending Jerusalem. Although the precise design of these devices is unknown, they are designed to defend the city with arrows and larger rocks. The language suggests that the design and construction of these devices requires skill and ingenuity. No other king in Chronicles uses such devices.

Devices for Throwing Rocks

Some scholars have identified these devices as catapults; however, catapults did not exist in the eighth century B.C., nor would they have likely existed in the region until centuries later. Others have identified the devices as structures where soldiers on the wall of the city could shoot arrows and hurl stones while protected. Eighth-century images of Sennacherib's invasion of Lachish portray such devices, although it is not clear whether such devices were found there or not.

One should not think of the "large stones" as boulders. These stones are large compared to the stones used in slings (mentioned in 26:14), but still small enough that a soldier using both hands could throw one of them down upon the enemies outside the city walls (for a somewhat similar situation, see Judg. 9:53).

26:15b. This verse closes with a statement that Uzziah grows more famous because he is helped until he becomes strong. Even though the Chronicler does not specify who helps Uzziah here, in 26:7 he has already stated that YHWH helps Uzziah. Therefore, this verse is picking up on a keyword in the first part of Uzziah's reign to explain the cause of Uzziah's success.

Second Chronicles 26:15 closely resembles 26:8. These verses form bookends around the Chronicler's description of Uzziah's building projects within his kingdom. Two differences between the verses are worth examining. First, 26:15 says that Uzziah is helped marvelously. The Chronicler does not attribute Uzziah's success to some aspect of Uzziah's personality or activity. His great success and fame result from the wonderful help he receives. Second, 26:15 indicates that Uzziah's fame spreads because he is helped until he becomes strong, whereas 26:8 says that his fame spreads because he is strong. The insertion of the word "until" (עַד) foreshadows a turning point in the narrative.

From this period of Uzziah's reign, the following picture emerges: Uzziah is a good king who seeks YHWH. Because he seeks YHWH, YHWH rewards him with success. Uzziah's success makes him a wealthy and influential king. Such a picture is common among good kings in Chronicles. However, Uzziah is also unique in a couple of ways: (1) he loves agriculture, and (2) he builds ingenious defensive structures. Even though the Chronicler's portrait of Uzziah clearly confirms his theological point that YHWH rewards Uzziah because Uzziah seeks him, Uzziah is still his own person, with unique accomplishments and characteristics.

Uzziah Transgresses and Suffers (26:16–23)

When Uzziah becomes arrogant and violates the temple's sanctity, God punishes him with a disease that makes him unclean.

26:16. Like other kings in Chronicles (e.g., Asa, Amaziah, Joash), Uzziah's reign falls into a period of faithfulness followed by unfaithfulness. YHWH blesses Uzziah greatly during his period of faithfulness so that he becomes a wealthy and influential person. Sometime during his fifty-two-year reign, while he is powerful (this is the sense of כְּחֶזְקָתוֹ here) he becomes arrogant (גָּבַהּ לִבּוֹ). Because he is arrogant, he acts corruptly and commits a violation against YHWH by entering the temple to offer up incense. The Chronicler uses his characteristic term מעל to describe Uzziah's violation of YHWH's regulations regarding ritual worship (see sidebar "Unfaithfulness Against YHWH"). According to Exodus 30:1–10 the incense altar is located within the holy place, where only the priests are allowed. Also, 1 Chronicles 6:49 (HB 34) explicitly restricts the burning of incense to the priests, according to what Moses commanded (cf. Exod. 30:7; Num. 16:40–41 [HB 17:5–6]). Therefore, Uzziah violates YHWH's sanctity in two ways: (1) he enters the restricted area of the temple where the incense altar is located, and (2) he attempts to offer up incense there. Because Uzziah commits this violation (מעל), he joins others whom YHWH punishes for committing מעל (e.g., Saul, Rehoboam, Ahaz, and the final generation before exile). From the Chronicler's description, a dark shadow begins to fall upon Uzziah's reign.

TRANSLATION ANALYSIS:

The phrase עַד־לְהַשְׁחִית is ambiguous. The ambiguity lies in the meaning of the infinitive לְהַשְׁחִית. The verb *hiphil* שחת may refer to destruction or to acting corruptly. For instance, 2 Chronicles 25:16 uses the term to refer to YHWH's decision to destroy Amaziah. At the same time, 2 Chronicles 27:2 comments that even though Jotham

did what was upright, the people acted corruptly. The latter example closely resembles Uzziah: just as the people worshipped improperly, Uzziah tried to do the same. Even though either is sense is possible, the latter appears to work best in context with the following logic: (1) Uzziah became arrogant, (2) his arrogance led to his corrupt activity, (3) that corrupt activity was a violation against YHWH, and (4) it took the form of entering the temple to offer up incense.

Designation for Restricted Area

There is no specific instruction stating that the הֵיכַל יְהוָה is restricted. In fact, the way in which the Chronicler uses the term within the temple construction account suggests that the phrase may not be limited to such an area. However, outside the temple construction account, the Chronicler uses the phrase three times. The first is here in 2 Chronicles 26:16. The second is 2 Chronicles 27:2, a passage that refers to this incident. The final passage (2 Chron. 29:16) describes how the priests went inside the temple (בֵית יְהוָה) to remove anything unclean from the הֵיכַל יְהוָה and place it in the temple's court. Each of these occurrences seems to emphasize the sanctity of this area and its restricted access, at least in parts of it.

26:17. To guard the sanctity of the temple and enforce the regulations regarding the role of the priests, the chief priest Azariah (here designated הַכֹּהֵן) and eighty other priests follow Uzziah to the incense altar. There are two possible related wordplays in this verse. First, the text describes the priests as "men of valor" (בְּנֵי־חָיִל). The phrase in some other contexts refers to warriors (Deut. 3:18; 1 Sam. 18:17; 2 Sam. 17:10; 1 Chron. 5:18; 2 Chron. 28:6). In fact, the word חַיִל occurs four other times during Uzziah's reign: in each case it refers to his military force (26:11, 12, 13 [twice]). That military force stood ready to help (עזר) the king (26:13). Now, however, Azariah (עֲזַרְיָהוּ, meaning "YHWH has helped") opposes the king with many men described like soldiers. The wordplays on חַיִל and עזר highlight the stark contrast between Uzziah's earlier reign and his decision now and show that YHWH helps those who seek him but opposes those who don't.

Significance of Eighty
In 2 Kings 10:24, Jehu commands a group of eighty men to ensure that no Baal worshipper escapes from the temple of Baal. The number appears to be sufficient for either preventing access to or preventing escape from a public building like a temple.

26:18. When the priests confront Uzziah, they warn him that what he has done is wrong, why it is wrong, what he should do now, and why he should do it. They state that it is wrong by showing him he has no right to do it. Also, it is wrong because it violates the sacred space of the sanctuary and the sacred role of the priests ("those consecrated"). As a result, he should now leave the sanctuary because he has committed a ritual violation and because his activity will not bring him honor from YHWH. In Chronicles honor is one of YHWH's typical blessings for kings who seek him (David, 1 Chron. 29:28; Solomon, 2 Chron. 1:12; Jehoshaphat, 2 Chron. 17:5; 18:1; Hezekiah, 2 Chron. 32:27, 33); Uzziah's actions threaten such blessing.

26:19a. Even though Uzziah has violated YHWH's law, he still has an opportunity to stop. He can leave the sanctuary. However, he responds in anger. His anger recalls another king's anger: Asa (2 Chron. 16:10). When the prophet Hanani confronts Asa for his political maneuvering with Aram, Asa becomes angry and imprisons the prophet. Later, he develops a disease in his feet (2 Chron. 16:12). One can discern that the Chronicler condemns this type of angry response because in both cases he records how the king suffers a disease following it.

TRANSLATION ANALYSIS:
The verb occurring in this verse not only refers to Uzziah's internal emotional state, but also his

actions. Translations such as the NIV "raging," NLT "raging," and NET "ranting and raving" bring out this aspect of the verb most clearly.

26:19b–20. As Uzziah responds to the priests in anger, a spot appears on his forehead. The priests notice the spot and look more carefully. They identify it as a skin disease (traditionally translated "leprosy," but the Hebrew term refers to a wider range of diseases than the contemporary English word "leprosy"). Once the priests and king recognize the spot as a skin disease, both the priests and Uzziah himself try to remove the king from the holy area as quickly as possible.

The text provides a reason for removing the king: "because YHWH struck him" (כִּי נִגְּעוֹ יְהוָה). The Chronicler may be communicating that since YHWH has punished the king with a disease, fear of further punishment motivates the king to hurry out. However, such a skin disease would also make Uzziah unclean. To keep the temple clean, the priests would need to remove the king. Most likely both fear and uncleanness motivate the king's hasty exit.

26:21. YHWH punishes Uzziah with a skin disease because he violates God's stipulations regarding the sanctity of the inner temple area and of the priests. Since the skin disease makes Uzziah unclean, he spends the rest of his life largely isolated from other people (this is the sense of "house of isolation" בֵּית הַחָפְשִׁית). The Chronicler points out an ironic point in Uzziah's downfall: the king who arrogantly enters the inner part of the temple is now completely cut off in humiliation from the entire temple for the rest of his life.

Since Uzziah is no longer able to carry out his royal duties, his son Jotham takes over the role of ruling the people as a royal steward. The role is similar to that of Joseph under Pharaoh, in which Joseph is granted authority like Pharaoh but does not occupy the throne (Gen. 41:40). Since Jotham is mentioned as ruling over the people while his father is still alive, it is no surprise that upon his father's death he becomes king.

26:22. Uzziah's reign concludes with the typical formula concerning the "rest of the acts of Uzziah, from first to last." Rather than alluding to a source that records the acts of the kings of Judah or Israel, the Chronicler states that the prophet Isaiah wrote these things down. The Chronicler mentions Isaiah to confirm that his account is trustworthy since a prophet, one who communicates YHWH's message, has preserved it.

Reference to Isaiah

The Chronicler sometimes refers to prophetic records of kings' reigns without referring to other sources (e.g., 2 Chron. 12:15; 13:22), but most often he refers to records concerning the kings, even if he cites a prophet (e.g., 2 Chron. 20:34; 32:32). In this case, the focus is entirely on Isaiah. Unfortunately, the book of Isaiah does not contain clear records about Uzziah's life. The only explicit reference to Uzziah recounts what happens during the year of his death (Isa. 6:1). Therefore, the Chronicler must be referring to something no longer available or no longer identified specifically with Uzziah.

26:23. Uzziah's reign closes in a typical manner: the Chronicler recounts that Uzziah dies, using the expression "Uzziah rested with his fathers," and that he is buried. At first glance it may appear that the text reads that Uzziah is buried right alongside the other kings because he dies with a skin disease. However, such an understanding does not make sense for two reasons: first, he would be buried among the kings either because he is a king or is honored like a king (e.g., Jehoiada, 2 Chron. 24:16); and second, his skin disease would not result in the honor of being buried alongside the other kings (as the priests warn Uzziah). Instead, what appears more likely is that the text distinguishes

Uzziah from the other kings. Uzziah is buried in the burial field which belongs to the kings (בִּשְׂדֵה הַקְּבוּרָה אֲשֶׁר לַמְּלָכִים) rather than among the tombs of the kings (בְּקִבְרוֹת הַמְּלָכִים). His burial places him among his royal ancestors but not among the royal tombs. Even though Uzziah did what was upright during the first part of his reign, YHWH punishes him and strips him of honor because he violates the sanctity of the temple and does not listen to the priests' warning. Upon Uzziah's death, his son Jotham becomes king.

Jotham Seeks YHWH and Succeeds (27:1–9)

Like Uzziah, Jotham seeks YHWH, but unlike Uzziah, Jotham does not violate the temple's sanctity; therefore, YHWH grants Jotham great success, even extending the work of his father.

27:1–2. Jotham's reign belongs alongside his father's reign, since the Chronicler explicitly and implicitly connects the kings together. After the Chronicler records the typical information introducing a king (his age when he becomes king, how long he rules, and the name of his mother), he provides a theological assessment of Jotham's reign. He explicitly compares Jotham to his father by recording that Jotham does what is right just as Uzziah did. He then explicitly contrasts them by recording that Jotham does not enter the inner part of the temple as Uzziah did. The Chronicler's assessment also contains implicit comparisons. Like Jotham, Uzziah also did what was right as his father Amaziah had done. However, Uzziah sought YHWH during the days of Zechariah; Jotham's obedience is not limited in this way. Furthermore, during Jotham's reign the people still acted corruptly (עוֹד הָעָם מַשְׁחִיתִים), while Uzziah's pride led to his corrupt act (2 Chron. 26:16, גָּבַהּ לִבּוֹ עַד־לְהַשְׁחִית), linking the two reigns together by a common word (*hiphil* שׁחת). Jotham is like his father, but also unlike him.

27:3–5. Because Jotham does what is upright, YHWH rewards him with success similar to his father Uzziah's. As Uzziah did, Jotham fortifies Jerusalem, extending the work of his father by rebuilding the Upper Gate of the temple and building up the wall around the Ophel (most likely the southern part of the city of David, the older fortification of Zion [cf. 1 Chron. 11:5]). As Uzziah did, Jotham builds cities and defensive structures beyond Jerusalem, again extending the work of his father by rebuilding cities in the hill country of Judah and constructing towers and forts in the wooded areas (בֶחֳרָשִׁים). As Uzziah did, Jotham fights and defeats his enemies and secures tribute from them, extending his father's work by securing the tribute from the Ammonites for three years. The similarities between Uzziah's and Jotham's successes suggest that the Chronicler presents Jotham in light of Uzziah. The different details show that Jotham fulfills or extends the work of his father.

Significance of Tribute Amount

The amount of silver in the tribute is quite high since Amaziah hired one hundred thousand soldiers for one hundred talents of silver (2 Chron. 25:6). However, Egypt imposes the same amount of tribute upon Jehoahaz (2 Chron. 36:3). Therefore, the amount makes sense within Chronicles. Furthermore, even though the amount of barley and wheat is large, it is half of what Solomon paid to Huram for aid in building the temple (cf. 2 Chron. 2:7–10 [HB 6–9]).

27:6. Jotham's successes lead to increased power and influence. Uzziah's successes had also led to his increased power and influence. The Chronicler uses the same term to describe their growing influence: "he grew powerful" (Uzziah: 26:8 הֶחֱזִיק; 26:15 חָזַק; Jotham: וַיִּתְחַזֵּק). The Chronicler spells out precisely why Jotham becomes powerful: "he ordered his ways before YHWH his God." In other words, Jotham faithfully obeys YHWH. Since Jotham faithfully obeys, YHWH rewards him.

TRANSLATION ANALYSIS:
The translations treat this phrase differently. Some translations (ESV, KJV, NASB, NKJV, NRSV) render the phrase more word-for-word; however, the resulting phrase is not a common English idiom. It is clear enough that the phrase carries a positive connotation, that is, Jotham does something good. However, the more precise sense of the phrase involves Jotham's faithful commitment. While the CSB ("he did not waver in obeying") and NIV ("he walked steadfastly") emphasize the faithful aspect and others like NET ("he was determined to please") and NLT ("careful to live in obedience") emphasize the commitment aspect, these translations closely approximate the sense of the Hebrew phrase.

27:7–8. Jotham's reign closes with the typical form, stating that the remainder of Jotham's activities are recorded in the book concerning the kings of Israel and Judah. Within the typical form, the Chronicler picks up on features of Jotham's reign by including Jotham's wars (alluding back to 27:5) and his ways (alluding back to 27:6). By including these terms, the Chronicler concisely brings Jotham's works to a close.

27:9. The Chronicler describes Jotham's death and burial in typical terms. Jotham "rests with his fathers" and is buried in the city of David. Upon his death, his son Ahaz becomes king.

Uzziah and Jotham emerge as two kings quite similar but quite different. Uzziah as a king who fears YHWH receives astounding rewards and accomplishments. Yet, Uzziah's reign is tragic as the good king becomes arrogant after YHWH has rewarded him for his earlier devotion. His life ends without honor, punished by YHWH. On the other hand, Jotham follows the early example of his father. He likewise receives great rewards because he obeys YHWH. However, unlike his father, Jotham remains faithful to YHWH in attitude and deed even when, like Uzziah, he becomes powerful. Where Uzziah failed, Jotham succeeds.

For the first readers, this contrast between Uzziah and Jotham would be encouraging. As the Chronicler's descriptions of David and Solomon demonstrate, the postexilic community was looking to restore what had been lost in exile. Previous generations had lost something when YHWH exiled them because of their disobedience, much like Uzziah. Now, even though the people maintained their identity as Israel through exile, their conditions changed. However, like Jotham, they could have hope that, if they remain faithful to YHWH, he will restore them and even extend the work that previous generations had started.

THEOLOGICAL FOCUS

Although God may reward past obedience, he still disciplines those who pridefully presume upon his sanctity; however, future obedience may restore such rewards.

Most of this passage focuses on the reign of Uzziah. If one looks only to his reign, then the passage appears to be a tragic story that addresses the theological themes of retribution, pride, and sanctity. One can see retribution play out between the two phases of his reign. While Uzziah seeks God, God rewards him with blessings. When Uzziah violates God's boundaries, God punishes him with disease. The Chronicler shows that God actively pursues justice as he rewards obedience and punishes disobedience. This principle extends beyond Uzziah and beyond Chronicles. Deuteronomy 28 makes clear that God's covenant with Israel operates on this same principle. Furthermore, as Paul states, "God is not mocked, for whatever one sows, that will he also reap" (Gal. 6:7 ESV).

Uzziah's reign also addresses human pride. The passage shows how sometimes even God's blessings become the occasion for human pride. Because Uzziah seeks God, God grants him wealth, strength, fame, and influence. One can observe this pattern elsewhere (e.g., Noah's deliverance becomes the occasion for his drunkenness; David's victories become the occasion for his adultery). Furthermore, Uzziah's reign illustrates that God opposes the proud (Prov. 3:34; James 4:6; 1 Peter 5:5). In this case, God's opposition takes the form of his priests and Levites as well as the disease that breaks out on Uzziah's forehead. What Uzziah gains from his obedience, he loses because of his pride.

Uzziah's reign also addresses divine sanctity. God's holiness entails several aspects (e.g., moral purity, overwhelming power, glorious presence) demonstrating that he is distinct from creature and creation. At the same time, God chooses to interact with what he has created. For this reason, God chooses some places, persons, practices, and objects to be closely associated with him so that they also become distinct from the rest of common experience. As a result, one cannot treat these chosen things improperly without serious consequences. Uzziah violates the sanctity of the Jerusalem temple, where God dwells. Paul reminds the Corinthians that because the Holy Spirit dwells with them that they are God's temple and "God will destroy anyone who destroys this [God's] temple" (1 Cor. 3:17 NLT). Although expressed differently, God sanctifies where he dwells, and violating that sanctity brings about serious consequences.

The theological focus of the passage expands when one considers the reigns of both Uzziah and Jotham. The passage still addresses retribution, pride, and sanctity. However, the message now includes hope and restoration after failure. In many ways, the two reigns follow the examples of Ezekiel 18. Uzziah, a righteous king, turns away from his righteousness and dies without honor because of the sin he commits (cf. Ezek. 18:24). However, his son lives righteously and therefore does not experience punishment for his father's sin or his own (cf. Ezek. 18:14–17). For this reason, Jotham's success provides a ray of hope following the tragic failure of Uzziah.

PREACHING AND TEACHING STRATEGIES

Exegetical and Theological Synthesis

The theme of a king starting out well but then failing is a constant theme that points to the need of a king who will not fail. Uzziah's pride and arrogance point us to the perfect king, Jesus. Uzziah is presented as a king who sought God for help. He was given that help through abundant blessings from God. He received the help, but somehow he began to think that he could help himself to whatever he chose. Tragically he chose to act as a priest and violated God's sanctity.

The concept of sanctity is hard for twenty-first-century people because we have so few things that are set apart as being worthy of special treatment. Perhaps the White House, the Supreme Court Building, or the Capitol Building could be thought of in this way, but each of these in the past few years have not been held as places worthy of honor and respect. Perhaps the sterile atmosphere of a surgical operating room gives us a sense of a sacred place; only the right people with the right preparation are allowed into that special room. Uzziah, in his pride, violated a spiritually sacred place and was punished for it by God's disciplining hand. But there is more to the story. God seems to extend Uzziah's reign through his son, Jotham.

Preaching Idea

Help from God doesn't mean we can help ourselves.

Contemporary Connections

What does it mean?

There are parallels between Uzziah and his father Amaziah. Amaziah's sin was the worship of other gods. Uzziah's sin was worshipping YHWH incorrectly. The discipline was appropriate for each sin: death, versus isolation due to skin disease. The point in both cases is that pride can undermine a successful walk with God.

We must ask ourselves from where Uzziah's pride came. God was clearly helping and blessing Uzziah's obedience during the first part of his reign, so much so that his fame "spread afar" and he became strong. It was when he became strong that things began to change in his heart. He became so successful as a king that he thought he had earned rights he did not have.

He thought that since he was so blessed, it allowed him to be more than a king; he wanted to be a priest. Perhaps he thought that if YHWH blessed him so abundantly, it must mean, "I have now achieved a certain level that puts me above God's laws. I know I am not a priest, but that is what I want to do, so it must be a good thing."

Several years ago, a good friend invited me to hunt on his beautiful Texas hill country ranch. It was a delightful place both in accommodations and natural beauty. He asked me to come four years in a row. I began to think that I would always be invited. The fifth year, when I wasn't invited, I had to check my feelings. I wanted to feel slighted and hurt because he didn't offer that blessing. I had begun to think that I deserved to be asked. In my pride I thought that I was his special friend who always got asked. In another setting, when an employer gives a bonus every year, the employee often begins to think of the bonus as an expected part of their salary.

God's help shouldn't lead to us to think that we have certain rights or privileges. An engaged couple is blessed with a great relationship and rationalizes that this great relationship that God gave them can be enjoyed more fully by living together before they are married. God's blessing led them to think they could help themselves to that which God, for now, had placed off limits. A pastor is greatly helped by God to build a healthy church. He is then invited to speak at conferences and write books. In the influence of fame, he begins to think that he has the power within himself to resist temptation and begins to flirt with an attractive assistant in the office.

God's help should not lead us to think that we can help ourselves to that that which God has forbidden.

Is it true?

When I was a boy back in the middle of the last century, I was often scolded not to run in church. In that era, the place where a local church gathered to worship was often called the sanctuary. Now it seems that these places are called worship centers, perhaps because the place of worship today often functions at other times as a gym or school cafeteria. The change in name also indicates a change in attitude toward a place designated for worship. Thus, it may be difficult for us to grasp why it was a big deal for a king to step into the holy place.

Perhaps a metaphor of a surgical room could help us bridge this gap. Hospitals have a cleaning policy for operating rooms. The one I checked had detailed instructions as to what cleaning equipment and supplies were to be used, followed by a nine-step cleaning process which must be followed after every surgery. Part of the policy includes the preparation of individuals who enter the operating room. There is a sanctity about an operating room. If the space is violated by someone who is not properly clothed and cleansed, that person is ushered out and the room may need to be made clean again. There are even times when the risk of infection is so great that personnel work in what is basically a spacesuit. This kind of "sanctity" we understand and expect. And if we are the one who is undergoing surgery, we demand it.

Consider an imaginary hospital administrator after he had successfully brought a failing hospital out of bankruptcy into financial stability. And then, even further, he attracted research teams and highly sought-after specialists, so that the once-failing hospital became a highly respected medical facility. After years of being affirmed by doctors and the governing board, and being given bonuses of more than six figures, this hospital administrator became

proud and decided that he wanted to witness an operation. So, he burst into the operating room to witness a surgery in process. That would be unthinkable, but that is akin to what Uzziah did.

Operating rooms are different and need to be thought about and treated differently. God is unique. No one is like him. One way he taught this to his chosen race was to set up strict guidelines about who could come into the building that housed his special presence.

Now what?

We must recognize that when we receive God's help, our standing before him doesn't change. We haven't earned any more love or privileges. In many situations in our lives, we can earn or pay for greater privileges. I was once given a first-class ticket on a flight because the airline had made some mistakes in my flight and wanted to make up for the error. I had never expected nor been able to fly first class. I almost wish I hadn't been given that privilege, because now I know what I am missing. When I fly now, I don't expect the airline to give another first-class ticket. Their upgrading my flight did not change my standing with the airline. When God helps and blesses, even with great abundance, it doesn't mean we have achieved a higher level of his love. We are God's children, and we are loved by him. His blessing and help may make us sense his love more, but he never loves us less or more. He fully loves all the time. So, we need to continue in dependence upon him.

His help in our lives is not like the help of others in our lives. If I asked my neighbor to help me unload a heavy piece of furniture, we both share the one hundred pounds, hopefully about fifty pounds each. But God's help is different. It is all from him. When his hand comes through others, or in some direct miraculous way, it is easy for us to see that it was completely his hand that helped. But even when we are able to work out our own problems, we must remember that our own abilities and strength came from him.

Receiving God's help comes out of a humble dependent and grateful relationship to him.

Another element we must not overlook is the consequences of violating God's sanctity. Of course, through Christ there is full forgiveness, but consequences remain. God in his grace still blessed Uzziah through his son Jotham. But it was a blessing enjoyed at a distance, lived through another.

Creativity in Presentation

The first part of Uzziah's reign is a straightforward narrative ending with his being aware of his strength. The second part of this pericope is a dramatic episode that needs to be presented in such a way that the congregation can feel the dynamics. One can present the successful part of his reign in a simple fashion, then give more attention to the drama of the second half. It might be helpful to use one of the many video illustrations of the Solomonic temple to help the congregation visualize the special nature of the holy place.

If one is prone to and skilled at storytelling, this section could be presented as a first-person narrative. Tell Uzziah's story from his point of view. Your presentation could include him rehearsing the great accomplishments of his reign. This could lead into his musing what it would be like to be a priest. Perhaps he wondered what the inside of the temple looked like. Then present the pivotal point of Uzziah deciding that he could violate God's sanctuary. Imagine what it might have been like for him to step into a place that he had never seen and was not supposed to see. One could include Uzziah thinking out loud about the temple: "As king, I have stood on the steps and looked into the holy place, but have always been stopped by the priest. But I am king. Surely, I have a greater rank than a priest." Then present the climactic confrontation by the priest and his breaking out with a skin rash. This is followed by his quick exit from the temple, and the resulting discipline of an isolated life. Yet God's mercy is evident in giving him the blessing of at least watching his son be blessed. Another possibility would be to present the story from Jotham's point of view. Here is one possible structure:

- Present the story
  - Present the first part of Uzziah's reign (26:1–15).
  - Tell or act out the second part and Jotham's reign (26:16–27:9).
- Application: help from God doesn't mean we can help ourselves.

DISCUSSION QUESTIONS

1. What are some ways you have seen God's help come to other people?

2. How have you experienced God's help?

3. Have you ever received special attention? How?

4. How did that special attention make you feel?

5. How did you feel when the special attention stopped?

6. Does receiving help from God change our standing with him?

7. What are some places that seem sacred to you or others?

8. When do people feel it is right to violate those sacred places?

2 Chronicles 28:1–27

EXEGETICAL IDEA
When Ahaz stubbornly disobeyed YHWH, shut down YHWH's worship, and trusted in other kings and gods, he proved to be worse than the nation of Israel that listened to YHWH's warning, so YHWH punished him.

THEOLOGICAL FOCUS
Regardless of status, origin, or even past failure, God treats people according to their trust in him and obedience to him.

PREACHING IDEA
God's disciplining hand should lead us to obey.

PREACHING POINTERS
In this age of positive reinforcement in which there are no wrong answers, only those that still need some work, the harsh justice and discipline that God administers to Ahaz will be difficult to present. However, that is the thrust of the text. This is not a story that puts us over Ahaz in judgment so that we can shake our heads and say, "Isn't he terrible?". We need to see that the story also includes the positive example of the northern leaders who obey God. This passage gives us a choice to let sin govern our lives, or to trust and obey. Sin results in God's discipline, so choose to trust and obey.

REIGN OF AHAZ—A KING MORE WICKED THAN THE WICKED (28:1–27)

LITERARY STRUCTURE AND THEMES (28:1–27)

Following the reigns of several kings who are characterized as doing what is upright (Joash, Amaziah, Uzziah, Jotham), the Chronicler turns to the reign of Ahaz. Ahaz is wicked from beginning to end. The narrative begins almost immediately by describing Ahaz's unfaithfulness to YHWH in terms of violating specific commandments recorded in Mosaic law. Without interruption, the account records Ahaz's punishment. YHWH punishes Ahaz as Aram and Israel kill many from Judah, including some from the king's inner circle, and take others captive.

To this point, the narrative moves briskly, just describing the events. Then the narrative slows down by recounting a prophet's warning to Israel as they bring the Judahite captives back to Israel. The prophet confronts Israel, warning them that they are also guilty before YHWH. As a result, he commands them to return the captives, which they do.

Following the episode with the prophet and Israel, the narrative returns to Ahaz to show that he suffers further punishment as the Edomites, Philistines, and Assyrians attack Judah successfully. This punishment takes place even though Ahaz tries to negotiate Assyria's help. Finally, the last stage of Ahaz's reign recounts his further unfaithfulness to YHWH as he worships other gods, closes the Jerusalem temple doors, and sets up places to worship virtually everywhere else.

Two important structural features of this account point to its central message. First, the account has a concentric structure with the prophet's speech of warning in the middle. This structure focuses on the prophet's speech and the response to the speech as a central element of the narrative. This speech shows that despite Israel's past, they obey the prophet's warning and avert YHWH's wrath. Second, the account characterizes Ahaz the same way throughout the narrative: he does not change. Despite the trouble his disobedience brings, he stubbornly continues to disobey YHWH's commands. Ahaz looks much worse than Israel because he refuses to worship YHWH properly. As a result, YHWH punishes him.

- *Ahaz's Unfaithfulness (28:1–4)*
- *Ahaz's Punishment (28:5–8)*
- *A Prophet Confronts Israel (28:9–15)*
- *Ahaz's Further Punishment (28:16–21)*
- *Ahaz's Further Unfaithfulness (28:22–27)*

EXPOSITION (28:1–27)

Contemporary culture values good leadership. Good leaders strengthen groups; bad leaders destroy groups. However, such is not always the case, especially in contexts where there is a balance of power. One good or bad apple does not always have such a dramatic effect on the whole. In the ancient Near Eastern world, such a balance of power did not often exist. In many situations, a king held tremendous power and influence. Furthermore, the king was largely responsible for leading his nation in worshipping their god(s). A king's devotion or lack thereof could result in either prosperous or disastrous consequences for the king and the whole nation. The account of Ahaz's reign depicts the power and influence of the king along these lines. At the same time, it points to the responsibility for each person to respond to YHWH's word properly. The account creates a contrast between Ahaz and Judah, who forsake YHWH through their improper worship, and Israel, who despite their past misconduct obey YHWH's warning given through the prophet. As a result, YHWH punishes Ahaz and all Judah with him.

Ahaz's Unfaithfulness (28:1–4)
Ahaz follows bad examples as he violates YHWH's prohibitions recorded in Mosaic law.

28:1. The Chronicler begins the account of Ahaz's reign as he does with other kings: he states Ahaz's age when he becomes king, how long he rules, and how he measures up in YHWH's estimation. Two features of this introduction stand out. First, the Chronicler contrasts Ahaz's conduct with David's as a hint to how serious Ahaz's wickedness is. The Chronicler only compares two other kings to David when he introduces them: Hezekiah and Josiah. The Chronicler highlights how upright Hezekiah and Josiah act, especially as they purify and restore the temple and celebrate the Passover. They are the two best kings after David and Solomon. In contrast, Ahaz is the most consistently wicked king. He disobeys YHWH throughout his reign, ending it by closing the doors to YHWH's temple, destroying the temple implements, and building altars and high places to worship other gods.

David as Standard
Even though the Chronicler is following Kings virtually verbatim, it is still significant that he mentions David here. Kings uses David as a standard to measure many of the kings of Judah (Abijah/Abijam, 1 Kings 15:3; Asa, 1 Kings 15:11; Amaziah, 2 Kings 14:3). Chronicles removes all these cited references to David. For this reason, it still appears that by mentioning David the Chronicler intends more than just to follow his source in Kings.

Second, Ahaz rules a long time as a wicked king. In Chronicles, good kings rule for a long time while wicked kings rule for a short time. However, wicked Ahaz rules for the same length of time as his upright father Jotham. Even though the Chronicler demonstrates repeatedly that YHWH rewards righteous kings with a long reign and punishes wicked kings with a short reign, there are exceptions. The exceptions show that YHWH acts consistently throughout history but not mechanically. He is still free to act as he pleases (Ben Zvi 2006a, 161–66).

28:2a. After the Chronicler introduces Ahaz as a wicked king, he describes Ahaz's wicked conduct. Ahaz follows the religious practices of Israel's kings. Identifying Ahaz with Israel highlights how wicked Ahaz is. The Chronicler has already shown that YHWH is not with Israel (2 Chron. 25:7) and that the wicked kings preceding Ahaz also have followed the kings of Israel (Jehoram, 2 Chron. 21:6; Ahaziah, 2 Chron. 22:3).

28:2b–4. The Chronicler mentions three activities of Ahaz's pagan worship that resemble the Israelite kings: (1) he makes metal images for the Baals, (2) he sacrifices specifically in the Valley of Ben Hinnom, including offering up his sons, and (3) he sacrifices at the high places and other illicit sites. These activities violate YHWH's covenant. Not only does the law condemn such activities (e.g., for metal images [מַסֵּכוֹת], Exod. 34:17; Lev. 19:4; for passing children through fire, Deut. 12:31; 18:10; for these pagan sites, Deut. 12:2), it also points out what happens to those who practice them. YHWH will dispossess those who practice them, just as he has dispossessed the nations who preceded Israel in the land (2 Chron. 28:3). One expects that since Ahaz practices these wicked activities, YHWH will punish him by threatening his possession of the land.

The meaning of this expression is debated. On the one hand, the expression appears to refer to child sacrifice. The debate centers on how literally one takes many of the expressions. For a summary of the discussion, see Cogan and Tadmor 1988, 266–67. For an argument that child sacrifice did take place regularly in the ANE, including Judah, see Stavrakopoulou 2004, 207–99.

Ahaz's Punishment (28:5–8)
YHWH hands Ahaz and Judah over to their enemies as punishment for their sin.

28:5. As one would expect, YHWH responds to Ahaz by punishing him. The Chronicler explicitly states that YHWH hands Ahaz over to his enemies. He mentions first the king of Aram and then the king of Israel. It may appear that the Chronicler has presented the attacks of these kings as separate events; however, the verse's grammar and syntax portray them as related parts of a single event. The Chronicler presents the attack against Ahaz as a joint campaign of the kings of Aram and Israel. At first, the Chronicler leaves out nearly all the details: the names of the kings, the numbers killed or taken captive, the places of combat, the length of the campaign, and the rest. His initial description is a general statement summarizing the entire attack and, most importantly, providing the theological reason for it: YHWH handed Judah over.

Related Events in Hebrew Narrative
In Hebrew narrative the following construction portrays two distinct verbs as parts of a single action: *wayyiqtol* followed by a clause beginning with וֹ followed by something other than the verb and then a *qatal* verb having the same root as the *wayyiqtol* verb. One may use the designation *wayyiqtol, waw + x + qatal*. Genesis 1:5 illustrates this construction well. The verse begins with וַיִּקְרָא (*wayyiqtol* of root קרא) followed by וְלַחֹשֶׁךְ קָרָא (*waw + x + qatal* of root קרא). The two

verbs do not represent separate events, but two parts of a single action, naming day and night. In 2 Chronicles 28:5 the *wayyiqtol* verb is וַיִּתְּנֵהוּ, then four clauses later, it reads וְגַם־בְּיַד־מֶלֶךְ יִשְׂרָאֵל נִתַּן. Both verbs derive from the root נתן. Therefore, when YHWH hands Judah over to Aram, he is also handing them over to Israel. Even though the Chronicler has presented this attack differently, his presentation is consistent with the simpler statement in 2 Kings 16:5.

Another aspect of his statement describing Ahaz's punishment is the relationship between the king and his nation. By using different grammatical forms, the Chronicler identifies the actions and consequences of the king with those of the nation. For instance, the text states that YHWH hands Ahaz over to "the king of Aram," followed by "they defeated him and took captives from him." Even though the natural subject of the verbs "defeated" and "took captives" is the king of Aram, the verbs have a plural ending, referring to Aram as a whole. Furthermore, 28:5 limits the defeat and capture to King Ahaz ("they defeated him and took captives from him"), but 28:6 states that these things happened because "they [Judah] abandoned YHWH, God of their fathers." By shifting between the king and the nation, the Chronicler communicates that even though a king may greatly influence a nation, YHWH holds the members of a nation accountable for their actions as well (Ben Zvi 2006a, 220–22). If only reading 28:5, one may conclude that Ahaz sinned but Judah suffered the punishment; 28:6 balances that perspective by showing that Judah as a people sinned also.

28:6–8. Even though the text mentions Aram, it focuses on Israel. It specifies the attacking king as Pekah, the son of Remaliah, and highlights one of his warriors, an Ephraimite named Zichri. It provides other details to show how extensive and swift the attack is. Israel kills large numbers of competent warriors, kills high-ranking officials of the king, and captures large numbers of women and children. By showing that an unusually large number of people were killed or captured in such a short period of time (cf. number killed and captured in the days of Amaziah, 2 Chron. 25:11–13; also excursus "Troop Numbers in Judah"), the Chronicler confirms that YHWH was behind the battle. Only his involvement can explain Judah's swift and severe defeat.

Role of Officials

The role of Ahaz's high-ranking officials is not clear. As the king's son, Maaseiah likely would have some duties in the kingdom's administration; however, the text is silent on this point and on the point whether he is the heir apparent before his death. The third title "second to the king" (מִשְׁנֵה הַמֶּלֶךְ) implies an official with authority second only to the king, but the text provides no direct evidence for the official's function. The second title, "prince of the house" (נְגִיד הַבָּיִת), is ambiguous because it is not clear whether "the house" (הַבָּיִת) refers to the palace or the temple. The title נְגִיד בֵּית הָאֱלֹהִים occurs four times in the OT; however, the title הַנָּגִיד לְבֵית יְהוּדָה also occurs in 2 Chronicles 19:11, in which it designates a royal official. It mostly likely designates a royal official here also, since the other two titles point to similar types of officials.

The Chronicler points out that both Aram (28:5) and Israel (28:8) take captives from Judah. This point draws on how the Chronicler describes Ahaz's sinful activities: he performs the same abominable practices as the nations who preceded Israel in the land. The captives are a sign that just as YHWH dispossessed the previous nations in the land because of their sinful activities, he now (partly) dispossesses Judah from the same land. The Chronicler will come back to this point in 28:17–18.

This section draws another point from how the Chronicler describes Ahaz's sinful activities: Ahaz follows the ways of Israel's kings. The way

the Chronicler portrays Judah's defeat under Ahaz resembles the way he describes Israel's defeat under Jeroboam. When Jeroboam rules over Israel, he prepares a large military force to face Judah's king Abijah in combat. Before the battle begins, Abijah warns Jeroboam that Judah has not forsaken (עזב) YHWH, the God of their fathers, but that Israel has (2 Chron. 13:10–11). Despite the warning Jeroboam attacks, but God hands Israel over to Judah so that Abijah and his people severely defeat them (וַיִּתְּנֵם אֱלֹהִים בְּיָדָם: וַיַּכּוּ בָהֶם אֲבִיָּה וְעַמּוֹ מַכָּה רַבָּה) 2 Chron. 13:16b–17a).

Virtually the same language describes Ahaz's defeat (וְגַם בְּיַד־מֶלֶךְ יִשְׂרָאֵל נִתָּן וַיַּךְ־בּוֹ מַכָּה גְדוֹלָה, 28:5); the significant difference is that Israel now defeats Judah because Judah has forsaken YHWH, the God of their fathers (בְּעָזְבָם אֶת־יְהוָה אֱלֹהֵי אֲבוֹתָם, 28:6). Since Ahaz has walked in the way of Israel's kings, Judah now plays the role of Israel.

A Prophet Confronts Israel (28:9–15)

When the prophet confronts Israel for treating Judah harshly, Israel accepts the warning and returns their Judahite captives.

28:9–10. As mentioned, Judah has acted wickedly like Israel. Now the narrative explores whether Israel will act wickedly as it has previously. As Israel returns to their capital with Judah's captives and spoils of war, the prophet Oded confronts them to warn them that YHWH is angry with what they are doing. Oded points out that Israel is also guilty before YHWH. The text does not explicitly identify why Israel is guilty. The immediate context of Oded's speech seems to indicate that Israel transgresses by killing so many Judahites in such a terrible rage as well as planning to enslave their captives. According to this interpretation, because they have already killed so many and planned to enslave so many others they are guilty before YHWH and should relent against Judah. However, if one looks beyond Oded's speech, one finds another reason for Israel to relent. Judah has provoked YHWH's anger by worshipping other gods with forbidden idols in forbidden places; Israel has committed the same violations. Therefore, since they are guilty of the same offenses that has led YHWH to judge Judah, Israel should relent because the situation could easily be inverted. At this point, Israel should show mercy, since they have committed the same types of transgressions as Judah (e.g., 2 Chron. 11:14–15; 13:8–9).

28:11. Because of Israel's guilt, the prophet commands them to return their Judahite captives. Here, as elsewhere in Chronicles, the prophet's warning plays an important role. Even if someone has already committed a transgression, YHWH rewards the one who obeys a prophet's warning but punishes the one who does not. As Oded warns them, YHWH is angry with them. As a result, they can avoid YHWH's punishment by returning their captives. Despite their past guilt, Israel has a choice to make: either ignore the prophet's warning or follow his command.

The verse points to an aspect of how the Chronicler understands the relationships between Judah and Israel and between YHWH and the two nations. The prophet Oded points out that Judahite captives are "relatives" or "brothers" (אַחִים) of Israel. Elsewhere in the narrative (28:8, 15), the Chronicler uses the same language. Even though Chronicles records how the northern kingdom Israel begins as a separate kingdom when it rebels against the Davidic king (2 Chron. 10:19; 13:6–8), the Chronicler still considers the northern tribes to be related to Judah. Even though they have a separate identity as a kingdom, they are not outsiders to Judah; they are brothers. Furthermore, the tribes of both nations are included among YHWH's people. YHWH is the God of their ancestors: in 28:6 "their ancestors" refers to Judah's ancestors, but in 28:9 it refers to Israel's ancestors. Both nations have the same ancestors; therefore, both nations have the same God: YHWH. Even when they are faithless and disobedient (as Judah often was and as Israel almost always was), they are still his people and he is still their God. This point is especially important for a people who are returning from exile: YHWH did not abandon them in the past, despite exile, so they can have confidence that he won't in the future.

28:12–15. Given Israel's faithless past, one might expect them to ignore the prophet's warning, but they don't. Surprisingly, they follow the prophet's warning. Their obedience to the prophet contrasts to the disobedience of Ahaz and Judah. There is another point of difference between Judah and Israel: the king disappears from Israel (Ben Zvi 2006a, 223–24). From the time Oded confronts Israel to the time Israel returns the captives, no king appears. Instead, leaders from the tribe of Ephraim step up to ensure that the army obeys Oded's warning. They start by confronting the army, warning them not to bring the captives into Samaria. Their words echo the prophet Oded by pointing to Israel's existing guilt and condemning the plan to enslave their captives. As a result, the army leaves the captives and the spoils of war to them. These leaders then take care of the captives, ironically, by using the spoils of war to provide for their basic needs of nutrition, health, clothing, and, if needed, transportation. After providing the captives' needs, the leaders return them to Jericho.

TRANSLATION ANALYSIS:
The decision to interpret the leaders of 28:15 as referring to the leaders listed in 28:12 is based on taking the phrase "the men designated by name" (הָאֲנָשִׁים אֲשֶׁר־נִקְּבוּ בְשֵׁמוֹת) as referring back to those listed in 28:12 rather than to another group not mentioned elsewhere in the narrative. This interpretation is consistent with most translations except for NET. The phrase "designated by name" occurs in several contexts. In Numbers 1:17 it refers back to those just mentioned in the text. However, in 1 Chronicles 12:32; 16:41; and 2 Chronicles 31:19, it appears to

refer to other persons not already mentioned in the text. However, the other passages in Chronicles each occur with a purpose for their designation. In this case, as in Numbers 1:17, the text does not specify for what purpose these men are designated; therefore, it seems most likely that the phrase refers back to the leaders mentioned in 2 Chronicles 28:12.

This turn of events is even more surprising when one looks at another passage involving Israelite soldiers without mentioning Israel's king: 2 Chronicles 25:6–10, 13. Judah's king Amaziah hires a group of Israelite mercenaries (specifically called "sons of Ephraim" בְּנֵי אֶפְרַיִם), but dismisses them after a man of God warns him not to include them in his army. This group of soldiers then attacks several cities, killing thousands and taking the spoils of war. None of the verses concerning the Israelite mercenaries mentions the Israelite king, yet the mercenaries act in a way that is opposite of Israel's leaders during Ahaz's day. The contrast highlights how the roles of Judah and Israel have changed during the reign of Ahaz (see Ben Zvi 2006a, 223–25).

Furthermore, the narrative does not intend to condemn the idea of a king; instead, it shows that the people can and should respond obediently to YHWH's word regardless of who may be reigning over them. This message is especially appropriate in the Chronicler's context when no Davidic king sits on the throne. Instead, the people constitute a small province in a foreign empire. Just as previously sinful Israel was able to hear and obey YHWH's warning, so also all exilic Israel, which suffered the punishment of exile because of their transgressions, still has the opportunity and responsibility to heed YHWH's words. One reason for the Chronicler to write the book is to call YHWH's people to obey his word even under less-than-ideal conditions, such as a period of foreign domination without a Davidic king.

This section is the centerpiece of Ahaz's reign. The Chronicler has placed this narrative showing how Israel obeys the prophet to contrast Israel's role with Ahaz's. Up to this point in Chronicles, the northern kingdom has played the role of a wicked rebel. However, in this case even the wicked rebel is willing to obey the prophet's warning. When Israel obeys that warning, they act contrary to their pasts. Even so, Ahaz does not change, as the next section reveals.

Ahaz's Further Punishment (28:16–21)
Judah continues to suffer military defeat because of Ahaz's sin, even though Ahaz looks to Assyria for help.

28:16–18. After the text describes how Israel obeys the prophetic warning concerning the Judahite captives, it further describes how YHWH punishes Ahaz through other nations. It begins by stating that Ahaz turned to Assyria for help, although it does not immediately state the result of his action. Instead, it moves on to other nations that defeat Judah in battle, likely foreshadowing how Assyria will respond to Ahaz's call for help. Using virtually the same vocabulary, Edom does to Judah what Aram and Israel have already done (28:5): they strike them and take captives (וַיַּכּוּ בִיהוּדָה וַיִּשְׁבּוּ־שֶׁבִי). The Philistines raid (פשט) several cities, even occupying them. In both cases the threat of exile hangs over the narrative, as Judah's enemies capture them and dispossess them of their land.

> **Temporal Sequence**
> Second Chronicles 28:16 begins with the phrase "at that time" (בָּעֵת הַהִיא). This phrase is not referring specifically to the time when the captives return to Jericho, but generally to the period described in 28:5–8 when Aram and Israel attack Judah. The use of this phrase in 28:16 and the shift in focus to the prophet Oded in 28:9 signal that 28:9–15 its distinct from their surroundings. For this reason, 28:16 refers back to 28:5–8 rather than 28:9–15.

If one looks at the Edomites and Philistines throughout Chronicles, one finds that the relation between Judah and these nations reflects Judah's devotion to YHWH. For instance, the upright kings David (1 Chron. 18:11–13), Jehoshaphat (2 Chron. 20:22–23), and Amaziah (2 Chron. 25:11–12) defeat the Edomites, but the Edomites successfully rebel against the wicked King Jehoram (2 Chron. 21:8–10). Likewise, the upright kings David (1 Chron. 18:1) and Uzziah (2 Chron. 26:6–7) defeat the Philistines, but the Philistines defeat and kill the wicked King Saul (1 Chron. 10:1–7). As seen elsewhere in Chronicles, this pattern of God's activity shows that YHWH consistently rewards those kings who follow him and punishes those who do not. Since Ahaz acts wickedly, one expects that YHWH is punishing him through military defeat.

28:19. This verse explains that what is happening to Judah results from YHWH's humbling them because Ahaz has committed transgressions (see sidebar "Unfaithfulness Against YHWH") and let others commit transgressions. Two features of this verse highlight Ahaz's sinfulness. First, many manuscripts designate Ahaz as the king of Israel here. This designation may be an attempt to show that Ahaz is acting as Israel. Second, when the text describes Ahaz as letting others commit transgressions (*hiphil* פרע), it uses the same language to describe Aaron's role during the golden calf incident at Mount Sinai (Exod. 32:25). Ahaz leads Judah to worship improperly, violating YHWH's commands regarding worship, in a way similar to building the golden calf at Mount Sinai.

TRANSLATION ANALYSIS:
Translating this verse presents three noticeable issues. First, translations differ slightly concerning the translation of כנע. Some translations (KJV, NKJV, NRSV) use the expression "to bring low," whereas most translations (CSB, ESV, NASB, NIV, NLT) use the expression "to

humble." The verb כנע occurs frequently in Chronicles and captures one the book's main theological ideas: humility before YHWH. Several passages speak of people "humbling themselves" (*niphal* כנע) before YHWH (e.g., 2 Chron. 7:14; 12:6–7, 12; 32:26; 33:12; 34:27) while here YHWH "humbles" (*hiphil* כנע) Judah.

Second, even though BHS reads "king of Israel" (מֶלֶךְ־יִשְׂרָאֵל), several Hebrew manuscripts and the ancient translations read "king of Judah" (מֶלֶךְ־יְהוּדָה). Either reading is possible since in Chronicles the word "Israel" may be used more generically, and thus appear as a substitute for "Judah" (e.g., 2 Chron. 33:18). Furthermore, BHS may be an attempt to portray Ahaz in a negative light as a king of Israel.

Third, translations render the verb *hiphil* פרע in a variety of ways. The verb in the *qal* often refers to letting one's hair fall loosely or to leave something unattended. Based upon this evidence, many translations render the verb along the lines of throwing off restraint. Other translations emphasize the moral dimension of Ahaz's actions by rendering the verb along the lines of encouraging sin, wickedness, or moral decline. Given the context, a proper translation should bring out the moral dimension as well (see ESV, NET, NIV, NKJV, NLT).

28:20–21. The previous verse explains not only what precedes it but also what follows it. After describing how the Edomites and Philistines defeat Judah, the Chronicler returns his focus to Assyria. He includes just enough detail of what Assyria does to highlight that YHWH is at work in the situation with Assyria, because it does not happen as one would expect. Ahaz has already asked Assyria for help, so the narrative takes a surprising turn when the Assyrian king Tiglath-pileser arrives not to help Ahaz but to cause him further problems. Assyria's activity is even more surprising since Ahaz raids the treasuries of the temple, the king, and high-ranking officials as an incentive for the Assyrian king to help him, but it still does not help. Even though his plan to pay a stronger nation to help him makes sense (Ben Zvi 2006a, 217–20), not only does it not work but it also actually ends up causing him more trouble. This result is not a coincidence but a deliberate act of YHWH (28:19). YHWH frustrates Ahaz's plans in an ironic way, so that what Ahaz does to help himself results in hurting himself. The Chronicler is pointing out that YHWH controls history; he can even turn reasonable human plans on their heads to punish those who disobey him.

Treasuries of Officials

Other OT texts do not mention the treasuries of high-ranking officials. The mention of these officials here mirrors their mention earlier in the account. Second Chronicles 28:7 recounts that Zichri killed several high-ranking officials. The Chronicler seems to have included this information in 28:7 to show how extensive Judah's defeat was. The text here in 28:21 may be related to the same purpose. That is, Ahaz's plan to request Assyria for help affected the temple, the king, and the high-ranking officials.

Ahaz's Further Unfaithfulness (28:22–27)

Despite YHWH's punishment against Ahaz, Ahaz does not turn to YHWH but continues to commit more transgressions through improper worship.

28:22. Ahaz responds to all his problems by continuing to commit more transgression. This general statement draws on previous parts of the narrative. Just as Ahaz has committed transgression in the past (see מעל, 28:19), he does so even more now. Furthermore, in contrast to Israel, who has chosen not to add (יסף) to its own guilt (28:13), Ahaz does add (יסף) to his transgressions.

28:23. The following verses specify Ahaz's transgressions as false, forbidden worship.

First, Ahaz sacrifices to the foreign gods of Aram. The text does not say where, when, or how he sacrifices to them, but it does plainly state why he sacrifices to them: so that they will help him in his distress just as they helped Aram defeat him in battle. In other words, Ahaz sacrifices for the same reason he has reached out to Assyria: he wants help against his enemies. Furthermore, this action leads to the same result: what he has planned to help him adds to his trouble. On the surface what Ahaz proposes appears reasonable, but it does not correspond to what is really happening. The Aramean gods are not responsible for Ahaz's defeat; YHWH is. The text implies that although Ahaz appears reasonable and even wise (Ben Zvi 2006a, 217–20), he is wrong and wicked because he refuses to turn to YHWH (see 2 Chron. 7:14).

Designation of Gods

The text refers to the gods in two ways: "the gods of Damascus" (אֱלֹהֵי דַרְמֶשֶׂק) and "the gods of Aram's kings" (אֱלֹהֵי מַלְכֵי־אֲרָם). Commonly in the OT, the name of a nation and its capital city are interchanged.

28:24. Second, Ahaz ceases worship at YHWH's temple. He has already raided the temple treasuries to pay off Assyria (28:21), an activity that Chronicles condemns (Evans 2010, 37–40). At this point he destroys the temple's implements so that proper worship with the proper tools is no longer possible. Then he closes the doors. By closing the doors, he further confirms how wicked he is as a king. Not only does he disobey YHWH's commandments by worshipping other gods in forbidden ways in forbidden places (28:2–4), he also actively steers the people away from worshipping YHWH. The temple plays an important role in Chronicles as the focal point for YHWH's worship. For this reason, closing the doors of YHWH's temple is a serious offense because it also means "closing the door" on worshipping YHWH.

28:25. Third, as he closes the temple doors, he promotes worshipping other gods beyond the temple. The Chronicler describes Ahaz's false worship as pervasive. In Jerusalem Ahaz sets up altars on every corner throughout the city. Beyond Jerusalem, he sets up illegitimate worship sites in every single city throughout Judah. He constructs all these sites to make sacrifices to other gods. As expected, his false worship provokes YHWH to anger, as demonstrated by Judah's various military defeats.

Extent of Pagan Altars

The expression "on every corner of Jerusalem" (בְּכָל־פִּנָּה בִירוּשָׁלַם) metaphorically implies that Ahaz has constructed these altars throughout the city. They are located at the intersections where people pass by. The adulterous woman also lurks in these places (Prov. 7:12).

When surveying Ahaz's offenses in 28:24–25, one notices that the Chronicler has arranged the material in the following way: he moves from the temple, to Jerusalem, to all Judah. Ahaz closes the place that YHWH has chosen for his presence and his praise (cf. 2 Chron. 7:16), constructs altars throughout YHWH's chosen city Jerusalem (2 Chron. 6:6), and then sets up high places throughout all of Judah. This movement from the temple to the rest of the land reflects one aspect of the Chronicler's message: the temple lies at the heart of YHWH's worship. This message carries special significance in the postexilic setting of the book. Even though YHWH's people have been dispersed and can worship him in exile, the temple still plays a special role in promoting YHWH's worship. The Chronicler encourages consideration and support for this temple in his own day.

Nonchronological Arrangement of the Ahaz Narrative

Since geography explains how the Chronicler has arranged 28:24–25, it casts doubt on whether he intended these verses to be understood chronologically. In other words, it is unlikely that these offenses took place after all the other events recorded during Ahaz's reign. Instead, the Chronicler structures the narrative to reveal Ahaz's stubborn character. This fact also helps explain how the Chronicler can record that Ahaz sacrifices to the gods of Aram even though he has just mentioned Assyria.

The Chronicler makes it clear that regardless of what Ahaz experiences he will not turn to YHWH. It is not just that Ahaz turns to others along with YHWH; the Chronicler shows that Ahaz does not depend on YHWH at all, as illustrated by Ahaz's closing the doors of YHWH's temple. Ironically, the only one who can help Ahaz is the one he "shuts the door on." Instead, Ahaz looks to other sources for help: either an imperial power like Assyria, or supernatural powers like the gods of Aram. Even though Ahaz stubbornly forsakes YHWH and turns to others for help, YHWH does not destroy him or the people. Certainly, he punishes them both, but he does not destroy them completely. He allows for another day to come and another king to rule—perhaps a king better than Ahaz who can reverse the course of Israel's history.

28:26–27. The Chronicler concludes Ahaz's reign in a typical fashion. He refers to the book of the kings of Judah and Israel as a source for more information. He then records that Ahaz rested with his fathers, was buried in Jerusalem, though not in the kings' tombs, and that his son succeeded him. Even though Chronicles does not contain a clear-cut pattern showing that good kings have one type of burial whereas wicked kings have another (Schweitzer 2007, 119–25), the fact that Ahaz is not buried in the kings' tombs reflects the dishonor he earned as a wicked king. Therefore, from beginning to end, Ahaz is a king who does not do what is right and receives punishment because of it.

THEOLOGICAL FOCUS

Regardless of status, origin, or even past failure, God treats people according to their trust in him and obedience to him.

The message of this passage centers on a key contrast: the contrast between Judah, led by Ahaz, and Israel. The Chronicler contrasts the two kingdoms on several occasions, most notably 2 Chronicles 13, the account of Abijah's reign. However, in this case, the situation is different because of the roles that the kingdoms play. For example, in 2 Chronicles 13, Abijah calls Israel out for their illicit worship and their opposition to the Davidic king. He describes them as forsaking God and opposing God's kingdom. In contrast, Abijah shows how Judah remains faithful to God by worshipping him properly. With Ahaz, the roles are somewhat reversed. Judah forsakes God through their illicit worship, while Israel accepts a prophet's warning and does what is right. This surprising reversal of roles illustrates that national identity does not dictate obedience or disobedience. Even though God chose Judah as the place for his temple and the Davidic line as his royal representatives over the kingdom, their identity does not ensure that either the Davidic king or the people will obey. Furthermore, even though Israel's founding king Jeroboam leads the nation in idolatry from its beginning, Israel still may respond to God's word properly. The people's national identity does not determine their course of action (for another OT example, see the book of Jonah).

The contrast between Judah and Israel also points to how God treats these nations. When Ahaz leads Judah to forsake God, God punishes them. The text makes clear that Ahaz is not the only one to forsake God; the people join in with him. Even though Ahaz holds tremendous power as king, the people are still responsible along with him. Therefore, the punishment touches the king and the people. Regardless of political status, those who forsake God during Ahaz's reign suffer punishment. In contrast, when Israel obeys God's word, delivered by the prophet, they avoid God's wrath in that moment. In this way, God treats both kingdoms (and the groups within them) according to their obedience to him and trust in his word. The account reflects Ezekiel's point regarding God's judgment and individual responsibility: "Therefore, I [YHWH] will judge each person according to his conduct" (Ezek. 18:30a NET).

The New Testament picks up on this point, explicitly focusing on the role of faith. The apostle Paul describes the gospel as "the power of God for salvation to everyone who believes, first to the Jew, and also to the Greek" (Rom. 1:16 CSB). In other words, ethnic identity does not determine whether God saves or not—faith does. In fact, neither ethnic identity, social status, nor gender determines one's relationship to God; instead, those united with Christ through faith are God's children and are treated as such (Gal. 3:28–29). Even past sinfulness (for all have sinned, Rom. 3:23) does not determine one's fate, since God saves those who respond to him through faith and repentance. As a result, regardless of status, ethnicity, or even past sinfulness, God treats people according to their trust in him and obedience to him.

PREACHING AND TEACHING STRATEGIES

Exegetical and Theological Synthesis

In the middle of the account of this painfully evil king is the story of the soldiers of the northern kingdom who follow YHWH, in sharp contrast to Ahaz. He not only neglects following YHWH; even worse, he actively worships other gods to a degree unseen in all of Israel: Ahaz sacrifices children to his false gods. And it seems that those in his kingdom follow his lead. Here the writer inserts the story of individuals from the northern kingdom. It reminds us that when a leader is evil, we must not follow his lead. We are responsible to follow God no matter how evil the king, president, boss, spouse, parent, or pastor may be. Even if, like Ahaz, they have been in authority for a long period of time. Ahaz gives us the negative example of disobedience and despicable evil that is punished by God. However, even with such a terrible leader there is the positive example of obedience by those in the northern kingdom.

Preaching Idea

God's disciplining hand should lead us to obey.

Contemporary Connections

What does it mean?

All of us will have an Ahaz in our lives. It might be that teacher who put down a wrong grade for a student but refused to admit his mistake and correct the grade, or a boss who always took credit for the work of others. Tragically it may have been an abusive parent or sibling. There are leaders in our lives who seem to be evil, and perhaps they are. How is God going to deal with them? This passage affirms that God sees the evil and brings his wrath upon the wrongdoer. While it doesn't take away the pain we experience, we can at least know that God will bring justice upon the Ahazes in our lives. We could take this knowledge that God will punish evil and shake our heads and say with a smirk of satisfaction that God will get the bad guys—but then we would miss a great lesson.

This passage gives us a choice. We can trust God and follow his guidance as the men of Israel did, or we can be like Ahaz. None of us would choose to be an Ahaz, but do we choose to disobey? Do we choose to not trust God? Ahaz fought battles with nations, but he failed to fight the battle within himself: the battle against unbelief and sin. We need to acknowledge that there is an Ahaz in our own minds and hearts. Like Ahaz we commit sins, but unlike Ahaz we can trust the work of Jesus to forgive us. We can rely upon the Spirit to empower us to turn from sin.

Is it true?

It was raining again. It was the fourth rainy day in a row. As the preschool teacher was running out of inside games, she remembered one from her childhood and decided to give it a try. Gathering her fifteen children around her, she told them about this exciting new game, called "Follow the Leader." She assured them that everyone would have fun and get a turn being the leader. They sat in their customary circle and began. The first leader had them clapping hands, putting hands over their heads, and other fairly calm actions. The second and third leaders were not much different. The children were having fun and couldn't wait for their turn being the leader. It was entertaining and was helping with the rainy morning, until a highly creative and mildly impertinent child became the leader. He began by having them leave their seats and then jump on one foot. Then, though it was against preschool rules, he led them to stand on their chairs and jump up and down. Before the teacher realized what was happening the children were not only jumping on their chairs but, taking the cue from the leader, they started running around the room and yelling as though they had been set free. Being opportunistic, the children saw a chance to disobey some rules and get away with it. The game ended quickly when the teacher led the unwise student to time out and the rest of the class to a stern quiet time in their seats.

We will always have leaders, some good and some bad. How do we respond when a leader leads in the wrong way? How do we respond when a leader, like Ahaz, is not just wrong but actually evil?

If we are not sensitive to the Lord's leading and aware of his commands we can be led astray, and bad leaders can become an excuse to sin. Our rationalizing goes along the line that we can't be expected to act any better than the leader; if we had a better leader, we would not be acting so badly. Who could blame us? Poor leadership can take place in many forms: elected leadership, employers, parents, spouses, and even pastors. When the leadership is bad, we too can be opportunistic and excuse our sin. When a president is unfaithful to his wife, or lies, or is continually arrogant, our response could be, "Well, if he does these things, why shouldn't I?" When a father is cruel to his children and others, why should the child try to be any better? When a boss is dishonest with the government tax forms, shouldn't we feel free to be dishonest on our expense reimbursement forms? If my spouse is flirty, why shouldn't I be? When we see that God punishes Ahaz because of his lack of trust and disobedience, it serves as a negative example of what not to do and why.

Now what?

God designed us in such a way that much of what we learn is through imitation. We learn to speak by following the sounds and expressions of those around us. A child raised in the deep South thinks that "light" is pronounced "lat," and a child raised in New England learns later in life that the "r" in "car" is not silent. Before baseball games were televised, children had to be taught how to hold a bat. That changed after they watched Mickey Mantle on TV and followed his example. Following a leader is a part of life. The difficulty comes in knowing which examples are good and which are not. For this there must be some kind of standard outside of us. Our parents corrected our speech; a baseball coach corrected our batting stance. But who or what corrects our lives? It is the Word of God. For these soldiers the word came through the prophet Oded; for us, it is the written Word and the living Word. The apostle Paul tells us to imitate him as he imitates Christ.

A leader's sin is no excuse for me to sin. We must not let the sin of others cause us to sin. In the closing verses of this account, God's punishment of Ahaz is an additional reminder that God does respond to our disobedience. The preschool teacher has the time-out chair. So does God.

Creativity in Presentation

The structure of this story is a common rhetorical structure that has endured across the ages. It presents the negative and positive examples and then challenges us to choose the positive. Negative and positive examples given in this passage form a natural contrast. Ahaz's evil gives us the negative example: what not to do. The northern leaders restoring the captives in response to YHWH's directive gives us the positive example: what to do. God gives us the reason to not follow Ahaz: what *God* will do. The way the writer presents this has hints of a chiastic structure. It moves from the negative to the positive and then back to the negative. This exegetical structure can be followed in the sermon structure. The tragedy of Ahaz's life is motivation to not be like him. In our culture of positive reinforcement this type of negative motivation is not often used, but that is a major part of his story. It could be helpful to assist our listeners by showing that negative reinforcement is not always a bad thing. When we see a car crash, it prompts us to drive more carefully. Fifty years ago, smoking was seen as a positive thing, but the harshness of a disease brought on by smoking motivated our culture to change its view. So negative motivation can and does work.

Here is one possible structure in presenting the sermon:

- What not to do: Ahaz's unfaithfulness (28:1–4)
  - Why: Ahaz's punishment (28:5–8)
- What to do: A prophet confronts Israel (28:9–15)
- What not to do: Ahaz's further punishment (28:16–21)
  - Why: Ahaz's further unfaithfulness (28:22–27)
- God's disciplining hand should lead us to obey.

DISCUSSION QUESTIONS

1. List at least five areas in which we are led.

2. List five persons whom, at some level, you have followed or are following.

3. Share a time when a leader's example was very helpful.

4. Share a time when a leader's example was harmful.

5. When was a time when you had to do what was right, despite poor leadership?

6. What are some ways we can ensure that we are following Christ?

2 Chronicles 29:1–31:21

EXEGETICAL IDEA
When Hezekiah restored proper worship by addressing previous sins, uniting the people at the temple, and providing for future sacrifices, YHWH blessed all obedient Israel.

THEOLOGICAL FOCUS
God blesses worship that addresses past sins, promotes unity among believers, and provides for future ministry.

PREACHING IDEA
Restore and refresh the joy of worship.

PREACHING POINTERS
When the COVID pandemic hit, the church I was attending stopped having in-person worship services. We tried to continue to worship, sitting at home watching the leaders on a screen, listening to our own voices singing, and then working hard to stay focused on a message that seemed far away. Worship didn't stop; it was just very different. Perhaps that is the closest experience we have to the situation that Hezekiah had when he started his reign.

As the pandemic eased and in-person worship began to resume, it was like a fresh breeze. We could sing, pray, and listen to the Word with live people. Ahaz's wicked practices shut down the corporate worship of YHWH. This passage describes how worship of YHWH returned. It showed the first readers, and shows us, how our worship can be renewed and refreshed. They confessed sin, they celebrated the forgiveness and deliverance of Passover, and they provided for the advancement of future worship.

REIGN OF HEZEKIAH—PROMOTING PROPER WORSHIP AT THE TEMPLE (29:1–31:21)

LITERARY STRUCTURE AND THEMES (29:1–31:21)

From the time Hezekiah ascends the throne, he focuses his energies on leading the people to worship YHWH in the proper way. The account breaks down into three sections. Each section addresses a different topic and concludes with a positive comment regarding the previous events. The first section focuses on restoring worship at the temple. It looks to the past as Hezekiah addresses the wickedness of his father Ahaz. He reopens the temple, removes the defilements from it, and restarts the sacrificial service to YHWH. The section concludes by recounting how the people rejoice over restoring temple worship. The second section recounts how all Israel observes the Passover together at the temple. People from Judah and Israel come together at Jerusalem for the observance. The section concludes with all the people rejoicing and a comment reflecting that the entire Passover has finished. The third section looks to the future as it recounts how Hezekiah carries out certain appointments and procedures to ensure that the temple and its personnel have the resources to continue worship at the temple into the future. This section concludes by commending Hezekiah for all the measures he takes to promote the proper worship of YHWH at Jerusalem. Even though this commendation applies to the third section, it also characterizes Hezekiah's actions throughout chapters 29–31.

- ***Hezekiah Restores Worship at the Temple (29:1–36)***
- ***Hezekiah and All Israel Observe the Passover Together at the Temple (30:1–31:1)***
- ***Hezekiah Ensures Continued Worship at the Temple (31:2–21)***

EXPOSITION (29:1–31:21)

In the Old Testament's context, people generally conceived of religion and faith in terms of the community more than in terms of the individual. As a result, public religious practices served as more important signs for the religious outlook of a community than personal, private piety. For this reason, the reign of King Ahaz created a crisis for Judah's worship of YHWH. Ahaz either prevented or perverted Judah's practices so that they no longer represented worshipping YHWH at all. Into this setting, Hezekiah became Judah's new king.

These chapters show how Hezekiah addresses the crisis created by Ahaz's reign. In contrast to Ahaz, Hezekiah restores proper worship of YHWH at the Jerusalem temple according to the Mosaic law and the Davidic pattern. Because of his actions, the Chronicler presents Hezekiah as a sort of second David and second Solomon (see Throntveit 2003, 105–21). Like both these kings, Hezekiah leads all the tribes of Israel to worship together in Jerusalem at the place that YHWH has chosen. Hezekiah fulfills this task by addressing the people's previous sins, uniting all the people in reinstituting the proper practices for worshipping YHWH at the Jerusalem temple, and providing the resources and structure to promote that worship into the future.

Hezekiah Restores Worship at the Temple (29:1–36)

At the start of his reign, Hezekiah restores the proper worship of YHWH at the Jerusalem temple by commanding the priests and Levites to clean out the temple, by offering sacrifices, and by reinstituting the Levitical musical service.

29:1–2. The Chronicler introduces Hezekiah's reign in a typical fashion: he lists Hezekiah's age when he becomes king (twenty-five years old), how long he reigns (twenty-nine years), the name of his mother (Abijah, daughter of Zechariah), and the theological evaluation of his reign. The Chronicler evaluates Hezekiah's activity as that which is acceptable to YHWH and then compares him to his ancestor David, the standard model of a good king.

29:3–18. Following the introduction to Hezekiah's reign, the Chronicler jumps into the specific measures that Hezekiah takes to restore the proper worship of YHWH. These measures focus on the place of worship: the Jerusalem temple. The first step is to reopen and clean out the temple from any religious impurity. Reopening the temple is a simple matter of opening its doors and repairing them (29:3). To clean out the temple, Hezekiah calls together a group of priests and Levites who recruit other priests and Levites to help them clean out the temple. These priests and Levites sanctify themselves and then spend sixteen days cleaning out the temple and sanctifying its various locations, furnishings, and implements. Once they finish, they report to Hezekiah that the temple is cleaned out (29:18). Thus, they complete the first step of restoring proper worship.

Significance of Doors

There is a double-sided nature to the doors of the temple. On one hand, the temple requires doors to separate it from the rest of the world. As a holy place, it is distinct from other normal, common places. On the other hand, opening the doors signifies an invitation to come to the temple. In other words, the doors of the temple are both an invitation to come and a barrier from coming. They foster worship while also preserving the temple's sanctity.

Several ancient Near Eastern texts associate opening the doors of a temple with restoring ritual worship within that temple. The Chronicler seems to intend the same sense here. Other ancient Near Eastern texts associate building or repairing the temple doors with an act of repentance or propitiation. Again, the Chronicler apparently intends the same sense here, since he later records Hezekiah's concern to appease YHWH's wrath (2 Chron. 29:10). See Payne 2017, 88–155, 245, 247–49.

29:3. The Chronicler emphasizes that Hezekiah carries out this task at the beginning of his reign. The Chronicler describes these events as taking place during the first month of the first year of Hezekiah's reign. By mentioning the first month of the first year of Hezekiah's reign, the Chronicler intends to show how urgently Hezekiah went about the task of restoring proper worship.

Timing of Events

The timing of these events is ambiguous; it may refer to the month of Hezekiah's coronation or it may refer to the first month of the calendar year in which Hezekiah was king. The latter interpretation is more likely because the following narrative states that the people were unable to observe the Passover at the regular time during the first month of the year (2 Chron. 30:3). Even if a period of time passes between Hezekiah's coronation and these measures to restore worship, the Chronicler intends to present Hezekiah's enthusiasm to restore temple worship.

29:4–11. The Chronicler explains why this task of restoring worship is so important by recording Hezekiah's speech to the priests and Levites. The speech refers to "our fathers" (אֲבוֹתֵינוּ) to show how Judah's past disobedience to YHWH leads to their present circumstances. He characterizes their disobedience using terms found repeatedly in Chronicles: they transgress, do what is evil according to YHWH's estimation, and forsake YHWH (for the first expression, see sidebar "Unfaithfulness Against YHWH"; for the second expression, see 2 Chron. 21:6; 22:4; 33:2, 6, 22; 36:5, 9; for the third expression, see 2 Chron. 7:19, 22; 12:1, 5; 13:10, 11; 15:2; 21:10; 24:18, 20, 24; 28:6; 34:25). These terms often illustrate the Chronicler's theological concern to show that YHWH rewards obedience and punishes disobedience. In this case, "our fathers" specifically disobey YHWH by turning away from YHWH's temple through closing its doors, extinguishing its lamps, and ceasing to offer incense and sacrifices to YHWH. In other words, they stopped the temple's normal ritual worship. As a result, the people find themselves in a terrible situation as an object of scorn and derision: "our fathers" have died by the sword, while the women and children have been taken as captives. Since past neglect of temple worship brought about the present situation, the remedy lies in restoring temple worship. In this way, Hezekiah hopes that YHWH's "fierce wrath may turn away."

Hezekiah Making a Covenant

Hezekiah states that he intends to make a covenant with YHWH; however, the text does not record that he ever makes a covenant. One may argue that Hezekiah does formally make a covenant even though the text does not record it. Certainly, this action would be in line with others who implement reforms during their reigns (e.g., Asa, 2 Chron. 15:12; Jehoiada, 2 Chron. 23:16; Josiah, 2 Chron. 34:31).

However, in this case, the language of covenant is more likely metaphorical rather than literal. Hezekiah is speaking of a commitment to YHWH to restore temple worship rather than a formal agreement (cf. 2 Chron. 23:1, 3).

Even though Hezekiah's speech clearly deals with his present situation in Judah and Jerusalem, it uses language that extends beyond this situation. For instance, rather than blaming closing the temple doors on Ahaz directly (2 Chron. 28:24), Hezekiah speaks of "our fathers." This language covers not only Ahaz but others of Judah as well. Furthermore, when Hezekiah describes the current situation, he speaks of the people becoming an object of scorn and derision. Jeremiah uses this same language to describe how the Babylonians destroy Judah and Jerusalem during the period of exile (e.g., Jer. 15:4; 24:9; 29:18; 34:17). The language drives home the point that if Israel fails to maintain temple worship, YHWH will judge them.

29:11–19. The priests and Levites are essential for the task of cleaning out the temple. As Hezekiah reminds them, YHWH chose them to oversee and perform the ritual worship in his holy presence. For this reason, even though the temple is a holy place forbidden for most people to enter, the priests and Levites are permitted to enter its various sacred locations. However, before they can begin, they must sanctify themselves to ensure that they do not violate the temple's sanctity. The text shows that the priests and Levites preserve the temple's sanctity by sanctifying themselves and remaining in the areas where they are permitted. For this reason, the priests go into the sanctuary itself to bring out all the filth to the courtyard where the Levites then remove it from the temple and the city. Once they finish the task of cleaning the temple, they report their success to the king.

Priestly and Levitical Tasks

Hezekiah reminds the priests and Levites of three tasks that YHWH has chosen them to do: to stand before him to serve him (לַעֲמֹד לְפָנָיו לְשָׁרְתוֹ), to be servants (מְשָׁרְתִים), and to be sacrificers (מַקְטִרִים). Most likely, the first task is a general expression applicable to both priests and Levites. It indicates that both groups perform certain worship tasks within the temple, the place of YHWH's presence. The root שרת occurs again in the second task because this time it refers more specifically to the Levites (cf. 2 Chron. 23:6). The third task applies to the priests (1 Chron. 23:13).

29:20–36. After the priests and Levites report that they have cleaned out the temple and sanctified it, the second step of restoring proper worship begins. This step includes three related activities: (1) Hezekiah and Jerusalem's leaders offer public sacrifices on behalf of the people (29:21–24), (2) Hezekiah reinstitutes the Levitical musical service alongside the sacrifices (29:25–30), and (3) the people bring individual offerings to YHWH (29:31–36).

29:21–24. The public offerings consist of burnt offerings and sin offerings. Hezekiah commanded the priests to offer these sacrifices to restore the community to YHWH. The Chronicler specifies further by referring to the elements of the community involved in bringing about YHWH's wrath: (1) the kingdom, that is, the kings, especially Ahaz who closed the doors of the temple, (2) the sanctuary since its worship ceased, and (3) the people as a whole who participated in pagan practices and ceased worshipping YHWH. The Chronicler describes the rituals for both the burnt and sin offerings, concluding that the sacrifices remove sin from the altar and atone for all Israel. In this case, "all Israel" refers to all the tribes, not just to the kingdom of Judah. Since the northern kingdom no longer exists, Hezekiah takes the first opportunity to restore all Israel to YHWH so that they may reunite in worshipping him.

29:25–30. The second activity involves reinstituting the Levitical music service. First, the Chronicler emphasizes the role that David plays in establishing the musical service. David organizes the musicians, supplies the instruments, and provides the lyrics. The Chronicler characterizes this activity as prophetic, assigning it a divine source and authority. For instance, 29:25 mentions David, Gad, and Nathan as providing the organization for the music "from YHWH through his prophets," while 29:30 mentions the words of David and Asaph, characterizing Asaph as the seer. Second, the Chronicler shows how the musical service coincides with the sacrifices. After the offerings have been slaughtered and their blood applied to the altar, the priests present the offerings to burn completely on the altar (Kleinig 1993, 101–4). The priests signal this presentation with the blowing of the trumpets (see Num. 10 for other uses of priestly trumpets) while the Levites begin singing, with musical accompaniment. The music finishes when the burnt offering finishes. As part of this activity, the people also bow down before YHWH, likely as a sign that YHWH has accepted their offerings and as a result is now present before them. The music also promotes an atmosphere of joy as YHWH accepts their offering.

Bowing Down and Worshipping

Besides 2 Chronicles 29:30, the only other passage in Chronicles to use both terms "to bow" (קדד) and "to bow, pay homage, worship" (חוה) is 2 Chronicles 7:3. This passage describes how the people react to YHWH's glory filling the temple after Solomon's prayer of dedication. In other words, just as the people acknowledged YHWH's acceptance and presence in the temple when it was constructed, the people acknowledge YHWH's acceptance and presence in the temple after its restoration.

29:31–36. The third activity involves the people bringing individual offerings to

YHWH. Hezekiah invites the people to bring in sacrifices and thank offerings but, as with David's invitation to the people (1 Chron. 29:5–9), the people give beyond expectation, bringing those sacrifices as well as burnt offerings. In fact, the people are so generous that the priests cannot handle the quantity. For this reason, the Levites step in to help skin the animals for sacrifice until more priests have sanctified themselves for the task.

Hezekiah and David

The text signals the connection to David in a couple of ways. First, Hezekiah applies the expression מִלֵּאתֶם יֶדְכֶם ("filled your hand"; translations usually render it something like "consecrated yourselves") to the people. Elsewhere, except for here and 1 Chronicles 29:5 the term refers to the consecration of priests. Second, the Chronicler describes those who bring the burnt offerings as נְדִיב לֵב ("willing of heart"). The verbal form of this word occurs in 1 Chronicles 29:6 (וַיִּתְנַדְּבוּ).

29:35–36. As a result of Hezekiah's initiative to clean out the temple, offer the public offerings at the temple, reinstitute the temple's musical service, and invite the people to offer sacrifices—which they do generously—the temple service to YHWH is restored. Then, as is typical in Chronicles, the people's obedience results in their joy. In fact, the Chronicler emphasizes how quickly these events took place and attributes their quick pace to YHWH's activity.

Hezekiah and All Israel Observe the Passover Together at the Temple (30:1–31:1)

After restoring proper worship at the temple, Hezekiah, Judah, and Israel observe the Passover in Jerusalem.

30:1–5. After showing that proper worship has resumed at the temple, the Chronicler recounts how all Israel observes the Passover at Jerusalem. The account begins by stating generally that Hezekiah invites all Israel and Judah to participate in the Passover at Jerusalem. The passage then provides more detail regarding this invitation (for this literary technique, see Kalimi 2005b, 369–77). The statements work together to highlight the Chronicler's message.

Three important points emerge. First, the Chronicler emphasizes that Hezekiah invites all Israel, both northern and southern tribes. The Chronicler refers generally to all Israel, represented by the individual tribes of Ephraim and Manasseh. Furthermore, he communicates the full extent of all Israel by referring in detail to Beersheba and Dan, the typical representatives of the southernmost and northernmost cities among all the tribes.

30:1–6. Second, the Chronicler points out the dynamic between Hezekiah's leadership and the people's involvement. The Chronicler states that Hezekiah sends out the messengers; however, the important decision-making takes place among the king, his officials, and the people. The whole group considers when to observe the Passover and issues the invitation to observe it at Jerusalem. The situation here closely resembles Israel's decision to assemble all Israel to bring up the ark of God under David (1 Chron. 13:1–4). For both kings, their predecessors have neglected an aspect of worship (for David, the ark, 1 Chron. 13:3; for Hezekiah, the Passover, 2 Chron. 30:5). In this way, the Chronicler portrays Hezekiah as a strong leader, like David, while also demonstrating the importance of the people in preserving, maintaining, and, when needed, restoring proper worship.

TRANSLATION ANALYSIS:
The Chronicler portrays previous kings as neglecting the Passover (30:5). Although some translations render the expression לְרֹב in terms of the quantity of those celebrating (e.g., "in great numbers" NASB, NIV, NLT, NRSV; "on a nationwide scale" NET), the expression more likely refers to the frequency of observing Passover. The

people had not often kept it; in fact, this passage is the first in Chronicles to mention Passover specifically, even if it is assumed to be observed with the Feast of Unleavened Bread. By celebrating the Passover, Hezekiah is continuing to do what his ancestors have neglected to do in worshipping YHWH properly.

Celebrating Passover and Bringing the Ark

Further similarities between the accounts of Hezekiah's celebrating Passover and David's transferring the ark are as follows: both kings establish or reestablish YHWH's proper worship for all Israel, both kings "take counsel" (*niphal* יעץ) with the people (1 Chron. 13:1), in both the people assemble in Jerusalem (1 Chron. 13:2), and in both the proposed plan is pleasing (יָשַׁר) to everyone involved (1 Chron. 13:4).

Third, the Chronicler emphasizes when and where the Passover will take place. Since the Passover will take place at the temple in Jerusalem (based on Deut. 16:2), the people cannot observe it at the prescribed time (fourteenth day of first month; cf. Exod. 12:6; Lev. 23:5; Num. 9:3; 28:16) because the people are not present in Jerusalem. Furthermore, since the restoration of temple service has happened so quickly (2 Chron. 29:37), an insufficient number of priests have sanctified themselves. For these reasons, the Chronicler records that the whole group decides to delay the Passover until the second month. The choice of the second month likely relies on the Pentateuch's account of a somewhat similar situation (cf. Num. 9:6–12). Therefore, regarding when and where the Passover takes place, the Chronicler's description appears to draw on passages from the Mosaic law.

30:6–9. Since the assembly decides to invite all Israel to observe Passover in Jerusalem, Hezekiah sends messengers throughout the land to proclaim this invitation alongside written letters. Even though the messengers go

throughout all the land, the invitation addresses the northern tribes more specifically. The way the Chronicler preserves this invitation highlights three important points. First, the people from Israel and Judah share a common heritage with a common God. The invitation repeatedly uses familial language: "sons of Israel," "fathers," and "brothers." Furthermore, the invitation refers to YHWH as "God of Abraham, Isaac, and Israel" as well as the more generic "God of their fathers." Although Israel and Judah may represent distinct political realities, the people of these states are one common people, the sons of Israel, and therefore brothers. Furthermore, the invitation highlights that YHWH has established a connection with this common people from their beginning with the patriarchs. As a result, Hezekiah is not a foreigner inviting them to worship a foreign god; instead, he is a brother inviting them to worship their own God.

Israel vs. Jacob

The use of the name Israel in the series "Abraham, Isaac, and Israel" reflects the Chronicler's preference for the name Israel over Jacob. In fact, the series more often occurs as "Abraham, Isaac, and Jacob" within the Old Testament (e.g., Exod. 3:6, 15, 16; 4:5; Deut. 6:10; 9:5; 29:12). However, by using the name Israel the Chronicler highlights the common heritage of the all the tribes, that is, all the sons of Israel (בְּנֵי יִשְׂרָאֵל).

Second, the invitation highlights how bad the situation in Israel is. The language paints the portrait of Israel as an exiled people, destroyed by a series of Assyrian kings with only a few surviving. It closely resembles how Hezekiah describes the situation in Judah before he cleans out the temple (2 Chron. 29:5–11). In both cases, their fathers act faithlessly, so that YHWH delivers them to destruction. Although the Chronicler does not specify their disobedience, he implies it when he records that the people should yield to YHWH by coming to the Jerusalem temple to worship YHWH. When

Israel became a distinct political state, its first king Jeroboam led them to turn away from the temple and to worship idols (2 Chron. 13:8–9). Now that the political state of Israel, founded by the rebel against the Davidic king Jeroboam (2 Chron. 13:6–7), is in shambles, the most significant barrier to Israel's proper worship of YHWH has also been removed. The door is open for the Davidic king to reunite all Israel in its worship of YHWH at the temple in Jerusalem.

Third, the invitation highlights Israel's possible future hope, which lies in returning to YHWH. For Israel to return to YHWH (or repent) involves submitting themselves to him, coming to the temple in Jerusalem, and worshipping him (exclusively). In other words, what YHWH requires of Israel is what Judah, led by Hezekiah, has already done and is doing. YHWH has already given them joy by enabling them to accomplish their task quickly (2 Chron. 29:36). Therefore, when the text describes YHWH as "gracious and compassionate," it not only draws on a common confession (e.g., Exod. 34:6–7; Neh. 9:17; Pss. 86:15; 103:8; Joel 2:13; Jonah 4:2) but also on Judah's experience previously recorded in the narrative. Furthermore, if Israel returns to YHWH, YHWH will return to them, that is, he will "pay attention" to their situation to do something about it (see similar language in Zech. 1:3–4). Generically, the text describes what YHWH will do as YHWH's wrath turning away; however, specifically, the text speaks of granting the people compassion from their captors and returning them to the land. This hope builds on the promise of 2 Chronicles 7:14, where the people's repentance leads to their restoration.

30:10–12. Israel's response to this invitation is mixed. Many within the northern tribes mock and ridicule the messengers; however, several people accept the invitation, described in the text as humbling themselves and coming to Jerusalem. The former group resembles the generation of King Zedekiah, who mocks and ridicules God's messengers and finally receives YHWH's judgment of exile (2 Chron. 36:16). The latter group exemplifies the kind of repentance that YHWH calls for (2 Chron. 7:14). Despite the mixed response of the northern tribes, Judah's response is unanimous and unambiguous. YHWH enables the people to come together to follow through on the invitation to observe the Passover. Furthermore, the Chronicler indicates that the invitation reveals YHWH's will, indicated by the phrase "by the word of YHWH."

What YHWH Provides and Expects

Judah's response provides an insight into the Chronicler's understanding of retribution, that is, the teaching that YHWH rewards obedience and punishes disobedience. Although the Chronicler affirms this principle repeatedly, he also qualifies it in this case. YHWH demands that both Israel and Judah obey the invitation to come to Jerusalem, but he also empowers all Judah to obey it. See also comments on 1 Chronicles 22:12 and the "Covenant" section in the introduction.

30:13–14. Before those gathered observe the Passover, they clean out Jerusalem. To clean it out, the people remove the altars erected by Ahaz (2 Chron. 28:24) along with illicit altars for burning incense. They follow a course of action like that taken in 2 Chronicles 29 regarding the temple: first they clean it out, then they offer sacrifices and praise.

30:15–20. Once they have prepared Jerusalem, they begin observing the Passover. The Chronicler shows how they address two problems that arise. First, since the Passover was delayed because an insufficient number of priests had sanctified themselves, the priests feel ashamed and, as a result, sanctify themselves and offer up burnt offerings for themselves. At that point, they are ready to assume their positions to perform the Passover rituals. Second, many of those journeying from the northern tribes are ritually unclean. The people take two measures to deal with these problems: (1) the Levites step in to slaughter the animals, and (2) Hezekiah prays that YHWH will not hold the northerners' impurity against them. Hezekiah prays for them because even though they do not sacrifice the offerings, they participate in the Passover by eating them. However, Leviticus 7:20–21 states specifically that an unclean person who eats a sacrifice will be cut off from the people. Therefore, Hezekiah intercedes, praying that YHWH will value their commitment to follow YHWH and exempt them from the prescribed judgment. YHWH proves that he is gracious and compassionate (30:9) by listening to Hezekiah's prayer and forgiving the people. In this case, the Chronicler alludes to 2 Chronicles 7:14 by using the term רפא (often translated "heal") to speak of forgiving the people, just as 2 Chronicles 7:14 uses the term to speak of restoring the land.

In fact, nearly all the elements of 2 Chronicles 7:14 appear in this narrative as the northern tribes humble themselves (30:11), Hezekiah prays (30:18), the people seek God (30:19), and YHWH hears and heals (30:20). These allusions reveal that this narrative serves as a concrete example of the pattern of repentance and restoration outlined in 2 Chronicles 7:14. What may be surprising is that this concrete example involves those from the northern tribes and superseding purity regulations. These surprising elements indicate that even though the Chronicler highly values worshipping YHWH according to what is prescribed in the law, he recognizes that at times one may worship YHWH sincerely even when violating certain purity regulations.

30:21–27. The rest of the chapter highlights the positive results of observing Passover. The people continue by observing the closely related Feast of Unleavened Bread for seven days. During this time, the people enthusiastically celebrate by making offerings, eating them

together, and giving YHWH thanks. The people even extend their celebration for another seven days beyond what is prescribed. The Chronicler highlights that everyone gathered in Jerusalem—those from the southern tribes, the northern tribes, and even the foreign residents who lived among them—experiences great joy.

Furthermore, the Chronicler presents the priests and Levites as finally getting it completely right. Now, the priests and Levites praise YHWH through music with such skill and insight that Hezekiah takes notice. The priests sanctify themselves in sufficient numbers to handle the large crowd for the entire period of the celebrations. The priests bless the people (cf. Deut. 26:15; 27:12–14; Josh. 8:33), a blessing that YHWH accepts. Finally, Hezekiah looks like Solomon because nothing like this Passover has taken place since Solomon's time as king. The Chronicler emphasizes the significance of Solomon (and therefore Hezekiah) by describing him as "son of David, king of Israel." This kind of joy in Israel results from a Davidic king (Solomon or Hezekiah) bringing all Israel together to worship YHWH at the newly (re)opened temple in Jerusalem.

Musicians' Skill and Insight

Second Chronicles 30:22 describes the Levites with the expression מַשְׂכִּילִים שֵׂכֶל־טוֹב לַיהוָה ("who performed skillfully before the Lord" CSB; "who taught the good knowledge of the Lord" NKJV). This phrase is probably intentionally ambiguous. It may refer to the skill of musical performance, as well as their insight into YHWH and his work as exhibited through their songs (see Kleinig 1993, 76).

31:1. The Chronicler shows how the people conclude the Passover: they destroy all the illicit sites and objects of worship. This activity extends beyond the political boundaries of Hezekiah's rule to Ephraim and Manasseh. In this way, the people deal with the sins of the past, starting at the temple, then in Jerusalem, and now throughout the tribes of Israel. Once this work is finished, the people return to their homes.

Hezekiah Ensures Continued Worship at the Temple (31:2–21)

After recording how Hezekiah reinstates the worship at the temple and brings all Israel together to observe the Passover, the Chronicler turns his focus to how Hezekiah will maintain that worship in the future by reappointing the priests and Levites both according to the established organization and their functions, setting aside his royal contribution for certain temple offerings, charging the storehouses to hold the contributions, and appointing officers to oversee the collection and distribution of the contributions to the priests and Levites.

31:2–21. Certain features of this account tie into other passages in the Old Testament. When Hezekiah reestablishes the divisions of priests and Levites, he follows the example of Solomon based on the pattern set up by David (1 Chron. 23:6; 2 Chron. 8:14). Furthermore, he establishes their duties as outlined by David (cf. 1 Chron. 16:4; 23:13). When Hezekiah contributes the offerings, he fulfills the expectations of Ezekiel 45:17 while providing the types of sacrifices required by the law (cf. Num. 28–29). When Hezekiah and the people contribute so much, they also look like David and his generation (1 Chron. 29:2–8). When Hezekiah commands that storerooms be prepared, he follows the pattern that David has established (1 Chron. 28:12). These verses show how Hezekiah responds to his specific historical circumstances in light of the law and the precedents established by David and Solomon, the kings over all Israel.

Two other themes the Chronicler emphasizes are blessing and faithfulness. The Chronicler uses the theme of blessing in this narrative to show how YHWH rewards those who obey him and how his blessing leads others to bless. Hezekiah and his officials respond to the people's generosity by blessing YHWH and blessing the people. At the same time, when Hezekiah inquires about the piles of offerings, the priest responds that the offering is so abundant because YHWH has blessed his people. In other words, YHWH has rewarded the people because of their obedience. This blessing, however, also requires fidelity on the part of those who oversee the offerings and their distribution. The Chronicler repeatedly points out that the Levites perform their duties faithfully (31:12, 15, 18). For the priests and Levites to serve continually in the temple, the people must continue to bring offerings and those who oversee the distribution of those offerings must act faithfully (see Neh. 13:10–13).

31:14–19. The Chronicler elaborates on the distribution of offerings. These verses present some text-critical and syntactical challenges in the details, but the overall point remains clear: Hezekiah organizes several Levitical officers to oversee the faithful distribution of the offerings to the priests and the Levites. Among the details, the Chronicler distinguishes among priests and Levites and among those who are serving at the temple and those who are staying in their allocated cities. The priests receive their distributions for each individual male three years old and above. The Levites receive their distributions for each Levite twenty years old and above, along with the members of their household. In this way, Hezekiah establishes a system for providing continual support for the priests and Levites.

31:20–21. The Chronicler closes out his description of all the measures Hezekiah takes for all Israel to worship YHWH properly at the temple in Jerusalem by evaluating the work theologically and commenting on its results. The Chronicler describes Hezekiah's work uniquely: it is good, upright, and faithful. No other king receives a commendation with this combination of positive elements. Furthermore, the Chronicler comments on Hezekiah's mindset regarding this work: He did it wholeheartedly. Hezekiah's work involves the temple service (e.g., 2 Chron. 29:35), according to the law (e.g., 2 Chron. 31:3), according to the commandment (e.g., 2 Chron. 29:25) to follow YHWH, one of the Chronicler's typical expressions for obeying YHWH. Finally, the Chronicler presents the result of Hezekiah's obedience: success. As is typical in Chronicles, YHWH rewards obedience with success. Hezekiah is another example of this pattern.

The first readers knew firsthand the conditions of exile. They had been scattered into various neighboring lands under the cruel hands of the Assyrians and Babylonians. Many of them longed to return to their ancestral land. Even those who did not return hoped to find compassion among the populations in which they lived. The Chronicler communicates to this community several important reminders. First, the narrative demonstrates the importance of dealing with past sins. Before all Israel could worship YHWH properly, they had to remove the filth of the past. Second, the narrative demonstrates that the condition for realizing the hopes of return lies in worshipping YHWH at the Jerusalem temple according to his command. In this way, Hezekiah's invitation to all Israel to observe the Passover reaches beyond his days to the postexilic community itself and provides a strong impetus for supporting and visiting the Jerusalem temple (see Guy 2019, 201). Third, the narrative demonstrates that YHWH will reward those who care for the priests and Levites through generous offerings and faithful distribution. The postexilic community experienced problems in these areas (Neh. 13:10–13), so the Chronicler's account would encourage them to continue giving so that the priests and Levites could continue fulfilling their duties of offering sacrifices and praise to YHWH. Finally, the narrative encourages the community to continue looking for another Davidic king who would rule over all Israel, uniting them in their worship of YHWH alone according to his law.

THEOLOGICAL FOCUS

God blesses worship that addresses past sins, promotes unity among believers, and provides for future ministry.

This passage presents Hezekiah as a great king. Like David and Solomon before him, he unites all Israel in worship to God at the Jerusalem temple. However, before he can bring Israel to Jerusalem to worship God, he must address Israel's past sins. Others in the postexilic period follow the same pattern. When Daniel considers Jeremiah's prophecy of restoration, he confesses Israel's sin before asking God to restore the temple and the land (Dan. 9:2–19). After the reading of the law during the days of Ezra and Nehemiah, all the people gather to confess their sin before they ask God to deliver them from their difficult circumstances (Neh. 9:1–32).

Like the situation during Hezekiah's day, the prayers in Daniel and Nehemiah apply to all Israel; however, the same pattern applies to individuals. Psalm 51 records when David confesses his sin and then calls on God to restore him. Jesus tells the parable of a tax collector who is justified after he cries out for God to have mercy on him because he is a sinner. James 5:16 encourages the readers to confess their sins and pray so that they may be healed. John summarizes the pattern as follows: "If we confess our sins, he is faithful and righteous to forgive us our sins and to cleanse us from all unrighteousness" (1 John 1:9 CSB). Restoration requires reckoning with past sins.

After dealing with Israel's past sins, Hezekiah invites all God's people to gather at Jerusalem to worship God together. This picture of all Israel united in worship runs throughout Chronicles, especially in the reigns of David and Solomon. This picture likely represents what the Chronicler desires for his postexilic community. However, the picture of God's people united stretches far beyond the postexilic community. The New Testament repeatedly speaks of the unity of God's people. Jesus prays that all those who believe will experience unity analogous to the unity of the Father and the Son (John 17:20–21). Paul reminds the churches that even though they are many, they are united as God's people (e.g., Rom. 12:4–5; Gal. 3:28; Eph. 2:14–22). Furthermore, their unity is important for proper worship. In 1 Corinthians 11, Paul corrects those who create divisions within the congregation during the eating of the Lord's Supper. God condemns their practice because it is not really worship. Proper worship leads to unity.

This question of proper, united worship also looks beyond a single church or generation. In Philippians Paul encourages the church to remain united (e.g., 2:1–4), but their unity is not for its own sake. Their unity promotes the gospel (see Black 1995, 16) because it reflects the work that God has done to make them one people and promotes the spread of the gospel as they partner with Paul and others. In this way, united worship not only pleases God when it takes place; it also promotes the gospel among those who may not believe so that they may become future worshippers as well.

Although many of the specific historical circumstances have changed, the portrait that Chronicles paints of God's people during the days of Hezekiah reflects the desired portrait of God's people throughout time: those who have addressed their sins, presently worship God together, and promote the advancement of God's work into future generations.

PREACHING AND TEACHING STRATEGIES

Exegetical and Theological Synthesis
One of Ahaz's last acts was to close the doors of the temple; one of Hezekiah's first acts was to reopen them. Hezekiah's reign started with this courageous and delightful act that expressed his heart that sought after YHWH. The narrative only gets better as we walk through these three chapters, which describe a stunning revival in Judah that even extended into the northern kingdom.

Hezekiah's actions were not novel or creative on his part. He was only obeying God's revealed will in the Torah. The blessings that accompanied his obedience were not out of reach for any of the previous kings. They were always there, but unbelief and disobedience prevented them from receiving and enjoying the blessings that God had provided. Obedience and trust don't earn the blessing of God; the blessing of God is always there. Our obedience and trust put us in a position to enjoy those blessings. Hezekiah was not making a deal with God that if he obeyed, then God would bless. The blessings had already been promised (2 Chron 7:13–14); trust and obedience opened the door to them.

The progression of the revival of YHWH worship is exemplary for us. It began with acknowledging and confessing their sin and the accompanying consecration of individuals and places. Then they observed Passover, celebrating God's forgiveness and deliverance that promoted unity. This was followed by making provision for continued worship and the great joy in seeing God provide. To return, to refresh, or even to begin worshipping God, we need to (1) confess our sin, (2) embrace the forgiveness and deliverance that comes through faith in Christ, and (3) live in his love, making provision to continue worshipping him and him alone.

Preaching Idea
Restore and refresh the joy of worship.

Contemporary Connections

What does it mean?
The engine had gas; I had even checked the spark plug. Why wouldn't it start? The online registration seemed simple, so why did it keep rejecting it when I clicked on "submit"? I had the right amount of meat drippings, flour, and milk, so why did my gravy always have lumps? In each of these situations, there is an order that must be followed. If you choke an engine too much, it won't start. If you don't fill in each

blank on the form, the computer won't accept a registration. If you don't mix the right ratio of flour and drippings before adding the milk, the gravy will have lumps.

Likewise, genuine worship requires the right steps. Hezekiah and his people confessed their own sins and the sins of their fathers. Then they celebrated Passover, which reaffirms that YHWH had passed over their sins and delivered them. The resulting unity and joy came as they saw God's abundant provision for worship and for their lives. The whole process was astounding in light of past kings' actions and leadership. The people's renewed worship extended as they went throughout the land, ridding it of idols and setting up of structures for ongoing YHWH worship.

These steps should at some level influence the order of our private and public worship. This is not to say that there is a strict step-by-step list of things that must be followed, but there is a general progression demonstrated for us. Whether it is a private time of prayer or a gathering of thousands to worship, confession of sin should lead to focus on the Passover lamb, Jesus. This is followed by taking action that comes out of our worship, which is obedience to God's will.

Is it true?

The first readers must have wondered and marveled at the joyful celebration described by the Chronicler. Perhaps they wondered if they could have worship like this. This positive story certainly encouraged them that they could have their worship renewed and refreshed. Hezekiah led the nation from a closed temple and despicable practices to this astonishing revival. It wasn't just a mild correction; it was a complete overhaul and change of direction. If God could do it in Hezekiah's time, he could do it in the lives of these first readers in postexilic Israel. And he can restore and refresh worship in our own lives.

When we have a dullness in our worship or when there is obvious sin in our lives, we know that we need this refreshment. Other times, the refreshing of our worship comes when we are not expecting it. Fifteen years into ministry I was leading a Thanksgiving communion service. In the middle of distributing the elements, the Spirit of God began to disturb my spirit. Somehow in that very moment, my self-centered motivation became very evident to me. I began to see that I was working hard at pastoring, leading my family, and loving my wife so that people would respect me and affirm me. As the Spirit helped me see my sin, he also empowered me to confess it before the Father. As I led the congregation to reflect on the sacrifice of the Lamb for us, I was overwhelmed by his forgiveness. I struggled to finish the service. This began a fresh season of renewed joy in worship. I wasn't even aware that my worship had become somewhat routine and more of a duty, rather than a joyful expression of our great God. Worship must begin with confession of sin, which leads to embracing the sacrificial work of Christ on our behalf and a renewed joy in worship.

God wants to renew and refresh our worship. He even wants those who have never worshipped him to come and worship. He calls us to confess sin, put our trust in the sacrifice and resurrection of Jesus, and live in the unity and joy that true worship brings.

Now what?

These three steps are not a formula to get God to do something for us. Worship logically includes confession, trust, and obedience. The refreshing comes from God. His restoring worship in Israel resulted in a radical cultural revolution. Refreshing our worship may not look like this. It can be a very private renewing of the heart, or it can be a time of public confession in a local church body. Our side of restoring worship is confession and embracing Jesus's work. The joy, unity, and provision come from God in ways that are unique for each situation.

Our ongoing responsibility is to provide for continued worship. Perhaps changes need to be made in a schedule so that adequate time for private worship can take place, maybe even something as simple as rising earlier in the morning for prayer and meditating on his Word. Providing for ongoing worship could mean setting aside Sunday as a day primarily for worship rather than recreation or yard work. It means daily examining our lives and striving to live in joyful obedience to God's clear commands.

Sometimes our worship needs to be renewed and refreshed, but we simply don't realize it. It might be good to take some time to evaluate our private and corporate worship. If prayer and meditating on the Word is a dull routine instead of a joy and privilege, perhaps we need our worship refreshed. If Sunday is a day for our obligatory attendance at a church meeting instead of an event that is a highlight of our week, perhaps our worship of God needs to be renewed.

When an engine sputters and almost stops, it is clear that it needs some work. When the gravy has lumps, changes need to be made. We need to ask ourselves if our worship is just sputtering along. Does it seem like our worship has some lumps in it—that it just doesn't feel right? Our worship of God can, and should, be renewed and refreshed.

Creativity in Presentation

In the previous section I suggested a first-person storytelling method of getting the story across. This pericope could be handled in the same way with a little more creativity. It could be told from the perspective of Isaiah the prophet, who must have been thrilled at the revival. The story is told so well in the text that it could form the script. Some editing would be helpful, such as summarizing the long lists of names. As the story is told, the ever-increasing joy can be built. Imagine the doors of the temple being closed for years. Then, one bright morning as the sun begins to warm the city, a group of priests pries open the doors, stuck from unuse. Here is one possible structure:

- Tell the story
  - Restoring worship at the temple (29:1–36)
  - Observing the Passover together at the temple (30:1–31:1)
  - Ensuring continued worship at the temple (31:2–21)
- Apply the story
  - Confess sin
  - Celebrate the work of the Passover Lamb (Jesus)
  - Continue to ensure that worship continues

This passage can be preached in one sermon, or it can be divided easily into three sermons. If the three sermons are preached, emphasizing the individual parts of renewing worship, it could be helpful to preach a fourth sermon that emphasizes the progression.

DISCUSSION QUESTIONS

1. When was worship something you didn't want to do? What do you think contributed to that attitude?

2. Describe a worship service that was particularly memorable or important to you. How did that service affect you?

3. What must take place before we can confess sins? When we confess sin, what are we admitting?

4. The Jews had to tear down idols. What idols exist in our culture today? Are any of these idols in our lives? How can we tear those idols down?

5. What changes can you make to ensure you will continue to worship God?

2 Chronicles 32:1–33

EXEGETICAL IDEA
YHWH acted as the true God when he responded to Hezekiah in war and sickness.

THEOLOGICAL FOCUS
YHWH is the only true God with the power to deliver those who trust him from any opposing force, whether spiritual or physical.

PREACHING IDEA
God's unending power requires our perpetual dependence.

PREACHING POINTERS
Was it too good to be true? Hezekiah's reign was filled with the obedience that came from a heart that sought after God. Would he, as other kings, become proud and end his reign in disobedience? That is what seems to have happened. The Assyrians attack—God delivers, and Hezekiah become proud. Thus, he joins the list of disappointing kings. But it doesn't end that way. He is confronted about his pride, repents, and humbles himself before YHWH. When God displays his enduring power, our response should be continued and total dependence upon him.

REIGN OF HEZEKIAH—YHWH RESPONDS TO PRAYER IN WAR AND SICKNESS (32:1–33)

LITERARY STRUCTURE AND THEMES (32:1–33)

After the Chronicler commends Hezekiah for his activity in cleaning out the temple, reestablishing its service, and securing its future use, the Chronicler changes course to show how Hezekiah acts in matters other than the temple. Hezekiah faces two significant challenges in the latter part of his reign: an Assyrian invasion and a deadly disease. The two challenges form the main sections of the chapter, followed by a brief conclusion to Hezekiah's reign.

Facing the Assyrian invasion, Hezekiah and the people of Jerusalem prove to be faithful to YHWH. Judah prepares for a siege against Jerusalem, while Hezekiah encourages them to trust YHWH to fight for them. The Assyrians insult and disrespect both Hezekiah and YHWH while also trying to intimidate the people of Jerusalem. Hezekiah and Isaiah the prophet pray to YHWH; as the true God, YHWH responds miraculously. YHWH delivers the people by destroying the Assyrian army. Ashamed, the Assyrian king returns home, where he dies by the hand of his own sons in the temple of his god. In contrast, other nations honor YHWH and Hezekiah.

Following the account, Hezekiah falls deathly sick. Again, Hezekiah prays, and again YHWH, as the true God, responds miraculously. Although Hezekiah's (and Judah's) pride provokes YHWH's wrath, Hezekiah and the people humble themselves before YHWH so that he relents from his anger. Hezekiah again experiences a period of prosperity and honor because YHWH grants him great wealth. In fact, Hezekiah succeeds in everything he does, even as YHWH tests him to discern his true intentions.

Hezekiah's reign concludes by recounting that Hezekiah dies in peace and receives an honorable burial. His son Manasseh becomes king after him.

- **Assyrian Invasion and Its Results (32:1–23)**
  - ◦ *Judah's Preparation (32:1–8)*
  - ◦ *Assyria's Intimidation and Insults (32:9–19)*
  - ◦ *YHWH's Deliverance (32:20–23)*
- **Hezekiah's Sickness and Its Results (32:24–31)**
- **Conclusion of Hezekiah's Reign (32:32–33)**

EXPOSITION (32:1–33)

Although people in the ancient world faced many threats, two of the most significant and pervasive were war and sickness. They understood both to have a religious aspect. For war, people living in the ancient Near East believed that their deity would fight for them in battle. Therefore, a battle between nations also represented a conflict between the nations' gods. In many cases, ancient Near Eastern peoples interpreted their victory as a sign that their deity was more powerful than that of the defeated nation. As a result, the victor could boast in themselves and in their deity. At the same time, nations often did not interpret a defeat as a sign of weakness for their deity. Instead, they understood that they had angered the deity because of their lack of devotion. Such a defeat would cause them to reconsider their worship to determine if they were performing it correctly.

For sickness, ancient Near Eastern people often believed that sickness was a form of divine punishment. Often, they believed that some unseen spiritual force lay behind the sickness itself. Therefore, curing the sickness demonstrated that the one bringing about the healing held power over this type of spiritual force.

This chapter addresses both threats as it recounts part of Hezekiah's reign. Regarding war, the narrative confirms that Hezekiah acted properly in worshipping YHWH and that YHWH is truly God, unlike the gods of other nations. Regarding sickness, the narrative confirms that YHWH holds power over disease, since he heals Hezekiah after he humbles himself. Therefore, the account highlights that YHWH is truly God when he delivers Hezekiah in war and sickness.

Assyrian Invasion and Its Results (32:1–23)

When Assyria invades Judah, Hezekiah trusts YHWH, and YHWH demonstrates that he is the only true God.

32:1–23. The Chronicler's account of the Assyrian invasion accomplishes two primary purposes: (1) to confirm Hezekiah's trust in YHWH, and (2) to demonstrate that YHWH is the only true God. Hezekiah reveals his trust by directing the people to trust YHWH to fight the battle (32:7–8) even while they prepare for a coming siege on Jerusalem. Then, the Chronicler shows how the Assyrians question both Hezekiah's devotion to YHWH and YHWH's ability to rescue his people from them. The Chronicler records repeated insults against Hezekiah and YHWH. In their insults, they treat YHWH like any other god. However, Hezekiah proves his devotion to YHWH by crying out to him for help. Furthermore, YHWH proves that he is the only true God by annihilating the powerful Assyrian army. In the aftermath of this conflict, both YHWH and Hezekiah receive many gifts in honor of what they have done.

Judah's Preparation (2 Chron. 32:1–8)

32:1. Following Hezekiah's faithful deeds recorded in chapters 29–31, Sennacherib, the Assyrian king, invades Judah. This sequence seems out of place in Chronicles. Chronicles repeatedly illustrates how the principle of retribution works out among YHWH's people (for retribution, see "Covenant" sections in the introduction). Based on that principle, an invasion would serve as punishment for some type of disobedient behavior. However, in this case, the Chronicler qualifies that principle to show that even those who obey may face an invasion. The question at this point is how Hezekiah will respond.

Foreign Invasions

The Chronicler records other instances where an obedient king faces a foreign invasion: Asa (2 Chron. 14:9 [HB 8]) and Jehoshaphat (2 Chron. 20:1). Wicked kings who face invasion include Rehoboam (2 Chron. 12:2), Jehoram (2 Chron. 21:16–17), Ahaz (multiple attacks recorded in 2 Chron. 28), Manasseh (2 Chron. 33:11), and Judah's final kings (Jehoahaz, Jehoiakim, Jehoiachin, and Zedekiah; 2 Chron. 36).

32:2–6. The Chronicler describes how Hezekiah responds by recording what he does and what he says. Regarding his actions, first, Hezekiah consults with others to create a preparation plan for a coming siege on Jerusalem. The plan involves removing water sources outside the city so that the Assyrians will not have easy access to water. Not only do many people create the plan, but they also carry it out.

Importance of Supplies During Sieges

Sieging an ancient city was often a matter of supplies. The number of supplies, especially food and water, determined how long the invader could fight and how long the defender could hold out. The Assyrians even allude to this fact when they speak of Jerusalem dying from hunger and thirst (32:11). By limiting the water supply for the Assyrian invaders, the people of Jerusalem increased their chances of overcoming a siege.

Second, Hezekiah fortifies Jerusalem by strengthening the city wall and its defensive towers, adding another wall around Jerusalem, reinforcing the terraces around the city of David, and manufacturing many weapons and shields.

The Millo

The Hebrew word מִלּוֹא, most likely meaning "fill," refers to some type of structure associated with the older fortification within Jerusalem called the city of David (cf. 1 Chron. 11:7–8). The word may refer to several terraces built up around the old fortification (*HALOT* s.v. "מִלּוֹא" 587). In Hezekiah's case, improving the structure would help Jerusalem withstand a siege.

Third, Hezekiah organizes his fighting forces. Each of these activities fits the pattern for good kings elsewhere in Chronicles: good kings promote popular support (e.g., David, 1 Chron. 12:38 [HB 39]; 15:28; Solomon, 1 Chron. 29:23), fortify their territory (e.g., Asa, 2 Chron. 14:6–7; Jehoshaphat, 2 Chron. 17:2, 12–13), and organize their armies (e.g., Asa, 2 Chron. 14:8; Jehoshaphat, 2 Chron. 17:14–19; Uzziah, 2 Chron. 26:11–14). Therefore, even in these preparations, the Chronicler presents Hezekiah as following YHWH.

Hezekiah's Military Organization

This event differs somewhat from other accounts of military organization. Other accounts present lists of officers and positions for a standing army. In this case, Hezekiah's action appears ad hoc and probably includes more than the standing army; he likely assigns military officers over everyone who would defend the city, not just the regular army (see Japhet 1993, 984). Even so, the Chronicler still commends Hezekiah in this way, even if not in a stereotyped manner.

32:7–8. Next, the Chronicler turns to what Hezekiah says. As he gathers the people before him, he encourages them to remain strong and brave. Hezekiah's confidence stems from his accurate understanding of the situation. Even though the Assyrian king has a large army, they are just weak humans. In contrast, Jerusalem needs only one divine defender: YHWH their great God, who is able and willing to help them and fight for them. The people believe Hezekiah and support him.

Hezekiah's Speech in Old Testament Language

Hezekiah's speech resembles several other passages in the Hebrew Bible. The first half of 32:7 resembles Deuteronomy 31:6 to a large extent ("Be strong and courageous; don't be terrified or afraid of them. For it is the LORD your God who goes with you," CSB). It also resembles Jahaziel's response to Jehoshaphat in the face of invasion ("'Do not be afraid or discouraged because of this vast number, for the battle is not yours, but God's,'" 2 Chron. 20:15 CSB). The latter part of 32:7 resembles Elisha's words to his servant when surrounded by the Arameans ("Do not be afraid, for there are more with us than there are with them," 2 Kings 6:16 NRSV).

One of the recurring ironies in Chronicles is that even though the Chronicler records that good kings consistently fortify their territories, organize large armies, and produce large quantities of military equipment as a result of YHWH's blessing, these forces rarely fight. Instead, the Chronicler records that YHWH fights for them, not even mentioning the king's forces. This irony arises in this case also. Hezekiah trusts that YHWH will fight for Jerusalem, yet at the same time he enlists the people to prepare themselves for the battle. Apparently for the Chronicler, trusting YHWH to fight and taking steps to prepare for battle do not contradict one another.

TRANSLATION ANALYSIS:
The expression "arm of flesh" (זְרוֹעַ בָּשָׂר) describes the Assyrian king's source of power. In this context, זְרוֹעַ ("arm") carries the sense of power while בָּשָׂר ("flesh") refers to the mortal constitution of humans. The emphasis here is that Sennacherib's source of power is only mortal, whereas Judah's source of power is divine. For this reason, some translations (e.g., CSB, NET) render the phrase as "human strength." One finds this same contrast in Jeremiah 17:5.

Assyria's Intimidation and Insults (2 Chron. 32:9–19)

32:9–12. While Sennacherib and his full military force remain near Lachish, presumably carrying out his plan to take Judah's fortified cities, he sends messengers to intimidate the people of Jerusalem so that he might conquer the city more easily. Their intimidation begins by casting doubt on Hezekiah. They state that Hezekiah is leading the people on a path to their own destruction because he is confident that YHWH will save the city. However, as they see it, YHWH has no reason to support Hezekiah since Hezekiah has torn down sites throughout Judah dedicated to worshipping YHWH. In fact, he has limited Judah's sacrificial worship to the temple in Jerusalem. In this way, the messengers call into question Hezekiah's devotion to YHWH and the temple's exclusive role in worship.

TRANSLATION ANALYSIS:
Most translations (CSB, ESV, NIV, NKJV, NLT, NRSV) understand the messengers to be asking the object of the people's trust, understanding the phrase עַל־מָה as "upon what." However, this phrase occurs often with the sense of "why?" Interpreting the phrase in this way simplifies the syntax. The NET follows this approach, translating the question as "Why are you so confident that you remain in Jerusalem while it is under siege?"

32:13–16. After the messengers question why YHWH would be motivated to save Jerusalem, they doubt whether he is able to save Jerusalem. The messengers compare YHWH to the gods of the other nations that the Assyrians have conquered. They imply that other nations have trusted in their gods (as Judah trusts YHWH), but none of those gods ever saved the people. They doubt that YHWH is any different. They treat him as though he is simply another human-made idol (32:19).

At the same time, during these attacks on Hezekiah and YHWH, the messengers portray the Assyrian kings as the most powerful force in their known world. Everywhere they attack, they conquer, without exception.

Assyrian Kings as a Threat

The Chronicler often speaks of the kings of Assyria whenever he does not name a specific king (cf. 2 Chron. 30:6). This use is likely intentional, signifying that Assyria "is not one single king, but an existential threat to the world of the nations" (Japhet 1993, 988). In this context, the text presents these kings as Sennacherib and his predecessors (designated in Hebrew as אֲבוֹת "fathers").

32:17–19. The Assyrians continue their efforts to intimidate Jerusalem by using different tactics. Targeting the officials in the city, they resort to letters that mock YHWH as a powerless god who cannot stand against the Assyrian king's power. Targeting the rest of the citizens, they address the people standing upon the city walls in the people's language. Whomever they target, their message is the same: YHWH will not save Jerusalem.

Judah's Language

The Chronicler designates the language in which the messengers speak as יְהוּדִית. The designation associates the language specifically with Judah; therefore, it is probably best to understand it as the language characteristic of Judah. Biblical Hebrew does betray certain differences that most likely result from geography: a northern (Israelite) dialect and a southern (Judahite) dialect. Although it is possible that the term specifies the southern dialect of Hebrew, it is not necessary.

Even though the Chronicler lists various tactics and targets, in 32:16, through a subtle choice of language he clarifies the true nature of the conflict. He calls the Assyrian messengers Sennacherib's servants while he calls Hezekiah YHWH's servant. This comment shows that the battle is not between Sennacherib and Hezekiah. The real battle is between the Assyrian king (presented as the most powerful force in their world) and YHWH; the messengers and Hezekiah are simply servants.

Servant of YHWH

The Chronicler refers to only a small number of people as YHWH's servant (עֶבֶד): Moses, Israel, David, and Hezekiah. By using this designation, the Chronicler further confirms Hezekiah's important role as a good king, following David and Solomon.

In another subtle way, the Chronicler clarifies who YHWH is. He describes YHWH as God in four different ways in these verses: "the God" (הָאֱלֹהִים), "God of Israel," "God of Hezekiah," and "God of Jerusalem." In its current context, the first designation reveals YHWH as the true God, indicated in English with a capital letter ("God"). In this sense, YHWH embodies what the word אֱלֹהִים represents. In the conflict, the word keys in on YHWH's divine power, especially in contrast to Assyria's "fleshly strength" (32:7). By using this designation, the Chronicler anticipates the result of the conflict between the Assyrian king and YHWH. The latter designations specify YHWH's relation as God to someone else. Not only is YHWH the powerful God in an abstract sense, but he is also God in the specific sense of Israel, Hezekiah, and the city of Jerusalem. As Japhet states, "All these

[designations of God] should be understood in their very specific context: this major threat to the people of Israel, to king Hezekiah, and to the city of Jerusalem, will come to nothing because the Lord is very specifically their God" (1993, 989). Each designation clarifies that YHWH is able and willing to save Jerusalem from Assyria.

For the first readers, these verses would address several of their concerns. First, it raises the question whether Jerusalem is the exclusive site for cultic worship. In various ways, the postexilic people struggled to maintain and support the second temple in Jerusalem as the exclusive site for proper ritual worship. This narrative confirms that the exclusive role of Jerusalem's temple honors YHWH as God, even if it requires closing other sites dedicated to him. Second, it raises the question whether trusting YHWH is worth it. The messengers claim that Hezekiah's trust in YHWH will lead the people to destruction. Just as arrogant Assyria had experienced victory after victory, some arrogant, irreverent individuals during the postexilic period experienced tremendous success. Such success led others to claim that serving YHWH did no good (Mal. 3:14–15). This narrative affirms that trusting YHWH ultimately leads to success and deliverance; therefore, it encourages the postexilic community to remain faithful to YHWH.

YHWH's Deliverance (2 Chron. 32:20–23)

32:20–23. After a period of Assyrian intimidation, Hezekiah prays, along with the prophet Isaiah, crying out to YHWH in heaven. In response, YHWH dispatches an angel who annihilates the Assyrian army at various levels of command (skilled warriors, commanders, and high-ranking officers) so that Sennacherib is no longer able to wage war. Defeated, Sennacherib returns home humiliated. Ironically, Sennacherib dies where he should be most secure: in his own land, in the temple of his own god, by the hand of his own offspring. The arrogant, blaspheming, powerful, conquering king of Assyria is obviously no match for YHWH. YHWH demonstrates that he truly is God, much more powerful than any mortal king.

Connection to Exodus

The Hebrew Bible contains another passage in which YHWH's angel "annihilates" (*hiphil* כחד) Israel's enemies. Exodus 23:20–23 describes how YHWH will send an angel before Israel in order to destroy the peoples who live in the land that YHWH has promised Israel. Just as YHWH sent an angel to ensure that Israel would possess the land from their enemies, he sends an angel to protect this land from their enemies.

The first readers needed to know that YHWH would do more than just bring them into the land. They needed to know that he would also protect it, no matter the threat. Although Jerusalem would become an important city economically and politically, during the early parts of the postexilic period Jerusalem was a small, struggling, insignificant city. This passage encourages those readers to trust YHWH instead of another god or nation because YHWH is willing and able to protect the people and the city regardless of what opposition might arise.

Throughout these verses, the Chronicler describes Hezekiah following the pattern of good kings in Chronicles. Like Asa (2 Chron. 14:10) and Jehoshaphat (2 Chron. 20:9), Hezekiah cries out to YHWH for deliverance, and YHWH delivers. Like Solomon (1 Chron. 22:9, 18), Asa (2 Chron. 14:5–6), and Jehoshaphat (2 Chron. 20:30), Judah experiences peace all around. Like Solomon (e.g., 2 Chron. 9:24) and Jehoshaphat (2 Chron. 17:5), other nations bring gifts to Hezekiah.

TRANSLATION ANALYSIS:
Regarding the last clause of 32:22, the translations generally fall into two categories. Some translate the verb either as "guided" (NASB), "provided" (ESV), or "took care of" (NIV), while others translate the verb as "gave rest"

or "made secure." The two categories of translations arise because of a textual variant in the text's transmission. MT reads וַיְנַהֲלֵם, a *piel* impf. *waw*-consecutive from the root נהל. The root נהל occurs infrequently in the Hebrew Bible, about ten times. LXX and Vulgate seem to reflect another Hebrew reading: וַיָּנַח לָהֶם "he gave them rest." MT appears to be a misreading of a form originally similar to that reflected in LXX and Vulgate. LXX's reading makes better sense and coincides well with other passages in Chronicles that speak about YHWH's helping a good king (e.g., 1 Chron. 22:9, 18; 23:25; 2 Chron. 14:5, 6; 15:15; 20:30).

32:23. The Chronicler clearly presents Hezekiah as a good king. However, the unit closes with a statement that could foreshadow trouble to come: Hezekiah is exalted in the estimation of all the nations. The statement itself is positive; the other nations think highly of Hezekiah. However, in other passages in Chronicles, good kings who become wealthy, famous, and respected also become arrogant. The statement raises the question whether the pattern will apply in Hezekiah's case as well.

Hezekiah's Sickness and Its Results (32:24–31)

Because Hezekiah becomes arrogant, he falls sick; however, when he humbles himself, YHWH miraculously restores his well-being.

32:24–31. Up to this point, the Chronicler's portrait of Hezekiah is clearly positive, since Hezekiah stays true to YHWH through religious reforms (2 Chron. 29–31) and foreign invasion (2 Chron. 32:1–23). However, after the invasion, the portrait becomes more complex. Several questions arise concerning how the Chronicler intends to present the sequence of events. For instance, does Hezekiah's illness take place before Sennacherib's invasion, during it, or after it? Does Hezekiah become ill because he is arrogant, or does he become arrogant after he receives a sign from YHWH? The following interpretation of the sequence of events depends largely on the decision to see the events as part of a pattern within Chronicles rather than as a break from such a pattern. This pattern consists of the following elements: (1) YHWH blesses a king for his obedience, (2) the king becomes arrogant and (3) the king's arrogance angers YHWH.

A Pattern Among Kings

The sequence of Hezekiah's actions follows a pattern observed in 2 Chronicles: (1) YHWH blesses a king for his obedience, (2) the king becomes arrogant, and (3) the king's arrogance angers YHWH. The pattern emerges most clearly during the reign of Uzziah (2 Chron. 26). One feature of the pattern that connects Hezekiah to Uzziah is the Chronicler's expression to describe each king's arrogance: the king has a "high heart" (נבה לב). The expression describes only Hezekiah (32:25) and Uzziah (26:16). Even though Uzziah's reign constitutes the clearest example of the pattern in Chronicles, other kings exemplify the pattern using different terminology, such as Amaziah (2 Chron. 25), and perhaps Jehoshaphat (2 Chron. 17–18).

32:24. Regarding the timing of Hezekiah's illness, the text simply states that it occurs "in those days." "Those days" likely refer to the end of the previous verse, that is, the days in which the nations hold Hezekiah in high esteem. Therefore, the Chronicler seems to indicate that the illness takes place after YHWH defeats the Assyrian army.

32:24–26. Regarding the cause of Hezekiah's illness, based on the pattern presented earlier, one would expect Hezekiah's pride to lead to his illness. The challenge to this interpretation is the sequence of verbs themselves since the Chronicler speaks of Hezekiah's illness, prayer, and receiving a sign before his arrogance. However, the verbal sequence may indicate that 32:24

presents a general statement summarizing the events while the subsequent verses spell out in more detail the general statement (see also 2 Chron. 30:1–10a; Kalimi 2005b, 369–77).

If such is the case, then the Chronicler accomplishes two purposes by including this general statement at the beginning of the story. First, it is a compact statement illustrating the Chronicler's principle of retribution and YHWH's gracious response to repentance. Following Hezekiah's exaltation, he becomes ill, but responds properly by praying. In response to his prayer, YHWH graciously responds by giving a sign, apparently of Hezekiah's healing. Second, the statement highlights the role of the sign in the coming verses. Even though the Chronicler does not specify the nature of the sign, the word itself most often refers to a supernatural wonder. Based on Kings, the sign most likely refers to the shadow moving backward, confirming that Hezekiah would recover from his illness (2 Kings 20:8–11). Here, when YHWH gives the sign, he acts as the gracious, supernatural God that he is. Furthermore, the narrative refers to this sign in 2 Chronicles 32:31, where it prompts the Babylonians to visit Hezekiah.

Following the general statement, the narrative provides further details regarding Hezekiah's illness. It explains more explicitly that Hezekiah has become proud. The Chronicler identifies this pride as failing to respond to YHWH appropriately for what he has done on his behalf, that is, delivering him from the Assyrian king. The text does not specify how Hezekiah fails to respond properly, but it does report that Hezekiah's pride angers YHWH. YHWH's anger extends beyond Hezekiah to include Judah and Jerusalem. For this reason, it appears that Judah and Jerusalem share in the same type of pride: failing to honor YHWH for saving them from Sennacherib. In this way, this narrative follows the pattern laid out earlier: YHWH blesses the king, the king becomes proud, and the king's pride angers YHWH.

YHWH's Benefit to Hezekiah

The text speaks of the "benefit/kindness" (גְּמוּל) that YHWH provides for Hezekiah. The text is ambiguous regarding what this benefit entails; however, two options are most likely in the context: deliverance from Assyria or the sign of Hezekiah's healing. In the commentary, I have chosen the first alternative, primarily because it fits better with a pattern within Chronicles. However, the first option also helps explain why YHWH becomes angry with Judah and Jerusalem alongside Hezekiah, since the whole nation benefits from YHWH delivering Jerusalem from the Assyrians. If Hezekiah becomes proud after he receives YHWH's sign of his healing, then it is more difficult to explain how that pride applies to all the people.

At this point, the narrative takes a turn away from the pattern. Instead of an expected downfall, the people of Judah, represented by Hezekiah and the inhabitants of Jerusalem, humble themselves so that YHWH is no longer angry with them. This activity alludes back to 2 Chronicles 7:13–14 in which YHWH promises that if the land experiences various types of hardship and the people respond by humbling themselves, praying, seeking YHWH's face, and turning from their evil ways, then YHWH will listen, forgive their sin, and heal their land. This allusion is significant because it presents Hezekiah and his generation as model repentant sinners. In other words, not only does Hezekiah embody the characteristics of a righteous king, but he also embodies the characteristics of a repentant king.

32:27–29. As a result of the people humbling themselves, YHWH is no longer angry with them. He blesses Hezekiah with benefits typical of good kings: great wealth and honor (wealth and honor describe the reigns of David [1 Chron. 29:28], Solomon [2 Chron. 2:12; 9:22], and Jehoshaphat [2 Chron. 17:5; 18:1]). The Chronicler illustrates this wealth and honor in three ways.

First, he addresses Hezekiah's great wealth. In fact, Hezekiah receives so much wealth in precious materials, agricultural plant products, and livestock that he must build places to hold them all. The Chronicler explains that Hezekiah has so much wealth because YHWH gives it to him. Here again, YHWH acts as God, this time by rewarding Hezekiah with tremendous wealth.

32:30. Second, the Chronicler points to Hezekiah's successful city development plan. The Chronicler describes Hezekiah as the person who redirects waters around Jerusalem so that they provide water for the city itself. This activity reminds one of the efforts to remove water sources for the Assyrians to use during a siege (32:3–4), but it may not represent the same event (see Japhet 1993, 982). What the Chronicler describes here in detail may be a further development of the activity that preceded the Assyrian invasion. Still, the Chronicler presents this activity as an example of Hezekiah's other works; he states that Hezekiah succeeds in all his works. This comment connects the first part of Hezekiah's reign to this latter part, since the Chronicler has earlier said that Hezekiah succeeds in all his work regarding his devotion to YHWH in his worship practices (2 Chron. 31:21). Therefore, in matters related both to cultic and noncultic matters, Hezekiah succeeds because he trusts and obeys YHWH.

32:31. Third, the Chronicler alludes to an episode involving a group of Babylonian envoys. The envoys visit Hezekiah to learn more about the miraculous sign that has occurred, apparently referring to 32:24. Again, the Chronicler does not record what the sign entails; he is only concerned in relating it to Hezekiah. The Chronicler states that YHWH uses the visit to test Hezekiah. Although the Chronicler does not specify whether Hezekiah passes the test or not, the context provides clues that he does. The previous verse states that Hezekiah succeeds in all his works while the following verse characterizes Hezekiah's actions in general as his faithful deeds. Not only does Hezekiah appear as a good king, but YHWH again acts as God by examining Hezekiah's heart, something that only God does (see 1 Chron. 28:9; 29:17; 2 Chron. 6:30).

Hezekiah's Test

The Chronicler states that YHWH "left Hezekiah alone" (עזב) to test him. In this context, the verb does not carry connotations of abandonment. Rather, the Chronicler likely has in mind that for that moment, YHWH refrained from actively protecting and guiding Hezekiah. Job also endures a similar type of test to determine his devotion to YHWH.

Despite the positive picture that emerges after the people humble themselves, the Chronicler provides a hint that things may not stay this way. In 32:26, the Chronicler states that YHWH is not angry with Judah while Hezekiah lives. This time limit opens the door that YHWH may become angry with Judah in the future. In fact, the next generation of Judah, under Hezekiah's son Manasseh, turns away from YHWH and experiences his wrath (2 Chron. 33:1–11). Ultimately, YHWH pours out his wrath upon Judah and Jerusalem until it is destroyed (see 2 Chron. 36:16). During that time of destruction, Zedekiah does not humble himself (2 Chron. 36:12). In contrast, Hezekiah humbles himself and avoids such a fate.

As a people devastated by the Babylonian exile, the postexilic community could find both encouragement and warning in this passage. Just as Hezekiah's generation chooses its fate, whether YHWH's blessing because of their trust and obedience or his anger because of their pride, so also the first readers could choose their fate. Even though previous generations had forsaken YHWH and suffered judgment, this generation could obey and experience YHWH's blessing. On the other hand, for those who were returning to the land and experiencing a measure of restoration, the passage is a warning that past obedience does not cover up present sin. The community needed to remain focused on trusting YHWH. One can see the postexilic community's struggle to trust YHWH when rebuilding the temple (Hag. 1:2–8), maintaining its sanctity, and supporting its staff (see Neh. 13). In their context, this passage calls the first readers to humble themselves and to continue supporting the temple.

Conclusion of Hezekiah's Reign (32:32–33)

The Chronicler closes out Hezekiah's reign by confirming that he is a good king who has trusted and followed YHWH.

Following his custom, the Chronicler includes further sources for information regarding Hezekiah. In this case, he mentions the vision of the prophet Isaiah, the son of Amoz. Even though the title corresponds to the beginning of the book of Isaiah ("vision of Isaiah, son of Amoz," Isa. 1:1), this work does not correspond to the biblical book because it is included within the Book of the Kings of Judah and Israel. The reference still indicates that the Chronicler likely uses material found within Isaiah's book (for possible allusions to Isaiah, see Warhurst 2011, 165–75) and presents the prophet as a reliable interpreter and recorder of history (see "Genre" section in the introduction for the relation of prophets to history).

In the conclusion to Hezekiah's reign, the Chronicler reinforces the image of Hezekiah as a good king. He designates Hezekiah's activities as his faithful deeds, highlighting Hezekiah's devotion to YHWH as exhibited through his actions. The Chronicler also describes his burial in positive terms. Like other good kings, the people bury Hezekiah among his ancestors; however, Hezekiah seems to surpass other kings because he lies in a tomb distinguished from the others. Like the good kings Asa (2 Chron. 16:14) and Josiah (2 Chron. 35:24b–25), the people honor him in his death. This honor contrasts sharply with the wicked king Jehoram, whom no one honors or even regrets that he has died (2 Chron. 21:19–20).

THEOLOGICAL FOCUS

YHWH is the only true God, with the power to deliver those who trust him from any opposing force, whether spiritual or physical.

During the Chronicler's final chapter describing Hezekiah's reign, Hezekiah faces two threats pervasive in the ancient Near Eastern world: war and sickness. In both cases, God delivers Hezekiah. Just the fact that God delivers Hezekiah speaks to God's power and his kindness to act for the benefit of his people. However, the text emphasizes these points through its details. Regarding the Assyrian invasion, God proves that his power far exceeds that of the worthless god Sennacherib was worshipping. Not only does God defeat the Assyrians, but he does it with a far inferior military force. Furthermore, God needs only to dispatch an angel to strike Assyria once and the entire force is destroyed. In contrast, Sennacherib's god cannot even protect the king from his own sons within the god's temple. The presentation confirms that there is no force mighty enough to defeat God.

The New Testament shows how this power of God secures victory for God's people through Jesus Christ. As Paul says, "This power he exercised in Christ when he raised him from the dead and seated him at his right hand in the heavenly realms far above every rule and authority and power and dominion and every name that is named, not only in this age but also in the one to come" (Eph. 1:20–21 NET). Therefore, those who are in Christ, God's people, have no reason to fear the earthly and spiritual forces that oppose them. Their victory is secure.

The victory over the Assyrians also affirms how Hezekiah worships God. In 2 Chronicles 29–31, Hezekiah purges the land of illicit objects and removes illicit sites of worship. The Assyrians accuse Hezekiah of worshipping God improperly because of these activities. However,

God's victory over Assyria confirms that Hezekiah's measures are proper. Even though the Assyrians interpret Hezekiah's worship as too exclusive, God confirms that exclusive worship is proper for him because he alone is God.

During this chapter, the Chronicler presents a good, though not perfect, king who remains loyal to YHWH during military conflict and humbles himself when confronted with his pride. However, even greater than this good king is YHWH, the one and only true God. YHWH demonstrates that he is God through his power to overcome the mighty Assyrian army and through his mercy to restore a haughty king and his people. Furthermore, YHWH proves to be the victorious fighter, the miraculous healer, the abundant giver, and the one who discerns the inner thoughts of a person. The Chronicler surely intends for this account of YHWH's deeds to lead its readers to praise YHWH, the true God. For the first readers, he encourages them to praise him in the Jerusalem temple, for successive generations, in spirit and truth.

PREACHING AND TEACHING STRATEGIES

Exegetical and Theological Synthesis

For years Hezekiah had enjoyed God's power through the blessings that God had poured out upon him and Judah. In this chapter Hezekiah sees God's destructive power against the Assyrians, but he does not respond well. The Chronicler only says that his heart was proud. How could he be proud? Did he think that the vastly superior army just went away on their own initiative? Or worse, did he think that he had power over them? Somehow his response to God's powerful intervention was pride in himself. Apparently, the exaltation he received from people he kept for himself and did not pass on to God. If we had been there, how we would have responded? When we see God's power at work through us our response should be continued and total dependence upon him.

Preaching Idea

God's unending power requires our perpetual dependence.

Contemporary Connections

What does it mean?

We need to always depend upon God's great power. Pastors and teachers, when rightly relating to our Lord, depend on his power to work through them and even in spite of them. All believers should strive to trust that God is working through them to accomplish his good will. Their prayer should be that God would work powerfully to exalt himself in this world. This was exemplified by Hezekiah. When we have this total trust and dependence, we often get to see God's powerful hand. When he works and graciously lets us see his blessings, how will we respond?

Dr. James Eaves, former professor of evangelism at Southwestern Baptist Theological Seminary, was a naval historian during early 1950s. He was part of the team assigned to record a historical account of the testing of the hydrogen bomb in the remotest part of the Pacific Ocean. Though he was not specific as to which test he performed, he recounted what he remembered and what he could tell. The bomb was detonated on an uninhabited island, where structures had been erected and derelict ships were anchored nearby to measure the damage. At a safe distance from the center of the blast, cameras were set up both on ships and in aircraft.

After weeks of preparation, all was ready. The bomb exploded. The various teams waited until it was safe and then flew over the island to observe the destruction. As Dr. Eaves told it, the observation crews saw no sign of the prepositioned structures or ships. In fact, they couldn't find the island. James was stunned. What kind of power had they discovered and harnessed? He felt a sobering dread and fear that humans could invent such terrifying power. He thought surely those around him would respond with humility and sobriety at the catastrophic, destructive power that they had just witnessed. But when they returned to base and the initial reports were written, the commanding officers threw a beer bash: a celebration for a job well done. How do we respond when we see displays of great power?

Is it true?

The thirty-year-old carpenter didn't want to come to church, but his girlfriend kept pushing him, so to please her he went. Unexpectedly, he was so touched during the sermon that after the service he pulled the pastor aside. With watery eyes he asked if he and his girlfriend could talk with him. They went to a small prayer room. Tears began to fall as he confessed to pushing his girlfriend to live with him. The girlfriend, a believer in Christ, also shed tears of repentance. Right then, he confessed his trust in Christ and surrendered to him as savior. He vowed that they would stop living together until they got married. God's great power was displayed in their lives.

The pastor responded as Hezekiah did. He was so pleased that his sermon was so powerful and that his years of training and hard work had paid off. He thought, "I've got to write this up for the alumni magazine." Lord, protect us from such arrogance. Yet this can be our response when we see God's great power at work through our lives.

God graciously would not let Hezekiah exalt himself for long, and struck him with a grave illness. Once again God's power was displayed to Hezekiah in this very personal way. How would he respond? God's hand was again gracious in that Hezekiah realized that he had no power apart from what God let him experience. Thus, Hezekiah humbled himself, and the nation followed his example. God healed and blessed both the king and the nation. In the end, they responded correctly to God's power.

Now what?

We celebrate events in our lives such as winning a cross-country race, making the honor roll, rebuilding a 1957 Chevy, completing a master's degree, hiring the one hundredth employee in the business we built from scratch, taking the family picture with all the grandkids, or inviting guests to a fiftieth wedding anniversary. In these celebrations of great success, we must never forget that these things are God's work—through us, but these successes and grand events are still his work. Each celebratory event is a display of his great power. Our response to his power is to exalt him.

Notice that the text tells us that Hezekiah's heart was proud and that he did not respond as he should have. The Chronicler doesn't tell us how he responded. The point is that arrogance was in his heart, expressed or not. Perhaps on the surface we give God the credit, but internally we are quite pleased with ourselves more than being amazed at God's power.

My mother, a practicing nurse in the 1940s, told the story of the response of her hospital's staff to the powerful effects of penicillin. They had heard about this new wonder drug that had been in development for more than ten years and its use in World War II. But no one at her hospital had seen its effectiveness. A patient with a severe staph infection, who was at death's door, was treated with this new drug. By the next morning he had recovered. This man, who everyone thought would be dead by morning, was sitting up in bed having breakfast. The hospital staff had never seen anything like this. Everyone was so excited and found some kind of reason to go down that wing of the hospital, just to get a glimpse of the man who had experienced the power of this drug. When we see God's power at work, we must be sure that our hearts want to go "down that wing," just to see what he has done.

Creativity in Presentation

A narrative like this has a plot that is easy to follow: crisis, preparation to face it, the conflict escalates, and then an outside force solves the crisis. The story stands on its own with little explanation needed. The text can be emphasized in several ways. One is to tell the story rather than read it. This will require mastering the story and practicing good storytelling skills. Then from the text, highlight and explain key elements that lead to the main thrust of the passage. Another way is to explain these key elements first and then read the story.

While the plot is universal, the setting and characters of the ancient world are outside of our experience. The spectacular and almost storybook ending of Sennacherib's siege is so different than our daily lives, it makes it difficult to apply. How can we identify with a king? How could he possibly take any pride in this miracle? The preacher/teacher will need to create or tell stories of success that are closer to people's lives, perhaps from the list mentioned above. Paint verbal pictures of these more common stories of success along with the feelings and emotions associated with them. Highlight that our most natural response is to let the attention stay upon us. We need to respond to God's display of power with praise for him and continued obedience.

A scene from the Disney version of *The Chronicles of Narnia: Prince Caspian* illustrates relying upon God's power quite well. Toward the end of the film, the army of the usurping king comes up against the rightful kings of Narnia, who are weaker and outnumbered. The bad guys come to a bridge and are about to cross, meaning defeat for the good guys. At the end of the bridge Lucy, a mere child, stands unwaveringly. She pulls out a small dagger to stop the advance of the enemy. Everyone can't imagine what she is doing—until the powerful lion Aslan, the creator of Narnia, steps up behind her. When he roars in power, it changes everything.

Here is one possible structure for your sermon:

- Present the text
  - God's power over the Assyrians (32:1–23)
  - God's power over Hezekiah (32:24–33)
    - Hezekiah's pride and humble repentance (32:24–26)
    - God's blessing (32:27–33)
- Apply the text
  - God's unending power requires our perpetual dependence.

DISCUSSION QUESTIONS

1. What events have you celebrated?

2. What did those celebrations look like?

3. Why do we tend to take credit during these types of events?

4. How do the comments of others affect us?

5. How was God's power at work in the events leading up to the celebrations?

6. What are some ways to ensure that we respond correctly to God's power?

2 Chronicles 33:1–25

EXEGETICAL IDEA

The Lord forgave and restored King Manasseh, who directly violated God's covenant, when he humbled himself before the Lord, but did not forgive his son Amon when he did not humble himself.

THEOLOGICAL FOCUS

The Lord forgives and restores even the most disobedient when they humble themselves and repent, but judges those who arrogantly continue in sin.

PREACHING IDEA

God's grace isn't just amazing—it's astonishing.

PREACHING POINTERS

The author is proving to us that there is no evil so terrible that it is beyond God's surprising grace. It is easy to say that God forgives even the worst sin, but when faced with the extreme evil of Manasseh, do we really believe that God will forgive him? When greed overtakes one's life, when the spouse cheats again, when drugs are taken again and again, will God forgive them? When I find myself having blatantly disobeyed God in some harmful act or thought, will God forgive me? God included this story in his record to shout to us in terms we could not miss—that no matter how horrible my sin, he offers forgiveness and restoration. We can always humbly turn to him.

REIGNS OF MANASSEH AND AMON—THE DIFFERENCE HUMILITY CAN MAKE (33:1–25)

LITERARY STRUCTURE AND THEMES (33:1–25)

Following the reign of Hezekiah (2 Chron. 29–32), the Chronicler turns to Judah's next two kings: Manasseh and Amon. The passage follows several typical elements, including an introduction and conclusion to each king's reign. The narrative focuses on Manasseh. The main body recounts Manasseh's reign in two major sections: his period of wickedness and punishment (33:1–11), and his period of repentance and restoration (33:12–17). During Manasseh's period of wickedness and punishment, the text presents Manasseh as specifically violating the commandments of YHWH's law. The description has a geographical focus, as the point of view moves back and forth between Jerusalem and the rest of Judah. Manasseh's disobedience leads to his eventual exile into Babylon by the Assyrians. Manasseh's humble plea for YHWH's assistance changes the tone of the narrative and leads to his period of repentance and restoration. It forms the center of Manasseh's reign (Abadie 2003, 96). Manasseh acknowledges that YHWH is God and begins to act accordingly.

After the conclusion of Manasseh's reign, the Chronicler addresses Amon. Amon's reign is almost a footnote to Manasseh's reign, occupying only five verses in total (33:21–25). However, this short account contrasts Manasseh and Amon, focusing on the role of humility in either restoration (Manasseh) or final punishment (Amon).

- *Manasseh's Wickedness and Punishment (33:1–11)*
- *Manasseh's Repentance and Restoration (33:12–17)*
- *Conclusion of Manasseh's Reign (33:18–20)*
- *Amon's Reign (33:21–25)*

EXPOSITION (33:1–25)

Compared to much of the contemporary world, the people of the ancient Near East would appear to be quite obsessed with religious rituals. The religious beliefs in the region required regular offerings and sacrifices from the people. Kings and others would dedicate land and materials to construct temples and other sites so that the people could engage in rituals at those places. Members of the community became priests of various sorts at sites considered holy so that they could practice regular rituals. Although the OT distinguishes itself from other ancient Near Eastern religions in several ways, it still includes more rituals than are customary in contemporary practice. From a contemporary perspective, one could think that such ancient religion is only ritualistic, human work performed to gain divine favor. However, the accounts of Manasseh and Amon contradict such a characterization. Although both kings practice rituals forbidden by Mosaic law, their fates end up quite different. The difference is a result of their attitude and action toward God. After YHWH punishes Manasseh, Manasseh humbles himself before YHWH, and YHWH restores him. In contrast, Amon does not humble himself, so he suffers under YHWH's punishment.

Manasseh's Wickedness and Punishment (33:1–11)

Manasseh is the most wicked king of all Israel because he directly violates YHWH's law and defiles his temple.

33:1–2a. The Chronicler begins his description of Manasseh's reign by stating his age and length of his rule. Manasseh became king at an early age (twelve) and ruled fifty-five years. His reign endured longer than any other in Israel. Despite the length of his reign, the Chronicler states that Manasseh did what was evil from YHWH's point of view.

33:2b–9. The Chronicler outlines the reasons for his assessment of Manasseh's activity. He begins by connecting Manasseh's activity to the detestable practices of the nations who occupied the land of Israel before YHWH gave it to them. YHWH dispossessed these nations, in part, because of their detestable practices (Deut. 18:12). The Chronicler uses the language of the Pentateuch (see Lev. 18:24; 20:23; Deut. 18:9) to drive this point home. Second Chronicles 33:2 has a corresponding element in 33:9. These verses frame the description of Manasseh's wicked deeds with a general assessment relating his deeds to those of other nations (33:2, "he did evil . . . according to the detestable practices of the nations YHWH had driven out"; 33:9, "[doing] more evil than the nations YHWH had destroyed"). Within the frame formed by 33:2, 9, the Chronicler alternates between activities beyond the temple and activities within the temple. Second Chronicles 33:3, 6 describe what Manasseh does beyond the temple while 33:4–5, 7–8 describe what Manasseh does within the temple.

33:3. The Chronicler begins to enumerate Manasseh's specific offenses. The number and nature of the offenses portray Manasseh as the most wicked king of Judah. The first three offenses are related directly to the religious acts of his upright father Hezekiah. Hezekiah obeys the stipulations of Deuteronomy (Deut. 7:5; 12:3): He tears down the high places, cuts down the Asherah poles, and tears down the altars (2 Chron. 31:1). In contrast, Manasseh builds the high places, makes Asherah poles, and erects altars. By contrasting these two kings in this way, the Chronicler implies that Manasseh is at least as evil as Hezekiah is upright (cf. 2 Chron. 32:32).

Asherah

Second Chronicles 33:3 uses the word אֲשֵׁרוֹת. The term is difficult to translate because of its ambiguity. Each of the uses is most likely related to a goddess worshipped in the ANE. The singular אֲשֵׁרָה is most likely the name for this goddess. However, the word may be used in three other ways: (1) as a generic term referring to goddesses, (2) as an image representing either Asherah or another goddess, or (3) as a cultic object, most likely a wooden pole, related to the way in which the goddess was worshipped (*HALOT* s.v. "אֲשֵׁרָה" 99). Perhaps because of the ambiguity, some translations prefer to transliterate the word as *Asheroth* (ESV). Most translations understand the word to refer to cultic objects, especially in Chronicles (see Frevel 1991, 263–71). The differences in translation reflect which aspect of the cultic object they pick up in translation. Many pick up on the wooden material used for the object ("poles" CSB, NIV, NLT, NRSV; "wooden" NKJV; "groves" KJV). Some pick up the connection to Asherah (CSB, NIV, NLT) while others only the fact that the object is used in worship ("sacred" NRSV; "images" NKJV).

Manasseh goes beyond overturning the upright deeds of his father. He continues to disobey the laws of Deuteronomy by worshipping the host of heaven (Deut. 4:19; 17:3). Chronicles does not mention that anyone else besides Manasseh worships the host of heaven. Manasseh has forsaken YHWH in ways that surpass other kings. Like other kings he worships false gods/idols in false ways, but he also worships the sun, moon, and stars. Chronicles uses typical vocabulary to describe how Manasseh acts toward the heavenly bodies: he bows down (וַיִּשְׁתַּחוּ) and serves (וַיַּעֲבֹד) them (see comments on 2 Chron. 7:19–22). Chronicles does not give a specific location where Manasseh committed these evil deeds, but it states that he built and erected multiple sites and images. The implication is that Manasseh committed these violations throughout Judah, beyond Jerusalem and its temple.

Host of Heaven

The phrase "host of heaven" (צְבָא הַשָּׁמַיִם) requires some explanation to unpack conceptually. Its basic sense refers to those that occupy the heavens. In some contexts, these heavenly occupants are spiritual beings. Second Chronicles 18:18 describes the צְבָא הַשָּׁמַיִם as those who stand beside YHWH, apparently functioning like a divine council (cf. Ps. 82:1). In other contexts, the phrase clearly refers to visible objects in the sky. Deuteronomy 4:19 states that the Israelites will see the sun, moon, and the stars—that is, all the host of heaven (וְרָאִיתָ אֶת־הַשֶּׁמֶשׁ וְאֶת־הַיָּרֵחַ וְאֶת־הַכּוֹכָבִים כֹּל צְבָא הַשָּׁמַיִם). Although to the modern reader spiritual beings and visible lights in the sky may have little to do with each other, in many cultures, worshipping the sun, moon, and stars as gods is customary.

33:4–5, 7. The text already shows enough of Manasseh's disobedience to the law, especially as expressed in Deuteronomy (Deut. 4:19; 7:5; 12:3; 17:3), to condemn him, but his evil continues further. He brings his corrupt worship into the temple, the house of God itself. He builds altars that are dedicated to other deities, including altars set up for the worship of the sun, moon, and stars. He also erects an idolatrous image (פֶּסֶל הַסֶּמֶל). Although the text does not specify precisely what the image represents, given the parallel passage in Kings (2 Kings 21:7) it likely represents a female deity thought to accompany YHWH. Since the idol intends to represent the companion to YHWH so that the people may make requests from it (Dohmen 1984, 263–66), its presence threatens YHWH's exclusive worship in the temple, thereby provoking him to jealousy (see "image" סֶמֶל in Ezek. 8:5). The language describing Manasseh's evil activity emphasizes the plurality of both the objects and means of Manasseh's worship. Manasseh does not worship the invisible YHWH and him alone; rather, he worships various foreign images that are human-made objects.

33:6. Manasseh disobeys other laws as well. In Deuteronomy 18:10–11, Moses warns the people not to pass their children through fire (see sidebar "Passing Children Through Fire") or to practice various divining and magical arts. Manasseh does both. By violating these stipulations nearly word for word, Manasseh provokes YHWH's anger. Manasseh's false worship still correlates to the worship of Ahaz, even though Chronicles does not make an explicit connection between Manasseh and Ahaz (as 2 Kings 21:3 does). Ahaz makes images for the Baals (2 Chron. 28:2), makes his sons pass through fire (2 Chron. 28:3), and sacrifices at the high places (2 Chron. 28:4). However, Manasseh's disobedience exceeds even that of Ahaz. He violates more laws and defiles the temple itself by building altars and setting up an idol within it.

Manasseh vs. Deuteronomy's Law

Expression in 2 Chronicles 33:6	Expression in Deuteronomy 18:10–11
וְהוּא הֶעֱבִיר אֶת־בָּנָיו בָּאֵשׁ בְּגֵי בֶן־הִנֹּם וְעוֹנֵן וְנִחֵשׁ וְכִשֵּׁף וְעָשָׂה אוֹב וְיִדְּעוֹנִי	לֹא־יִמָּצֵא בְךָ מַעֲבִיר בְּנוֹ־וּבִתּוֹ בָּאֵשׁ קֹסֵם קְסָמִים מְעוֹנֵן וּמְנַחֵשׁ וּמְכַשֵּׁף ¹¹וְחֹבֵר חָבֶר וְשֹׁאֵל אוֹב וְיִדְּעֹנִי וְדֹרֵשׁ אֶל־הַמֵּתִים
He passed his sons through fire in the Valley of Ben-Hinnom, interpreted omens, practiced divination and sorcery, and dealt with necromancers and familiar spirits.	Let there not be found among you one who passes his son or daughter through fire, tells fortunes, interprets omens, practices divination and sorcery, consults a necromancer or familiar spirit, or inquires the dead.
--	קֹסֵם קְסָמִים
וְעוֹנֵן	מְעוֹנֵן
וְנִחֵשׁ	וּמְנַחֵשׁ
וְכִשֵּׁף	וּמְכַשֵּׁף
וְעָשָׂה אוֹב וְיִדְּעוֹנִי	וְשֹׁאֵל אוֹב וְיִדְּעֹנִי
--	וְחֹבֵר חָבֶר
--	וְדֹרֵשׁ אֶל־הַמֵּתִים

Although there are some differences between the two texts, the texts share enough similarity to suggest that the Chronicler is intentionally alluding to Deuteronomy.

33:8. The text heightens the seriousness of Manasseh's activity by drawing on the promises of Deuteronomy (Deut. 12:5, 11) that YHWH would choose a place for his name (not another's name, given the context) to dwell. The temple was built for his name because he chose Jerusalem as the place for it to dwell (2 Chron. 6:6; 7:16). Twice, Chronicles mentions that Manasseh violates the house of God: first by building altars, and then by erecting the idolatrous image within it. When Chronicles repeats the point, it heightens the seriousness of the offense. Furthermore, the second mention draws in the seriousness of its consequences because YHWH promises that with the temple he will not "remove the feet of Israel again from the land that he appointed for their fathers, only if they are careful to do everything [he] commanded them." What is at stake with the temple is keeping Israel in the land. Corrupting the temple raises the possibility of serious punishment: exile from the land.

33:9. The Chronicler summarizes Manasseh's activity with an eye to exile. After the Chronicler states that Manasseh's wickedness influences the people to sin as well, he mentions the nations that YHWH has driven out before Israel entered the land. In fact, both assessments of Manasseh's activity (33:2, 9), which frame the enumeration of his offenses, mention these nations. By connecting Manasseh's activity with the practices of these nations, the Chronicler raises a question for the reader: Since YHWH has removed those nations from the land because of their detestable practices, will he also remove all Israel from the land? Exile casts a long shadow over Manasseh's reign.

33:10. Throughout Chronicles, the Chronicler points out YHWH's typical way of dealing with his people. If his people sin, YHWH sends a prophet (or some type of prophetic figure) to warn them to stop. If his people ignore the warning, God punishes them through a disaster, often a military defeat (e.g., Rehoboam, 2 Chron. 12:1–5; Amaziah, 2 Chron. 25:14–24; see "Covenant" section in the introduction). YHWH responds to Manasseh's sins according to this pattern, although with some variation. Chronicles states only that YHWH speaks to them; it does not specify the means. Chronicles likely implies that prophets are the means, since in Chronicles YHWH typically sends prophets to give warnings, and the conclusion to Manasseh's reign refers to the words of prophetic figures ("seers" הַחֹזִים in 2 Chron. 33:18) who speak to Manasseh. Therefore, most likely YHWH speaks by his prophets to warn Manasseh and the people; however, the Chronicler's shorthand expression for prophetic warning is immediate and direct (the expression וַיְדַבֵּר יהוה אֶל "YHWH spoke to" almost always occurs with Moses as its object; Ben Zvi 2013, 131). YHWH speaks to them, but they do not listen to him. Unlike other sinners described in Chronicles, who disobey YHWH's commandments in an indirect way or defile worship out there on the high places or disregard YHWH's messenger, Manasseh stands out as a king who disobeys, dishonors, and disregards YHWH "to his face." Furthermore, Manasseh leads all Israel to engage in this disobedience with him.

33:11. As a result of Manasseh's disobedience, YHWH punishes him by bringing leaders of Assyria's army to capture him with hooks (חֹחִים) and take him to Babylon in shackles (נְחֻשְׁתַּיִם). Even though the account lacks several details, it includes the means of his bondage. The first term (חֹחַ) and a related term (חָח) refer to a hook or barb, usually placed in the nose or mouth. These terms for a hook or barb occur in contexts that describe defeat and humiliation (e.g., 2 Kings 19:28 // Isa. 37:29; Ezek. 19:4, 9; 29:4; 38:4). One particularly clear example of its use in this way is 2 Kings 19:28 // Isaiah 37:29, in which YHWH proclaims that he will put a hook in Sennacherib's nose and return him from where he came because he has spoken arrogantly against YHWH. Including this term to describe how Assyria binds Manasseh highlights the nature of YHWH's judgment toward him. The second term that describes how Assyria binds Manasseh also depicts defeat and humiliation; however, a further reason explains its occurrence. The Chronicler's description of Manasseh's capture draws closely on 2 Chronicles 36:6, almost quoting the latter half of the verse: "He [Nebuchanezzar, King of Babylon] bound him [Jehoiakim] in shackles to bring him to Babylon." Jehoiakim's capture represents an early stage in the Babylonian exile.

Manasseh's Punishment

YHWH punishes Manasseh by sending military leaders from Assyria to bind Manasseh in chains and exile him to Babylon. Manasseh's punishment resembles other texts in Chronicles. First Chronicles 5:25–26 similarly describes how Assyria rose up against the tribes of Reuben and Gad and the half-tribe of Manasseh to take them into exile as punishment for their unfaithfulness (מעל) toward YHWH. As mentioned earlier, this passage also nearly quotes 2 Chronicles 36:6, a passage that describes Jehoiakim's capture in shackles and exile to Babylon. By drawing on these two passages (1 Chron. 5:25–26; 2 Chron. 36:6), the Chronicler shows that YHWH's character remains consistent because Manasseh's punishment is in line with YHWH's activity from the beginning of Chronicles to its end.

When Chronicles describes how Assyria comes against Judah, it passes over the details regarding all the people and focuses on Manasseh: he experiences capture and exile. At the same time, the text states that Assyria attacks all the people. It appears that the Chronicler is balancing two different purposes. First, he is concerned to show that Manasseh's direct disobedience, especially in defiling the temple, is punished directly by YHWH. Second, he is concerned to show how Manasseh serves as a model for the entire people. As mentioned earlier, exile hangs over this first part of Manasseh's account. However, the warning of exile is not directed to the individual king alone. As 33:8 points out, exile represents a possible future reality for the nation. When the Chronicler describes Manasseh's disobedience and punishment, he weaves these two aspects (individual and national) together in a sophisticated way. At the individual level, Manasseh suffers for his disobedience in an immediate, direct way. At the national level, Manasseh serves as a model for the entire people whose disobedience will lead them as a nation into exile.

Manasseh's Repentance and Restoration (33:12–17)
After Manasseh humbles himself and prays to YHWH, YHWH restores Manasseh to his throne, as Manasseh recognizes that YHWH is the only true God and worships him alone.

33:12–13a. Here, the course of Manasseh's life takes a surprising, dramatic turn. From the moment that Chronicles states that Manasseh has done evil up to this point, the narrative follows a predictable course: the enumeration of Manasseh's and Judah's sins, YHWH's warning, disregard for the warning, and then YHWH's judgment. When King Ahaz commits

wicked deeds and disregards YHWH's warning, YHWH punishes him. As mentioned earlier, Manasseh commits the same wicked deeds that Ahaz commits, and a bit more. However, in the time of Ahaz's trouble (וּבְעֵת הָצֵר לֹו) brought on by YHWH's judgment, Ahaz determines to commit even more wickedness (2 Chron. 28:22); but in the time of Manasseh's trouble (וּכְהָצֵר לֹו) brought on by YHWH's judgment, Manasseh humbly turns to YHWH. The contrast is hard to miss.

Chronicles describes when Manasseh turns to YHWH by using three expressions: he entreats YHWH (*piel* חלה), humbles himself greatly (*niphal* כנע), and prays (*hithpael* פלל). These expressions do not represent three distinct actions; rather, they represent different aspects of the same activity. Manasseh prays (the means of his activity) to entreat YHWH (the purpose of his activity), and in so doing humbles himself (the attitude of his activity). The text emphasizes his attitude: it states that he humbles himself sincerely (מְאֹד). The centerpiece of Manasseh's turning to YHWH is his humbling himself.

33:13b. Because Manasseh humbles himself, YHWH responds by restoring him to his rule in Jerusalem. The Chronicler makes clear that YHWH responds by using two expressions with quite similar meanings: YHWH is moved by Manasseh's plea for mercy (וַיֵּעָתֵר לֹו), and he listens to Manasseh's supplication for favor (וַיִּשְׁמַע תְּחִנָּתֹו). As a result, YHWH restores Manasseh to his rule in Jerusalem. Chronicles includes two elements when it describes Manasseh's restoration: Jerusalem and his kingdom. These two elements draw attention to significant themes in Chronicles: Jerusalem (where YHWH's name dwells in the temple), the Davidic king, and the relationship between them. How these themes are developed in this context will be discussed below.

When YHWH restores Manasseh, he knows that YHWH is God. This confession raises the question of what the Chronicler intends by using הָאֱלֹהִים ("the God" or just "God"). The word אֱלֹהִים (God or gods) carries the sense of what is divine—that is, something or someone that is superhuman, with power to control matters that humans cannot. The distinctive use of the article indicates that YHWH is אֱלֹהִים unlike all other אֱלֹהִים. In other words, Manasseh realizes that only YHWH embodies all that the word אֱלֹהִים is intended to convey. Since the verb וַיֵּדַע ("he recognized") occurs in the wayyiqtol tense, it implies that Manasseh realizes that YHWH is God because of YHWH's restoring him. Even though YHWH sent prophets to warn him and then punishes him by using Assyria to exile him, he does not recognize YHWH as God until YHWH saves him from his punishment. Because YHWH hears Manasseh and restores him, he "is the only one that fits the description of what 'God' is, and ought to be able to do" (De Vries 1989, 398). In this case the proof that YHWH is the God, unlike other so-called gods, is not that he speaks or judges but that he listens and restores. Chronicles emphasizes this side of God's activity as a message of hope for those first readers whose ancestors experienced exile as YHWH's judgment.

Although unexpected, Manasseh's surprising turn to YHWH and its results make sense in the context of Chronicles. Second Chronicles 7:13–14 describes what Israel should do in times of distress (drought, locust plague, pestilence) for YHWH to restore them and their land. It states that the people should humble themselves (niphal כנע), pray (hithpael פלל), seek YHWH's face (piel בקש), and turn from their wicked ways (qal שוב). Although the language does not correspond precisely, Chronicles shows how Manasseh does this activity: He entreats YHWH's face (piel חלה), he humbles himself (niphal כנע), and he prays (hithpael פלל). Each element of 2 Chronicles 7:14 has a counterpart in Manasseh's actions (2 Chron. 33:12–13) except for one: turn from wicked ways (qal שוב). However, even this element has a

less obvious counterpart because the Chronicler uses a different form of the same term (hiphil שוב) to describe YHWH's returning Manasseh to his throne. Manasseh's turning to YHWH is recounted later (33:15–16).

33:14. YHWH's response to Manasseh also makes sense within Chronicles. Second Chronicles 7:14 states that after Israel turns to YHWH, he will hear, forgive, and heal their land. Even though not all the same expressions occur in 2 Chronicles 33, YHWH hears and returns Manasseh to his reign in Jerusalem. After Manasseh returns to Jerusalem, he builds further fortifications around Jerusalem and allocates military forces for the fortified cities throughout Judah. In several passages Chronicles describes how a king builds up the military defenses of Jerusalem and Judah. Each of these passages occurs in contexts that demonstrate YHWH's favor upon the king. Manasseh's military preparations are a concrete description of YHWH's restoring Manasseh; they are a concrete realization of YHWH's commitment to Israel as expressed in 2 Chronicles 7:14.

33:15–17. Now the Chronicler shows how Manasseh turns from his wicked ways (see 2 Chron. 7:14). Rather than simply stating that Manasseh turns from them, the Chronicler describes Manasseh's concrete actions: (1) he destroys the foreign idols, the image, and the altars in the temple; (2) he restores worship to YHWH; and (3) he commands all of Israel to worship YHWH. These verses contain several parallels to the previous section recording Manasseh's wickedness. The evil deeds that Manasseh has committed, he reverses, at least in part. The account emphasizes what he does in the temple. He destroys the altars he built for other gods (and presumably for the host of heaven). He also destroys the (female) image he set up as a companion with YHWH. After he destroys them, he throws them out of Jerusalem, presumably to remove the defilement from the temple area (see Lev. 14:40).

Although Manasseh turns from his wicked ways by destroying the implements of false worship in Jerusalem and restoring proper worship in the temple, he does not complete the work for all Judah. Beyond Jerusalem, Chronicles does not record that Manasseh destroys anything. Instead, it shows that Manasseh commands the people to worship YHWH instead of the Baals. Beyond the temple, Manasseh does not destroy the high places, the sacred poles, or idols that he earlier rebuilt, even though he commands the people to worship YHWH. The task of removing false worship from all Judah is left for another to complete.

Conclusion of Manasseh's Reign (33:18–20)

33:18–19. As he does for other kings, the Chronicler finishes describing Manasseh with a concluding notice consisting of an assessment of Manasseh's activity, references to other sources for information, and a burial notice. Even though he follows his typical formula, he highlights points important for the way he portrays Manasseh. The concluding notice summarizes the reign of Manasseh in reverse order from its presentation except that it begins by mentioning Manasseh's prayer, not his return, and then restarts in 33:19, again mentioning Manasseh's prayer and YHWH's hearing him. If one leaves out the restart at the beginning of 33:19, the following sequence occurs: (1) prayer, (2) words of the prophets, (3) his sin, (4) his faithlessness, (5) the high places he built, and (6) the sacred poles and idols he set up. His activity is then brought around to the front again with the brief notice "before he humbled himself" (לִפְנֵי הִכָּנְעֹו).

TRANSLATION ANALYSIS:
In MT, the concluding notice includes two source citations for further information: the affairs of Israel's kings (דִּבְרֵי מַלְכֵי יִשְׂרָאֵל), and the words of Hozai (חֹוזָי). Both source citations

contain textual variants. The first citation reads "words of his prayer" (λόγων προσευχῆς αὐτοῦ) in LXX; that is, the phrase "kings of Israel" and the following conjunction at the start of 33:19 are not included in LXX. Likely, MT is the better reading since the phrase in LXX may be explained as a line that dropped out accidentally (Allen 1974, 2:55). The second citation reads "words of the seers" (τῶν λόγων τῶν ὁρώντων) in LXX and one Hebrew manuscript. The one Hebrew manuscript, which reads חוזים, raises doubts regarding the validity of the MT reading, especially since MT includes a name that is not mentioned anywhere else in the Old Testament and is so similar to a title used commonly in source citations (seer; cf. 1 Chron. 29:29; 2 Chron. 9:29; 12:15; 29:30 MT). At the same time, the reading of חוזים is problematic because one would expect the word to be definite (as it is in LXX), thus החוזים. The MT reading likely develops when the ו of the original reading חֹוזָיו drops out through haplography, since the following word (וישכב) also begins with a ו. LXX transmits the text by relating it to 33:18, in which the phrase "words the seers" (λόγοι τῶν ὁρώντων) already occurred. If חֹוזָיו is the original reading, then the antecedent for the third-person masculine singular suffix is most likely "Manasseh" and would therefore refer back to 33:18, that is, the seers who addressed Manasseh.

The concluding notice draws attention to Manasseh's wickedness, even though the first and last word regarding Manasseh's activity is his prayer and humility. Both Manasseh's wickedness and his prayer are important for the Chronicler to point out as he transitions from Manasseh's reign to Amon's. By drawing out Manasseh's wickedness, he can compare Manasseh and Amon to one another ("Amon did evil in the sight of YHWH just as his father Manasseh did," 33:22). By mentioning Manasseh's prayer and humility, he can contrast Manasseh and Amon to one another

("Amon did not humble himself before YHWH like Manasseh his father did," 33:23).

The Chronicler closes the account of Manasseh with a standard idiom for death, "Manasseh rested with his fathers" (Glatt-Gilad 2001, 203; Halpern and Vanderhooft 1991, 183–90; R. Klein 2012, 149), and the mention of his burial in his house. The Chronicler does not record any other king's burial site as his house. Even though some scholars have emphasized the location and manner of burial as an indication of the Chronicler's assessment of a king, such does not appear to be the case (See Schweitzer 2007, 119–25). The mention of Manasseh's burial "in his house" (בֵּיתוֹ) likely functions to compare and contrast Manasseh further with his son Amon. Conspirators kill a young Amon "in his house" (בְּבֵיתוֹ) while an old Manasseh rests in his burial site "in his house" (בֵּיתוֹ).

Amon's Reign (33:21–25)

33:21–25. The brief account of Amon's reign raises several points of comparison and contrast between Amon and his father Manasseh. Some of these points are implicit. For instance, following Manasseh's long reign, his son Amon reigns only for a short time, two years. Also, the manner of their deaths is quite different. Whereas Manasseh "rests" with his fathers and is buried in his house, Amon is violently assassinated in his house and no burial is even mentioned.

33:22. Chronicles explicitly compares Amon and Manasseh by stating that Amon does evil in YHWH's sight just as his father had done. The evil that it identifies is the worship of all the idols (הַפְּסִילִים) that Manasseh has made. The Chronicler's expression ties together the entire chapter and helps position these kings in relation to others. Earlier, in nearest proximity it connects to the summary of Manasseh's reign (33:19). Because it refers to Manasseh's making the idols, it also connects

to the beginning of Manasseh's reign in which he constructed altars and idols outside of Jerusalem (33:3).

33:23. Chronicles also explicitly contrasts the two kings. The focus of the contrast is humility before YHWH. As seen previously, Chronicles emphasizes that Manasseh humbled himself before YHWH. In contrast, Amon does not. Instead, he continues in wickedness.

> **Continuing in Wickedness—Multiplying Guilt**
> A wide range of translations render the Hebrew expression הִרְבָּה אַשְׁמָה. A proper translation requires a careful balance of two aspects. On the one hand, the translation should reveal the distinct connotation of אַשְׁמָה in relation to other words pertaining to misconduct (e.g., עָוֹן, חַטָּאת). Translating the word as "guilt" addresses this concern well. On the other hand, the translation should correspond to English usage. In a legal sense, the word "guilt" in English is not a term of degree: one is either guilty or not guilty. For this reason, translating הִרְבָּה אַשְׁמָה as "multiplying or increasing guilt" is inadequate. Amon does not become guiltier of one offense; rather, the phrase in this context means that he commits additional acts that make him guilty of a great number of offenses.

33:24–25. Amon dies at the hands of his own servants. Chronicles does not specify why his servants conspire against him. Although one may wonder what political or economic reasons may have prompted the servants to conspire, the true reason Amon dies is that he commits evil deeds by worshipping idols and not humbling himself before YHWH. As in the similar cases of Joash (2 Chron. 24:25) and Amaziah (2 Chron. 25:27), a king's wicked actions lead to the punishment of conspiracy. The account of Amon closes out with the notice that the people of the land kill the conspirators and hand over the throne to Josiah.

THEOLOGICAL FOCUS

The Lord forgives and restores even the most disobedient when they humble themselves and repent, but judges those who arrogantly continue in sin.

This passage presents a dramatic picture of Manasseh's radical transformation from Judah's worst king to follower and reformer for the God of Israel. This transformation takes place when Manasseh humbles himself. His act of humbling himself is not some general statement that Manasseh boasts less or the like; it communicates his act of repentance, abandoning his own resources, confessing his own wrongdoing, and depending on God to restore him. Jesus illustrates the same type of repentance when he tells the parable of a boasting Pharisee and humble tax collector. The proud Pharisee thanks God that he is not a sinner like others. The humble tax collector cries out for God's mercy. The Pharisee is not justified before God, but the tax collector is (Luke 18:9–14). In fact, Jesus calls for this type of repentance during his entire ministry (Matt. 4:17; Mark 1:15; Luke 5:32).

Paul's preaching and ministry also calls for this same type of repentance (Acts 20:21; 26:20). God calls Paul to this ministry in part because

Paul, the worst sinner as a blasphemer, persecutor, and insolent person, experiences the mercy of God when he repents (1 Tim. 1:13–15). Manasseh, Paul, and the teaching of Jesus illustrate that God forgives and restores even the most disobedient when they humble themselves and repent, but he judges those who continue in their arrogance.

This passage points to another theological point as well. As one examines how Chronicles describes Manasseh's reign, one can hardly overlook the similarities between Manasseh and Israel as a whole. Several similarities have already been pointed out above: (1) like Israel, Manasseh directly disobeys God by violating the law of Moses, (2) like Israel, Assyria attacks Manasseh, and (3) like Israel, Manasseh is exiled to Babylon in chains. Furthermore, Chronicles connects Manasseh's restoration to 2 Chronicles 7:14, a passage that deals with all Israel. One may wonder why the Chronicler connects 2 Chronicles 7:14 with the life of an individual Judahite king.

Manasseh serves as an individual modeling Israel's corporate fate, or at least their possible fate, if they turn to God as Manasseh does. The Chronicler's portrayal of Manasseh serves as an example on two levels: individual and corporate. At the individual level, he represents hope that God can restore the worst of sinners who humbly turns to God. Manasseh models how that individual restoration includes realizing that YHWH is God and experiencing his favor as illustrated through military fortification. At the corporate level, Manasseh represents hope that God can restore a nation after it humbly turns to God. This restoration also includes a realization that YHWH is God and experiencing God's favor; however, the fact that Manasseh returns to his kingdom in Jerusalem takes on a greater significance at the corporate level.

Manasseh's kingdom in Jerusalem emphasizes the two institutions that dominate the textual landscape of Chronicles: Davidic monarchy and Jerusalem temple. Manasseh's actions following his return from exile focus on those two aspects: his military actions are a picture of strengthening his power as king, and his religious reforms involve the Jerusalem temple. In other words, Manasseh's restoration points to Israel's return from exile and reestablishment of the Davidic monarchy and Jerusalem temple. At the same time, Chronicles shows how Manasseh does not complete the pattern fully because, even though he turns from his wicked ways, he does not finish the process. He is a model of repentance and restoration, just not a perfect one. As a result, the text points beyond Manasseh to a future reality in which a Davidic king will rule over his people, leading them in proper worship. God's people will be like Manasseh himself, those who humble themselves and repent before God. In contrast, those who are stubborn and unrepentant store up wrath for themselves until the day of God's judgment (Rom. 2:5). On that day, God will fulfill all his promises, restore all that has been broken, and carry out justice fully and finally.

PREACHING AND TEACHING STRATEGIES

Exegetical and Theological Synthesis

God's story of Manasseh and Amon shows us that there is no evil so horrible that it is beyond God's astonishing grace of forgiveness and restoration. Up to this point in Chronicles the disobedient kings, such as Ahaz, were warned by God and judged. So, as Manasseh's extreme evil unfolds, we anticipate and likely even desire that same end of judgment. A surprising turn occurs when Manasseh humbles himself and pleads with YHWH for mercy. Our surprise turns to astonishment and even anger when God forgives and even restores him. We want Manasseh to be punished, not forgiven. It just doesn't seem right that Manasseh's horrendous sins could be forgiven.

But God's surprising forgiveness and restoration of Manasseh is not void of human responsibility. The author blatantly points out that Amon, Manasseh's son, was just as evil as his father, if not more. We wonder if Amon too will turn to God at the last minute and be forgiven and restored as his father was. In stark contrast to Manasseh, Amon does not humble himself. Rather than being restored in his house as Manasseh was, Amon is killed in his house. The astonishing grace of God comes to those who in humility turn to God.

Preaching Idea

God's grace isn't just amazing—it's astonishing.

Contemporary Connections

What does it mean?

The story surfaces the same emotions that we feel when a huge 4x4 truck speeds by and then cuts in front of us. As we watch him whip from lane to lane, barely missing the bumper of a minivan, we see a patrol car. Our astonishment increases when the officer seems to ignore the blatant and reckless breaking of the law. We want this guy to get caught and feel deeply that it is not right that he gets away. We feel the same way about Manasseh. We want to see the very evil king punished.

The author is proving to us that there is no evil so astonishing that it is beyond God's surprising grace. It is easy to say that God forgives even the worst sin, but when faced with the extreme evil of Manasseh, do we really believe that God will forgive him?

At some level, all Christians have some understanding of God's grace. The challenge of this passage is to verify and deepen that belief. Grace is familiar to us, but when the depth of grace that this passage teaches is more firmly grasped, that depth should make grace be more than amazing. Grace is astonishing.

Many of those to whom we preach love to sing the old hymn "Amazing Grace." The news clips of noteworthy funerals seem to always show bagpipes playing this hymn. Popular singers each seem to have their own version of it, and even the purely secular public television network graces us with a documentary of its history. In our culture of tolerance and acceptance, the word "grace" is very familiar. Our familiarity with so-called grace inoculates us from its true meaning. The grace part of this story will strike a favorable, though somewhat unbelievable, chord with our congregation. The great difficulty will be speaking about why grace is necessary: our sin. The burden for the teacher/preacher of this passage is to help the congregation believe that their sin is just as deserving of judgment as Manasseh's and Amon's sin. This passage takes grace beyond amazement to astonishment. It takes a familiar word and makes it almost unbelievable.

Is it true?

In order for us to appreciate the astonishing grace of God, we must first grasp how far we miss God's standard. We like to think that we are not so bad, but Manasseh and Amon serve as models of what each of us is capable of doing. Most of us are not outwardly displaying terrible evil, but inwardly we all have hearts that are desperately wicked. When we honestly view our sinfulness, God's grace becomes astonishing.

It is not that we have committed the same exact sins that Manasseh committed, but that we have hearts that could commit terrible sins. The same root of Manasseh's sin grows in us. We may not be as bad as we can be, but we are as bad-off as we can be. God gives us a picture of Manasseh so that we can more clearly see ourselves.

Since our culture has minimized sin, we must take the time to explain and demonstrate that we do sin. Tim Keller, who preached to the cutting edge of our culture in New York City, suggested in his lectures on preaching that to communicate sin to our culture, we should focus on the unfilled potential in each of us. Why haven't we lived up to all that we could be? This is not to minimize that we are totally

depraved, but that same depravity is very clever at sidestepping guilt. Focusing on shortcomings that even our sin-ignoring culture can grasp is a way of finding a break in the wall. This acknowledgement of sin can then be expanded to ask the *why* questions and bring up examples. Why didn't we speak up for that coworker? Why did we lie to our spouse? Why don't we care more about those hurting around us? We can lead our people to admit that we all fall very short of what we should be. Along with Manasseh, we are accountable to God regarding our sin.

Our congregations are more apt to embrace the concept of accountability. Most likely they have been part of a team, whether in the workplace, on the athletic field, or in the arts. They understand that a team needs to have accountability. Teams that make money, win games, and produce quality entertainment have coaches and members with high expectations who hold each other accountable. When we fall short on a team, we expect the coach or fellow member to correct us and to exhort us to improve and not make the same mistake over and over again. In a much greater way, God holds us accountable to his expectations.

Now what?

The presentation of God's restoration will need to be celebrated. This restoration should be grasped and accepted by our people. However, in any congregation there are many who have been hurt terribly. Some lost jobs because of greedy bosses. Others saw a spouse leave for another person. Tragically, there are many who struggle every day with the memory of sexual abuse. When hurting people read about Manasseh, there is a strong possibility that they will see in Manasseh that person who was evil toward them. It is important to explain that Manasseh did endure God's strong hand of discipline and suffered consequences that lingered throughout his life. It could be wise, at least, to acknowledge our frustration of wanting that person to be punished, but it should stop there.

This frustration should lead us to the severe price that Christ paid for us. Manasseh's evil was judged. Pain and suffering were poured out in measure on Jesus.

It is astonishing that, when we humble ourselves before God in repentance, he forgives and restores. Manasseh entreated the Lord, humbled himself before God, and prayed. This is not three steps to salvation; this is one act of faith with three elements. The turning of Manasseh is an expression of his faith. He called out to God, humbled himself, and prayed. The story continues and shows that his faith was not without works. His rebuilding and attempt at purification of Judah's worship is evidence of his sincere faith. When his horrific deeds are put in contrast to his restoration, astonishment should grow in us. Yes, God really forgave Manasseh, and yes, God can really forgive me.

Creativity in Presentation

God designed our minds to more quickly embrace that which we discover, so rather than a direct condemnation of us he paints a picture for us to look at. God tells us a story and lets us discover the message. We can let the Chronicler's method affect our method of presentation.

Let the message be more impactful through the power of a story. Work at presenting the story effectively. The hero of the story is not Manasseh and certainly not Amon. The hero is God. He is the one who called out to Manasseh. He is the one who brought the Assyrians, and they then brought Manasseh into captivity. He is the one before whom Manasseh humbles himself. He is the one who restores Manasseh to his house. And he is the one who judges Amon.

The plot has unexpected turns in it that keep us wondering what will happen next. Help your listeners to expect and even want Manasseh to be judged. Then, express the surprise as you reveal the unexpected turns in the plot when he humbles himself and God forgives. Then, as you move into the story of Amon, again set your listeners up, this time to expect that he, like his father, will turn to God. But again, the plot changes; Amon does not humble himself and suffers the consequences.

A possible conclusion to the sermon is a final unexpected turn: the connection between us and these kings. We are just as evil as they were. As we more fully acknowledge our own horrible sin, we have a choice: to be like Manasseh or Amon. Will we humble ourselves and be astonished at God's forgiveness, or will we continue in our sin and face his consequences? Here is one possible structure:

- Present the story
  - Manasseh's reign
    - Manasseh's wickedness and punishment (33:1–11)
    - Manasseh's repentance and restoration (33:12–20)
  - Amon's reign (33:21–25)
    - Amon's wickedness (33:21–22)
    - Amon's lack of repentance and severe consequences (33:23–25)
- Apply the story
  - God's grace isn't just amazing—it's astonishing.

DISCUSSION QUESTIONS

1. What makes something astonishing?

2. Why do many people think that grace is earned?

3. What are some ways that people could feel about Manasseh being restored?

4. At what places in the story do you identify with Manasseh?

5. When are you not astonished by God's grace?

2 Chronicles 34:1–35:27

EXEGETICAL IDEA
Josiah followed YHWH and obeyed the law to an exemplary degree, but because of Judah's coming exile and Josiah's ignoring God's warning, Josiah experienced a surprising death instead of typical royal blessings.

THEOLOGICAL FOCUS
God accomplishes his plans in a way that is just both to his people as a whole and to individuals.

PREACHING IDEA
Don't drop the ball—trust the one who never does.

PREACHING POINTERS
At first glance, this story is only about finishing well. Josiah is wonderful up to the last few days of his life. Certainly, this is part of the message, but there is another part that is the motivation for us to finish well. This passage also teaches us that God will always accomplish his plans. Josiah's obedience or disobedience did not alter God's plans for him or for the nation. We can always trust our great God because he will always keep his promises. He will always accomplish his will, no matter what we do. God's good and just hand is not dependent upon us.

REIGN OF JOSIAH—A RIGHTEOUS KING FACES INEVITABLE JUDGMENT (34:1–35:27)

LITERARY STRUCTURE AND THEMES (34:1–35:27)

Josiah's reign contrasts sharply to the previous reigns of Manasseh and Amon. The previous kings forsook YHWH and acted wickedly (even though Manasseh later repented). In contrast, Josiah follows YHWH and acts righteously. Only when recounting how Josiah dies does the narrative cast any shadow on him.

The account breaks down into five sections. Each section concludes either with a report to the king or a comment regarding the previous action. During the first part of Josiah's reign, he leads Judah in restoring the land and temple. The previous generations of false worship defiled the land through the presence of the illicit objects and sites, while the lack of attention to the Jerusalem temple left it in disrepair. Josiah orders the objects destroyed and the temple repaired. The unit concludes when an official reports that the workers have finished the work assigned. Then, the narrative turns to the law discovered during the temple restoration. Josiah hears the law and asks for confirmation regarding its judgment for Judah. He sends officials to a prophetess who confirms that God will judge Judah. The unit concludes by recounting that the officials report their results to Josiah.

Despite the coming judgment, Josiah leads the people in making a covenant to observe the law discovered. The unit concludes by commenting that the covenant works, because the people do not forsake YHWH during Josiah's lifetime. The next unit recounts one way the people obey the law: they observe the Passover.

The unit concludes by commenting that Josiah observes the Passover unlike any other king in Israel's history.

The final unit recounts Josiah's death. Surprisingly, Josiah dies as a result of war with an Egyptian king. The king warns Josiah, but Josiah ignores the warning. Still, the unit concludes by pointing to Josiah's faithful actions according to the law.

- *Josiah Restores Land and Temple (34:1–17)*
- *Josiah Hears the Law and Its Judgment (34:18–28)*
- *Josiah Makes a Covenant to Observe the Law (34:29–33)*
- *Josiah Observes Passover (35:1–19)*
- *Josiah's Death (35:20–27)*

EXPOSITION (34:1–35:27)

In contrast to contemporary American culture, the Old Testament, along with other ancient Near Eastern cultures, focuses more on the community than the individual. This focus comes to light when considering God's covenants. Even when YHWH establishes a covenant with specific individuals, a larger community is in view: God's covenant with Abraham includes the promise of a great nation; God's covenant with David includes the promise of a long-lasting dynasty. Furthermore, God's covenant at Sinai relates to Israel as a nation. The heart of that covenant is that Israel is YHWH's people while YHWH is Israel's God. God's covenant with Israel outlines the blessings for the people if they obey, and the curses (especially exile) if they disobey. At the same time, based on that same covenant, God deals with individuals. As Chronicles illustrates again and again, God rewards those who obey what the covenant commands and punishes those who disobey (see the "Covenant" section in the introduction).

The Chronicler's account of Josiah arises from this backdrop. On the one hand, YHWH plans to punish Judah because of their wickedness. On the other hand, Josiah is a good king who worships YHWH properly, according to Mosaic law. The narrative shows how these corporate and individual elements play out for Josiah and for Judah. In the end, Josiah receives honor upon his death so that he does not witness YHWH's coming wrath; however, Josiah does not experience typical royal blessings both because of YHWH's coming wrath and because in his final days he does not pay attention to YHWH's warning.

Josiah Restores Land and Temple (34:1–17)
Josiah begins his reign righteously by purging the land from illicit, false worship and by repairing the Jerusalem temple.

34:1–3. The first few verses of Josiah's reign describe Josiah as a king as righteous as David. Not only does Josiah follow the ways of David, but he also does not stray from them. The Chronicler does not associate another king after Solomon so closely to David. Since David serves as a model for a righteous king, comparing Josiah to David in this way presents Josiah as one of the best kings of Israel (along with Hezekiah and, possibly, Jehoshaphat; see commentary on each). The Chronicler substantiates this claim by showing how eager Josiah is to serve YHWH completely. Even as a vulnerable young man, Josiah begins to follow YHWH. As soon as he reaches "adulthood" (the age of twenty, the twelfth year of his reign), he begins his religious reforms throughout Israel.

Adulthood in Ancient Judah
Second Chronicles 34:3 describes Josiah at age sixteen as a "youth" (נַעַר). The term most often carries connotations of vulnerability as one leaves his father's house (Leeb 2000, 94–95). It is not clear that ancient Judah thought of childhood and adulthood the same way that contemporary culture does; however, twenty years of age was the typical age at which males could fulfill certain duties within society (e.g., military or priestly service; see also 1 Chron. 23:24, 27; 2 Chron. 25:5; 31:17). In Josiah's case, his first act as an adult is to purge his people and land of their illicit worship.

34:4–7. After giving a sense of Josiah's character, the narrative focuses on what he does. He purges from Israel the illicit objects used repeatedly in their worship of other gods. While describing this purge, the Chronicler highlights the extensive nature of Josiah's activity. Like other good kings, Josiah targets a wide range of illicit objects: the high places, altars for Baal worship, wooden Asherah poles, molten images, carved images, and structures housing any of these objects.

Structures for Illicit Objects
In 34:4, the Chronicler speaks of הַחַמָּנִים that stood "over them" (לְמַעְלָה מֵעֲלֵיהֶם). Although translations generally render the word הַחַמָּנִים "incense altars," the word more likely refers to small chapels set up over the altars. In the case of 2 Chronicles 34:4, the sense of "over them" (לְמַעְלָה מֵעֲלֵיהֶם) becomes clearer, since the chapels would cover the altar (R. Klein 2012, 497). See also R. Klein 2012, 215, for further discussion.

Unlike other good kings, Josiah also targets those who worship using these objects: he spreads the remains of the destroyed objects upon the graves of these worshippers and burns the bones of the pagan priests upon their own altars to defile the sites so that they are unfit for future use. Geographically, Josiah targets all Israel. He begins in Jerusalem and Judah but then extends his activity to the northern tribes, represented by the largest tribes (Manasseh and Ephraim), the southernmost tribe (Simeon), and the northernmost tribe (Naphtali). The Chronicler points out that Josiah removes these objects through all the land of Israel. The expression "land of Israel" occurs only during the reigns of David, Solomon, Hezekiah, and Josiah, putting Josiah among a small group of great kings (Dillard 1987, 279). Once Josiah finishes this work throughout Israel, he returns to Jerusalem, implying that he is personally involved in cleansing the land (R. Klein 2012, 499).

The Chronicler presents Josiah as obeying YHWH's law directly. As an example, the Chronicler describes how Josiah destroys illicit worship objects using language almost identical to Exodus 34:13 and Deuteronomy 7:5; 12:3. As a result, it is not surprising that the Chronicler states that Josiah follows what is written in the law of YHWH (2 Chron. 35:26).

34:8–9. After removing the objects of false worship, Josiah turns his attention to the temple to repair it, since his predecessors have ruined it. The way Josiah gathers resources for the repairs resembles the measures of Joash (2 Chron. 24:4–13); however, Josiah implements the measures more fully. Joash tells the priests and Levites to gather resources throughout Judah for the temple repairs; however, the Levites fail to follow through. As a result, Joash places a chest at the temple so that visitors may deposit the money there. In contrast, during Josiah's reign, the Levites gather resources from all Israel (as Joash proposed), bringing them into the temple (as Joash ordered) to distribute them to those doing the repairs. The picture suggests that the people during Josiah's reign follow the proper procedure. This picture anticipates the Passover observance in 2 Chronicles 35.

TRANSLATION ANALYSIS:
The Chronicler provides a comprehensive listing of the groups constituting Israel during the days of Josiah: Manasseh and Ephraim, all those who remain from Israel, all Judah, Benjamin, and the inhabitants of Jerusalem. Some translations render the final expression differently because of the text's transmission. The *qere* reads וַיֵּשְׁבוּ יְרוּשָׁלָ͏ִם ("they returned to Jerusalem," KJV, NKJV). The *ketiv* reads וְיֹשְׁבֵי יְרוּשָׁלָ͏ִם ("and the inhabitants of Jerusalem," CSB, ESV, NASB, NIV, NRSV). One can see that the only difference between the readings occurs at the end of the first word: י or ו. Since the *ketiv* makes good sense in context and since the *qere* reading could easily originate from misreading ו for י, the *ketiv* is more likely.

> ### Josiah and Joash
> Josiah actually shares much in common with Joash: (1) he is also a Judahite king who rises to the throne as a boy, (2) his reign follows a period of Israel's unfaithfulness to YHWH, (3) he repairs the temple, (4) he stands at his position in the temple while making a covenant with the people, and (5) he dies after he fails to listen to YHWH's word (Dillard 1987, 282).

34:10–17. Regarding the repairs, the Chronicler shows that each group involved handles them properly. First, the Levites supervise the repair work according to their assigned positions (e.g., musicians, scribes, officials, and gatekeepers; see 1 Chron. 23:4). Second, the craftsmen carry out the work with integrity. Third, those who oversee the resources for the repairs distribute them to those doing the work, ensuring they are justly compensated. Finally, Shaphan the scribe reports to Josiah that the workers are completing the tasks assigned by the king and have been properly compensated for the work. This integrity throughout the process throws a positive light both on the temple itself and on Josiah who leads its repair.

Josiah Hears the Law and Its Judgment (34:18–28)

When Josiah hears the Mosaic law, he mourns because he expects coming judgment; the prophetess Huldah confirms that YHWH will judge the people, but Josiah will not experience it.

34:18–21. During the temple repairs, the priest Hilkiah discovers "the book of YHWH's law given by Moses." Hilkiah passes it along to the scribe Shaphan; Shaphan passes it on to Josiah and reads it to the king. When Josiah hears it, he tears his clothes. As a cultural practice in Josiah's time, tearing one's clothes expresses intense emotional distress. For Josiah, the reading of the law reveals that Judah is in extreme danger of YHWH's punishment because, despite Josiah's efforts to cleanse the land and temple, Judah has disobeyed the law. In his distress he sends a delegation to inquire of YHWH for him and the people concerning what the law says. Josiah might be interested in confirming that the discovered book is authentic, but he is more likely concerned with knowing what can be done to avoid YHWH's coming judgment and how soon it might come (see R. Klein 2012, 503–4; for the suggestion that Josiah may also have desired prophetic intervention, Japhet 1993, 1032).

Identity of Josiah's Book

Scholars have long debated the specific identity of the book that Shaphan reads, especially in light of the parallel passage in 2 Kings 22. Generally, the book in Kings is considered to be Deuteronomy (or some hypothetical early version of it). However, the book in 2 Chronicles 34 is generally considered to be the entire Pentateuch (Genesis–Deuteronomy). One argument for identifying the book differently in each parallel text involves how each text describes Shaphan's reading. In Kings, the book functions as the object of the verb (וַיִּקְרָאֵהוּ, object marked by pronominal suffix); in Chronicles, it functions as the object of the preposition ב (וַיִּקְרָא־בוֹ). Although one can

---

interpret the expression in Chronicles to indicate that he read "in the book"—that is, he read part of it—such a specific contrast between "reading it" and "reading in it" is unlikely (cf. Deut. 17:19; 31:11). In both texts, the author focuses on the origin and authority of the book rather than its specific identity.

34:22–25. To accomplish the task, the delegation meets the prophetess Huldah. She is apparently a prominent woman, being the wife of Shallum, the official responsible for the wardrobe, and living in a certain part of Jerusalem. When she delivers YHWH's word to the delegation, she confirms Josiah's concerns: YHWH is about to punish Judah. He will punish them because of their disobedience, specifically worshipping other gods through idols. In fact, YHWH will bring disaster on Judah, taking the form of the curses promised in the law (see esp. Deut. 28:15–68; also Lev. 26:14–39). These curses include destruction, defeat, humiliation, and suffering, and will culminate in exile. Furthermore, the situation appears to be inevitable; using imagery typical of Jeremiah (Jer. 4:4; 7:20; 17:27; 21:12), the text states that once YHWH's anger catches fire against Judah, it will not go out.

TRANSLATION ANALYSIS:
Translations differ in how they render the verb וְנִתְּךָ. Most translations treat the verb as "poured out." In the *qal* stem, the verb most often carries this sense. In other stems, the verb is associated with melting (cf. Ezek. 22:20–22). Furthermore, the parallel in 2 Kings 22:17 uses the וְנִצְּתָה "kindled," and the imagery of burning works better with the following phrase: "it will not be extinguished." As a result, one may render the verb as "ignite" (NET).

Idols as Human Products

In 2 Chronicles 34:25, the text speaks of the "works of their hands" (מַעֲשֵׂי יְדֵיהֶם). Although this expression can refer generally to the product of

538

a person's work, in this case, it more likely refers specifically to idols because the text focuses on forsaking YHWH in order to worship other gods. Furthermore, Chronicles uses the similar phrase מַעֲשֵׂה יְדֵי הָאָדָם ("works of human hands") elsewhere for idols (2 Chron. 32:19).

34:26–28. In contrast, what YHWH says to Josiah is more positive. YHWH affirms how Josiah has responded to hearing the law: Josiah shows no stubbornness but sincerely humbles himself by weeping and tearing his clothes. As a result, YHWH listens to Josiah's response and promises him that he will not experience the coming disaster against Judah, because he will be gathered to his fathers and buried in peace. This promise also indicates that the judgment against Judah is inevitable. Even Josiah's humble response does not change Judah's disastrous fate; it only delays it (cf. Hezekiah and the people in 2 Chron. 32:26). By this point YHWH has made up his mind concerning Judah's fate; it is now only a matter of time.

TRANSLATION ANALYSIS:
Concerning Josiah, 34:27 reads, "Your heart was tender" (רַךְ־לְבָבְךָ). A number of translations (CSB, ESV, NASB, NKJV) render the phrase as "your heart was tender." Most often in the Hebrew OT the verb describes fear or a lack of courage. In this case, however, the emphasis lies not on fear but on responsiveness. In other words, the text communicates that Josiah was not stubborn toward the law but accepted its judgment. Other translations try to capture this more specific sense by rendering the phrase as "you displayed a sensitive spirit" (NET), "your heart was responsive" (NIV), "you were sorry" (NLT), or "your heart was penitent" (NRSV).

34:28. While Judah's fate seems clear, Josiah's is less so. The text states that Josiah will be gathered to his fathers and to his grave in peace. One may understand the expression to indicate that Josiah will die a peaceful death and receive

a proper burial among his ancestors' tombs; however, this promise may be more or less specific. One can understand the promise of dying in peace more generally, so that it is fulfilled if Josiah does not see Judah's coming disaster (e.g., Dillard 1987, 282). One can understand it more specifically as indicating only that Josiah will not die "at the hands of a combatant or assassin" (Merrill 2015, 586). To summarize, the language of the text leaves open how this promise to Josiah may be fulfilled.

Regardless of Josiah's precise fate, the text is clearer that Josiah's death and burial are a reward for his proper response to the law. In Josiah's death, YHWH spares him from the coming disaster about to strike all Judah. Like Hezekiah before him (2 Chron. 32:26), Josiah's humble response to YHWH ensures that YHWH will not destroy Judah and exile the survivors while Josiah is alive.

Josiah Makes a Covenant to Observe the Law (34:29–33)

Josiah delays the coming judgment by leading all the people to commit to obey Mosaic law, through worshipping YHWH exclusively and properly.

34:29–32. Even after Josiah's delegation informs him of the seemingly inevitable judgment coming to Judah, he implements nationwide reform. After he joins all the people of Judah at the temple, he reads the book discovered there earlier. At this point, the text presents Josiah like Moses. Just as Moses in Exodus 24:7 reads the book of the covenant while the people listen, Josiah reads the book of the covenant while the people listen. Furthermore, as the people at Sinai agree to obey what YHWH commands in the book (Exod. 24:3, 7), so also the people in Jerusalem agree to obey what YHWH commands in the book (for further similarities, see Hahn 2012, 184). The Chronicler may compare Josiah to Moses both in order to present Josiah in a positive light and to anticipate and validate

Josiah's authority in determining certain details of Passover observance (see below on 2 Chron. 35:1–19).

34:31–33. Once Josiah reads the book of the covenant, he makes a covenant to obey everything commanded in the book. Josiah's covenant is not a covenant with YHWH, but a formal commitment, attested by YHWH ("before YHWH"), to honor the covenant recorded in the book of the covenant, a covenant between YHWH and the people. The text summarizes the demands of the book's covenant as following YHWH and keeping his commandments, his laws, and his statutes wholeheartedly. Josiah follows through on this commitment by removing every idolatrous object from all the areas belonging to the people of Israel and requiring everyone living in the land to worship YHWH alone. Josiah, like Hezekiah, exercises authority over all Israel, not just Judah and Jerusalem. Therefore, during his reign, the people do not stray from following YHWH, just as Josiah does not stray (cf. 2 Chron. 34:2). In this way, Josiah and the people fulfill the demands found in the book of the covenant, acting in line with the covenant YHWH made with them.

Comprehensive Obedience to the Law

In 34:31, the Chronicler likely lists the various types of stipulations in the covenant to emphasize that Josiah is committing to comprehensive obedience. Furthermore, the vocabulary here reflects David's words to Solomon (1 Chron. 29:19). Even though this expression is heavily influenced by Deuteronomy, where the terms occur frequently, only Deuteronomy 6:17 has all three terms together.

Throughout this section, Josiah takes the lead in bringing about reform. Contrary to the Chronicler's general concern to highlight how the people participate in important events, this narrative assigns almost all the activity to Josiah himself. Josiah gathers the elders, reads the book of the covenant, makes the covenant, makes those present agree to the covenant, removes the idolatrous objects from all Israel, and requires Israel to worship YHWH alone. Huldah's prophecy helps explain this focus on Josiah's activity. As stated earlier, Huldah's prophecy reveals both that YHWH will punish Judah and that Josiah's humility delays that punishment. The narrative shows that during Josiah's reign, Judah remains faithful to YHWH and therefore is not punished. However, by focusing on Josiah, the text holds out little, if any, hope that Judah as a people will remain loyal to YHWH after Josiah dies. In this way, the stage is still set to see Huldah's prophecy come about.

Josiah Observes Passover (35:1–19)
Josiah and the people observe the Passover in a fully developed form following the appropriate authorities of YHWH, Moses, David, Solomon, Josiah, law, and even tradition.

35:1–17. Following Josiah's reforms, the narrative recounts how Josiah and the people observe the Passover. Again, Josiah takes the lead in observing the Passover. In fact, at first, the text only mentions Josiah as observing the Passover (35:1). Furthermore, Josiah prepares the priests (35:2) and Levites (35:3–6) and contributes sacrifices for the occasion (35:7). Even when the people observe the Passover and offer sacrifices, they do so as Josiah commands them (35:16). Even during this national celebration, the text focuses on Josiah's initiative (see above).

35:1–9. The Chronicler begins his account by showing how Josiah prepares for the Passover. First, he posts the priests to their stations and encourages them in the work they do during the observance. Second, he clarifies the role of the Levites. Following the example of David (cf. 1 Chron. 23:26), Josiah expands the Levites' roles. Since they no longer need to carry the ark as prescribed in the law, Josiah assigns them the task of serving both YHWH and the people, by organizing themselves according to Israel's family divisions, slaughtering the Passover lambs, and helping their fellow Levites and the priests carry out their duties as assigned by the law of Moses. In other words, the Levites are responsible to step in where needed. Third, Josiah and his officials provide animals for the sacrifices. Josiah takes the lead by providing thirty thousand sheep or goats and another three thousand bulls for the people to offer as Passover sacrifices and other offerings. His temple officials and Levitical leaders provide for the priests and Levites, contributing almost a third of what he provides.

Distribution of Passover

Second Chronicles 35:5 suggests that certain Levitical family divisions were assigned to family divisions from the other tribes. The text does not include all the details; however, it seems that at least the Levites would skin the Passover lambs and distribute the remains to the family divisions so that families could then present the animal for sacrifice. The priests would burn some portions of the animal on the altar as a burnt offering while the Levites would cook the other portions so that the families could eat the meat together.

35:10–16. Once the preparations are complete, the priests and Levites take their positions and begin sacrificing the Passover lambs. For this Passover, the Chronicler focuses on the participants and their responsibilities. The priests sprinkle the blood from the Passover lambs and burn the remains of the animals that the people do not eat. The singers, here called the sons of Asaph, remain in their designated areas, apparently performing their music as the sacrifices take place. The gatekeepers maintain their assigned positions at the gates, apparently ensuring the safety and sanctity of the area. The people receive the slaughtered animals and then present portions of them to the priests as burnt offerings, to be entirely burned on the altar. In everything else, the Levites fill in, carrying out what Josiah has assigned them (35:3–6). They slaughter the lambs, flay them (35:11), distribute the parts of the animals burned as a sacrifice to the family divisions (35:12), cook the meat of the sacrifices (35:13), and ensure that the priests, singers, and gatekeepers are free to carry out their assigned responsibilities (35:14–15).

Participants in Passover

Second Chronicles 35:5, 7, 12, and 13 use the expression בְּנֵי הָעָם ("sons of the people") for the people who are neither priests, Levites, nor the king. For this reason, many translations (CSB, ESV, NASB, NKJV) render the phrase as "laypeople." Other translations just render the phrase simply as "people (NET, NIV, NLT, NRSV). The sense of the phrase is likely "common people," that is, the people not marked out specially during this occasion; cf. Jer. 17:19; 26:23.

Regarding the nature of the Passover itself, Josiah's observance contrasts to the Passover described in the law. For example, in the law, the people provide their own sacrifices; here, Josiah and his officials provide them. Also, Mosaic law does not assign specific tasks for priests or Levites; here, the priests and Levites perform most of the tasks for the ritual (see Shaver 1989, 110–16). At the same time, despite these differences, the account mentions repeatedly that various authorities validate Josiah's current practices. By the written authority of David and Solomon (see 1 Chron. 28:19), Josiah commands the Levites to organize themselves by divisions (35:4). By the authority of David and his musical prophets Asaph, Heman, and Jeduthun (all called seers: Asaph, 2 Chron. 29:30; Heman, 1 Chron. 25:5; Jeduthun, here), the singers take their positions during the Passover. As commanded in the law, the people offer the Passover animals as burnt offerings to YHWH (35:12). Furthermore, the entire Passover observation takes place as Josiah the king commands it (35:16). The Chronicler emphasizes that Josiah's Passover takes place according to the recognized authorities regulating the cultic life of Israel. The differences between the Passover in the law and Josiah's Passover reflect changes in the circumstances (e.g., Davidic king and Jerusalem temple). The Chronicler's account respects the authority of the law while affirming the authority of the king (David or Josiah) to adapt specific ritual applications to address changing circumstances.

Applying Passover Regulations

Despite differences between Josiah's Passover and the Passover in the law, the Chronicler still treats the specifics of the law as the guide for Passover practice. For instance, 35:13 describes how the Levites cook the meat for the Passover. Most English translations state that they roasted the Passover meat with fire; however, this translation obscures an interpretive challenge. Exodus 12:8–9 commands the sons of Israel to eat the meat roasted (צְלִי), not raw or boiled in water (בָּשֵׁל מְבֻשָּׁל בַּמָּיִם); however, Deuteronomy 16:7 commands the sons of Israel to cook the meat, using the same word (בשל) prohibited in Exodus 12:9. Most often when the verb בשל occurs, it clearly refers to boiling meat rather than roasting (Ben Zvi gives a number of reasons for understanding the verb as "to boil" rather than the general sense of "to cook"; 2006b, 240–41); however, one may argue that the word בשל refers to food preparation in general and boiling in particular only when stated that the preparation takes place with water (so Kilchör 2013, 483–86). In either case, the text reveals that

the Chronicler has combined the language and sense of both Pentateuchal passages to show that Josiah observes the Passover properly ("as prescribed" כַּמִּשְׁפָּט), that is, according to how these passages are interpreted together (see Schniedewind 1999, 173–78).

35:18–19. At the end of the account, the Chronicler comments that this Passover is unlike any Passover that takes place during the time of the monarchy (35:18). The Chronicler likely makes this statement because Josiah's Passover is the fully developed form of the observance at the Jerusalem temple. This point becomes clearer when comparing Josiah's Passover to Hezekiah's. During Hezekiah's Passover, the king and people needed to take several measures because the people were not ready (e.g., Passover takes place a month later, the Levites step in to help the priests because an insufficient number of priests are prepared, the Levites slaughter the Passover lambs because many people are not prepared, Hezekiah prays for those who are still unclean). In contrast, Josiah's Passover happens as it should. It takes place at the right time according to the law (fourteenth day of first month; 35:1, 16, 17). It falls in line with various authoritative sources: Moses, YHWH, David, Solomon, Josiah, law, and even tradition (מִשְׁפָּט; for this translation, see Schniedewind 1999, 173–78). Furthermore, it makes some of the ad hoc measures of Hezekiah's Passover (e.g., the Levites slaughtering the Passover sacrifices) standard practice. In this way, Josiah's Passover completes his reforms and finalizes the form of the Passover before exile (Jonker 2003, 57–60). In this way, the Chronicler presents this Passover as unique.

Mention of Samuel

In 35:18, the Chronicler mentions Samuel specifically. The Chronicler likely has many reasons for mentioning Samuel specifically. First, Samuel marks the end of the period of the judges. Second, since Josiah's Passover emphasizes the expanded role of the Levites, he may mention Samuel as a Levitical prophet (Dillard 1987, 291), perhaps even suggesting that the Levites participated in sacrificing the Passover animals before the rise of the monarchy (R. Klein 2012, 523).

Josiah's Death (35:20–27)

Josiah confronts Pharaoh Neco but dies in combat, like other kings, both because he does not listen to God's warning through Neco and because his death spares him from the coming exile.

35:20–24. After Josiah and the people complete the reforms and observe the Passover, a foreign king, Pharaoh Neco, invades the land. This situation is not unique in Chronicles: Asa, Jehoshaphat, and Hezekiah face a foreign invader after completing religious reforms. In each previous case, the king repels the foreign invader when he trusts YHWH to fight for him. Given Josiah's track record, one expects him to do the same. However, he does not. The narrative recounts how he dies after he confronts Neco on the battlefield.

Three observations may help explain this strange turn of events. First, as Josiah's encounter with Neco develops, it begins to look less like the other examples. For instance, unlike previous encounters, Neco does not intend to fight against Josiah or besiege any of Judah's cities. Instead, he is passing through Judah to fight his enemy at Carchemish. Furthermore, when Neco sends messengers, he does not act like Sennacherib, boasting of his own strength and treating YHWH as a powerless idol. Instead, he warns Josiah not to stand in the way of what God is doing; otherwise, God will destroy him. Unlike previous encounters, Neco speaks for God when he warns Josiah not to fight. This final point is especially important for changing the course of Josiah's reign.

Second, the Chronicler presents Josiah in a negative light during these final verses of his reign. Josiah resembles wicked Ahab (2 Chron. 18:28–33): both ignore God's warning by going to battle, both prepare for battle by disguising themselves, both are wounded by archers during the battle, and both ask to be removed from battle because of their injuries. This comparison suggests that Josiah dies because he ignores YHWH's warning through Neco.

Third, the account of Josiah's death plays into Huldah's prophecy concerning him. As stated previously, Huldah prophesies that because of Josiah's humility before YHWH, he would not see the coming disaster against Jerusalem and Judah but would "be gathered to his grave in peace." In this way, Josiah's death is his reward. However, Josiah dies as a result of battle, not exactly "in peace."

There are two approaches to resolving this tension between the prophecy and what happens. The first approach focuses on the negative picture of Josiah. This approach argues that since Josiah behaves like Ahab and ignores God's warning through Neco, Josiah forfeits the prophesied reward. Rather than dying "in peace," Josiah dies from battle.

dead in his chariot at Ramoth-gilead (2 Chron. 18:34), but Josiah escapes the battlefield to return to an honorable death and burial in Jerusalem. Interestingly, Ahab's ally at Ramoth-gilead, Jehoshaphat, narrowly escapes death to return to Jerusalem "in peace" (בְּשָׁלוֹם; 2 Chron. 19:1). Because Jehoshaphat ignores YHWH's warning against fighting at Ramoth-gilead, Jehoshaphat loses the battle and almost loses his life; however, because of Jehoshaphat's past reforms, he returns to Jerusalem in peace (cf. 2 Chron. 19:1–3). In this way, Josiah contrasts sharply to Ahab, but more closely resembles Jehoshaphat.

35:25–27. The second approach focuses on the sense of being gathered to his grave "in peace." The text suggests two ways in which Josiah is gathered to his grave "in peace." First, unlike the kings who follow Josiah, Josiah rules independently. "Josiah dies 'in peace' because he dies immediately before the imperial rule of Judah begins" (Janzen 2017, 154–56). Second, Josiah dies in Jerusalem and receives an honorable burial there. His death in Jerusalem ironically fits the picture of dying "in peace" because ירושלם ("Jerusalem," i.e., "Foundation of Peace") is a play on the word בשלום ("in peace"; see Mitchell 2006, 421–27). Furthermore, the Chronicler emphasizes the honor Josiah receives at his burial. Josiah receives the unique distinction in Chronicles of the people, including the prophet Jeremiah, composing and passing on songs mourning his death. This honor in burial is the only obvious blessing that the Chronicler records for Josiah and likely serves as part of the reward that Huldah prophesies. The honor fits Josiah, since even the final comment about him characterizes him as performing faithful deeds according to YHWH's law (35:26).

Laments of Jeremiah

The Old Testament does not preserve these songs as a collection. Based on their content, they are not the book of Lamentations, even though they are called laments (קִינוֹת) and are recorded in a

book of laments. The songs may exist in some form as individual psalms or parts of other psalms.

Another important point should be mentioned regarding Huldah's prophecy: since Huldah prophesies Josiah's death, his death constitutes a part of YHWH's plan to reward Josiah but still punish Judah. Other passages in which a king does not listen confirm this point explicitly. Rehoboam does not listen to the people as a part of YHWH's plan to divide the tribes into two nations, as Ahijah prophesied to Jeroboam (2 Chron. 10:15–16). Amaziah does not listen to Joash's warning as a part of YHWH's plan to destroy him (2 Chron. 35:16, 20). In a similar way, Josiah does not listen to Neco's warning as a part of YHWH's plan to destroy Judah—a plan that is delayed until Josiah dies, since Huldah has prophesied that Josiah will not see the destruction.

Based on the observations made above, I suggest the following. First, since Neco communicates God's warning to Josiah, Josiah disobeys God. Showing how Josiah resembles Ahab in the battle confirms this point. Second, because Josiah disobeys, YHWH punishes him during the battle, since Josiah is wounded in a way similar to Ahab. Third, Josiah's death and burial in Jerusalem fulfills Huldah's prophecy, even if in an ironic or unexpected manner. Fourth, Josiah's death is a part of YHWH's plan to reward Josiah but also to punish Judah.

For the first readers, on the one hand, Josiah's reign provides a model for worshipping YHWH properly. It encourages the community to hold on to authorities from the past (e.g., the law of Moses and the instructions of David) while adapting to changing circumstances. On the other hand, Josiah's account shows that despite his faithfulness (35:26), he does not experience blessing as one might expect. As the postexilic community struggled to rebuild their homes, farms, cities, and institutions, some of them faithfully served YHWH. The Chronicler's repeated emphasis on God's retribution may prove disheartening to such readers: If YHWH rewards the faithful, then why is the community struggling so much? Josiah's reign shows that YHWH sometimes works more mysteriously and indirectly. For instance, Josiah receives his blessing only in his burial. Even his death serves both as a reward for his faithfulness and punishment for his disobedience. The proper response to YHWH's mysterious ways is continued faithfulness to him (Ristau 2009, 242–44).

THEOLOGICAL FOCUS

God accomplishes his plans in a way that is just, both to his people as a whole and to individuals.

In many ways, Josiah embodies the characteristics of a good king in Chronicles: he seeks God from an early age, removes all kinds of illicit worship objects from all Israel, repairs God's temple, leads the people to serve God, and obeys what is written in God law. Typically, in Chronicles, kings who possess these characteristics receive numerous blessings from God: wealth, fame, an organized army, fortification of cities, victory over enemies, and rest. This observation fits in with a prominent theme in Chronicles: retribution; that is, God rewards obedience but punishes disobedience. However, since Josiah does not experience these blessings, his reign complicates a simple presentation of retribution as it addresses how human action interacts with God's will.

Hanging over Josiah's reign, especially the latter half, is Judah's coming exile. Once Josiah hears the reading of the book of the law discovered in the temple, the narrative turns to God's wrath upon Israel and the coming disaster that his wrath will bring. The narrative presents this disaster as inevitable because of Israel's past sins, but it also promises that Josiah will not experience it. The narrative then confirms that Josiah does not experience it because he dies as a result of fighting Pharaoh Neco. Even though Neco, speaking for God, warns Josiah not to attack, he does not listen. On the one hand, Josiah dies because he does not listen to God. On the other hand, Josiah does not experience the coming exile and receives great honors upon his death. Furthermore, the way is clear for God to bring about Judah's judgment, which God soon does (2 Chron. 36).

The Chronicler's account of Josiah's reign explores how human action interacts with YHWH's will in a sophisticated manner. Furthermore, the account demonstrates how the actions of an individual can play into God's plan for his people. At the corporate level, Josiah's righteous rule delays God's judgment so that Israel can observe the Passover in a fully standardized form, building on the authorities of Moses, David, Solomon, and Josiah. At the individual level, Josiah has an honorable burial so that he does not experience Judah's exile. At the same time, at the corporate level, Josiah's ignoring of the warning from Neco clears the way for God to punish Judah. At the individual level, Josiah dies from a wound in battle much like the wicked kings Saul and Ahab. This activity reveals that God is just at both the corporate and individual levels and that God is not dependent on Josiah's obedience or disobedience in order to accomplish his plans concerning his people.

PREACHING AND TEACHING STRATEGIES

Exegetical and Theological Synthesis

While we need to learn from the life of Josiah to be faithful to the end, there is another message: God's plans are not dependent upon individuals. The coming exile was part of God's plan. Josiah's obedience may have delayed the exile, but in God's plan Judah was about to be severely disciplined. This could be taken as a discouragement that God will bring about his plan, no matter what we do. But that is the point of encouragement. We can always fully trust him because his plans are not dependent upon us. Even when we have failed, God's plan will not fail. And when we have had great success, our trust is not in what we do but in what God does.

Preaching Idea
Don't drop the ball—trust the one who never does.

Contemporary Connections

What does it mean?
Those who first heard this message of Josiah's reign surely had mixed emotions and reactions. On the one hand, they were motivated to listen and obey God as Josiah had done. Yet they must have been disappointed that Josiah dropped the ball and suffered great consequences. They needed encouragement. These first readers lived with opposition to obeying the law of God. These listeners either were still in exile living in a pagan nation or were those trying to reestablish Israel as their homeland. Both faced opposition to the worship and obedience to YHWH. At the beginning of Josiah's reign, the nation was not just turning away from God but was running away from him toward idols of fertility goddesses and prosperity gods. Yet, Josiah followed and obeyed YHWH.

The exiles needed an example, and so do we. Josiah's total and even radical commitment to God's law is exemplary for us. The struggle for us is twofold. The first is just like Josiah's. We must stay the course and not drop the ball of obedience even in the face of our culture's opposition to God: redefining marriage, sex before marriage, sanctity of life, oppression of others for financial gain, seeking happiness in material things, on and on the list goes. But there is a second struggle for us. Josiah was the king. He could make national changes because he was in authority. We are not. Our obedience, our carrying the ball well, means that we live respectfully while holding to our beliefs and practices in a loving and caring way.

But then, Josiah dropped the ball. This disappointing aspect of his life teaches us to never stop trusting and following our Lord and his commands. God's revelation to Josiah came from the written law, but it also came in two other ways: Huldah, a woman prophetess, and then from Neco the Egyptian king. Though these were unusual, the writer presents them as valid sources for Josiah. I heard long ago that all truth is God's truth. These two unusual voices were valid sources of truth.

Is it true?
Hold on to the football until you hear the whistle. It has happened more times than you would think: after a long pass, or run, or perhaps an interception, the player who has the ball is running thinking that a touchdown is a sure thing. But the celebration begins too early and the unbelievable happens. The player, who appears to be the hero, lets go of the ball, thinking he has already crossed the plane of the goal line, or he slows down and pridefully coasts the last few yards, only to be tackled by an unexpected opponent. Josiah dropped the ball just before the goal line when he did not listen to God's directive and acted in defiance of God. He attacked the army of Neco of Egypt even after God made it clear that this was not his will. This was no small thing, for it resulted in Josiah's early death. His burial was a blessing.

Part of the thrust of this passage only makes sense if we believe that there is more to life than this physical world in which we now live. Because of Josiah's heart for God and the obedience that verified this devotion, God made a promise to him that he would not see Judah destroyed. God fulfilled his promise through an early and untimely death. Josiah's burial was both a punishment and a blessing. God's grace and punishment to Josiah is seen in one event: his death. Shortly after Josiah's death the nation died as well, brutally conquered by the Babylonians. Thus, we can fully trust our Lord who rightly disciplined Josiah and yet still blessed him.

Our Lord keeps his promises and always does what is right.

Now what?

Josiah's death was a blessing that teaches us that no human is worthy of our full-hearted trust. Those who saw the real-time events unfold and those of us who hear the story of Josiah might began to think that Josiah was the king that would bring in God's promise of a peaceful and powerful kingdom. Clearly, Josiah was not that king. Interestingly Josiah's burial being a blessing is an allusion to another whose burial was a blessing. The death, burial, and resurrection of our Lord Jesus shows us a king who did not and does not drop the ball. He alone is the one who deserves our fullest trust for guidance in this life and security of blessings in the life to come. We should trust him all our days.

We must not look at retirement as a time to change our focus. I have heard retirees rejoice that they finally get to do what they want to do. When we age, we often have to slow down, but not to do just what we want, but to always do what God wants. Our obedience to work must not be set aside. The type of work may change, but our focus must still be faithfulness to God's call on our lives to serve in his kingdom. Don't drop the ball in retirement.

An itinerant Bible teacher/evangelist once told me that temptations increased after a meeting that had very good responses from those attending. He was tempted after working faithfully and seeing God work mightily to see himself as a great success. However, another temptation threatened him: he found it easier to think that in a time of physical rest, which he needed, he could also rest from obedience. Perhaps Josiah was tempted in the same way. After years of struggling to lead Judah away from national sins he forgot to continue his struggle against his own sin. When we are promoted unexpectedly, when after a successful sermon or lesson we are flooded with affirmations, when our financial decisions are wonderfully successful, we must not drop the ball and forget to listen to and obey the Lord. Don't drop the ball in seasons of success.

And don't drop the ball when confronted with sin. When there is a failure due to sin one could choose to repent and turn from the sin, but not return to a life of ministry. After a moral failure, a Christian leader may have to adjust the area of service. But ministry should continue. Don't drop the ball in seasons of failure.

Creativity in Presentation

Presenting the story of an ancient king is always a challenge. One way to create tension is by telling your listeners that the end of this story is going to produce a mixture of emotions. At the end of the story, we could shed a sorrowful tear because evil seems to win—or we could feel our eyes watering because God's goodness eventually prevails. It is not wrong to tell a story that leaves us confused. It is a real story that happened, and God has seen fit to give us this account for a reason. The tension for this story comes near the end. Josiah drops the ball and is killed. So how is that both God's wrath and God's blessing? It is a story about a burial being a blessing. The mystery of how a burial can be a blessing needs to be highlighted, because that is a major point of the story. God's plans will succeed no matter what we do. That is why we can always trust him.

The above illustration of football players celebrating early and dropping the ball might be presented using video clips from football replays; one will need to be sure that copyright laws are observed. Or one could re-create the event, being sure to re-create the emotions of a team thinking that a win is about to be pulled out in a miraculous way, only to have that emotional high crumble. Here is one possible structure:

- Introduction: let listeners know that this story has a perplexing end
- Present the text
  - Restoring land and temple (34:1–17)
  - Hearing the law and its judgment (34:18–28)
  - Making a covenant to observe the law (34:29–33)
  - Observing Passover (35:1–19)
  - Josiah's death (35:20–27)
- Apply the text
  - Don't drop the ball—trust the one who never does.

DISCUSSION QUESTIONS

1. What are the hard parts of turning back to God in obedience after a failure?

2. When do people feel they have the right to be "a little disobedient"?

3. What is it about being successful that makes us think wrongly about ourselves?

4. Why do we tend to put our full trust in a person or a human institution?

5. Where do you think our culture is farthest away from God's law?

6. How should you respond to our changing culture:
   - to a same-sex couple who moves in across the street?
   - to a boss who wants you to put the job ahead of your family?
   - to our choice of entertainment?

2 Chronicles 36:1–23

EXEGETICAL IDEA
Even though YHWH justly judged Judah and Jerusalem for not listening to him, he held out hope for the future.

THEOLOGICAL FOCUS
Judgment is not God's final word for his people.

PREACHING IDEA
Our sins are many; his mercy is more.

PREACHING POINTERS
The books of 1–2 Chronicles all point to God's people being able to properly worship him under the leadership of a perfect king. Jesus is our perfect eternal king who enables us to worship God as we should. This closing pericope shows us, once again, that human kings are not sufficient to lead us or enable us to properly worship God. The rebellious sins of Judah and her kings remind us that we too are sinful. Sin leads to God's sure and just judgment, but in his love God offers us mercy.

REIGNS OF JUDAH'S FINAL KINGS—JUDAH'S JUDGMENT AND FUTURE HOPE (36:1–23)

LITERARY STRUCTURE AND THEMES (36:1–23)

Before the Chronicler describes Judah's exile and Cyrus's edict, he briefly describes the reigns of Judah's final four kings before exile, leaving out virtually all details except how old they were when becoming king, how long they ruled, how they were each removed as king, and how their reigns negatively affected Judah, especially the temple. Since the Chronicler gives so few details, one may more easily discern two primary concerns regarding each king's reign: (1) the king's exile, and (2) Judah's loss of wealth, most often relating to the temple. This pattern repeats for the reigns of Jehoahaz, Jehoiakim, and Jehoiachin. Before the pattern culminates, the Chronicler shows the wickedness and stubbornness of Judah during the reign of Zedekiah. Because of Zedekiah's stubborn refusal to honor YHWH, YHWH finally brings Judah's judgment by sending Babylon to plunder and destroy Jerusalem and to kill or exile the people. However, the Chronicler offers Judah hope. He points to the end of punishment and a promise of restoration by recording Cyrus's edict allowing the people to return and build the temple.

Another feature that points to the Chronicler's sense of hope is that despite the Chronicler's negative picture of each king, he does not recount their deaths. Furthermore, he shows that the items used in temple worship are taken away but not destroyed. The Chronicler emphasizes the common fate of the monarchy and the temple (Dillard 1987, 297). As the king goes into exile without any

final word concerning his fate, the temple's resources also go into exile without any final word concerning their fate. The Chronicler leaves the door open for both to be restored.

- **Reigns of Jehoahaz, Jehoiakim, and Jehoiachin (36:1–10)**
- **Reign of Zedekiah (36:11–14)**
- **Judah's Judgment and Exile (36:15–21)**
- **Judah's Hope (36:22–23)**

EXPOSITION (36:1–23)

Many factors revealed an ancient Near Eastern nation's well-being, or lack thereof (e.g., military strength, social rest, economic development). Underlying many of these factors was the degree to which foreign nations directed the nation's affairs: the greater the foreign influence, the weaker the nation. In the final days of Judah as a political state, the Chronicler focuses on the increasing influence of foreign nations on Judah. During this time, Judah is subject to foreign powers. Egypt and then Babylon depose kings, impose special taxes, and plunder their treasures. Judah's weakness is a result of their wickedness, but through all these events Judah still acts wickedly. YHWH finally brings Judah's judgment by sending Babylon to plunder and destroy Jerusalem and to kill or exile the people. Even though YHWH justly judges Judah and Jerusalem for their wickedness, the Chronicler ends his book with a note of hope as he points to the end of this punishment and a promise of restoration, through Cyrus's edict allowing the people to return and build the temple.

Reigns of Jehoahaz, Jehoiakim, and Jehoiachin (36:1–10)

As the kings of Jehoahaz, Jehoiakim, and Jehoiachin do what is evil, YHWH punishes Judah by sending its wealth and king to other lands.

36:1–4. After Josiah dies in combat against Pharaoh Neco, Judah declines quickly. With the few details that the Chronicler provides regarding each king's reign, he emphasizes how other nations assume authority over Judah. Therefore, even though the people of Judah make Josiah's son Jehoahaz king, the Egyptian pharaoh removes him from the throne after only three months and exiles him to Egypt. He also requires Judah to pay him tribute. His influence continues as he makes Eliakim, Jehoahaz's older brother, king and then changes Eliakim's name to Jehoiakim. Although these names are quite similar (only replacing the element אֵל "God" with יהו "YHWH"), in this context the name change demonstrates Egypt's authority.

36:5–8. Even though Egypt shows its authority at the beginning of Jehoiakim's reign, Babylon assumes control through the rest of his reign. The king of Babylon attacks him, restrains him with chains to lead him to exile in Babylon, and plunders some of the temple's items to display them in his palace. The Chronicler connects these events to Jehoiakim's conduct, since immediately before and after recording them the Chronicler summarizes Jehoiakim's conduct as what YHWH considers evil and as "abominations" (תּוֹעֵבוֹת). The use of "abominations" here anticipates its use later in the passage (36:14).

TRANSLATION ANALYSIS:

The Hebrew text uses the word הֵיכָל to describe where Nebuchadnezzar put the temple's items. This word may refer either to a palace or a temple. English translations split rather evenly: several translate it as "temple" (e.g., CSB, NASB, NIV, NKJV), while several others as "palace" (ESV, NET, NLT, NRSV). Determining the proper translation is difficult. First, Chronicles only uses הֵיכָל to refer to a temple. Second, other passages in the OT (Ezra 1:7; Dan. 1:2) speak of Nebuchadnezzar depositing the temple's items in the temple of his god(s). However, those passages may refer to the items' final destination from which they are later restored (cf. Ezra 1:7 in particular), or the Chronicler's statement may be a more general expression than Ezra 1:7 or Daniel 1:2 (Japhet 1993, 1064). Third, the possessive "his" does not apply as well to a temple as it does to a palace. For example, "his" house, which also could refer to a palace or a temple, would definitely refer to Nebuchadnezzar's palace and not a temple. I have chosen "palace," giving priority to the linguistic argument of the third point.

Jehoiakim's Fate

Elsewhere in the OT, there is little evidence that Jehoiakim ever went into exile in Babylon. The Chronicler's language is ambiguous in this regard because it does not state that Nebuchadnezzar took him to Babylon, only that he bound him to do so. Regardless of whether Jehoiakim went to Babylon, the Chronicler's concern is to present Jehoiakim's fate in terms of exile while still keeping his fate open, since the Chronicler does not specify how Jehoiakim spends the rest of his days.

Even though the Chronicler records that Nebuchadnezzar captures Jehoiakim and plunders the temple, he does not record Jehoiakim's final fate. This point becomes even more significant as one looks at the language used to describe Jehoiakim's capture and apparent exile to Babylon. The Chronicler uses virtually identical language to describe Manasseh's capture and exile to Babylon (2 Chron. 33:11 וַיַּאַסְרֻהוּ בַּנְחֻשְׁתַּיִם וַיּוֹלִיכֻהוּ בָּבֶלָה // 2 Chron. 36:6 וַיַּאַסְרֵהוּ בַּנְחֻשְׁתַּיִם לְהֹלִיכוֹ בָּבֶלָה). Even though Manasseh (like Jehoiakim) deserves this fate because of the abominations he commits (2 Chron. 33:2), exile is not his final fate. Instead, after he humbles himself before YHWH, YHWH restores him to his rule in Jerusalem. Even though the Chronicler provides no hint that Jehoiakim similarly humbles himself before YHWH, the fact that he does not specify Jehoiakim's final fate at all leaves open such a possibility (see Begg 1987, 83).

36:9–10. After Nebuchadnezzar takes Jehoiakim into exile, his son Jehoiachin rules for a very brief time. He becomes king at only eighteen years of age and reigns only three months. The Chronicler says very little about Jehoiachin; however, he makes two significant points: (1) Jehoiachin does what YHWH considers evil, and (2) as a result Nebuchadnezzar brings both Jehoiachin and some of the valuable temple items to Babylon. As with the other kings, the Chronicler provides few details regarding Jehoiachin, especially his final fate. However, the king appears elsewhere in Chronicles. In 1 Chronicles 3:17, he appears by his other name, Jeconiah. This verse describes him as "the prisoner" (אסיר) and begins the list of his descendants. By listing Jehoiachin's descendants, the Chronicler shows that the continued existence of the Davidic line is more than just a possibility; it is a reality preserved in the line of Jehoiachin, even though he was a Babylonian prisoner because YHWH judged him (Begg 1987, 82). In this way, the Chronicler encourages his first readers to continue hoping and waiting for a Davidic king to rule again.

TRANSLATION ANALYSIS:
Some translations (KJV, NASB, NKJV, NRSV) record that Jehoiachin was eight years old when he became king because MT reads "eight" here. However, several Hebrew manuscripts record the age as eighteen, and this reading corresponds to 2 Kings 24:8 and 3 Esdras 1:41. The MT here likely results from the word "ten" falling out and then being reinserted by a scribe to describe the length of the king's reign (requiring the addition of "days") instead of his age.

The relationship between Jehoiachin and Zedekiah is not entirely clear. MT 2 Chronicles 36:10 refers to Zedekiah as Jehoiachin's "brother/relative" (אָחִיו); however, MT 2 Kings 24:17 refers to Zedekiah as Jehoiachin's uncle (דֹּד). Jeremiah 37:1 also suggests that Zedekiah is Jehoiachin's uncle. LXX 2 Chronicles 36:10 preserves a reading of "brother of his father" (אֲחִי אָבִיו), corresponding also to MT 2 Kings 24:17 and Jeremiah 37:1. Translations deal with this issue in one of three ways: (1) they render אָח as "brother" (CSB, ESV, KJV, NRSV), (2) they accept the reading of LXX and render it as "uncle" (NIV, NLT), or (3) they render אָח in a more general sense as "kinsman" or "relative" (NASB, NET). In all three cases, it is possible to reconcile MT 2 Chronicles 36:10 with MT 2 Kings 24:17 and Jeremiah 37:1; however, the latter two options are the clearest in English.

Reign of Zedekiah (36:11–14)
Zedekiah stubbornly resists YHWH's word and rebels against Nebuchadnezzar.

36:11–12. After Nebuchadnezzar exiles Jehoiachin, he installs Zedekiah as king. The Chronicler provides two general statements to describe Zedekiah's behavior: he does what YHWH considers wicked, and he stubbornly resists YHWH's authority by stiffening his neck and hardening his heart. The Chronicler emphasizes the latter point by providing specific examples of Zedekiah's stubbornness. First, Zedekiah refuses to humble himself before YHWH's prophet Jeremiah. By describing Zedekiah in this way, the Chronicler picks up on key themes in his work. Beginning in 2 Chronicles 7:14, humbling oneself leads to experiencing restoration (see Rehoboam, 2 Chron. 12:6–7, 12; Hezekiah, 2 Chron. 32:26; Manasseh, 2 Chron. 33:12–13) while not humbling oneself leads to disaster (e.g., Amon, 2 Chron. 33:23–24). As demonstrated in these passages, humbling oneself involves both one's attitude toward YHWH as well as the activities that reflect that attitude (praying, kneeling, confessing, obeying, etc.). Furthermore, the Chronicler ties in Zedekiah's attitude toward YHWH with that of YHWH's prophet Jeremiah. Prophets and prophetic warnings are another key theme in Chronicles. The Chronicler shows throughout Israel's history that YHWH has sent prophets to warn people to return to YHWH or else suffer judgment. When the people accept the warning, YHWH relents (e.g., 2 Chron. 12:6–7, 12); however, when they do not, YHWH carries through on his judgment (e.g., 2 Chron. 21:12–19; 25:14–24). YHWH sends Jeremiah to warn Zedekiah to return to YHWH or suffer exile and destruction. Since Zedekiah does not accept Jeremiah's warnings, he suffers disaster as expected.

36:13. Second, Zedekiah stubbornly rebels against the Babylonian king Nebuchadnezzar. This stubborn rebellion ties into Jeremiah's prophetic word, since Jeremiah instructs Zedekiah to surrender to the Babylonians (Jer. 38:17). Furthermore, the Chronicler points out that Zedekiah also violates an oath he made in God's name. Anyone who violates such an oath, especially an oath made in God's name, should only expect to suffer (see Ezek. 17:13–19)—and Zedekiah does.

During the reign of Judah's last king before exile, the Chronicler emphasizes how Zedekiah refuses to acknowledge YHWH's authority and power both by ignoring Jeremiah's warnings and by violating the oath he made in God's name. Zedekiah provides a negative example for the first readers to consider as they navigate their lives under foreign rule. Zedekiah refuses to listen to YHWH's prophets and rebels against the foreign authority placed over him. The first readers would have the same options available to them: they could ignore YHWH's prophets (as recorded in the Scriptures) and rebel against the Persian Empire. However, they should expect the

same fate as Zedekiah: disaster. At the same time, the reigns of Jehoiakim and Jehoiachin encourage them to wait and hope for another Davidic king to rise. The Chronicler provides a balance for these first readers: they should accept YHWH's choice to have the Persian king rule over them, while also waiting for YHWH to restore the people and the Davidic dynasty sometime in the future.

36:14. After the Chronicler describes Zedekiah's wickedness, he turns his attention to the priests and the people. He describes their wickedness using the phrase הִרְבּוּ לִמְעָול־מַעַל כְּכֹל תֹּעֲבוֹת הַגּוֹיִם, often translated with a sense of becoming more unfaithful by imitating other nations in certain practices (thus, "All the officers of the priests and the people likewise were exceedingly unfaithful, following all the abominations of the nations," 2 Chron. 36:14a ESV). This unfaithfulness (מַעַל) entails worshipping in a prohibited manner. Examples of such prohibited worship include worshipping other gods, bringing in pagan cultic objects for worship, utilizing magic, or violating sacred space. The following phrase supports this more specific sense comparing it to the "abominations of the nations" (תֹּעֲבוֹת הַגּוֹיִם). This phrase occurs elsewhere in Chronicles where it refers to a king's activities that violate specific stipulations of Mosaic law regarding worship or magical practices (2 Chron. 28:3 regarding Ahaz; 2 Chron. 33:2 regarding Manasseh). Therefore, the Chronicler paints a picture of the priests and people repeatedly violating YHWH's regulations for worship, like those recorded in the law of Moses.

TRANSLATION ANALYSIS:
Since officials play such a significant role in Chronicles, one would expect them to be included so that the text would read "officials of Judah, priests, and the people." LXX contains this variant reading, which is the more likely reading; however, MT still makes sense. Perhaps for this reason, English translations follow MT.

The Chronicler uses the verb הִרְבּוּ to demonstrate the multitude of these violations. In two other similar contexts, the Chronicler uses this same verb. In 2 Chronicles 33:6, the Chronicler states that Manasseh increased (הִרְבָּה) doing what was evil in YHWH's estimation. In 2 Chronicles 33:23, the Chronicler states that Amon increased (הִרְבָּה) guilt. In all three instances, the verb does not indicate that they performed actions that were worse than others; instead, it indicates that they performed these actions more repeatedly. See sidebar "Continuing in Wickedness—Multiplying Guilt."

Because the priests and people repeatedly violate YHWH's regulations concerning worship, they defile (וַיְטַמְּאוּ) YHWH's temple. When the Chronicler mentions the temple's defilement, he foreshadows its coming trouble. Repeatedly throughout Chronicles, when the people worship improperly, the temple suffers. For instance, during Athaliah's reign, her followers raid the temple to support their worship of Baal (2 Chron. 24:7), and during Ahaz's reign, he closes the temple's doors to promote worshipping other gods (2 Chron. 28:24–25). Since the people during Zedekiah's reign again worship improperly, it is not surprising that the temple suffers. At the same time, it does not signal the temple's final fate. Following the reigns of Athaliah and Ahaz, a good king (Joash after Athaliah; Hezekiah after Ahaz) comes along to restore the temple. The Chronicler even records how Hezekiah commissions the priests to remove the defilement (טֻמְאָה) from the temple (2 Chron. 29:15–16). Therefore, even though the people defile the temple, there is hope that it may still be restored.

At the same time, the Chronicler reminds the reader that YHWH has consecrated this temple. The contrast between the people defiling the temple and YHWH consecrating it is striking. It looks back to what YHWH says to Solomon right after the temple's dedication (2 Chron. 7:15–22). In that speech YHWH affirms that he has consecrated this temple in Jerusalem and will hear the prayers made there. At the same time, he warns Solomon that if he does not follow him, he will destroy the temple. Here, the Chronicler reinforces this point just before he records the temple's destruction (36:19). This observation contradicts anyone who thinks that the temple is safe just because YHWH has consecrated it. Before the Chronicler's time, Jeremiah spoke out against those who said that Judah would remain safe because of YHWH's temple (Jer. 7:3–15). Jeremiah warned them that their actions would determine their fate in the land; YHWH's choice to consecrate the temple would not. The Chronicler makes this same point here to prevent those during the time of the rebuilt temple from making the same mistake.

Judah's Judgment and Exile (36:15–21)

Because of Judah's sin and refusal to heed YHWH's repeated warnings, YHWH sends Babylon to judge the land.

36:15. As a response to the wickedness of the king, the priests, and the people, YHWH repeatedly sends his messengers. Although his messengers include prophets, they are not limited to those with prophetic titles (such as seer, visionary, man of God, or prophet; see Schniedewind 1995, 53–54). Instead, a look through Chronicles reveals that YHWH's messengers consist of those who communicate his message, whether through spontaneous inspiration (such as the priest Zechariah, 2 Chron. 24:20) or through typical prophetic means (such as the prophet Oded, 2 Chron. 28:9–11). When YHWH sends a messenger, the messenger warns his audience that disaster is coming unless they stop their wicked activity (for more information regarding this pattern, see "Covenant" section in the introduction). In other words, the messenger's task is to call others to return to YHWH so that they may avoid punishment. This picture of the messenger makes sense of how the Chronicler describes YHWH's motive for sending them. YHWH sends them because of his compassion for his people and his temple. YHWH desires that the people will listen to his messengers and repent so that he doesn't have to punish them by exiling them and destroying his temple.

Jeremiah and Judah's Last Days

The language of repeatedly sending messengers in 36:15 closely resembles several passages in Jeremiah. Jeremiah's prophecies play an important role in the final verses of Chronicles, where three times the text explicitly mentions the prophecies (36:12, 21, 22). One can detect some of Jeremiah's implicit influence in 36:15.

36:16. However, the people do not listen. Instead, they respond in three ways: they mock God's messengers, despise God's words, and laugh at God's prophets. One may interpret these three phrases as essentially saying the same thing, without making any distinction between God's messengers, prophets, or words. However, this threefold description emphasizes Israel's stubborn reaction against YHWH's repeated attempts to warn them through every means available. By including his messengers (most likely those without a prophetic title who speak through spontaneous inspiration), his words (such as his written word in the law of Moses), and his prophets (such as Jeremiah), the Chronicler shows that "Israel [has] rejected every avenue through which God's word came" (Schniedewind 1995, 82). Since the people repeatedly reject YHWH's warnings of coming disaster and his invitation to repent, he eventually becomes angry enough that there is no turning back from punishing the people. In this sense there is no remedy (מרפה) for Israel.

36:17–20. Because YHWH's wrath rises up (*qal* עלה), he raises up (*hiphil* עלה) the Babylonian king to carry out his punishment against Judah. The Chronicler points out that the Babylonian

king kills, plunders, destroys, and exiles. First, he kills many, showing no mercy. The Chronicler speaks metaphorically to show how extensively the Babylonian king kills Judah's population. He kills male and female, young and old, even those who seek refuge inside the temple. In this way, YHWH's former compassion (36:15) contrasts to his thorough judgment, in which he hands over all his people to the Babylonians without compassion.

Comprehensiveness of Destruction

The Chronicler illustrates the comprehensiveness of Babylon's destruction in two ways. First, he speaks of those who go to the sanctuary. Apparently, they seek refuge in the holy place of the temple; however, the Chronicler has already pointed out that the people have defiled the temple (36:14), so it provides no refuge for them. Second, he speaks of young males and females as well as the elderly. Mentioning these opposites (male and female, young and old) creates a figure of speech to represent figuratively all the people. In other words, the Babylonian king not only killed Judah's soldiers, even if they sought refuge in the temple, but he killed everyone, even those who would not fight at all.

36:18. Second, the Babylonian king plunders. The Chronicler emphasizes that the Babylonians plunder Judah thoroughly. When he recounts that the Babylonians plunder the vessels used in the temple for worship, he mentions the large and small vessels. The Chronicler speaks figuratively to indicate that the Babylonians take all the vessels: small, large, and everything in between. When he reports that the Babylonians plunder the treasuries of Judah, he mentions not only the treasuries of the temple and king but also the treasuries of the officials. Since the Chronicler does not mention the treasuries of the officials elsewhere, their mention here confirms how extensive the Babylonian activity is.

36:19. Third, the Babylonian king destroys. The Chronicler shows his interest in the temple by mentioning it first. In fact, the Chronicler focuses on the temple through each step of what the Babylonian king does. He shows how the king's actions toward the temple escalate: first, he kills those seeking refuge in the temple; second, he plunders its equipment and treasuries; and finally, he burns it. Not only does he destroy the temple but he also destroys Jerusalem's walls, its fortified citadels, and any of its remaining items of value. All these structures and items would contribute to the city's prestige, prosperity, and peace, so it seems logical that the Chronicler would include them while describing Jerusalem's destruction.

However, these structures are important to the Chronicler for deeper reasons. YHWH's temple symbolizes his favor toward Jerusalem and Israel. When YHWH destroys the temple, he destroys this symbol because he is intensely angry with his people because of the seriousness, pervasiveness, and persistence of their sin. In a sense the city walls extend the boundaries of the temple to the city's edge. Therefore, they not only protect the inhabitants but more importantly symbolize YHWH's favor toward the city. One can detect this connection between the temple and the city walls in Psalm 51:18–19 (HB 20–21) and in the book of Nehemiah (Oeming 2012, 138–48). As a result, when the Chronicler recounts that the Babylonian king destroys the temple and the city walls, he is showing that the king has destroyed the entire area connected to his holy dwelling place.

36:20–21. Fourth, the king exiles those who survive his attack. He exiles them to Babylon where, as a conquered people, they serve the Babylonian king and his successors. Earlier the Babylonian king exiled Jehoiakim (36:6) and Jehoiachin (36:10) to Babylon and brought the temple implements (36:7, 18) and Jerusalem's treasures (36:18) there. However, now YHWH's

judgment extends fully to all the people when the king exiles those who survive his attack.

The Babylonian king's activity culminates in exile. Even though exile is a terrible form of YHWH's judgment it has a silver lining, which the Chronicler begins to point out. Unlike total annihilation, exile leaves open the possibility of return. Even though those exiled become servants, they only serve the Babylonians until the Persian Empire arises. Their time of servitude is limited. Furthermore, the Chronicler points out that the exile allows the land of Israel to make up for the Sabbath rests it has not experienced.

TRANSLATION ANALYSIS:
The Hebrew text speaks of the land and its Sabbaths with the following: עַד־רָצְתָה הָאָרֶץ אֶת־שַׁבְּתוֹתֶיהָ. The verb רצה represents two homonyms. One homonym carries the sense of "enjoying, being favorable to," while the second carries the sense of "paying back, redeeming, restoring" (*HALOT* s.v. "רצה" 1280–82). Although many translations (CSB, ESV, NASB, NIV, NKJV, NLT) render the verb as the first homonym ("enjoyed"), the word is more likely the second homonym, translated either as "made up for" (NRSV) or "paid back" (NJPS) since this passage draws on Leviticus 26:34–35 where the land makes up for all the Sabbaths it did not have while Israel lived in it.

The Chronicler shows how these events correspond to what YHWH has already announced. For instance, Jeremiah 27:7a reads, "All nations will serve him [Nebuchadnezzar], his son, and his grandson until the time for his own land comes" (CSB), and the Chronicler, living after Babylon's downfall, specifies that the Persian Empire brings the end to Babylonian dominance. He also alludes to Jeremiah 25:11–12 and 29:10 by referring to the seventy years in which Israel will remain under Babylonian rule. Beyond Jeremiah, he alludes to what YHWH has said to Moses on Mt. Sinai, recorded in Leviticus

26:34–35, 43. YHWH describes how he will punish Israel if they do not obey him. Part of this punishment is exile and desolation of the land. During this time of desolation, the land will make up for its Sabbath rests that the people do not observe while they live in the land. The Chronicler connects these warning passages to show that YHWH is just, punishing Israel for its wickedness, just as he said that he would. Therefore, both the Law and Prophets warn Israel of their coming fate so that "no one can say that Israel suffered this fate without warning" (Rudolph 1955, 338). At the same time, YHWH is gracious, limiting his punishment to a predetermined time (seventy years).

TRANSLATION ANALYSIS:
Even though *YHWH* limits the period of desolation, he does not cut it short. Even though some translations render the final phrase in 36:21 (לִמְלֹאות שִׁבְעִים שָׁנָה) as "to fulfill seventy years," apparently meaning to fulfill the prophecy of seventy years, the phrase more likely indicates that the full period of YHWH's judgment has passed. Some translations capture this sense by rendering the phrase as "until seventy years were complete" (NASB) or "until seventy years were completed" (NIV, NJPS).

Interpreting the Seventy Years

Although one may interpret the seventy years literally and precisely, there are number of reasons to consider it symbolic or at least approximate. First, the numbers seven and ten often signify completion. Second, seventy years signifies a human lifespan (cf. Ps 90:10); therefore, restoration can occur once every person living at the time of destruction has died. Third, the Chronicler associates the time period with an indefinite amount of time in which the land has not enjoyed its Sabbaths. Fourth, other ANE texts describe the length of a city's destruction as seventy years. See Renz 2000, 42.

Judah's Hope (36:22–23)

Following judgment YHWH raises up Cyrus to open the way for restoring the people to the land and rebuilding the temple in Jerusalem.

36:22. Since the Chronicler associates the seventy years of exile with the period of Babylonian dominance, once the Persian Empire arises under Cyrus, the way is clear for YHWH to begin restoring his people to the land. Within the first year of Cyrus's reign, YHWH prompts him to issue a proclamation, even in writing, throughout his empire. The Chronicler links this proclamation with Jeremiah's prophecy. One may interpret the text to mean that fulfilling Jeremiah's prophecy is the reason that YHWH prompts Cyrus to issue the proclamation; however, given the preceding context it seems more likely that the fulfillment of Jeremiah's prophecy is the condition for the proclamation (see the discussion in Frolov 2004, 596–98). In other words the prophecy that the Chronicler has in mind is the prophecy regarding Babylon's downfall (e.g., Jer. 25:12). This downfall marks the end of Israel's punishment. Only after the punishment is complete does YHWH begin restoring his people.

36:23. The Chronicler makes clear that YHWH is at work in all these events. YHWH raises up a foreign king to punish Israel for its wickedness; YHWH also raises up a foreign king to end that punishment and begin restoring Israel. Cyrus begins his proclamation by acknowledging YHWH's role in his rise to power and his obligation to see YHWH's temple built. It is hardly a coincidence that just as a foreign king (Huram of Tyre) participates in building the first temple, so also a foreign king (Cyrus) participates in building the second temple. Furthermore, Cyrus's blessing that YHWH will be with those who return to build the temple looks back to David's words to Solomon: "Now, my son, the LORD be with you, so that you may succeed in building the house of the LORD your God, as he has spoken concerning you" (1 Chron. 22:11 ESV). In these various ways, the Chronicler demonstrates explicitly and implicitly that YHWH is controlling Israel's fate.

The final words of Chronicles are words of hope. Cyrus's proclamation provides hope because it reminds the people that YHWH is at work in international affairs (raising up Cyrus), that he still cares for his temple (by appointing Cyrus to rebuild it), that YHWH's presence should empower the people to rebuild it, and that the people are free to return to Jerusalem to rebuild it. This hope is because YHWH is at work. It is true that YHWH has brought full punishment (seventy years) against Israel for its wickedness and its failure to listen to his repeated warnings. Nowhere (not only in this passage but throughout the book) does the Chronicler minimize the requirement to punish sin, but the Chronicler shows that there is hope after punishment—or perhaps even better, punishment does not have to be the final word. He offers a way to restore any and every generation of YHWH's people if they will humble themselves and repent (2 Chron. 7:14). He also provides a clear example of YHWH's willingness to bring about this restoration. At the same time, Chronicles does not end with a sense of completion. The book closes midsentence both literally (see Ezra 1:3) and thematically. YHWH hasn't returned the people, the temple hasn't been rebuilt, nor does a son of David rule on the throne. This openness is part of the point. Even though Chronicles is a book recounting the past, it is really about the future. It looks forward to a day in which YHWH will accomplish everything he has promised for his people in the return from exile (e.g., Deut. 30; Ezek. 36–37; Jer. 30–33; Dan. 9).

The closing of the book also allows for continuity between the past, present, and future, since those people and items carried into exile may return and preserve the past while building the present, awaiting the future. For the first readers of Chronicles, past, present, and future are important. The past reminds them who they are as YHWH's people; how just, consistent, faithful, and merciful YHWH has been as a covenant partner; and how inconsistent they have been. The present is the time for them to obey so that they may experience YHWH's reward rather than his punishment. They hope for the future because they know that YHWH will one day restore them as a people living in the land, worshipping at the temple, and following the Davidic king. This connection between past, present, and future helps explain why Chronicles begins with genealogies (who they are), repeatedly illustrating how YHWH rewards obedience and punishes disobedience (how they should now obey) and ends the work with a sense of hope (what they should await).

THEOLOGICAL FOCUS

Judgment is not God's final word for his people.

This passage recounts the end of Judah as a political state. It interprets this historical event as God's judgment against them. Theologically, this passage highlights two aspects of God's character: his justice and his mercy. Despite the distinction between justice and mercy, the presentation does not separate the two as though God is first just and then merciful. His justice and mercy flow together in his actions throughout the passage.

If one looks beyond the specific historical circumstances of Judah's end, this text presents insights into God's judgment. First, God judges those with no excuse. In the case of Judah, they knowingly and stubbornly resist God's authority. The passage repeatedly speaks of Judah doing what is evil. The passage does not elaborate much on what this evil entails except in the case of Zedekiah's reign, but given how quickly the Chronicler treats Jehoahaz, Jehoiakim, and Jehoiachin, it is reasonable to think that the wickedness under Zedekiah exemplifies the wickedness of these kings as well. The Chronicler presents Zedekiah as a stubborn rebel because not only does he do what is wicked, he does so knowingly and repeatedly. As the text points out, Zedekiah refuses to submit to God's instructions spoken by the prophet Jeremiah and rebels against the Babylonian king to whom he had pledged his allegiance with an oath in God's name (36:12–13). This type of stubborn rebellion deserves God's judgment. At the same time, in Romans Paul shows that both Jews and Gentiles are without excuse, either through what God has revealed in his word (Rom. 2:17–23) or in nature (Rom. 1:20–21). As a result, God is merciful in clearly communicating his instructions and just in judging such rebellion.

Second, God judges those who forsake him in worship. When God judges Judah, the Chronicler emphasizes that not only does Zedekiah behave as a stubborn rebel but that the priests and the people violate God's commands by engaging in wicked practices. Judah's wickedness is not limited to the kings or some other small group. Judah's wickedness encompasses all the people, including their religious leaders. The people do not maintain their covenant relationship as God's people. Therefore, God's judgment extends to those who are faithless. The situation is similar to what Jesus describes in John 15. Those who remain faithful to Jesus flourish, but those who do not, perish (John 15:5–6). God is jealous for his people, so when they forsake him he is just in his judgment.

Third, God judges those who ignore his warnings. Judah refuses to listen to God's warnings. God, in his compassion, sends messengers again and again to warn the people of their wicked ways that lead to disastrous consequences. Rather than accepting these warnings, the people despise and mock God's messengers. As is the case elsewhere in Chronicles, choosing to ignore God's warnings presented by his messengers leads to disaster (e.g., Asa, Jehoash, Amaziah, and Manasseh). In fact, this pattern of God's warning runs throughout the Bible. Chronicles portrays these messengers as proclaiming God's warnings based on what God has revealed. This activity continues as God has called and continues to call people to proclaim what God has revealed through Scripture. Their warnings are a sign both of God's mercy in offering the warning and of God's justice as he judges those who stubbornly ignore those warnings.

The passage demonstrates that God is right for judging Judah. As a result, God is also right for judging those who behave like Judah. At the same time, God's judgment is not the last word for Judah. The closing statements of the book (36:21–23) highlight the hope that awaits God's people. In the context of Chronicles, the statements point to the renewal of the land through observing its sabbaths, the end of God's sentence of punishment (seventy years), the rebuilding of the temple, and the return of God's people. Beyond the specific historical circumstances of the Chronicler, these statements apply to those who are in Christ, as they point beyond this present age to God's glorious future in which he renews all creation (e.g., Rom. 8:19–22), brings an end to suffering (e.g., Rev. 21:4), dwells among his people (e.g., Rev. 21:3), and settles his people in the place he has prepared for them (Rev. 21:2). God secures this glorious future and preserves his people for that day. Therefore, God's final word to his people is never judgment but a glorious hope (e.g., Rom. 7:24–8:2; Eph. 2:1–7).

PREACHING AND TEACHING STRATEGIES

Exegetical and Theological Synthesis

God's judgment and mercy are distinct, yet he puts them together. However, there can be a separation because he has given us a choice as to whether we embrace his mercy or not. We don't have a choice about his judgment, but we do have a choice about his mercy. His mercy is always there, but it is up to us whether we want to experience it.

Zedekiah rejected God's mercy and received severe judgment. Jehoiachin was brought to Babylon under God's judgment, but the writer leaves open the possibility of restoration. It is as if God is saying to us: I am giving you the option; my judgment will come. It can stop there as it did with Zedekiah, or you can receive my merciful restoration by humbling yourselves before me and trusting me, just as Manasseh received my astonishing grace.

This trust is shown by our turning from sin and following God in obedience. For the first readers the object of trust was YHWH's provision of forgiveness, as expressed through the sacrifices. For us, the object is the fulfillment of that system. We trust in Jesus, his substitutionary death, and his life-giving resurrection.

God's judgment is coming, make no mistake. Our sin will be judged, and there will be consequences. But that is not how God ends the story of 1 and 2 Chronicles. God's judgment and mercy always go together. He offers his mercy and restoration to those who will receive it.

Preaching Idea

Our sins are many; his mercy is more.

Contemporary Connections

What does it mean?

Zedekiah's sins were judged. To put it in terms of the Torah, his sins found him out (Num. 32:23). Sins will be judged because God is just. One wonders if Zedekiah, in his own mind, justified his sin?

Zedekiah worshipped other gods and yet was left in power. He confused God's patience with God's judgment. It is easy to think that God's delay in judgment must mean that we got away with the sin. With new technology in criminal investigation, we hear of a criminal being brought to justice fifteen to twenty years after the crime. Did they think they had gotten away with the crime? When the judgment doesn't come immediately, we could think that it will not come. We deny that we have sinned because there has been no punishment—yet. Or perhaps Zedekiah thought his sins were not so bad; after all, look at Manasseh. We can think that God's justice will not come because our sins are not as bad as those around us.

While we can speculate about whether Zedekiah justified his sin, we do know that he rebelled against God. This is a chosen course of action that is clearly and blatantly against authority. When raising a child, a parent witnesses a day when a toddler chooses to rebel. The cute little person is told to stop running toward a street. They stop for a moment, look back at the parents, smile, and then continue running toward danger, prompting quick action by the parent. The cuteness doesn't hide the rebelliousness.

Judgment will come whether we are blatantly rebelling or justifying our sins. In either case God's mercy is waiting for us when we humble ourselves, trust his grace, and receive his restoration.

Is it true?

Our view of judgment and mercy can be flawed. When we try to grasp God's justice and mercy, our understanding falls short.

Our judgment is flawed because we don't know everything. We cannot re-create the past, so being certain about a past crime or sin is subject to evidence. And the information we have surrounding a crime or sin is limited, so we may not have the full picture. A delightful Canadian production is the 1985 movie version of *Anne of Green Gables.* An orphan girl comes to live with an elderly brother and sister, Marilla and Matthew, on a trial basis. The thirteen-year-old girl, Anne, is falsely accused of stealing and losing Marilla's special brooch. Anne is judged because Marilla doesn't have all the facts. The resolution comes when the brooch is found on one of Marilla's shawls, and Anne is proven innocent. Because our judgment is flawed, we sometimes withhold it, and at times we should. God's judgment is not like ours. God's judgment always comes, and it is always just.

Our mercy is likewise flawed, because we don't know what is truly in a person's heart. If we knew for certain that a criminal would truly turn from a life of crime, our jails would be less crowded. Not only do we not know a person's true heart condition, but we also struggle with our own self-centered hearts. When we have been sinned against, mercy is not our first response. We first judge, which we assume is accurate, and that quickly turns into revenge. We judge without mercy. So, our mercy has its limits. God's mercy does not.

Now what?

How could this passage lead to anything less than our examining our hearts and actions? Where are we rebelling against God's authority and the authorities he has put into my life? At some level each of us has rebelled against parents, teachers, or some other authority, so we know that we can and do rebel.

There are some of us who know the exact point of our rebellion against God. For couples who are not married: Are you living together, or being too physically intimate? For the underpaid employee: Are you stealing little things from your employer to make up for your low pay? Are you habitually lying to benefit yourself? Have you offended a brother and sister and know that God wants you to go to them to seek reconciliation? Whatever the act of rebellion, we must humble ourselves, turn away from that specific sin, and turn to God.

Some of us need to ask the Spirit to examine our hearts and be open to his convicting work. If we think that we don't need to do this, then the Spirit has already revealed the sin of pride. In the words of Psalm 139:23–24 (NASB), "Try me . . . and see if there be any hurtful way in me."

A specific act of rebellion may already be known, or it might be revealed to us by the Holy Spirit or a brother or sister in Christ. Once the rebellion is known, our response must be to humble ourselves and trust God's mercy. He is eager to restore.

God's merciful restoration can give a couple the joy of truly respecting each other and increasing the great anticipation of being married. God's restoration can give an underpaid employee satisfaction that goes far deeper than a stolen ream of paper. God's restoration can bring the inner peace of speaking the truth. God judged the nation of Judah and restored her. God's judgment for my rebellion was placed on the cross. God's merciful restoration places me in sweet fellowship with him, now and forever. As the lyrics of a popular worship song remind us, our sins are many, but his mercy is more.

Creativity in Presentation

This closing narrative of the book can be effectively presented in two parts. The first part is depressing and disappointing. It presents the sin and judgment that God brought upon Judah. This first portion is a tragedy and should be presented as such. The second part is the wonderful promise of restoration. Judgment into mercy is the flow of thought.

To highlight the contrast between harsh judgment and the joy of God's merciful promise of restoration, the introduction should not give away the second part of the narrative. Since this is an inductive structure, present the first part and let it sound as if the sermon/lesson is almost finished. Then introduce the second part by saying that God doesn't end the story with his judgment. This is a type of unexpected ending that highlights the joy and hope that God offers. It is important to create the mood of tragedy in the first part, so that the joy of God's mercy will be desired and then experienced.

Here is one possible structure:

- The reason for judgment
  - The evil reigns of the kings
    - Jehoahaz's, Jehoiakim's, and Jehoiachin's rebellion (36:1–10)
    - Zedekiah's rebellion (36:11–13)
    - The people's rebellion (36:14)

- The evil in our lives
  - Known/unknown
  - Ignored/denied
- God's judgment will come
  - Babylon's destruction of Judah (36:15–21)
  - Consequences of sin
  - We will stand before God
- God's merciful promise of restoration
  - Cyrus's proclamation (36:22–23)
  - Our restoration
    - God's mercy and restoration through the cross
    - God's mercy and restoration for each day
- Our sins are many; his mercy is more.

DISCUSSION QUESTIONS

1. How do you remember rebelling against your parents?

2. What do you remember about how you felt toward them while you rebelled?

3. If you are a parent, how did you feel when your children blatantly rebelled against you?

4. Have you ever judged incorrectly? How?

5. Why do we hesitate to show mercy?

6. Do we hold judgment and mercy together as God does? Why or why not?

7. Describe when you experienced a restoration of a relationship.

8. What was required to restore that relationship?

REFERENCES

Abadie, Philippe. 2003. "From the Impious Manasseh (2 Kings 21) to the Convert Manasseh (2 Chronicles 33): Theological Rewriting by the Chronicler." In *The Chronicler as Theologian: Essays in Honor of Ralph W. Klein*, edited by M. Patrick Graham, Steven L. McKenzie, and Gary N. Knoppers, 89–104. JSOTSup 371. London: T&T Clark.

Ackroyd, Peter. 1977. "The Chronicler as Exegete." *JSOT* 2, no. 1:2–32. DOI: 10.1177/030908927600100201.

Allen, Leslie C. 1974. *The Greek Chronicles: The Relation of the Septuagint I and II Chronicles to the Massoretic Text*. VTSup 25. Leiden: Brill.

Amar, Itzhak. 2017. "The Characterization of Rehoboam and Jeroboam as a Reflection of the Chronicler's View of the Schism." *JHebS* 17:article 9. DOI: 10.5508/jhs.2017.v17.a9.

Barbiero, Gianni. 2013. "Psalm 132: A Prayer of 'Solomon.'" *CBQ* 75, no. 2:239–58.

Beentjes, Pancratius. 1993. "Tradition and Transformation: Aspects of Innerbiblical Interpretation in 2 Chronicles 20." *Bib* 74, no. 2:258–68.

Begg, Christopher. 1987. "The Fate of Judah's Four Last Kings in the Book of Chronicles." *OLP* 18:79–85.

Ben Zvi, Ehud. 1991. "Once the Lamp Has Been Kindled . . .: A Reconsideration of the Meaning of the MT *Nîr* in 1 Kgs 11:36; 15:4; 2 Kgs 8:19 and 2 Chr 21:7." *ABR* 39:19–30.

_____. 2006a. *History, Literature and Theology in the Book of Chronicles*. Bible World. New York: Routledge.

_____. 2006b. "Revisiting 'Boiling in Fire' in 2 Chronicles 35:13 and Related Passover Questions: Text, Exegetical Needs and Concerns, and General Implications." In *Biblical Interpretation in Judaism and Christianity*, edited by Isaac Kalimi and Peter Haas, 238–50. LHBOTS 439. London: T&T Clark.

_____. 2008. "A House of Treasures: The Account of Amaziah in 2 Chronicles 25—Observations and Implications." *SJOT* 22, no. 1:63–85. DOI: 10.1080/09018320802185077.

_____. 2013. "Reading Chronicles and Reshaping the Memory of Manasseh." In *Chronicling the Chronicler: The Book of Chronicles and Early Second Temple Historiography*, edited by Paul S. Evans and Tyler F. Williams, 121–40. Winona Lake, IN: Eisenbrauns. DOI: 10.5325/j.ctv18r6r1j.12.

Berner, Christoph. 2011. "The Egyptian Bondage and Solomon's Forced Labor: Literary Connections between Exodus 1–15 and 1 Kings 1–12?" In *Pentateuch, Hexateuch, Enneateuch? Identifying Literary Works in Genesis through Kings*, edited by Thomas B. Dozeman, Thomas Römer, and Konrad Schmid, 211–40. AIL 8. Atlanta: Society of Biblical Literature.

Black, David Alan. 1995. "The Discourse Structure of Philippians: A Study in Textlinguistics." *NovT* 37, no. 1:16–49. DOI: 10.1163/1568536952613703.

Blenkinsopp, Joseph. 2003. "Bethel in the Neo-Babylonian Period." In *Judah and the Judeans in the Neo-Babylonian Period*, edited by Oded Lipschits and Joseph Blenkinsopp, 93–107. Winona Lake, IN: Eisenbrauns. DOI: 10.5325/j.ctv1bxh3p2.8.

Boda, Mark J. 2004. *Haggai, Zechariah*. NIVAC. Grand Rapids: Zondervan.

_____. 2006. "From Dystopia to Myopia: Utopian (Re)Visions in Haggai and Zechariah 1–8." In *Utopia and Dystopia in Prophetic Literature*, edited by Ehud Ben Zvi, 210–48. PFES 92. Helsinki: Finnish Exegetical Society; Göttingen: Vandenhoeck & Ruprecht.

_____. 2010a. *1–2 Chronicles*. Cornerstone Biblical Commentary 5a. Carol Stream, IL: Tyndale House.

_____. 2010b. "Legitimizing the Temple: The Chronicler's Temple Building Account." In *From the Foundations to the Crenellations: Essays on Temple Building in the Ancient Near East and Hebrew Bible*, edited by Mark J. Boda and Jamie Novotny, 303–18. AOAT 366. Münster: Ugarit-Verlag.

_____. 2013. "Gazing through the Cloud of Incense: Davidic Dynasty and Temple Community in the Chronicler's Perspective." In *Chronicling the Chronicler: The Book of Chronicles and Early Second Temple Historiography*, edited by Paul S. Evans and Tyler F. Williams, 215–46. Winona Lake, IN: Eisenbrauns. DOI: 10.5325/j.ctv18r6r1j.16.

Bowen, Nancy R. 2001. "The Quest for the Historical *Gébîrâ*." CBQ 63, no. 4:597–618.

Braun, Roddy. 1976. "Solomon, the Chosen Temple Builder: The Significance of 1 Chronicles 22, 28, and 29 for the Theology of Chronicles." *JBL* 95, no. 4:581–90. DOI: 10.2307/3265573.

_____. 1986. *1 Chronicles*. WBC 14. Waco, TX: Word.

Bridge, Edward. 2011. "Self-abasement as an Expression of Thanks in the Hebrew Bible." *Bib* 92, no. 2:255–73.

Butler, Trent C. 1978. "A Forgotten Passage from a Forgotten Era (1 Chr. XVI 8–36)." *VT* 28, no. 2:142–50. DOI: 10.1163/156853378X00400.

Cogan, Mordechai. 1985. "The Chronicler's Use of Chronology as Illuminated by Neo-Assyrian Royal Inscriptions." In *Empirical Models for Biblical Criticism*, edited by Jeffrey H. Tigay, 197–209. Philadelphia: University of Pennsylvania Press.

Cogan, Mordechai, and Hayim Tadmor. 1988. *II Kings: A New Translation with Introduction and Commentary*. AB 11. Garden City, NY: Doubleday.

Cohen, Shaye J. D. 1984–1985. "Solomon and the Daughter of Pharaoh: Intermarriage, Conversion, and the Impurity of Women." *JANES* 16–17:23–37.

Cudworth, Troy D. 2014. "The Division of Israel's Kingdom in Chronicles: A Re-examination of the Usual Suspects." *Bib* 95, no. 4:498–523.

_____. 2016. *War in Chronicles: Temple Faithfulness and Israel's Place in the Land*. LHBOTS 627. London: Bloomsbury T&T Clark.

Curtis, Edward L., and Albert A. Madsen. 1910. *A Critical and Exegetical Commentary on the Books of Chronicles*. ICC. Edinburgh: T&T Clark.

Davies, Graham I. 1989. "'*Urwōt* in 1 Kings 5:6 (EVV 4:26) and the Assyrian Horse Lists." *JSS* 34, no. 1:25–38. DOI: 10.1093/jss/XXXIV.1.25.

Davis, Andrew R. 2019. *Reconstructing the Temple: The Royal Rhetoric of Temple Renovation in the Ancient Near East and Israel*. New York: Oxford University Press.

de Moor, Johannes C. 1976. "*Rāpi'ūma* – Rephaim" *ZAW* 88, no. 3:323–45. DOI: 10.1515/zatw.1976.88.3.323.

De Vries, Simon. 1988. "Moses and David as Cult Founders in Chronicles." *JBL* 207, no. 4:619–39. DOI: 10.2307/3267625.

_____. 1989. *1 and 2 Chronicles*. FOTL 11. Grand Rapids: Eerdmans.

Dillard, Raymond B. 1981. "The Chronicler's Solomon." *WTJ* 43, no. 2:289–300.

_____. 1987. *2 Chronicles*. WBC 15. Waco, TX: Word.

Dirksen, Peter B. 2005. *1 Chronicles*. HCOT. Leuven: Peeters.

Dohmen, Christoph. 1984. "Heißt סֶמֶל 'Bild, Statue'?" *ZAW* 96:263–66.

Duke, Rodney K. 1990. *The Persuasive Appeal of the Chronicler: A Rhetorical Analysis.* BLS 25. Sheffield: Almond Press.

Dutcher-Walls, Patricia. 1996. *Narrative Art, Political Rhetoric: The Case of Athaliah and Joash.* JSOTSup 209. Sheffield: Sheffield Academic.

Ellis, Richard S. 1968. *Foundation Deposits in Ancient Mesopotamia.* YNER 2. New Haven, CT: Yale University Press.

Endres, John C. 2001. "Joyful Worship in Second Temple Judaism." In *Passion, Vitality, and Foment: The Dynamics of Second Temple Judaism*, edited by Lamontte M. Luker, 155–88. Harrisburg, PA: Trinity Press International.

Evans, Paul S. 2010. "The Function of the Chronicler's Temple Despoliation Notices in Light of Imperial Realities in Yehud." *JBL* 129, no. 1:31–47. DOI: 10.2307/27821003.

Foster, Richard. 1988. *Celebration of Discipline: The Path to Spiritual Growth.* San Francisco: Harper Collins.

Fouts, David. 1994. "Another Look at Large Numbers in Assyrian Royal Inscriptions." *JNES* 53, no. 3:205–11.

———. 1997. "A Defense of the Hyperbolic Interpretation of Large Numbers in the Old Testament." *JETS* 40, no. 3:377–87.

Fox, Michael V. 2009. *Proverbs 10–31: A New Translation with Introduction and Commentary.* AB 18B. New Haven, CT: Yale University Press.

Fox, Nili S. 2018. "Kingship and the State in Ancient Israel." In *Behind the Scenes of the Old Testament: Cultural, Social, and Historical Contexts*, edited by Jonathan S. Greer, John W. Hilber, and John H. Walton, 475–81. Grand Rapids: Baker Academic.

Frederick, Thomas V., Yvonne Thai, and Scott Dunbar. 2021. "Coping with Pastoral Burnout Using Christian Contemplative Practices." *Religions* 12:378. DOI: 10.3390/rel12060378.

Fretheim, Terence E. 1984. *The Suffering of God: An Old Testament Perspective.* OBT 14. Philadelphia: Fortress.

Frevel, Christian. 1991. "Die Elimination der Göttin aus dem Weltbild des Chronisten." *ZAW* 103:263–71.

Friedman, Richard Elliott. 1980. "The Tabernacle in the Temple." *BA* 43, no. 4:241–48. DOI: 10.2307/3209799.

Frisch, Amos. 2000. "Jeroboam and the Division of the Kingdom: Mapping Contrasting Biblical Accounts." *JANES* 27:15–29.

———. 2011. "The Attitude toward Jerusalem in Two Rebellion Narratives: A Literary and Theological Investigation." *BN* 150:35–48.

Frolov, Serge. 2004. "The Prophecy of Jeremiah in Esr 1,1." *ZAW* 116, no. 4:595–601. DOI: 10.1515/zatw.2004.116.4.595.

Giffone, Benjamin D. 2016. *"Sit at My Right Hand": The Chronicler's Portrait of the Tribe of Benjamin in the Social Context of Yehud.* LHBOTS 628. London: T&T Clark.

Gilhooley, Andrew M. 2020. *The Edict of Cyrus and Notions of Restoration in Ezra-Nehemiah and Chronicles.* HBM 89. Sheffield: Sheffield Phoenix.

Glatt-Gilad, David A. 2001. "Regnal Formulae as a Historiographic Device in the Book of Chronicles." *RB* 108, no. 2:184–209.

Graham, M. Patrick. 1993. "Aspects of the Structure and Rhetoric of 2 Chronicles 25." In *History and Interpretation: Essays in Honour of John H. Hayes*, edited by M. Patrick Graham, William P. Brown, and Jeffrey K. Kuan, 78–89. JSOTSup 173. Sheffield: Sheffield Academic.

Grayson, A. Kirk. 1995. "Eunuchs in Power: Their Role in the Assyrian Bureaucracy." In *Vom Alten Orient zum Alten Testament: Festschrift für Wolfram Freiherrn von Soden zum 85. Geburtstag am 19. Juni 1993*, edited by Manfried Dietrich and Oswald Loretz, 85–98. AOAT 240. Kevelaer:

Butzon & Bercker; Neukirchen-Vluyn: Neukirchener Verlag.

Greene, Joseph R. 2018. "Did God Dwell in the Second Temple? Clarifying the Relationship between Theophany and Temple Dwelling." *JETS* 61, no. 4:767–84.

Gunn, David M., and Danna Nolan Fewell. 1993. *Narrative in the Hebrew Bible*. Oxford: Oxford University Press.

Guy, Jordan. 2019. *United in Exile, Reunited in Restoration: The Chronicler's Agenda*. HBM 81. Sheffield: Sheffield Phoenix.

Hahn, Scott W. 2012. *The Kingdom of God as Liturgical Empire: A Theological Commentary on 1–2 Chronicles*. Grand Rapids: Baker Academic.

Halpern, Baruch, and David S. Vanderhooft. 1991. "The Editions of Kings in the 7th–6th Centuries BCE." *HUCA* 62:179–244.

Harris, R. Laird, Gleason L. Archer Jr., and Bruce K. Waltke, eds. 1980. *TWOT* s.v. "חֶסֶד" 1:305–7.

Hasel, Gerhard. 1983. "Health and Healing in the Old Testament." *AUSS* 21, no. 3:191–202.

Heiser, Michael. 2015. *The Unseen Realm*. Bellingham WA: Lexham Press.

Hoskins, Paul M. 2007. *Jesus as the Fulfillment of the Temple in the Gospel of John*. PBM. Eugene, OR: Wipf & Stock.

Huffmon, Herbert B. 1966. "The Treaty Background of Hebrew *Yāda*'." *BASOR* 181:31–37. DOI: 10.2307/1356118.

Hundley, Michael B. 2013. *Gods in Dwellings: Temples and Divine Presence in the Ancient Near East*. WAWSup 3. Atlanta: Society of Biblical Literature.

Hwang, Sunwoo. 2017. "Coexistence of Unconditionality and Conditionality of the Davidic Covenant in Chronicles." *HeyJ* 58, no. 2:239–46. DOI: 10.1111/j.1468-2265.2012.00775.x.

Janzen, David. 2017. *Chronicles and the Politics of Davidic Restoration: A Quiet Revolution*. LHBOTS 655. London: T&T Clark.

_____. 2018. "A Monument and a Name: The Primary Purpose of Chronicles' Genealogies." *JSOT* 43, no. 1:45–66. DOI: 10.1177/0309089215702885.

Japhet, Sara. 1968. "The Supposed Common Authorship of Chronicles and Ezra-Nehemiah Investigated Anew." *VT* 18:330–71.

_____. 1993. *I & II Chronicles: A Commentary*. OTL. Louisville: Westminster John Knox.

_____. 2009. *The Ideology of the Book of Chronicles and Its Place in Biblical Thought*. Winona Lake, IN: Eisenbrauns.

Jeon, Yong Ho. 2013. *Impeccable Solomon? A Study of Solomon's Faults in Chronicles*. Eugene, OR: Pickwick.

Jonker, Louis C. 2003. *Reflections of King Josiah in Chronicles: Late Stages of the Josiah Reception in 2 Chr 34f*. Textpragmatische Studien zur Hebräischen Bibel 2. Gütersloh: Gütersloher Verlagshaus.

_____. 2013a. *1 & 2 Chronicles*. Understanding the Bible. Grand Rapids: Baker.

_____. 2013b. "Of Jebus, Jerusalem, and Benjamin: The Chronicler's *Sondergut* in 1 Chronicles 21 against the Background of the Late Persian Era in Yehud." In *Chronicling the Chronicler: The Book of Chronicles and Early Second Temple Historiography*, edited by Paul S. Evans and Tyler F. Williams, 81–102. Winona Lake, IN: Eisenbrauns. DOI: 10.5325/j.ctv18r6r1j.10.

_____. 2016. "'My Wife Must Not Live in King David's Palace' (2 Chr 8:11): A Contribution to the Diachronic Study of Intermarriage Traditions in the Hebrew Bible." *JBL* 135, no. 1:35–47. DOI: 10.15699/jbl.1344.2016.2870.

Kalimi, Isaac. 1995. "Paronomasia in the Book of Chronicles." *JSOT* 20, no. 67 (September): 27–41. DOI: 10.1177/030908929502006702.

_____. 2005a. *An Ancient Israelite Historian: Studies in the Chronicler, His Time, Place and Writing*. SSN 46. Assen: Van Gorcum.

_____. 2005b. *The Reshaping of Ancient Israelite History in Chronicles*. Winona Lake, IN: Eisenbrauns.

_____. 2019. *Writing and Rewriting the Story of Solomon in Ancient Israel.* Cambridge: Cambridge University Press.

Kapelrud, Arvid. 1963. "Temple Building, a Task for Gods and Kings." *Or* 32, no. 1:56–62.

Kauflin, Bob. 2008. *Worship Matters: Leading Others to Encounter the Greatness of God.* Wheaton, IL: Crossway.

Keel, Othmar, and Sylvia Schroer. 2015. *Creation: Biblical Theologies in the Context of the Ancient Near East.* Translated by Peter Daniels. Winona Lake, IN: Eisenbrauns.

Kelly, Brian. 2003. "'Retribution' Revisited: Covenant, Grace and Restoration." In *The Chronicler as Theologian: Essays in Honor of Ralph W. Klein*, edited by M. Patrick Graham, Steven L. McKenzie, and Gary N. Knoppers, 206–27. JSOTSup 371. London: T&T Clark.

Kilchör, Benjamin. 2013. "בשל – Das Essen ist bereit." *ZAW* 125, no. 3:483–86. DOI: 10.1515/zaw-2013-0030.

Kitchen, Kenneth A. 2003. *On the Reliability of the Old Testament.* Grand Rapids: Eerdmans.

Klein, Neriah. 2016. "Between Genealogy and Historiography: Er, Achar, and Saul in the Book of Chronicles." *VT* 66, no. 2:217–44.

_____. 2017. "The Chronicler's Code: The Rise and Fall of Judah's Army in the Book of Chronicles." *JHS* 17:article 3. DOI: 10.5508/jhs.2017.v17.a3.

Klein, Ralph W. 2000. "The Ironic End of Joash in Chronicles." In *For a Later Generation: The Transformation of Tradition in Israel, Early Judaism, and Early Christianity*, edited by Randal A. Argall, Beverly A. Bow, and Rodney A. Werline, 116–27. Harrisburg, PA: Trinity Press International.

_____. 2006. *1 Chronicles: A Commentary.* Hermeneia. Minneapolis: Fortress.

_____. 2012. *2 Chronicles: A Commentary.* Hermeneia. Minneapolis: Fortress.

Kleinig, John W. 1993. *The Lord's Song: The Basis, Function and Significance of Choral Music in Chronicles.* JSOTSup 156. Sheffield: Sheffield Academic.

Knapp, Andrew. 2015. *Royal Apologetic in the Ancient Near East.* WAWSup 4. Atlanta: SBL Press.

Knoppers, Gary N. 1990. "Rehoboam in Chronicles: Villain or Victim?" *JBL* 109, no. 3:423–40. DOI: 10.2307/3267050.

_____. 1991. "Reform and Regression: The Chronicler's Presentation of Jehoshaphat." *Bib* 72, no. 4:500–524.

_____. 1994. "Dissonance and Disaster in the Legend of Kirta." *JAOS* 114, no. 4:572–82. DOI: 10.2307/606163.

_____. 1995. "Prayer and Propaganda: Solomon's Dedication of the Temple and the Deuteronomist's Program." *CBQ* 57, no. 2:229–54.

_____. 1996. "'YHWH Is Not with Israel': Alliances as a Topos in Chronicles." *CBQ* 58, no. 4:601–26.

_____. 2001. "An Achaemenid Imperial Authorization of Torah in Yehud?" In *Persian and Torah: The Imperial Authorization of Torah*, edited by James W. Watts, 115–34. SymS 17. Atlanta: Society of Biblical Literature.

_____. 2003a. *1 Chronicles 1–9: A New Translation with Introduction and Commentary.* AB 12. New York: Doubleday.

_____. 2003b. "Greek Historiography and the Chronicler's History: A Reexamination." *JBL* 122, no. 4:627–50. DOI: 10.2307/3268069.

_____. 2004. *1 Chronicles 10–29: A New Translation with Introduction and Commentary.* AB 12a. New York: Doubleday.

_____. 2013. *Jews and Samaritans: The Origins and History of Their Early Relations.* Oxford: Oxford University Press.

_____. 2015. "More Than Friends? The Economic Relationship between Huram and Solomon Reconsidered." In *The Economy of Ancient Judah in Its Historical Context*, edited by Marvin Lloyd Miller, Ehud Ben Zvi, and Gary N. Knoppers, 51–76. Winona

Lake, IN: Eisenbrauns. DOI: 10.5325/j.ctv1bxh0x7.7.

———. 2019. *Judah and Samaria in Postmonarchic Times: Essays on Their Histories and Literatures.* FAT 129. Tübingen: Mohr Siebeck.

———. 2021. *Prophets, Priests, and Promises: Essays on the Deuteronomistic History, Chronicles, and Ezra-Nehemiah*, edited by Christl Maier and H. G. M. Williamson. VTSup 186. Leiden: Brill.

Koch, Klaus. 1965. "Das Verhältnis von Exegese und Verkündigung anhand eines Chroniktextes." *TLZ* 90, no. 9:659–70.

Koorevaar, Hendrik. 2015. "Chronicles as the Intended Conclusion to the Old Testament Canon." In *The Shape of the Writings*, edited by Julius Steinberg and Timothy J. Stone, 207–35. Siphrut 16. Winona Lake, IN: Eisenbrauns. DOI: 10.1515/9781575063744-012.

Leeb, Carolyn S. 2000. *Away from the Father's House: The Social Location of* na'ar *and* na'arah *in Ancient Israel.* JSOTSup 301. Sheffield: Sheffield Academic.

Levenson, Jon D. 1985. *Sinai & Zion: An Entry into the Jewish Bible.* San Francisco: Harper & Row.

Levin, Yigal. 2017. *The Chronicles of the Kings of Judah: 2 Chronicles 10–36; A New Translation and Commentary.* London: T&T Clark.

Lipschits, Oded. 2006. "Achaemenid Imperial Policy, Settlement Processes in Palestine, and the Status of Jerusalem in the Middle of the Fifth Century B.C.E." In *Judah and the Judeans in the Persian Period*, edited by Oded Lipschits and Manfred Oeming, 19–52. Winona Lake, IN: Eisenbrauns. DOI: 10.5325/j.ctv1bxgzgk.6.

Lohfink, Norbert. 1962. "Die deuteronomistische Darstellung des Übergangs der Führung Israels von Moses auf Josue." *Scholastik* 37:32–44. DOI: 10.15496/publikation-46883.

Lynch, Matthew. 2014a. "Mapping Monotheism: Modes of Monotheistic Rhetoric in the Hebrew Bible." *VT* 64, no. 1:47–68. DOI: 10.1163/15685330-12341141.

———. 2014b. *Monotheism and Institutions in the Book of Chronicles.* FAT 2/64. Tübingen: Mohr Siebeck.

Malamat, Abraham. 1963. "Kingship and Council in Israel and Sumer: A Parallel." *JNES* 22, no. 4: 247–53.

———. 1965. "Organs of Statecraft in the Israelite Monarchy." *BA* 28, no. 2:34–65. DOI: 10.2307/3211054.

Matthews, Victor. 1987. "Entrance Ways and Threshing Floors: Legally Significant Sites in the Ancient Near East." *Fides et historia* 19, no. 3:25–40.

McCarthy, Dennis J. 1971. "An Installation Genre?" *JBL* 90, no. 1:31–41. DOI: 10.2307/3262983.

McConville, J. G. 1984. *I & II Chronicles.* Daily Study Bible. Philadelphia: Westminster.

———. 1986. "1 Chronicles 28:9: Yahweh 'Seeks Out' Solomon." *JTS* 37, no. 1:105–8.

McKenzie, Steven L. 2004. *1–2 Chronicles.* AOTC. Nashville: Abingdon.

Merrill, Eugene H. 2015. *A Commentary on 1 & 2 Chronicles.* Kregel Exegetical Library. Grand Rapids: Kregel.

Mettinger, Tryggve N. D. 1971. *Solomonic State Officials: A Study of the Civil Government Officials of the Israelite Monarchy.* ConBOT 5. Lund: Gleerup.

———. 1976. *King and Messiah: The Civil and Sacral Legitimation of the Israelite Kings.* ConBOT 8. Lund: Gleerup.

Metzger, Martin. 1985. *Königsthron und Gottesthron: Thronformen und Throndarstellungen in Ägypten und im Vorderen Orient im dritten und zweiten Jahrtausend vor Christus und deren Beduetung für das Verständnis von Aussagen über den Thron im Alten Testament.* AOAT 15. Kevelaer: Butzon & Bercker; Neukirchen-Vluyn: Neukirchener Verlag.

Meyers, Carol. 1983. "Jachin and Boaz in Religious and Political Perspective." *CBQ* 45, no. 2:167–78.

Millard, Alan R. 1989. "Does the Bible Exaggerate King Solomon's Golden Wealth?" *BAR* 15, no. 3:20–31, 34.

Miller, Geoffrey. 2014. "The Wiles of the Lord: Divine Deception, Subtlety, and Mercy in I Reg 22." *ZAW* 126, no. 1:45–58. DOI: 10.1515/zaw-2014-0004.

Mitchell, Christine. 2006. "The Ironic Death of Josiah in 2 Chronicles." *CBQ* 68, no. 3:421–35.

Moberly, R. W. L. 2003. "Does God Lie to His Prophets? The Story of Micaiah ben Imlah as a Test Case." *HTR* 96, no. 1:1–23. DOI: 10.1017/S0017816003000312.

Mosis, Rudolph. 1973. *Untersuchungen zur Theologie des chronistischen Geschichtswerkes.* Freiburger theologische Studien 92. Freiburg: Herder.

Muffs, Yochanan. 1979. "Love and Joy as Metaphors of Volition in Hebrew and Related Literatures, Part II: The Joy of Giving." *JANES* 11, no. 1:91–111.

Noonan, Benjamin J. 2020. *Advances in the Study of Biblical Hebrew and Aramaic: New Insights for Reading the Old Testament.* Grand Rapids: Zondervan.

Nordheim, Eckhard von. 1977. "König und Tempel: Der Hintergrund des Tempelbauverbotes in 2 Samuel vii." *VT* 27, no. 4:434–53. DOI: 10.2307/1517059.

Oeming, Manfred. 2012. "The Real History: The Theological Ideas behind Nehemiah's Wall." In *New Perspectives on Ezra-Nehemiah: History and Historiography, Text, Literature, and Interpretation*, edited by Isaac Kalimi, 131–49. Winona Lake, IN: Eisenbrauns.

Payne, Randy C. 2017. "'He Opened the Doors of the House of Yahweh': Door Imagery in the Hebrew Bible in Light of Its Ancient Near Eastern Context." PhD diss., Southwestern Baptist Theological Seminary.

Pearson, Calvin. 2013. "'Lifting Holy Hands': Nuance, Nuisance, or Error? A Biblical Theology of the Practice of Lifting Hands in Worship." *Artistic Theologian* 2:26–36.

Peterson, Brian. 2018. "Did the Vassal Treaties of Esarhaddon Influence the Chronicler's Succession Narrative of Solomon?" *BBR* 28, no. 4:554–74. DOI: 10.5325/bullbiblrese.28.4.0554.

Plöger, Otto. 2000. "Speech and Prayer in the Deuteronomistic and the Chronicler's Histories." In *Reconsidering Israel and Judah: Recent Studies on the Deuteronomistic History*, edited by Gary N. Knoppers and J. Gordon McConville, 31–46. SBTS 8. Winona Lake, IN: Eisenbrauns.

Price, J. H. 2015. "The Conceptual Transfer of Human Agency to the Divine in the Second Temple Period: The Case of Saul's Suicide." *Shofar* 34, no. 1:107–30. DOI: 10.5703/shofar.34.1.107.

Prokop, Daniel. 2020. *The Pillars of the First Temple (1 Kgs 7, 15–22): A Study from Ancient Near Eastern, Biblical, Archaeological, and Iconographic Perspectives.* FAT 2/116. Tübingen: Mohr Siebeck.

Renz, Thomas. 2000. "Proclaiming the Future: History and Theology in Prophecies against Tyre." *TynBul* 51, no. 1:17–58. DOI: 10.53751/001c.30282.

Riley, William. 1993. *King and Cultus in Chronicles: Worship and the Reinterpretation of History.* JSOTSup 160. Sheffield: JSOT Press.

Ristau, Kenneth A. 2009. "Reading and Rereading Josiah: The Chronicler's Representation of Josiah for the Postexilic Community." In *Community Identity in Judean Historiography: Biblical and Comparative Perspectives*, edited by Gary N. Knoppers and Kenneth A. Ristau, 219–47. Winona Lake, IN: Eisenbrauns.

———. 2015. "'In the House of Judah, My Father's House': The Character of Joab in the Book of Chronicles." In *History, Memory,*

Hebrew Scriptures: A Festschrift for Ehud Ben Zvi, edited by Ian Douglas Wilson and Diana V. Edelman, 133–50. Winona Lake, IN: Eisenbrauns.

Rudolph, Wilhelm. 1955. *Chronikbücher*. HAT 21. Tübingen: Mohr.

Sailhamer, John. 1983. *First & Second Chronicles*. Everyman's Bible Commentary. Chicago: Moody.

Schmitt, Rüdiger. 2014. "War Rituals in the Old Testament: Prophets, Kings, and the Ritual Preparation for War." In *Warfare, Ritual, and Symbol in Biblical and Modern Contexts*, edited by Brad E. Kelle, Frank Ritchel Ames, and Jacob L. Wright, 149–61. AIL 18. Atlanta: Society of Biblical Literature. DOI: 10.2307/j.ctt6wqb3g.12.

Schniedewind, William M. 1995. *The Word of God in Transition: From Prophet to Exegete in the Second Temple Period*. JSOTSup 197. Sheffield: Sheffield Academic.

———. 1999. "The Chronicler as an Interpreter of Scripture." In *The Chronicler as Author*, edited by M. Patrick Graham and Steven L. McKenzie, 158–80. JSOTSup 263. Sheffield: JSOT Press.

Schweitzer, Steven J. 2007. *Reading Utopia in Chronicles*. LHBOTS 442. London: T&T Clark.

———. 2011. "Judging a Book by Its Citations: Sources and Authority in Chronicles." In *What Was Authoritative for Chronicles?*, edited by Ehud Ben Zvi and Diana Edelman, 37–66. Winona Lake, IN: Eisenbrauns. DOI: 10.5325/j.ctv1bxgxnp.6.

———. 2013. "The Genealogies of 1 Chronicles 1–9: Purposes, Forms, and the Utopian Identity of Israel." In *Chronicling the Chronicler: The Book of Chronicles and Early Second Temple Historiography*, edited by Paul S. Evans and Tyler F. Williams, 9–28. Winona Lake, IN: Eisenbrauns. DOI: 10.5325/j.ctv18r6r1j.6

———. 2016. "Exile, Empire, and Prophecy: Reframing Utopian Concerns in Chronicles."

In *Worlds That Could Not Be: Utopia in Chronicles, Ezra and Nehemiah*, edited by Steven J. Schweitzer and Frauke Uhlenbruch, 81–104. LHBOTS 620. London: Bloomsbury T&T Clark. DOI: 10.5040/9780567664068.ch-005.

Seevers, Boyd. 2013. *Warfare in the Old Testament: The Organization, Weapons, and Tactics of Ancient Near Eastern Armies*. Grand Rapids: Kregel.

Seow, Choon Leong. 1989. *Myth, Drama, and the Politics of David's Dance*. HSM 44. Atlanta: Scholars Press.

Shaver, Judson R. 1989. *Torah and the Chronicler's History Work: An Inquiry into the Chronicler's References to Laws, Festivals, and the Cultic Institutions in Relationship to Pentateuchal Legislation*. BJS 196. Atlanta: Scholars Press.

Shepherd, Michael B. 2016. *Textuality and the Bible*. Eugene, OR: Wipf & Stock.

Shin, Deuk-il. 2016. "The Translation of the Hebrew Term *Nīr*: 'David's Yoke'?" *TynBul* 67, no. 1:7–21. DOI: 10.53751/001c.29405.

Sklar, Jay. 2005. *Sin, Impurity, Sacrifice, Atonement: The Priestly Conceptions*. HBM 2. Sheffield: Sheffield Phoenix.

Smith, James K. A. 2016. *You Are What You Love: The Spiritual Power of Habit*. Grand Rapids: Brazos.

Sosik, Marcin. 2009. "*Gebira* at the Judean Court." *Scripta Judaica Cracoviensia* 7:7–13.

Sparks, James T. 2008. *The Chronicler's Genealogies: Towards an Understanding of 1 Chronicles 1–9*. AcBib 28. Atlanta: Society of Biblical Literature.

Stavrakopoulou, Francesca. 2004. *King Manasseh and Child Sacrifice: Biblical Distortions of Historical Realities*. BZAW 338. Berlin: de Gruyter.

Steins, Georg. 2015. "Torah-Binding and Canon Closure: On the Origin and Canonical Function of the Book of Chronicles." In *The Shape of the Writings*, edited by Julius

Steinberg and Timothy J. Stone, 237–80. Siphrut 16. Winona Lake, IN: Eisenbrauns. DOI: 10.5325/j.ctv1bxgzn5.14.

Stokes, Ryan E. 2009. "The Devil Made David Do It . . . Or *Did* He? The Nature, Identity, and Literary Origins of the *Satan* in 1 Chronicles 21:1." *JBL* 128, no. 1:91–106. DOI: 10.2307/25610168.

_____. 2019. *The Satan: How God's Executioner Became the Enemy.* Grand Rapids: Eerdmans.

Strawn, Brent A. 2003. "What is Stronger than a Lion? Leonine Image and Metaphor in the Hebrew Bible and the Ancient Near East." In Orbis Biblicus et Orientalis, 212 Fribourg: Academic Press.

Sweeney, Marvin A. 2007. *I & II Kings: A Commentary.* OTL. Louisville: Westminster John Knox.

Tadmor, Hayim. 1995. "Was the Biblical *sārîs* a Eunuch?" In *Solving Riddles and Untying Knots: Biblical, Epigraphic, and Semitic Studies in Honor of Jonas C. Greenfield*, edited by Ziony Zevit, Seymour Gitin, and Michael Sokoloff, 317–25. Winona Lake, IN: Eisenbrauns.

Talshir, David. 1988a. "The References to Ezra and the Books of Chronicles in B. Baba Bathra 15a." *VT* 38, no. 3:358–60. DOI: 10.1163/156853388X00148.

_____. 1988b. "A Reinvestigation of the Linguistic Relationship between Chronicles and Ezra-Nehemiah." *VT* 38, no. 2:165–93. DOI: 10.1163/156853388X00364.

Tate, Marvin. 1990. *Psalms 51–100.* WBC 20. Dallas: Word.

Taylor, Jonathan. 2011. "The Application of 2 Chronicles 7:13–15." *BSac* 168, no. 670:146–61.

Thames, John Tracy, Jr. 2011. "A New Discussion of the Meaning of the Phrase *'am hā'āreṣ* in the Hebrew Bible." *JBL* 130, no. 1:109–25. DOI: 10.2307/41304190.

Throntveit, Mark. 1982. "Linguistic Analysis and the Question of Authorship in Chronicles, Ezra and Nehemiah." *VT* 32, no. 2:201–16. DOI: 10.2307/1518445.

_____. 2003. "The Relationship of Hezekiah to David and Solomon in the Books of Chronicles." In *The Chronicler as Theologian: Essays in Honor of Ralph W. Klein*, edited by M. Patrick Graham, Steven L. McKenzie, and Gary N. Knoppers, 105–21. JSOTSup 371. London: T&T Clark.

Tiemeyer, Lena-Sofia. 2005. "Prophecy as a Way of Cancelling Prophecy: The Strategic Uses of Foreknowledge." *ZAW* 117, no. 3:329–50. DOI: 10.1515/zatw.2005.117.3.329.

Trimm, Charlie. 2017. *Fighting for the King and the Gods: A Survey of Warfare in the Ancient Near East.* RBS 88. Atlanta: SBL Press.

Van Seters, John. 1997. *In Search of History: Historiography in the Ancient World and the Origins of Biblical History.* Winona Lake, IN: Eisenbrauns.

Viezel, Eran. 2009a. "*Ezra katav sifro veyaḥas shel divrey ha-yamim 'ad lo . . . uman 'askeh? Neḥemiah ben-Ḥakalya*: On the Author of Chronicles in Bava Batra 15a." *JSQ* 16:243–54.

_____. 2009b. "Haggai, Zechariah and Malachi and Their Role in the Composition of Chronicles: The Origin of an Exegetical Tradition." *JJS* 60, no. 1:5–17. DOI: 10.18647/2848/JJS-2009.

Waltke, Bruce K. 2007. *An Old Testament Theology: An Exegetical, Canonical, and Thematic Approach.* Grand Rapids: Zondervan.

Warhurst, Amber K. 2011. "The Chronicler's Use of the Prophets." In *What Was Authoritative for Chronicles?*, edited by Ehud Ben Zvi and Diana Edelman, 165–81. Winona Lake, IN: Eisenbrauns. DOI: 10.5325/j.ctv1bxgxnp.13.

Watts, James W. 1992. *Psalm and Story: Inset Hymns in Hebrew Narrative.* JSOTSup 139. Sheffield: JSOT Press.

Weinfeld, Moshe. 1982. "The Counsel of the 'Elders' to Rehoboam and Its Implications." *Maarav* 3, no. 1:27–53. DOI: 10.1086/MAR198203102.

Wenham, Gordon. 1975. "Were David's Sons Priests?" *ZAW* 87, no. 1:79–82.

Whitney, Donald. 2014. *Spiritual Disciplines for the Christian Life*. Revised and updated. Colorado Springs: NavPress.

Willi, Thomas. 1972. *Die Chronik als Auslegung: Untersuchungen zur literarischen Gestaltung der historischen Überlieferung*. FRLANT 106. Göttingen: Vandenhoeck & Ruprecht.

Williams, Joshua E. 2019. "Creation in Chronicles: YHWH's Supremacy Manifested in Israel's Worship." *Southeastern Theological Review* 10, no. 2:77–95.

Williamson, H. G. M. 1976. "The Accession of Solomon in the Books of Chronicles." *VT* 26, no. 3:351–61. DOI: 10.1163/156853376X00510.

———. 1977. *Israel in the Books of Chronicles*. Cambridge: Cambridge University Press.

———. 1981. "'We Are Yours, O David': The Setting and Purpose of 1 Chronicles xii 1–23." In *Remembering All the Way . . . A Collection of Old Testament Studies Published on the Occasion of the Fortieth Anniversary of the Oudtestamentisch Werkgezelschap in Nederland*, edited by B. Albrektson, 164–76. OTS 21. Leiden: Brill.

———. 1982. *1 and 2 Chronicles*. NCBC. Grand Rapids: Eerdmans; London: Marshall, Morgan & Scott.

———. 2004. "Eschatology in Chronicles." In *Studies in Persian Period History and Historiography*, 162–95. FAT 38. Tübingen: Mohr Siebeck.

Wilson, Robert R. 1980. *Prophecy and Society in Ancient Israel*. Philadelphia: Fortress.

Wright, John W. 1990. "Guarding the Gates: 1 Chronicles 26:1–19 and the Roles of Gatekeepers in Chronicles." *JSOT* 48:69–81. DOI: 10.1177/030908929001504806.

———. 1991. "The Legacy of David in Chronicles: The Narrative Function of 1 Chronicles 23–27." *JBL* 110, no. 2:229–42. DOI: 10.2307/3267084.

———. 1993. "The Innocence of David in 1 Chronicles 21." *JSOT* 60:87–105. DOI: 10.1177/030908929301806007.

———. 2003. "Beyond Transcendence and Immanence: The Characterization of the Presence and Activity of God in the Book of Chronicles." In *The Chronicler as Theologian: Essays in Honor of Ralph W. Klein*, edited by M. Patrick Graham, Steven L. McKenzie, and Gary N. Knoppers, 240–67. JSOTSup 371. London: T&T Clark.

———. 2013. "Divine Retribution in Herodotus and the Book of Chronicles." In *Chronicling the Chronicler: The Book of Chronicles and Early Second Temple Historiography*, edited by Paul S. Evans and Tyler F. Williams, 195–214. Winona Lake, IN: Eisenbrauns. DOI: 10.5325/j.ctv18r6r1j.15.

Yamauchi, Edwin. 1980. "Was Nehemiah the Cupbearer a Eunuch?" *ZAW* 92, no. 1:132–42. DOI: 10.1515/zatw.1980.92.1.132.

Zucconi, Laura M. 2019. *Ancient Medicine: From Mesopotamia to Rome*. Grand Rapids: Eerdmans.

KERUX COMMENTARY SERIES